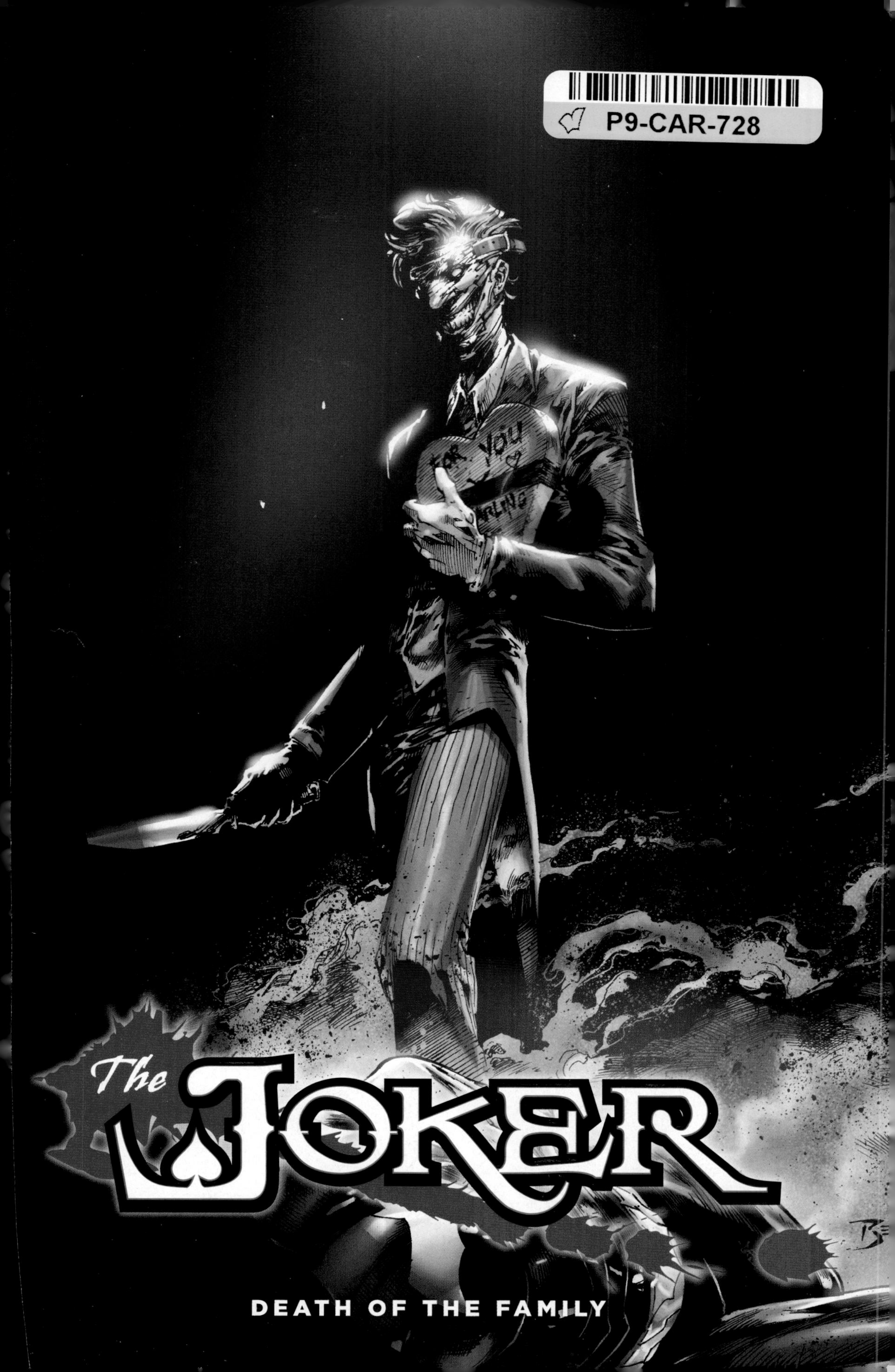
FOR YOU
The JOKER
DEATH OF THE FAMILY

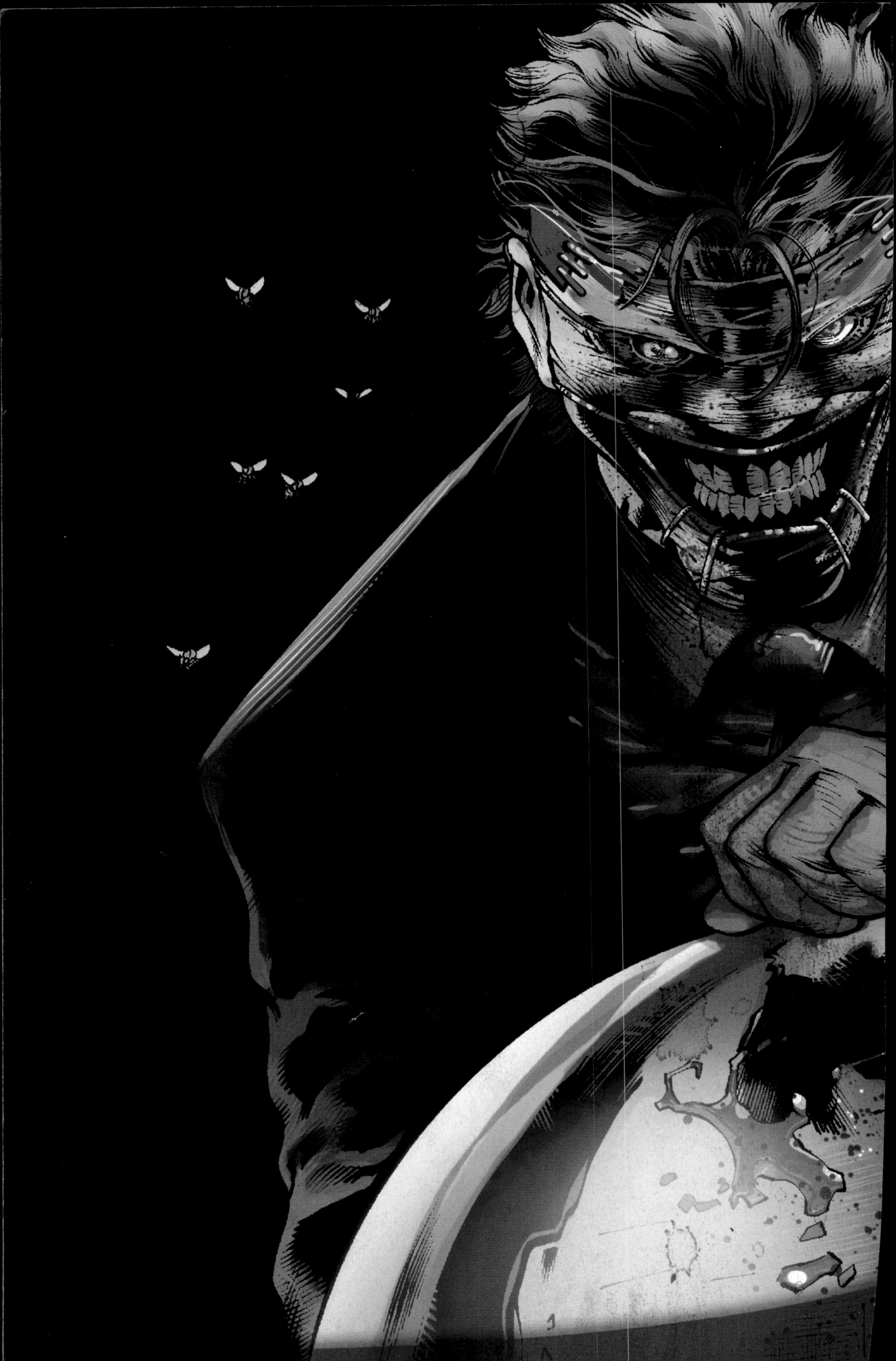

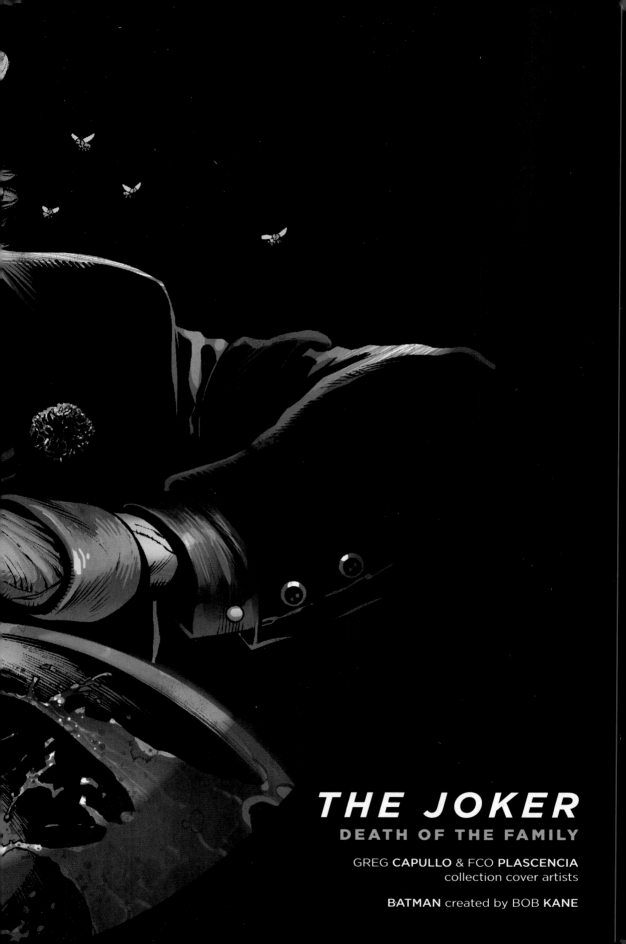

THE JOKER
DEATH OF THE FAMILY

GREG **CAPULLO** & FCO **PLASCENCIA**
collection cover artists

BATMAN created by BOB **KANE**

DRINK
JOE
JOE

MIKE MARTS RACHEL GLUCKSTERN BRIAN SMITH BRIAN CUNNINGHAM EDDIE BERGANZA Editors – Original Series
KATIE KUBERT RICKEY PURDIN Associate Editors – Original Series DARREN SHAN Assistant Editor – Original Series
PETER HAMBOUSSI Editor ROBIN WILDMAN Assistant Editor
ROBBIN BROSTERMAN Design Director – Books ROBBIE BIEDERMAN Publication Design

BOB HARRAS Senior VP – Editor-in-Chief, DC Comics

DIANE NELSON President DAN DIDIO and JIM LEE Co-Publishers
GEOFF JOHNS Chief Creative Officer
JOHN ROOD Executive VP – Sales, Marketing and Business Development
AMY GENKINS Senior VP – Business and Legal Affairs NAIRI GARDINER Senior VP – Finance
JEFF BOISON VP – Publishing Planning MARK CHIARELLO VP – Art Direction and Design
JOHN CUNNINGHAM VP – Marketing TERRI CUNNINGHAM VP – Editorial Administration
ALISON GILL Senior VP – Manufacturing and Operations HANK KANALZ Senior VP – Vertigo and Integrated Publishing
JAY KOGAN VP – Business and Legal Affairs, Publishing JACK MAHAN VP – Business Affairs, Talent
NICK NAPOLITANO VP – Manufacturing Administration SUE POHJA VP – Book Sales
COURTNEY SIMMONS Senior VP – Publicity BOB WAYNE Senior VP – Sales

JOKER: DEATH OF THE FAMILY

DC Comics, 1700 Broadway, New York, NY 10019
A Warner Bros. Entertainment Company.
Printed by RR Donnelley, Salem, VA, USA. 3/14/14. First Printing.
ISBN 978-1-4012-4646-4

Library of Congress Cataloging-in-Publication Data

Joker : Death of the Family.
pages cm
ISBN 978-1-4012-4235-0
1. Joker (Fictitious character)—Comic books, strips, etc. 2. Graphic novels.
PN6728.B36J646 2013
741.5'973—dc23
2013020541

SUSTAINABLE FORESTRY INITIATIVE
Certified Chain of Custody
At Least 20% Certified Forest Content
www.sfiprogram.org
SFI-01042

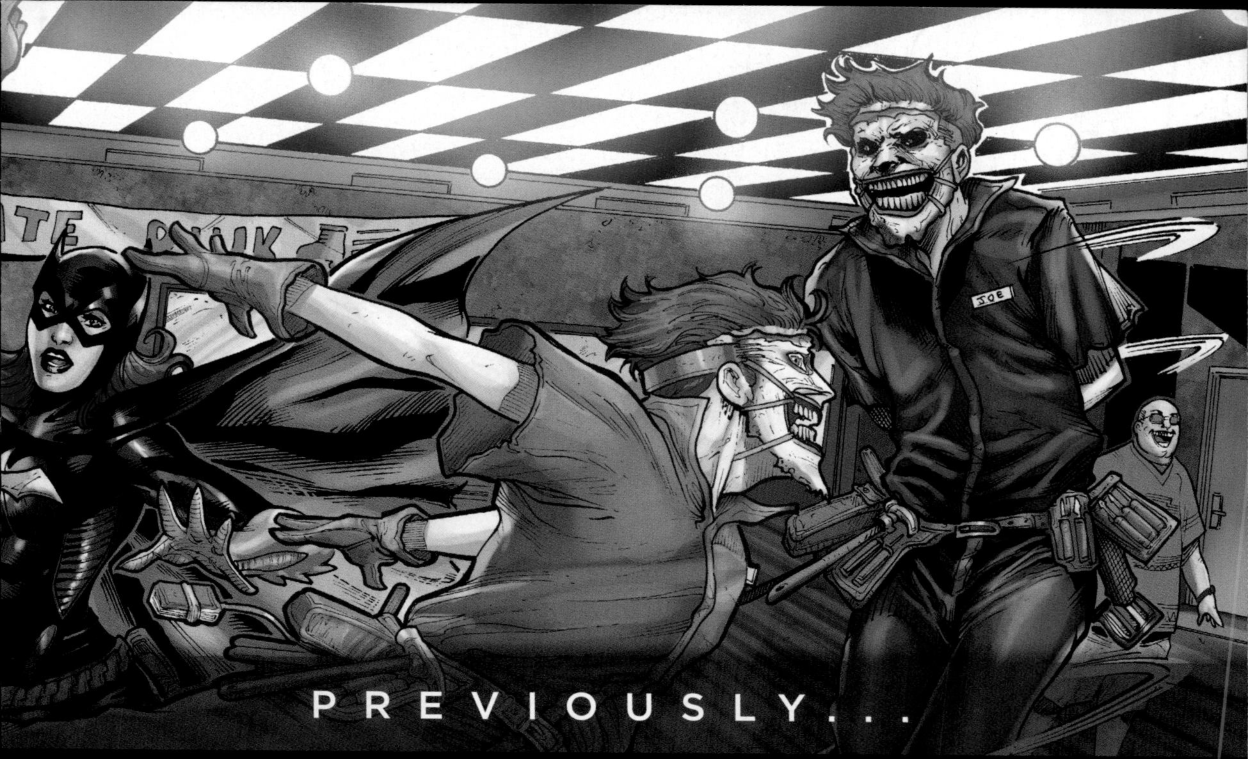
JOE

PREVIOUSLY...

A year ago, the Joker disappeared, seemingly forever. For his last terrifying stunt, he had the skin from his face removed, leaving it behind like a grisly calling card when he escaped Arkham Asylum. Afterwards, most believed him to be dead.

But they were wrong, and now he's back.

Wearing his decaying face like a mask, the Joker is in the midst of the most grisly murder spree Gotham has ever seen. He wants his "old friend" Batman to play along with him, but Batman has changed. The hero no longer works alone. He has an entire team of allies and friends.

But this family of Bats only weighs its leader down, making him weak and sentimental. To bring back the true Batman, the Joker will have to take them all out, one by one...

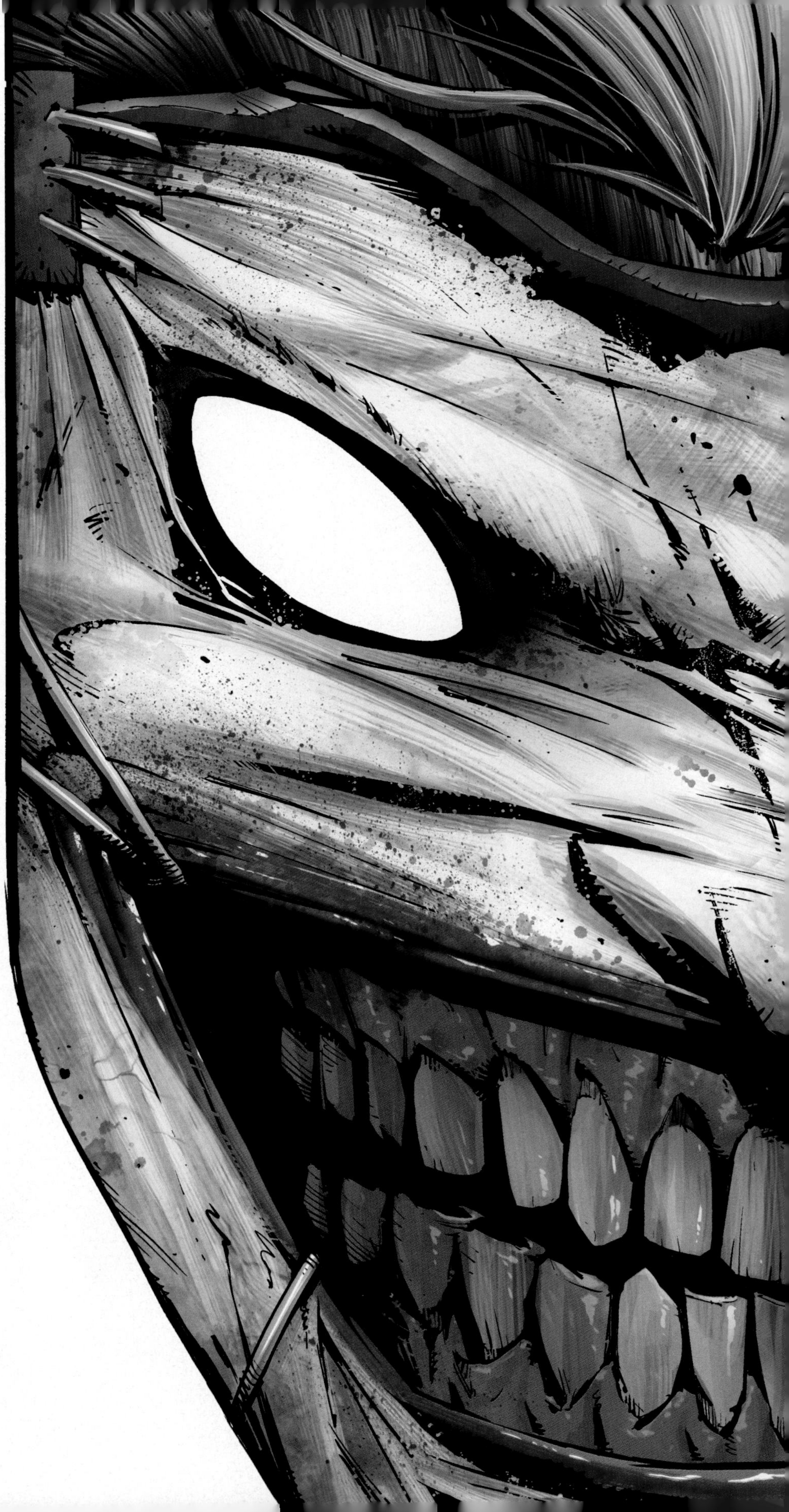

PART ONE
BATMAN

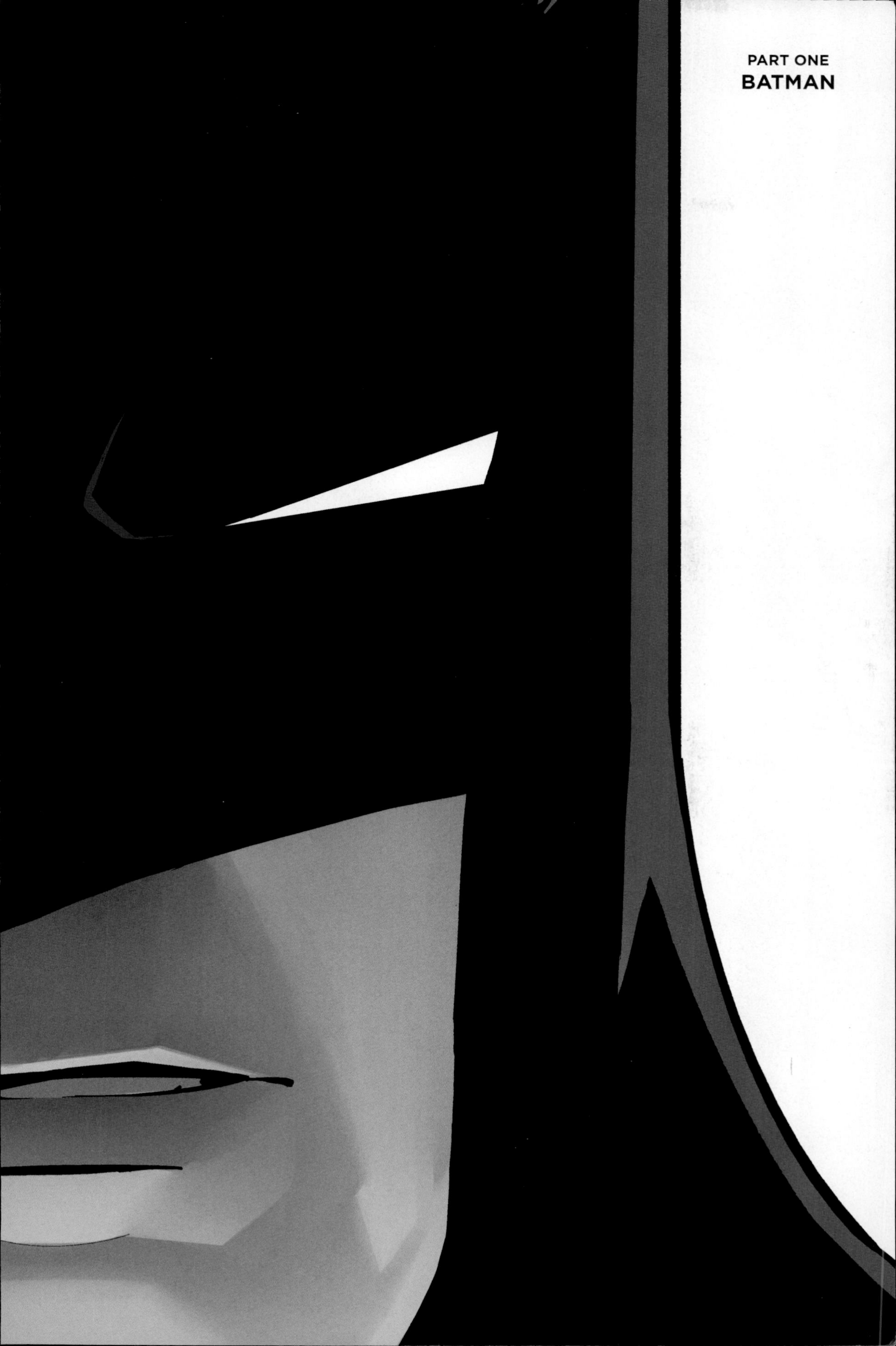

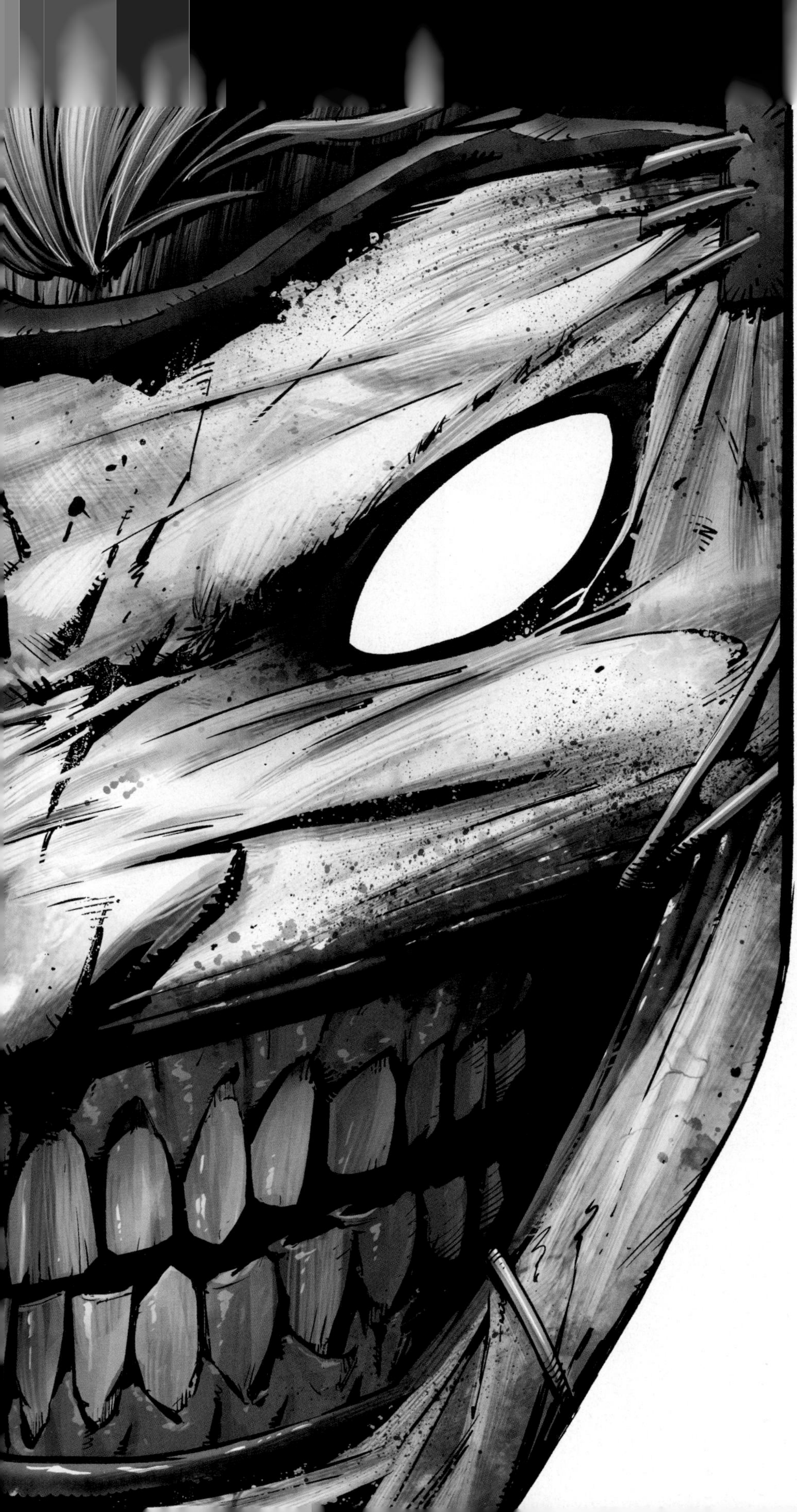

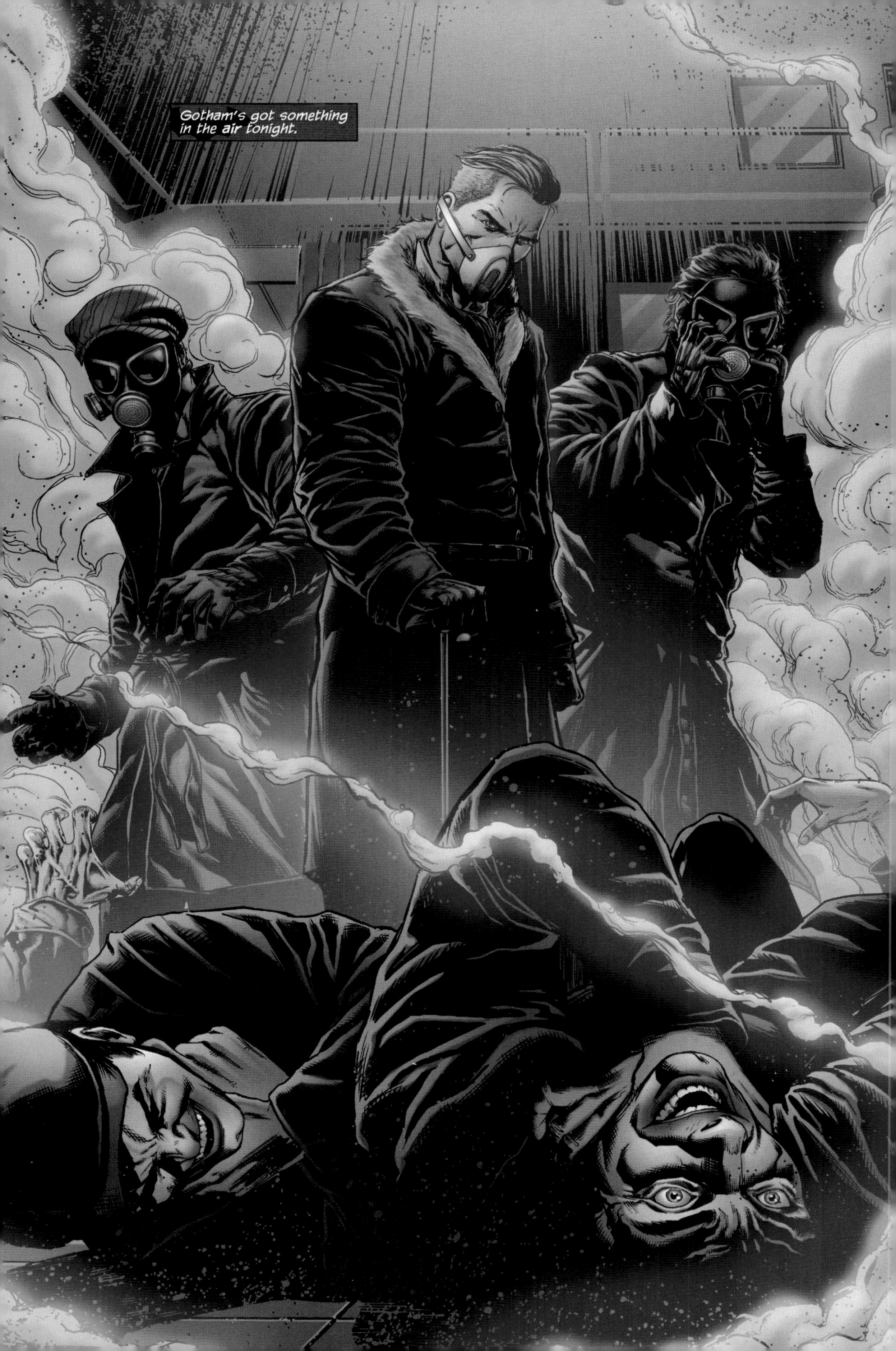
Gotham's got something in the air tonight.

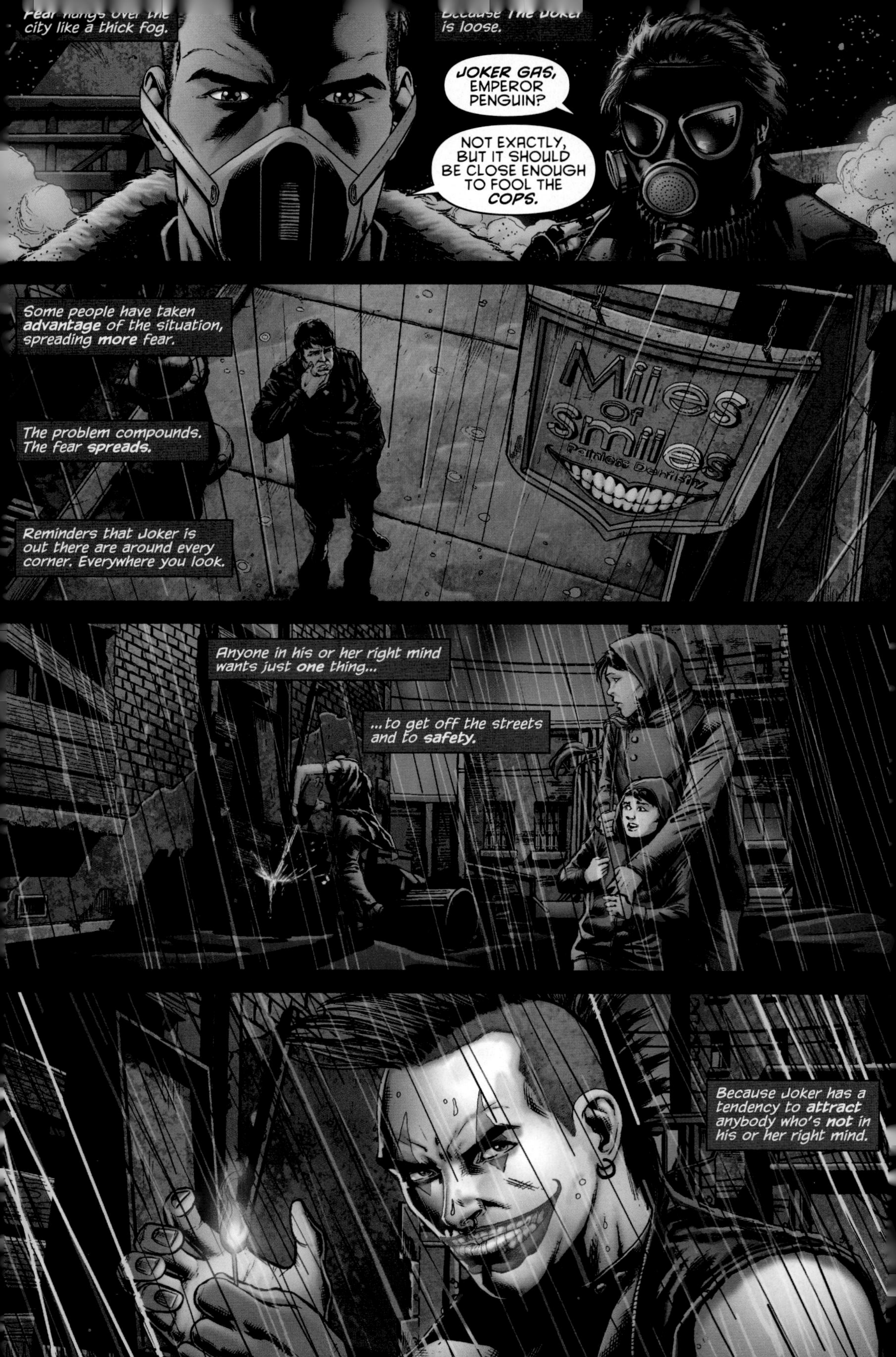
city like a thick fog.
is loose.
JOKER GAS, EMPEROR PENGUIN?
NOT EXACTLY, BUT IT SHOULD BE CLOSE ENOUGH TO FOOL THE COPS.
Some people have taken advantage of the situation, spreading more fear.
Miles of Smiles
Painless Dentistry
The problem compounds. The fear spreads.
Reminders that Joker is out there are around every corner. Everywhere you look.
Anyone in his or her right mind wants just one thing...
...to get off the streets and to safety.
Because Joker has a tendency to attract anybody who's not in his or her right mind.

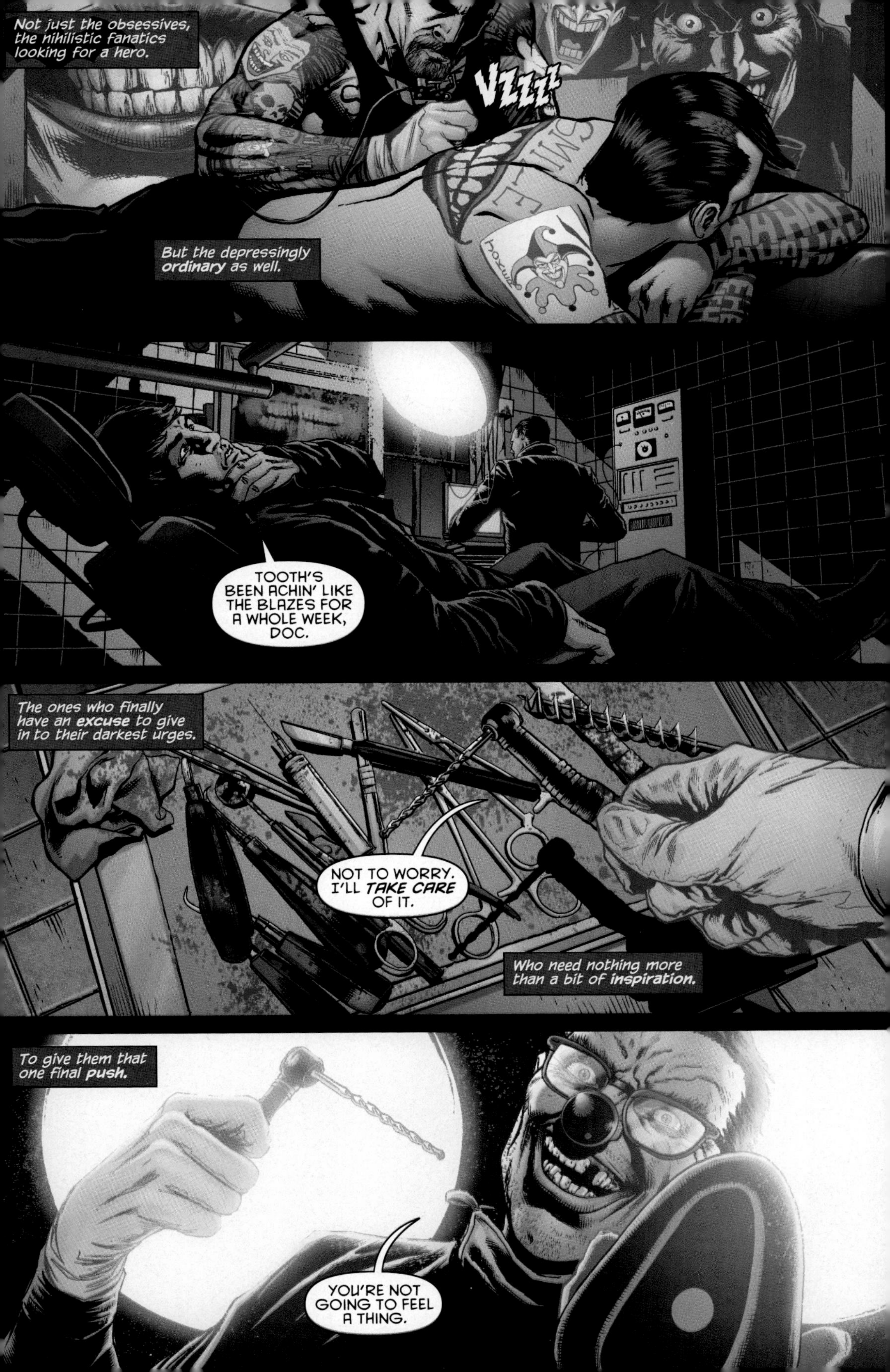
Not just the obsessives, the nihilistic fanatics looking for a hero.
VZZZZ
SMILE
But the depressingly ordinary as well.
TOOTH'S BEEN ACHIN' LIKE THE BLAZES FOR A WHOLE WEEK, DOC.
The ones who finally have an excuse to give in to their darkest urges.
NOT TO WORRY. I'LL TAKE CARE OF IT.
Who need nothing more than a bit of inspiration.
To give them that one final push.
YOU'RE NOT GOING TO FEEL A THING.

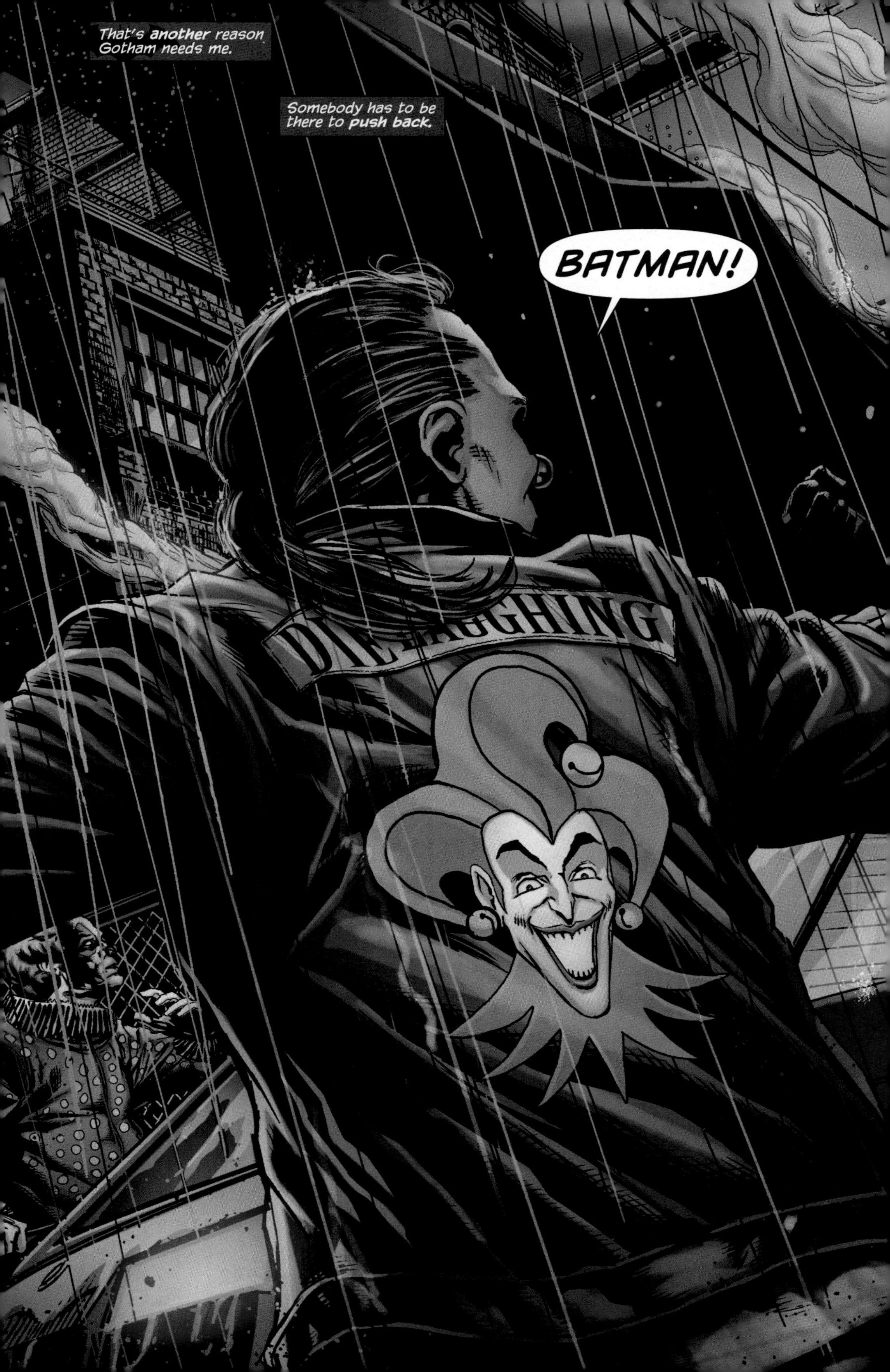
That's **another** reason Gotham needs me.
Somebody has to be there to **push back.**
BATMAN!

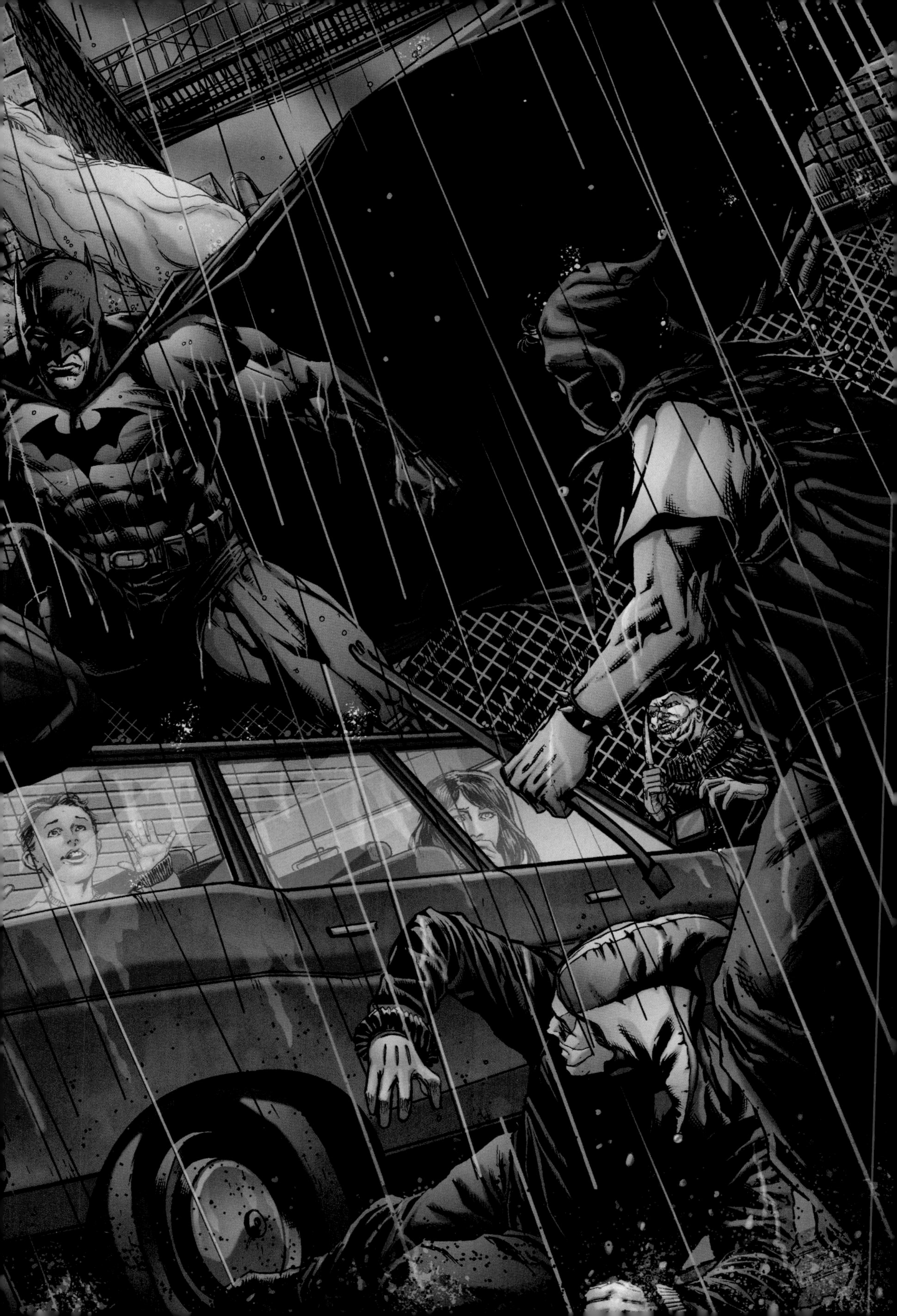

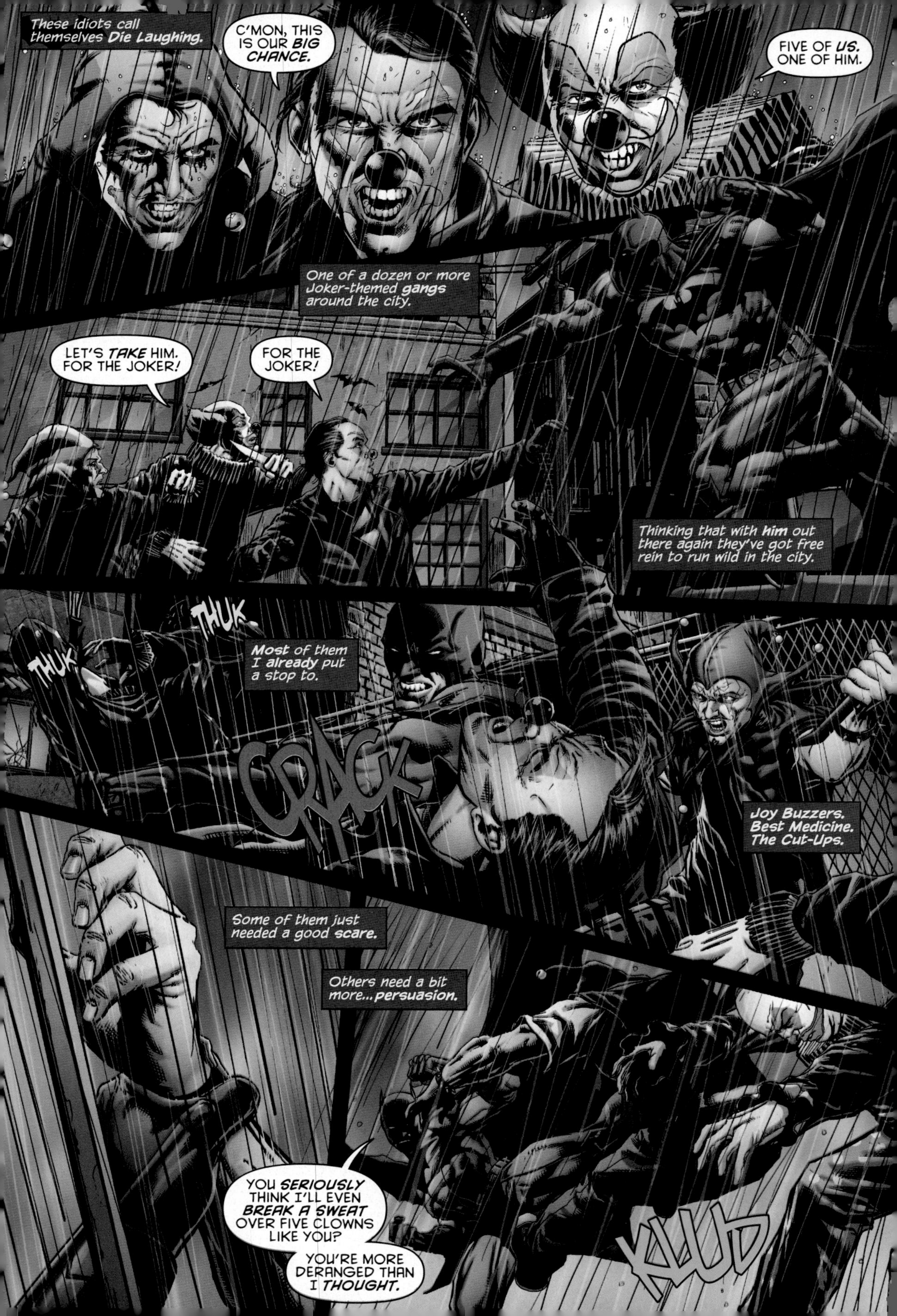
These idiots call themselves Die Laughing.
C'MON, THIS IS OUR BIG CHANCE.
FIVE OF US. ONE OF HIM.
One of a dozen or more Joker-themed gangs around the city.
LET'S TAKE HIM. FOR THE JOKER!
FOR THE JOKER!
Thinking that with him out there again they've got free rein to run wild in the city.
THUK
THUK
Most of them I already put a stop to.
CRACK
Joy Buzzers. Best Medicine. The Cut-Ups.
Some of them just needed a good scare.
Others need a bit more... persuasion.
YOU SERIOUSLY THINK I'LL EVEN BREAK A SWEAT OVER FIVE CLOWNS LIKE YOU?
YOU'RE MORE DERANGED THAN I THOUGHT.
KLUD

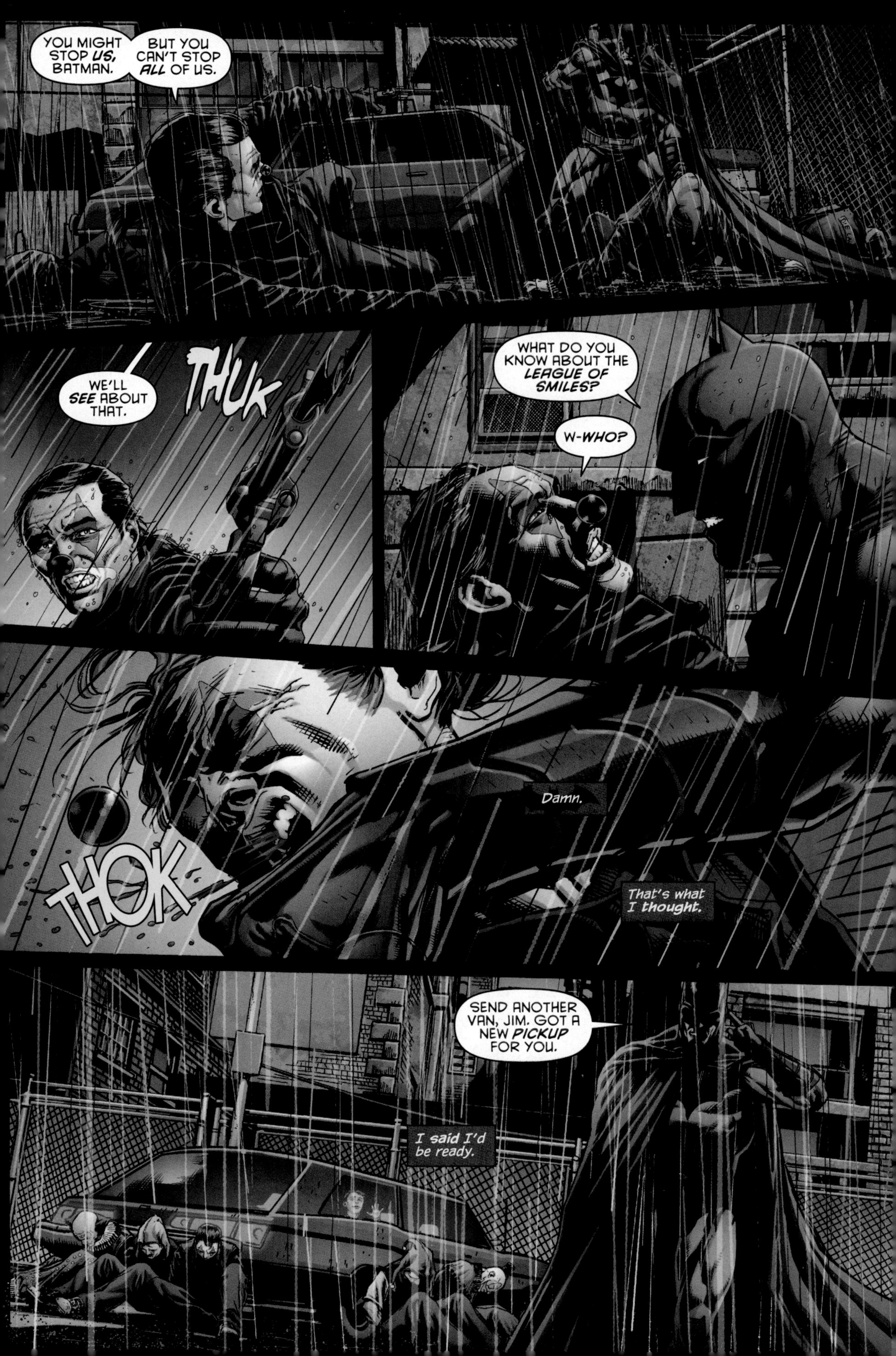

YOU MIGHT STOP US, BATMAN.
BUT YOU CAN'T STOP ALL OF US.
WE'LL SEE ABOUT THAT.
THUK
WHAT DO YOU KNOW ABOUT THE LEAGUE OF SMILES?
W-WHO?
Damn.
THOK
That's what I thought.
SEND ANOTHER VAN, JIM. GOT A NEW PICKUP FOR YOU.
I said I'd be ready.

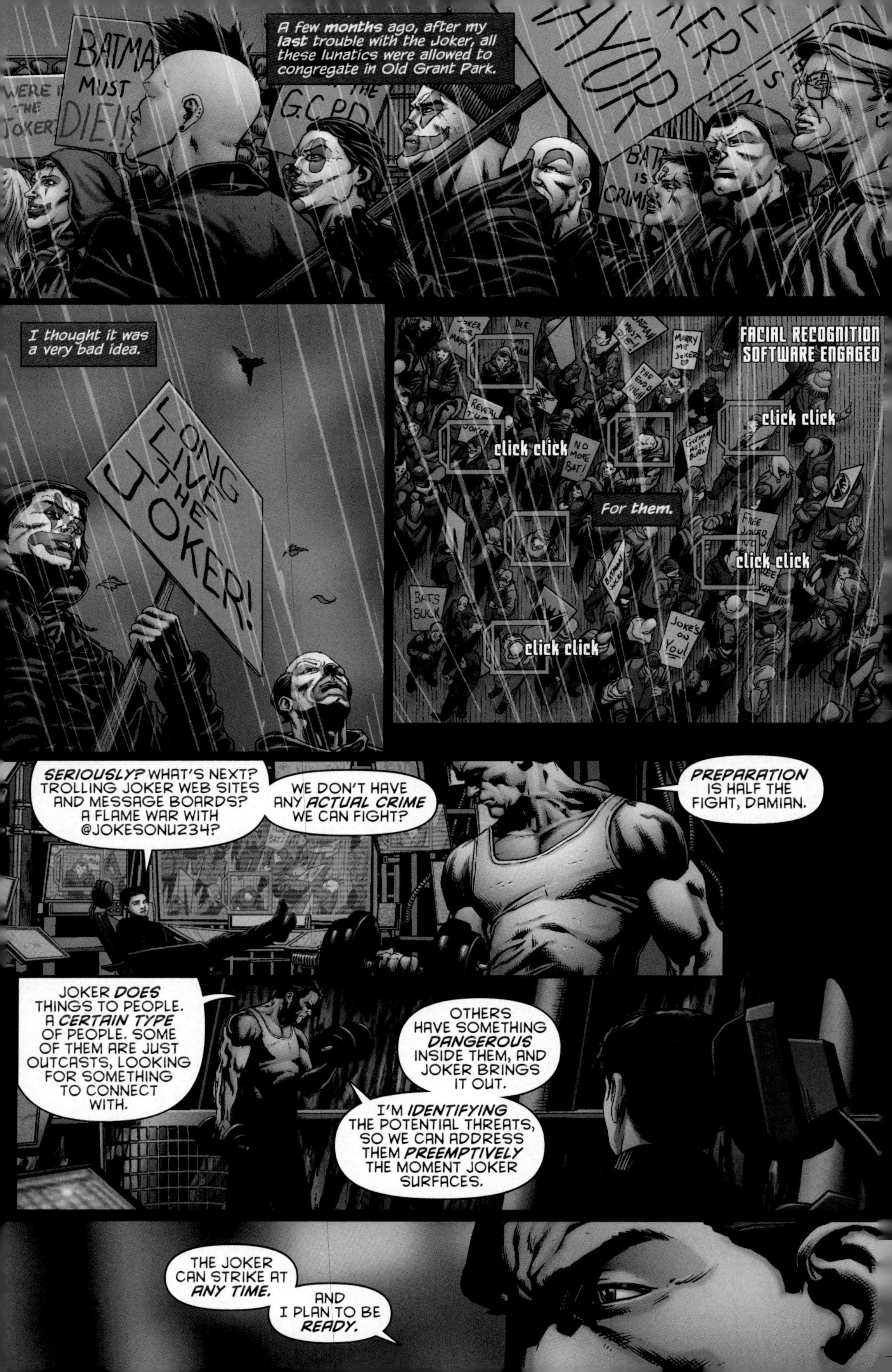

A few months ago, after my last trouble with the Joker, all these lunatics were allowed to congregate in Old Grant Park.
MUST DIE!!
G.C.P.D.
I thought it was a very bad idea.
LONG LIVE THE JOKER!
FACIAL RECOGNITION SOFTWARE ENGAGED
MARRY ME JOKER
NO MORE BAT!
GOTHAM MUST BURN
BATS SUCK
JOKE'S ON YOU!
click click
click click
For them.
click click
click click
SERIOUSLY? WHAT'S NEXT? TROLLING JOKER WEB SITES AND MESSAGE BOARDS? A FLAME WAR WITH @JOKESONU234?
WE DON'T HAVE ANY ACTUAL CRIME WE CAN FIGHT?
PREPARATION IS HALF THE FIGHT, DAMIAN.
JOKER DOES THINGS TO PEOPLE. A CERTAIN TYPE OF PEOPLE. SOME OF THEM ARE JUST OUTCASTS, LOOKING FOR SOMETHING TO CONNECT WITH.
OTHERS HAVE SOMETHING DANGEROUS INSIDE THEM, AND JOKER BRINGS IT OUT.
I'M IDENTIFYING THE POTENTIAL THREATS, SO WE CAN ADDRESS THEM PREEMPTIVELY THE MOMENT JOKER SURFACES.
THE JOKER CAN STRIKE AT ANY TIME.
AND I PLAN TO BE READY.

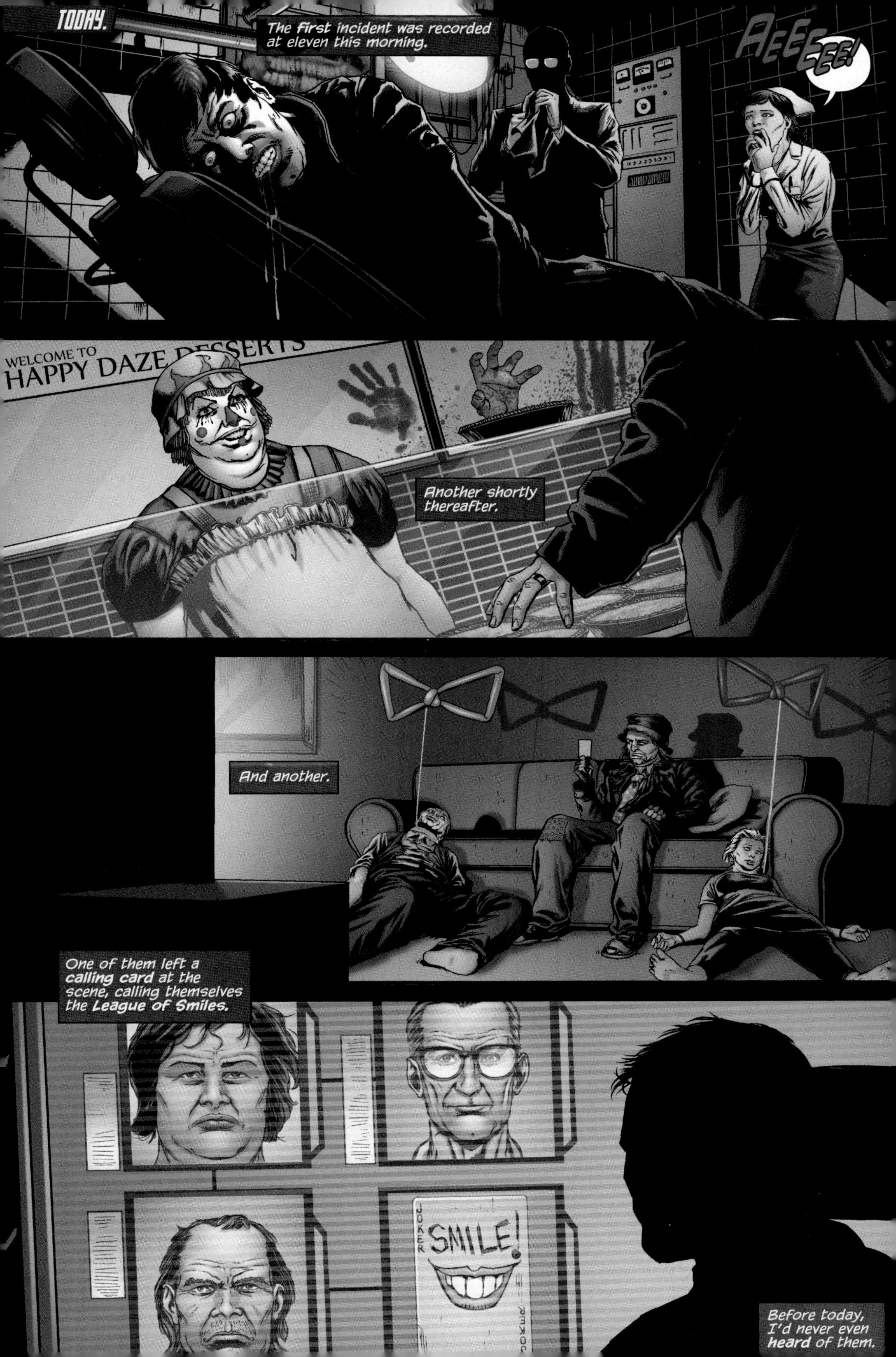
TODAY.
The first incident was recorded at eleven this morning.
AEEEEEE!
WELCOME TO HAPPY DAZE DESSERTS
Another shortly thereafter.
And another.
One of them left a calling card at the scene, calling themselves the League of Smiles.
JOKER
SMILE!
Before today, I'd never even heard of them.

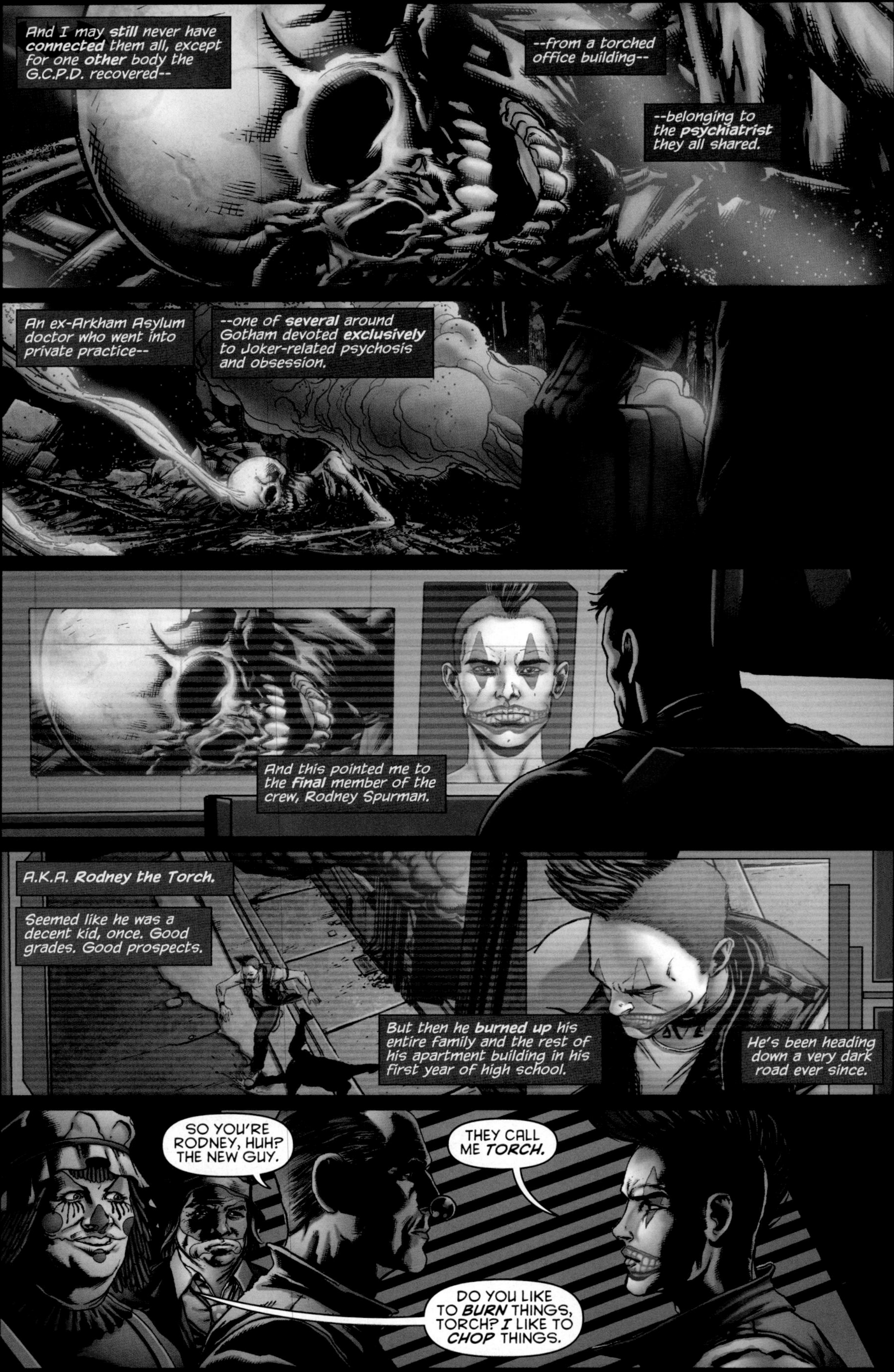
And I may still never have connected them all, except for one other body the G.C.P.D. recovered--
--from a torched office building--
--belonging to the psychiatrist they all shared.
An ex-Arkham Asylum doctor who went into private practice--
--one of several around Gotham devoted exclusively to Joker-related psychosis and obsession.
And this pointed me to the final member of the crew, Rodney Spurman.
A.K.A. Rodney the Torch.
Seemed like he was a decent kid, once. Good grades. Good prospects.
But then he burned up his entire family and the rest of his apartment building in his first year of high school.
He's been heading down a very dark road ever since.
SO YOU'RE RODNEY, HUH? THE NEW GUY.
THEY CALL ME TORCH.
DO YOU LIKE TO BURN THINGS, TORCH? I LIKE TO CHOP THINGS.

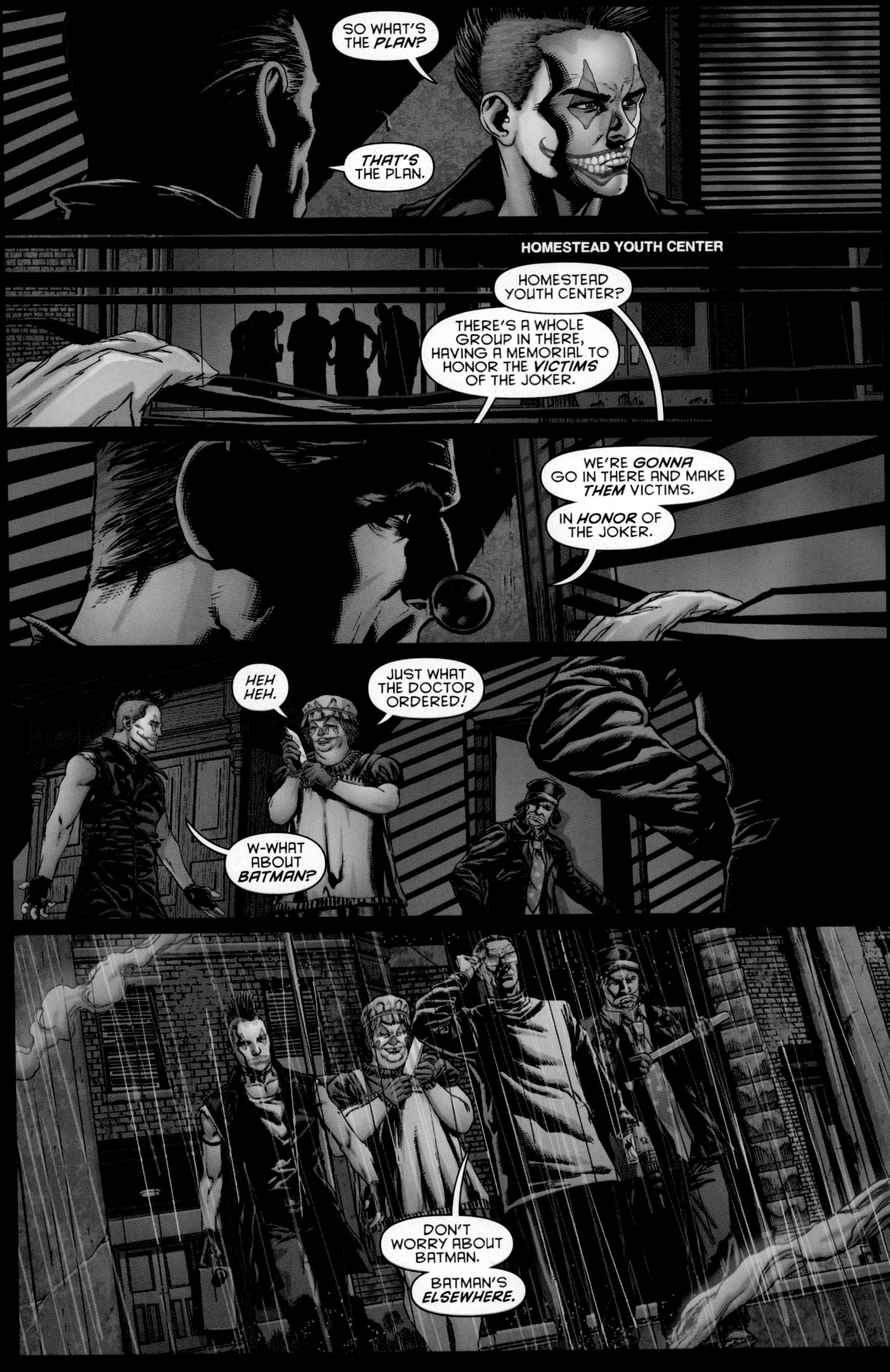
SO WHAT'S THE *PLAN?*
THAT'S THE PLAN.
HOMESTEAD YOUTH CENTER
HOMESTEAD YOUTH CENTER?
THERE'S A WHOLE GROUP IN THERE, HAVING A MEMORIAL TO HONOR THE *VICTIMS* OF THE JOKER.
WE'RE *GONNA* GO IN THERE AND MAKE *THEM* VICTIMS.
IN *HONOR* OF THE JOKER.
HEH HEH.
JUST WHAT THE DOCTOR ORDERED!
W-WHAT ABOUT *BATMAN?*
DON'T WORRY ABOUT BATMAN.
BATMAN'S *ELSEWHERE.*

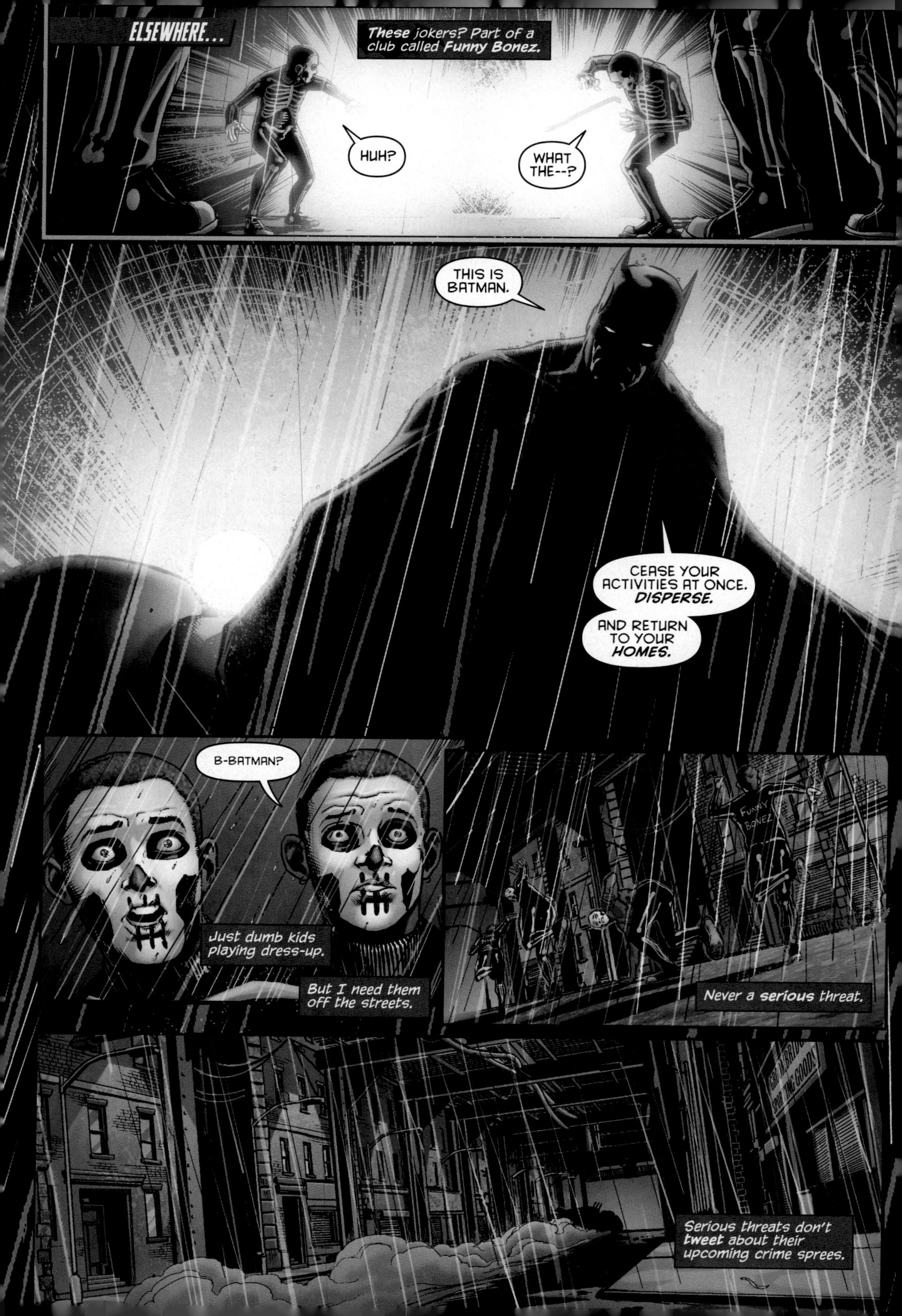
ELSEWHERE...
These jokers? Part of a club called Funny Bonez.
HUH?
WHAT THE--?
THIS IS BATMAN.
CEASE YOUR ACTIVITIES AT ONCE. DISPERSE.
AND RETURN TO YOUR HOMES.
B-BATMAN?
Just dumb kids playing dress-up.
But I need them off the streets.
FUNNY BONEZ
Never a serious threat.
Serious threats don't tweet about their upcoming crime sprees.

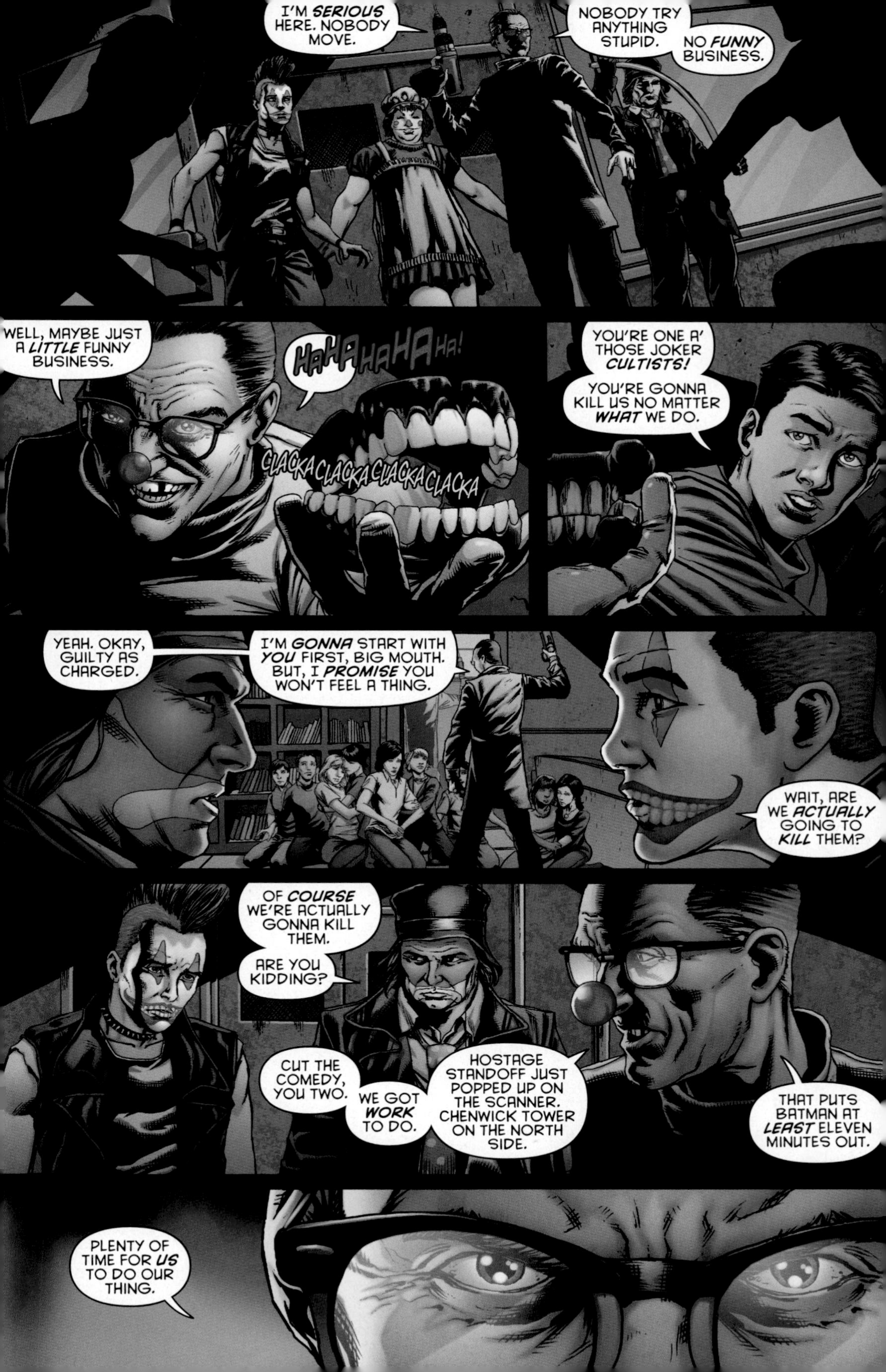
I'M SERIOUS HERE. NOBODY MOVE.
NOBODY TRY ANYTHING STUPID.
NO FUNNY BUSINESS.
WELL, MAYBE JUST A LITTLE FUNNY BUSINESS.
HAHAHAHAHAHA!
CLACKA CLACKA CLACKA CLACKA
YOU'RE ONE A' THOSE JOKER CULTISTS!
YOU'RE GONNA KILL US NO MATTER WHAT WE DO.
YEAH. OKAY, GUILTY AS CHARGED.
I'M GONNA START WITH YOU FIRST, BIG MOUTH. BUT, I PROMISE YOU WON'T FEEL A THING.
WAIT, ARE WE ACTUALLY GOING TO KILL THEM?
OF COURSE WE'RE ACTUALLY GONNA KILL THEM.
ARE YOU KIDDING?
CUT THE COMEDY, YOU TWO.
WE GOT WORK TO DO.
HOSTAGE STANDOFF JUST POPPED UP ON THE SCANNER. CHENWICK TOWER ON THE NORTH SIDE.
THAT PUTS BATMAN AT LEAST ELEVEN MINUTES OUT.
PLENTY OF TIME FOR US TO DO OUR THING.

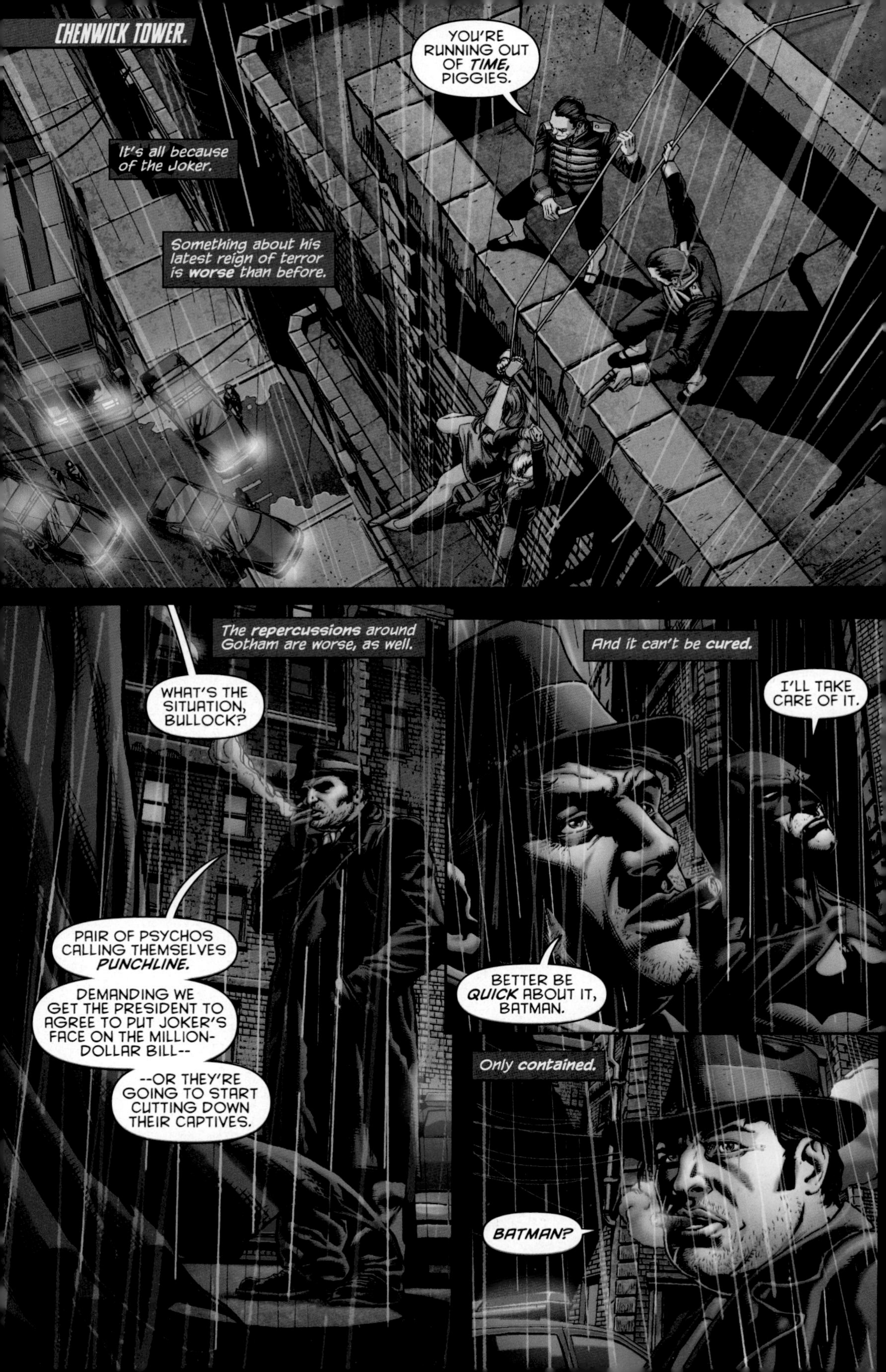
CHENWICK TOWER.
YOU'RE RUNNING OUT OF TIME, PIGGIES.
It's all because of the Joker.
Something about his latest reign of terror is worse than before.
The repercussions around Gotham are worse, as well.
WHAT'S THE SITUATION, BULLOCK?
PAIR OF PSYCHOS CALLING THEMSELVES PUNCHLINE.
DEMANDING WE GET THE PRESIDENT TO AGREE TO PUT JOKER'S FACE ON THE MILLION-DOLLAR BILL--
--OR THEY'RE GOING TO START CUTTING DOWN THEIR CAPTIVES.
And it can't be cured.
I'LL TAKE CARE OF IT.
BETTER BE QUICK ABOUT IT, BATMAN.
Only contained.
BATMAN?

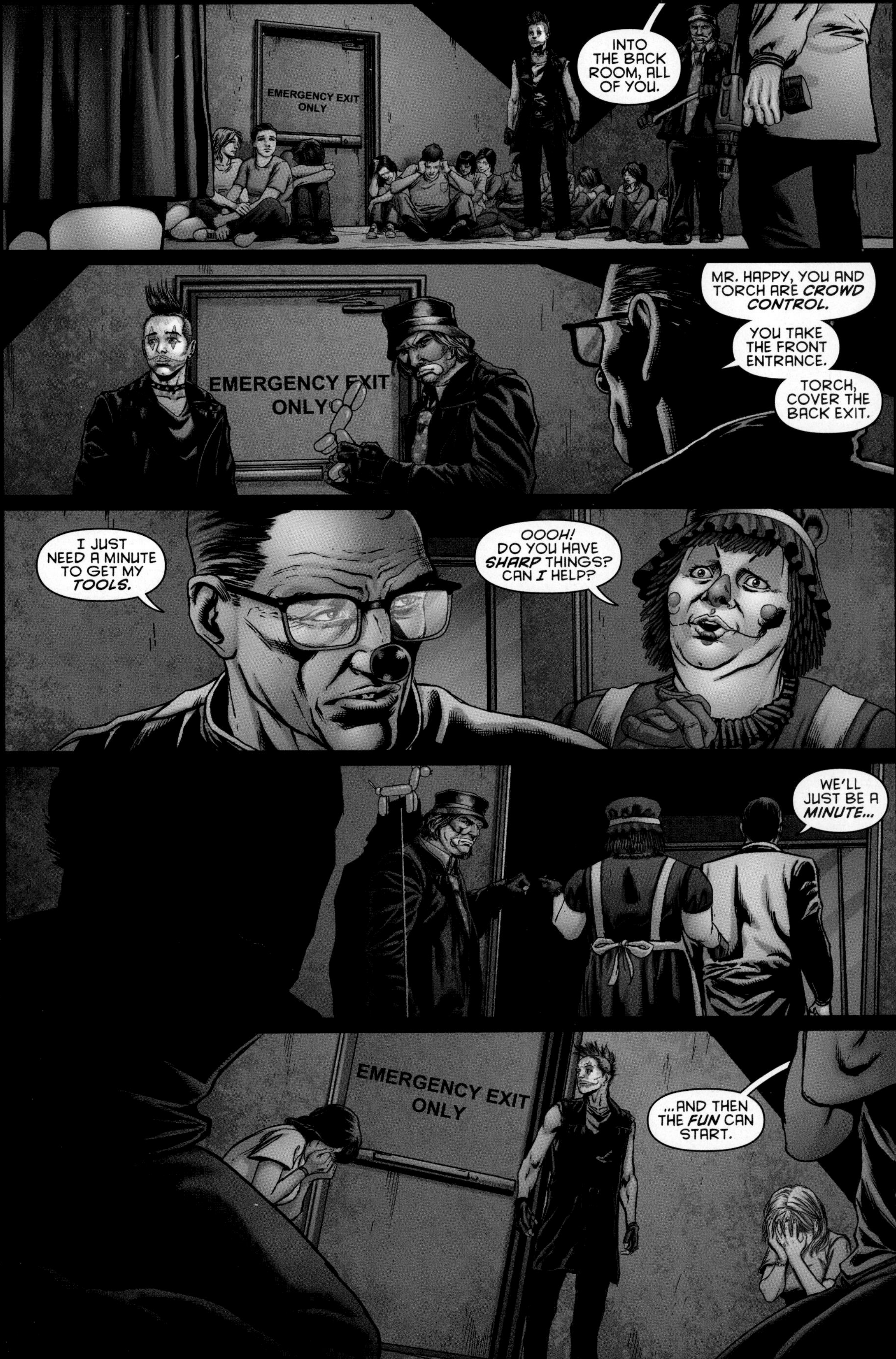
EMERGENCY EXIT ONLY
INTO THE BACK ROOM, ALL OF YOU.
MR. HAPPY, YOU AND TORCH ARE *CROWD CONTROL.*
YOU TAKE THE FRONT ENTRANCE.
TORCH, COVER THE BACK EXIT.
EMERGENCY EXIT ONLY
I JUST NEED A MINUTE TO GET MY *TOOLS.*
OOOH! DO YOU HAVE *SHARP* THINGS? CAN *I* HELP?
WE'LL JUST BE A *MINUTE*...
EMERGENCY EXIT ONLY
...AND THEN THE *FUN* CAN START.

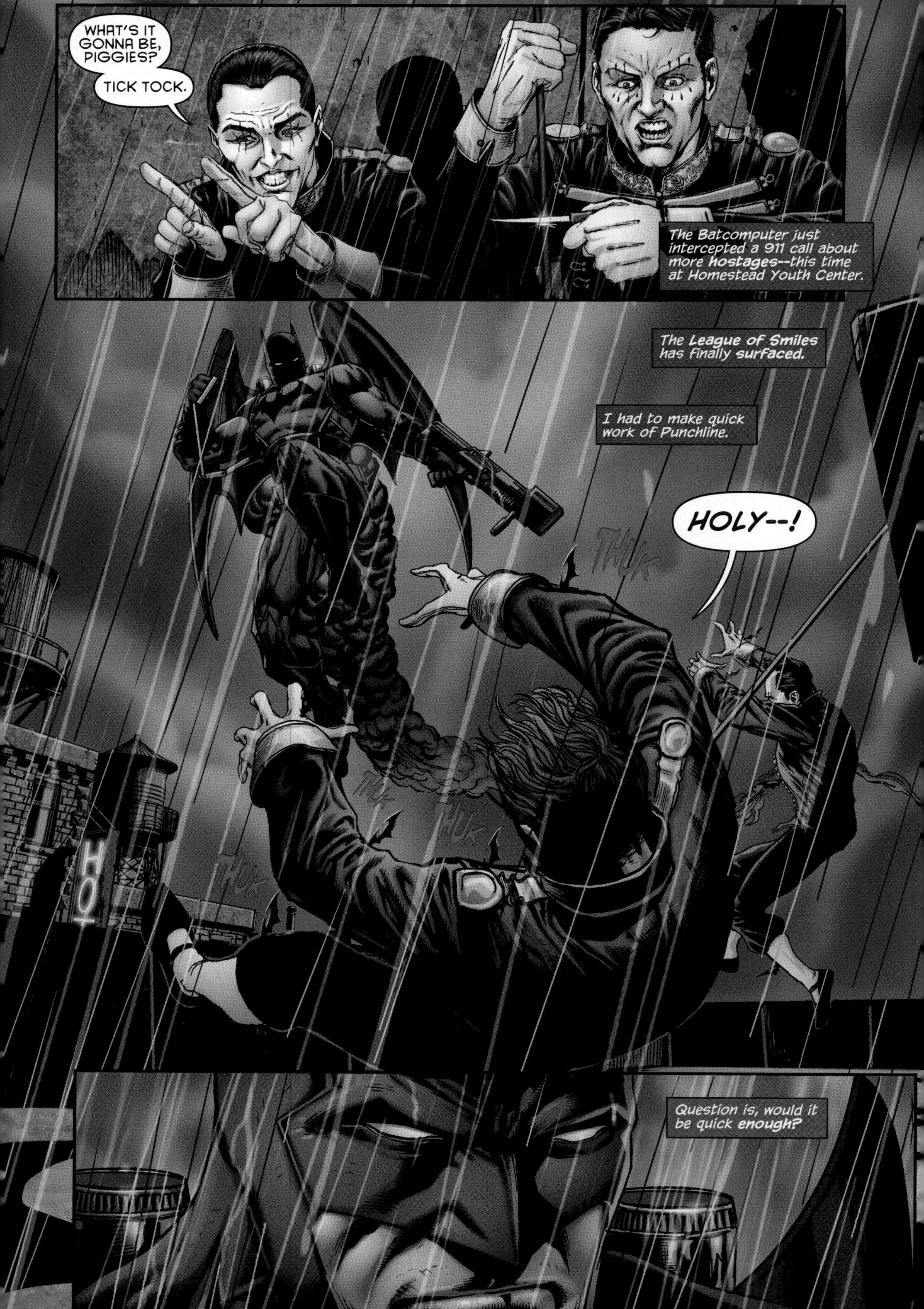
WHAT'S IT GONNA BE, PIGGIES?
TICK TOCK.
The Batcomputer just intercepted a 911 call about more hostages--this time at Homestead Youth Center.
The League of Smiles has finally surfaced.
I had to make quick work of Punchline.
HOLY--!
THUK
THUK
THUK
THUK
Question is, would it be quick enough?

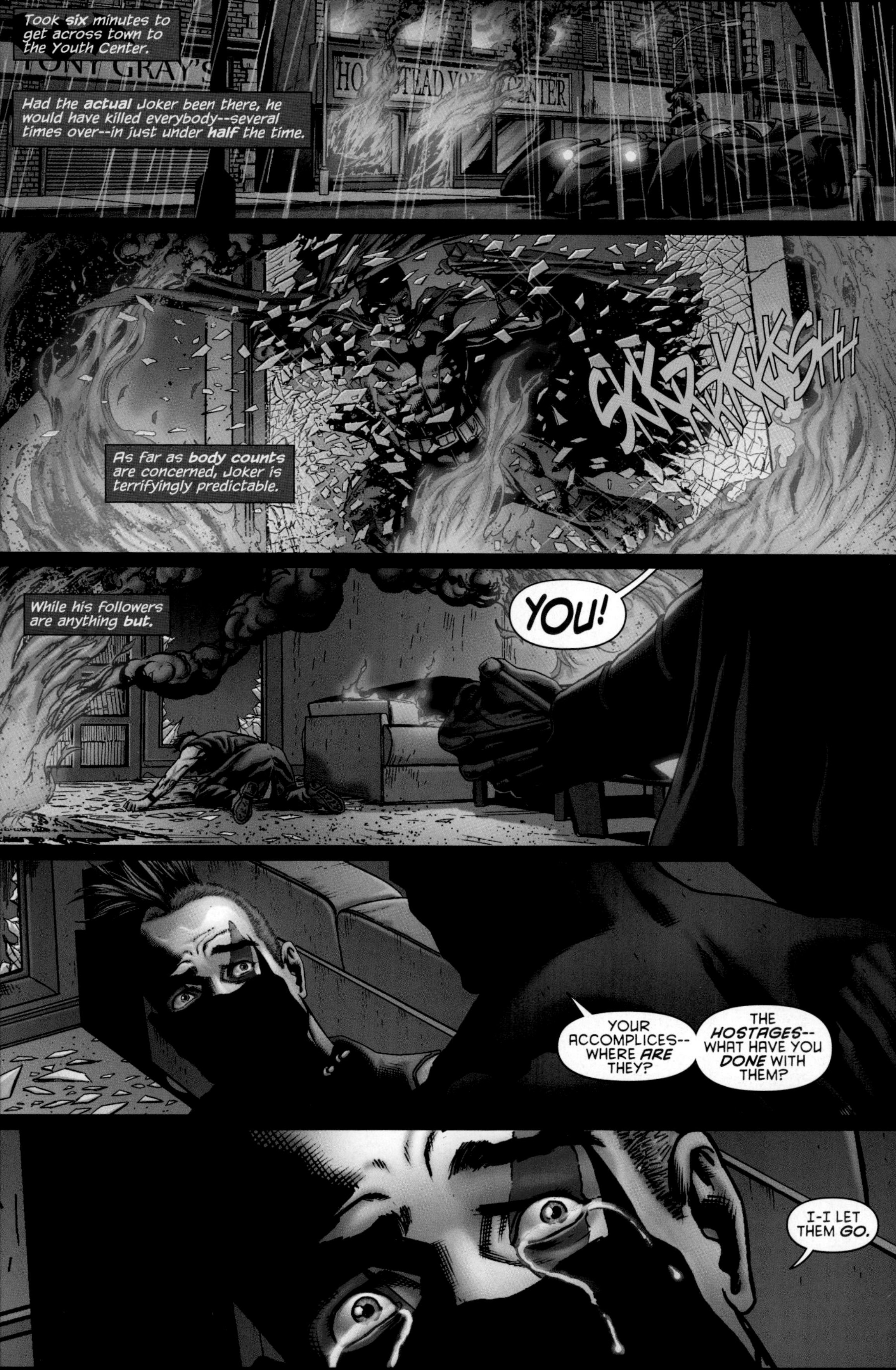
Took six minutes to get across town to the Youth Center.
Had the actual Joker been there, he would have killed everybody--several times over--in just under half the time.
CKKRRKKSHH
As far as body counts are concerned, Joker is terrifyingly predictable.
While his followers are anything but.
YOU!
YOUR ACCOMPLICES-- WHERE ARE THEY?
THE HOSTAGES-- WHAT HAVE YOU DONE WITH THEM?
I-I LET THEM GO.

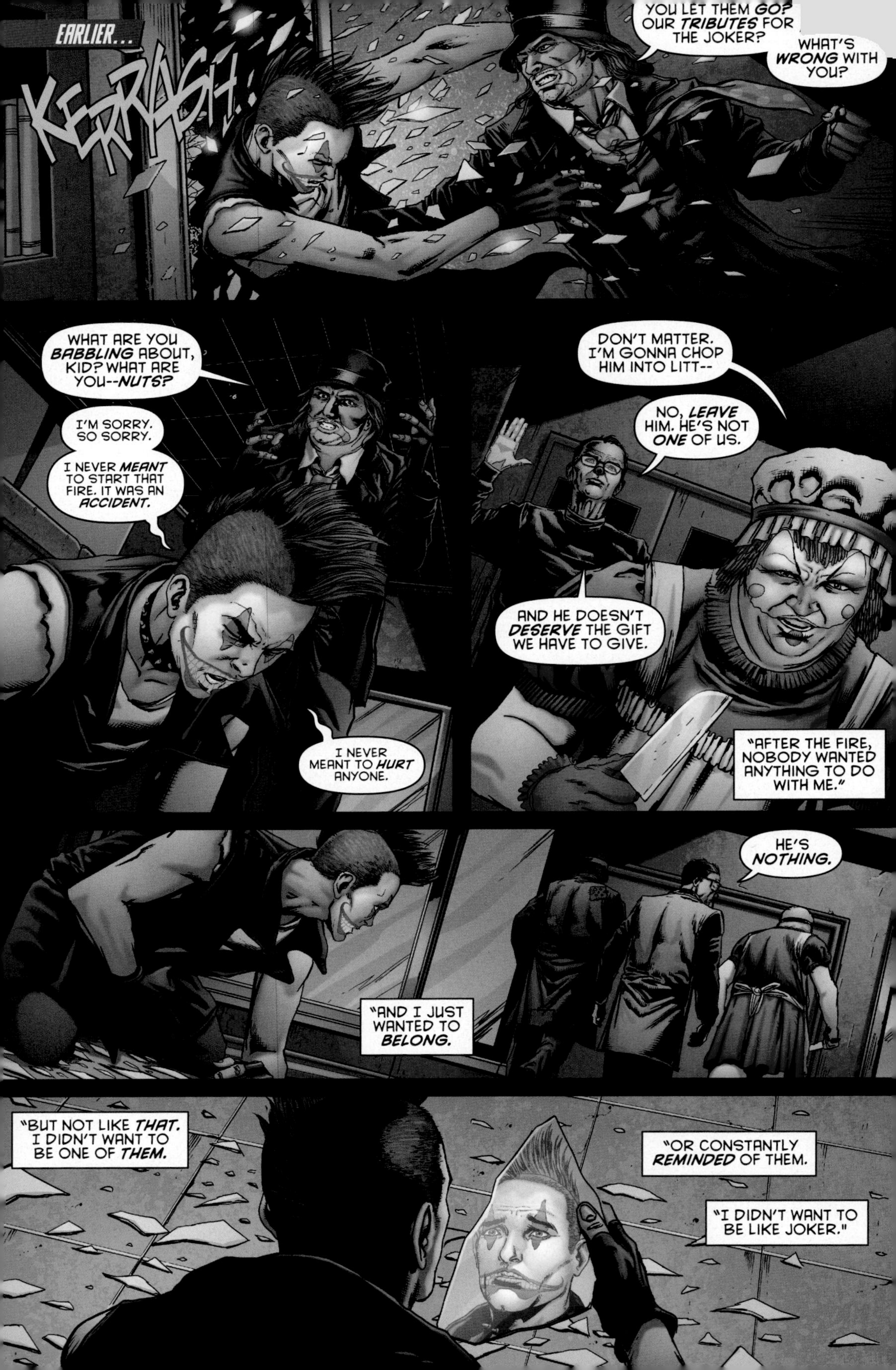
EARLIER...
KERRASH!
YOU LET THEM GO? OUR TRIBUTES FOR THE JOKER?
WHAT'S WRONG WITH YOU?
WHAT ARE YOU BABBLING ABOUT, KID? WHAT ARE YOU--NUTS?
I'M SORRY. SO SORRY.
I NEVER MEANT TO START THAT FIRE. IT WAS AN ACCIDENT.
I NEVER MEANT TO HURT ANYONE.
DON'T MATTER. I'M GONNA CHOP HIM INTO LITT--
NO, LEAVE HIM. HE'S NOT ONE OF US.
AND HE DOESN'T DESERVE THE GIFT WE HAVE TO GIVE.
"AFTER THE FIRE, NOBODY WANTED ANYTHING TO DO WITH ME."
"AND I JUST WANTED TO BELONG.
HE'S NOTHING.
"BUT NOT LIKE THAT. I DIDN'T WANT TO BE ONE OF THEM.
"OR CONSTANTLY REMINDED OF THEM.
"I DIDN'T WANT TO BE LIKE JOKER."

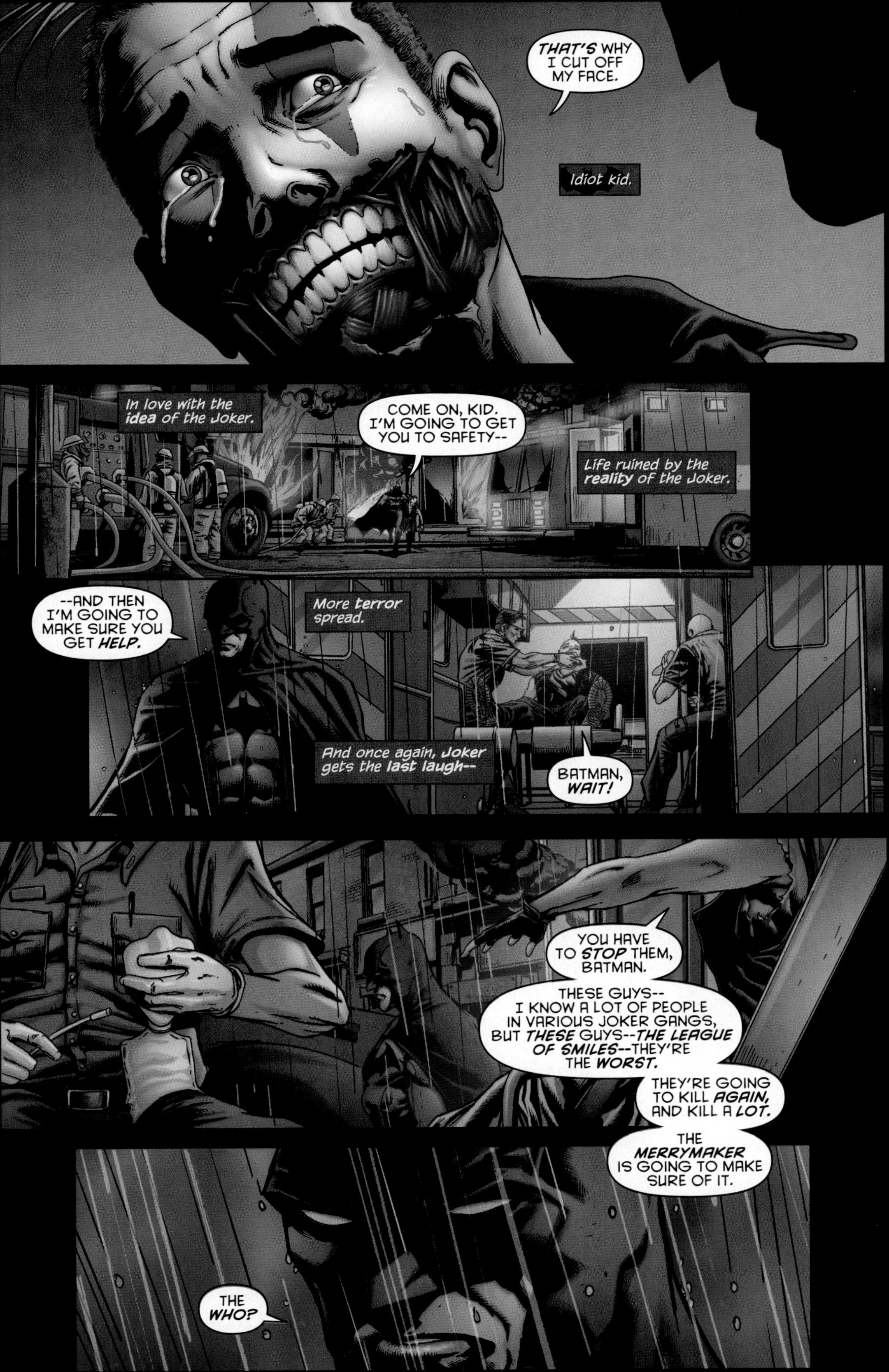
THAT'S WHY I CUT OFF MY FACE.
Idiot kid.
In love with the idea of the Joker.
COME ON, KID. I'M GOING TO GET YOU TO SAFETY--
Life ruined by the reality of the Joker.
--AND THEN I'M GOING TO MAKE SURE YOU GET HELP.
More terror spread.
And once again, Joker gets the last laugh--
BATMAN, WAIT!
YOU HAVE TO STOP THEM, BATMAN.
THESE GUYS-- I KNOW A LOT OF PEOPLE IN VARIOUS JOKER GANGS, BUT THESE GUYS--THE LEAGUE OF SMILES--THEY'RE THE WORST.
THEY'RE GOING TO KILL AGAIN, AND KILL A LOT.
THE MERRYMAKER IS GOING TO MAKE SURE OF IT.
THE WHO?

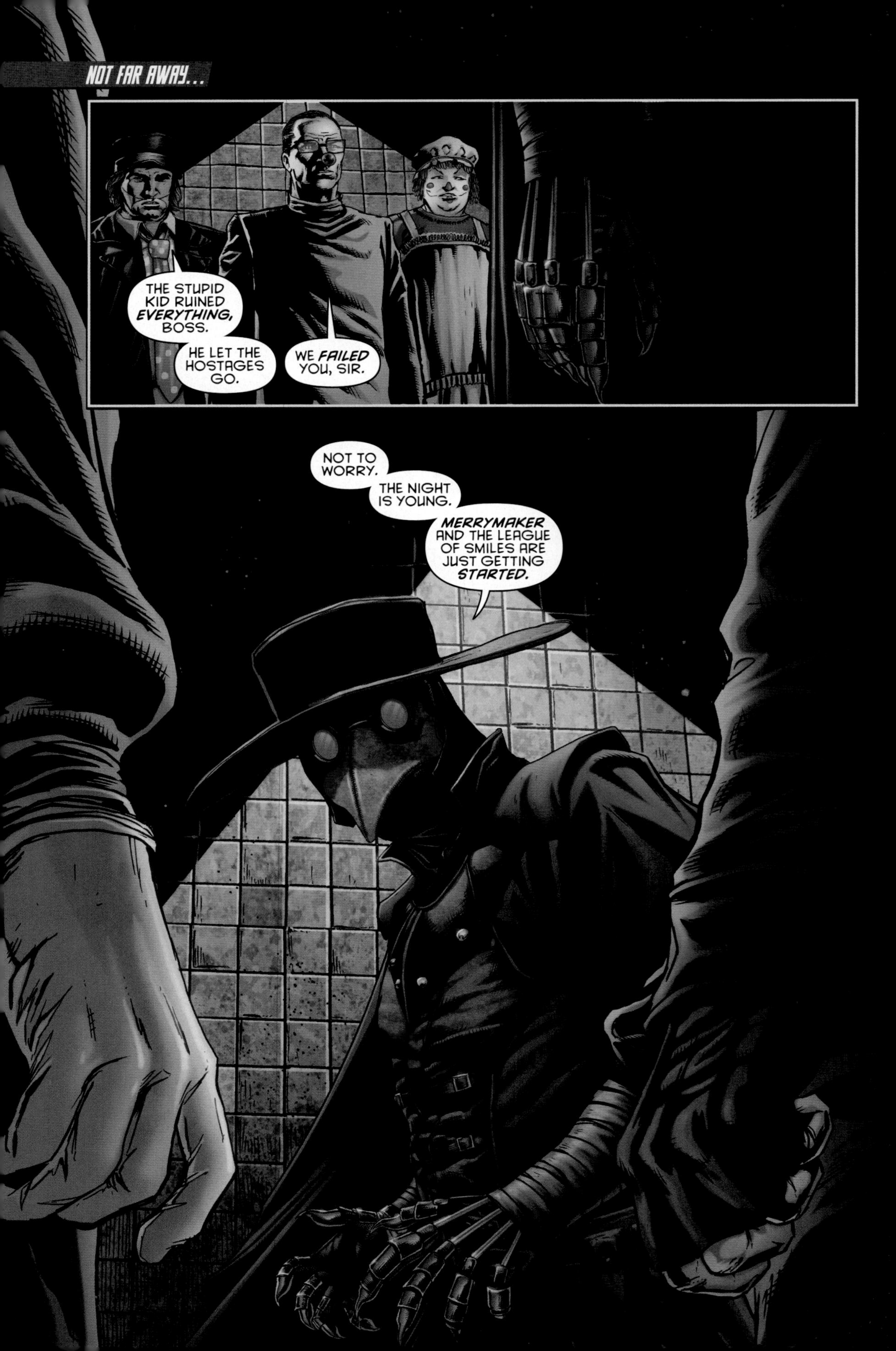
NOT FAR AWAY...
THE STUPID KID RUINED EVERYTHING, BOSS.
HE LET THE HOSTAGES GO.
WE FAILED YOU, SIR.
NOT TO WORRY.
THE NIGHT IS YOUNG.
MERRYMAKER AND THE LEAGUE OF SMILES ARE JUST GETTING STARTED.

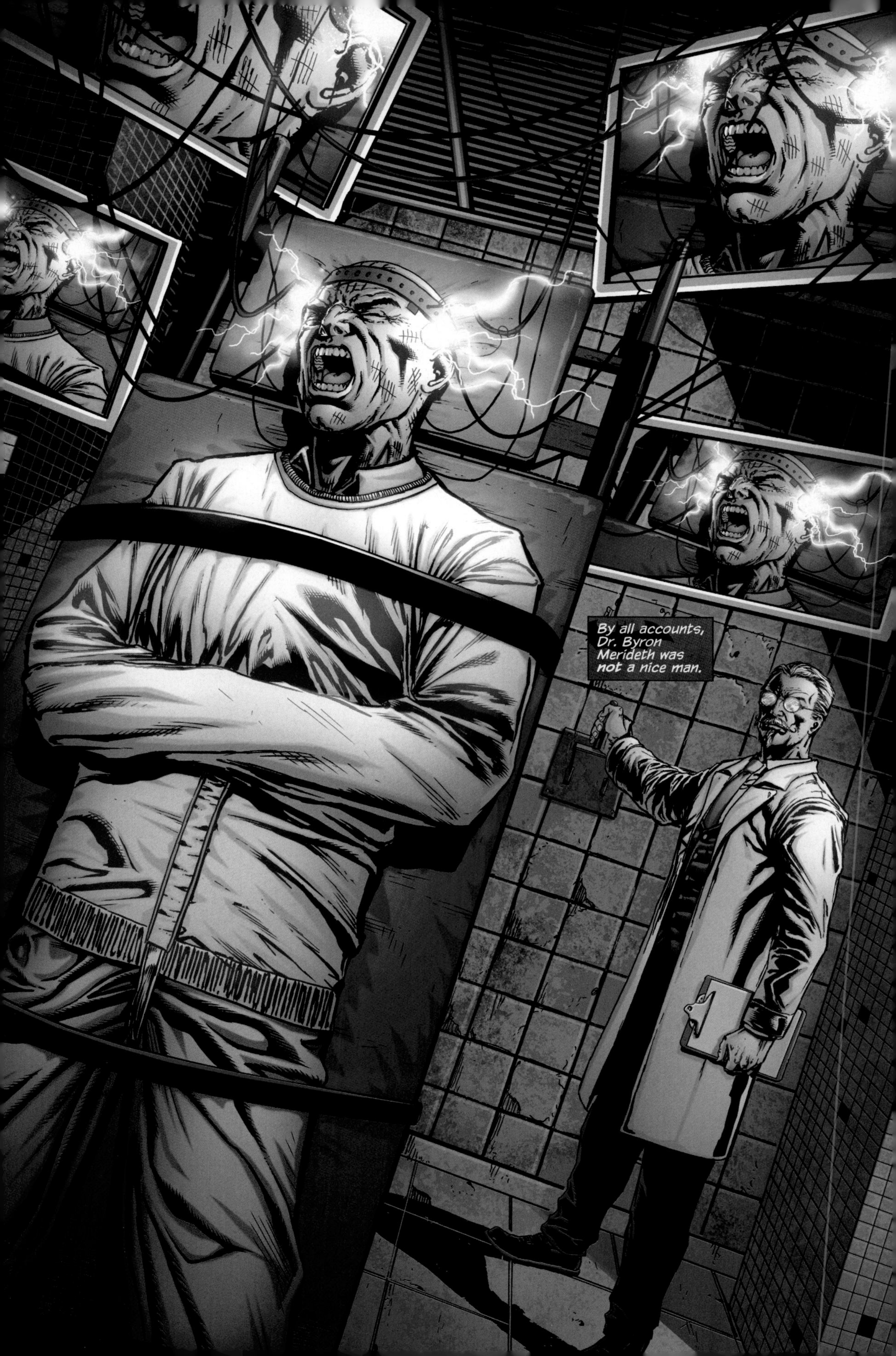
By all accounts, Dr. Byron Merideth was not a nice man.

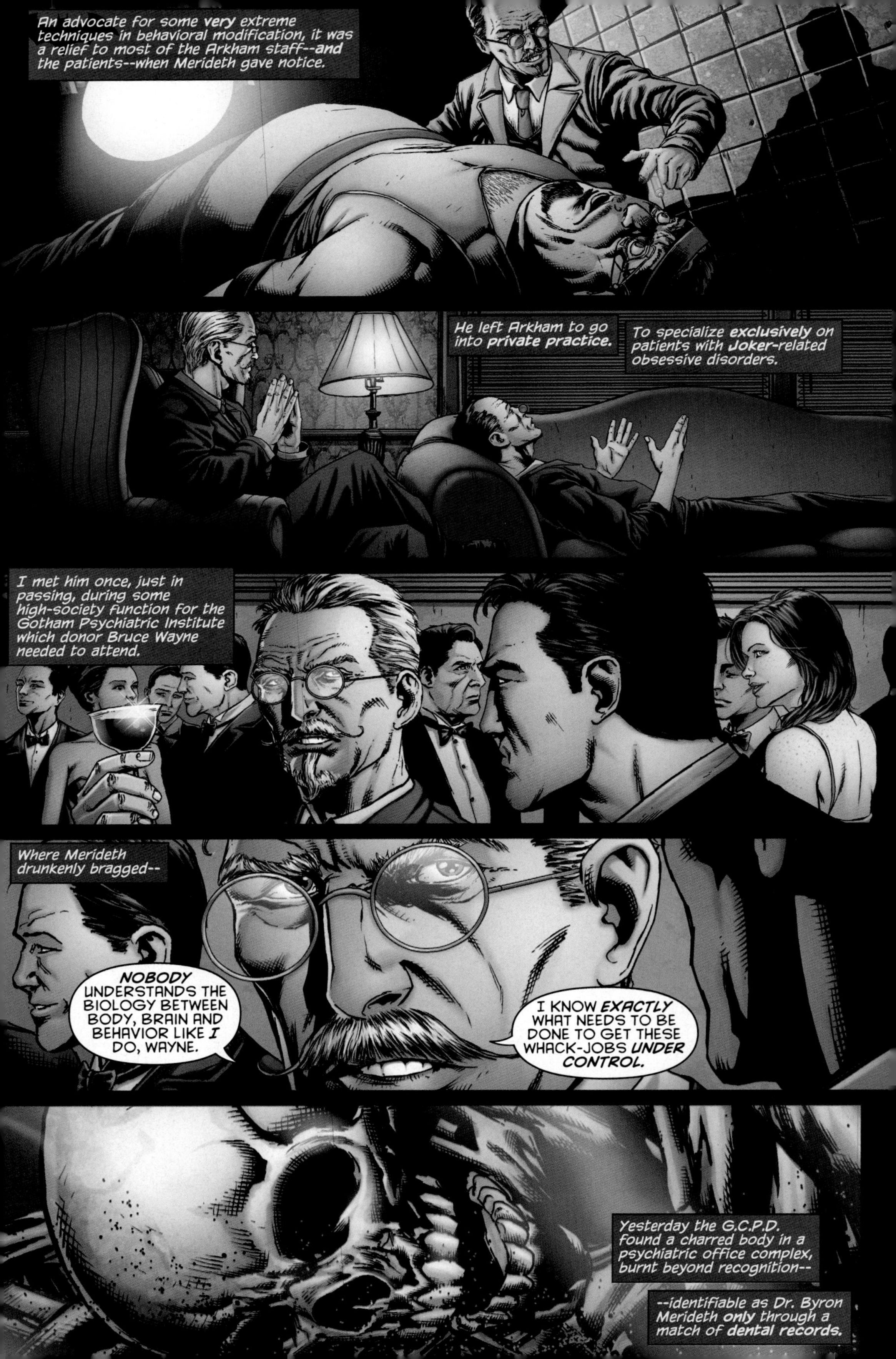
An advocate for some **very** extreme techniques in behavioral modification, it was a relief to most of the Arkham staff--**and** the patients--when Merideth gave notice.
He left Arkham to go into **private practice.**
To specialize **exclusively** on patients with **Joker**-related obsessive disorders.
I met him once, just in passing, during some high-society function for the Gotham Psychiatric Institute which donor Bruce Wayne needed to attend.
Where Merideth drunkenly bragged--
NOBODY UNDERSTANDS THE BIOLOGY BETWEEN BODY, BRAIN AND BEHAVIOR LIKE ***I*** DO, WAYNE.
I KNOW ***EXACTLY*** WHAT NEEDS TO BE DONE TO GET THESE WHACK-JOBS ***UNDER CONTROL.***
Yesterday the G.C.P.D. found a charred body in a psychiatric office complex, burnt beyond recognition--
--identifiable as Dr. Byron Merideth **only** through a match of **dental records.**

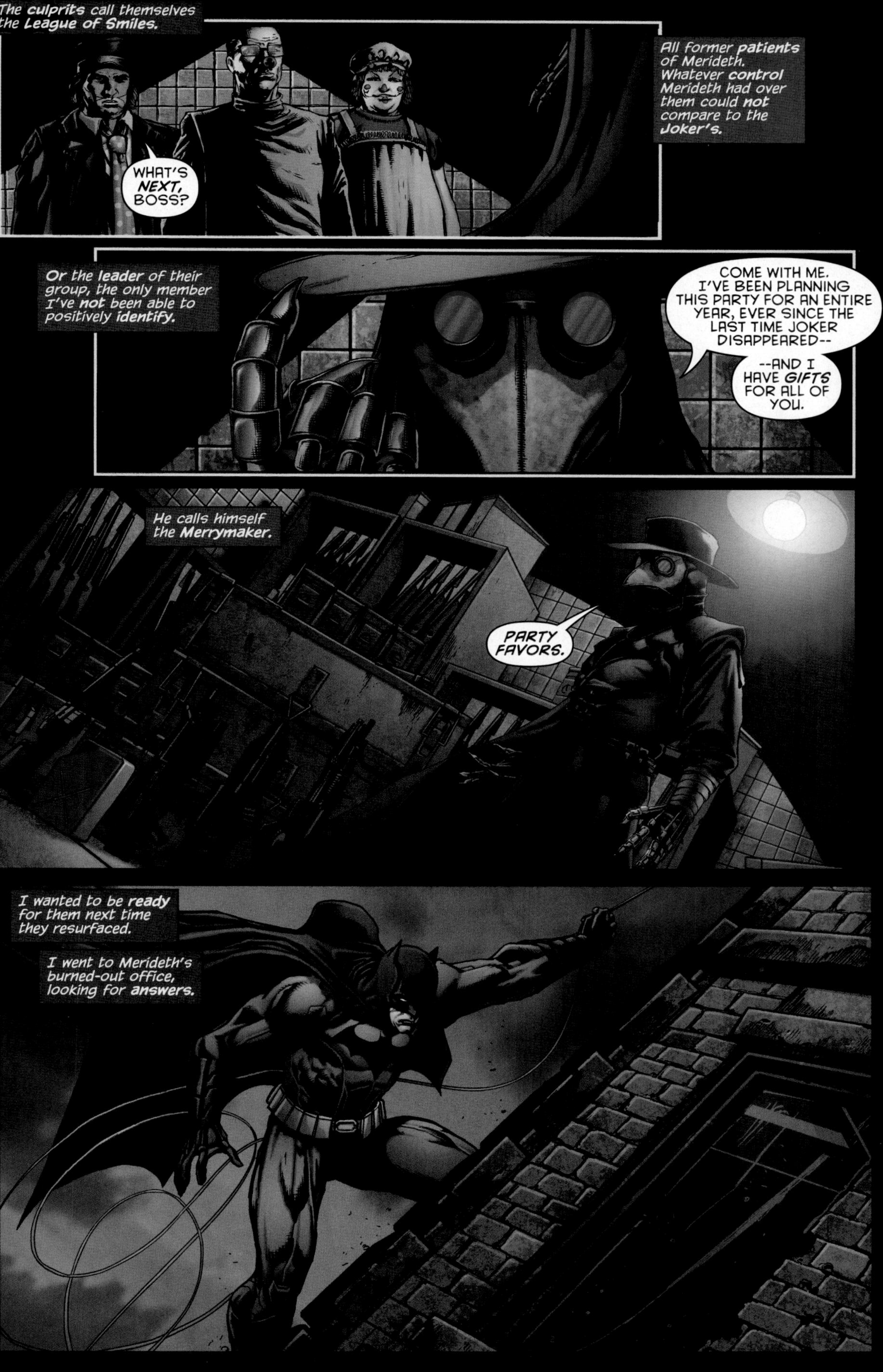

The culprits call themselves the League of Smiles.
All former patients of Merideth. Whatever control Merideth had over them could not compare to the Joker's.
WHAT'S NEXT, BOSS?
Or the leader of their group, the only member I've not been able to positively identify.
COME WITH ME. I'VE BEEN PLANNING THIS PARTY FOR AN ENTIRE YEAR, EVER SINCE THE LAST TIME JOKER DISAPPEARED--
--AND I HAVE GIFTS FOR ALL OF YOU.
He calls himself the Merrymaker.
PARTY FAVORS.
I wanted to be ready for them next time they resurfaced.
I went to Merideth's burned-out office, looking for answers.

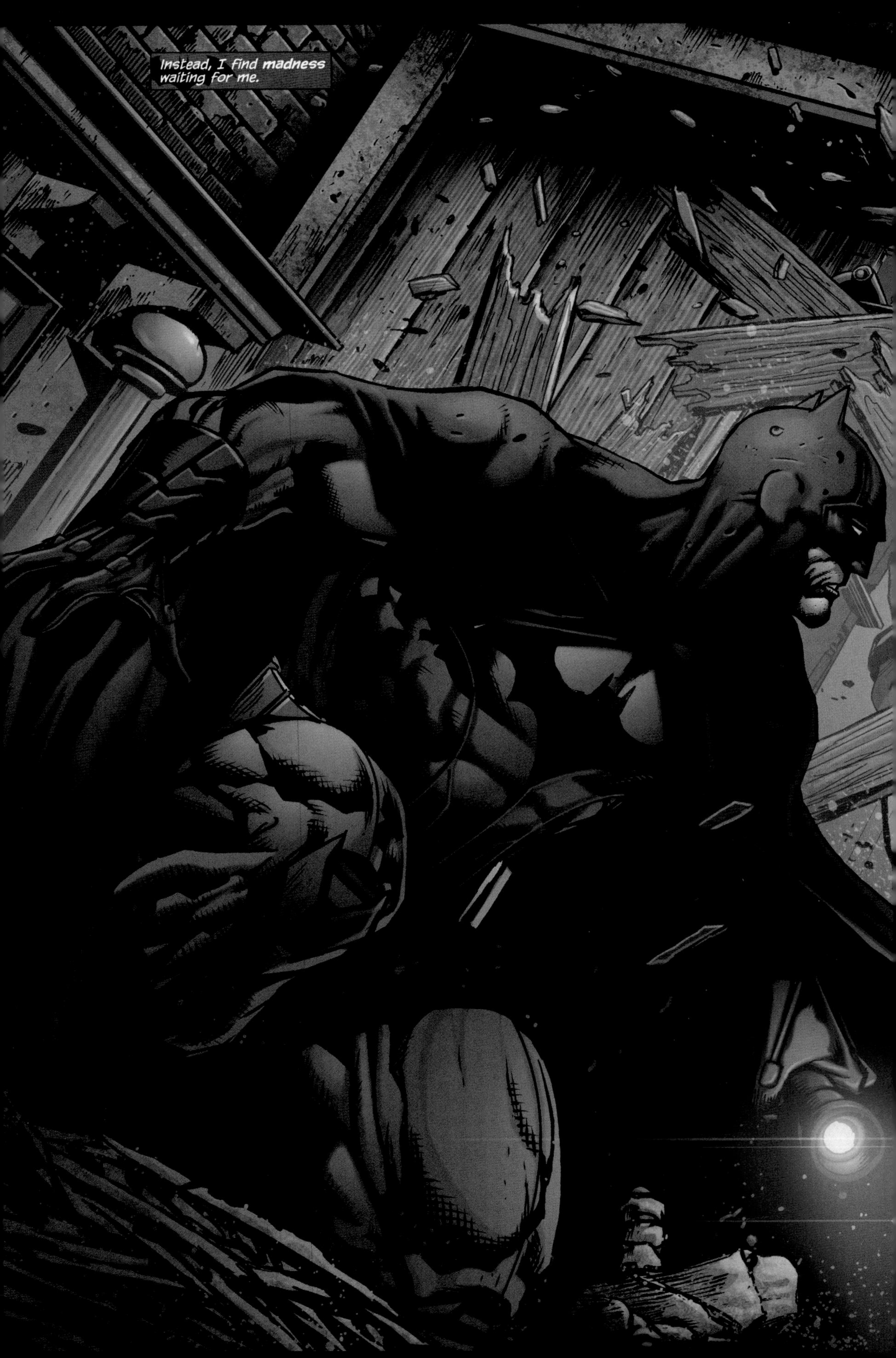
Instead, I find madness waiting for me.

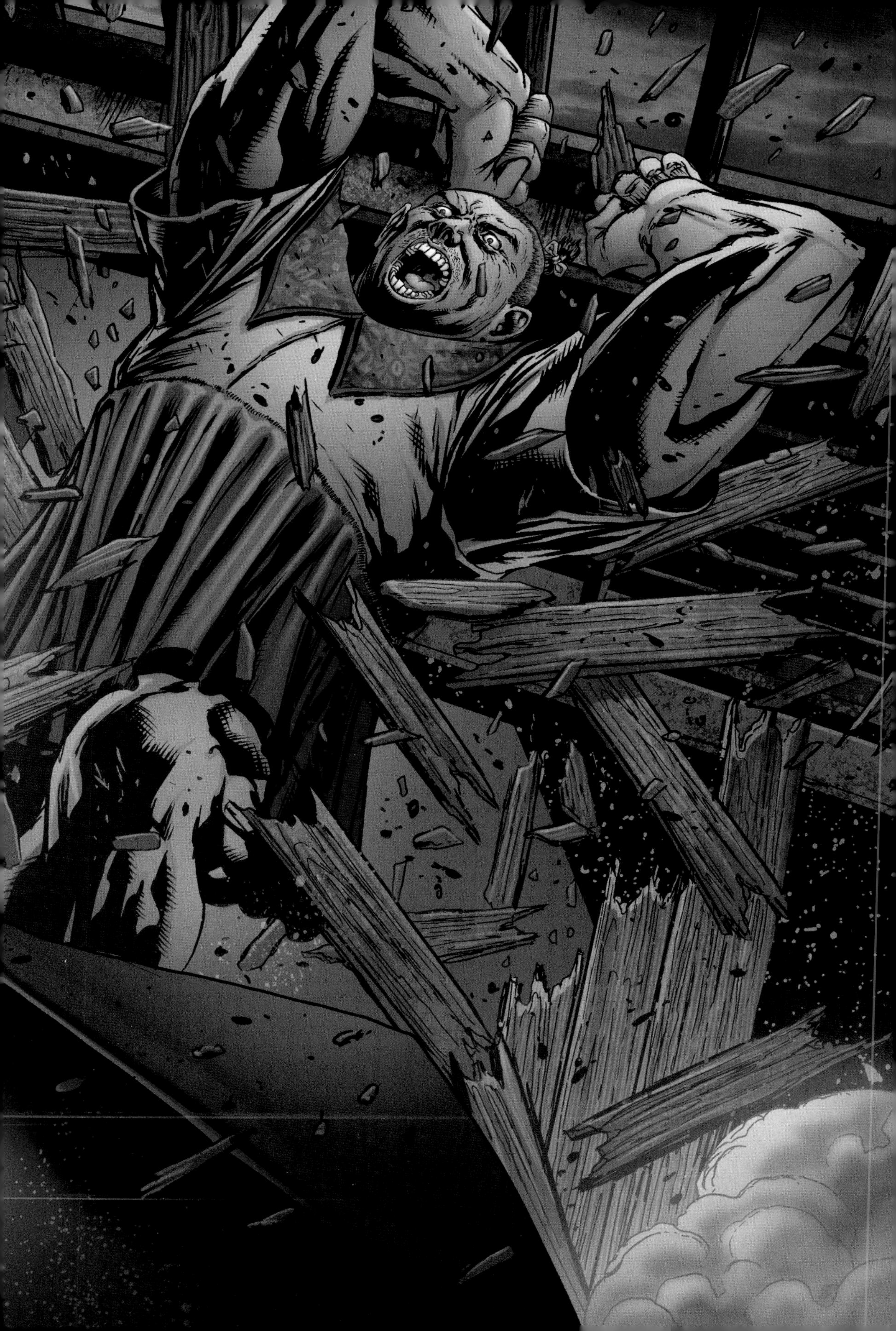

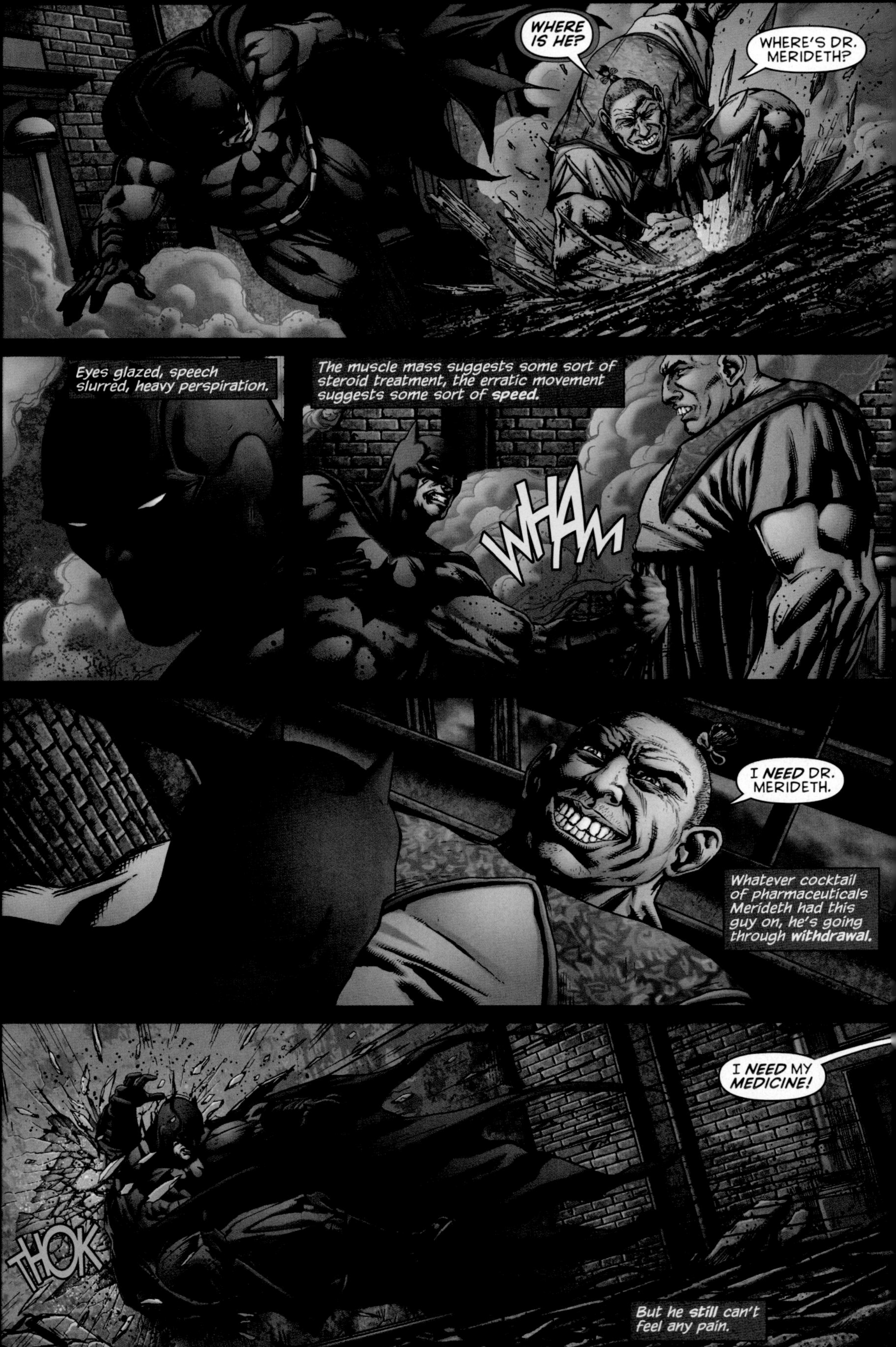
WHERE IS HE?
WHERE'S DR. MERIDETH?
Eyes glazed, speech slurred, heavy perspiration.
The muscle mass suggests some sort of steroid treatment, the erratic movement suggests some sort of **speed**.
WHAM
I **NEED** DR. MERIDETH.
Whatever cocktail of pharmaceuticals Merideth had this guy on, he's going through **withdrawal**.
I **NEED** MY **MEDICINE!**
THOK
But he **still** can't feel any pain.

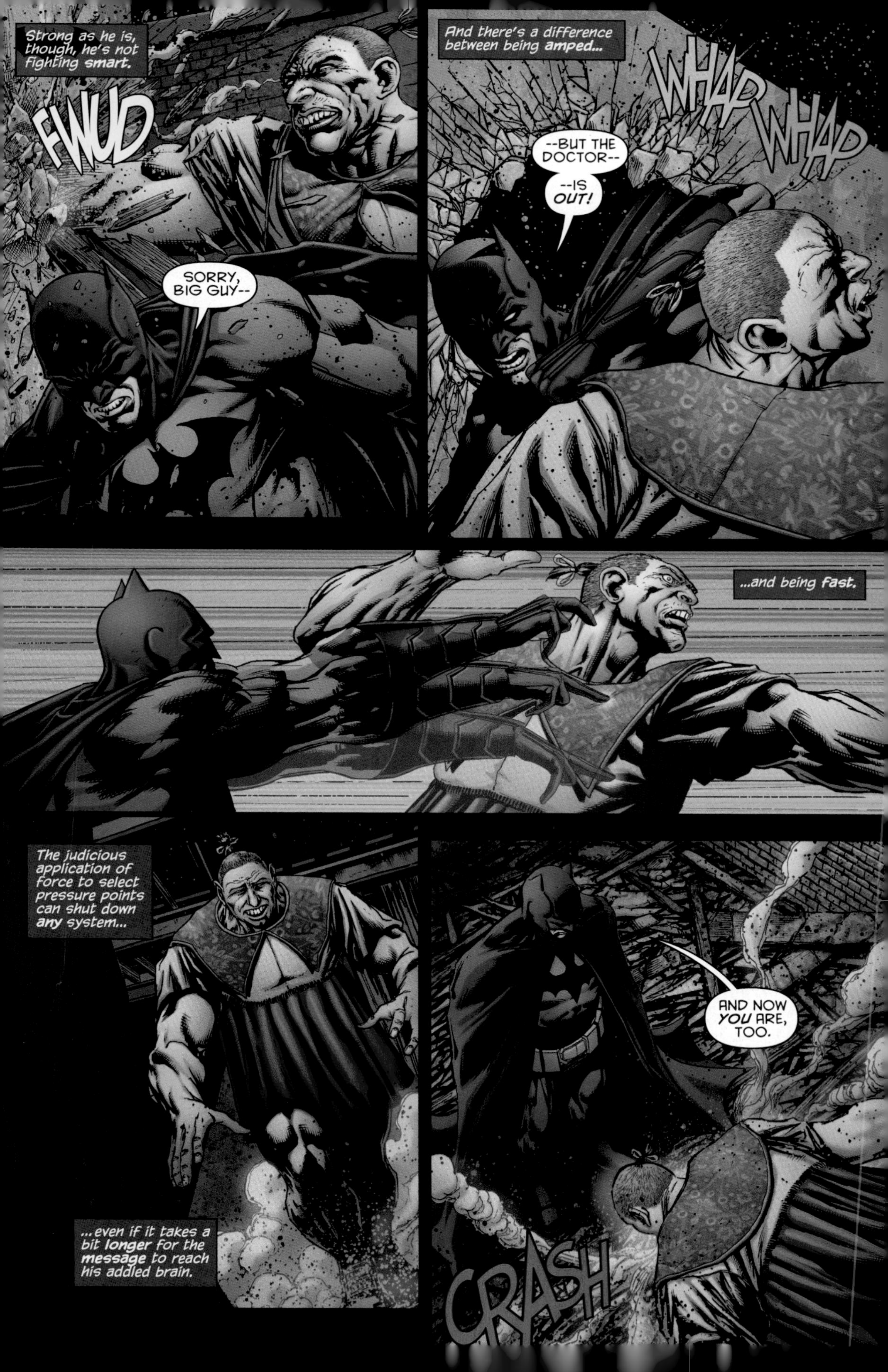
Strong as he is, though, he's not fighting smart.
FWUD
SORRY, BIG GUY--
And there's a difference between being amped...
WHAP WHAP
--BUT THE DOCTOR--
--IS OUT!
...and being fast.
The judicious application of force to select pressure points can shut down any system...
...even if it takes a bit longer for the message to reach his addled brain.
AND NOW YOU ARE, TOO.
CRASH

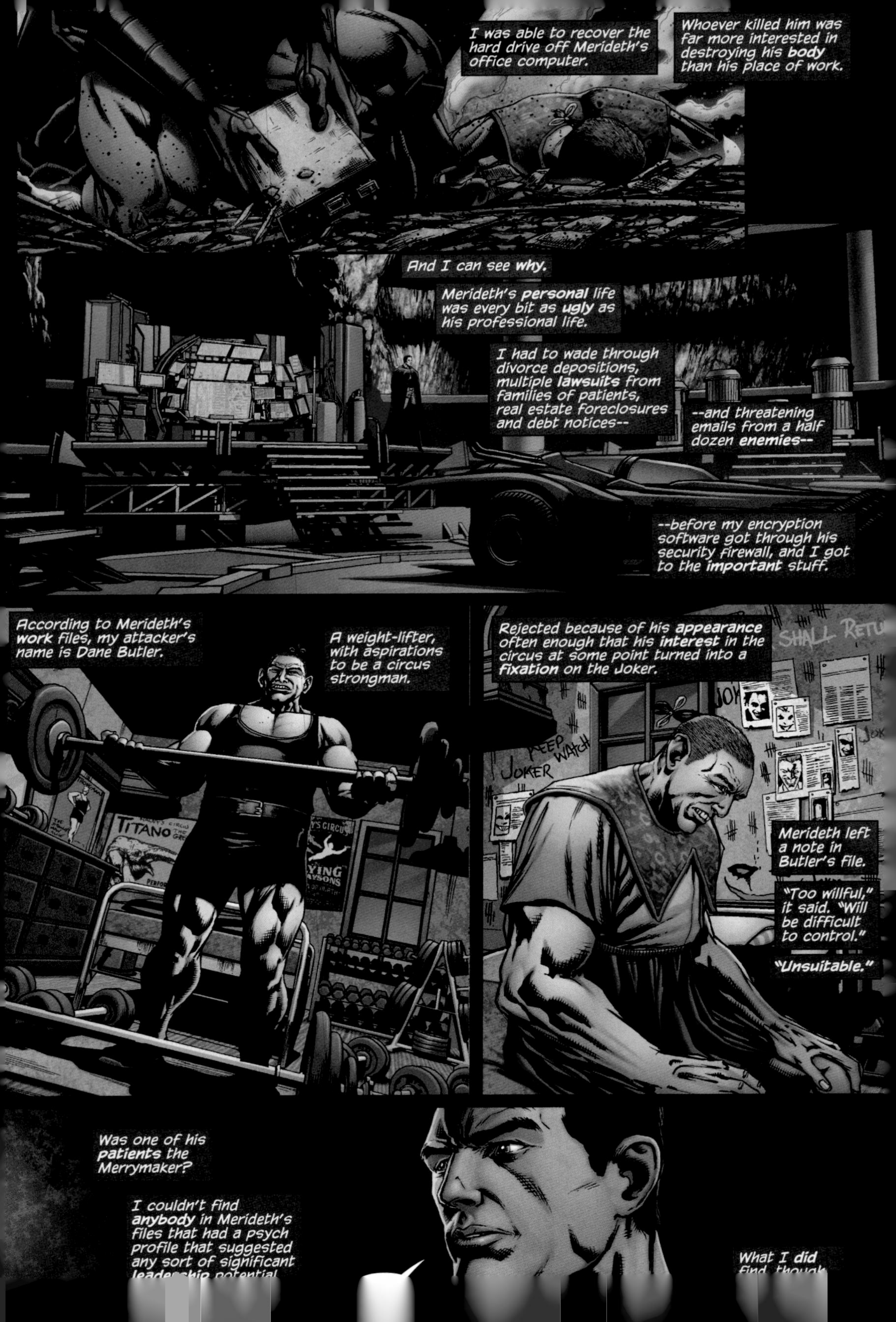

I was able to recover the hard drive off Merideth's office computer.
Whoever killed him was far more interested in destroying his **body** than his place of work.
And I can see **why.**
Merideth's **personal** life was every bit as **ugly** as his professional life.
I had to wade through divorce depositions, multiple **lawsuits** from families of patients, real estate foreclosures and debt notices--
--and threatening emails from a half dozen **enemies--**
--before my encryption software got through his security firewall, and I got to the **important** stuff.
According to Merideth's **work** files, my attacker's name is Dane Butler.
A weight-lifter, with aspirations to be a circus strongman.
TITANO
Rejected because of his **appearance** often enough that his **interest** in the circus at some point turned into a **fixation** on the Joker.
KEEP WATCH
JOKER
Merideth left a note in Butler's file.
"Too willful," it said. "Will be difficult to control."
"Unsuitable."
Was one of his **patients** the Merrymaker?
I couldn't find **anybody** in Merideth's files that had a psych profile that suggested any sort of significant
What I **did**

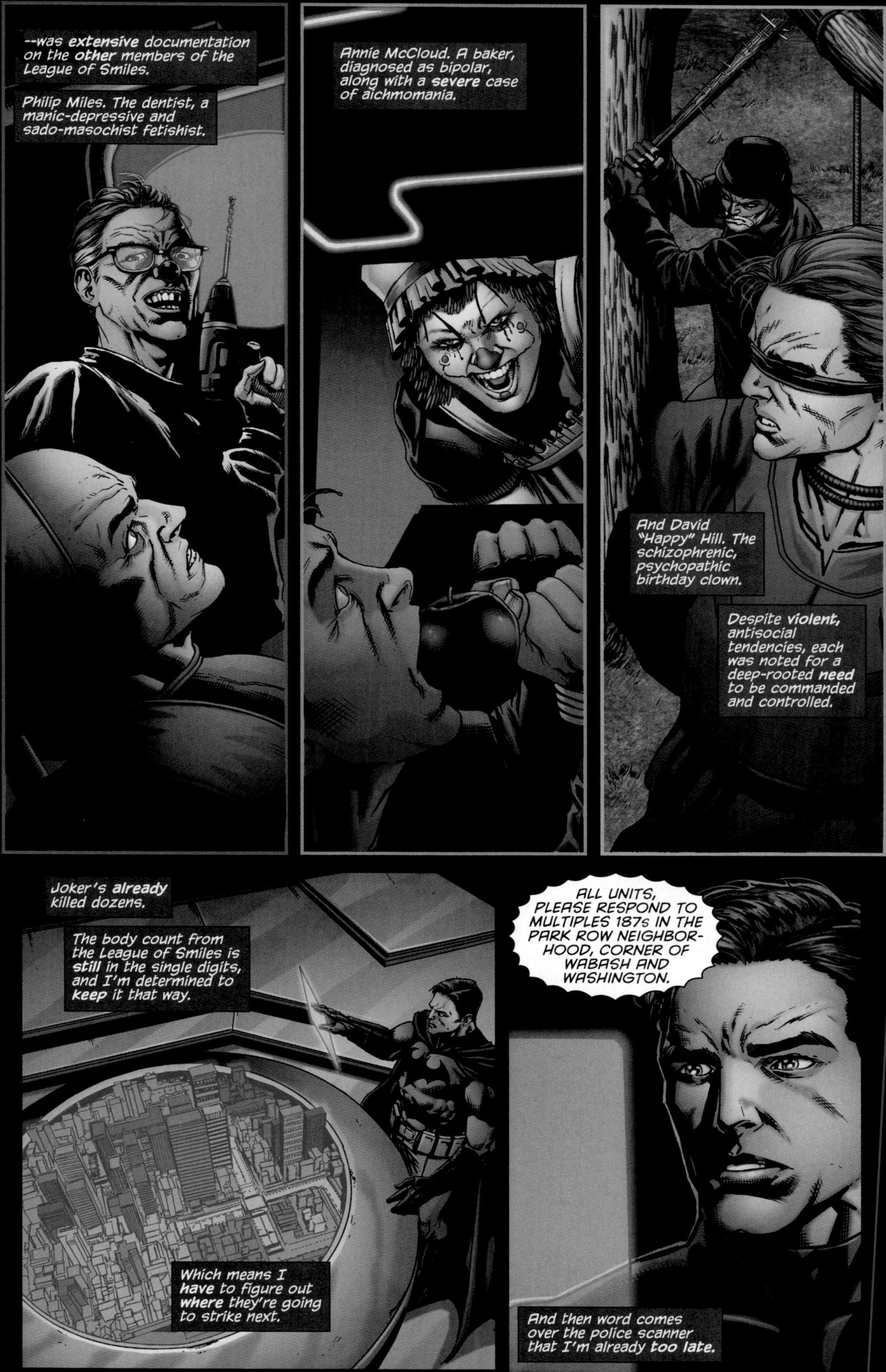
--was extensive documentation on the other members of the League of Smiles.
Philip Miles. The dentist, a manic-depressive and sado-masochist fetishist.
Annie McCloud. A baker, diagnosed as bipolar, along with a severe case of aichmomania.
And David "Happy" Hill. The schizophrenic, psychopathic birthday clown.
Despite violent, antisocial tendencies, each was noted for a deep-rooted need to be commanded and controlled.
Joker's already killed dozens.
The body count from the League of Smiles is still in the single digits, and I'm determined to keep it that way.
Which means I have to figure out where they're going to strike next.
ALL UNITS, PLEASE RESPOND TO MULTIPLES 187s IN THE PARK ROW NEIGHBORHOOD, CORNER OF WABASH AND WASHINGTON.
And then word comes over the police scanner that I'm already too late.

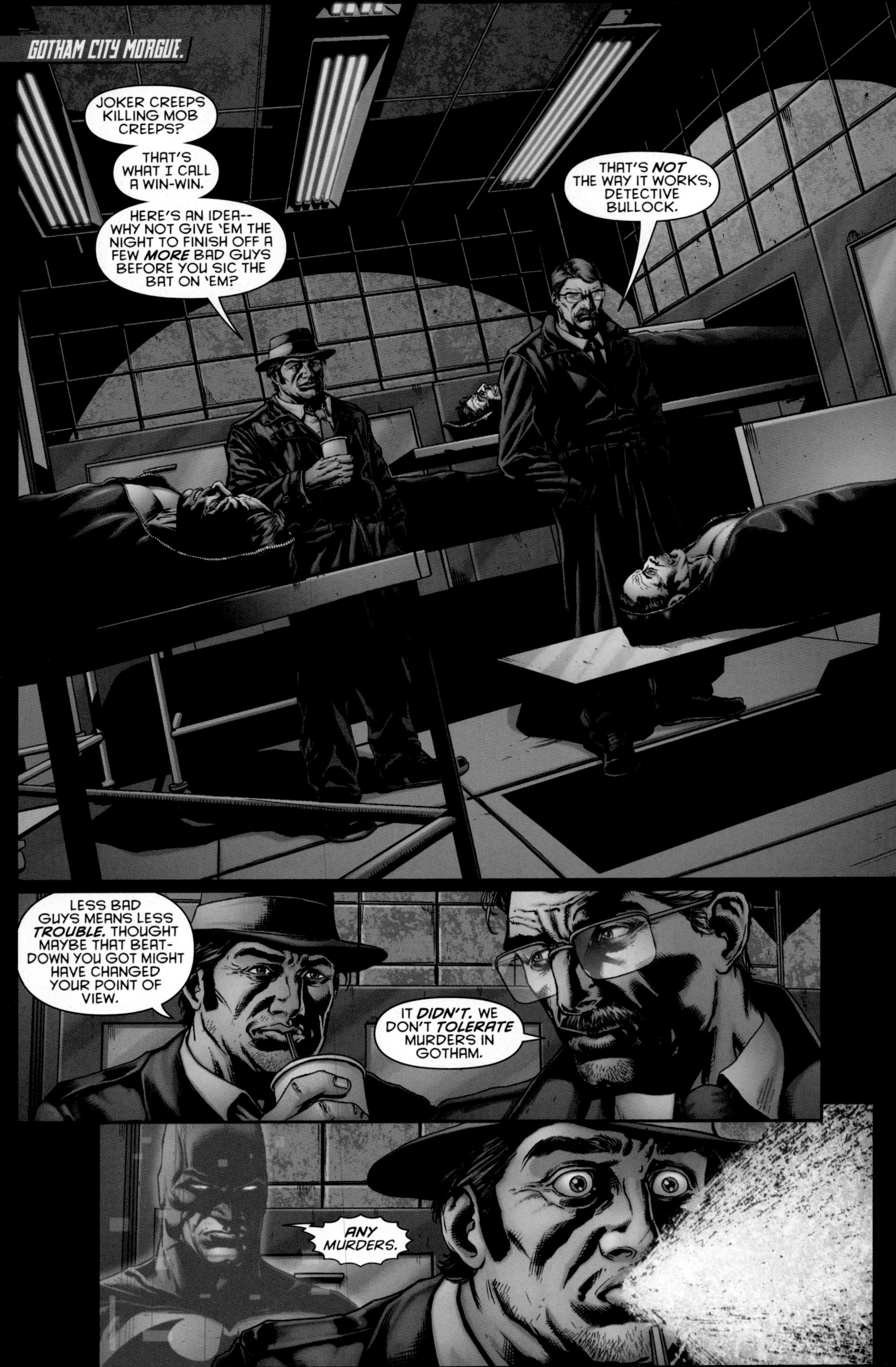
GOTHAM CITY MORGUE.
JOKER CREEPS KILLING MOB CREEPS?
THAT'S WHAT I CALL A WIN-WIN.
HERE'S AN IDEA-- WHY NOT GIVE 'EM THE NIGHT TO FINISH OFF A FEW MORE BAD GUYS BEFORE YOU SIC THE BAT ON 'EM?
THAT'S NOT THE WAY IT WORKS, DETECTIVE BULLOCK.
LESS BAD GUYS MEANS LESS TROUBLE. THOUGHT MAYBE THAT BEAT-DOWN YOU GOT MIGHT HAVE CHANGED YOUR POINT OF VIEW.
IT DIDN'T. WE DON'T TOLERATE MURDERS IN GOTHAM.
ANY MURDERS.

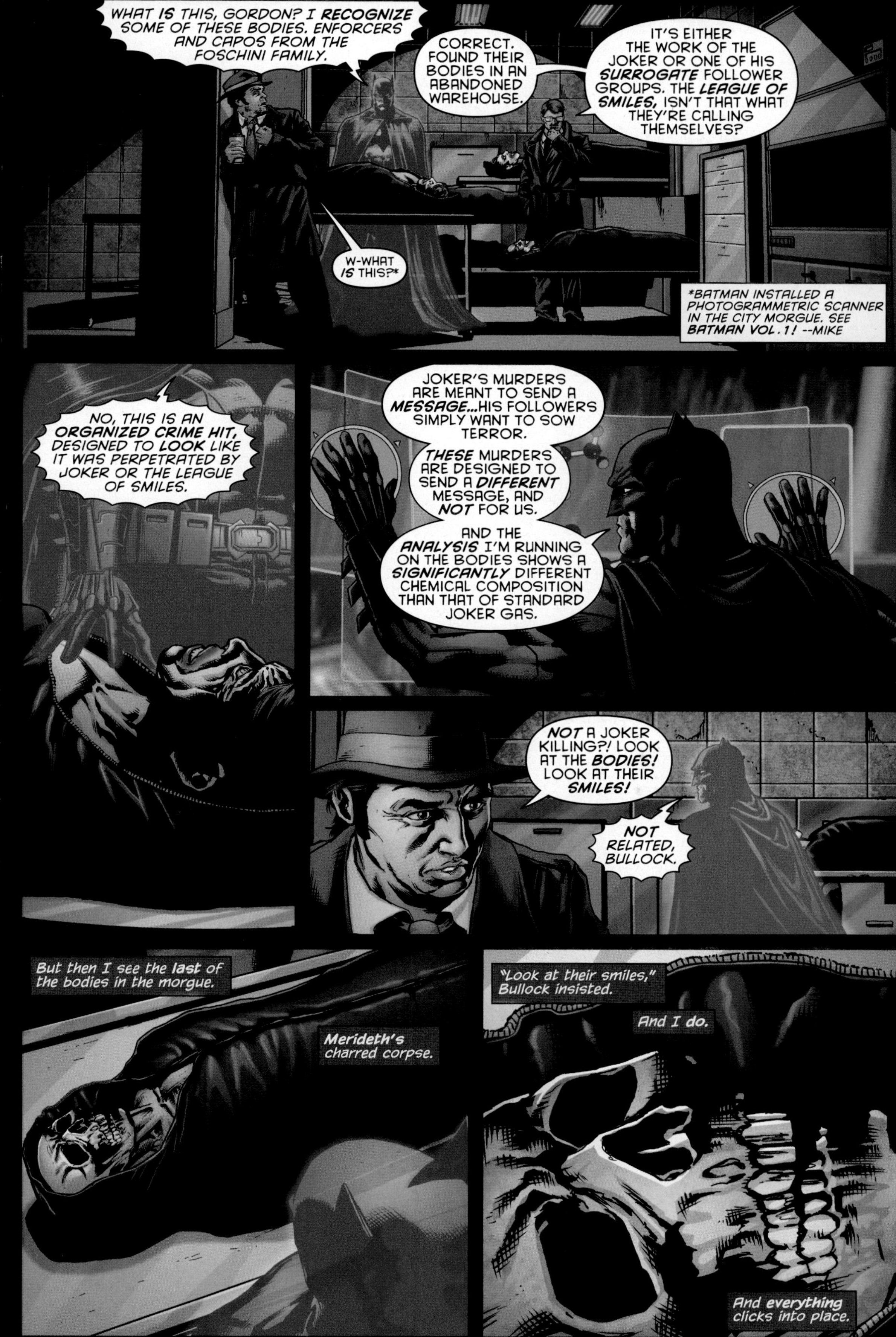
WHAT IS THIS, GORDON? I RECOGNIZE SOME OF THESE BODIES. ENFORCERS AND CAPOS FROM THE FOSCHINI FAMILY.
CORRECT. FOUND THEIR BODIES IN AN ABANDONED WAREHOUSE.
IT'S EITHER THE WORK OF THE JOKER OR ONE OF HIS SURROGATE FOLLOWER GROUPS. THE LEAGUE OF SMILES, ISN'T THAT WHAT THEY'RE CALLING THEMSELVES?
W-WHAT IS THIS?*
*BATMAN INSTALLED A PHOTOGRAMMETRIC SCANNER IN THE CITY MORGUE. SEE BATMAN VOL.1! --MIKE
NO, THIS IS AN ORGANIZED CRIME HIT, DESIGNED TO LOOK LIKE IT WAS PERPETRATED BY JOKER OR THE LEAGUE OF SMILES.
JOKER'S MURDERS ARE MEANT TO SEND A MESSAGE...HIS FOLLOWERS SIMPLY WANT TO SOW TERROR.
THESE MURDERS ARE DESIGNED TO SEND A DIFFERENT MESSAGE, AND NOT FOR US.
AND THE ANALYSIS I'M RUNNING ON THE BODIES SHOWS A SIGNIFICANTLY DIFFERENT CHEMICAL COMPOSITION THAN THAT OF STANDARD JOKER GAS.
NOT A JOKER KILLING?! LOOK AT THE BODIES! LOOK AT THEIR SMILES!
NOT RELATED, BULLOCK.
But then I see the last of the bodies in the morgue.
Merideth's charred corpse.
"Look at their smiles," Bullock insisted.
And I do.
And everything clicks into place.

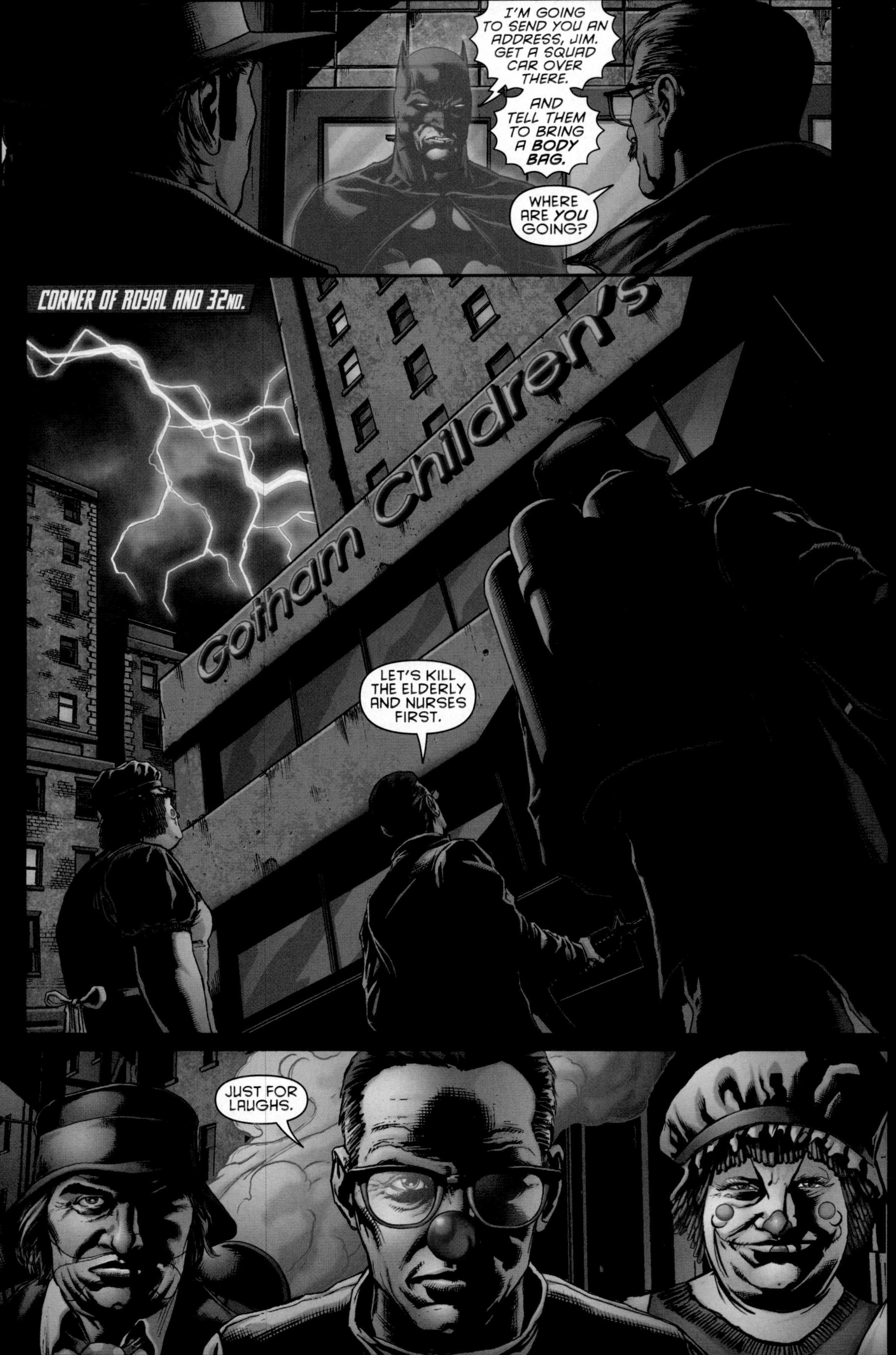
I'M GOING TO SEND YOU AN ADDRESS, JIM. GET A SQUAD CAR OVER THERE.
AND TELL THEM TO BRING A BODY BAG.
WHERE ARE YOU GOING?
CORNER OF ROYAL AND 32ND.
Gotham Children's
LET'S KILL THE ELDERLY AND NURSES FIRST.
JUST FOR LAUGHS.

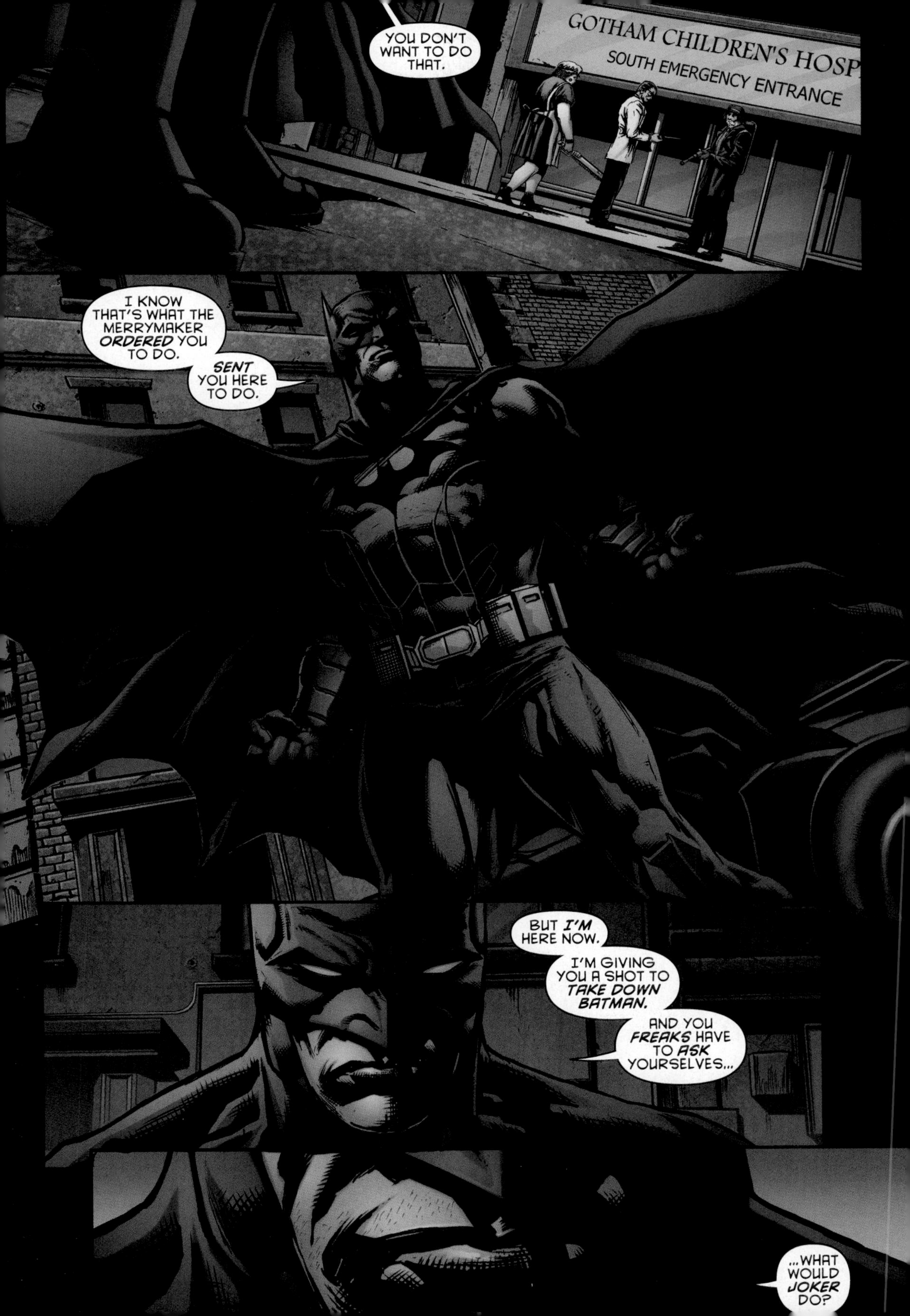
YOU DON'T WANT TO DO THAT.
GOTHAM CHILDREN'S HOSP
SOUTH EMERGENCY ENTRANCE
I KNOW THAT'S WHAT THE MERRYMAKER *ORDERED* YOU TO DO.
SENT YOU HERE TO DO.
BUT *I'M* HERE NOW.
I'M GIVING YOU A SHOT TO *TAKE DOWN BATMAN*.
AND YOU *FREAKS* HAVE TO *ASK* YOURSELVES...
...WHAT WOULD *JOKER* DO?

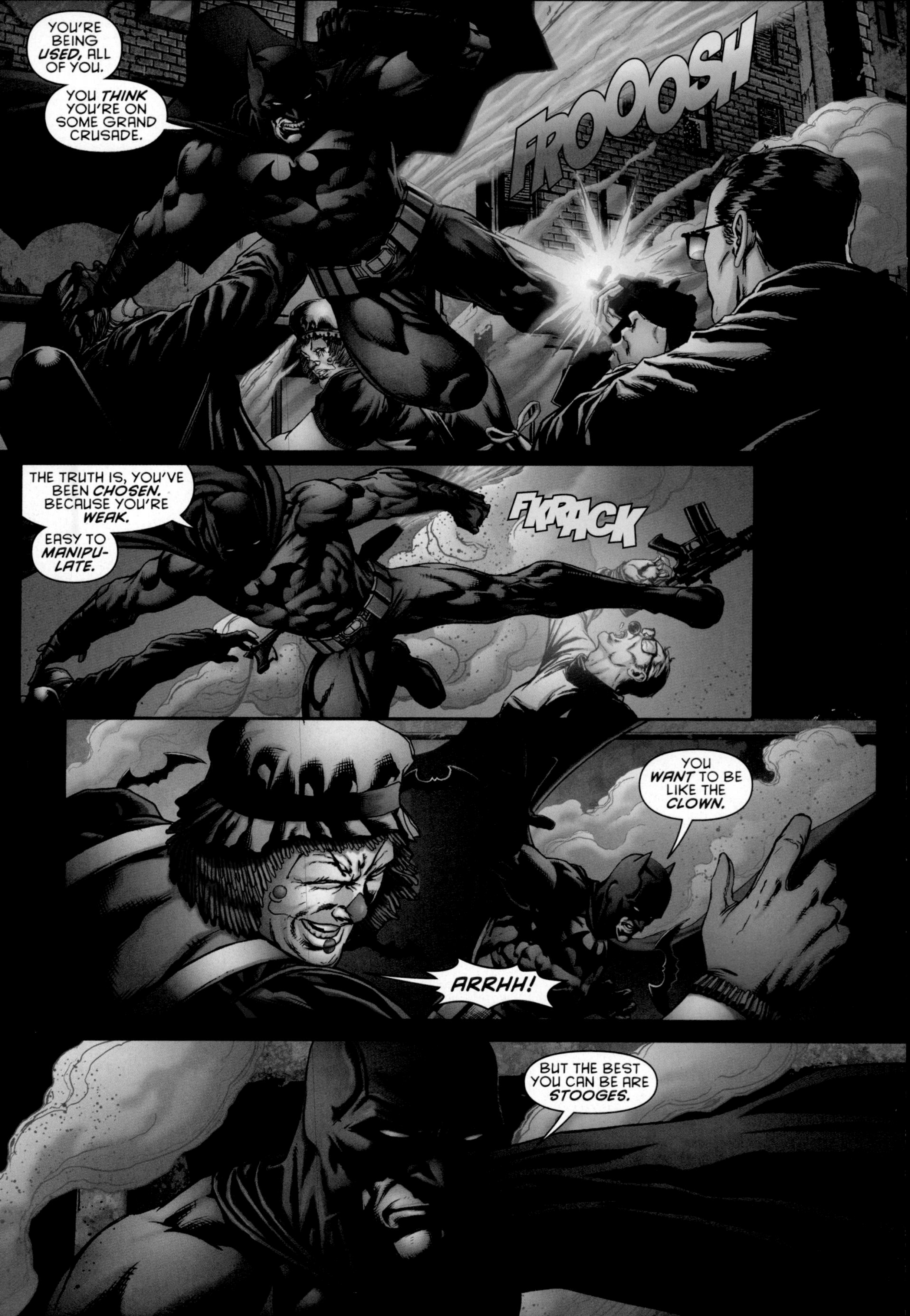

YOU'RE BEING USED, ALL OF YOU.
YOU THINK YOU'RE ON SOME GRAND CRUSADE.
FROOOSH
THE TRUTH IS, YOU'VE BEEN CHOSEN. BECAUSE YOU'RE WEAK.
EASY TO MANIPU-LATE.
FKRACK
YOU WANT TO BE LIKE THE CLOWN.
ARRHH!
BUT THE BEST YOU CAN BE ARE STOOGES.

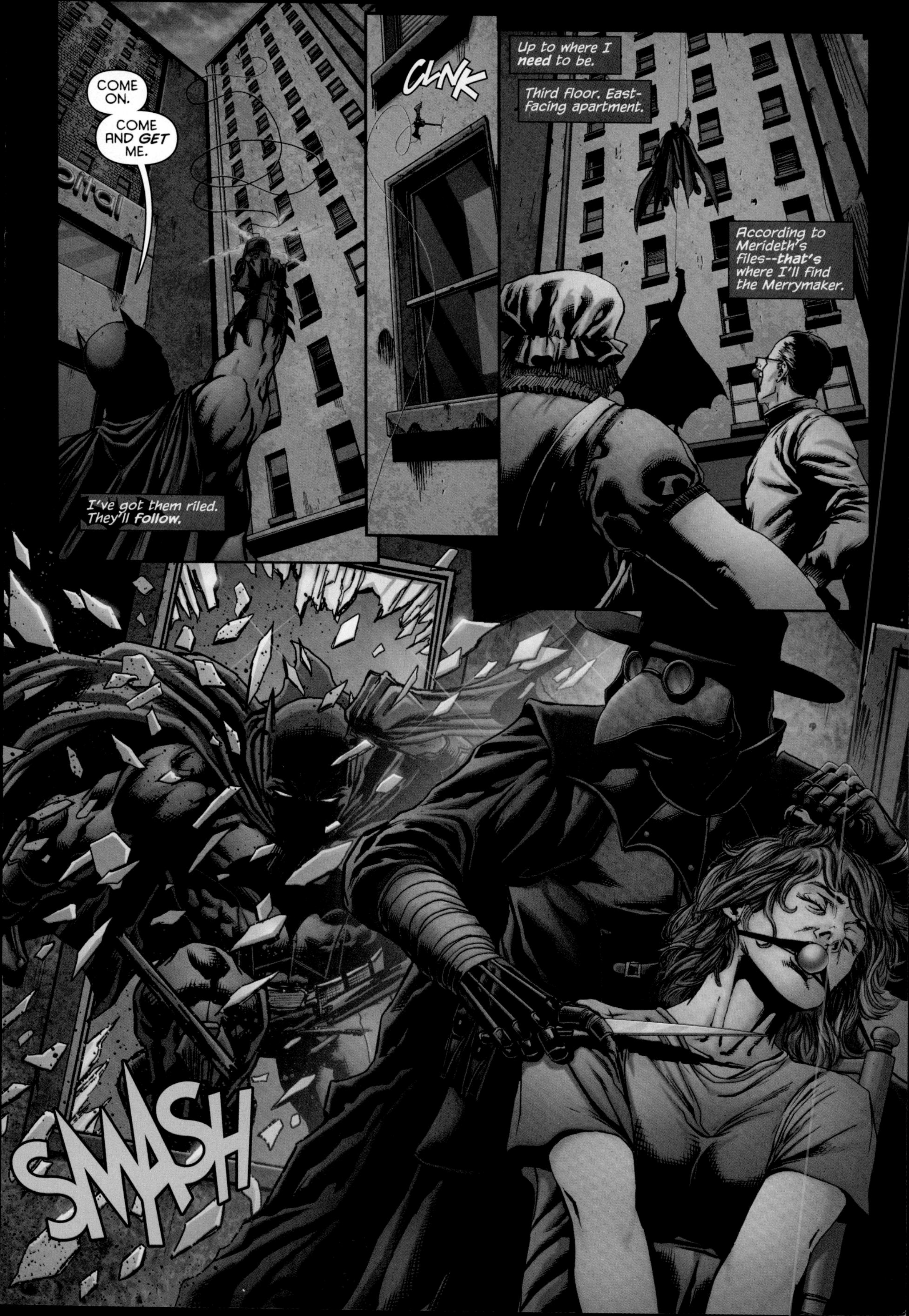
COME ON.
COME AND GET ME.
I've got them riled. They'll follow.
CLNK
Up to where I need to be.
Third floor. East-facing apartment.
According to Merideth's files--that's where I'll find the Merrymaker.
SMASH

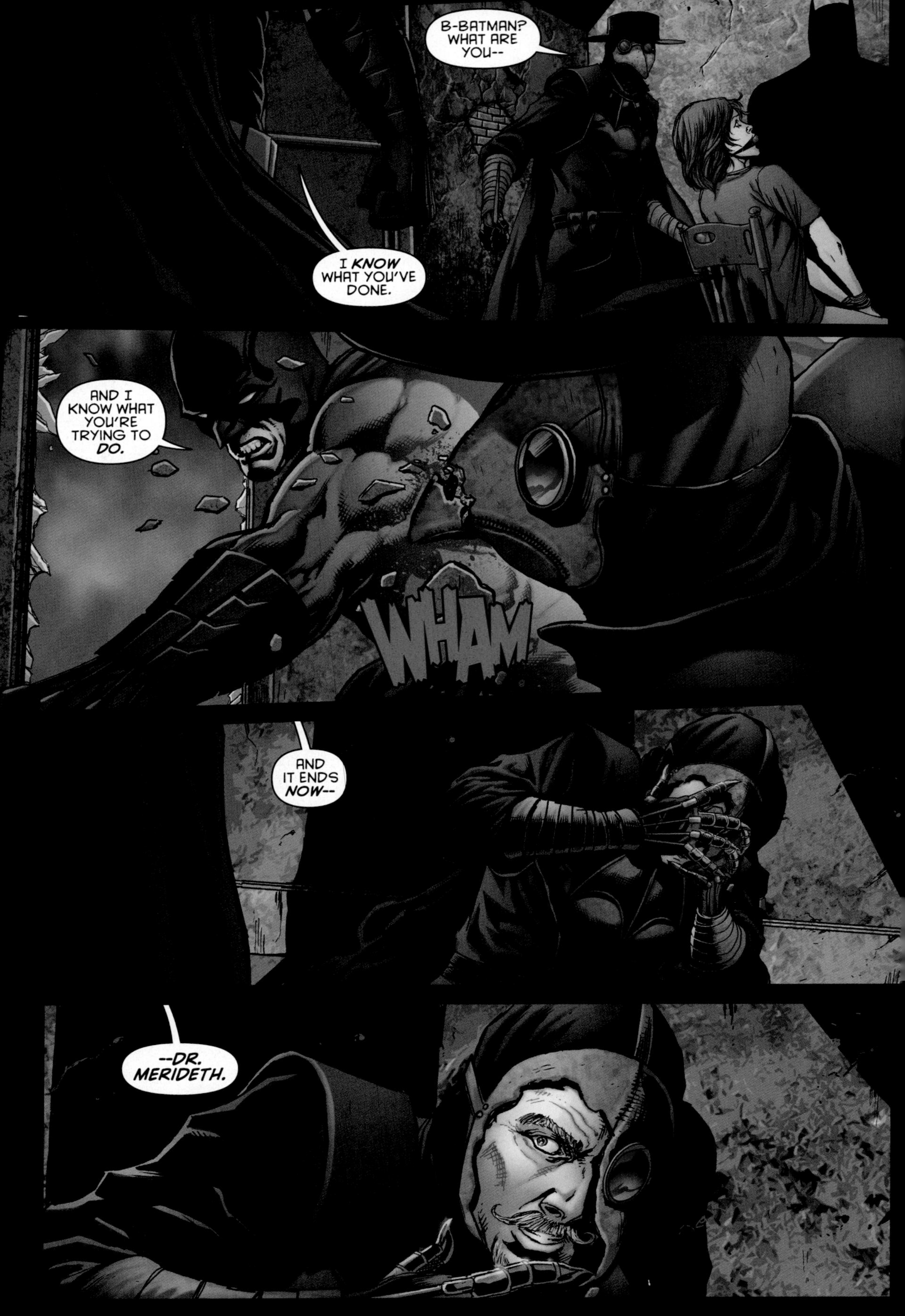
B-BATMAN? WHAT ARE YOU--
I KNOW WHAT YOU'VE DONE.
AND I KNOW WHAT YOU'RE TRYING TO DO.
WHAM
AND IT ENDS NOW--
--DR. MERIDETH.

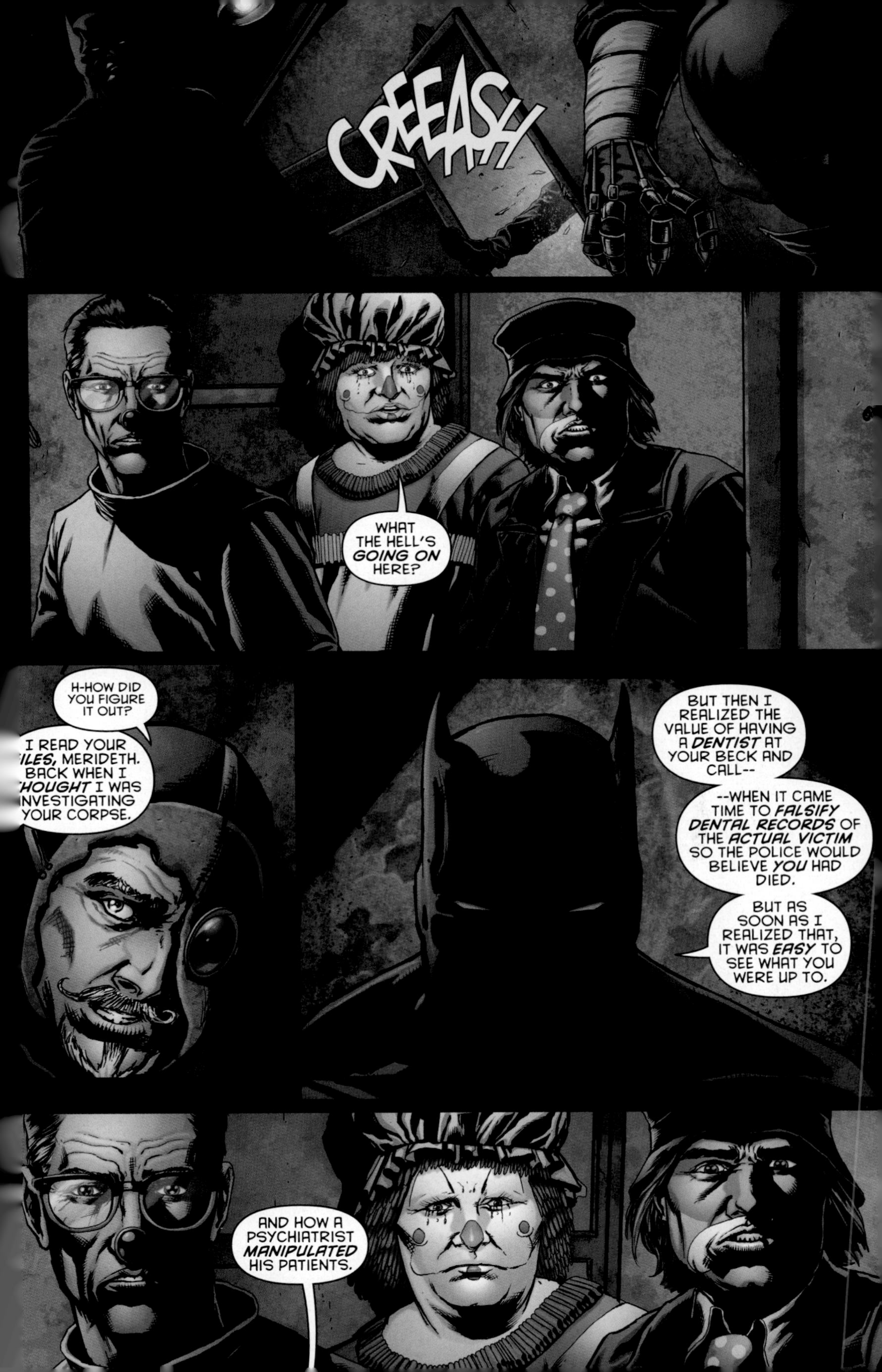

CREEASH
WHAT THE HELL'S GOING ON HERE?
H-HOW DID YOU FIGURE IT OUT?
I READ YOUR FILES, MERIDETH. BACK WHEN I THOUGHT I WAS INVESTIGATING YOUR CORPSE.
BUT THEN I REALIZED THE VALUE OF HAVING A DENTIST AT YOUR BECK AND CALL--
--WHEN IT CAME TIME TO FALSIFY DENTAL RECORDS OF THE ACTUAL VICTIM SO THE POLICE WOULD BELIEVE YOU HAD DIED.
BUT AS SOON AS I REALIZED THAT, IT WAS EASY TO SEE WHAT YOU WERE UP TO.
AND HOW A PSYCHIATRIST MANIPULATED HIS PATIENTS.

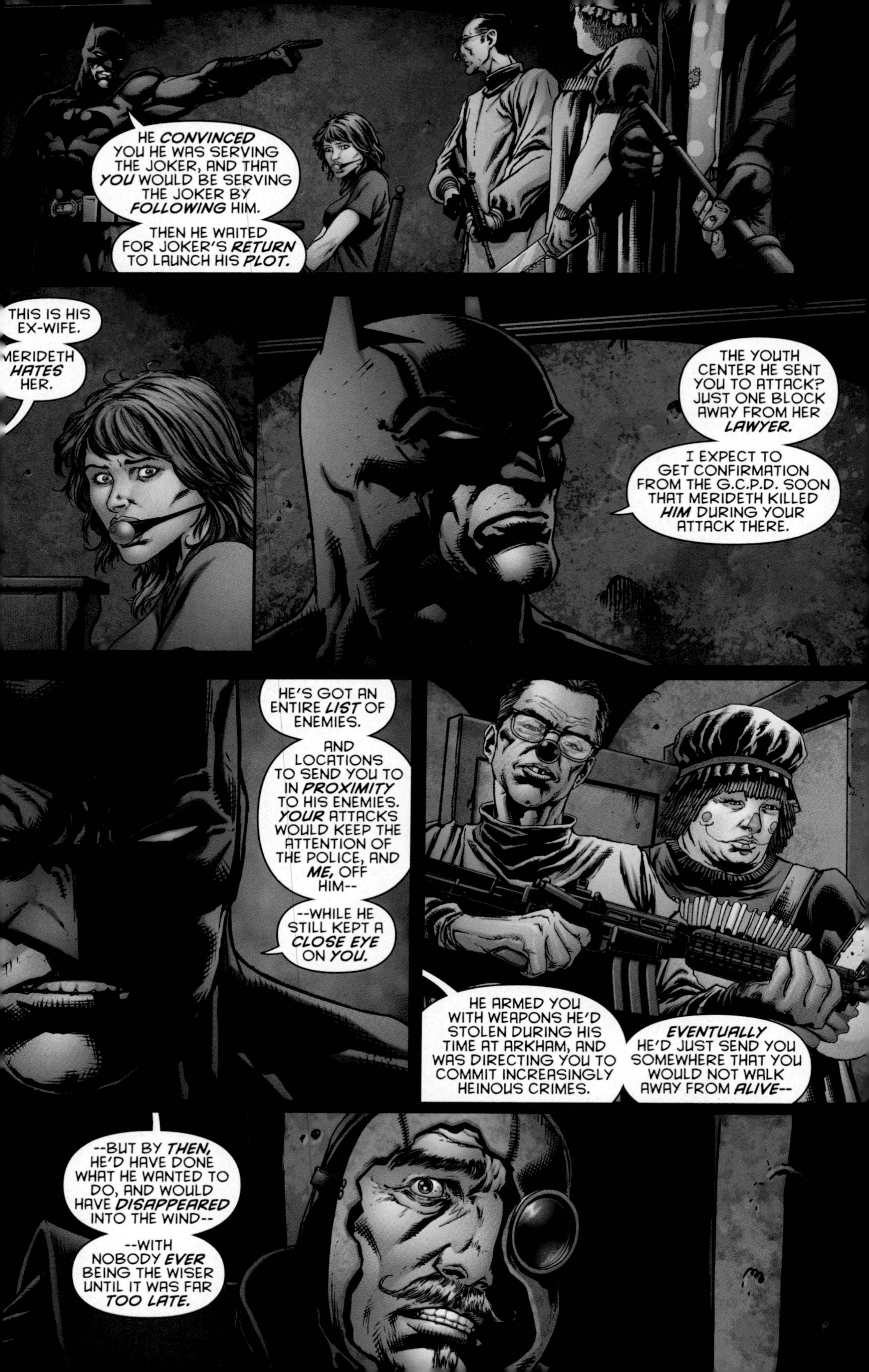
HE CONVINCED YOU HE WAS SERVING THE JOKER, AND THAT YOU WOULD BE SERVING THE JOKER BY FOLLOWING HIM.
THEN HE WAITED FOR JOKER'S RETURN TO LAUNCH HIS PLOT.
THIS IS HIS EX-WIFE.
MERIDETH HATES HER.
THE YOUTH CENTER HE SENT YOU TO ATTACK? JUST ONE BLOCK AWAY FROM HER LAWYER.
I EXPECT TO GET CONFIRMATION FROM THE G.C.P.D. SOON THAT MERIDETH KILLED HIM DURING YOUR ATTACK THERE.
HE'S GOT AN ENTIRE LIST OF ENEMIES.
AND LOCATIONS TO SEND YOU TO IN PROXIMITY TO HIS ENEMIES. YOUR ATTACKS WOULD KEEP THE ATTENTION OF THE POLICE, AND ME, OFF HIM--
--WHILE HE STILL KEPT A CLOSE EYE ON YOU.
HE ARMED YOU WITH WEAPONS HE'D STOLEN DURING HIS TIME AT ARKHAM, AND WAS DIRECTING YOU TO COMMIT INCREASINGLY HEINOUS CRIMES.
EVENTUALLY HE'D JUST SEND YOU SOMEWHERE THAT YOU WOULD NOT WALK AWAY FROM ALIVE--
--BUT BY THEN, HE'D HAVE DONE WHAT HE WANTED TO DO, AND WOULD HAVE DISAPPEARED INTO THE WIND--
--WITH NOBODY EVER BEING THE WISER UNTIL IT WAS FAR TOO LATE.

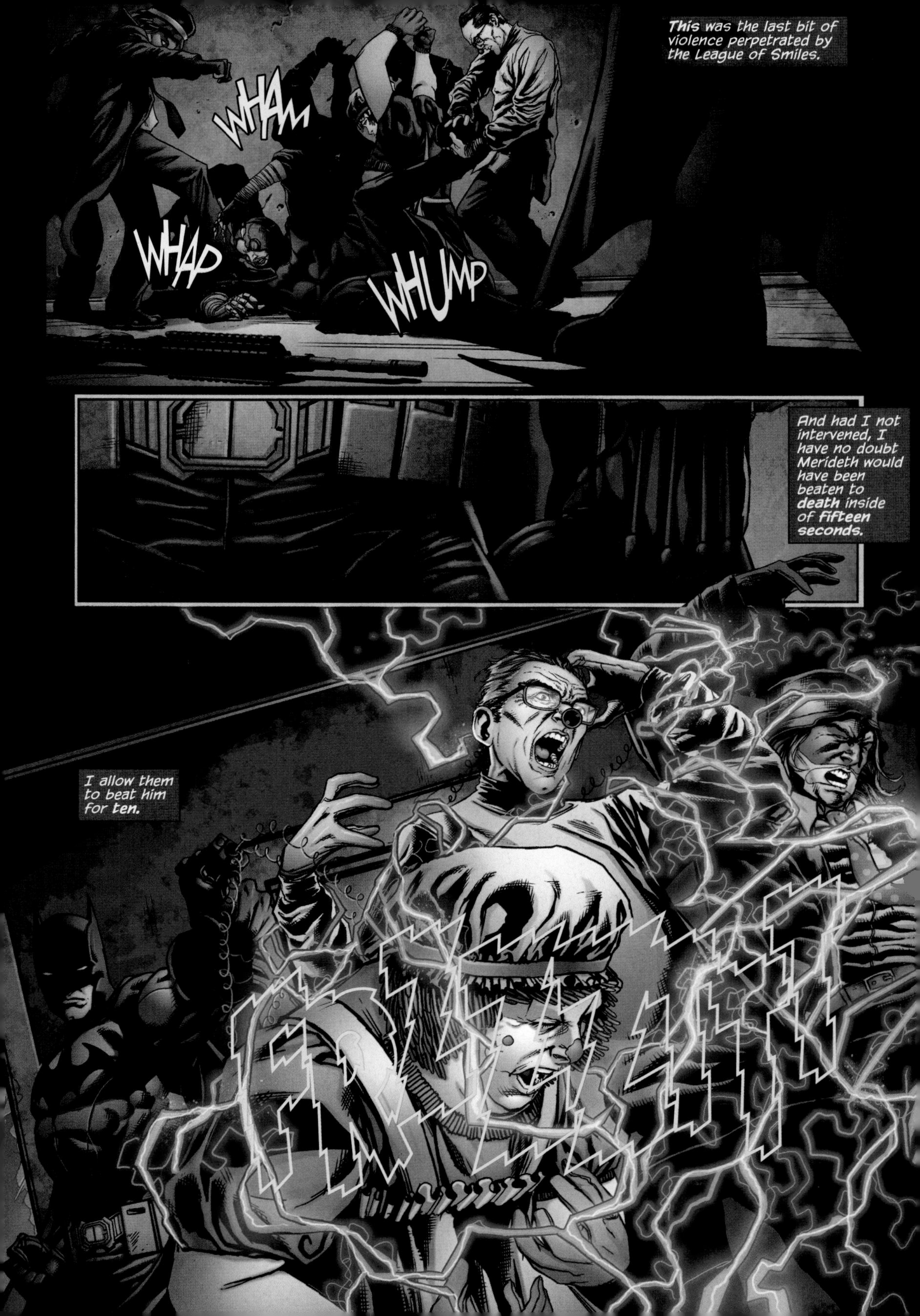

This was the last bit of violence perpetrated by the League of Smiles.
WHAM
WHAP
WHUMP
And had I not intervened, I have no doubt Merideth would have been beaten to **death** inside of **fifteen seconds**.
I allow them to beat him for **ten**.

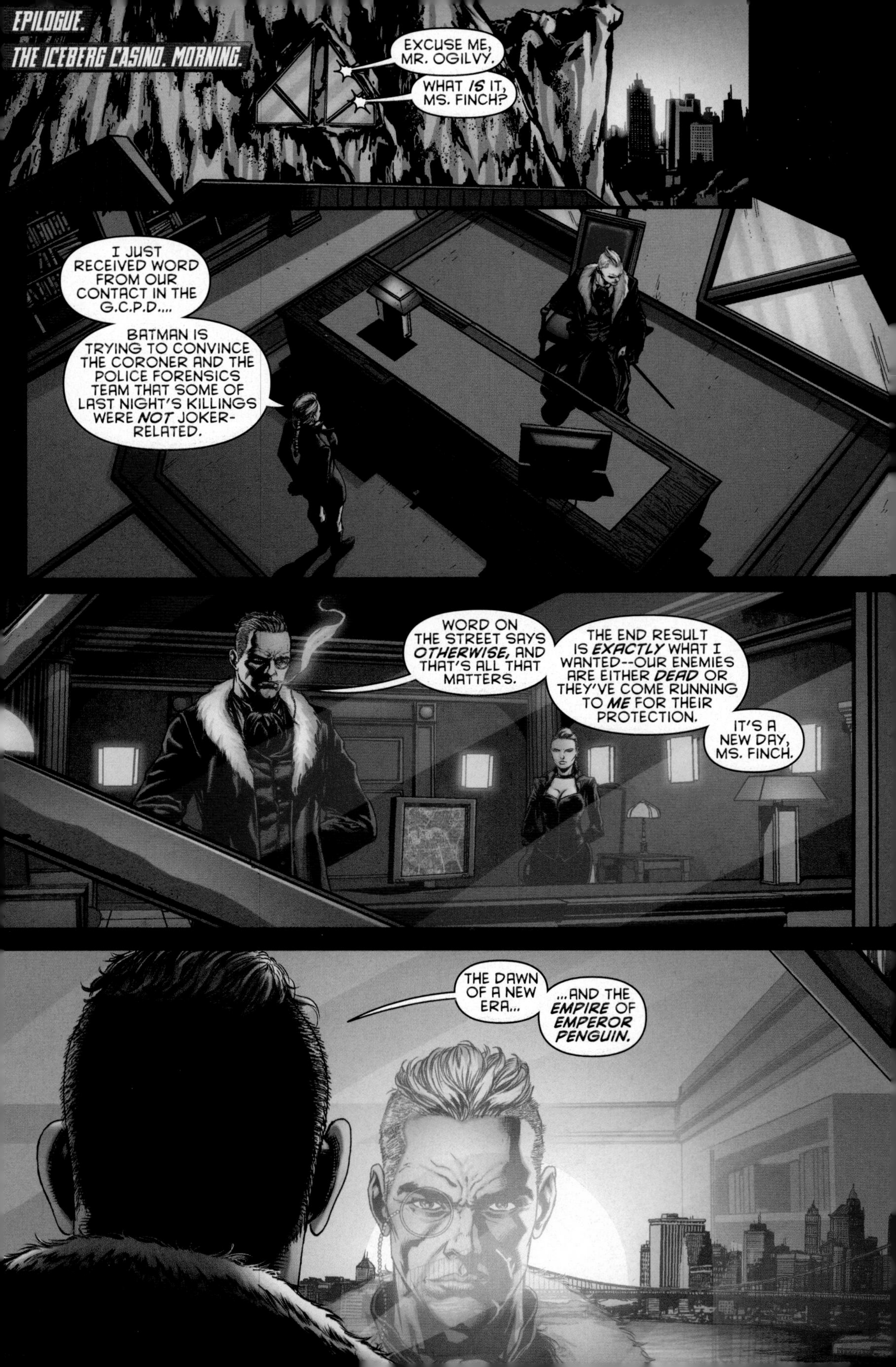
EPILOGUE.
THE ICEBERG CASINO. MORNING.
EXCUSE ME, MR. OGILVY.
WHAT IS IT, MS. FINCH?
I JUST RECEIVED WORD FROM OUR CONTACT IN THE G.C.P.D....
BATMAN IS TRYING TO CONVINCE THE CORONER AND THE POLICE FORENSICS TEAM THAT SOME OF LAST NIGHT'S KILLINGS WERE NOT JOKER-RELATED.
WORD ON THE STREET SAYS OTHERWISE, AND THAT'S ALL THAT MATTERS.
THE END RESULT IS EXACTLY WHAT I WANTED--OUR ENEMIES ARE EITHER DEAD OR THEY'VE COME RUNNING TO ME FOR THEIR PROTECTION.
IT'S A NEW DAY, MS. FINCH.
THE DAWN OF A NEW ERA...
...AND THE EMPIRE OF EMPEROR PENGUIN.

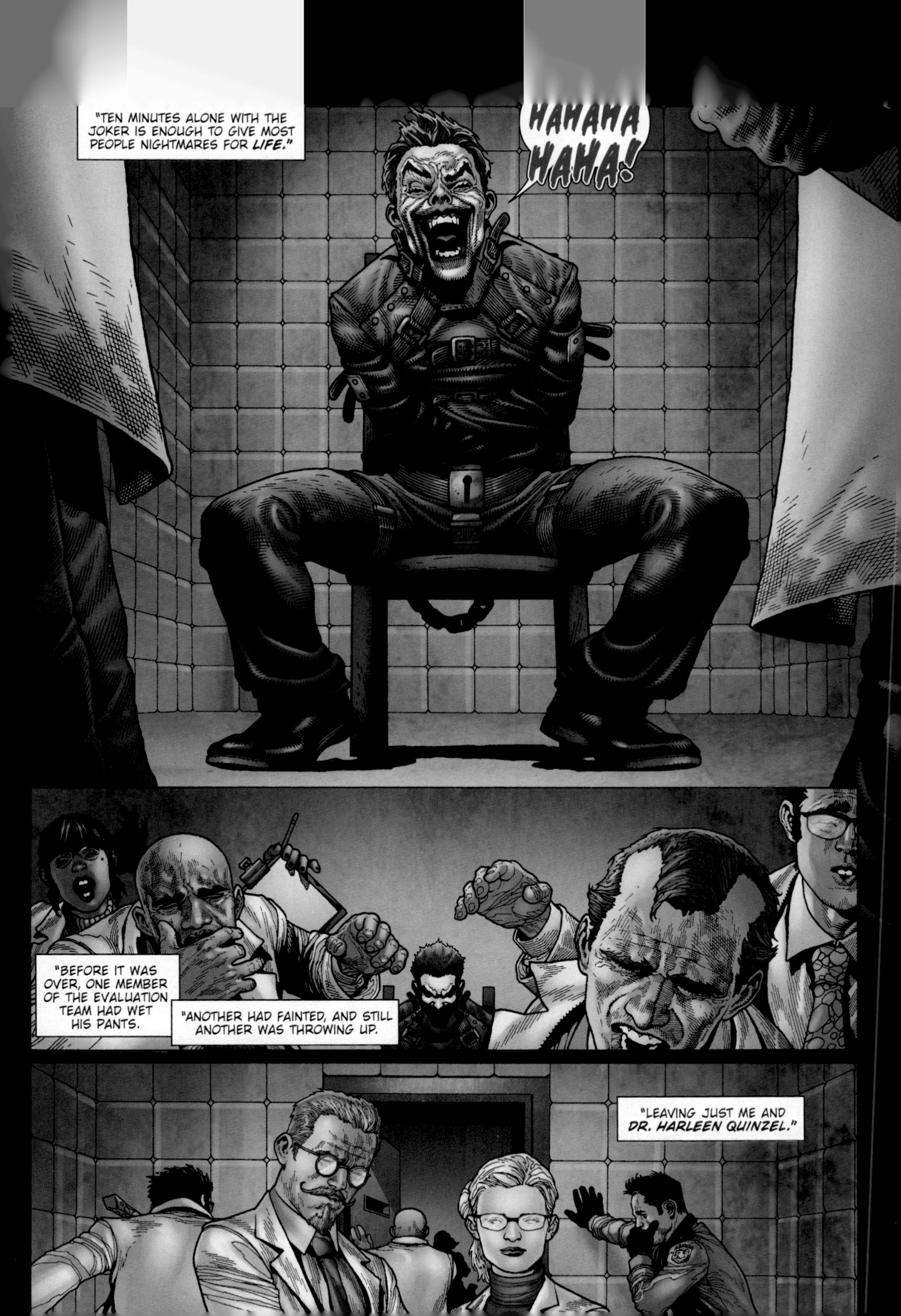
"TEN MINUTES ALONE WITH THE JOKER IS ENOUGH TO GIVE MOST PEOPLE NIGHTMARES FOR *LIFE.*"
HAHAHA HAHA!
"BEFORE IT WAS OVER, ONE MEMBER OF THE EVALUATION TEAM HAD WET HIS PANTS.
"ANOTHER HAD FAINTED, AND STILL ANOTHER WAS THROWING UP.
"LEAVING JUST ME AND *DR. HARLEEN QUINZEL.*"

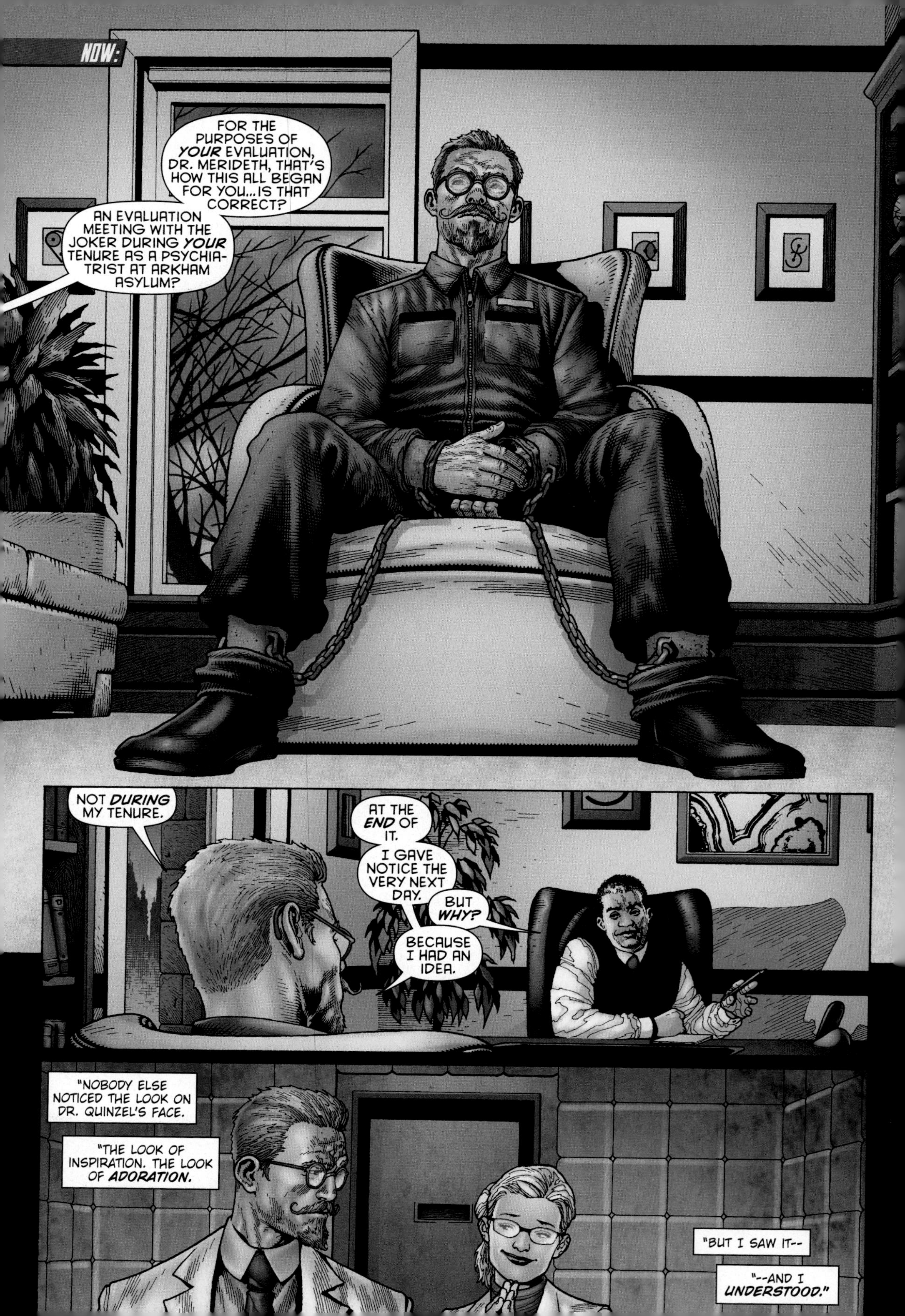
NOW:
FOR THE PURPOSES OF *YOUR* EVALUATION, DR. MERIDETH, THAT'S HOW THIS ALL BEGAN FOR YOU...IS THAT CORRECT?
AN EVALUATION MEETING WITH THE JOKER DURING *YOUR* TENURE AS A PSYCHIATRIST AT ARKHAM ASYLUM?
NOT *DURING* MY TENURE.
AT THE *END* OF IT.
I GAVE NOTICE THE VERY NEXT DAY.
BUT *WHY?*
BECAUSE I HAD AN IDEA.
"NOBODY ELSE NOTICED THE LOOK ON DR. QUINZEL'S FACE.
"THE LOOK OF INSPIRATION. THE LOOK OF *ADORATION.*
"BUT I SAW IT--
"--AND I *UNDERSTOOD.*"

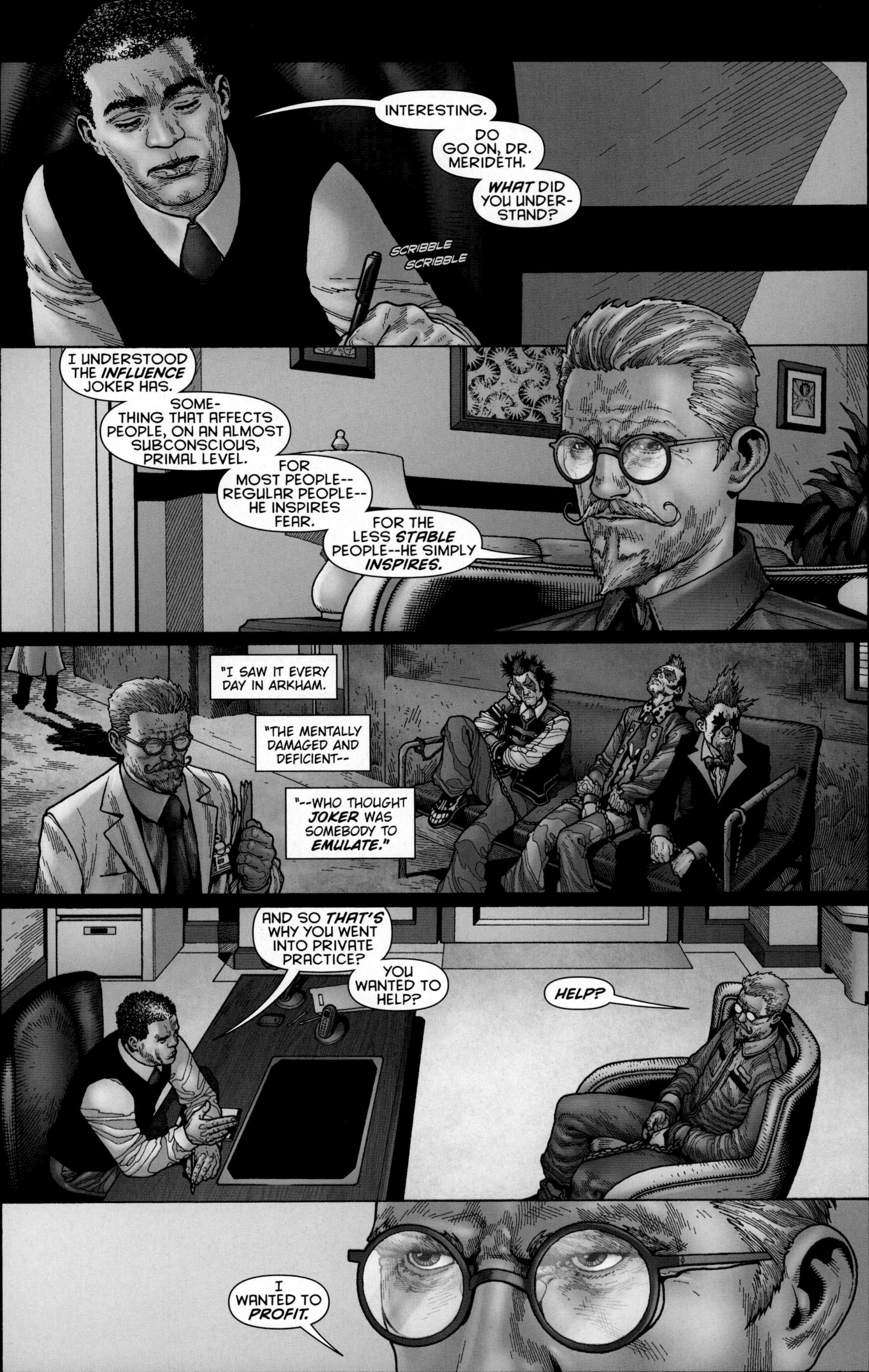
INTERESTING.
DO GO ON, DR. MERIDETH.
WHAT DID YOU UNDER-STAND?
SCRIBBLE SCRIBBLE
I UNDERSTOOD THE INFLUENCE JOKER HAS.
SOME-THING THAT AFFECTS PEOPLE, ON AN ALMOST SUBCONSCIOUS, PRIMAL LEVEL.
FOR MOST PEOPLE--REGULAR PEOPLE--HE INSPIRES FEAR.
FOR THE LESS STABLE PEOPLE--HE SIMPLY INSPIRES.
"I SAW IT EVERY DAY IN ARKHAM.
"THE MENTALLY DAMAGED AND DEFICIENT--
"--WHO THOUGHT JOKER WAS SOMEBODY TO EMULATE."
AND SO THAT'S WHY YOU WENT INTO PRIVATE PRACTICE?
YOU WANTED TO HELP?
HELP?
I WANTED TO PROFIT.

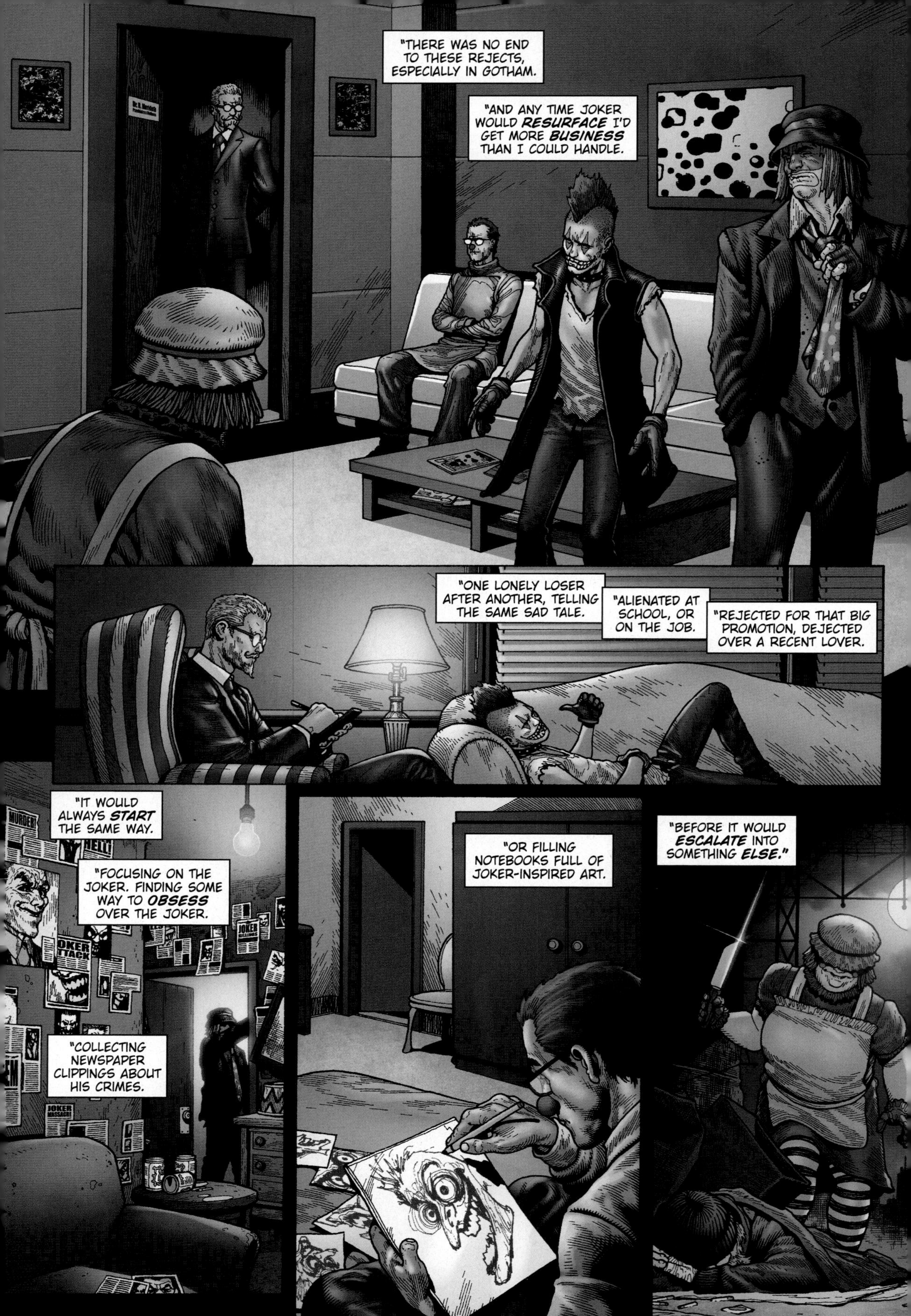
"THERE WAS NO END TO THESE REJECTS, ESPECIALLY IN GOTHAM.
"AND ANY TIME JOKER WOULD RESURFACE I'D GET MORE BUSINESS THAN I COULD HANDLE.
"ONE LONELY LOSER AFTER ANOTHER, TELLING THE SAME SAD TALE.
"ALIENATED AT SCHOOL, OR ON THE JOB.
"REJECTED FOR THAT BIG PROMOTION, DEJECTED OVER A RECENT LOVER.
"IT WOULD ALWAYS START THE SAME WAY.
"FOCUSING ON THE JOKER. FINDING SOME WAY TO OBSESS OVER THE JOKER.
"COLLECTING NEWSPAPER CLIPPINGS ABOUT HIS CRIMES.
"OR FILLING NOTEBOOKS FULL OF JOKER-INSPIRED ART.
"BEFORE IT WOULD ESCALATE INTO SOMETHING ELSE."

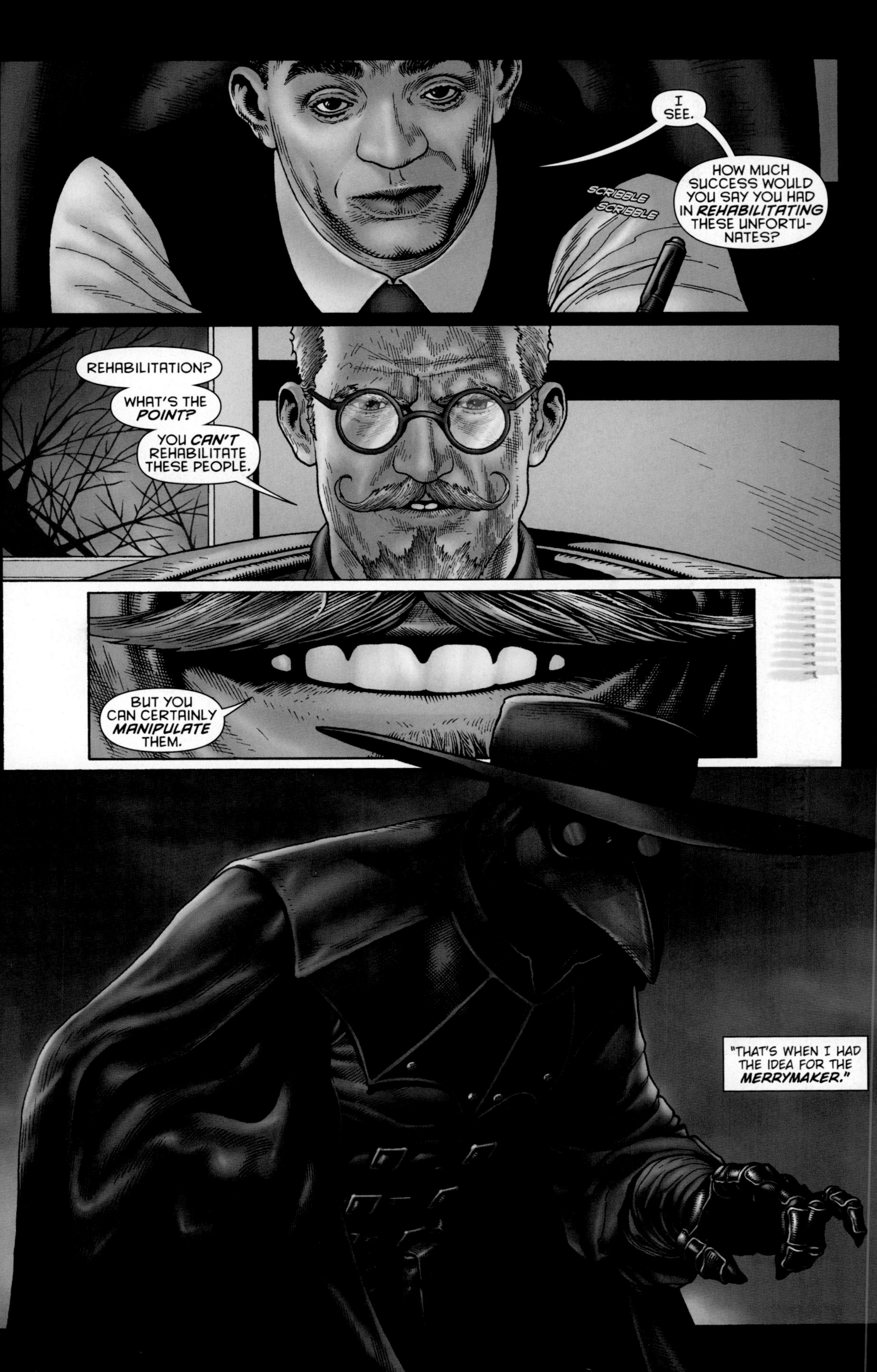

I SEE.
HOW MUCH SUCCESS WOULD YOU SAY YOU HAD IN REHABILITATING THESE UNFORTU-NATES?
SCRIBBLE SCRIBBLE
REHABILITATION?
WHAT'S THE POINT?
YOU CAN'T REHABILITATE THESE PEOPLE.
BUT YOU CAN CERTAINLY MANIPULATE THEM.
"THAT'S WHEN I HAD THE IDEA FOR THE MERRYMAKER."

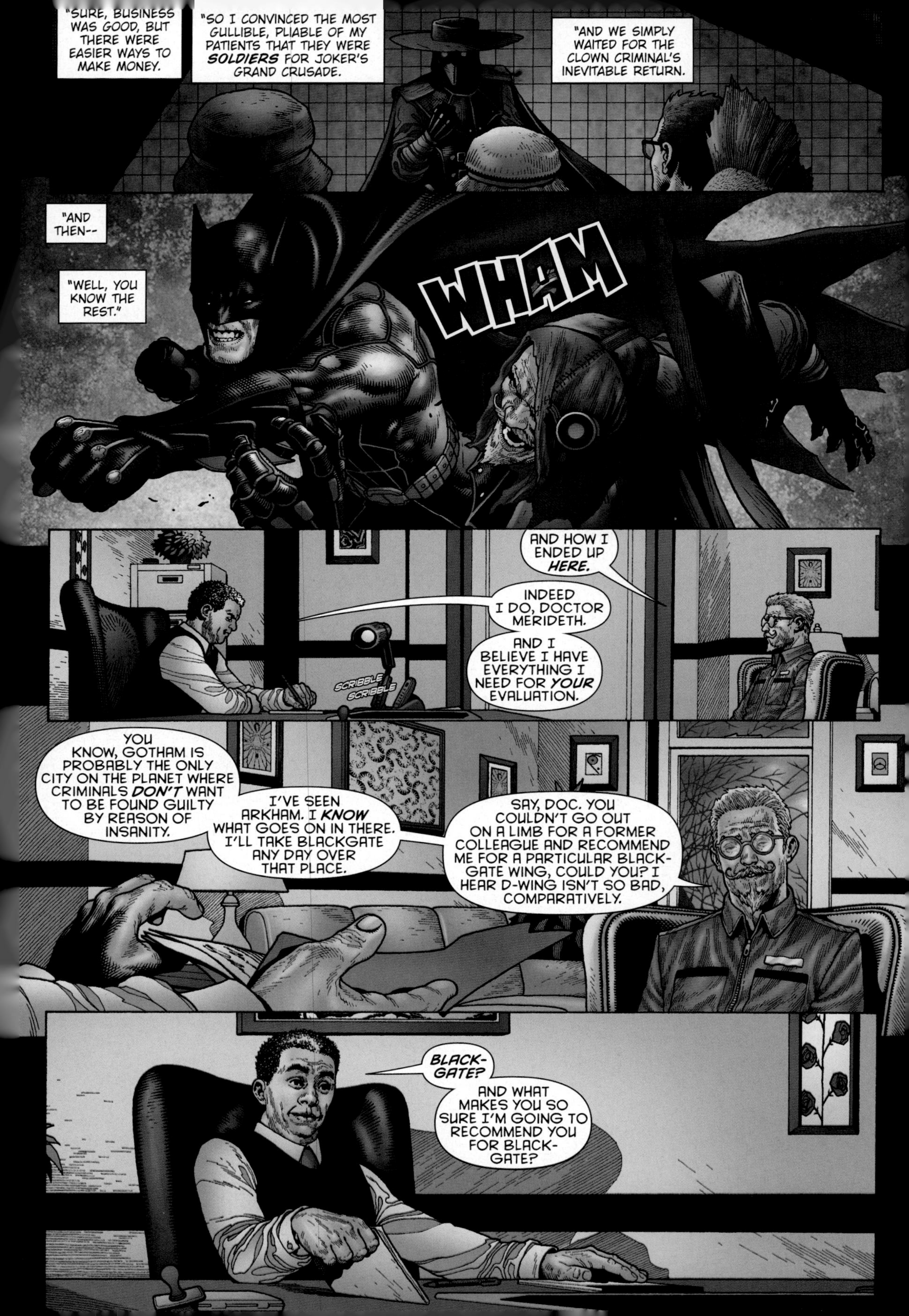
"SURE, BUSINESS WAS GOOD, BUT THERE WERE EASIER WAYS TO MAKE MONEY.
"SO I CONVINCED THE MOST GULLIBLE, PLIABLE OF MY PATIENTS THAT THEY WERE SOLDIERS FOR JOKER'S GRAND CRUSADE.
"AND WE SIMPLY WAITED FOR THE CLOWN CRIMINAL'S INEVITABLE RETURN.
"AND THEN--
"WELL, YOU KNOW THE REST."
WHAM
AND HOW I ENDED UP HERE.
INDEED I DO, DOCTOR MERIDETH.
AND I BELIEVE I HAVE EVERYTHING I NEED FOR YOUR EVALUATION.
SCRIBBLE SCRIBBLE
YOU KNOW, GOTHAM IS PROBABLY THE ONLY CITY ON THE PLANET WHERE CRIMINALS DON'T WANT TO BE FOUND GUILTY BY REASON OF INSANITY.
I'VE SEEN ARKHAM. I KNOW WHAT GOES ON IN THERE. I'LL TAKE BLACKGATE ANY DAY OVER THAT PLACE.
SAY, DOC. YOU COULDN'T GO OUT ON A LIMB FOR A FORMER COLLEAGUE AND RECOMMEND ME FOR A PARTICULAR BLACK-GATE WING, COULD YOU? I HEAR D-WING ISN'T SO BAD, COMPARATIVELY.
BLACK-GATE?
AND WHAT MAKES YOU SO SURE I'M GOING TO RECOMMEND YOU FOR BLACK-GATE?

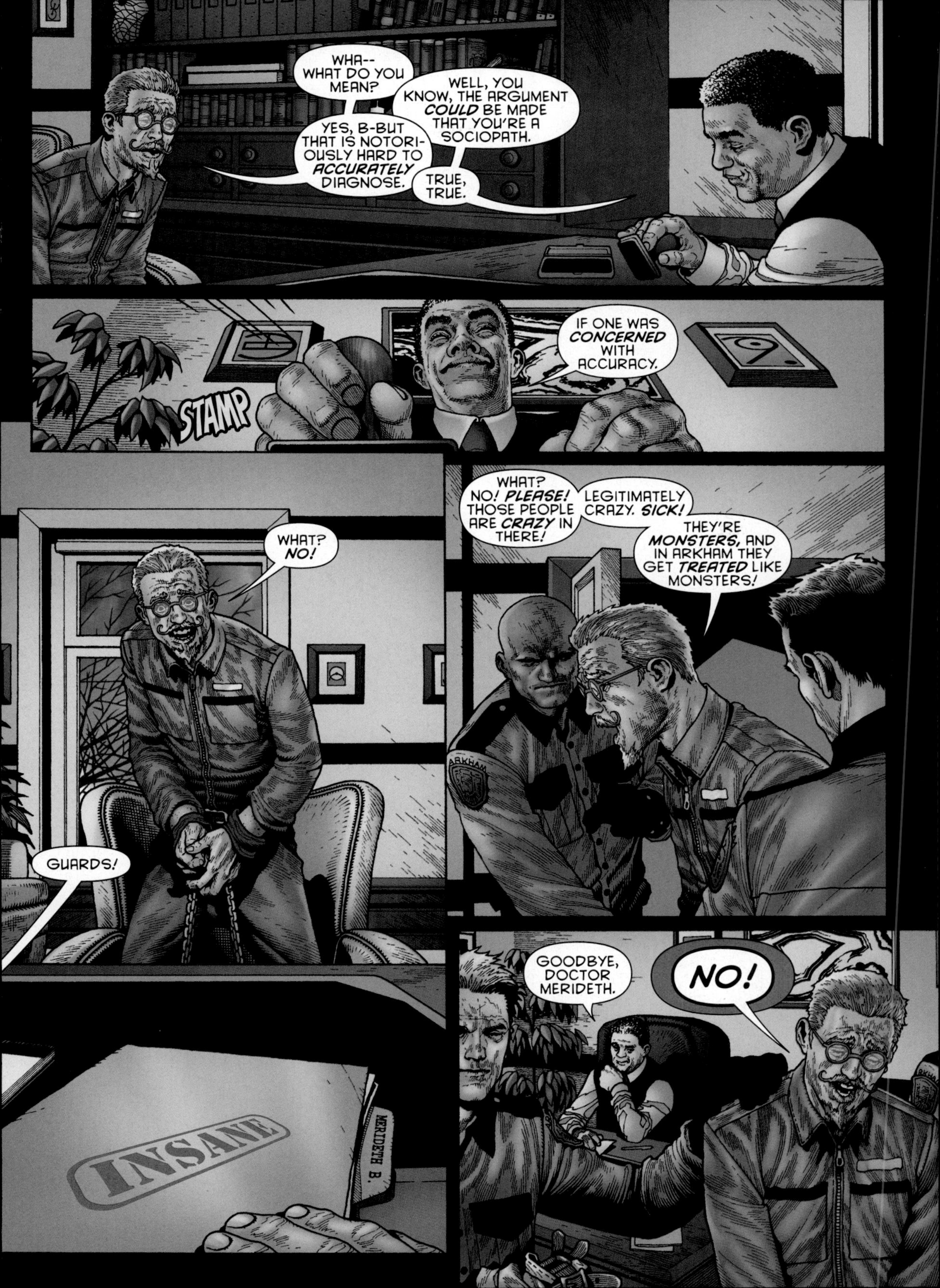
WHA-- WHAT DO YOU MEAN?
WELL, YOU KNOW, THE ARGUMENT *COULD* BE MADE THAT YOU'RE A SOCIOPATH.
YES, B-BUT THAT IS NOTORIOUSLY HARD TO *ACCURATELY* DIAGNOSE.
TRUE, TRUE.
IF ONE WAS *CONCERNED* WITH ACCURACY.
STAMP
WHAT? *NO!*
GUARDS!
WHAT? NO! *PLEASE!* THOSE PEOPLE ARE *CRAZY* IN THERE!
LEGITIMATELY CRAZY. *SICK!*
THEY'RE *MONSTERS,* AND IN ARKHAM THEY GET *TREATED* LIKE MONSTERS!
ARKHAM
INSANE
MERIDETH B.
GOODBYE, DOCTOR MERIDETH.
NO!

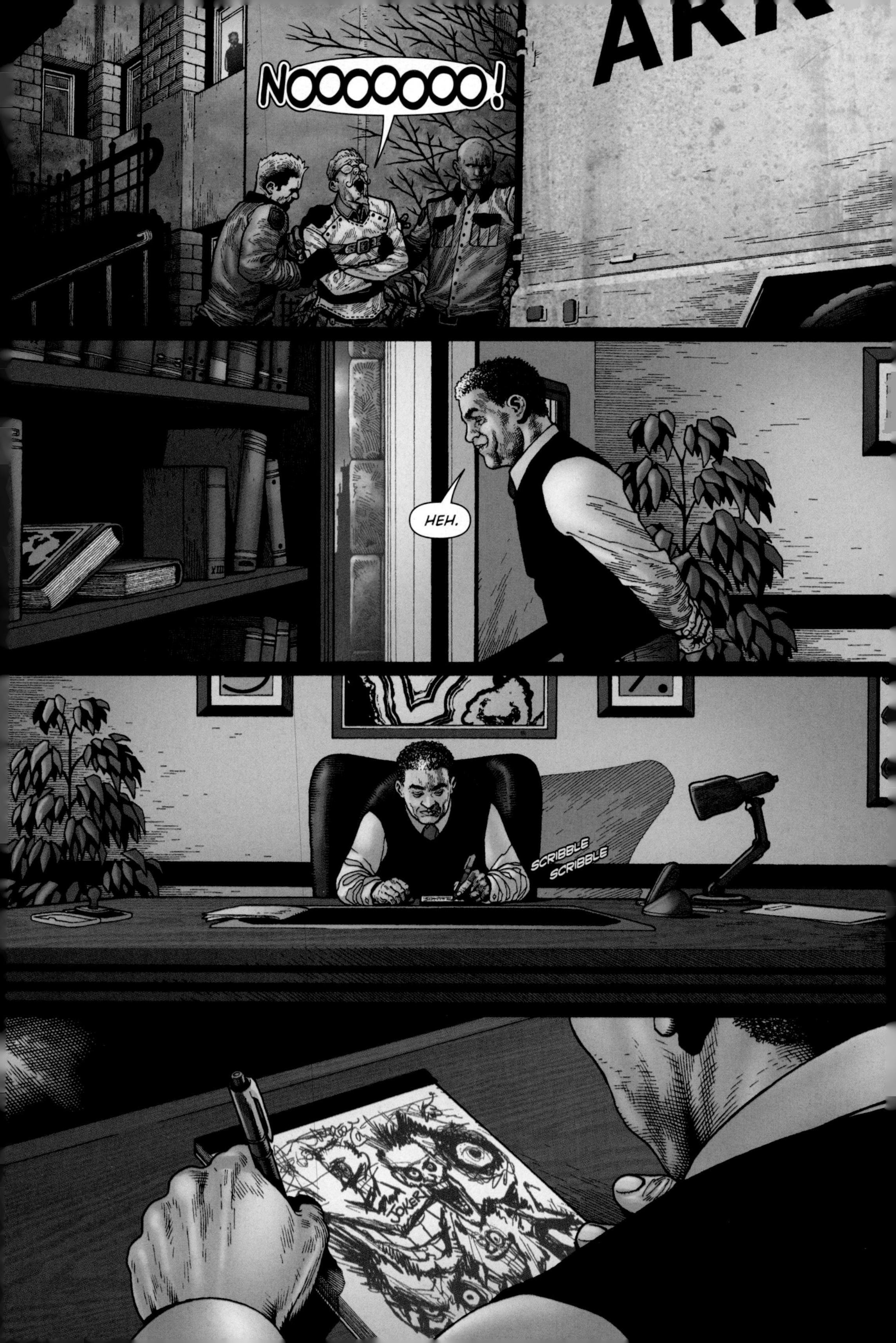

ARK
NOOOOOOO!
HEH.
SCRIBBLE SCRIBBLE
JOKER

PART TWO
CATWOMAN

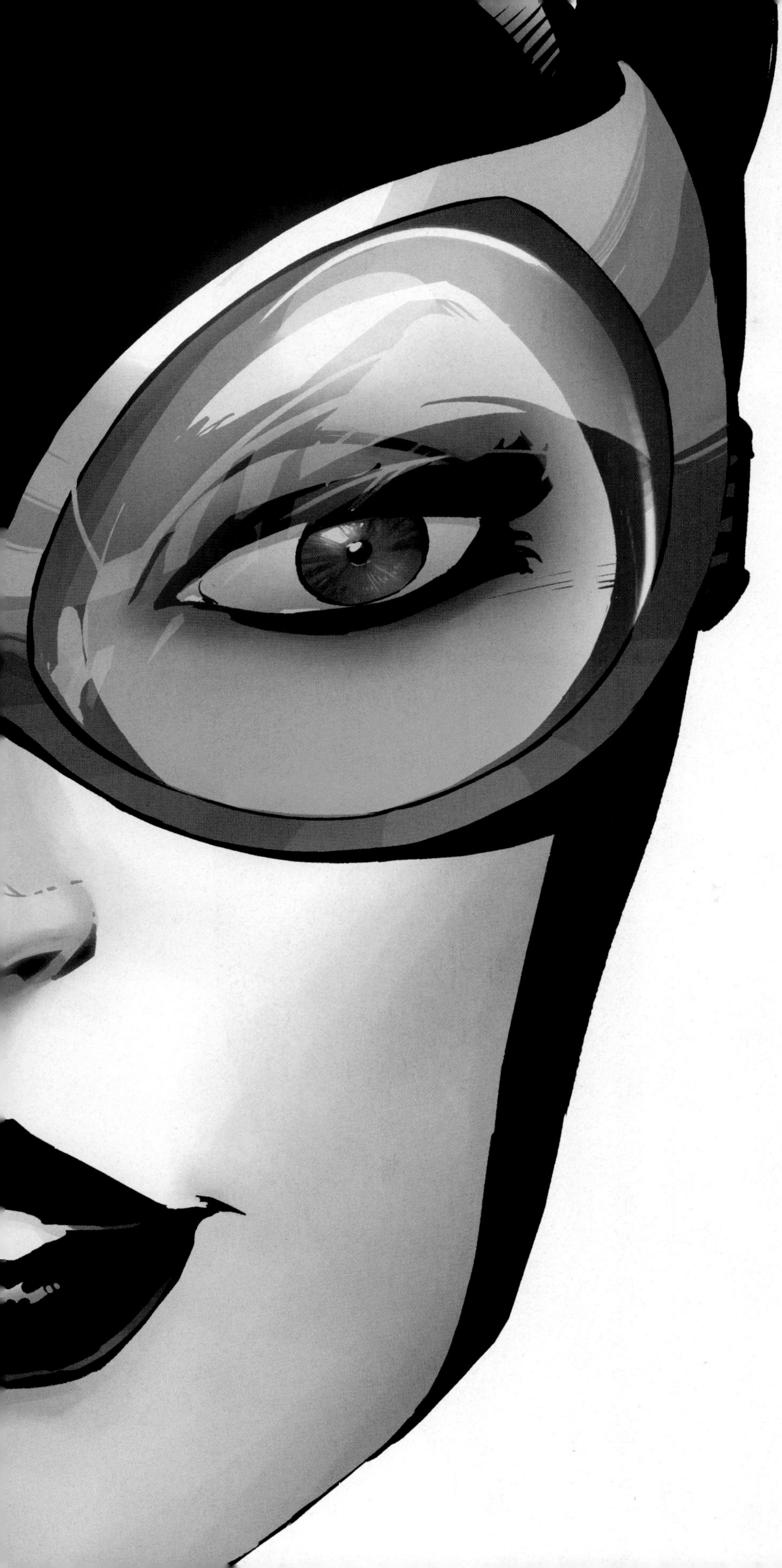

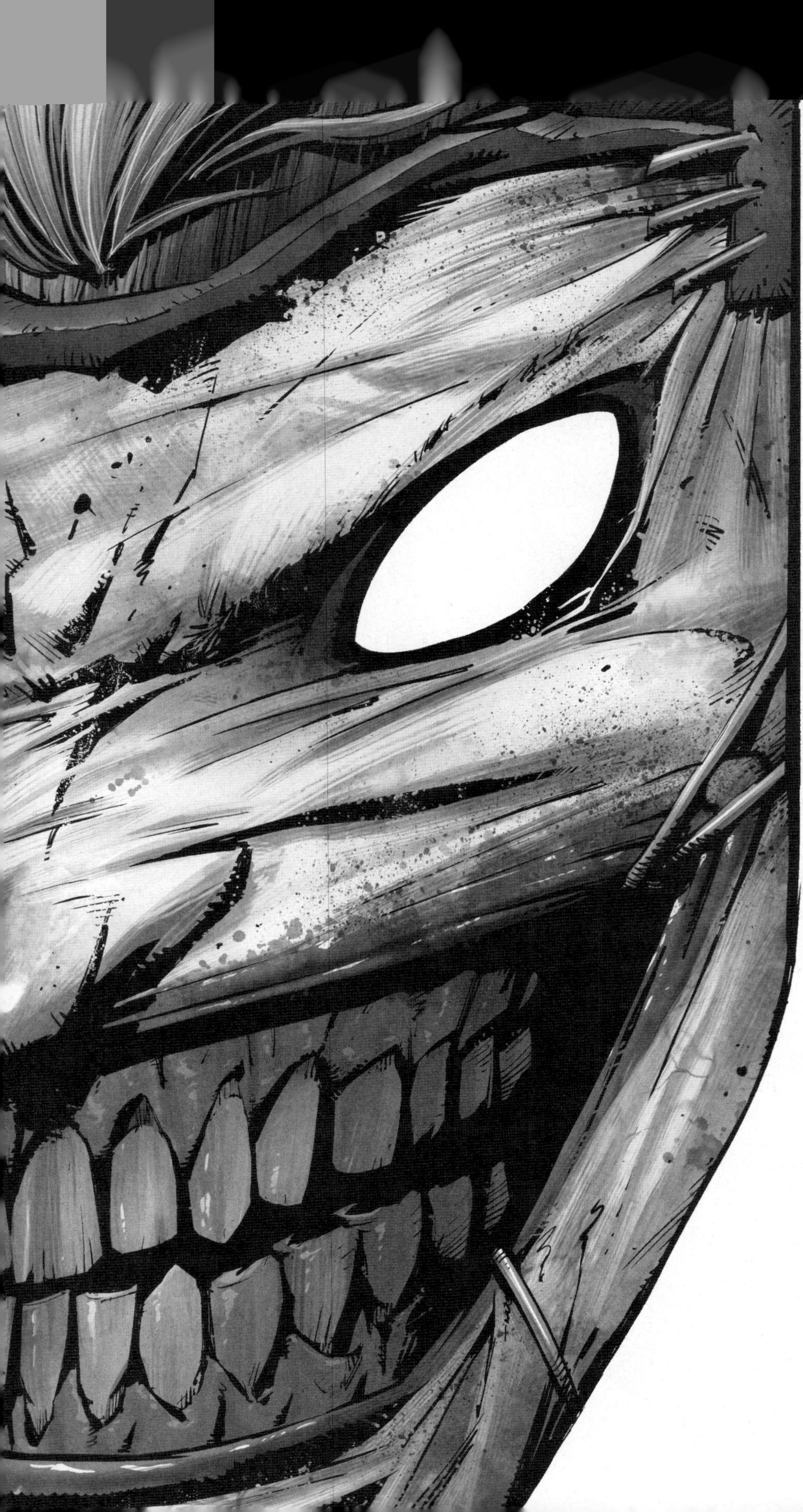

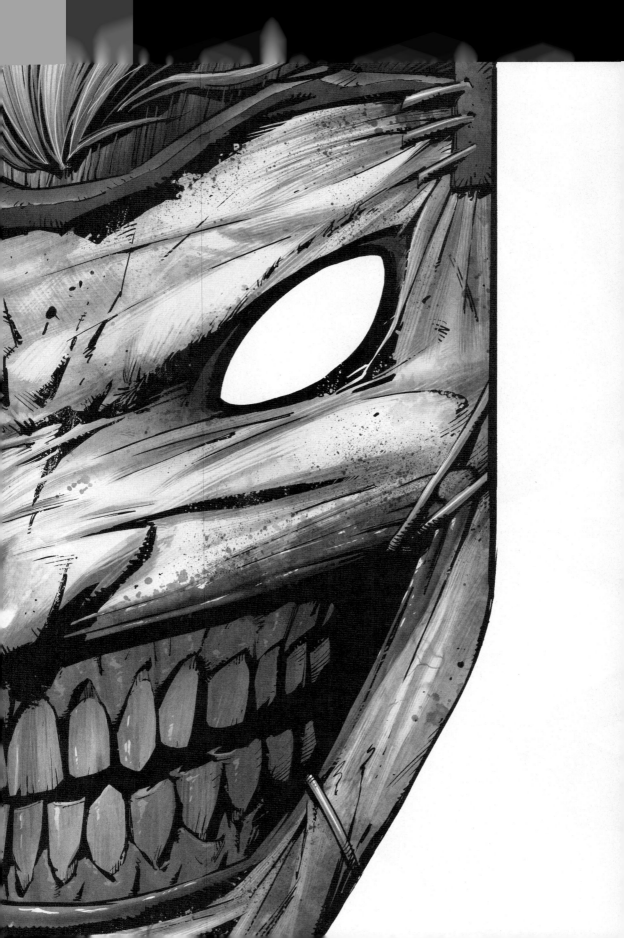

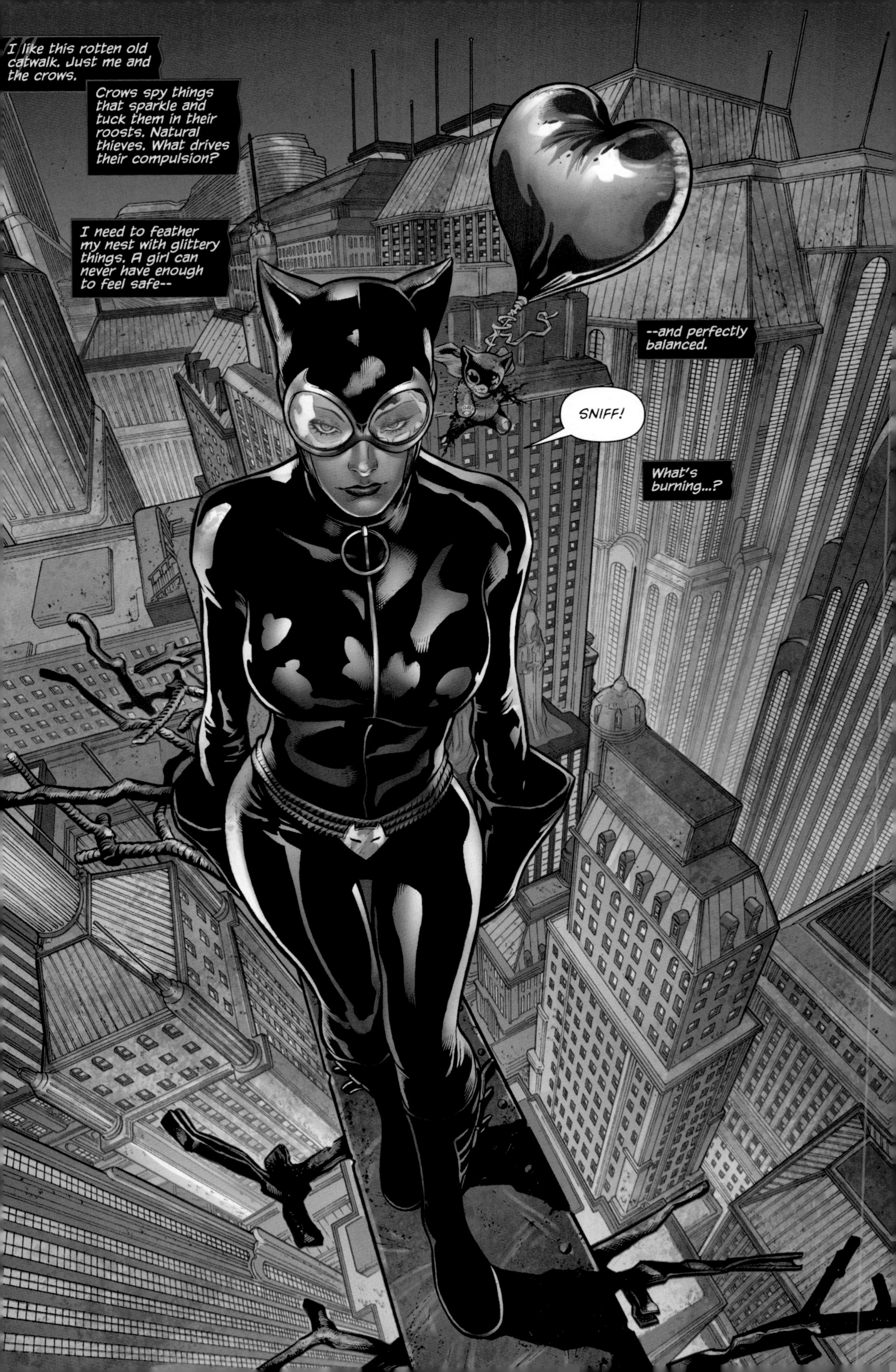
I like this rotten old catwalk. Just me and the crows.
Crows spy things that sparkle and tuck them in their roosts. Natural thieves. What drives their compulsion?
I need to feather my nest with glittery things. A girl can never have enough to feel safe--
--and perfectly balanced.
SNIFF!
What's burning...?

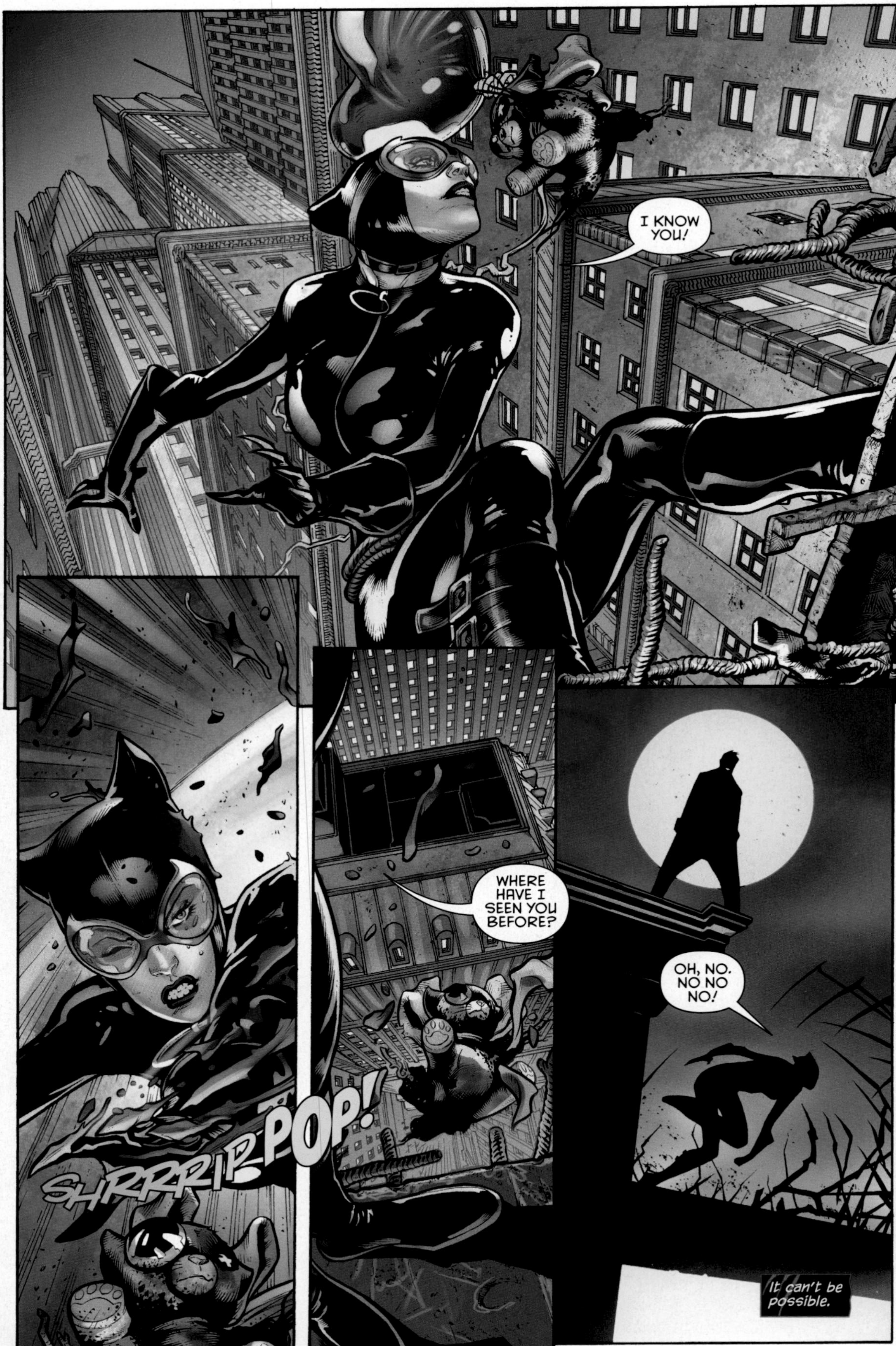
I KNOW YOU!
SHRRRIP
POP!
WHERE HAVE I SEEN YOU BEFORE?
OH, NO. NO NO NO!
It can't be possible.

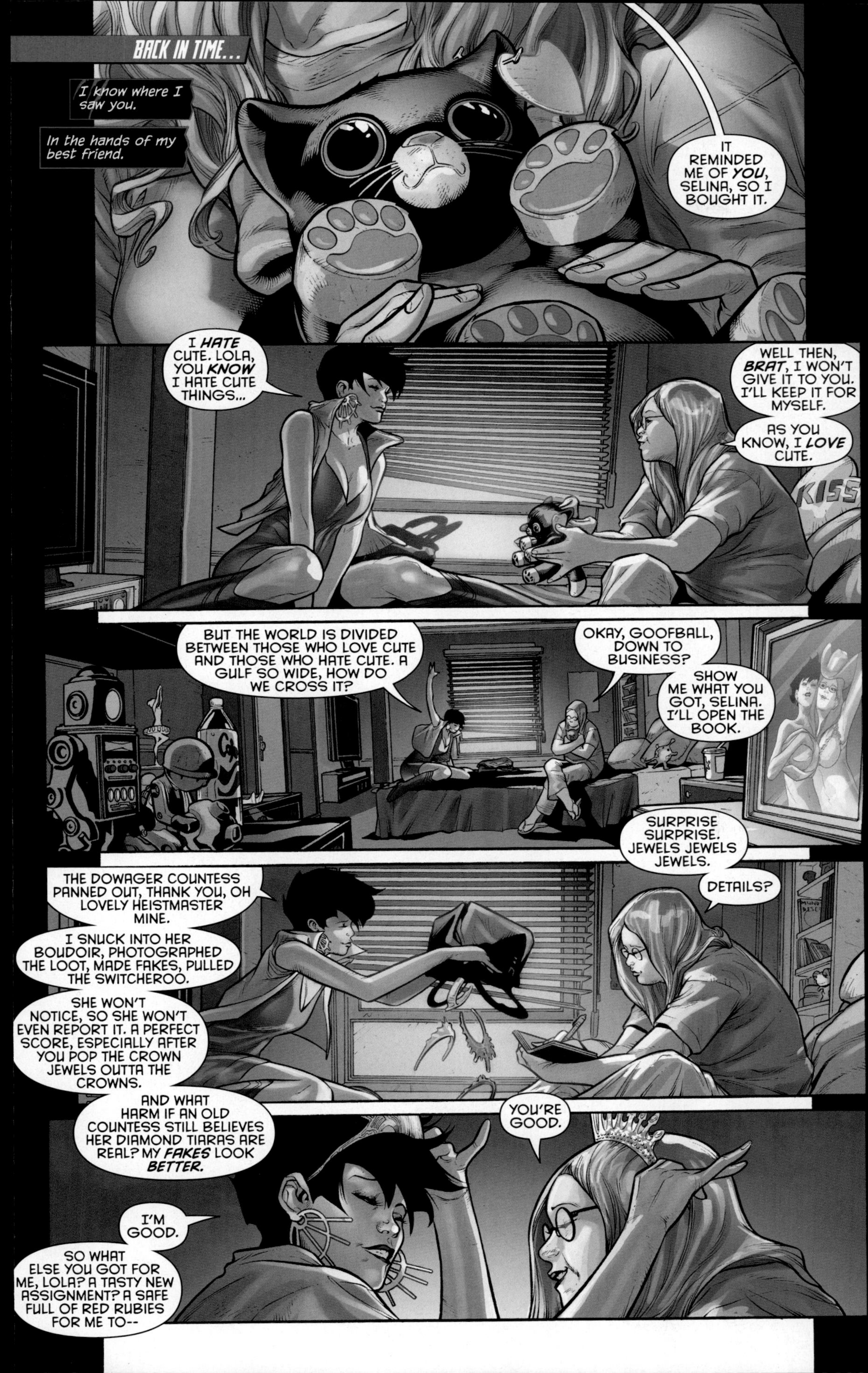
BACK IN TIME...
I know where I saw you.
In the hands of my best friend.
IT REMINDED ME OF YOU, SELINA, SO I BOUGHT IT.
I HATE CUTE. LOLA, YOU KNOW I HATE CUTE THINGS...
WELL THEN, BRAT, I WON'T GIVE IT TO YOU. I'LL KEEP IT FOR MYSELF.
AS YOU KNOW, I LOVE CUTE.
KISS
BUT THE WORLD IS DIVIDED BETWEEN THOSE WHO LOVE CUTE AND THOSE WHO HATE CUTE. A GULF SO WIDE, HOW DO WE CROSS IT?
OKAY, GOOFBALL, DOWN TO BUSINESS?
SHOW ME WHAT YOU GOT, SELINA. I'LL OPEN THE BOOK.
SURPRISE SURPRISE. JEWELS JEWELS JEWELS.
DETAILS?
THE DOWAGER COUNTESS PANNED OUT, THANK YOU, OH LOVELY HEISTMASTER MINE.
I SNUCK INTO HER BOUDOIR, PHOTOGRAPHED THE LOOT, MADE FAKES, PULLED THE SWITCHEROO.
SHE WON'T NOTICE, SO SHE WON'T EVEN REPORT IT. A PERFECT SCORE, ESPECIALLY AFTER YOU POP THE CROWN JEWELS OUTTA THE CROWNS.
AND WHAT HARM IF AN OLD COUNTESS STILL BELIEVES HER DIAMOND TIARAS ARE REAL? MY FAKES LOOK BETTER.
YOU'RE GOOD.
I'M GOOD.
SO WHAT ELSE YOU GOT FOR ME, LOLA? A TASTY NEW ASSIGNMENT? A SAFE FULL OF RED RUBIES FOR ME TO--

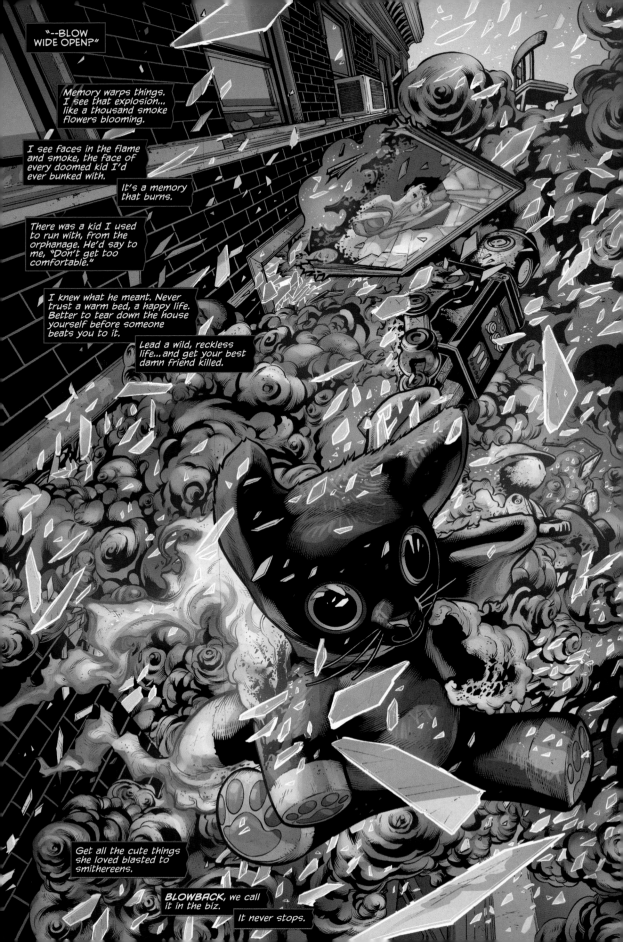

"--BLOW WIDE OPEN?"

Memory warps things. I see that explosion... like a thousand smoke flowers blooming.

I see faces in the flame and smoke, the face of every doomed kid I'd ever bunked with.

It's a memory that burns.

There was a kid I used to run with, from the orphanage. He'd say to me, "Don't get too comfortable."

I knew what he meant. Never trust a warm bed, a happy life. Better to tear down the house yourself before someone beats you to it.

Lead a wild, reckless life...and get your best damn friend killed.

Get all the cute things she loved blasted to smithereens.

BLOWBACK, we call it in the biz.

It never stops.

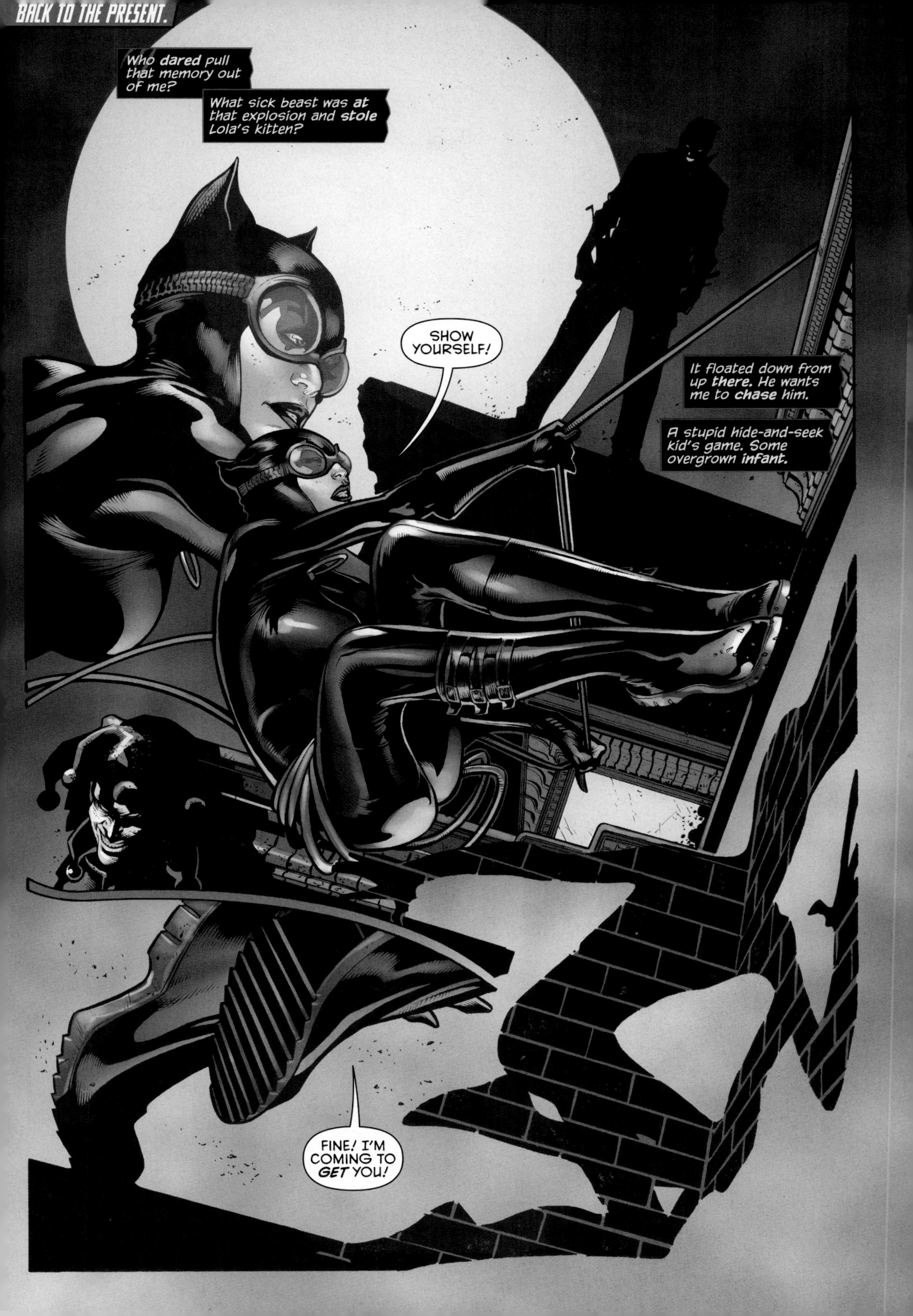
BACK TO THE PRESENT.
Who dared pull that memory out of me?
What sick beast was at that explosion and stole Lola's kitten?
SHOW YOURSELF!
It floated down from up there. He wants me to chase him.
A stupid hide-and-seek kid's game. Some overgrown infant.
FINE! I'M COMING TO GET YOU!

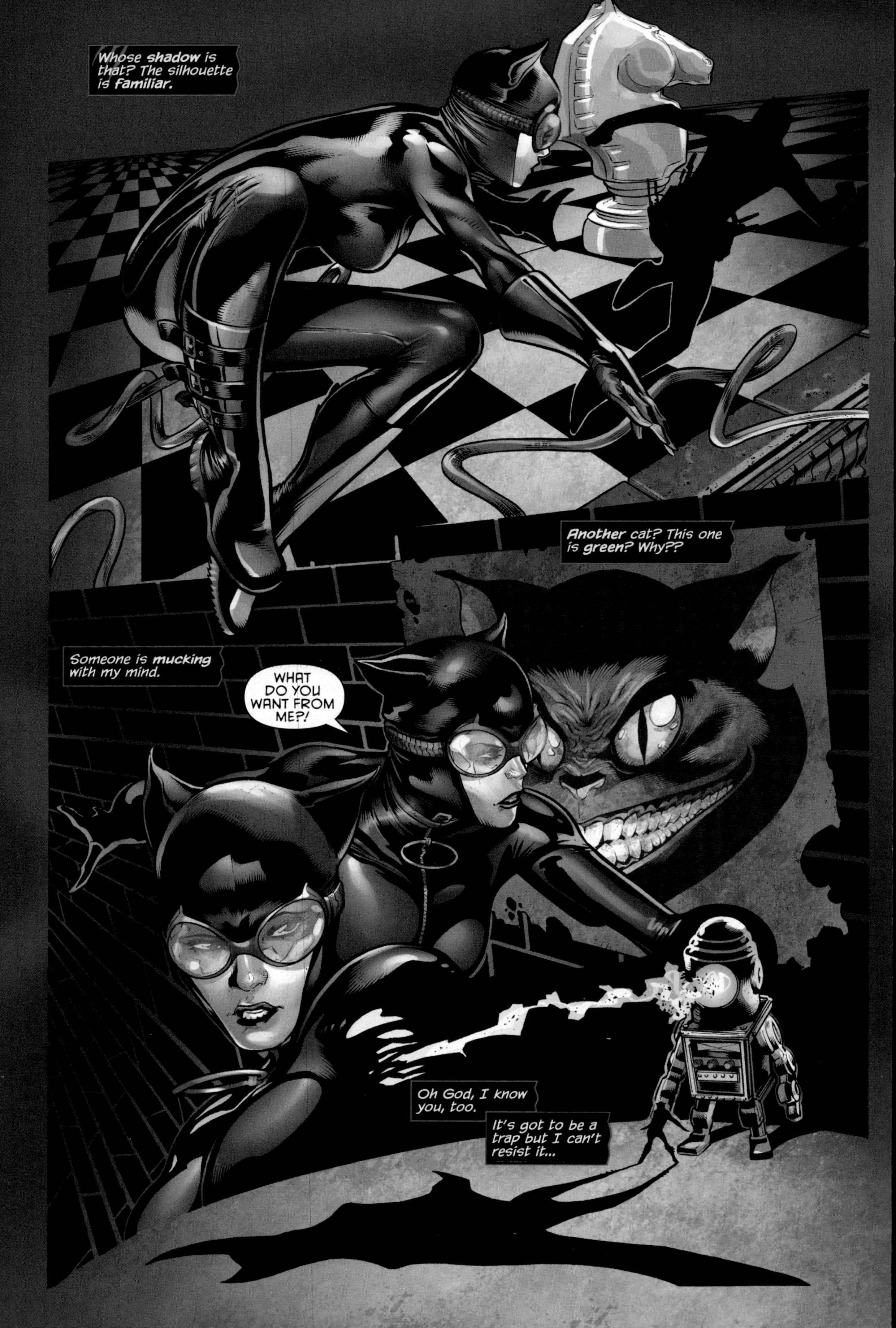
Whose **shadow** is that? The silhouette is **familiar.**
Another cat? This one is **green?** Why??
Someone is **mucking** with my mind.
WHAT DO YOU WANT FROM ME?!
Oh God, I know you, too.
It's got to be a trap but I can't resist it...

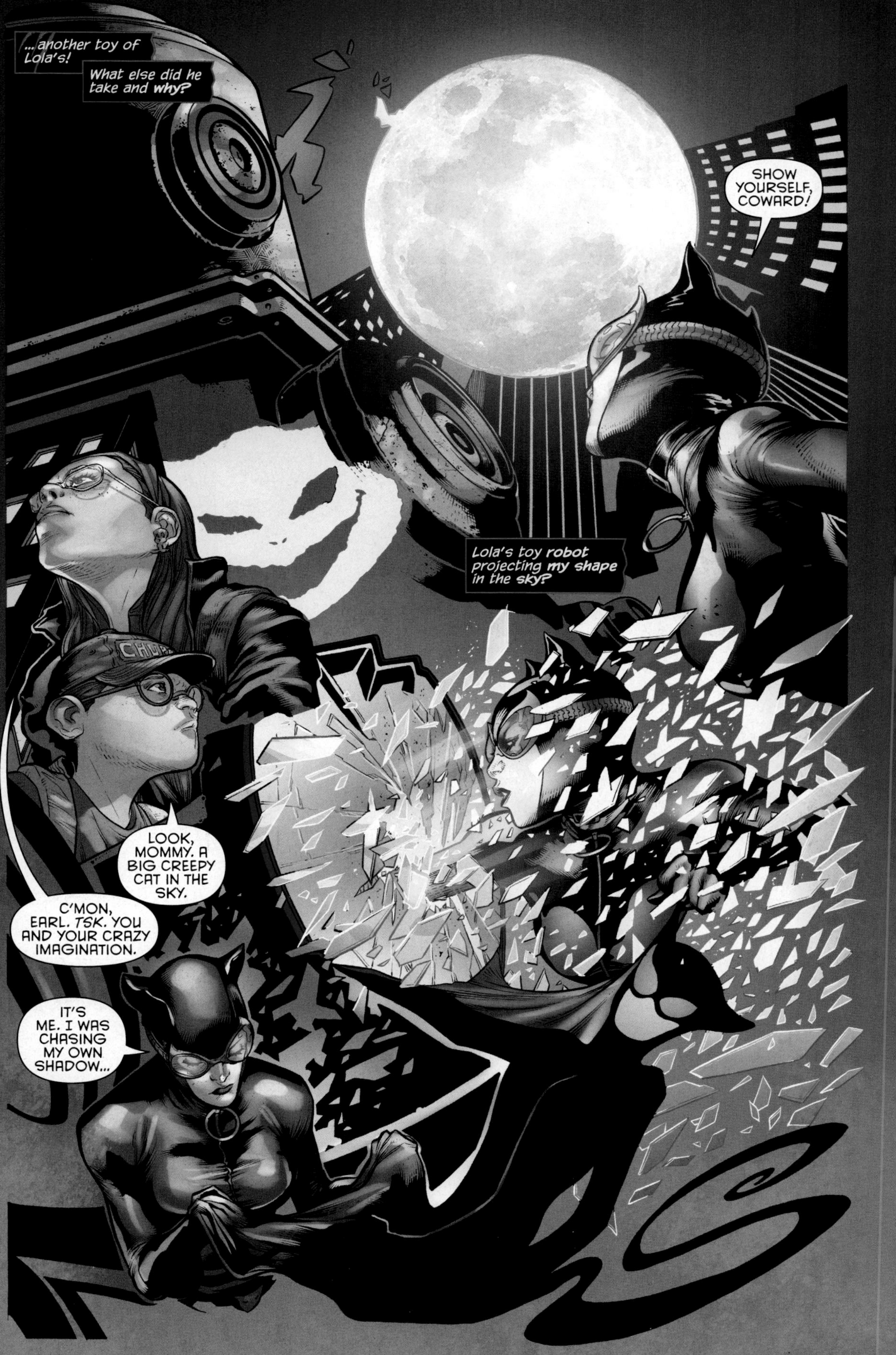
...another toy of Lola's!
What else did he take and why?
SHOW YOURSELF, COWARD!
Lola's toy robot projecting my shape in the sky?
LOOK, MOMMY. A BIG CREEPY CAT IN THE SKY.
C'MON, EARL. TSK. YOU AND YOUR CRAZY IMAGINATION.
IT'S ME. I WAS CHASING MY OWN SHADOW...

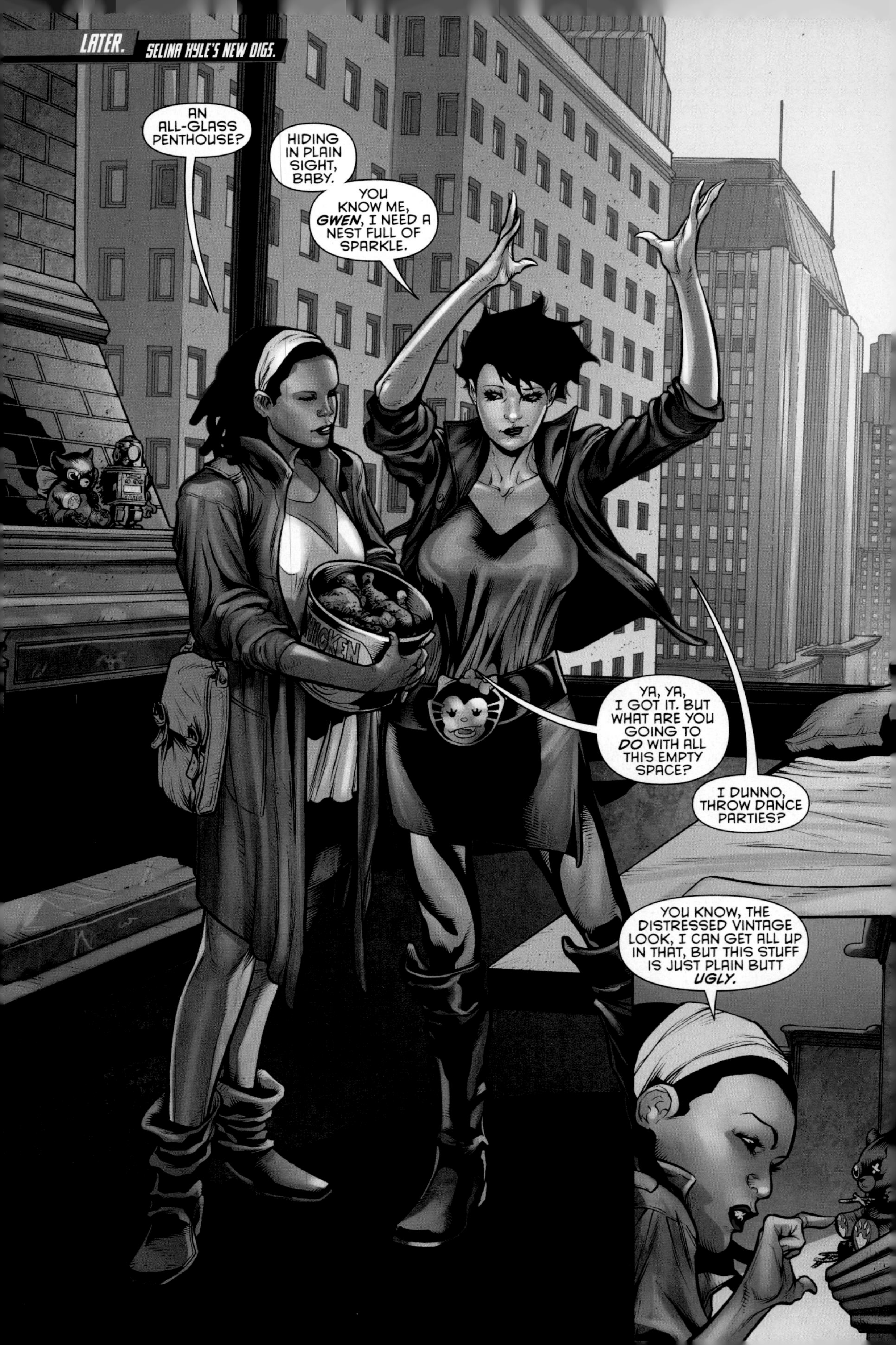
LATER.
SELINA KYLE'S NEW DIGS.
AN ALL-GLASS PENTHOUSE?
HIDING IN PLAIN SIGHT, BABY.
YOU KNOW ME, GWEN, I NEED A NEST FULL OF SPARKLE.
YA, YA, I GOT IT. BUT WHAT ARE YOU GOING TO DO WITH ALL THIS EMPTY SPACE?
I DUNNO, THROW DANCE PARTIES?
YOU KNOW, THE DISTRESSED VINTAGE LOOK, I CAN GET ALL UP IN THAT, BUT THIS STUFF IS JUST PLAIN BUTT UGLY.
CHICKEN

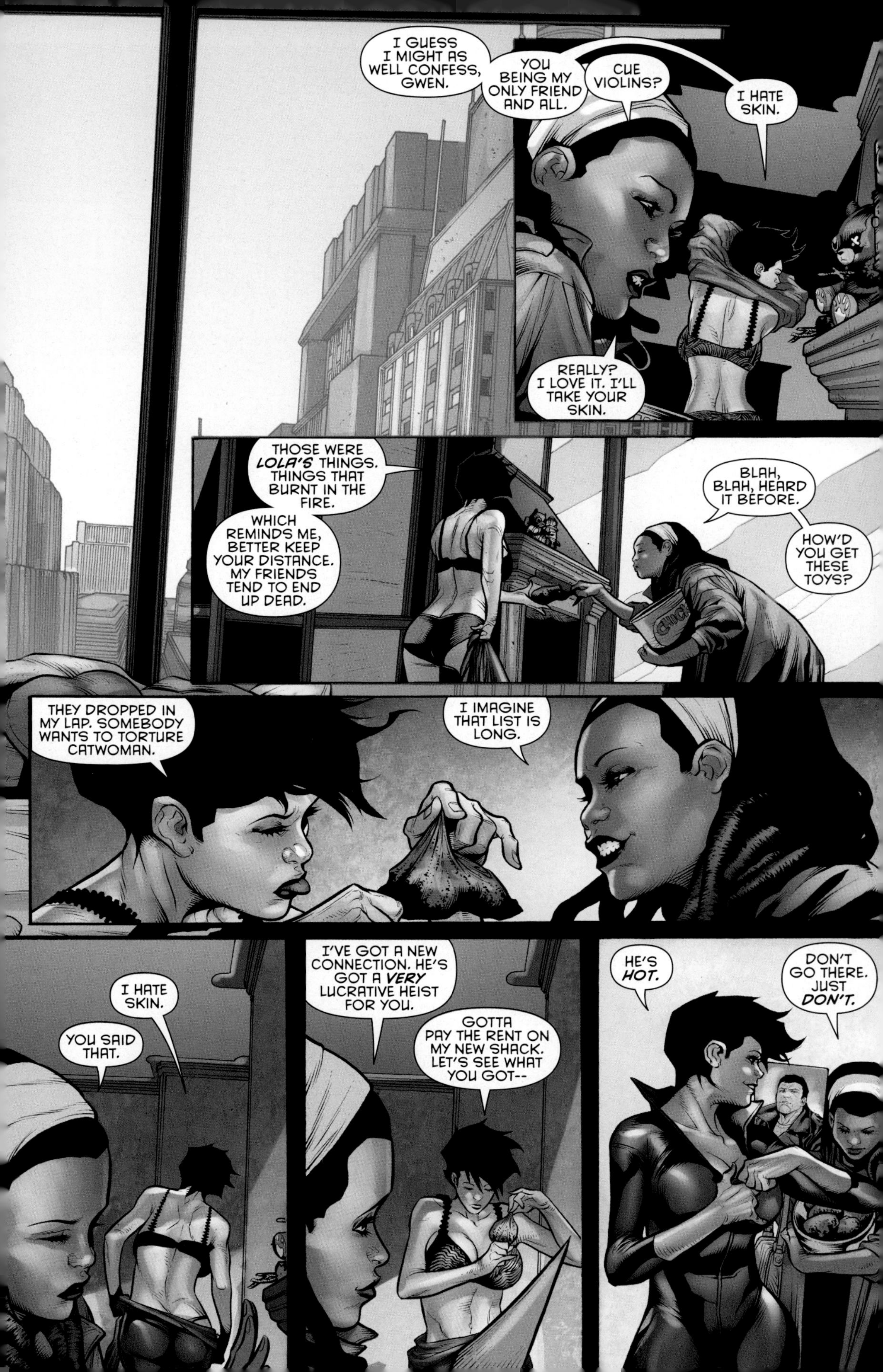
I GUESS I MIGHT AS WELL CONFESS, GWEN.
YOU BEING MY ONLY FRIEND AND ALL.
CUE VIOLINS?
I HATE SKIN.
REALLY? I LOVE IT. I'LL TAKE YOUR SKIN.
THOSE WERE *LOLA'S* THINGS. THINGS THAT BURNT IN THE FIRE.
WHICH REMINDS ME, BETTER KEEP YOUR DISTANCE. MY FRIENDS TEND TO END UP DEAD.
BLAH, BLAH, HEARD IT BEFORE.
HOW'D YOU GET THESE TOYS?
THEY DROPPED IN MY LAP. SOMEBODY WANTS TO TORTURE CATWOMAN.
I IMAGINE THAT LIST IS LONG.
I HATE SKIN.
YOU SAID THAT.
I'VE GOT A NEW CONNECTION. HE'S GOT A *VERY* LUCRATIVE HEIST FOR YOU.
GOTTA PAY THE RENT ON MY NEW SHACK. LET'S SEE WHAT YOU GOT--
HE'S *HOT.*
DON'T GO THERE. JUST *DON'T.*

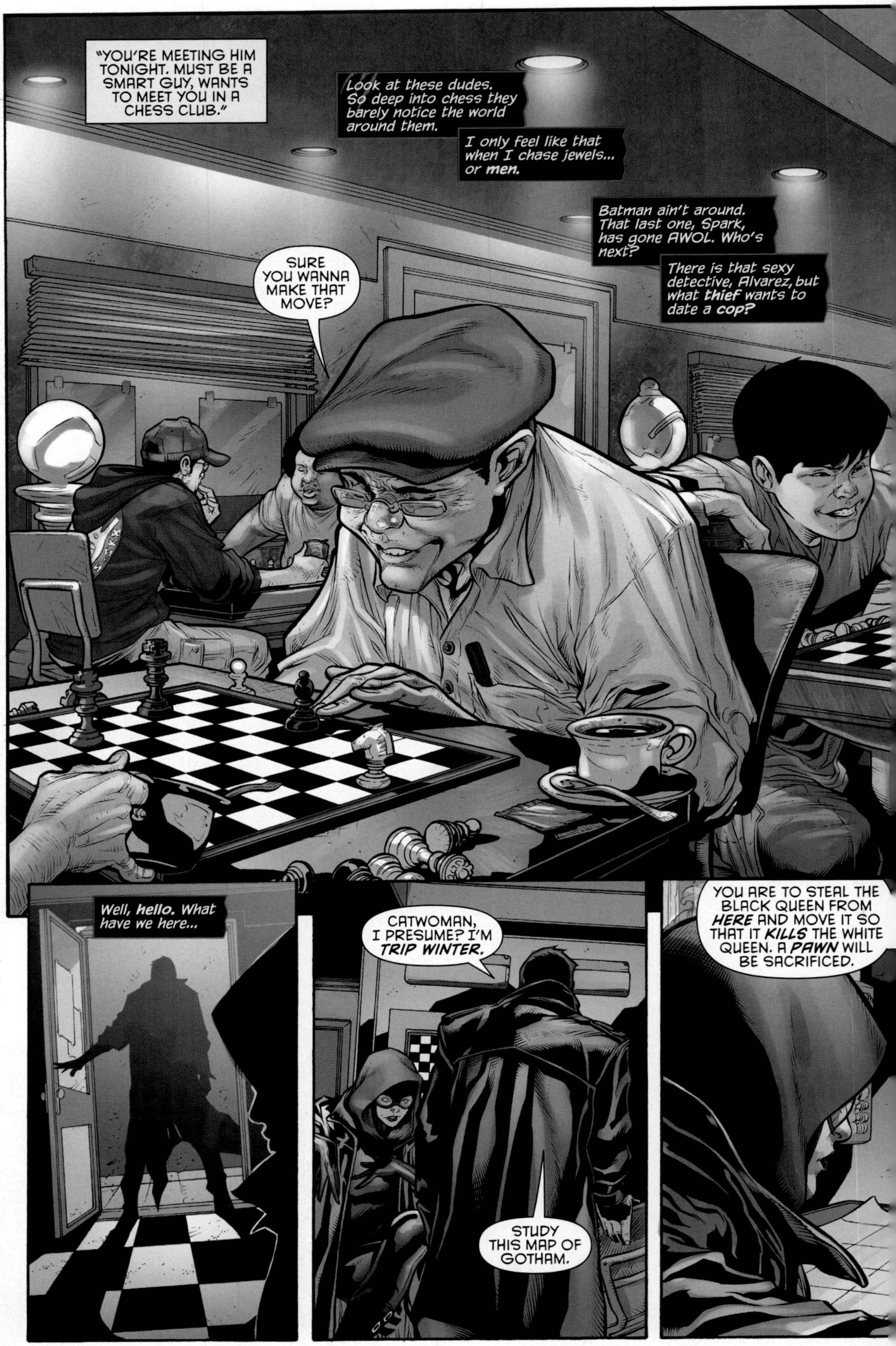
"YOU'RE MEETING HIM TONIGHT. MUST BE A SMART GUY, WANTS TO MEET YOU IN A CHESS CLUB."
Look at these dudes. So deep into chess they barely notice the world around them.
I only feel like that when I chase jewels... or men.
Batman ain't around. That last one, Spark, has gone AWOL. Who's next?
There is that sexy detective, Alvarez, but what thief wants to date a cop?
SURE YOU WANNA MAKE THAT MOVE?
Well, hello. What have we here...
CATWOMAN, I PRESUME? I'M TRIP WINTER.
STUDY THIS MAP OF GOTHAM.
YOU ARE TO STEAL THE BLACK QUEEN FROM HERE AND MOVE IT SO THAT IT KILLS THE WHITE QUEEN. A PAWN WILL BE SACRIFICED.

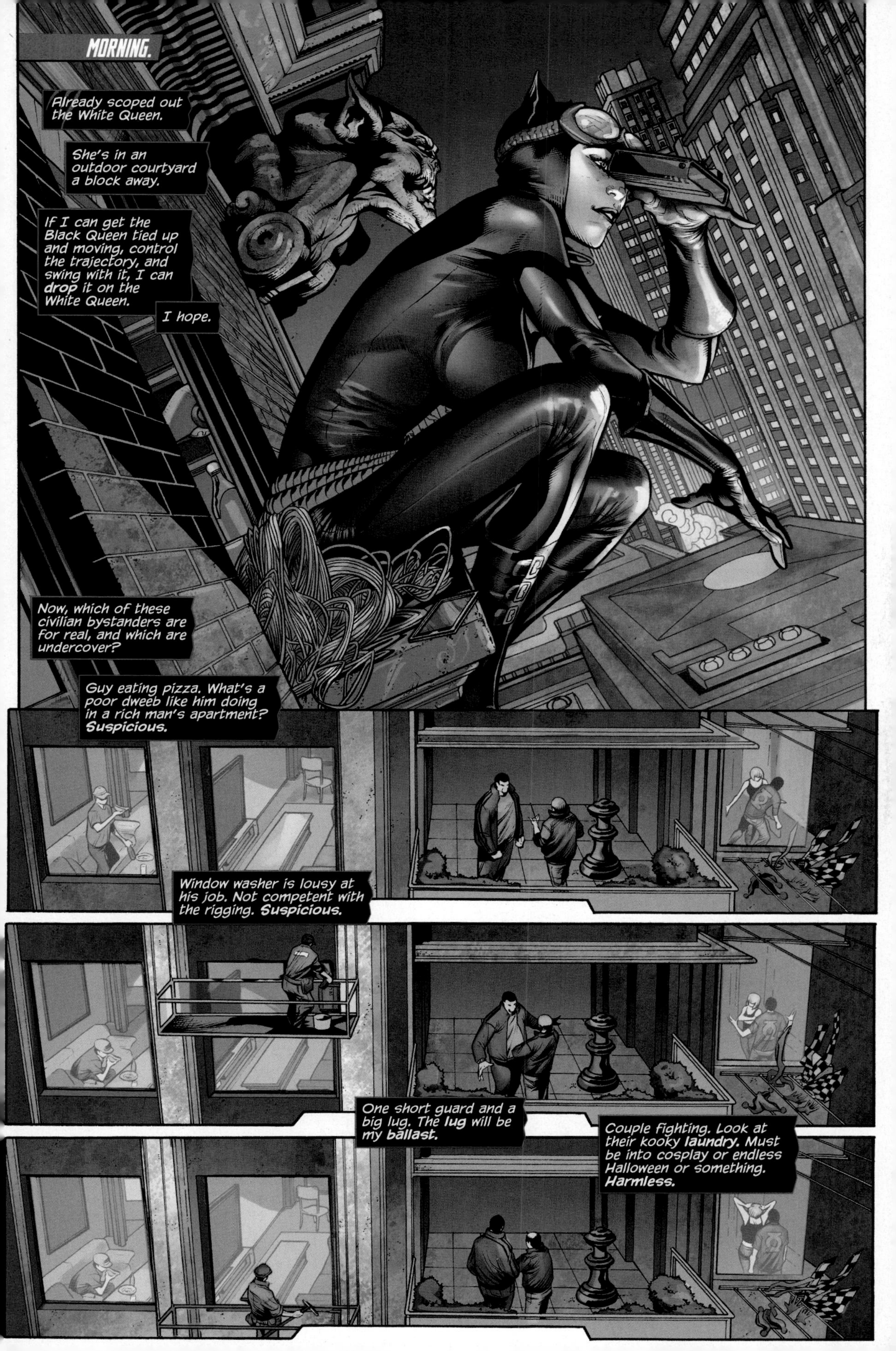
MORNING.
Already scoped out the White Queen.
She's in an outdoor courtyard a block away.
If I can get the Black Queen tied up and moving, control the trajectory, and swing with it, I can drop it on the White Queen.
I hope.
Now, which of these civilian bystanders are for real, and which are undercover?
Guy eating pizza. What's a poor dweeb like him doing in a rich man's apartment? Suspicious.
Window washer is lousy at his job. Not competent with the rigging. Suspicious.
One short guard and a big lug. The lug will be my ballast.
Couple fighting. Look at their kooky laundry. Must be into cosplay or endless Halloween or something. Harmless.

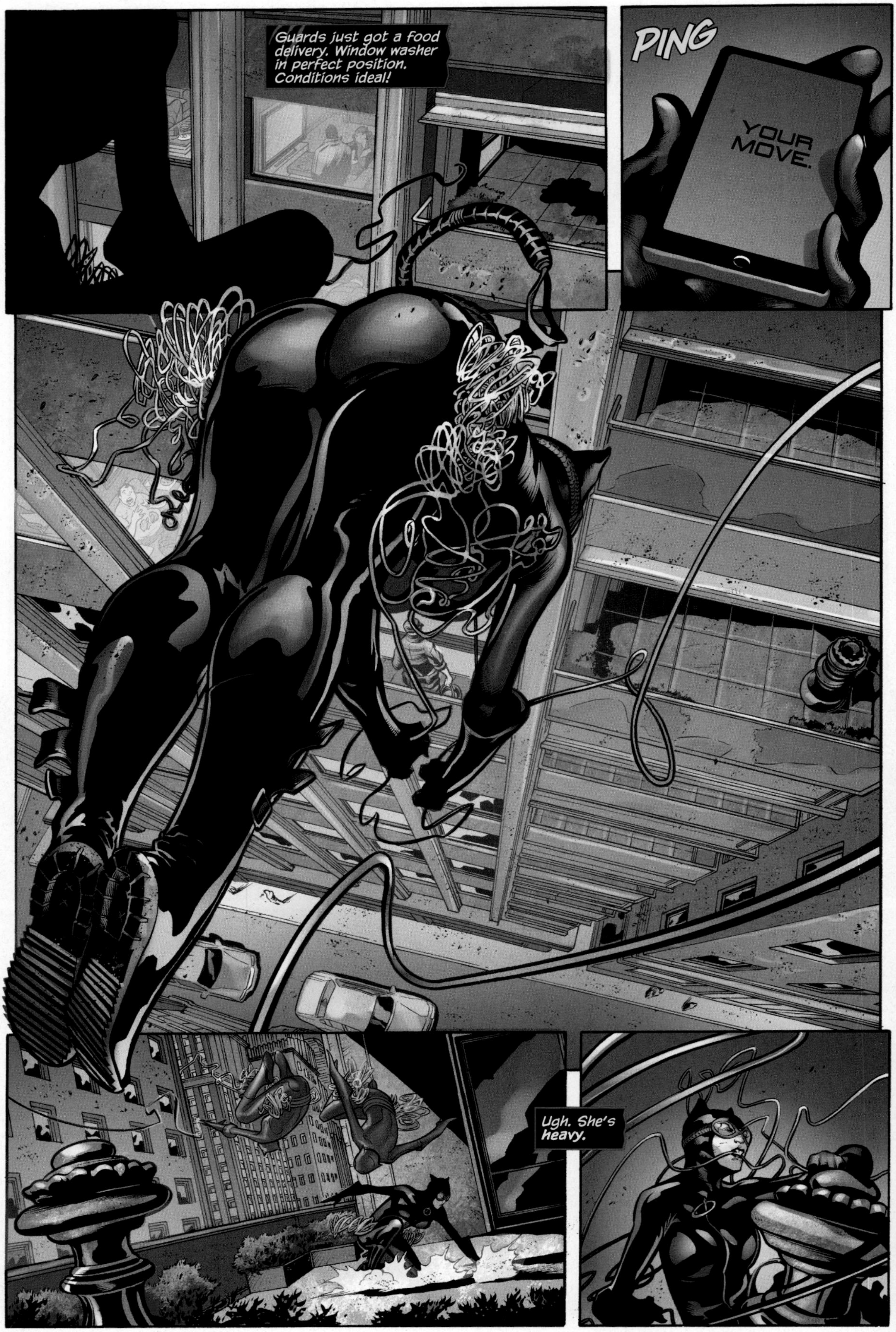
Guards just got a food delivery. Window washer in perfect position. Conditions ideal!
PING
YOUR MOVE.
Ugh. She's heavy.

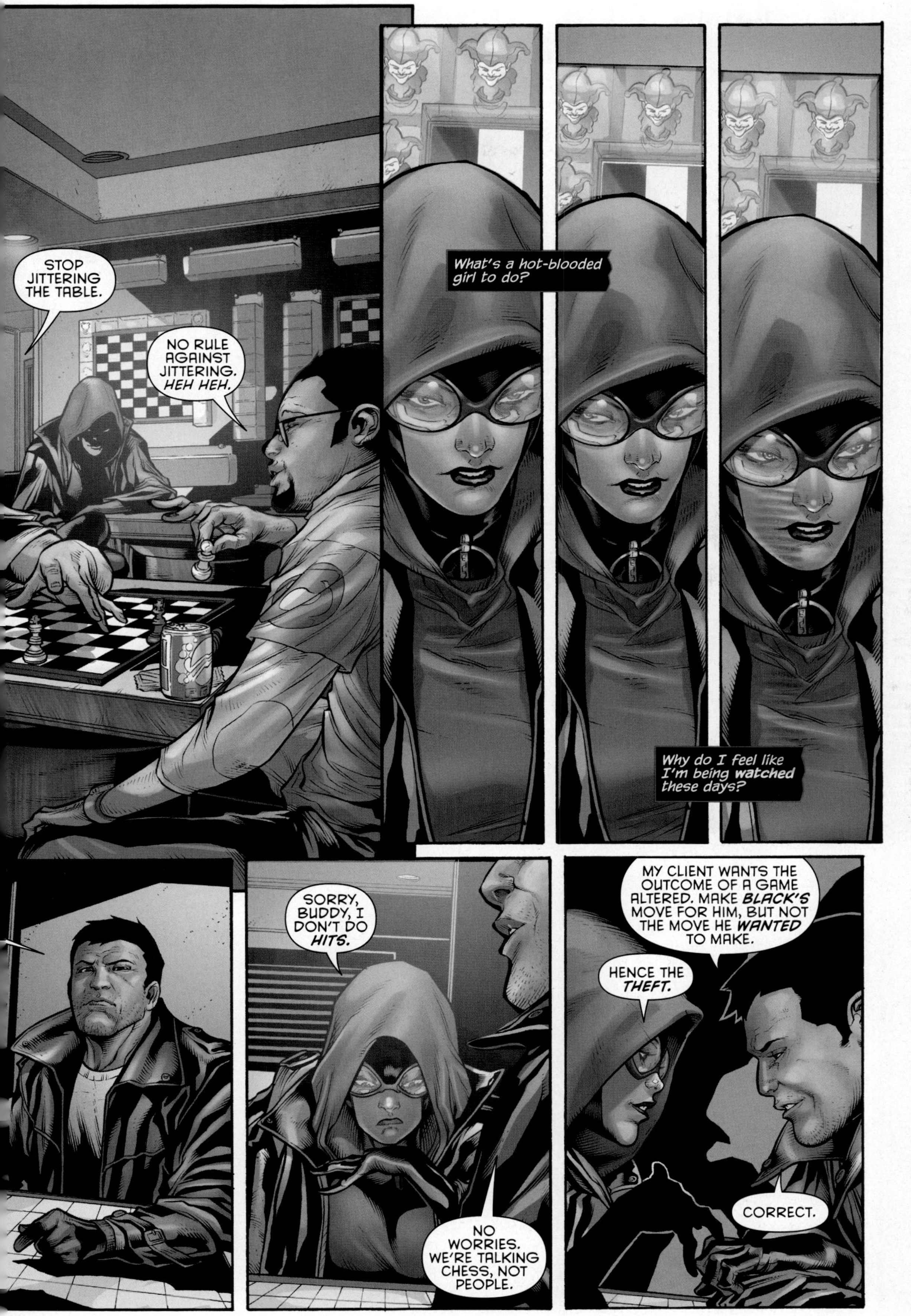
STOP JITTERING THE TABLE.
NO RULE AGAINST JITTERING. HEH HEH.
What's a hot-blooded girl to do?
Why do I feel like I'm being watched these days?
SORRY, BUDDY, I DON'T DO HITS.
NO WORRIES. WE'RE TALKING CHESS, NOT PEOPLE.
MY CLIENT WANTS THE OUTCOME OF A GAME ALTERED. MAKE BLACK'S MOVE FOR HIM, BUT NOT THE MOVE HE WANTED TO MAKE.
HENCE THE THEFT.
CORRECT.

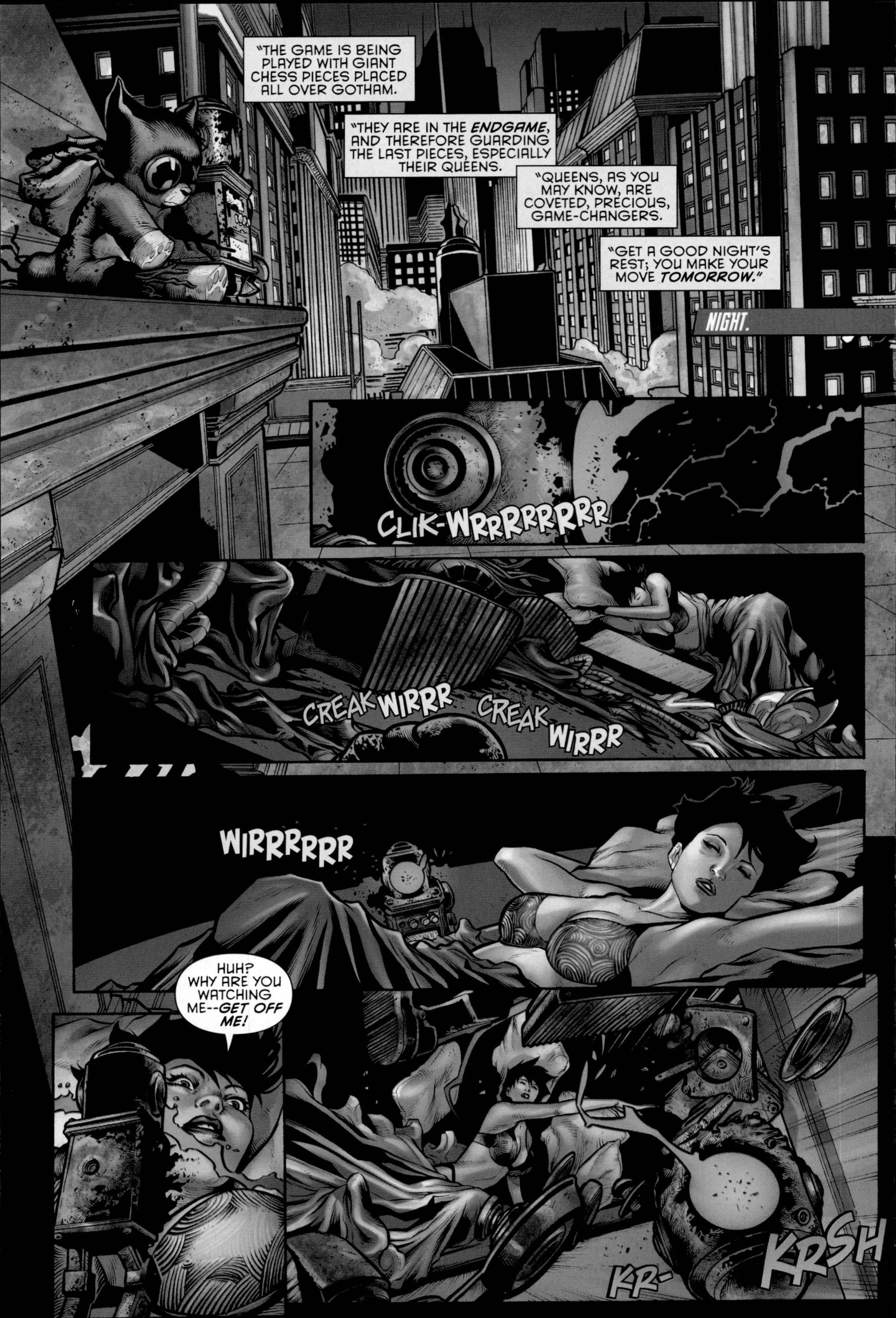

"THE GAME IS BEING PLAYED WITH GIANT CHESS PIECES PLACED ALL OVER GOTHAM.
"THEY ARE IN THE *ENDGAME*, AND THEREFORE GUARDING THE LAST PIECES, ESPECIALLY THEIR QUEENS.
"QUEENS, AS YOU MAY KNOW, ARE COVETED, PRECIOUS, GAME-CHANGERS.
"GET A GOOD NIGHT'S REST; YOU MAKE YOUR MOVE *TOMORROW*."
NIGHT.
CLIK-WRRRRRRR
CREAK WIRRR CREAK WIRRR
WIRRRRRR
HUH? WHY ARE YOU WATCHING ME--*GET OFF ME!*
KR- KRSH

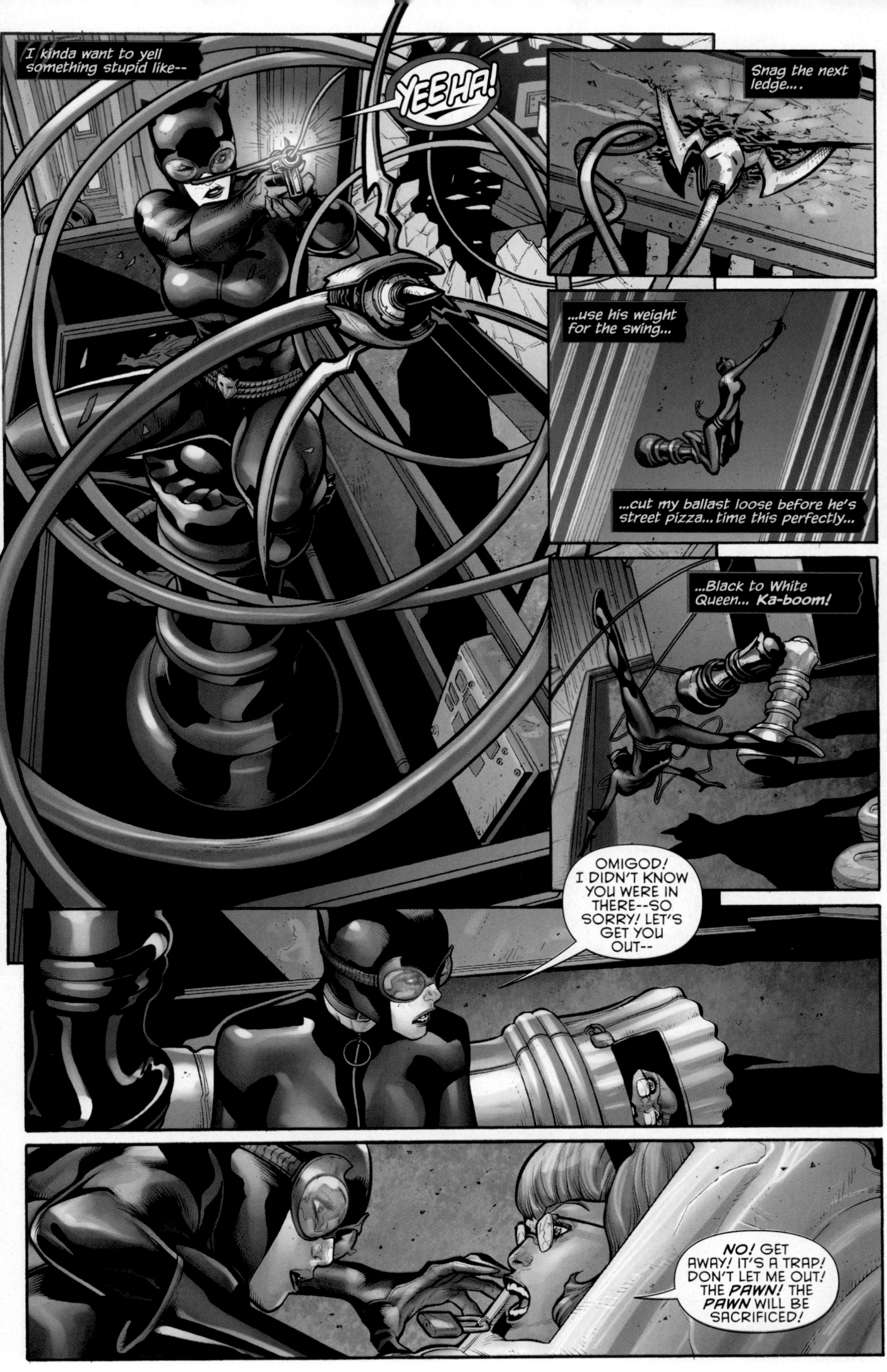
I kinda want to yell something stupid like--
YEEHA!
Snag the next ledge....
...use his weight for the swing...
...cut my ballast loose before he's street pizza...time this perfectly...
...Black to White Queen... Ka-boom!
OMIGOD! I DIDN'T KNOW YOU WERE IN THERE--SO SORRY! LET'S GET YOU OUT--
NO! GET AWAY! IT'S A TRAP! DON'T LET ME OUT! THE PAWN! THE PAWN WILL BE SACRIFICED!

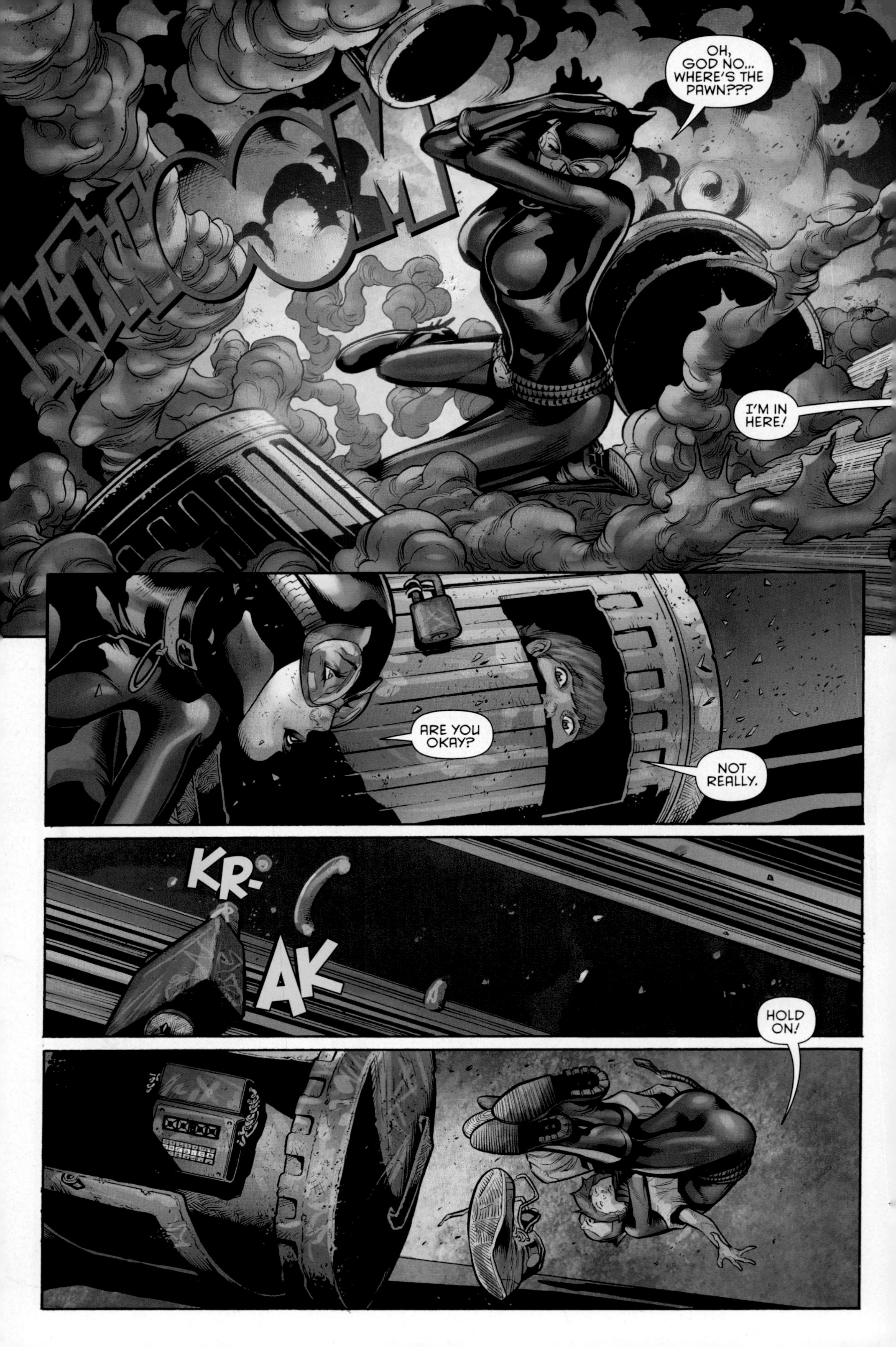
OH, GOD NO... WHERE'S THE PAWN???
I'M IN HERE!
ARE YOU OKAY?
NOT REALLY.
KR-AK
HOLD ON!

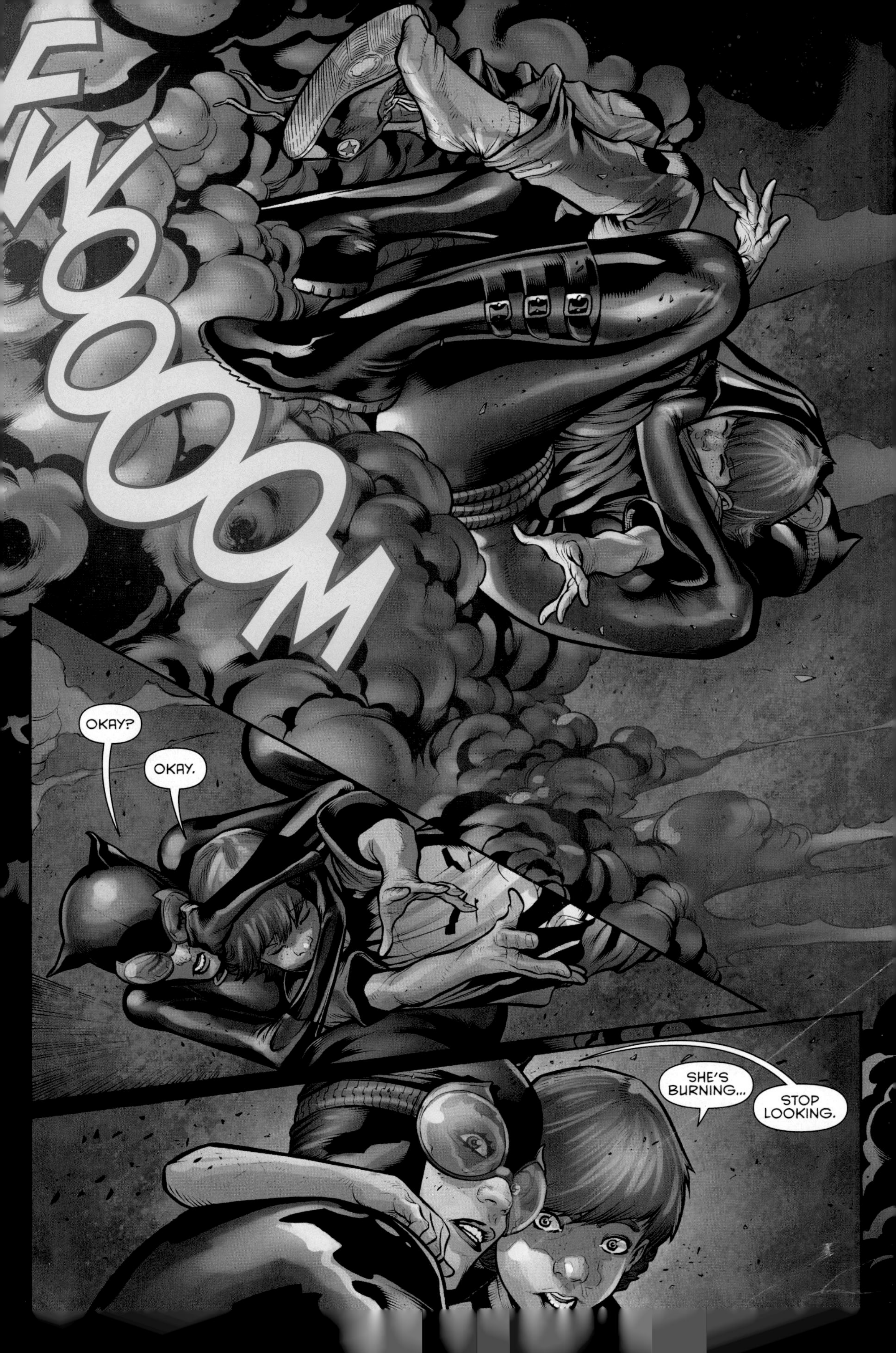
FWOOOOOM
OKAY?
OKAY.
SHE'S BURNING...
STOP LOOKING.

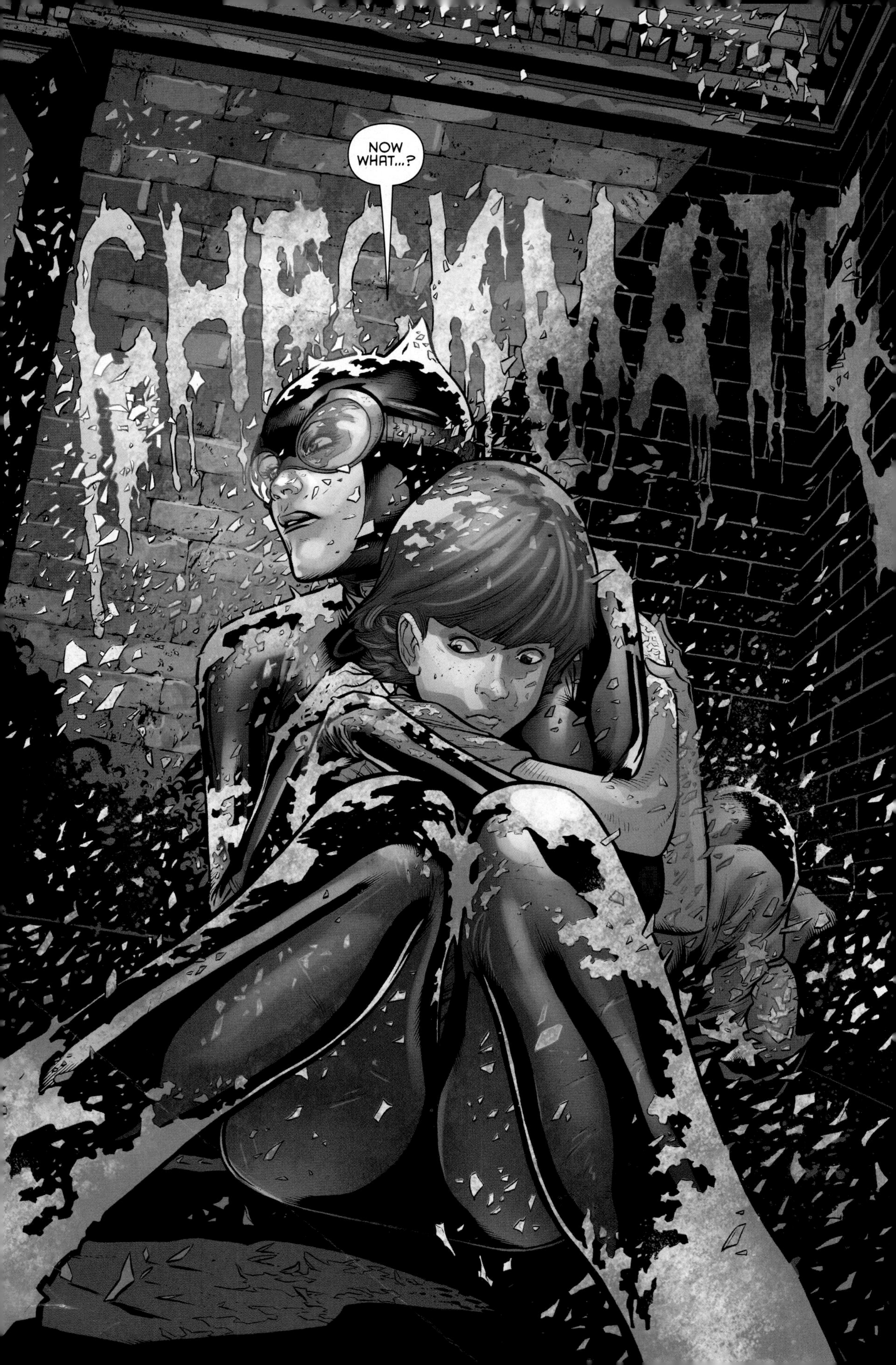
NOW WHAT...?

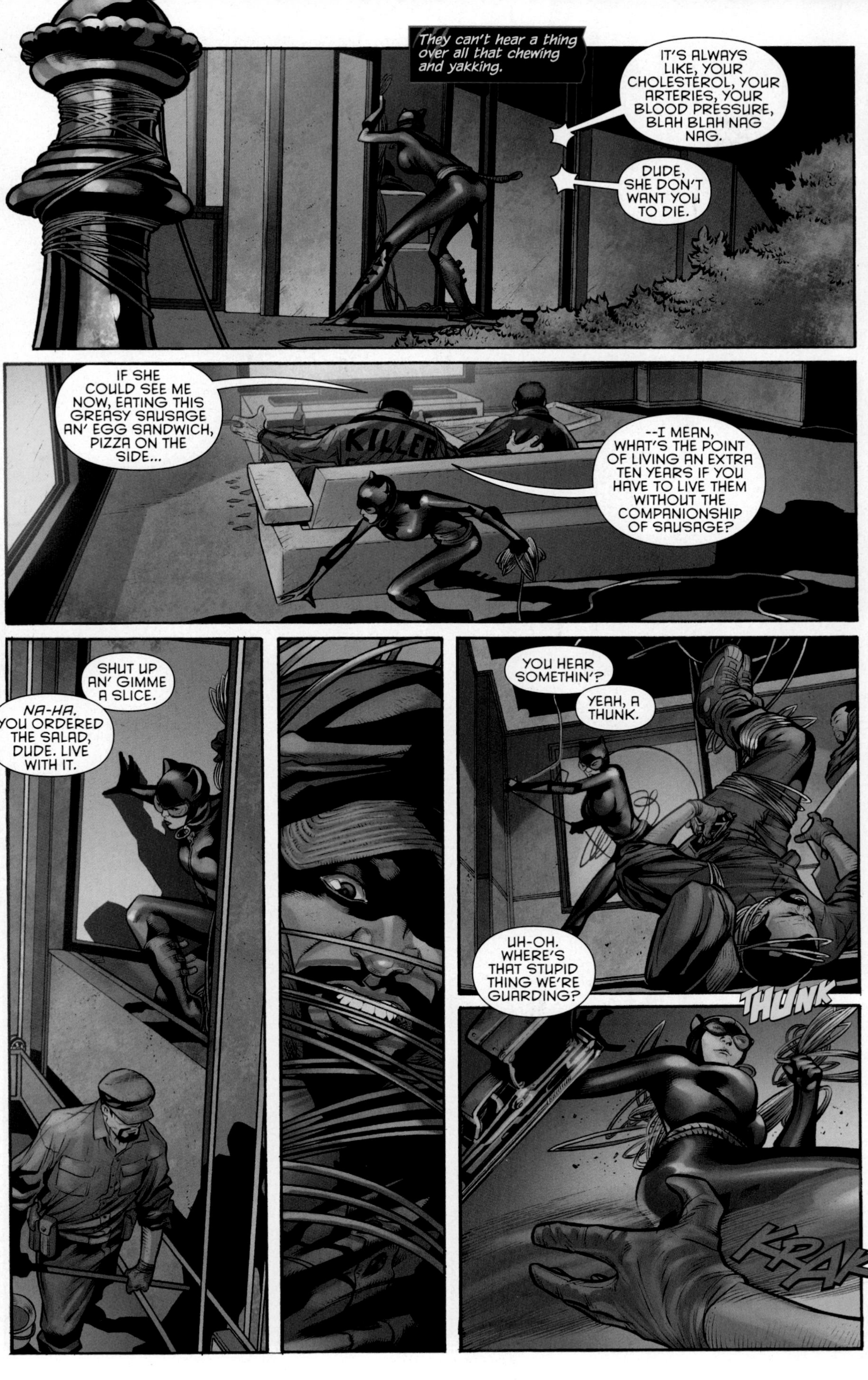
They can't hear a thing over all that chewing and yakking.
IT'S ALWAYS LIKE, YOUR CHOLESTEROL, YOUR ARTERIES, YOUR BLOOD PRESSURE, BLAH BLAH NAG NAG.
DUDE, SHE DON'T WANT YOU TO DIE.
IF SHE COULD SEE ME NOW, EATING THIS GREASY SAUSAGE AN' EGG SANDWICH, PIZZA ON THE SIDE...
KILLER
--I MEAN, WHAT'S THE POINT OF LIVING AN EXTRA TEN YEARS IF YOU HAVE TO LIVE THEM WITHOUT THE COMPANIONSHIP OF SAUSAGE?
SHUT UP AN' GIMME A SLICE.
NA-HA. YOU ORDERED THE SALAD, DUDE. LIVE WITH IT.
YOU HEAR SOMETHIN'?
YEAH, A THUNK.
UH-OH. WHERE'S THAT STUPID THING WE'RE GUARDING?
THUNK
KRAK

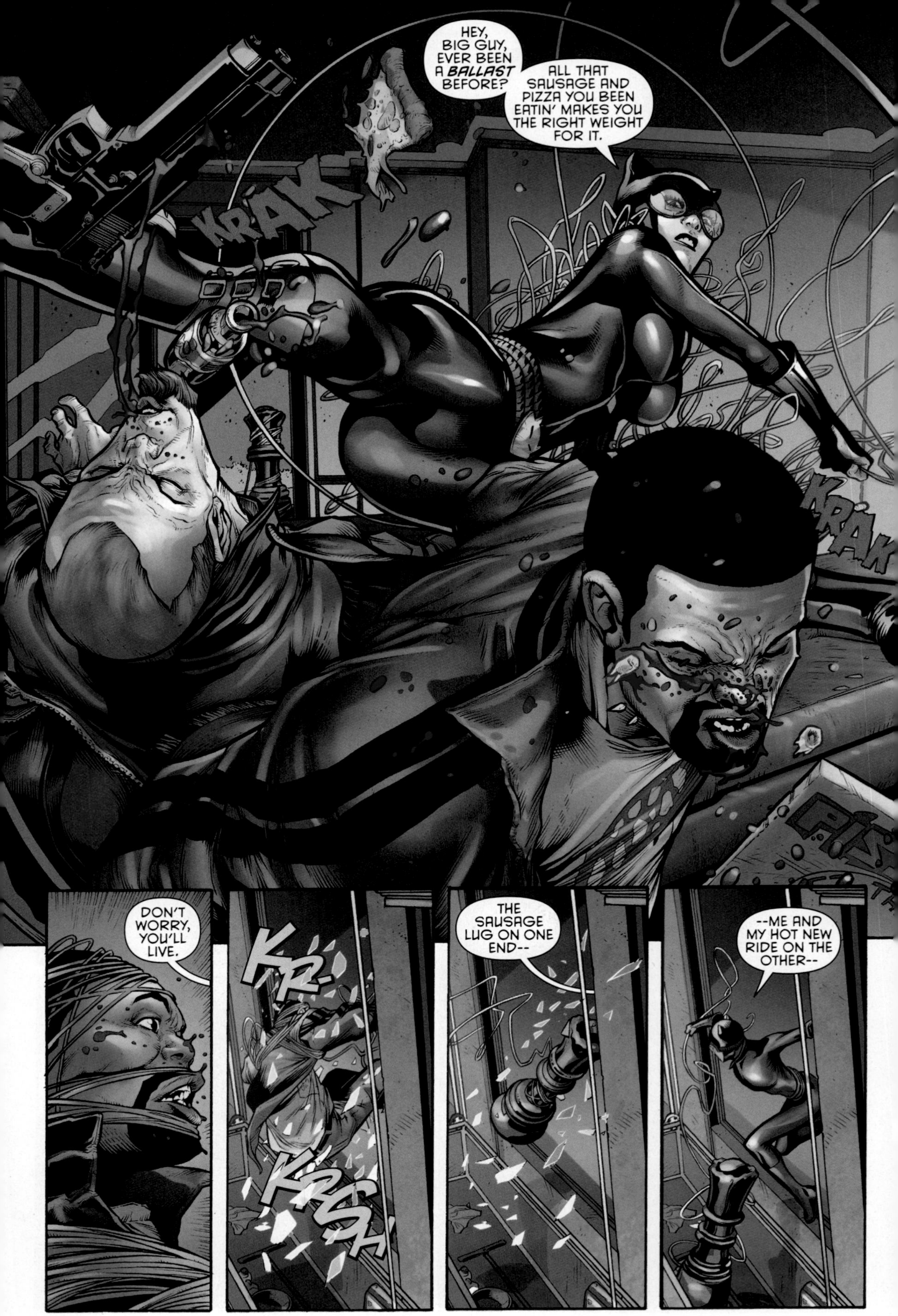
HEY, BIG GUY, EVER BEEN A *BALLAST* BEFORE?
ALL THAT SAUSAGE AND PIZZA YOU BEEN EATIN' MAKES YOU THE RIGHT WEIGHT FOR IT.
KRAK
KRAK
DON'T WORRY, YOU'LL LIVE.
THE SAUSAGE LUG ON ONE END--
--ME AND MY HOT NEW RIDE ON THE OTHER--

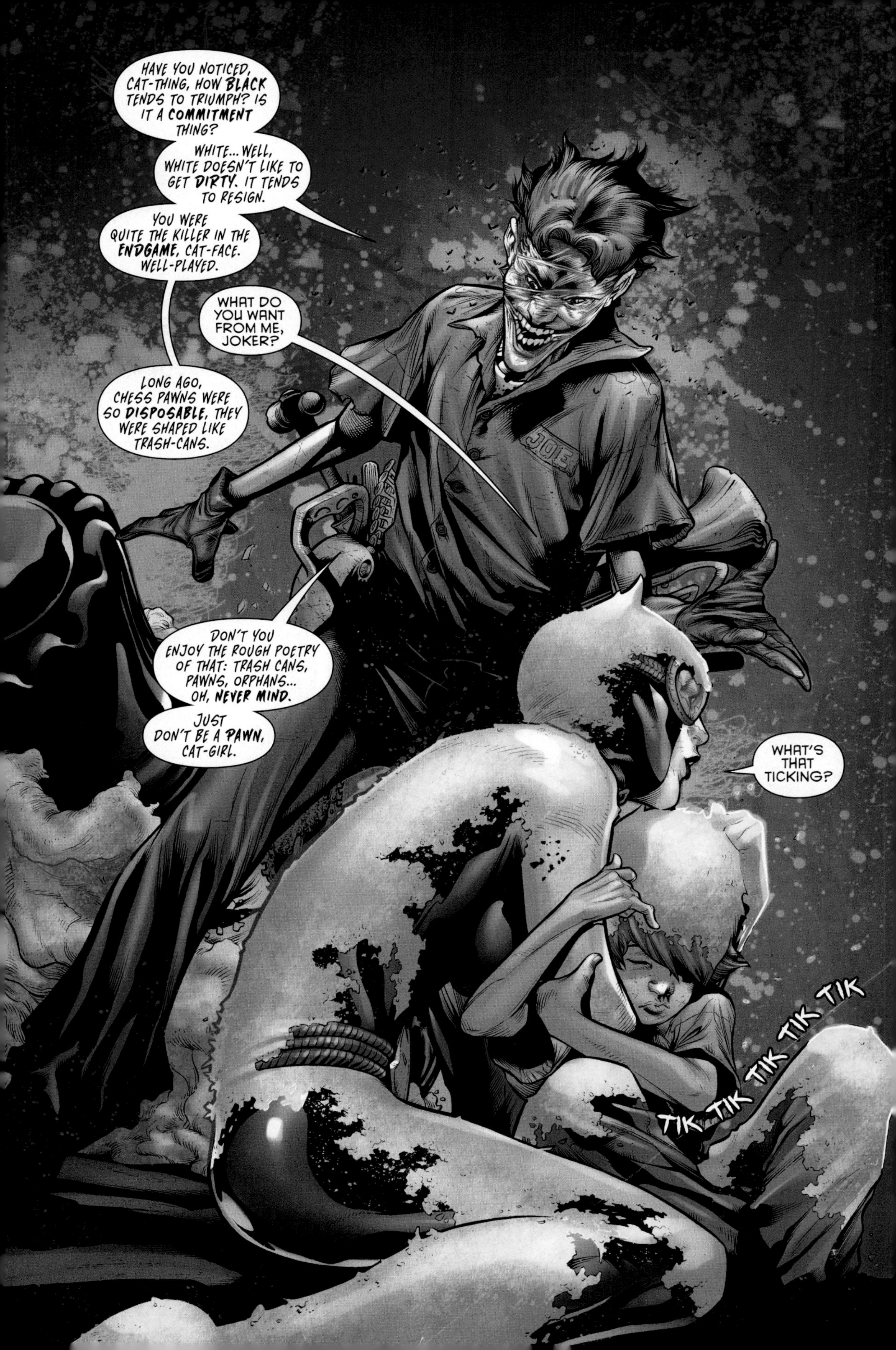
HAVE YOU NOTICED, CAT-THING, HOW BLACK TENDS TO TRIUMPH? IS IT A COMMITMENT THING?
WHITE... WELL, WHITE DOESN'T LIKE TO GET DIRTY. IT TENDS TO RESIGN.
YOU WERE QUITE THE KILLER IN THE ENDGAME, CAT-FACE. WELL-PLAYED.
WHAT DO YOU WANT FROM ME, JOKER?
LONG AGO, CHESS PAWNS WERE SO DISPOSABLE, THEY WERE SHAPED LIKE TRASH-CANS.
DON'T YOU ENJOY THE ROUGH POETRY OF THAT: TRASH CANS, PAWNS, ORPHANS... OH, NEVER MIND.
JUST DON'T BE A PAWN, CAT-GIRL.
WHAT'S THAT TICKING?
TIK TIK TIK TIK TIK

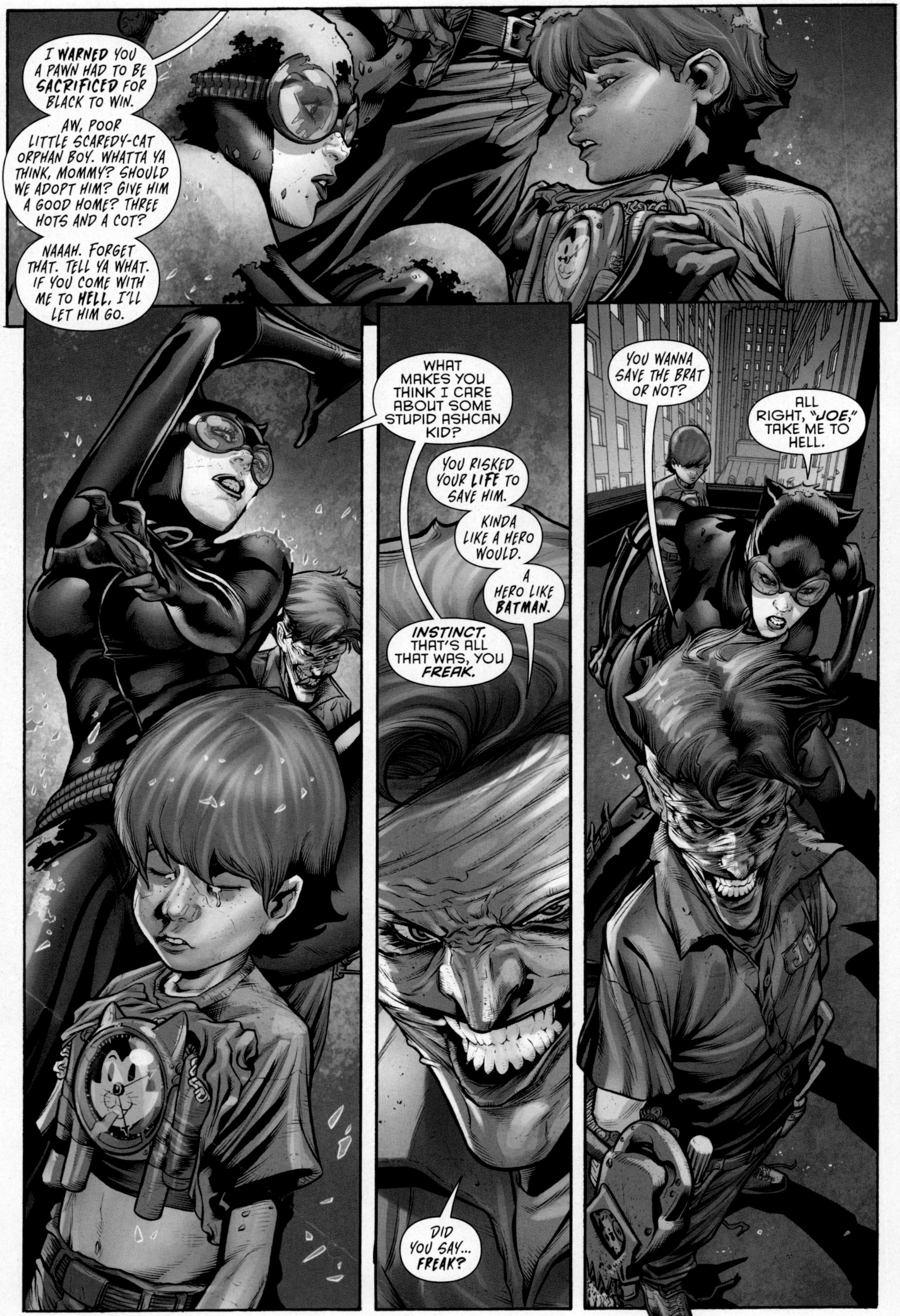
I WARNED YOU A PAWN HAD TO BE SACRIFICED FOR BLACK TO WIN.
AW, POOR LITTLE SCAREDY-CAT ORPHAN BOY. WHATTA YA THINK, MOMMY? SHOULD WE ADOPT HIM? GIVE HIM A GOOD HOME? THREE HOTS AND A COT?
NAAAH. FORGET THAT. TELL YA WHAT. IF YOU COME WITH ME TO HELL, I'LL LET HIM GO.
WHAT MAKES YOU THINK I CARE ABOUT SOME STUPID ASHCAN KID?
YOU RISKED YOUR LIFE TO SAVE HIM.
KINDA LIKE A HERO WOULD.
A HERO LIKE BATMAN.
INSTINCT. THAT'S ALL THAT WAS, YOU FREAK.
DID YOU SAY... FREAK?
YOU WANNA SAVE THE BRAT OR NOT?
ALL RIGHT, "JOE," TAKE ME TO HELL.

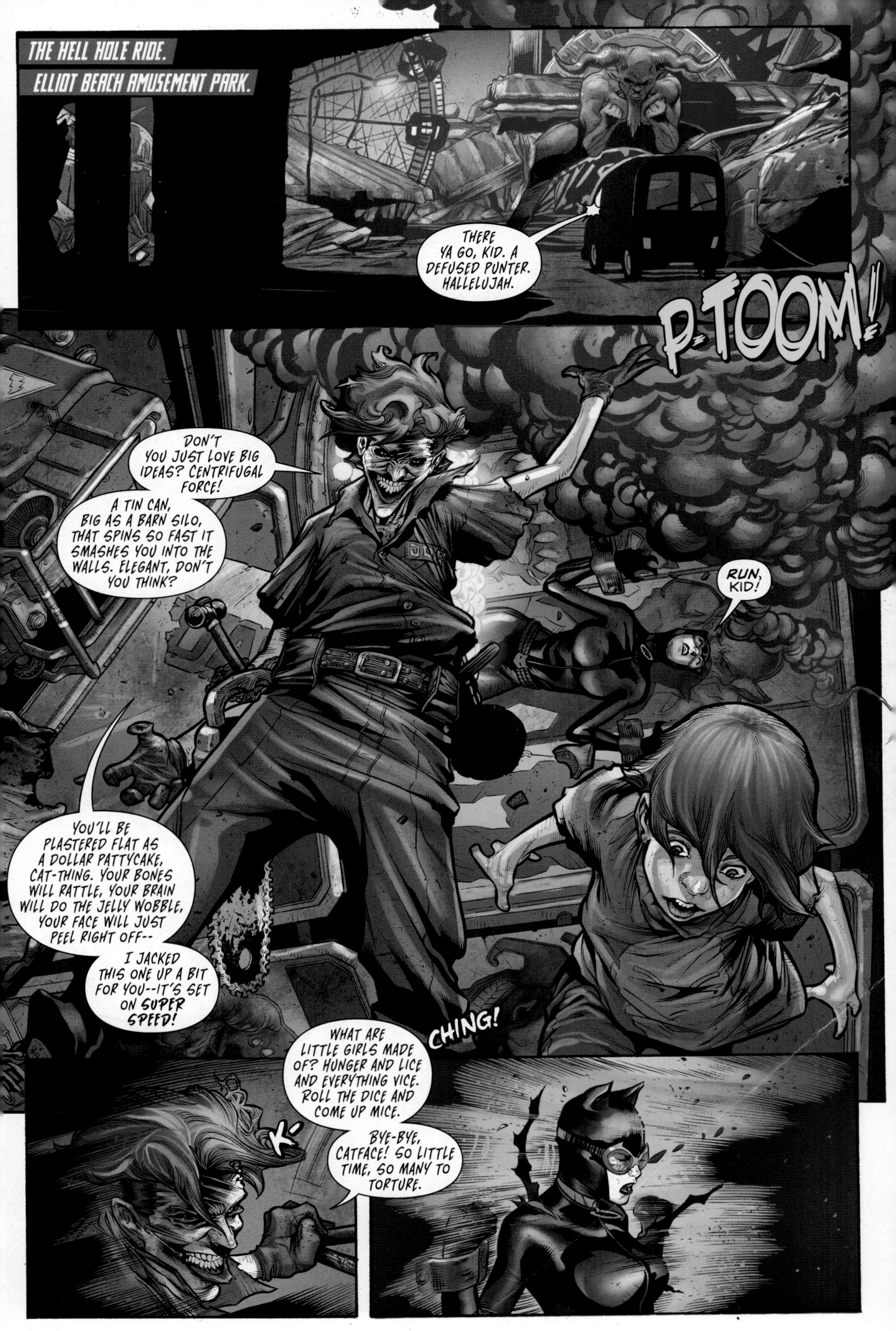
THE HELL HOLE RIDE.
ELLIOT BEACH AMUSEMENT PARK.
THERE YA GO, KID. A DEFUSED PUNTER. HALLELUJAH.
P-TOOM!
DON'T YOU JUST LOVE BIG IDEAS? CENTRIFUGAL FORCE!
A TIN CAN, BIG AS A BARN SILO, THAT SPINS SO FAST IT SMASHES YOU INTO THE WALLS. ELEGANT, DON'T YOU THINK?
RUN, KID!
YOU'LL BE PLASTERED FLAT AS A DOLLAR PATTYCAKE, CAT-THING. YOUR BONES WILL RATTLE, YOUR BRAIN WILL DO THE JELLY WOBBLE, YOUR FACE WILL JUST PEEL RIGHT OFF--
I JACKED THIS ONE UP A BIT FOR YOU--IT'S SET ON SUPER SPEED!
CHING!
WHAT ARE LITTLE GIRLS MADE OF? HUNGER AND LICE AND EVERYTHING VICE. ROLL THE DICE AND COME UP MICE.
BYE-BYE, CATFACE! SO LITTLE TIME, SO MANY TO TORTURE.
K-

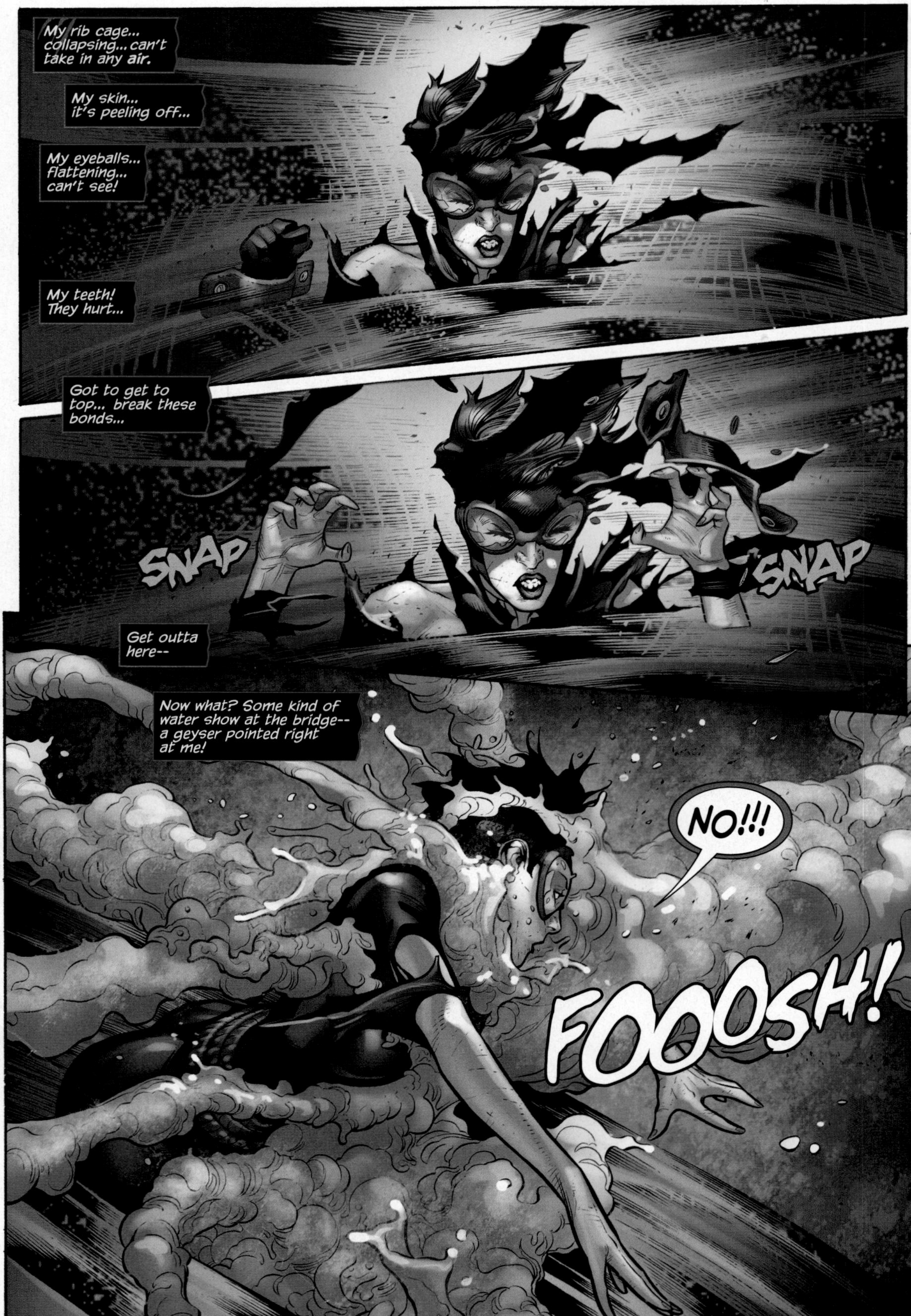

My rib cage... collapsing... can't take in any air.
My skin... it's peeling off...
My eyeballs... flattening... can't see!
My teeth! They hurt...
Got to get to top... break these bonds...
SNAP
SNAP
Get outta here--
Now what? Some kind of water show at the bridge-- a geyser pointed right at me!
NO!!!
FOOOSH!

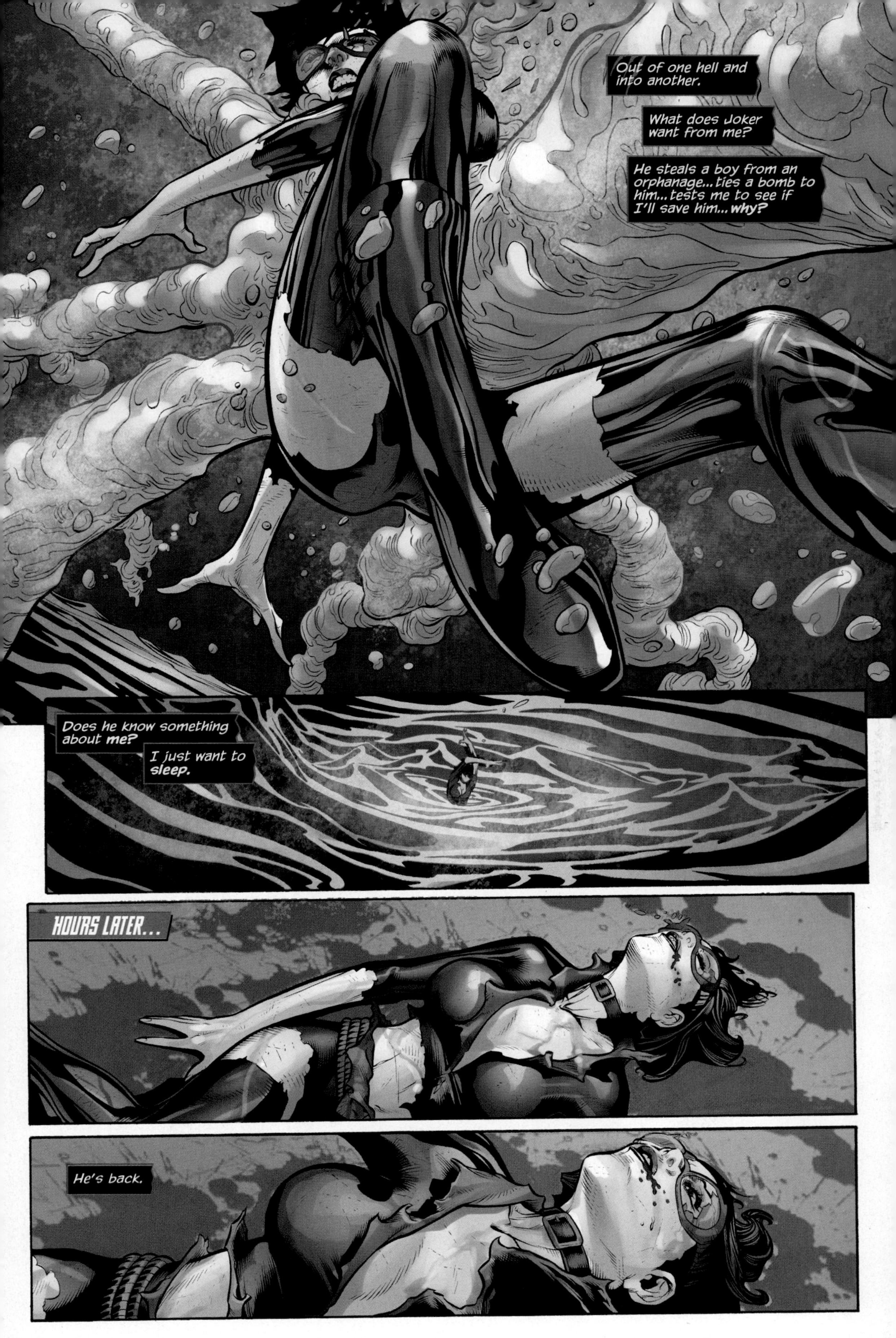
Out of one hell and into another.
What does Joker want from me?
He steals a boy from an orphanage...ties a bomb to him...tests me to see if I'll save him...why?
Does he know something about me?
I just want to sleep.
HOURS LATER...
He's back.

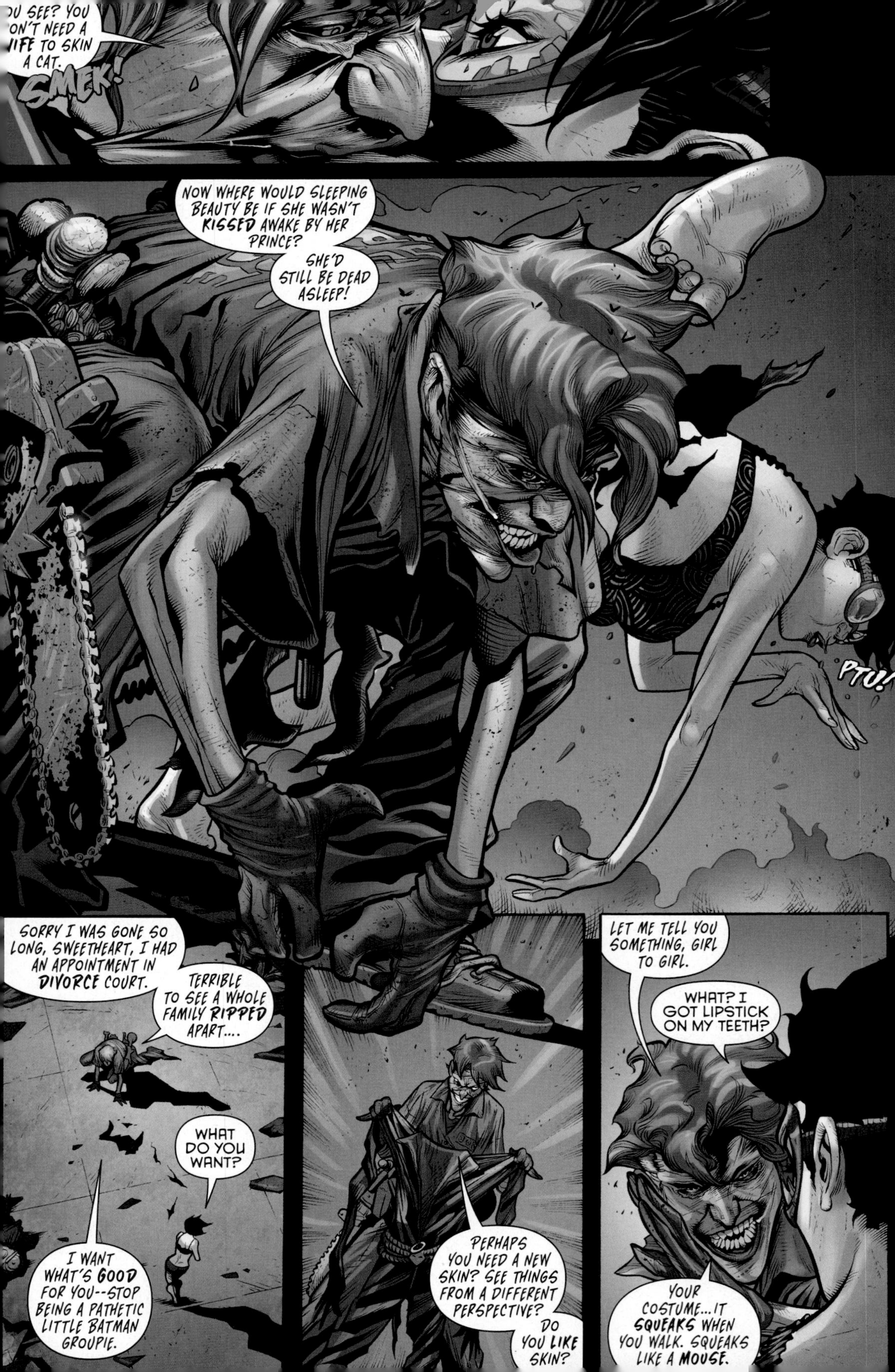

OU SEE? YOU
ON'T NEED A
IFE TO SKIN
A CAT.
SMEK!
NOW WHERE WOULD SLEEPING BEAUTY BE IF SHE WASN'T KISSED AWAKE BY HER PRINCE?
SHE'D STILL BE DEAD ASLEEP!
PTU!
SORRY I WAS GONE SO LONG, SWEETHEART, I HAD AN APPOINTMENT IN DIVORCE COURT.
TERRIBLE TO SEE A WHOLE FAMILY RIPPED APART....
WHAT DO YOU WANT?
I WANT WHAT'S GOOD FOR YOU--STOP BEING A PATHETIC LITTLE BATMAN GROUPIE.
PERHAPS YOU NEED A NEW SKIN? SEE THINGS FROM A DIFFERENT PERSPECTIVE?
DO YOU LIKE SKIN?
LET ME TELL YOU SOMETHING, GIRL TO GIRL.
WHAT? I GOT LIPSTICK ON MY TEETH?
YOUR COSTUME...IT SQUEAKS WHEN YOU WALK. SQUEAKS LIKE A MOUSE.

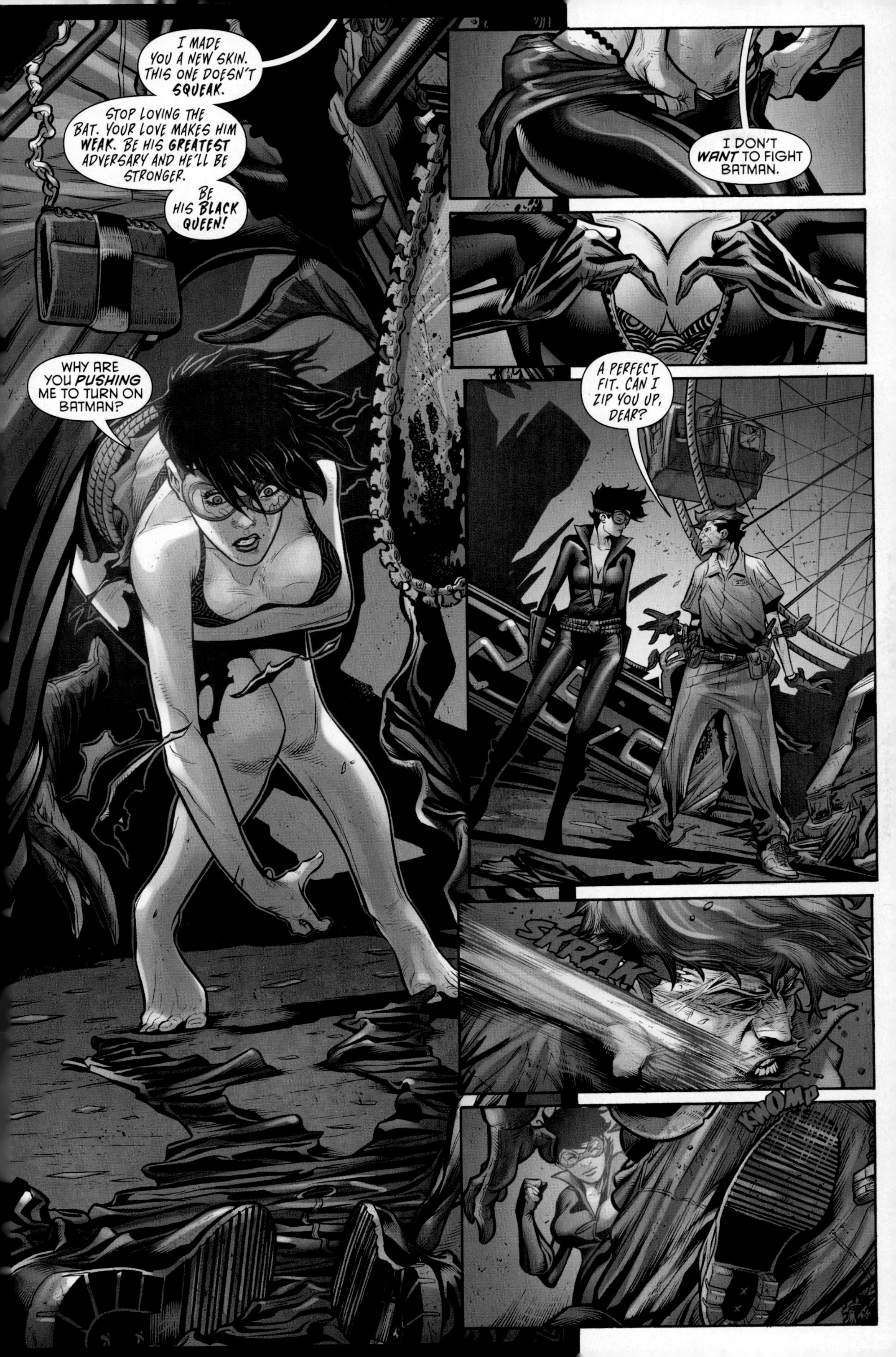
I MADE YOU A NEW SKIN. THIS ONE DOESN'T SQUEAK.
STOP LOVING THE BAT. YOUR LOVE MAKES HIM WEAK. BE HIS GREATEST ADVERSARY AND HE'LL BE STRONGER.
BE HIS BLACK QUEEN!
WHY ARE YOU PUSHING ME TO TURN ON BATMAN?
I DON'T WANT TO FIGHT BATMAN.
A PERFECT FIT. CAN I ZIP YOU UP, DEAR?
SKRAK
KWOMP

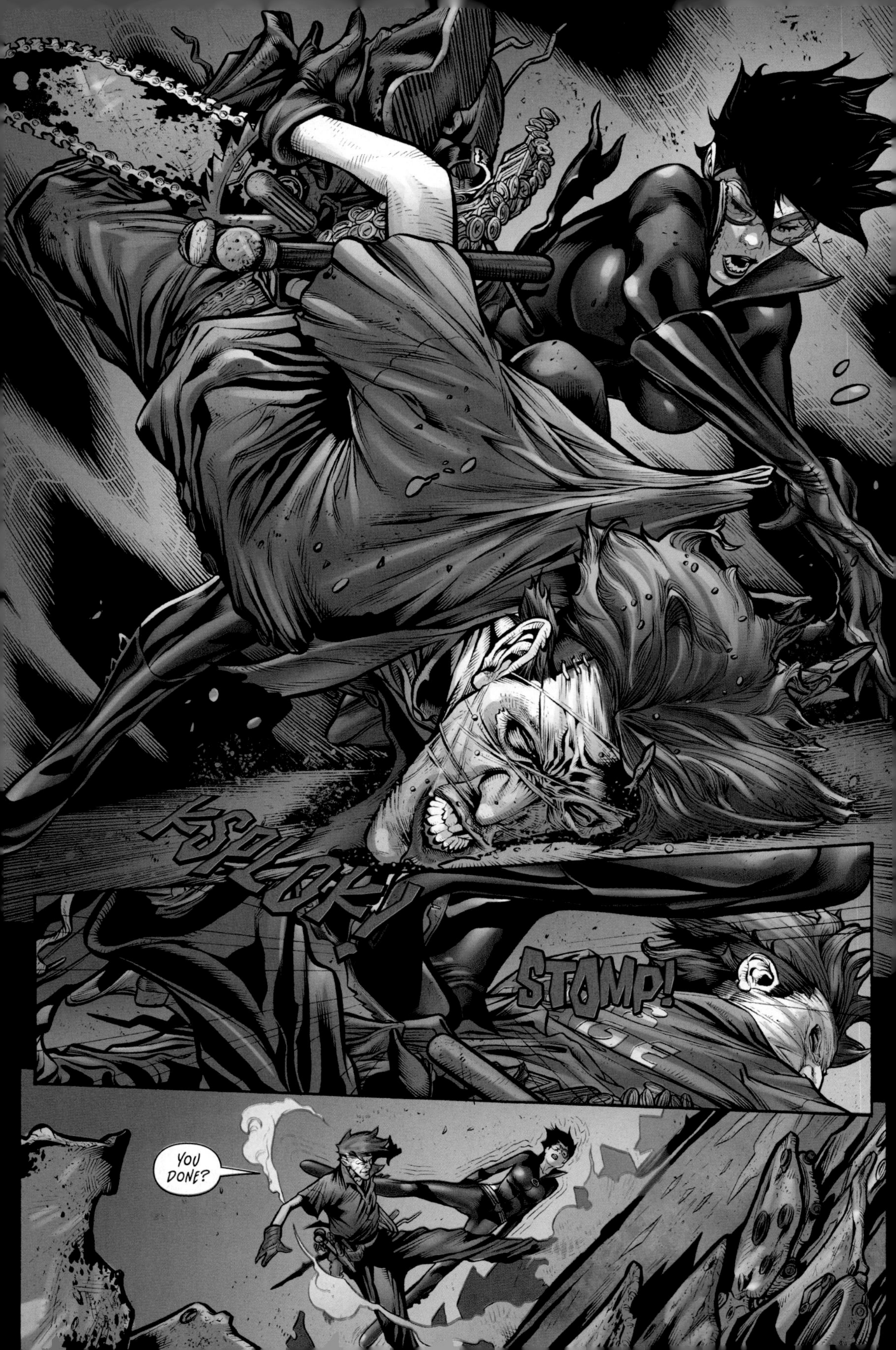
KSPLORK!
STOMP!
YOU DONE?

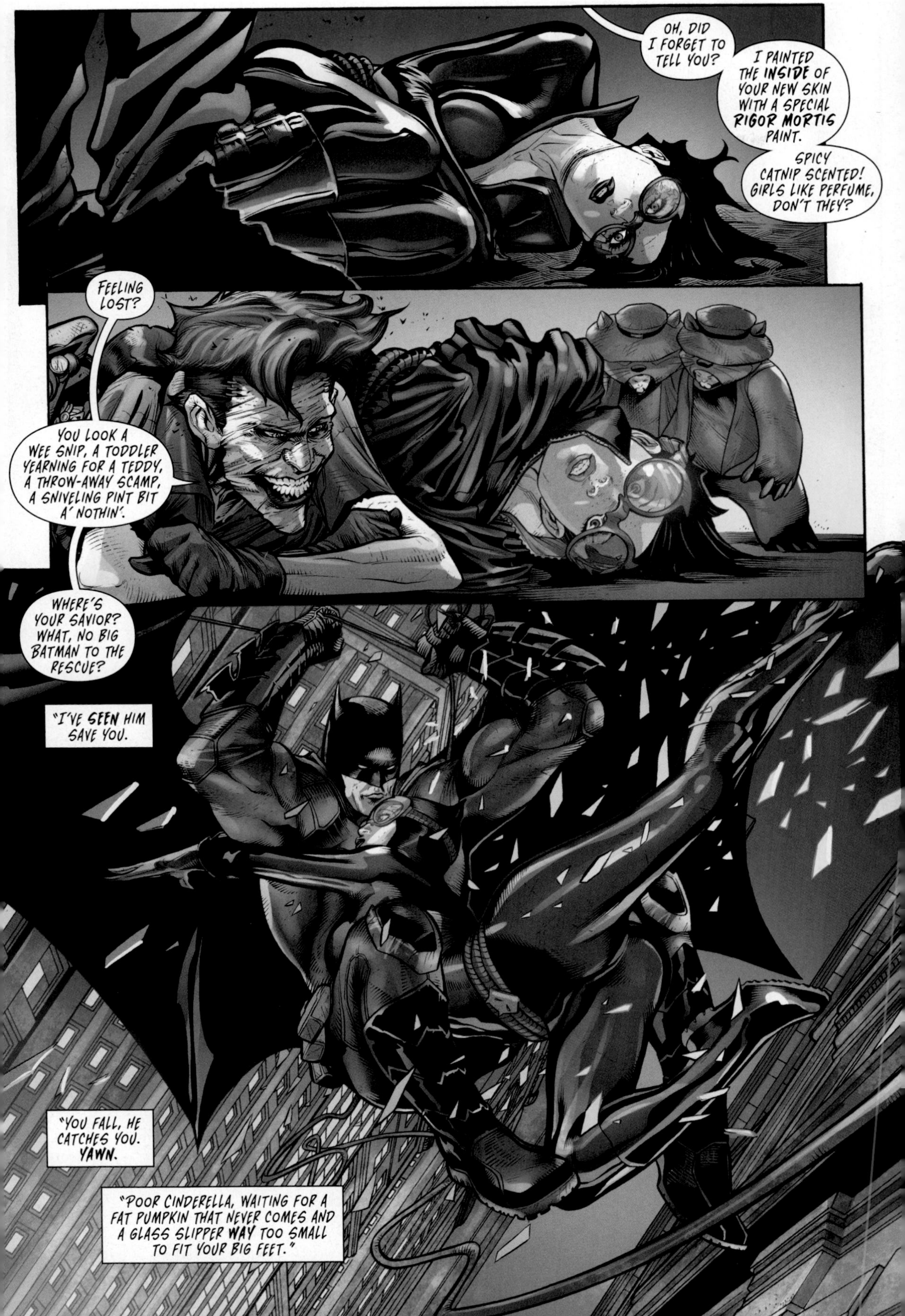
OH, DID I FORGET TO TELL YOU?
I PAINTED THE **INSIDE** OF YOUR NEW SKIN WITH A SPECIAL **RIGOR MORTIS** PAINT.
SPICY CATNIP SCENTED! GIRLS LIKE PERFUME, DON'T THEY?
FEELING LOST?
YOU LOOK A WEE SNIP, A TODDLER YEARNING FOR A TEDDY, A THROW-AWAY SCAMP, A SNIVELING PINT BIT A' NOTHIN'.
WHERE'S YOUR SAVIOR? WHAT, NO BIG BATMAN TO THE RESCUE?
"I'VE **SEEN** HIM SAVE YOU.
"YOU FALL, HE CATCHES YOU. **YAWN.**
"POOR CINDERELLA, WAITING FOR A FAT PUMPKIN THAT NEVER COMES AND A GLASS SLIPPER **WAY** TOO SMALL TO FIT YOUR BIG FEET."

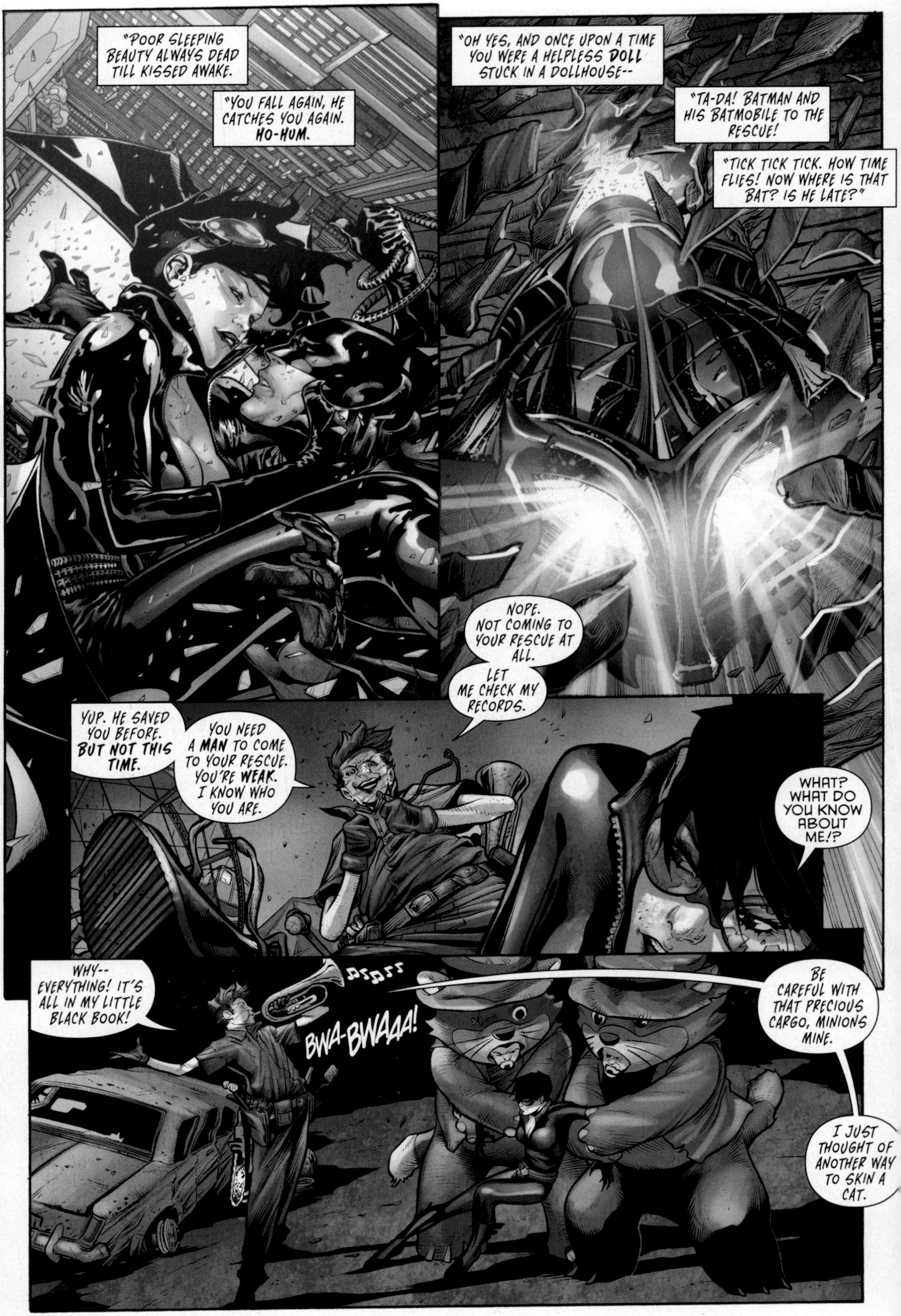
"POOR SLEEPING BEAUTY ALWAYS DEAD TILL KISSED AWAKE.
"YOU FALL AGAIN, HE CATCHES YOU AGAIN. HO-HUM.
"OH YES, AND ONCE UPON A TIME YOU WERE A HELPLESS DOLL STUCK IN A DOLLHOUSE--
"TA-DA! BATMAN AND HIS BATMOBILE TO THE RESCUE!
"TICK TICK TICK. HOW TIME FLIES! NOW WHERE IS THAT BAT? IS HE LATE?"
NOPE. NOT COMING TO YOUR RESCUE AT ALL.
LET ME CHECK MY RECORDS.
YUP. HE SAVED YOU BEFORE. BUT NOT THIS TIME.
YOU NEED A MAN TO COME TO YOUR RESCUE. YOU'RE WEAK. I KNOW WHO YOU ARE.
WHAT? WHAT DO YOU KNOW ABOUT ME!?
WHY-- EVERYTHING! IT'S ALL IN MY LITTLE BLACK BOOK!
BWA-BWAAA!
BE CAREFUL WITH THAT PRECIOUS CARGO, MINIONS MINE.
I JUST THOUGHT OF ANOTHER WAY TO SKIN A CAT.

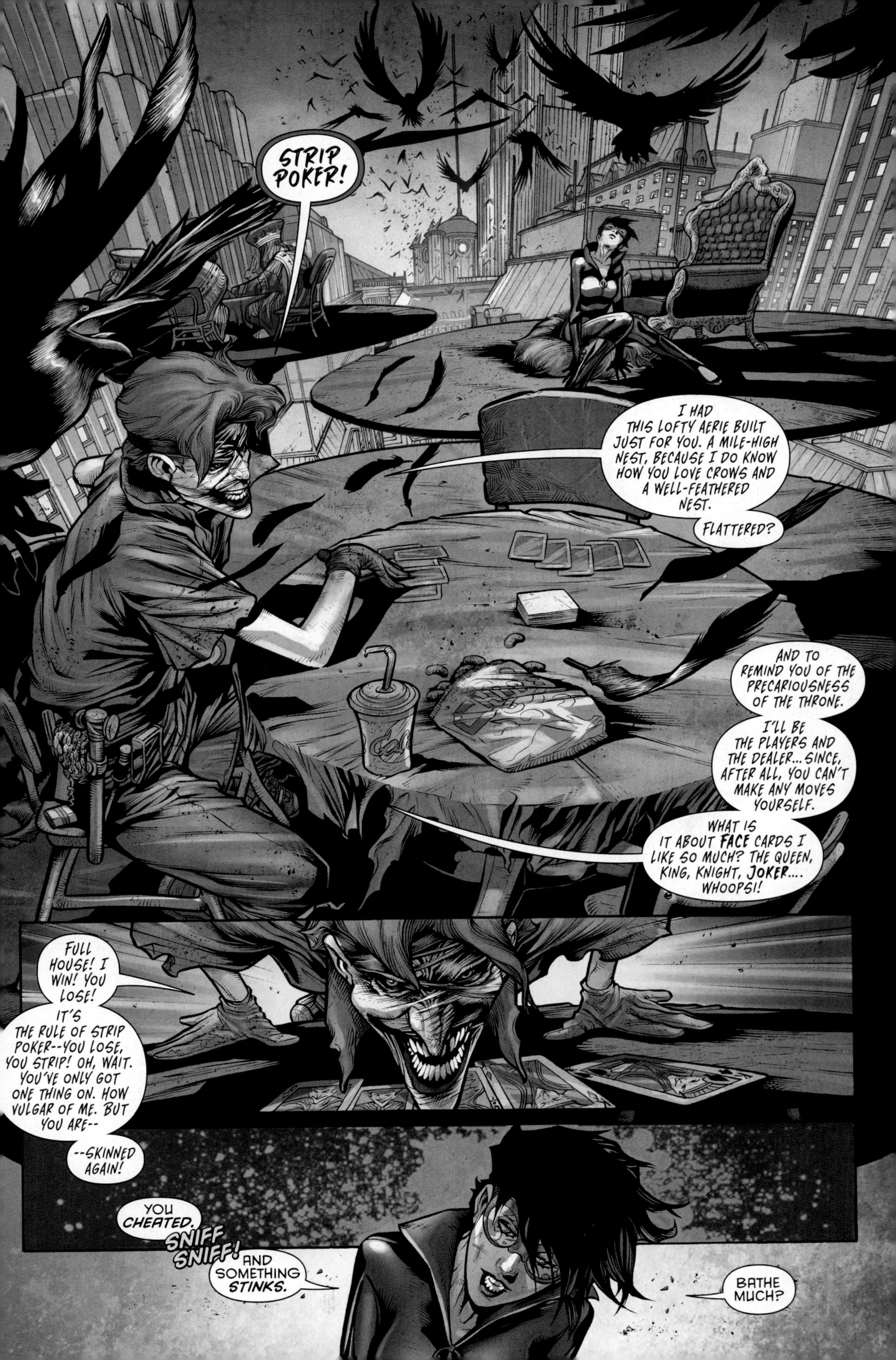
STRIP POKER!
I HAD THIS LOFTY AERIE BUILT JUST FOR YOU. A MILE-HIGH NEST, BECAUSE I DO KNOW HOW YOU LOVE CROWS AND A WELL-FEATHERED NEST.
FLATTERED?
AND TO REMIND YOU OF THE PRECARIOUSNESS OF THE THRONE.
I'LL BE THE PLAYERS AND THE DEALER... SINCE, AFTER ALL, YOU CAN'T MAKE ANY MOVES YOURSELF.
WHAT IS IT ABOUT FACE CARDS I LIKE SO MUCH? THE QUEEN, KING, KNIGHT, JOKER.... WHOOPS!!
FULL HOUSE! I WIN! YOU LOSE!
IT'S THE RULE OF STRIP POKER--YOU LOSE, YOU STRIP! OH, WAIT. YOU'VE ONLY GOT ONE THING ON. HOW VULGAR OF ME. BUT YOU ARE--
--SKINNED AGAIN!
YOU CHEATED.
SNIFF SNIFF!
AND SOMETHING STINKS.
BATHE MUCH?

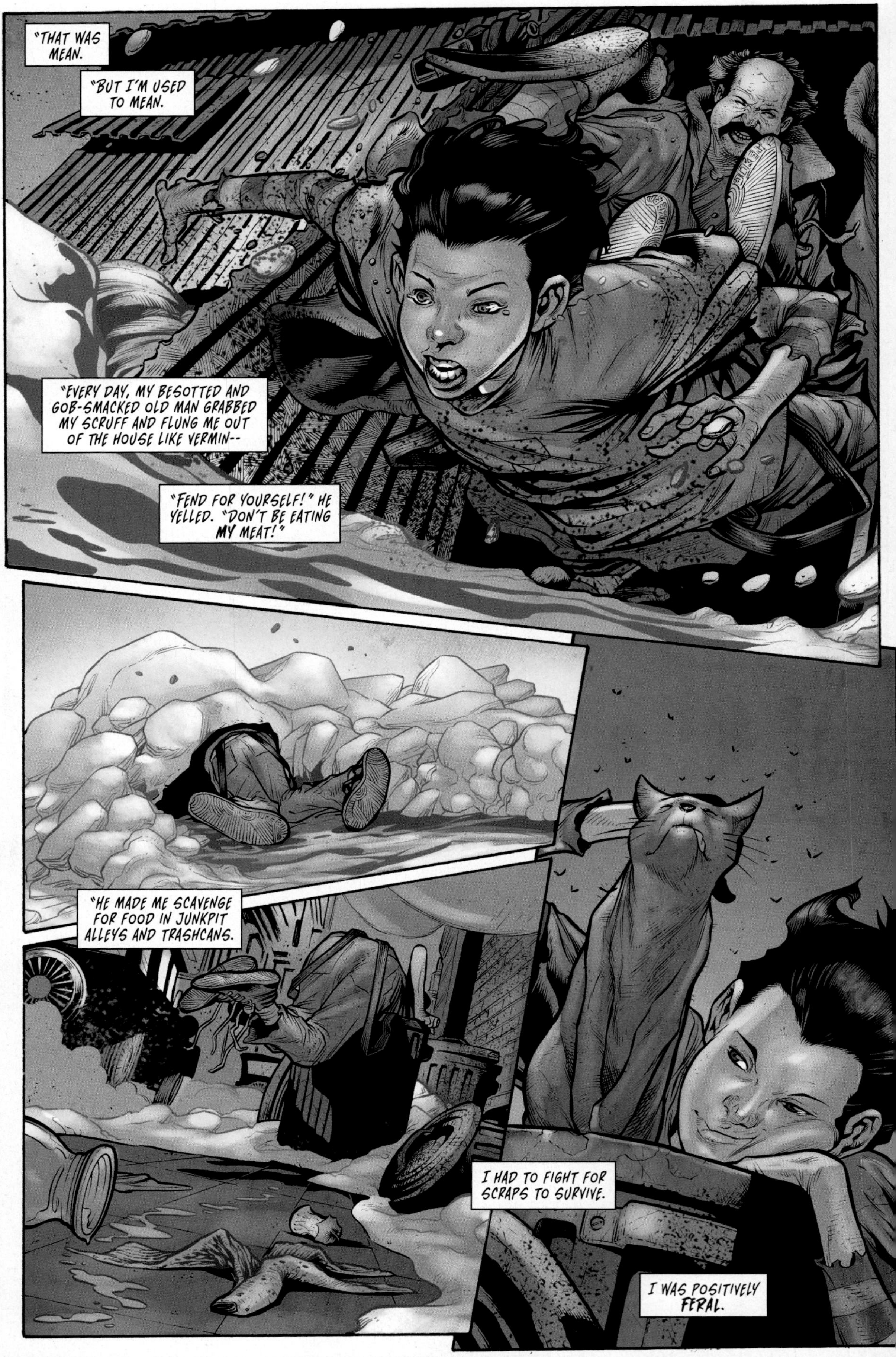
"THAT WAS MEAN.
"BUT I'M USED TO MEAN.
"EVERY DAY, MY BESOTTED AND GOB-SMACKED OLD MAN GRABBED MY SCRUFF AND FLUNG ME OUT OF THE HOUSE LIKE VERMIN--
"FEND FOR YOURSELF!" HE YELLED. "DON'T BE EATING MY MEAT!"
"HE MADE ME SCAVENGE FOR FOOD IN JUNKPIT ALLEYS AND TRASHCANS.
I HAD TO FIGHT FOR SCRAPS TO SURVIVE.
I WAS POSITIVELY FERAL.

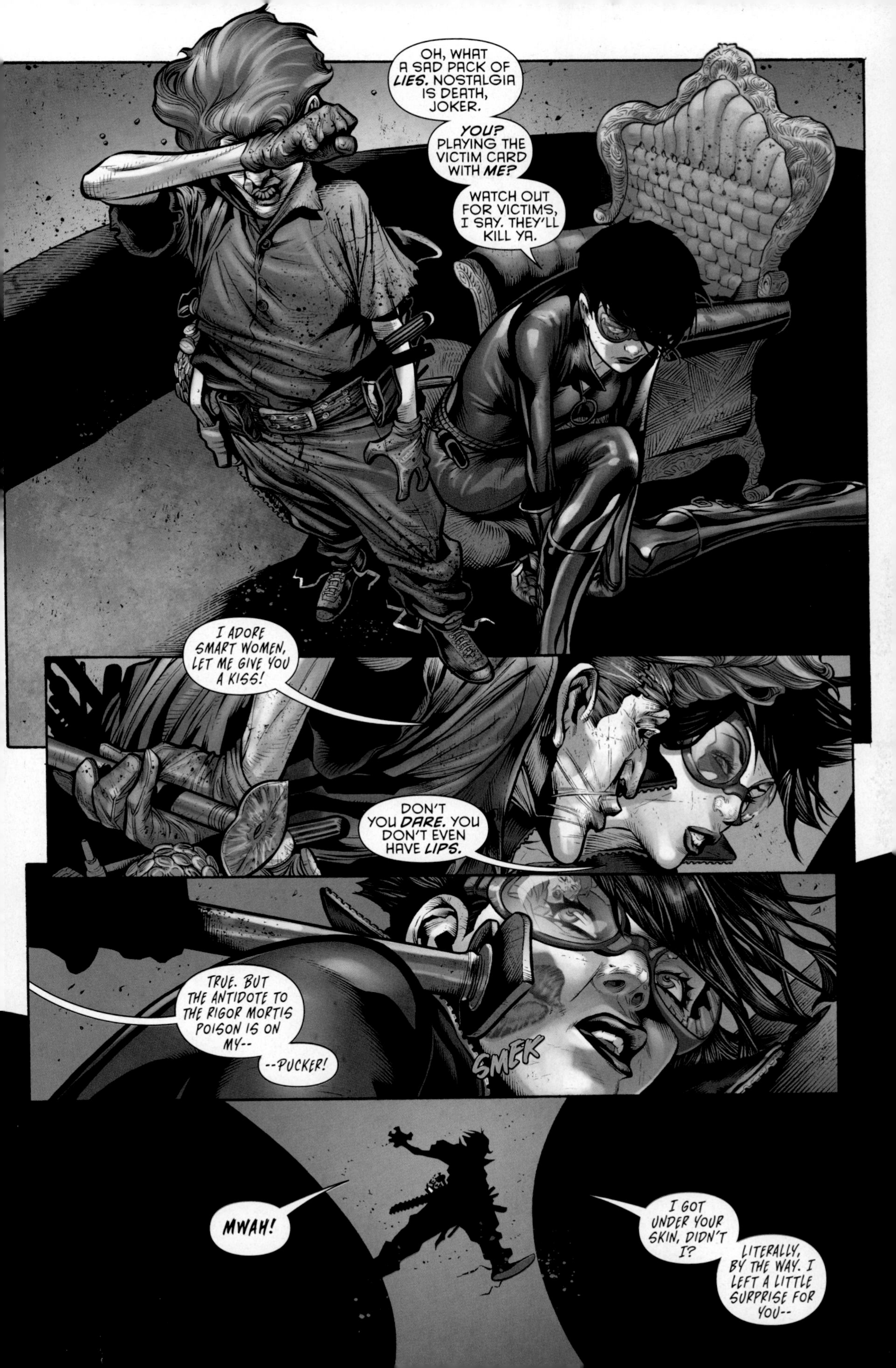
OH, WHAT A SAD PACK OF LIES. NOSTALGIA IS DEATH, JOKER.
YOU? PLAYING THE VICTIM CARD WITH ME?
WATCH OUT FOR VICTIMS, I SAY. THEY'LL KILL YA.
I ADORE SMART WOMEN, LET ME GIVE YOU A KISS!
DON'T YOU DARE. YOU DON'T EVEN HAVE LIPS.
TRUE. BUT THE ANTIDOTE TO THE RIGOR MORTIS POISON IS ON MY--
--PUCKER!
SMEK
MWAH!
I GOT UNDER YOUR SKIN, DIDN'T I?
LITERALLY, BY THE WAY. I LEFT A LITTLE SURPRISE FOR YOU--

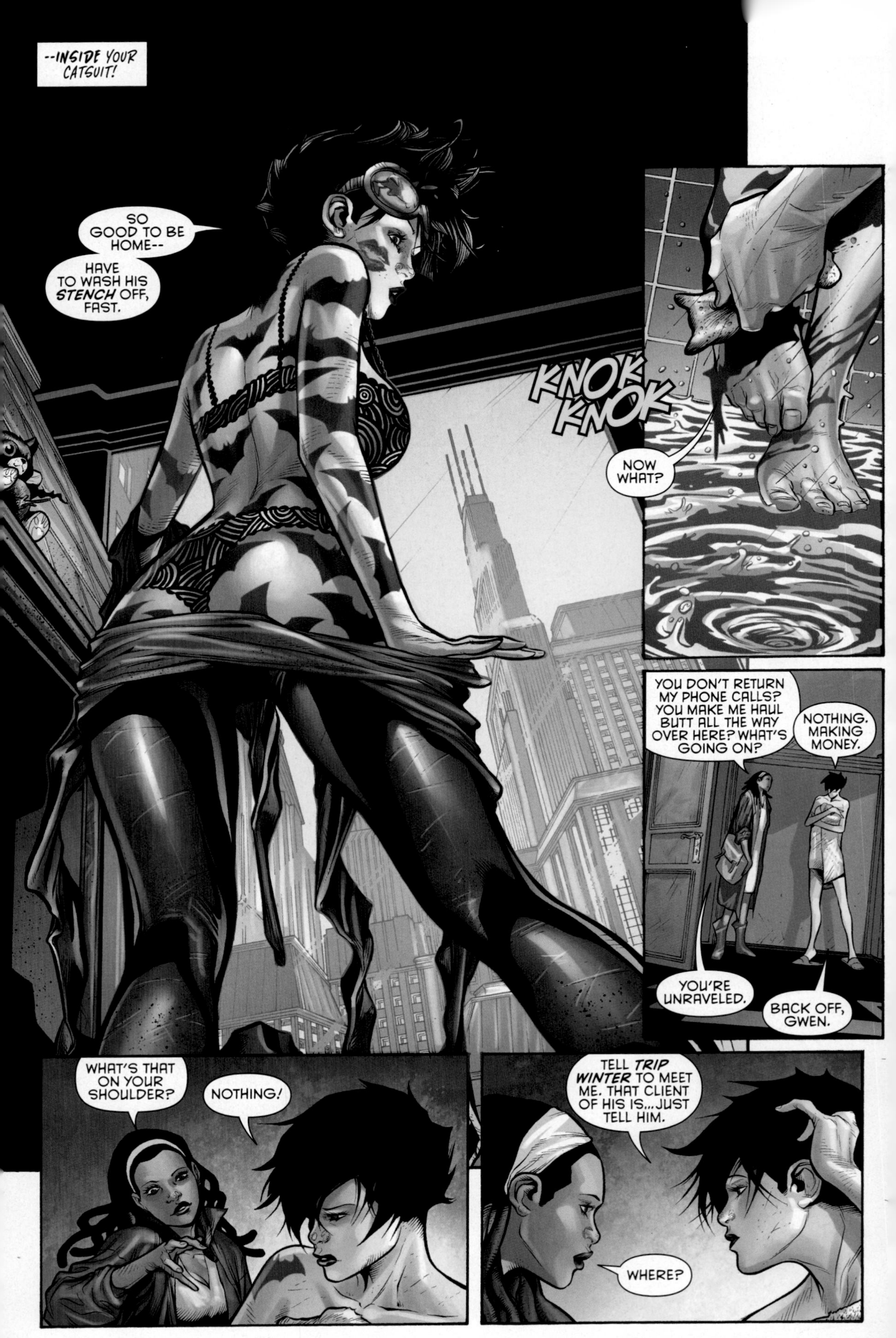
--INSIDE YOUR CATSUIT!
SO GOOD TO BE HOME--
HAVE TO WASH HIS STENCH OFF, FAST.
KNOK KNOK
NOW WHAT?
YOU DON'T RETURN MY PHONE CALLS? YOU MAKE ME HAUL BUTT ALL THE WAY OVER HERE? WHAT'S GOING ON?
NOTHING. MAKING MONEY.
YOU'RE UNRAVELED.
BACK OFF, GWEN.
WHAT'S THAT ON YOUR SHOULDER?
NOTHING!
TELL TRIP WINTER TO MEET ME. THAT CLIENT OF HIS IS...JUST TELL HIM.
WHERE?

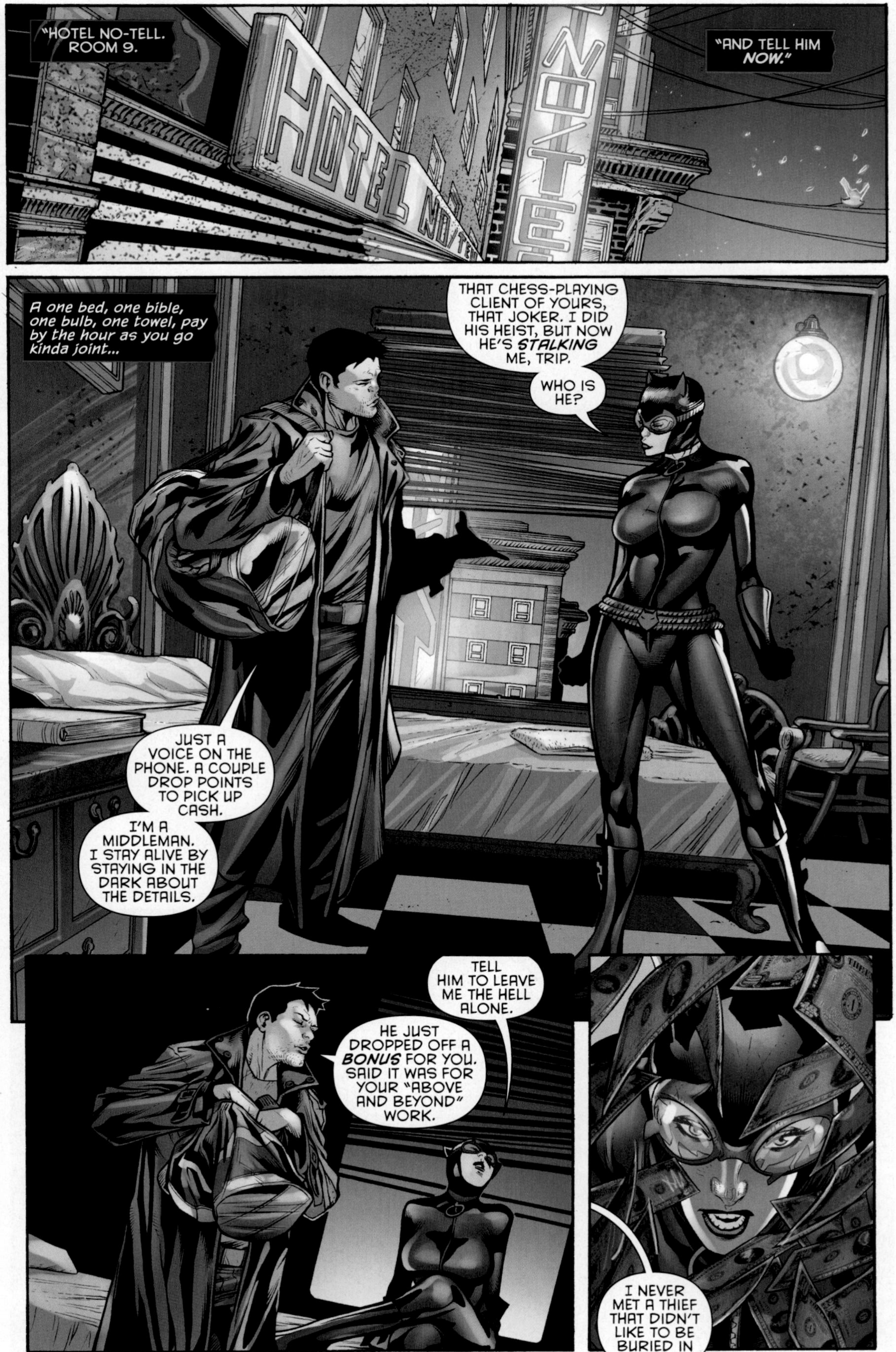
"HOTEL NO-TELL. ROOM 9.
"AND TELL HIM *NOW*."
HOTEL NO/TELL
NO/TEL
A one bed, one bible, one bulb, one towel, pay by the hour as you go kinda joint...
THAT CHESS-PLAYING CLIENT OF YOURS, THAT JOKER. I DID HIS HEIST, BUT NOW HE'S ***STALKING*** ME, TRIP.
WHO IS HE?
JUST A VOICE ON THE PHONE. A COUPLE DROP POINTS TO PICK UP CASH.
I'M A MIDDLEMAN. I STAY ALIVE BY STAYING IN THE DARK ABOUT THE DETAILS.
TELL HIM TO LEAVE ME THE HELL ALONE.
HE JUST DROPPED OFF A ***BONUS*** FOR YOU. SAID IT WAS FOR YOUR "ABOVE AND BEYOND" WORK.
I NEVER MET A THIEF THAT DIDN'T LIKE TO BE BURIED IN CASH.

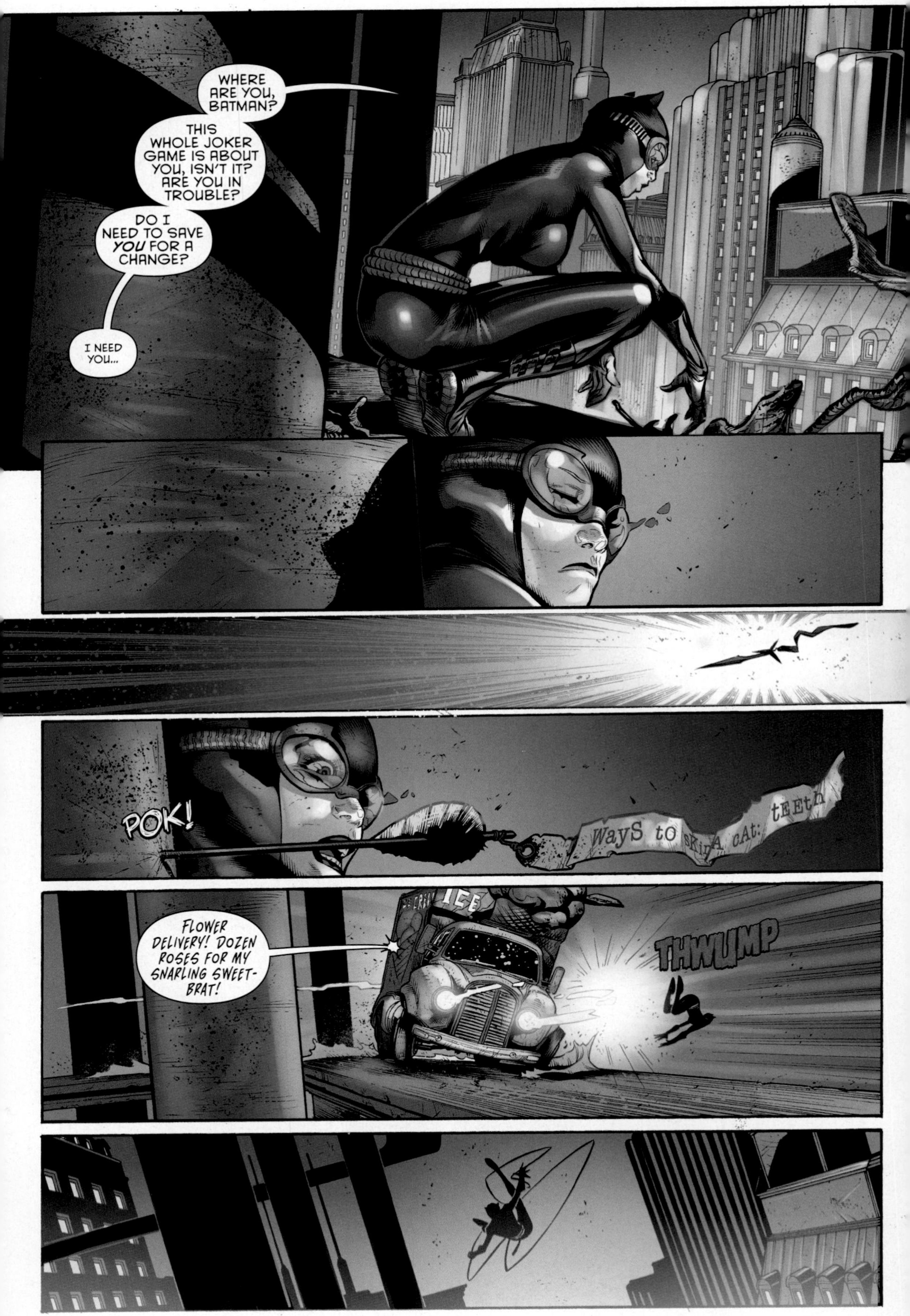
WHERE ARE YOU, BATMAN?
THIS WHOLE JOKER GAME IS ABOUT YOU, ISN'T IT? ARE YOU IN TROUBLE?
DO I NEED TO SAVE *YOU* FOR A CHANGE?
I NEED YOU...
POK!
WayS to sKin A cAt: tEEth
ICE
FLOWER DELIVERY! DOZEN ROSES FOR MY SNARLING SWEET-BRAT!
THWUMP

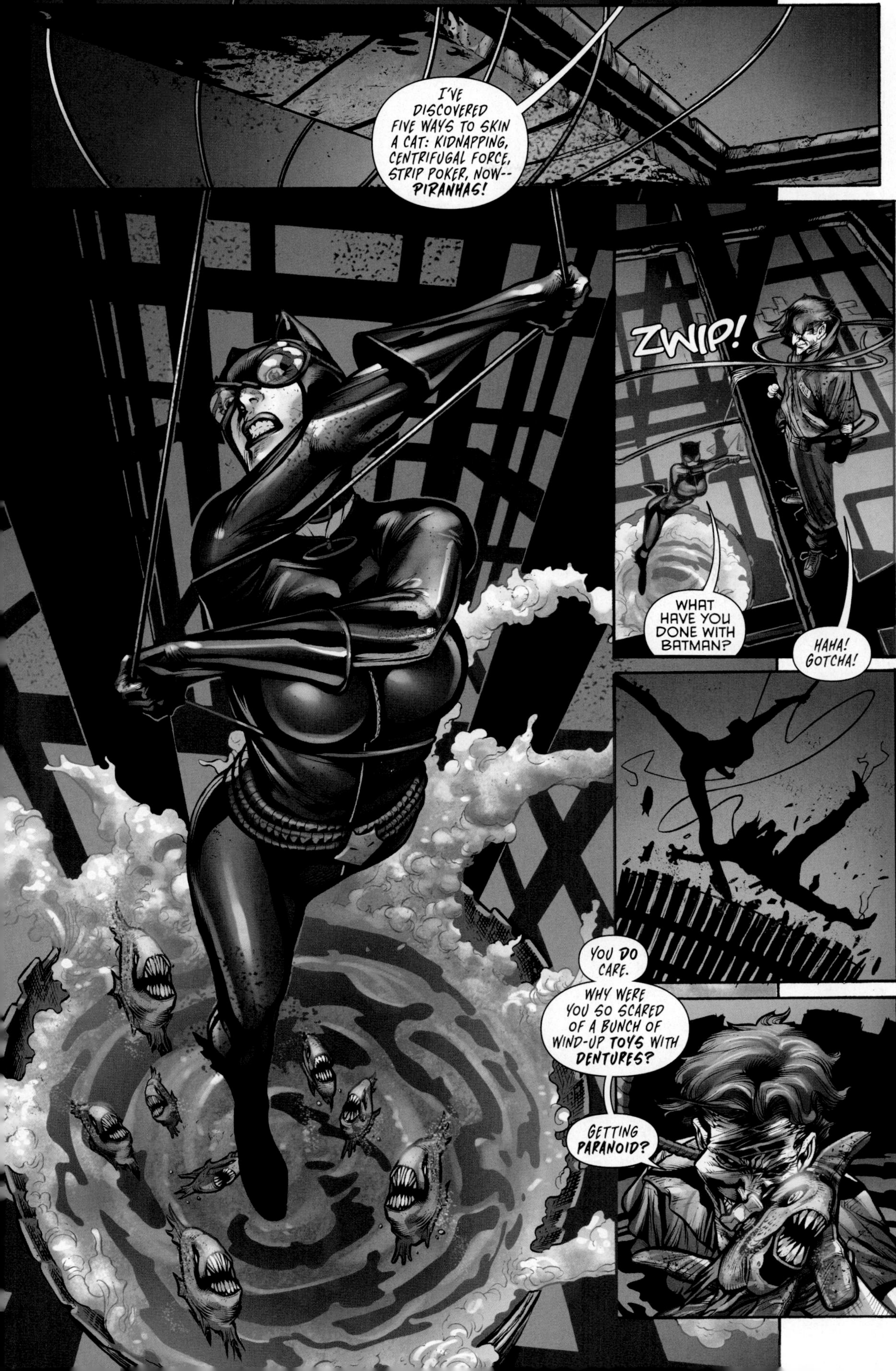
I'VE DISCOVERED FIVE WAYS TO SKIN A CAT: KIDNAPPING, CENTRIFUGAL FORCE, STRIP POKER, NOW-- PIRANHAS!
ZWIP!
WHAT HAVE YOU DONE WITH BATMAN?
HAHA! GOTCHA!
YOU DO CARE.
WHY WERE YOU SO SCARED OF A BUNCH OF WIND-UP TOYS WITH DENTURES?
GETTING PARANOID?

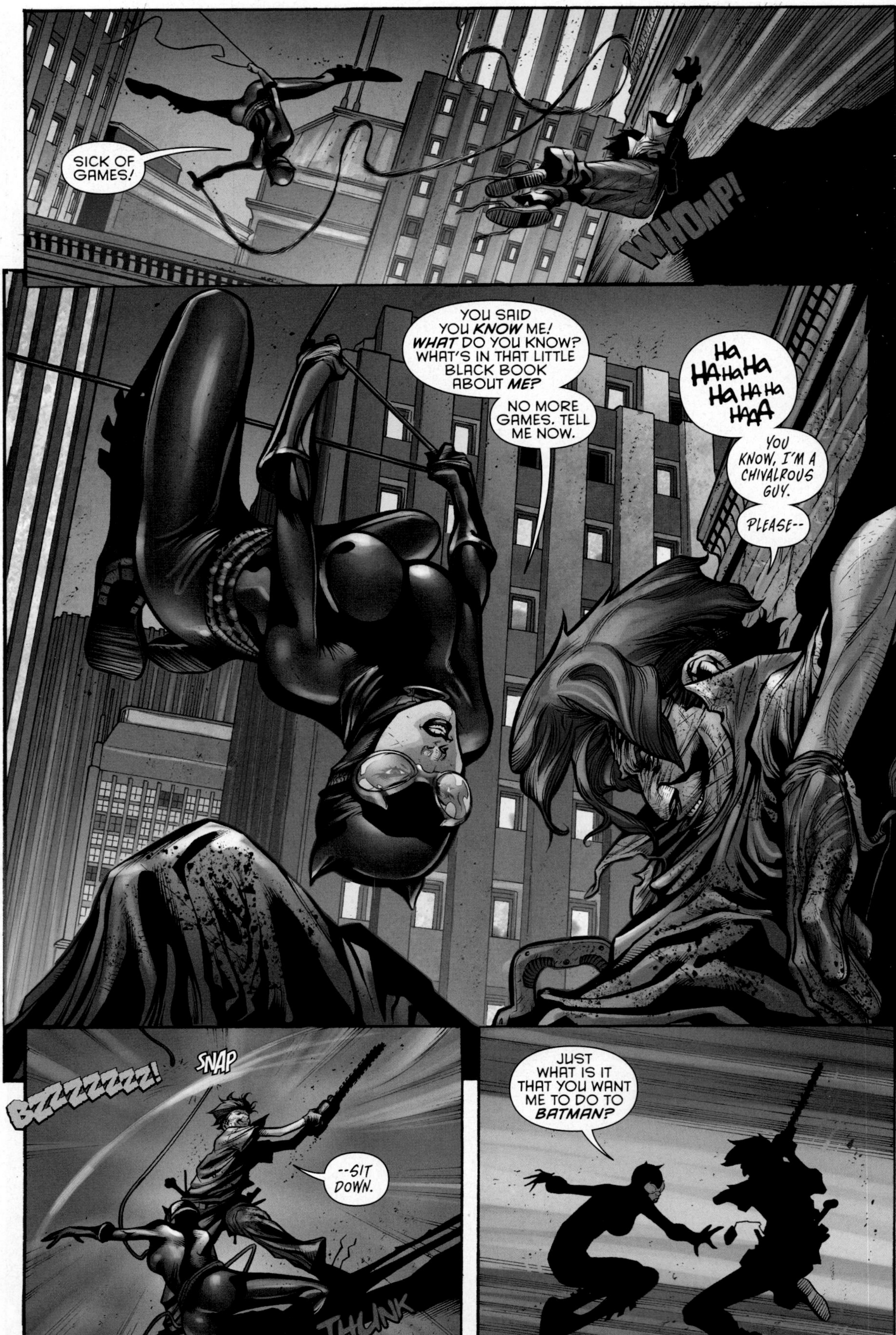
SICK OF GAMES!
WHOMP!
YOU SAID YOU KNOW ME! WHAT DO YOU KNOW? WHAT'S IN THAT LITTLE BLACK BOOK ABOUT ME?
NO MORE GAMES. TELL ME NOW.
Ha HaHaHa HaHaHa HAAA
YOU KNOW, I'M A CHIVALROUS GUY.
PLEASE--
SNAP
BZZZZZZZ!
--SIT DOWN.
THUNK
JUST WHAT IS IT THAT YOU WANT ME TO DO TO BATMAN?

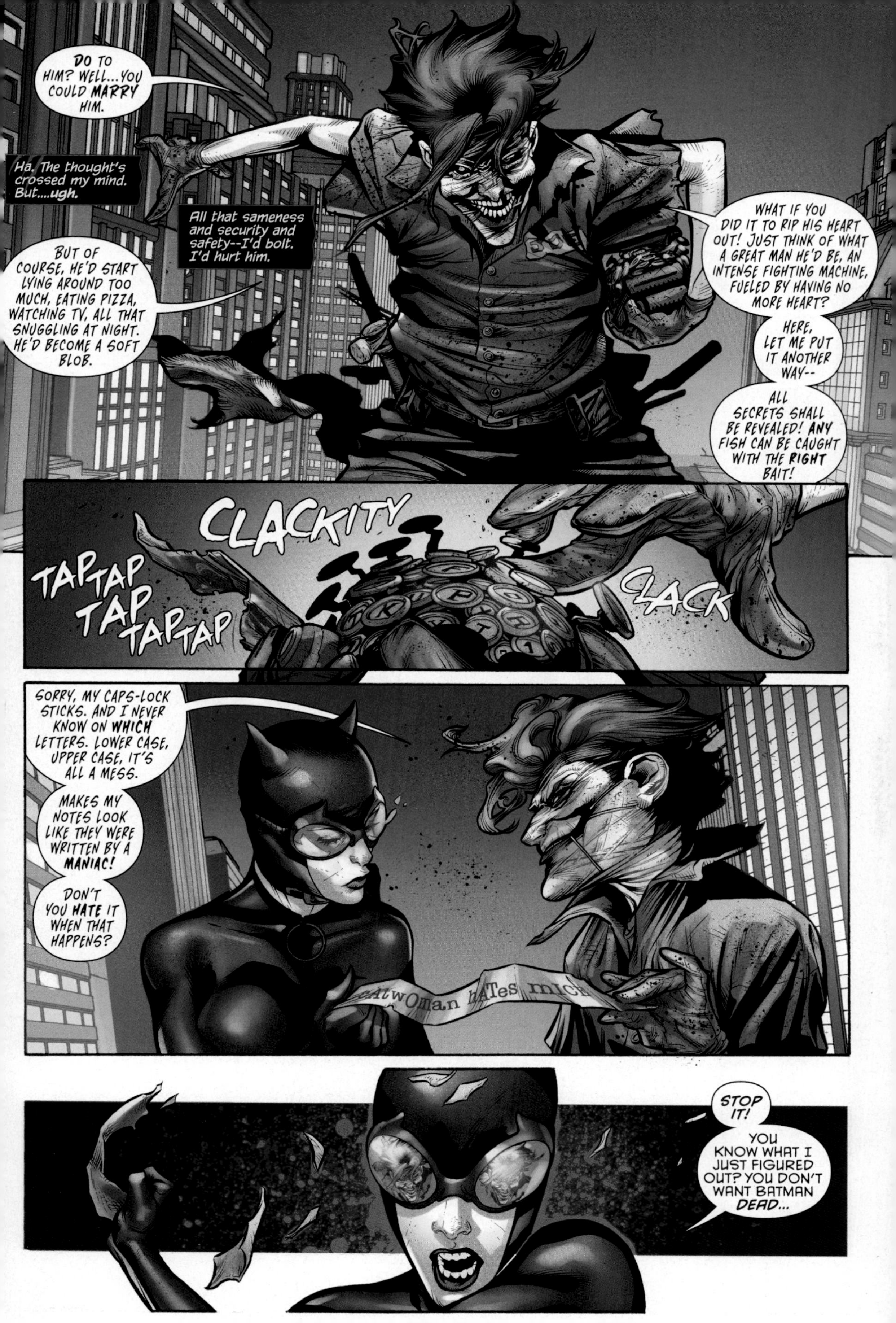
DO TO HIM? WELL...YOU COULD MARRY HIM.
Ha. The thought's crossed my mind. But....ugh.
All that sameness and security and safety--I'd bolt. I'd hurt him.
BUT OF COURSE, HE'D START LYING AROUND TOO MUCH, EATING PIZZA, WATCHING TV, ALL THAT SNUGGLING AT NIGHT. HE'D BECOME A SOFT BLOB.
WHAT IF YOU DID IT TO RIP HIS HEART OUT! JUST THINK OF WHAT A GREAT MAN HE'D BE, AN INTENSE FIGHTING MACHINE, FUELED BY HAVING NO MORE HEART?
HERE, LET ME PUT IT ANOTHER WAY--
ALL SECRETS SHALL BE REVEALED! ANY FISH CAN BE CAUGHT WITH THE RIGHT BAIT!
CLACKITY
TAPTAP TAP TAPTAP
CLACK
SORRY, MY CAPS-LOCK STICKS. AND I NEVER KNOW ON WHICH LETTERS. LOWER CASE, UPPER CASE, IT'S ALL A MESS.
MAKES MY NOTES LOOK LIKE THEY WERE WRITTEN BY A MANIAC!
DON'T YOU HATE IT WHEN THAT HAPPENS?
cAtwOman hATes mICE
STOP IT!
YOU KNOW WHAT I JUST FIGURED OUT? YOU DON'T WANT BATMAN DEAD...

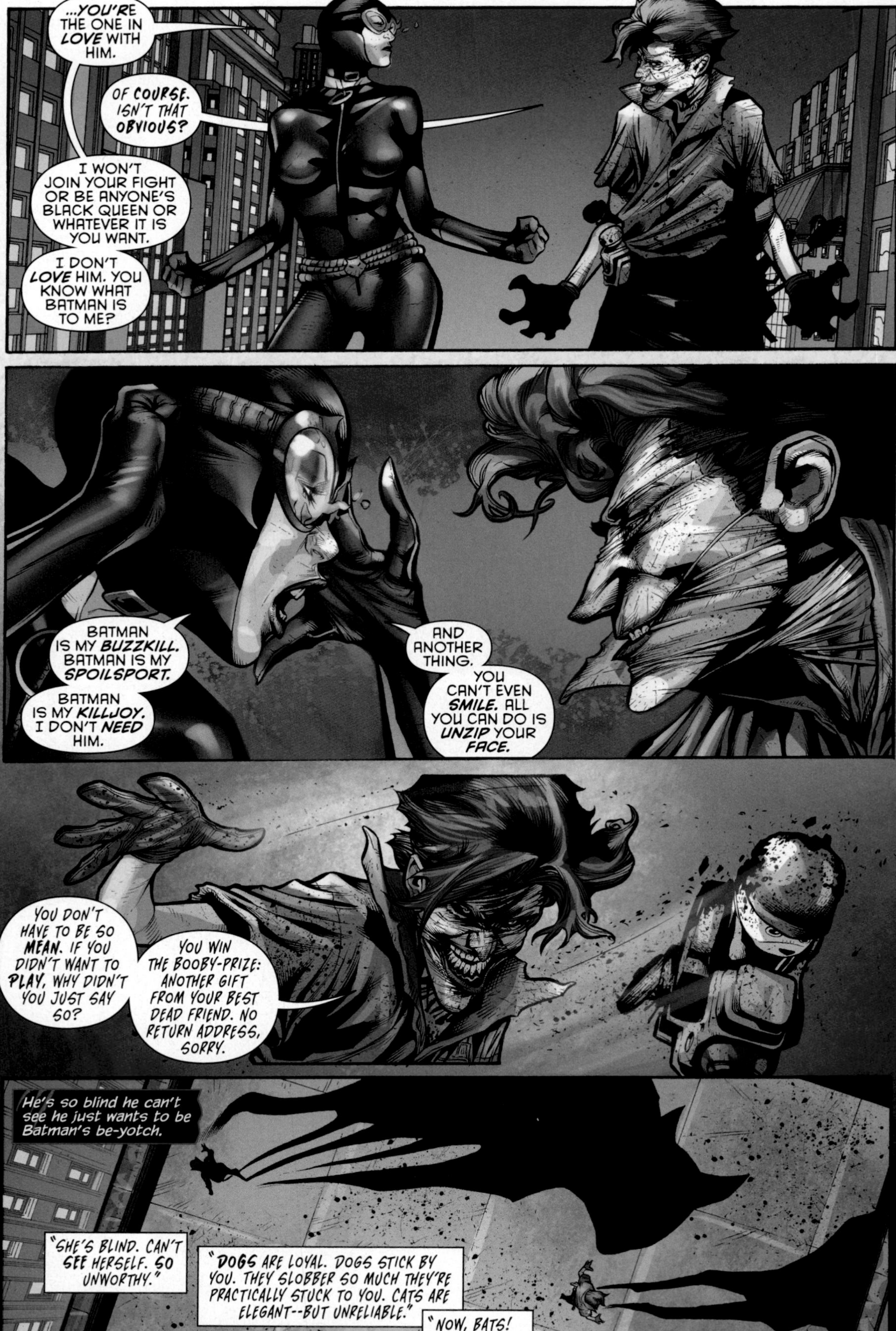
...YOU'RE THE ONE IN LOVE WITH HIM.
OF COURSE. ISN'T THAT OBVIOUS?
I WON'T JOIN YOUR FIGHT OR BE ANYONE'S BLACK QUEEN OR WHATEVER IT IS YOU WANT.
I DON'T LOVE HIM. YOU KNOW WHAT BATMAN IS TO ME?
BATMAN IS MY BUZZKILL. BATMAN IS MY SPOILSPORT.
BATMAN IS MY KILLJOY. I DON'T NEED HIM.
AND ANOTHER THING.
YOU CAN'T EVEN SMILE. ALL YOU CAN DO IS UNZIP YOUR FACE.
YOU DON'T HAVE TO BE SO MEAN. IF YOU DIDN'T WANT TO PLAY, WHY DIDN'T YOU JUST SAY SO?
YOU WIN THE BOOBY-PRIZE: ANOTHER GIFT FROM YOUR BEST DEAD FRIEND. NO RETURN ADDRESS, SORRY.
He's so blind he can't see he just wants to be Batman's be-yotch.
"SHE'S BLIND. CAN'T SEE HERSELF. SO UNWORTHY."
"DOGS ARE LOYAL. DOGS STICK BY YOU. THEY SLOBBER SO MUCH THEY'RE PRACTICALLY STUCK TO YOU. CATS ARE ELEGANT--BUT UNRELIABLE."
"NOW, BATS! THEY'RE FUN..."

PART THREE
HARLEY QUINN

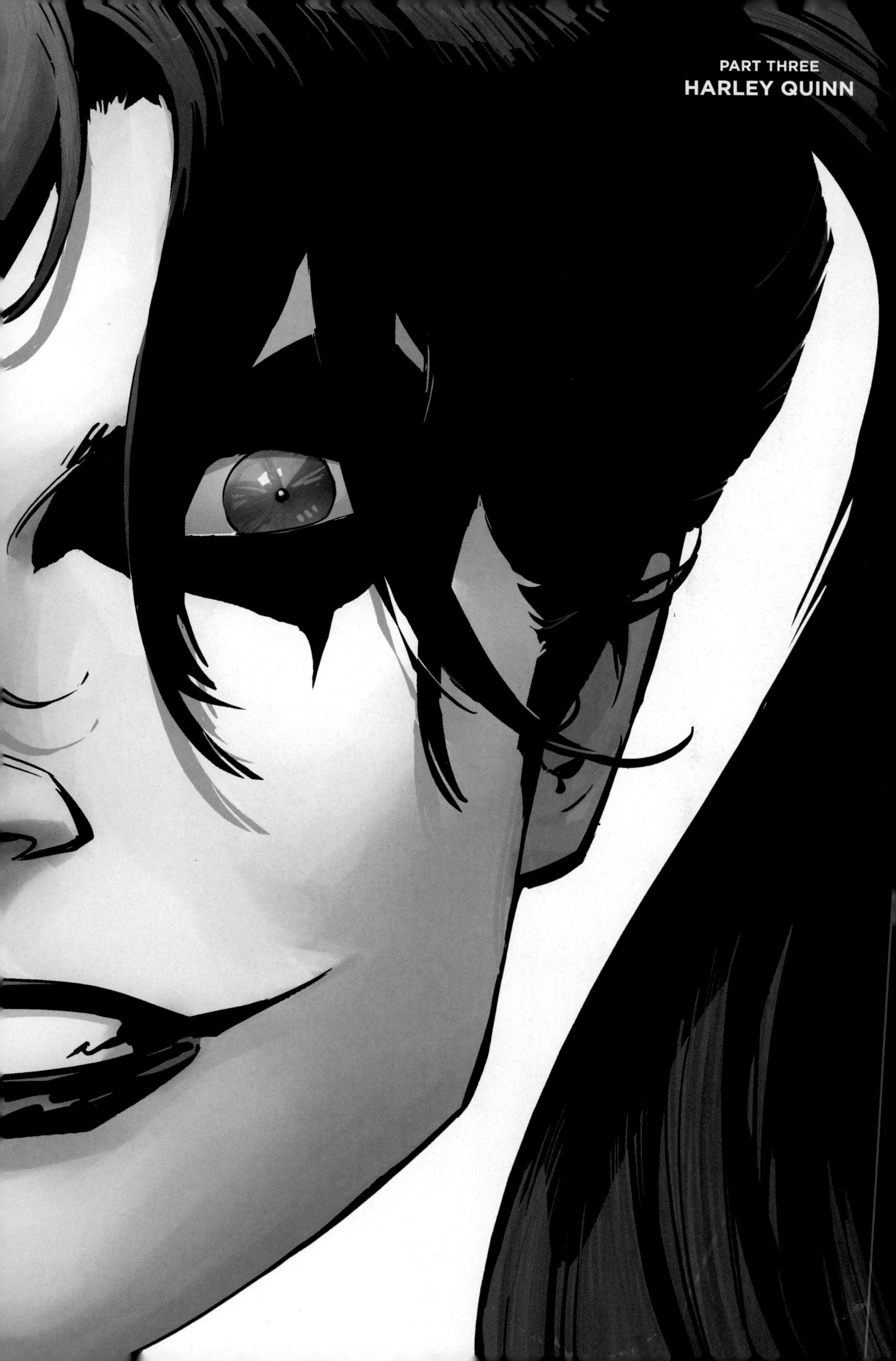

ADAM GLASS SCOTT SNYDER JAMES TYNION IV writers FERNANDO DAGNINO JOCK GREG CAPULLO JONATHAN GLAPION artists
MATT YACKEY JOCK FCO PLASCENCIA colorists JARED K. FLETCHER SAL CIPRIANO RICHARD STARKINGS COMICRAFT'S JIMMY BETANCOURT letterers

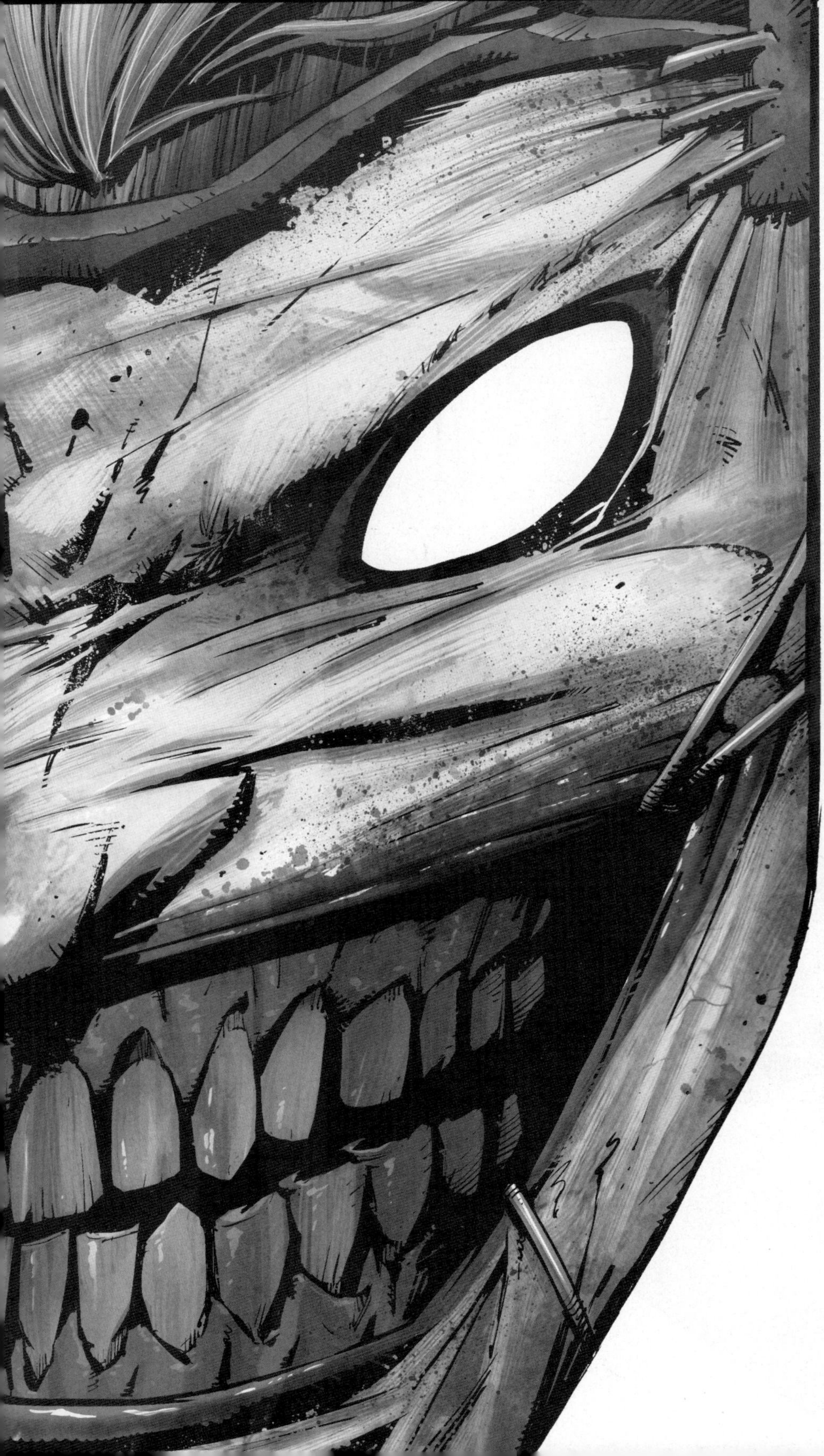

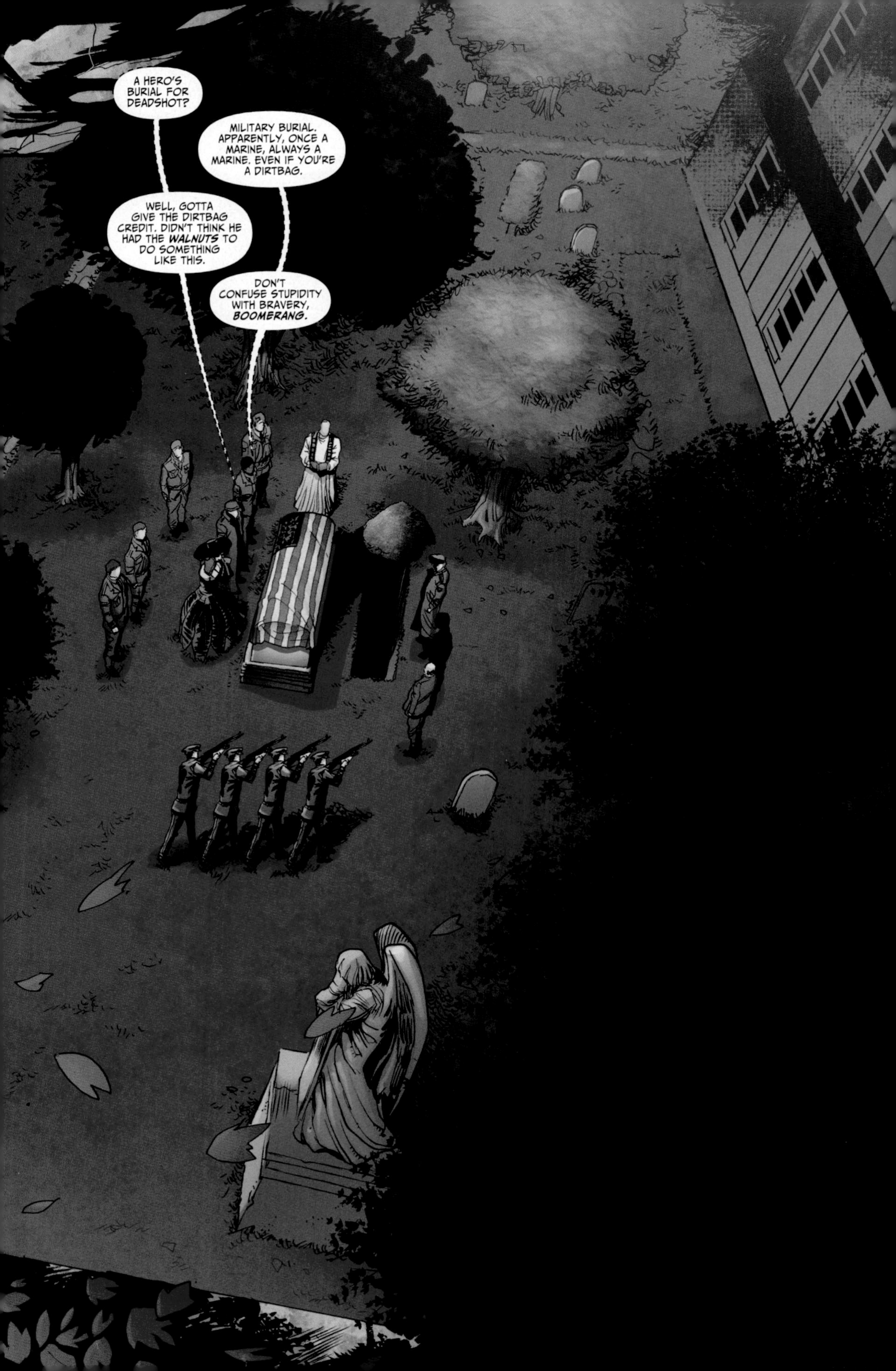
A HERO'S BURIAL FOR DEADSHOT?
MILITARY BURIAL. APPARENTLY, ONCE A MARINE, ALWAYS A MARINE. EVEN IF YOU'RE A DIRTBAG.
WELL, GOTTA GIVE THE DIRTBAG CREDIT. DIDN'T THINK HE HAD THE WALNUTS TO DO SOMETHING LIKE THIS.
DON'T CONFUSE STUPIDITY WITH BRAVERY, BOOMERANG.

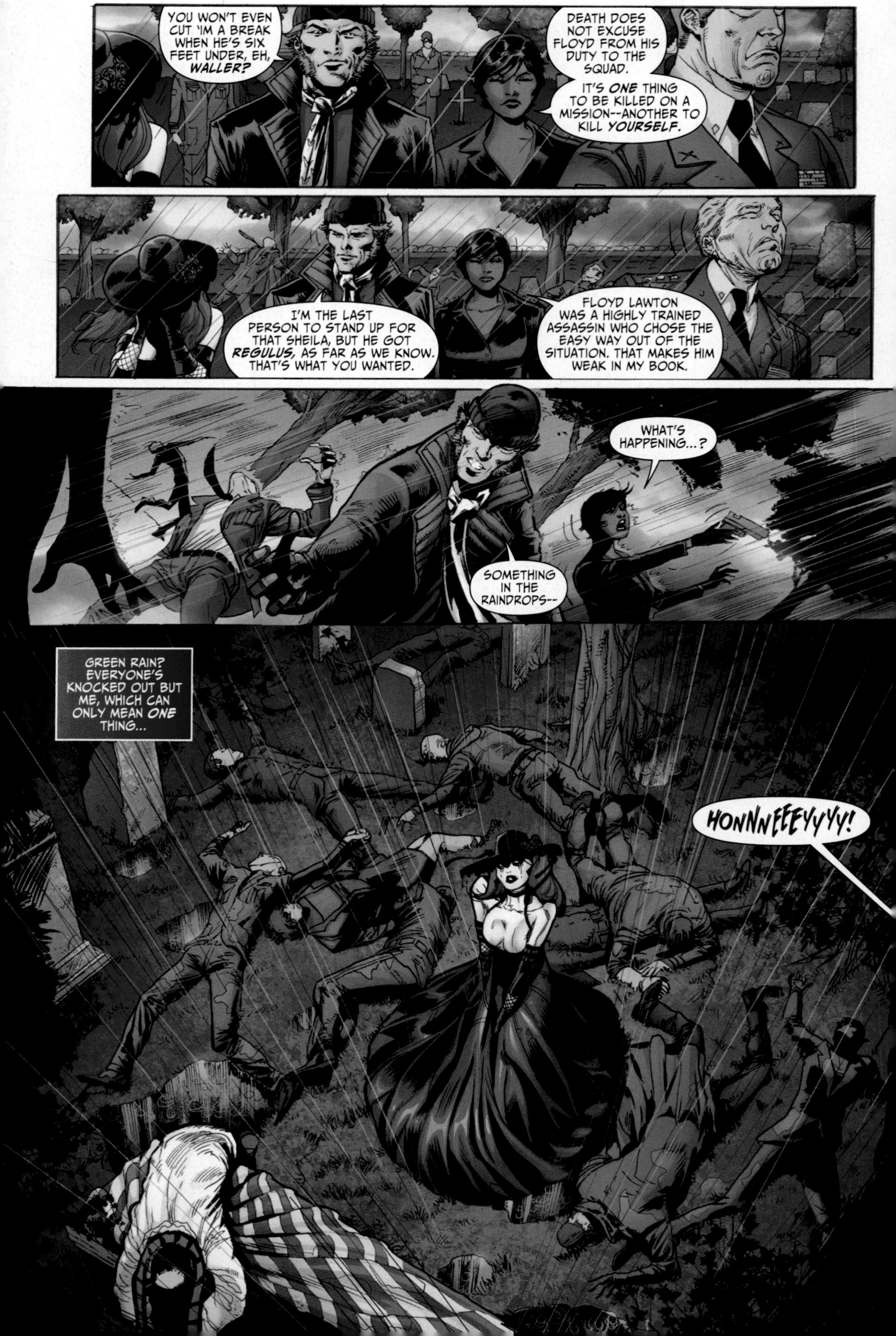
YOU WON'T EVEN CUT 'IM A BREAK WHEN HE'S SIX FEET UNDER, EH, WALLER?
DEATH DOES NOT EXCUSE FLOYD FROM HIS DUTY TO THE SQUAD.
IT'S ONE THING TO BE KILLED ON A MISSION--ANOTHER TO KILL YOURSELF.
I'M THE LAST PERSON TO STAND UP FOR THAT SHEILA, BUT HE GOT REGULUS, AS FAR AS WE KNOW. THAT'S WHAT YOU WANTED.
FLOYD LAWTON WAS A HIGHLY TRAINED ASSASSIN WHO CHOSE THE EASY WAY OUT OF THE SITUATION. THAT MAKES HIM WEAK IN MY BOOK.
WHAT'S HAPPENING...?
SOMETHING IN THE RAINDROPS--
GREEN RAIN? EVERYONE'S KNOCKED OUT BUT ME, WHICH CAN ONLY MEAN ONE THING...
HONNNEEEYYYY!

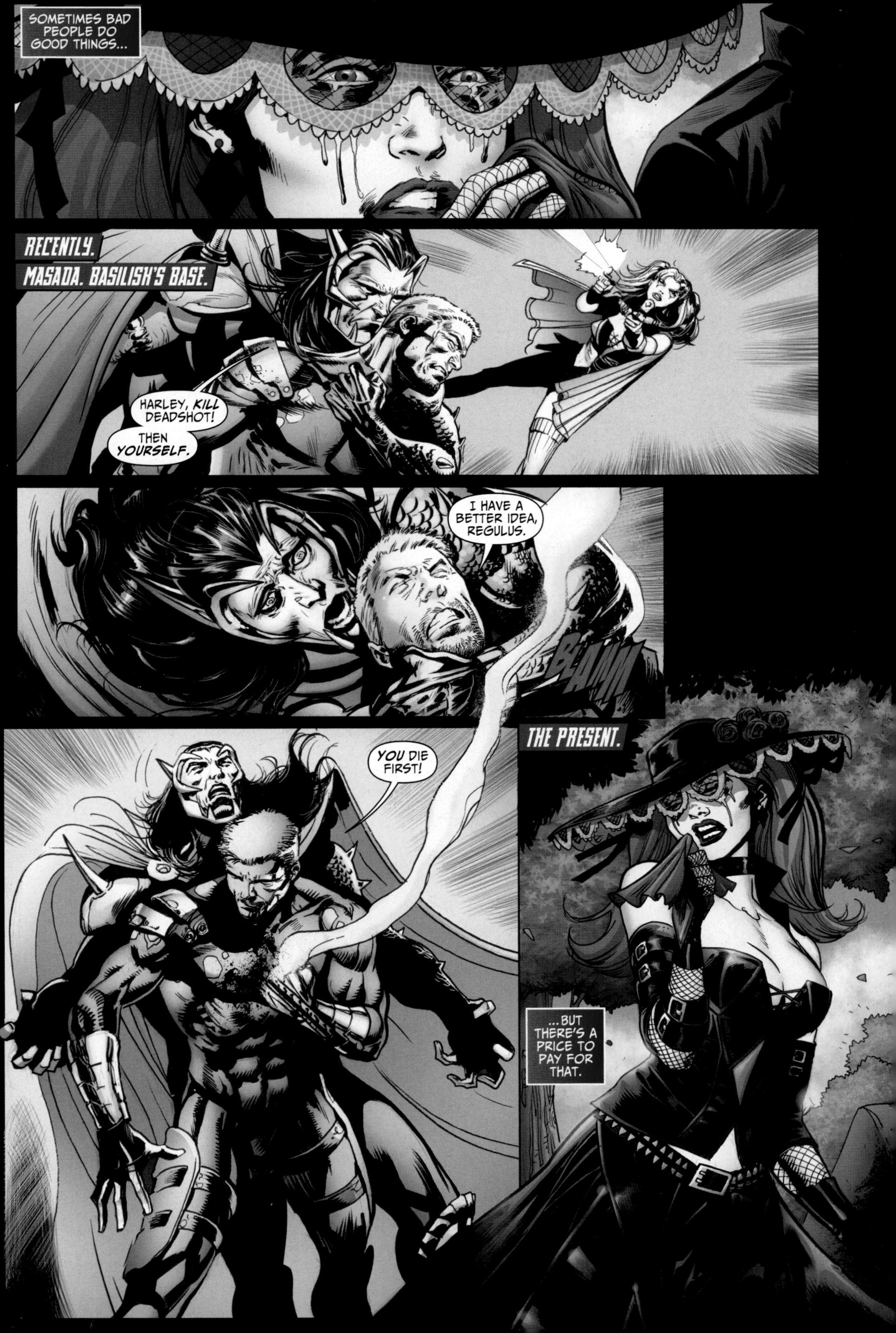
SOMETIMES BAD PEOPLE DO GOOD THINGS...
RECENTLY.
MASADA. BASILISK'S BASE.
HARLEY, KILL DEADSHOT!
THEN YOURSELF.
I HAVE A BETTER IDEA, REGULUS.
BLAMM
YOU DIE FIRST!
THE PRESENT.
...BUT THERE'S A PRICE TO PAY FOR THAT.

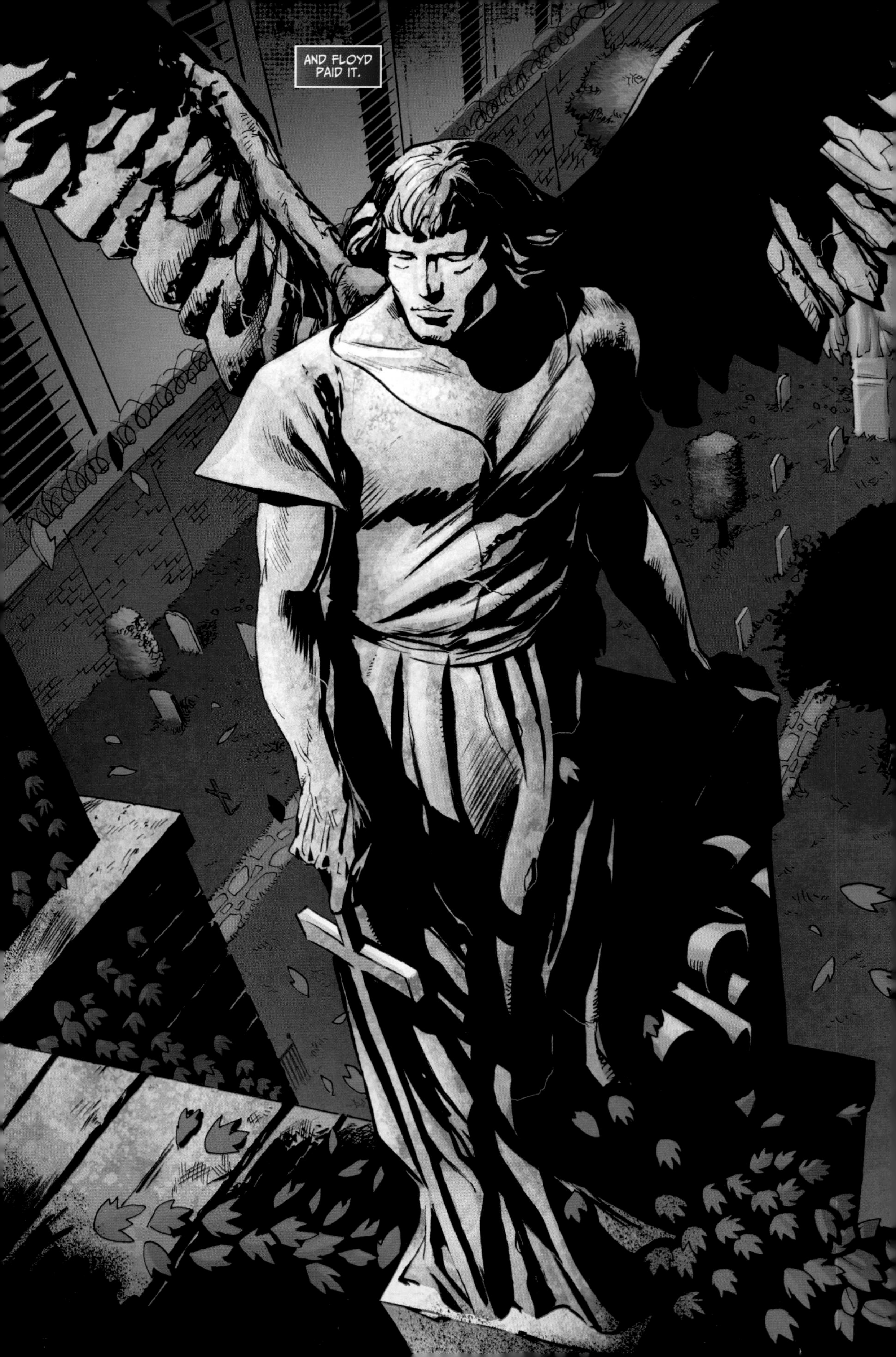
AND FLOYD PAID IT.

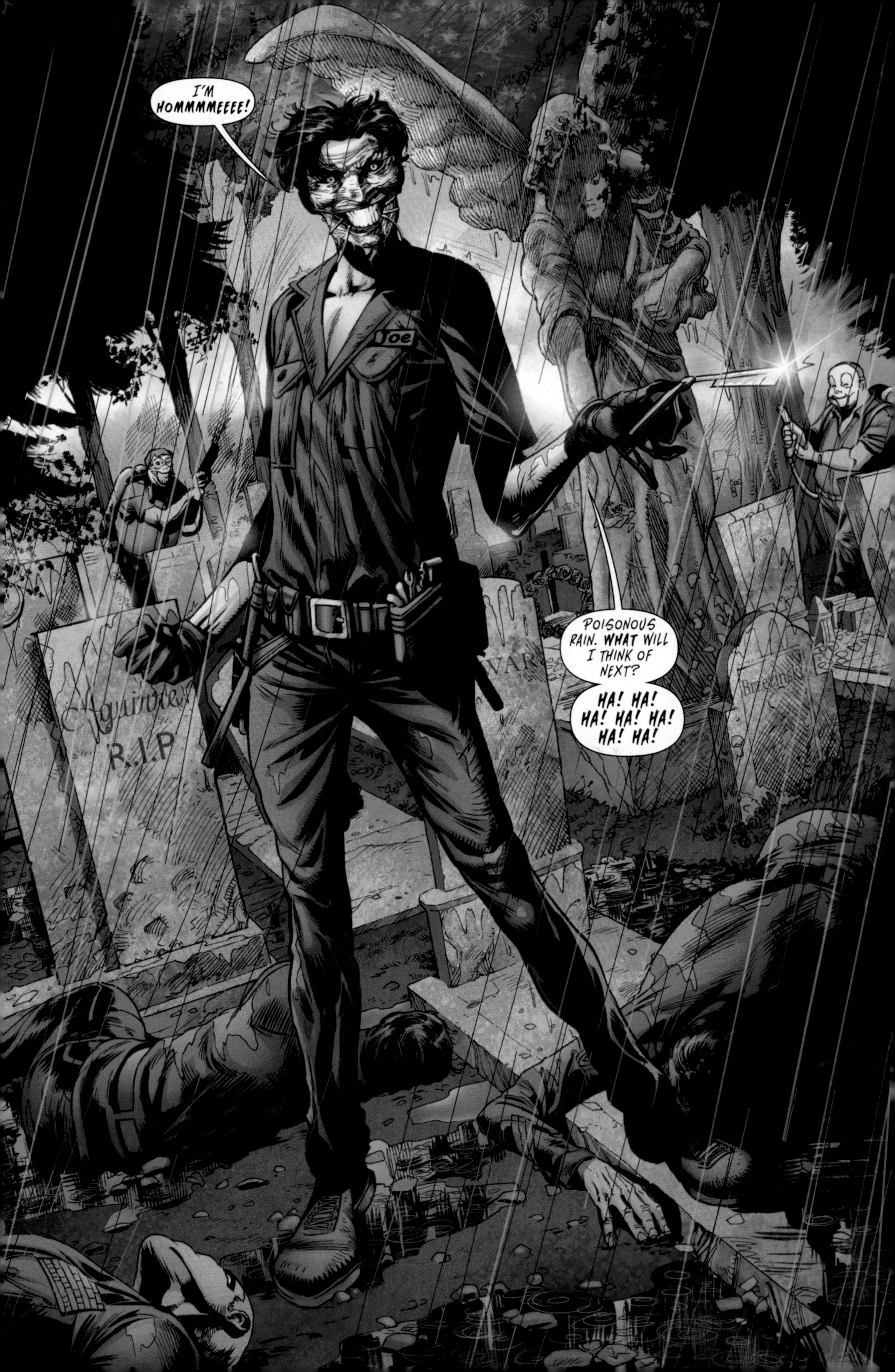
I'M HOMMMMEEEE!
POISONOUS RAIN. WHAT WILL I THINK OF NEXT?
HA! HA! HA! HA! HA! HA! HA!

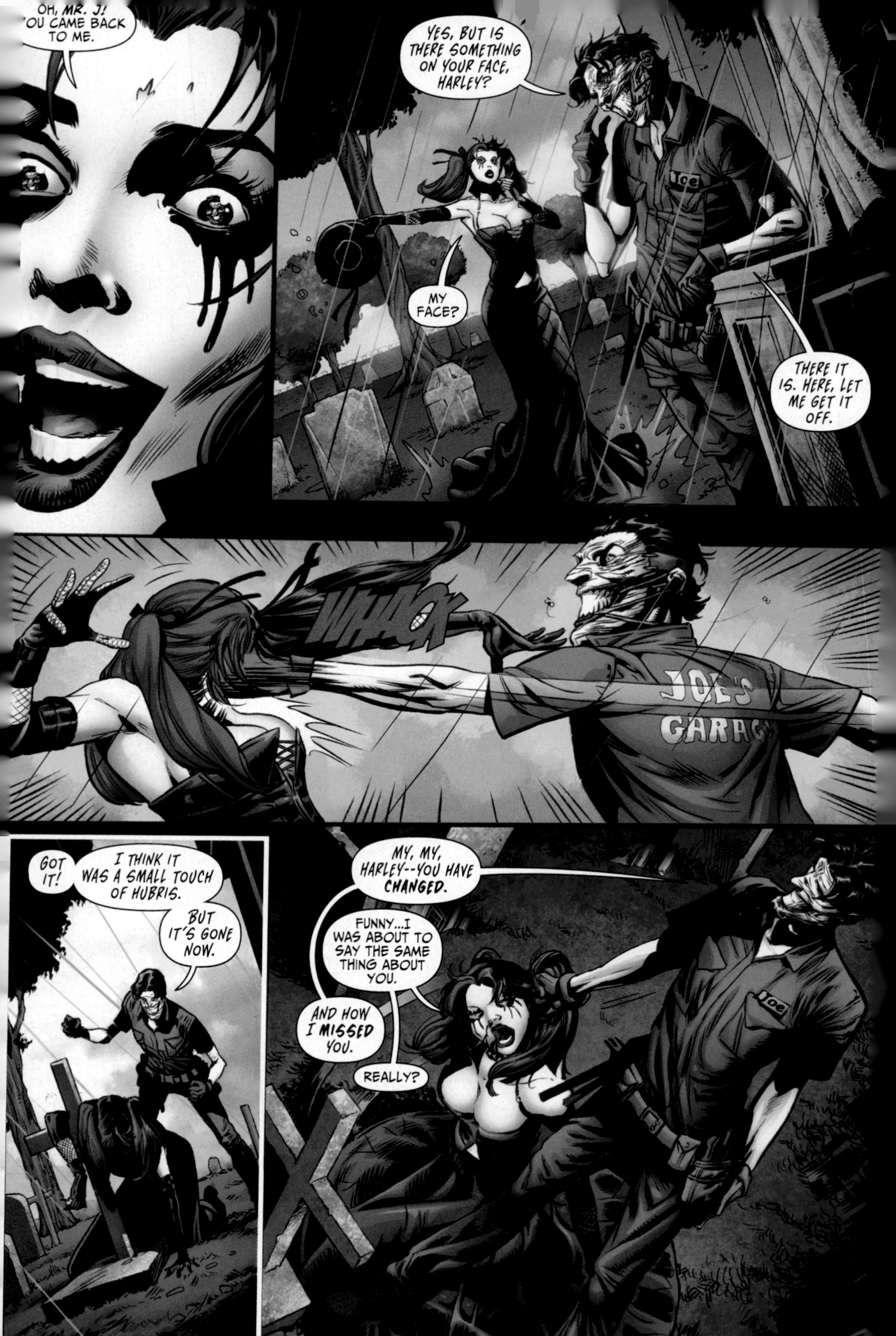
OH, MR. J! YOU CAME BACK TO ME.
YES, BUT IS THERE SOMETHING ON YOUR FACE, HARLEY?
MY FACE?
THERE IT IS. HERE, LET ME GET IT OFF.
JOE
WHACK
JOE'S GARAG
GOT IT!
I THINK IT WAS A SMALL TOUCH OF HUBRIS.
BUT IT'S GONE NOW.
MY, MY, HARLEY--YOU HAVE CHANGED.
FUNNY...I WAS ABOUT TO SAY THE SAME THING ABOUT YOU.
AND HOW I MISSED YOU.
REALLY?
JOE

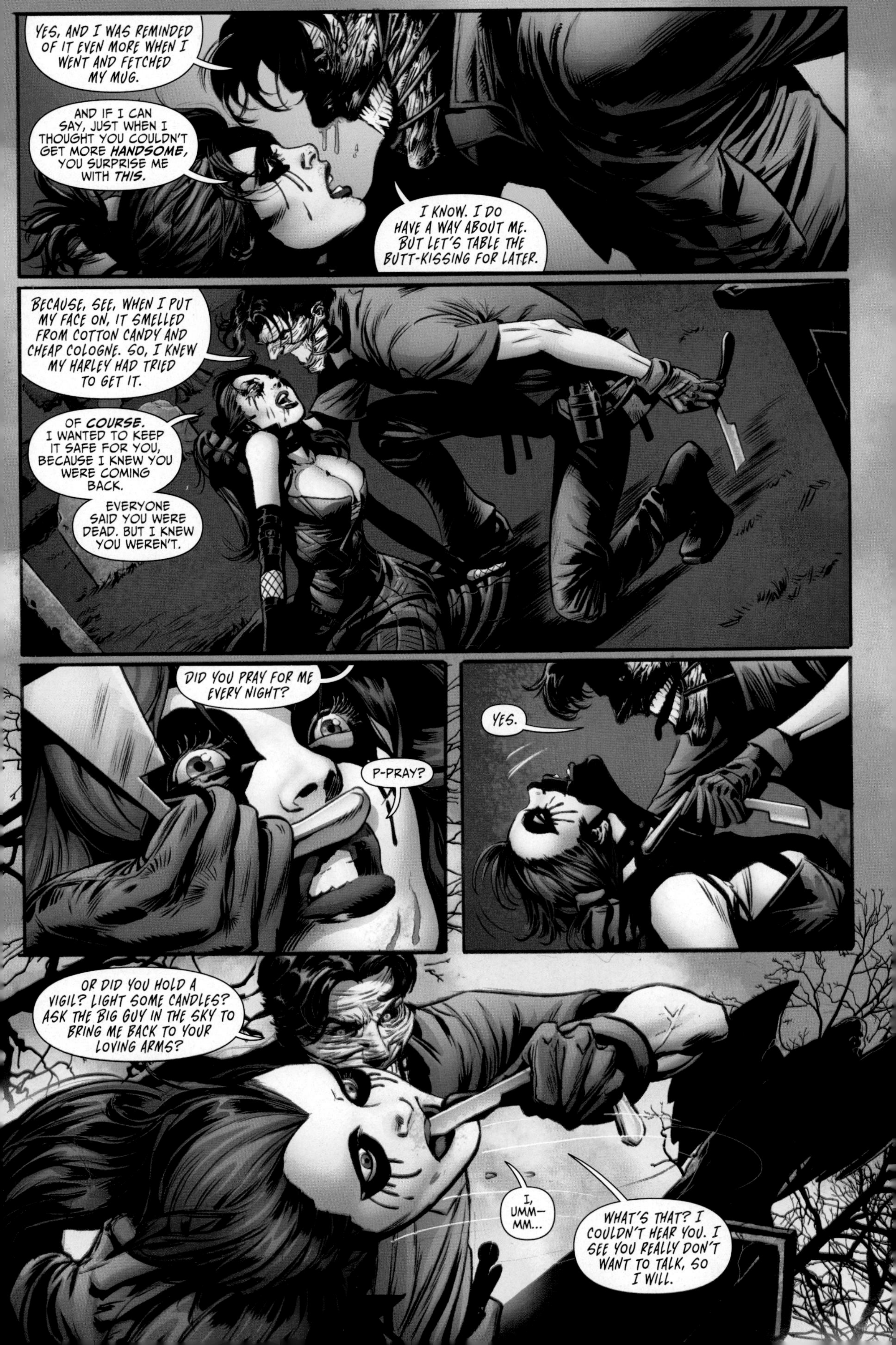
YES, AND I WAS REMINDED OF IT EVEN MORE WHEN I WENT AND FETCHED MY MUG.
AND IF I CAN SAY, JUST WHEN I THOUGHT YOU COULDN'T GET MORE *HANDSOME*, YOU SURPRISE ME WITH *THIS*.
I KNOW. I DO HAVE A WAY ABOUT ME. BUT LET'S TABLE THE BUTT-KISSING FOR LATER.
BECAUSE, SEE, WHEN I PUT MY FACE ON, IT SMELLED FROM COTTON CANDY AND CHEAP COLOGNE. SO, I KNEW MY HARLEY HAD TRIED TO GET IT.
OF *COURSE*. I WANTED TO KEEP IT SAFE FOR YOU, BECAUSE I KNEW YOU WERE COMING BACK.
EVERYONE SAID YOU WERE DEAD. BUT I KNEW YOU WEREN'T.
DID YOU PRAY FOR ME EVERY NIGHT?
P-PRAY?
YES.
OR DID YOU HOLD A VIGIL? LIGHT SOME CANDLES? ASK THE BIG GUY IN THE SKY TO BRING ME BACK TO YOUR LOVING ARMS?
I, UMM—MM...
WHAT'S THAT? I COULDN'T HEAR YOU. I SEE YOU REALLY DON'T WANT TO TALK, SO I WILL.

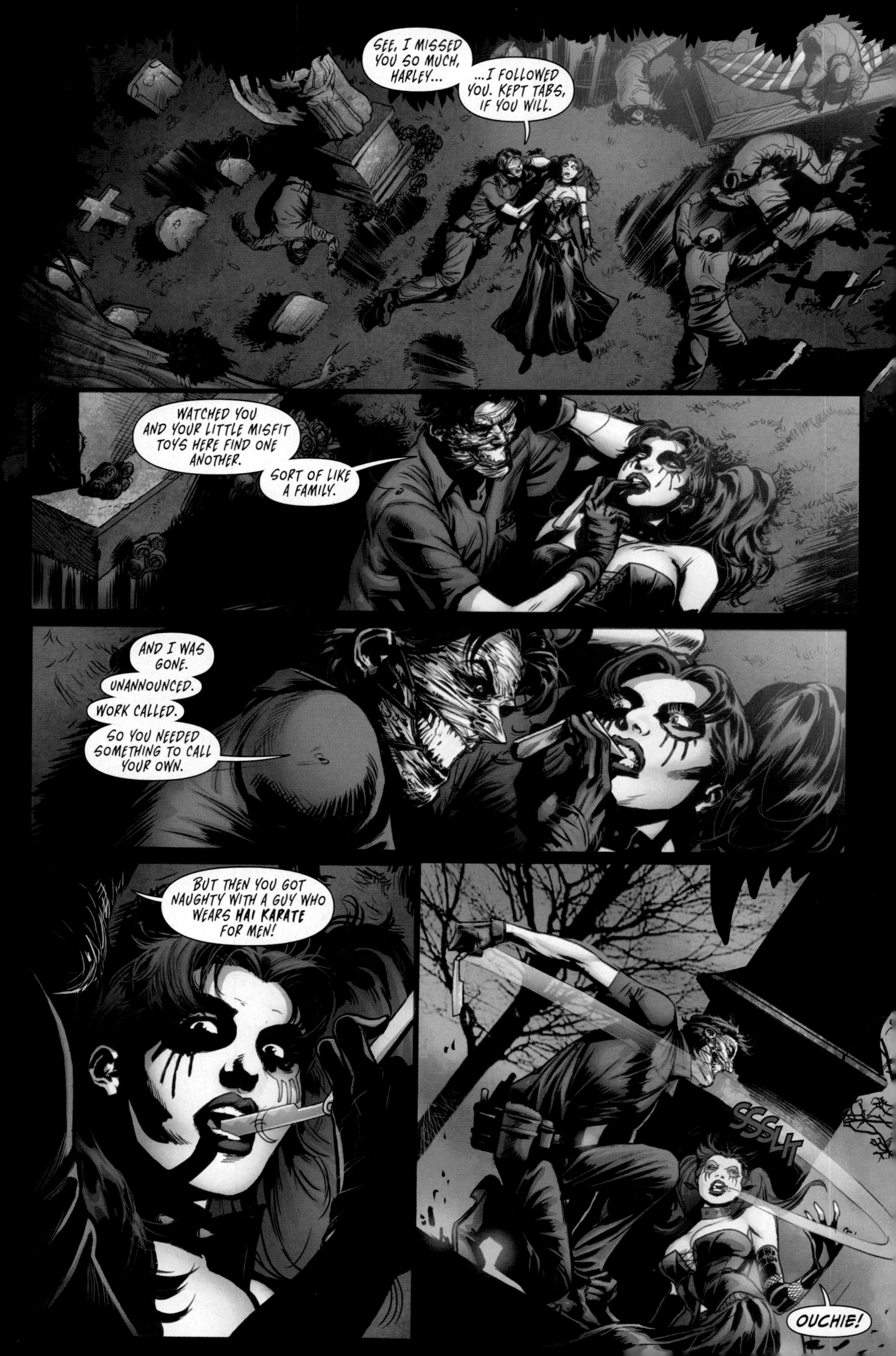
SEE, I MISSED YOU SO MUCH, HARLEY...
...I FOLLOWED YOU. KEPT TABS, IF YOU WILL.
WATCHED YOU AND YOUR LITTLE MISFIT TOYS HERE FIND ONE ANOTHER.
SORT OF LIKE A FAMILY.
AND I WAS GONE.
UNANNOUNCED.
WORK CALLED.
SO YOU NEEDED SOMETHING TO CALL YOUR OWN.
BUT THEN YOU GOT NAUGHTY WITH A GUY WHO WEARS **HAI KARATE** FOR MEN!
SSSLK
OUCHIE!

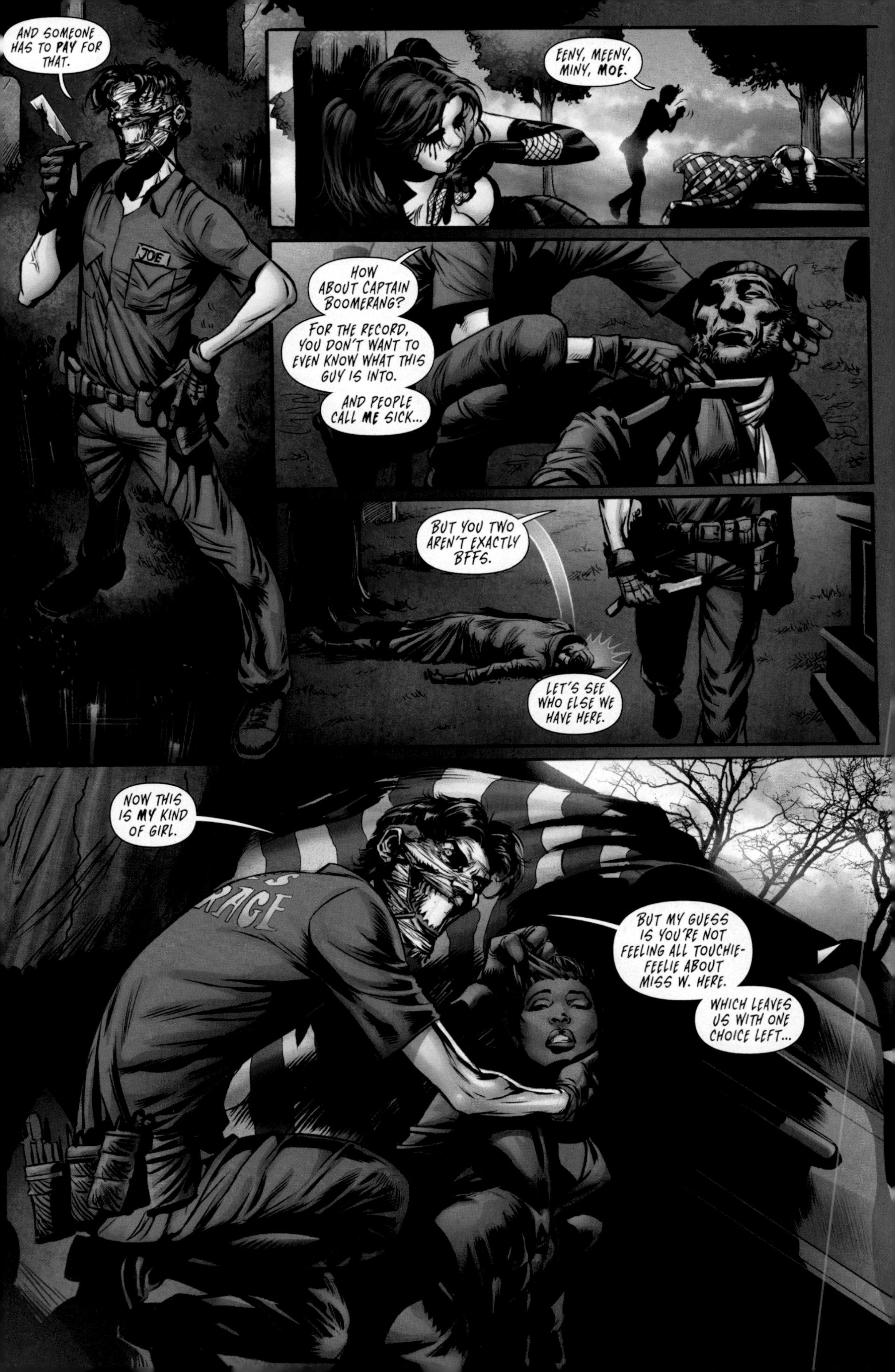
AND SOMEONE HAS TO PAY FOR THAT.
EENY, MEENY, MINY, MOE.
JOE
HOW ABOUT CAPTAIN BOOMERANG?
FOR THE RECORD, YOU DON'T WANT TO EVEN KNOW WHAT THIS GUY IS INTO.
AND PEOPLE CALL ME SICK...
BUT YOU TWO AREN'T EXACTLY BFFS.
LET'S SEE WHO ELSE WE HAVE HERE.
NOW THIS IS MY KIND OF GIRL.
BUT MY GUESS IS YOU'RE NOT FEELING ALL TOUCHIE-FEELIE ABOUT MISS W. HERE.
WHICH LEAVES US WITH ONE CHOICE LEFT...

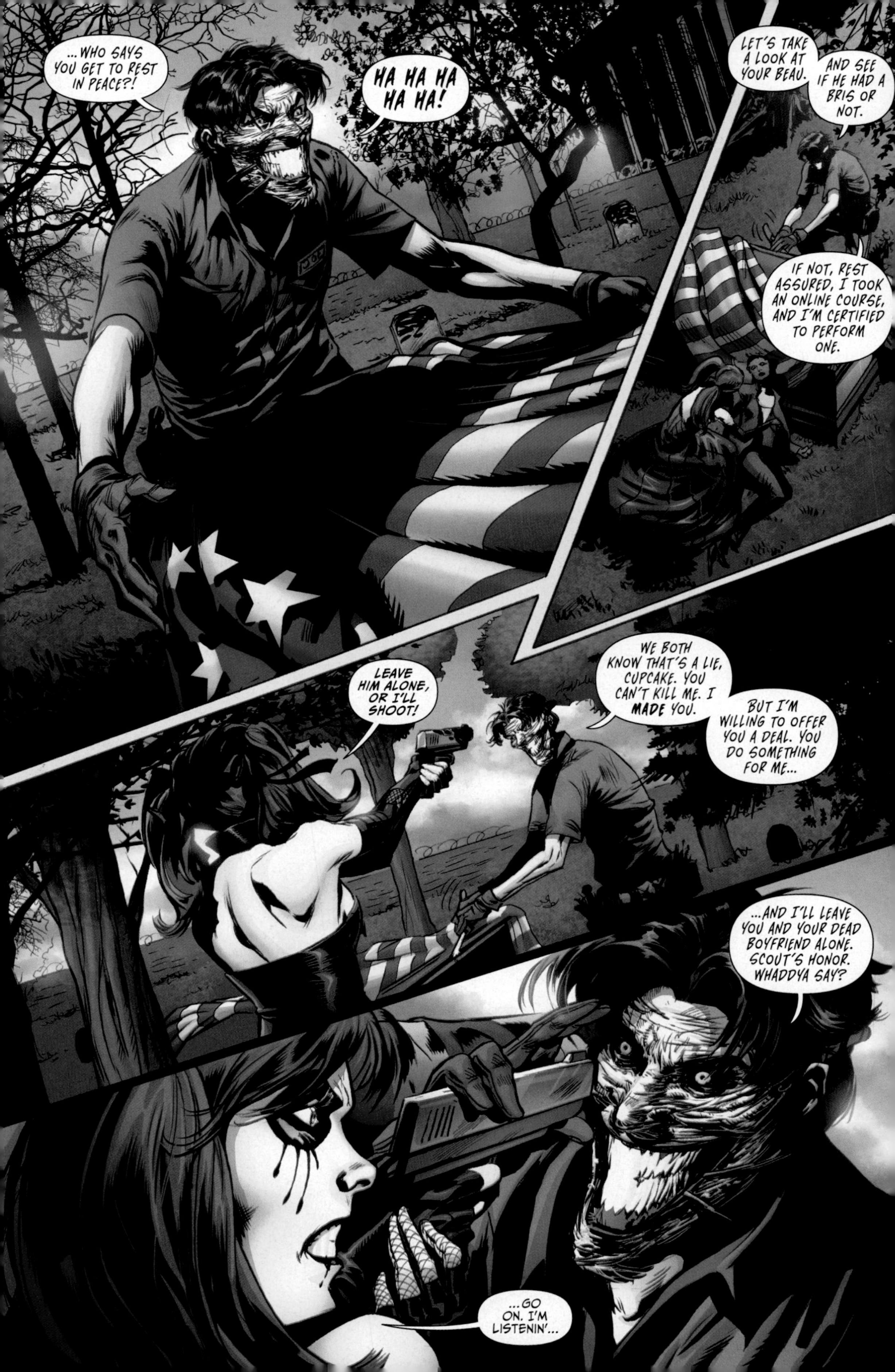
...WHO SAYS YOU GET TO REST IN PEACE?!
HA HA HA HA HA!
LET'S TAKE A LOOK AT YOUR BEAU.
AND SEE IF HE HAD A BRIS OR NOT.
IF NOT, REST ASSURED, I TOOK AN ONLINE COURSE, AND I'M CERTIFIED TO PERFORM ONE.
LEAVE HIM ALONE, OR I'LL SHOOT!
WE BOTH KNOW THAT'S A LIE, CUPCAKE. YOU CAN'T KILL ME. I MADE YOU.
BUT I'M WILLING TO OFFER YOU A DEAL. YOU DO SOMETHING FOR ME...
...AND I'LL LEAVE YOU AND YOUR DEAD BOYFRIEND ALONE. SCOUT'S HONOR. WHADDYA SAY?
...GO ON. I'M LISTENIN'...

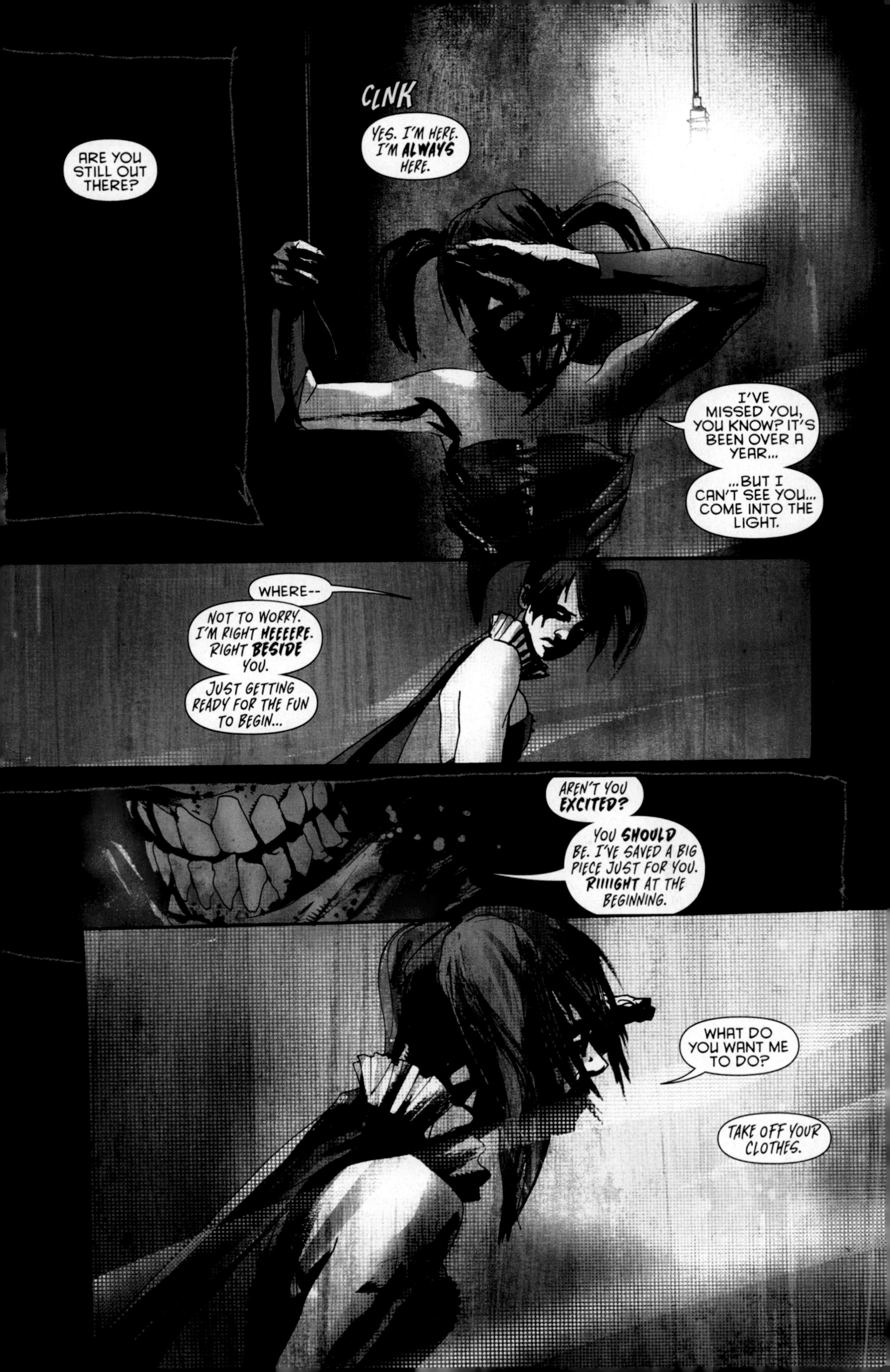
CLNK
ARE YOU STILL OUT THERE?
YES. I'M HERE. I'M ALWAYS HERE.
I'VE MISSED YOU, YOU KNOW? IT'S BEEN OVER A YEAR...
...BUT I CAN'T SEE YOU... COME INTO THE LIGHT.
WHERE--
NOT TO WORRY. I'M RIGHT HEEEERE. RIGHT BESIDE YOU.
JUST GETTING READY FOR THE FUN TO BEGIN...
AREN'T YOU EXCITED?
YOU SHOULD BE. I'VE SAVED A BIG PIECE JUST FOR YOU. RIIIIGHT AT THE BEGINNING.
WHAT DO YOU WANT ME TO DO?
TAKE OFF YOUR CLOTHES.

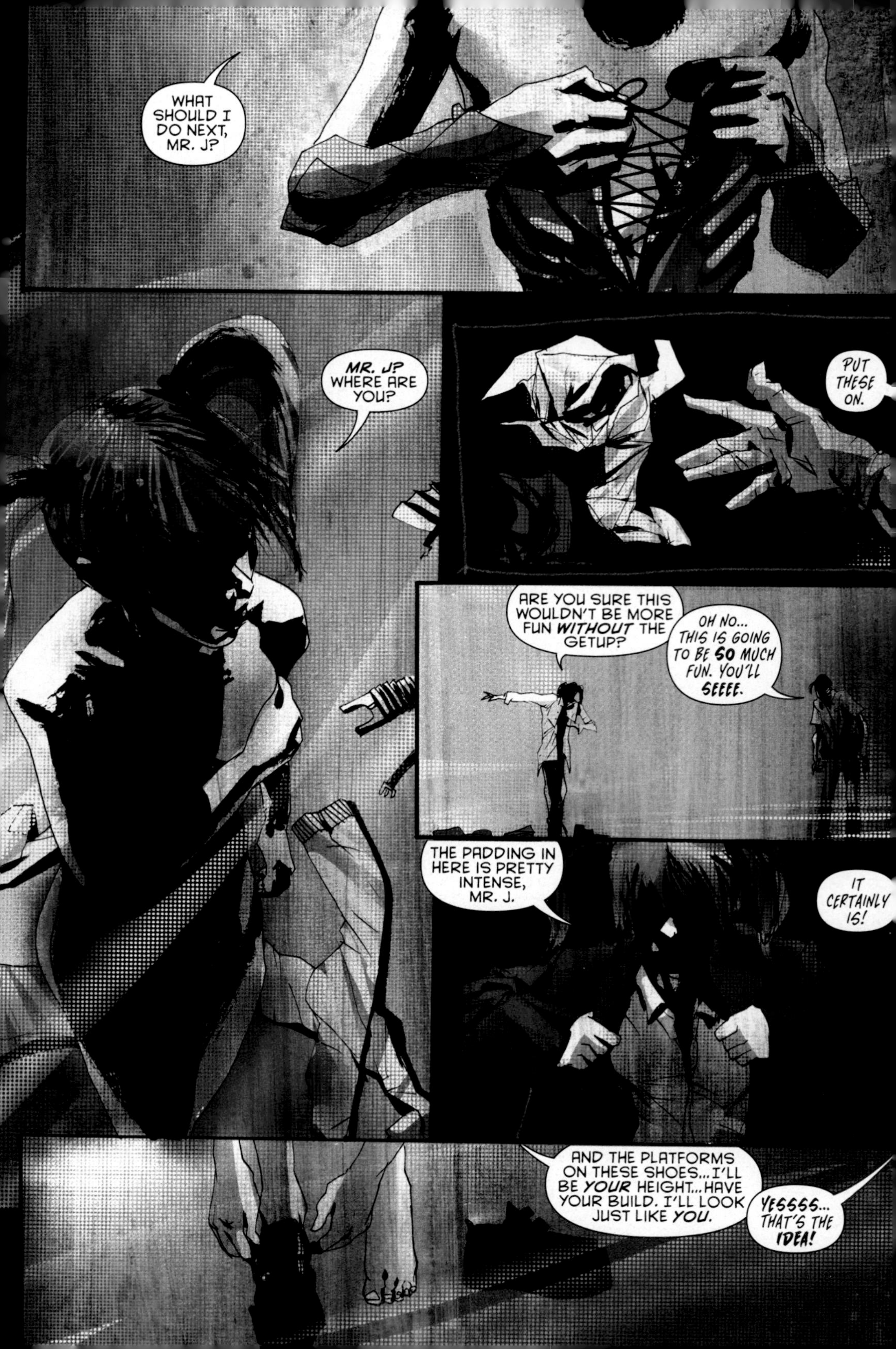
WHAT SHOULD I DO NEXT, MR. J?
MR. J? WHERE ARE YOU?
PUT THESE ON.
ARE YOU SURE THIS WOULDN'T BE MORE FUN WITHOUT THE GETUP?
OH NO... THIS IS GOING TO BE SO MUCH FUN. YOU'LL SEEEE.
THE PADDING IN HERE IS PRETTY INTENSE, MR. J.
IT CERTAINLY IS!
AND THE PLATFORMS ON THESE SHOES... I'LL BE YOUR HEIGHT... HAVE YOUR BUILD. I'LL LOOK JUST LIKE YOU.
YESSSS... THAT'S THE IDEA!

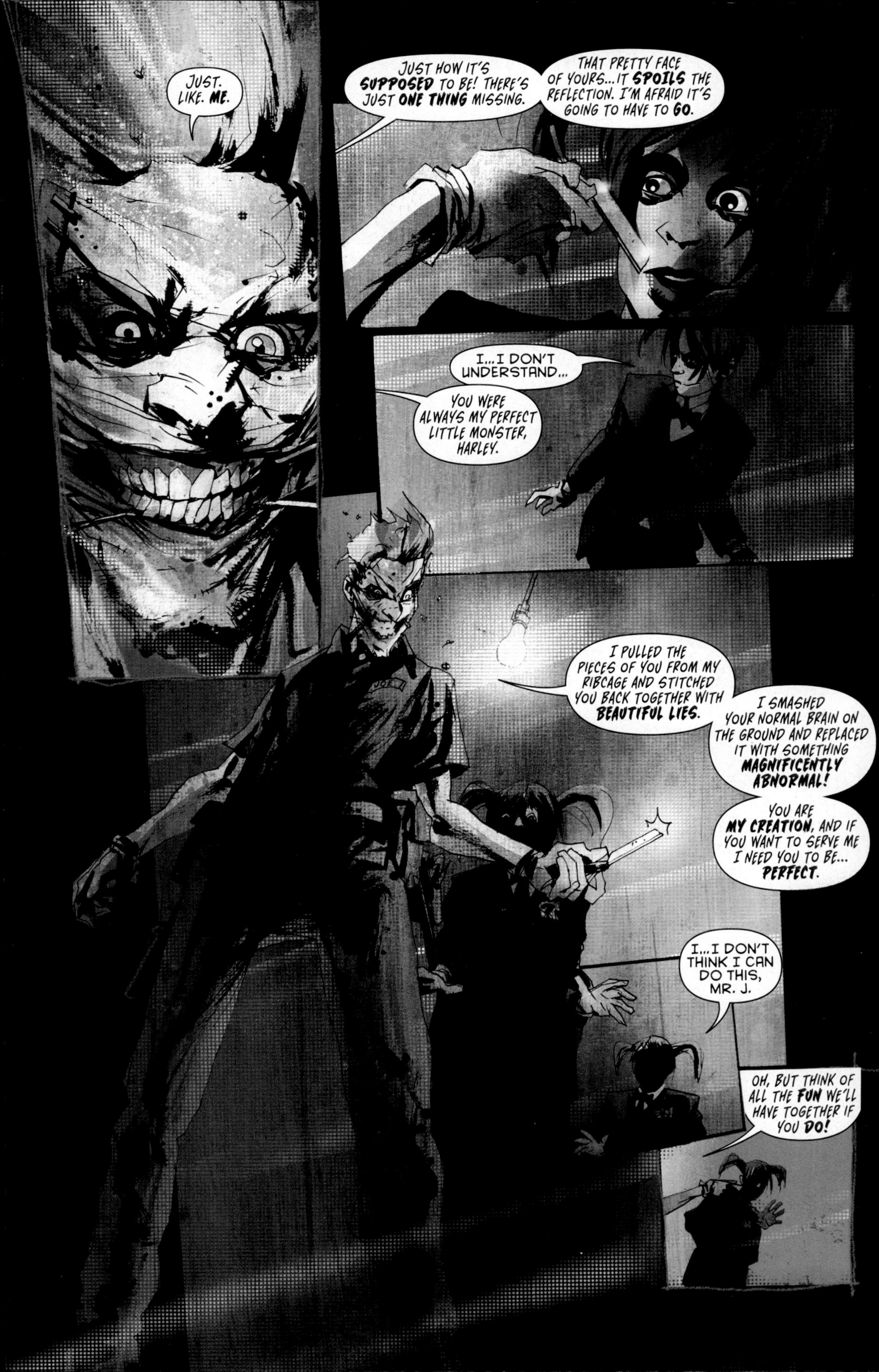
JUST. LIKE. ME.
JUST HOW IT'S SUPPOSED TO BE! THERE'S JUST ONE THING MISSING.
THAT PRETTY FACE OF YOURS... IT SPOILS THE REFLECTION. I'M AFRAID IT'S GOING TO HAVE TO GO.
I...I DON'T UNDERSTAND...
YOU WERE ALWAYS MY PERFECT LITTLE MONSTER, HARLEY.
I PULLED THE PIECES OF YOU FROM MY RIBCAGE AND STITCHED YOU BACK TOGETHER WITH BEAUTIFUL LIES.
I SMASHED YOUR NORMAL BRAIN ON THE GROUND AND REPLACED IT WITH SOMETHING MAGNIFICENTLY ABNORMAL!
YOU ARE MY CREATION, AND IF YOU WANT TO SERVE ME I NEED YOU TO BE... PERFECT.
I...I DON'T THINK I CAN DO THIS, MR. J.
OH, BUT THINK OF ALL THE FUN WE'LL HAVE TOGETHER IF YOU DO!

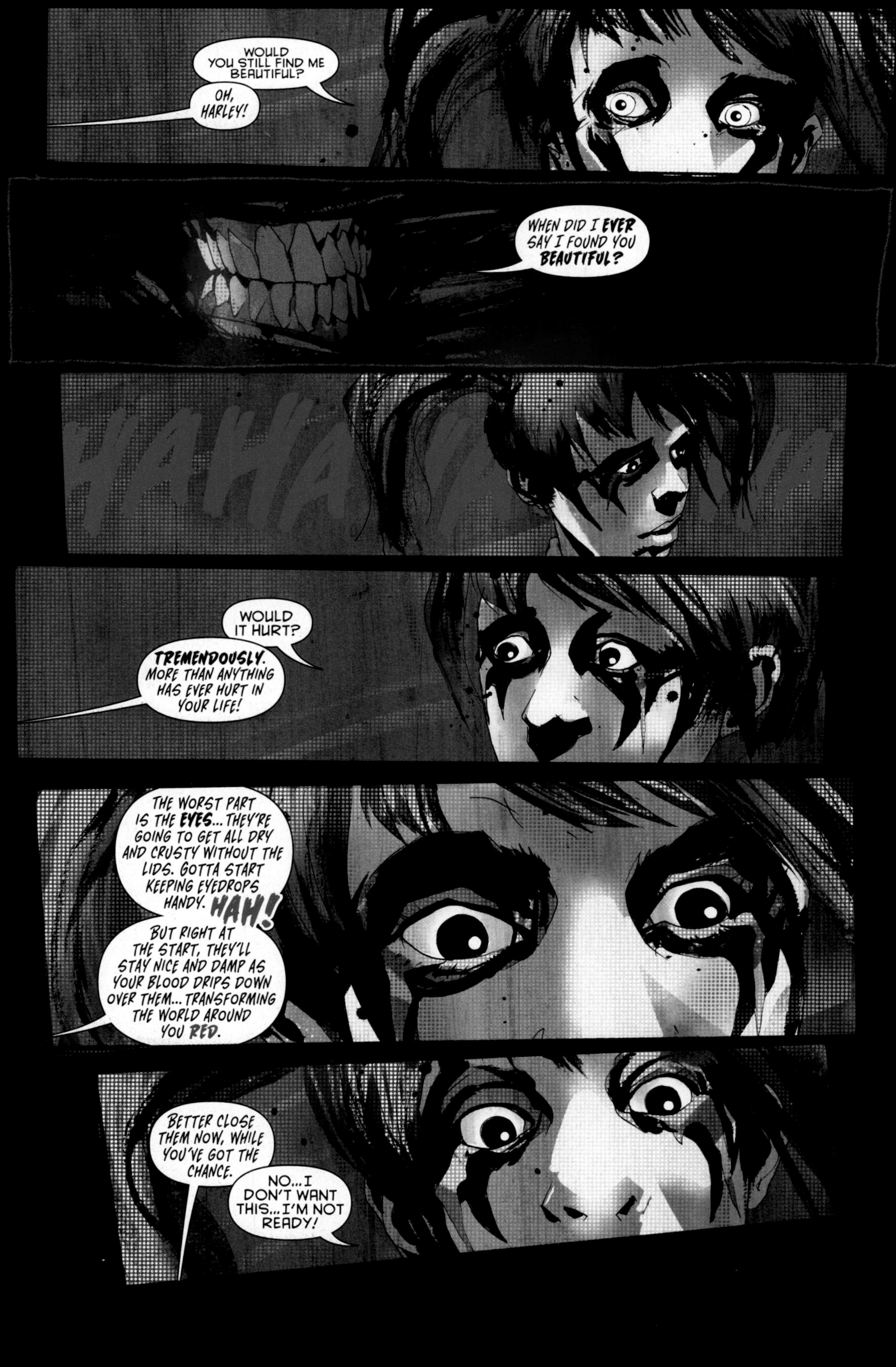
WOULD YOU STILL FIND ME BEAUTIFUL?
OH, HARLEY!
WHEN DID I EVER SAY I FOUND YOU BEAUTIFUL?
HAHA
WOULD IT HURT?
TREMENDOUSLY. MORE THAN ANYTHING HAS EVER HURT IN YOUR LIFE!
THE WORST PART IS THE EYES... THEY'RE GOING TO GET ALL DRY AND CRUSTY WITHOUT THE LIDS. GOTTA START KEEPING EYEDROPS HANDY. HAH!
BUT RIGHT AT THE START, THEY'LL STAY NICE AND DAMP AS YOUR BLOOD DRIPS DOWN OVER THEM... TRANSFORMING THE WORLD AROUND YOU RED.
BETTER CLOSE THEM NOW, WHILE YOU'VE GOT THE CHANCE.
NO... I DON'T WANT THIS... I'M NOT READY!

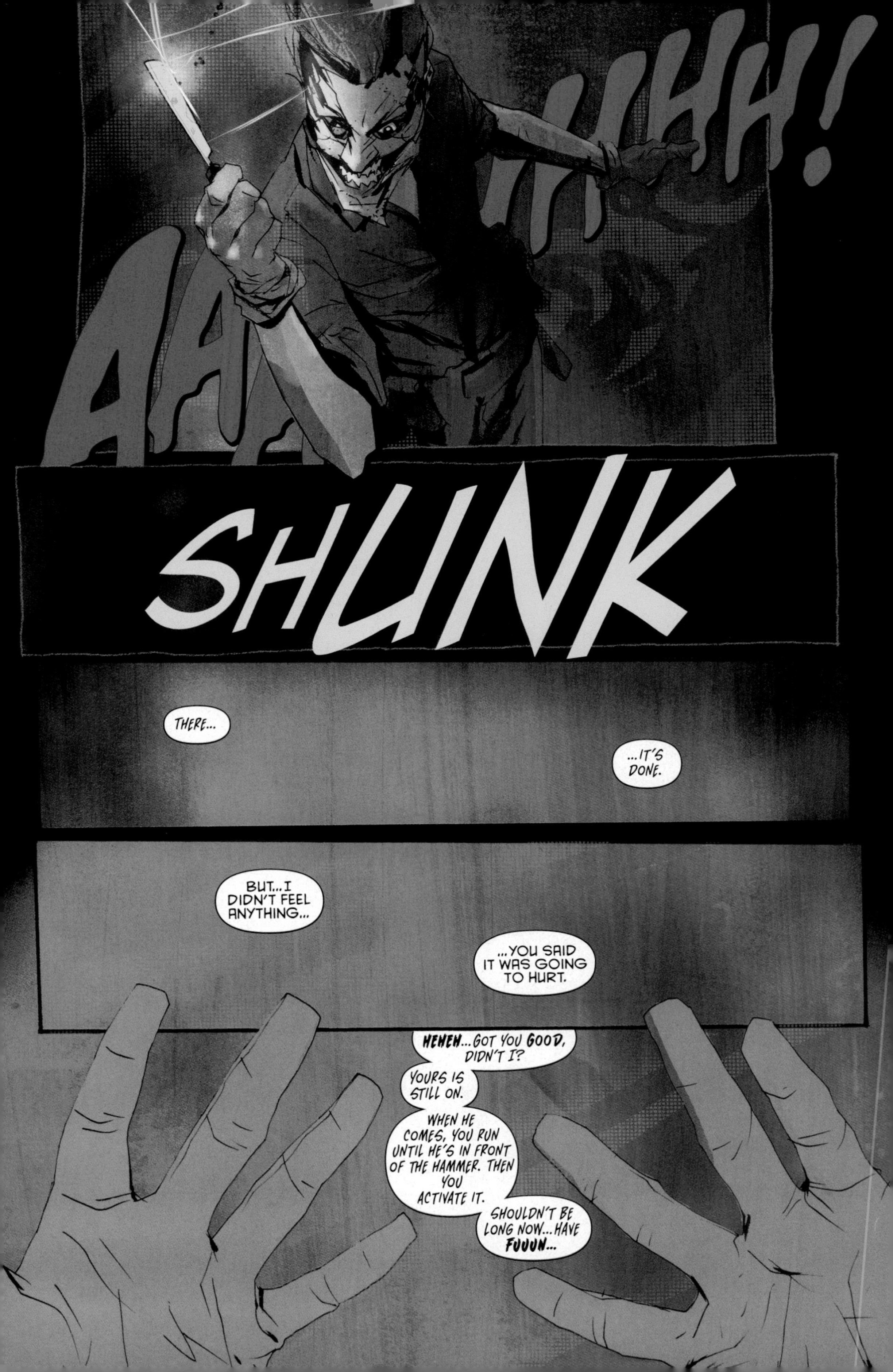
AAAHHH!
SHUNK
THERE...
...IT'S DONE.
BUT... I DIDN'T FEEL ANYTHING...
...YOU SAID IT WAS GOING TO HURT.
HEHEH... GOT YOU GOOD, DIDN'T I?
YOURS IS STILL ON.
WHEN HE COMES, YOU RUN UNTIL HE'S IN FRONT OF THE HAMMER. THEN YOU ACTIVATE IT.
SHOULDN'T BE LONG NOW... HAVE FUUUN...

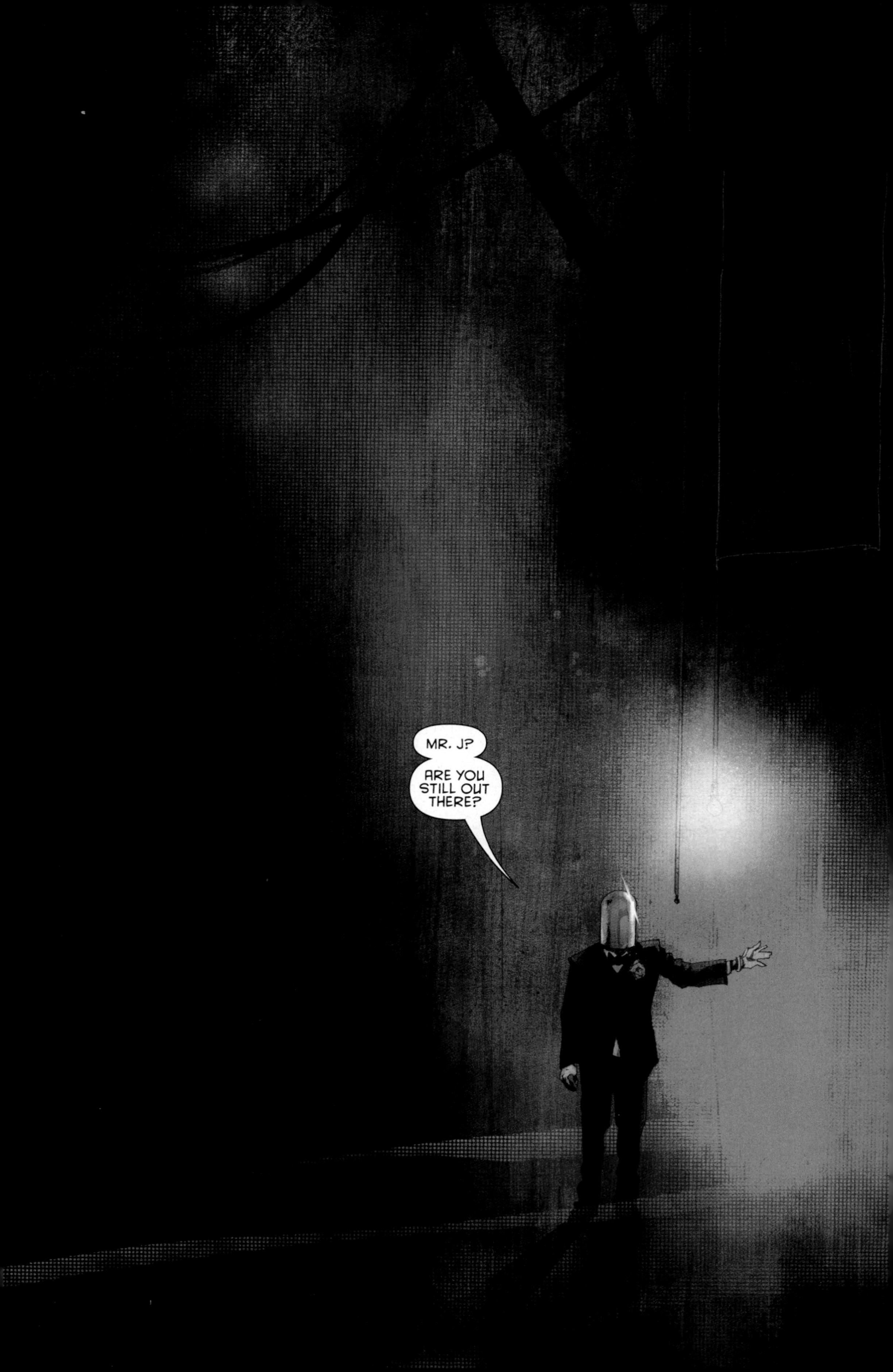
MR. J?
ARE YOU STILL OUT THERE?

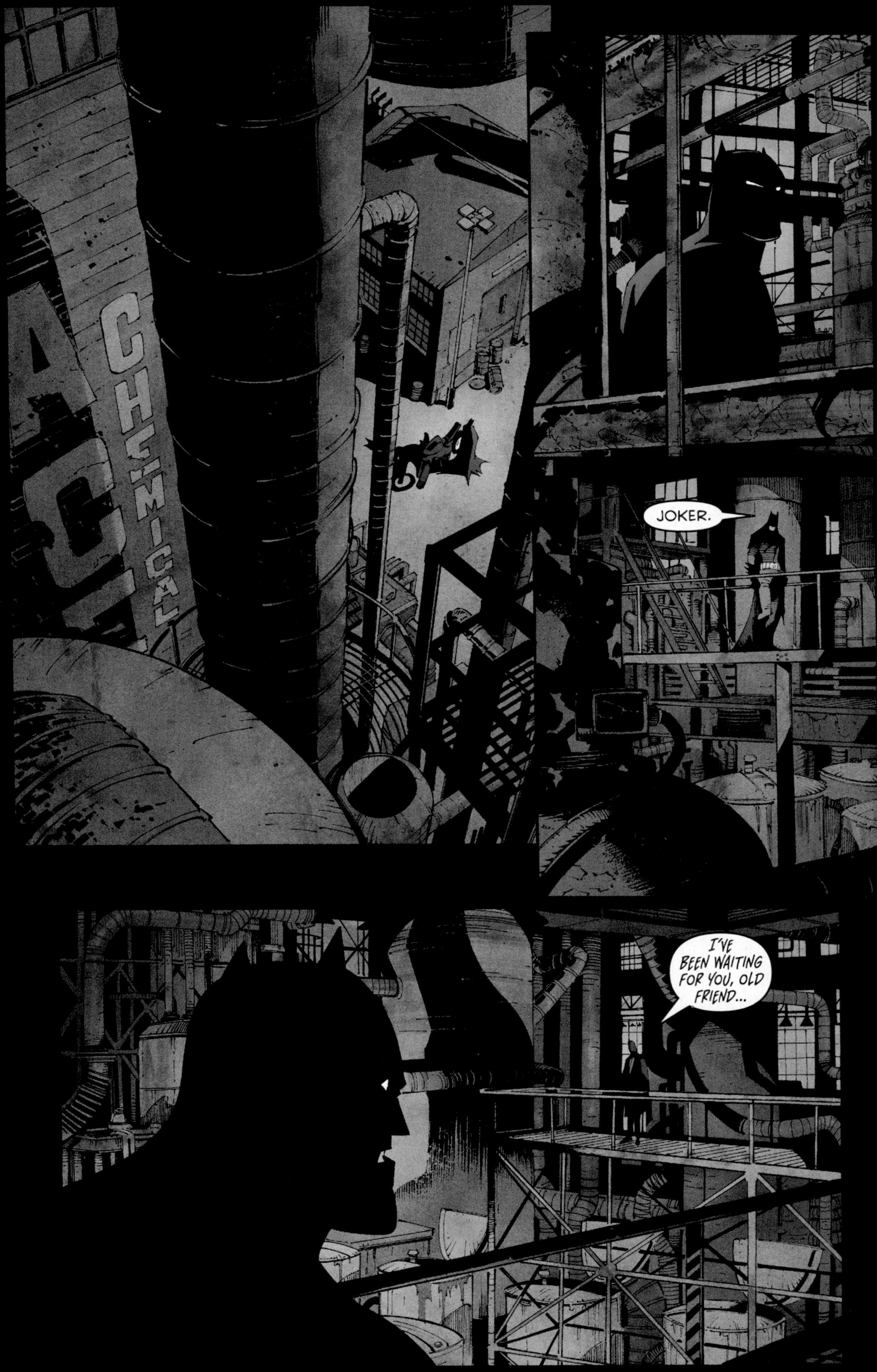
CHEMICAL
JOKER.
I'VE BEEN WAITING FOR YOU, OLD FRIEND...

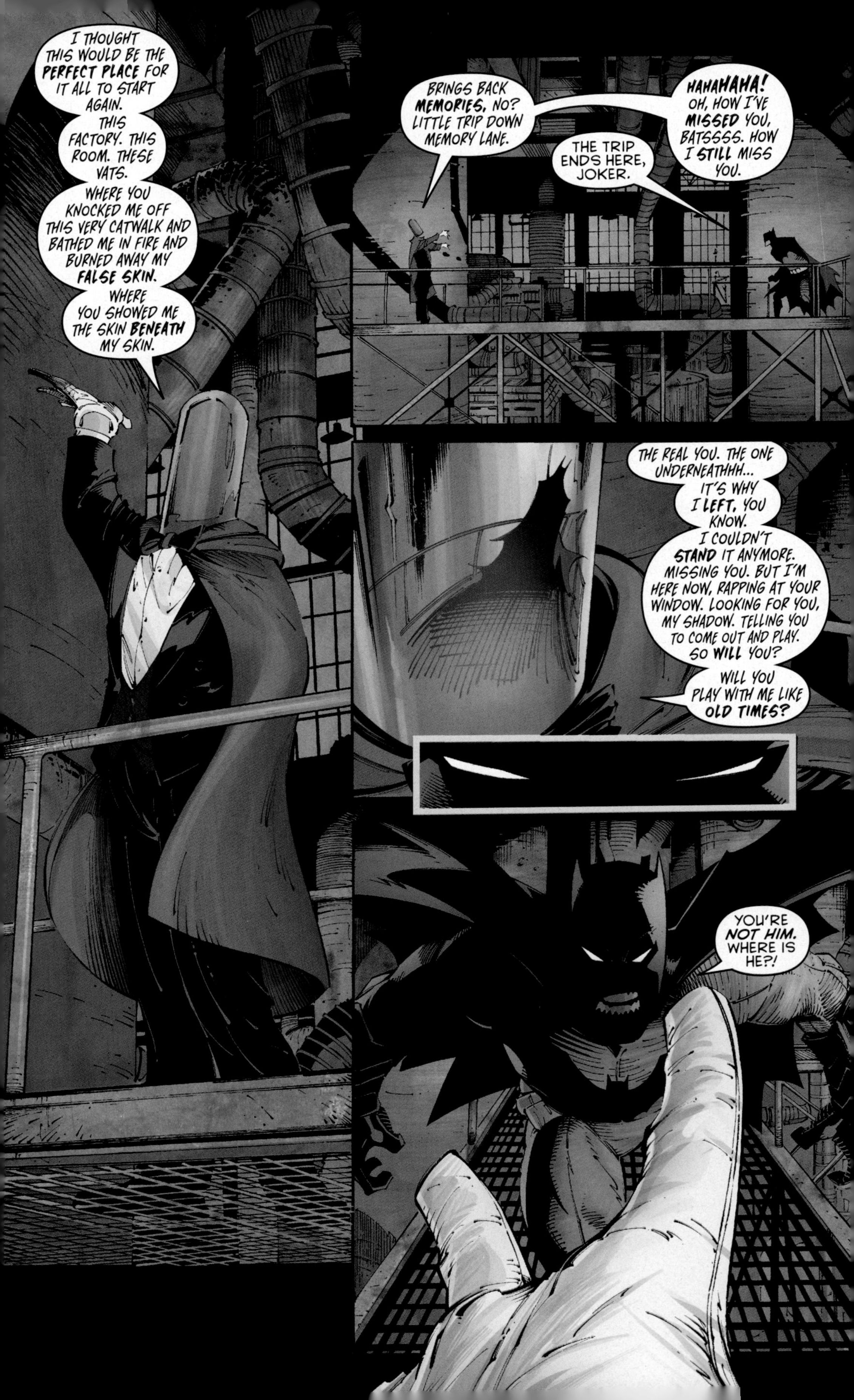
I THOUGHT THIS WOULD BE THE PERFECT PLACE FOR IT ALL TO START AGAIN.
THIS FACTORY. THIS ROOM. THESE VATS.
WHERE YOU KNOCKED ME OFF THIS VERY CATWALK AND BATHED ME IN FIRE AND BURNED AWAY MY FALSE SKIN.
WHERE YOU SHOWED ME THE SKIN BENEATH MY SKIN.
BRINGS BACK MEMORIES, NO? LITTLE TRIP DOWN MEMORY LANE.
THE TRIP ENDS HERE, JOKER.
HAHAHAHA! OH, HOW I'VE MISSED YOU, BATSSSS. HOW I STILL MISS YOU.
THE REAL YOU. THE ONE UNDERNEATHHH...
IT'S WHY I LEFT, YOU KNOW.
I COULDN'T STAND IT ANYMORE. MISSING YOU. BUT I'M HERE NOW, RAPPING AT YOUR WINDOW. LOOKING FOR YOU, MY SHADOW. TELLING YOU TO COME OUT AND PLAY. SO WILL YOU?
WILL YOU PLAY WITH ME LIKE OLD TIMES?
YOU'RE NOT HIM. WHERE IS HE?!

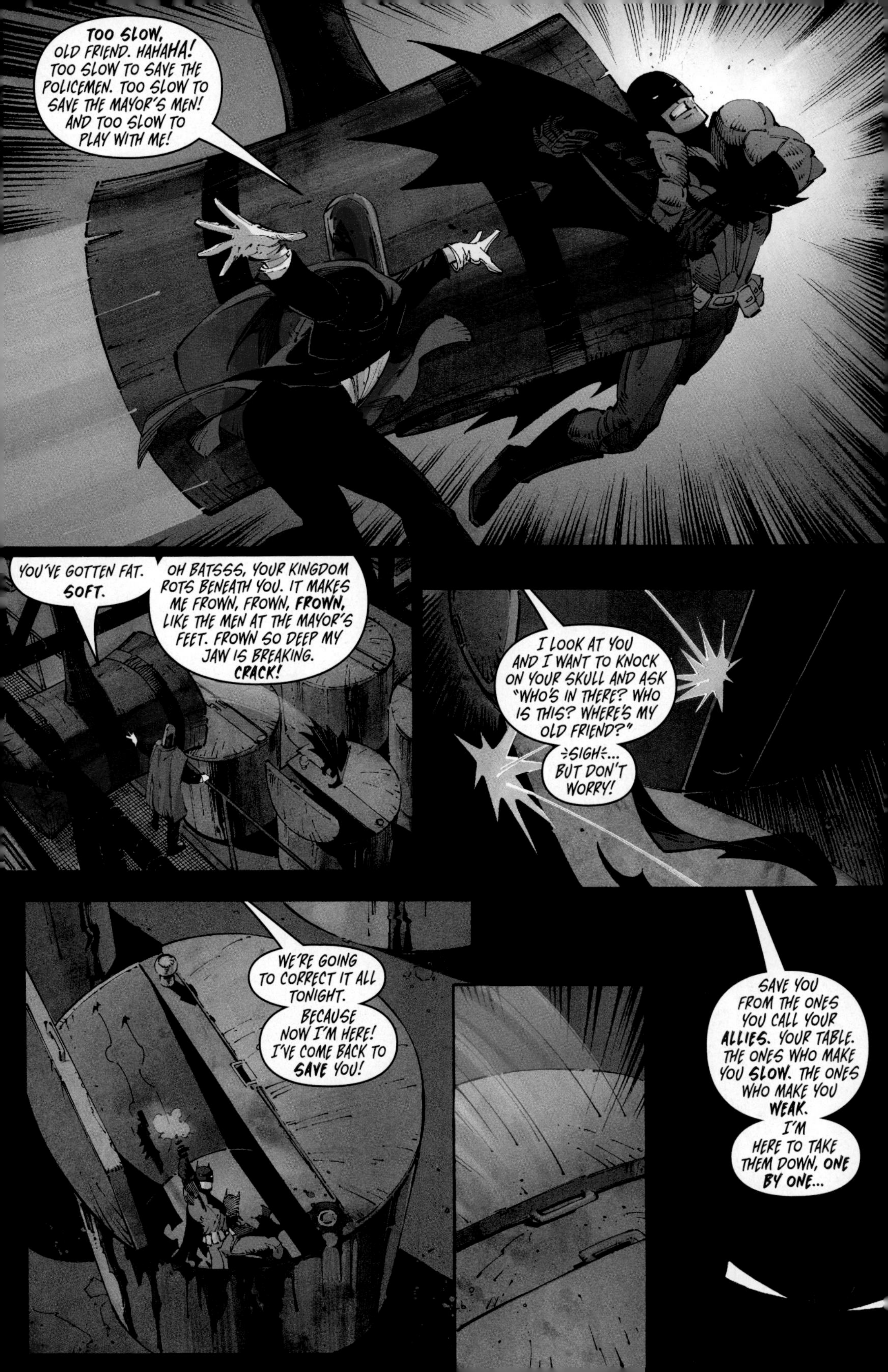
TOO SLOW, OLD FRIEND. HAHAHA! TOO SLOW TO SAVE THE POLICEMEN. TOO SLOW TO SAVE THE MAYOR'S MEN! AND TOO SLOW TO PLAY WITH ME!
YOU'VE GOTTEN FAT. SOFT.
OH BATSSS, YOUR KINGDOM ROTS BENEATH YOU. IT MAKES ME FROWN, FROWN, FROWN, LIKE THE MEN AT THE MAYOR'S FEET. FROWN SO DEEP MY JAW IS BREAKING. CRACK!
I LOOK AT YOU AND I WANT TO KNOCK ON YOUR SKULL AND ASK "WHO'S IN THERE? WHO IS THIS? WHERE'S MY OLD FRIEND?"
SIGH... BUT DON'T WORRY!
WE'RE GOING TO CORRECT IT ALL TONIGHT.
BECAUSE NOW I'M HERE! I'VE COME BACK TO SAVE YOU!
SAVE YOU FROM THE ONES YOU CALL YOUR ALLIES. YOUR TABLE. THE ONES WHO MAKE YOU SLOW. THE ONES WHO MAKE YOU WEAK.
I'M HERE TO TAKE THEM DOWN, ONE BY ONE...

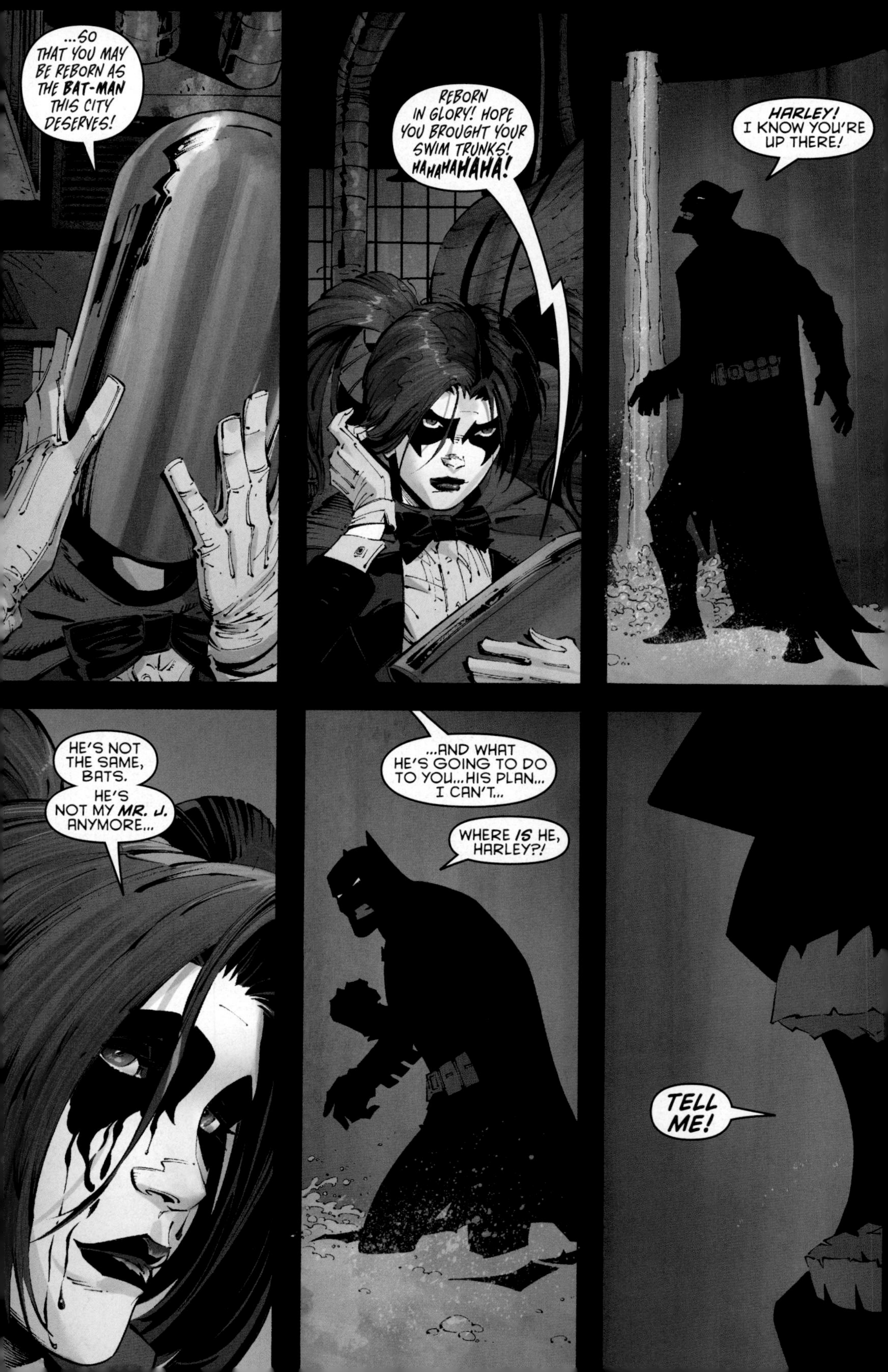
...SO THAT YOU MAY BE REBORN AS THE BAT-MAN THIS CITY DESERVES!
REBORN IN GLORY! HOPE YOU BROUGHT YOUR SWIM TRUNKS! HAHAHAHAHA!
HARLEY! I KNOW YOU'RE UP THERE!
HE'S NOT THE SAME, BATS.
HE'S NOT MY MR. J. ANYMORE...
...AND WHAT HE'S GOING TO DO TO YOU...HIS PLAN... I CAN'T...
WHERE IS HE, HARLEY?!
TELL ME!

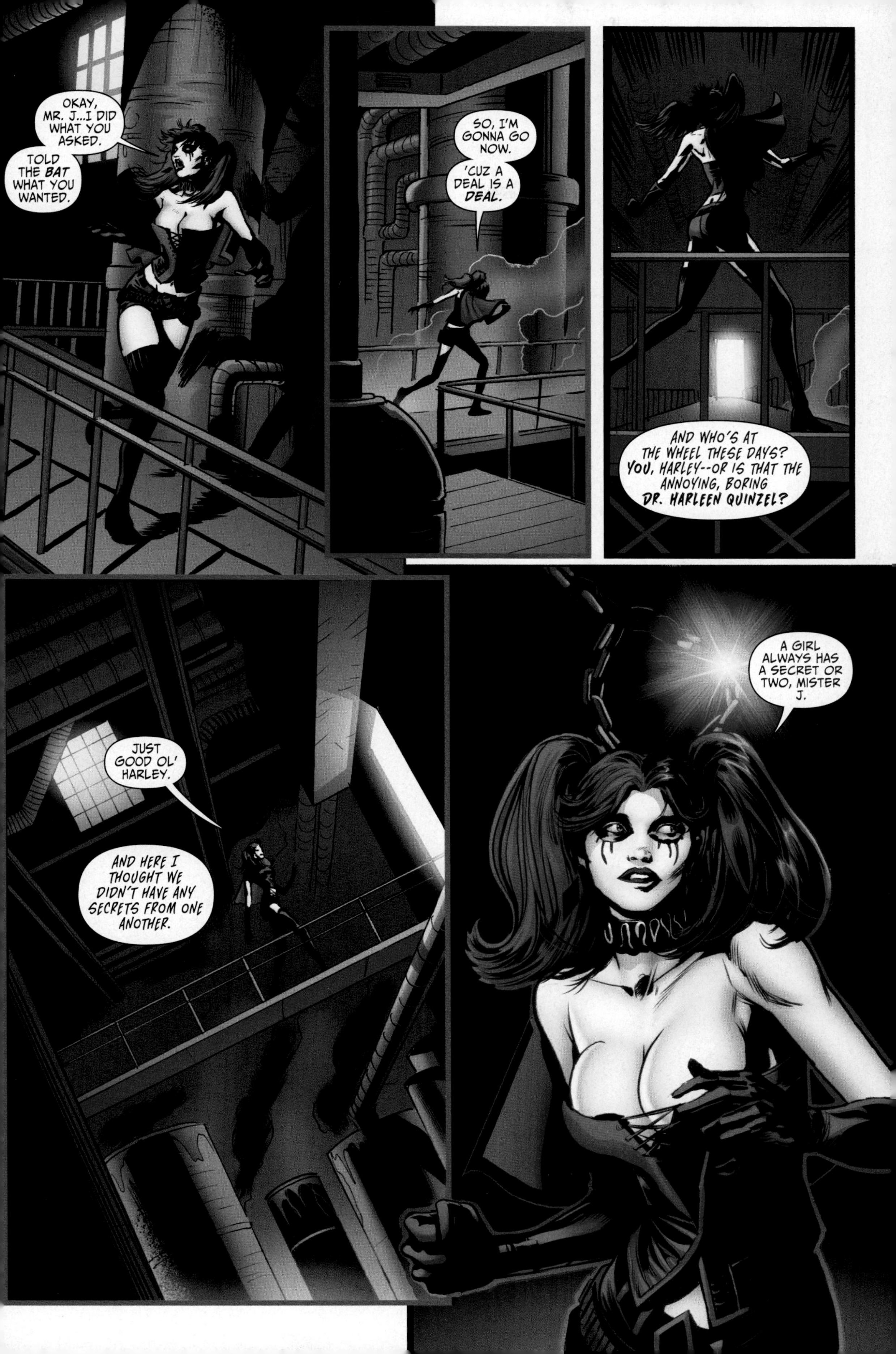
OKAY, MR. J...I DID WHAT YOU ASKED.
TOLD THE BAT WHAT YOU WANTED.
SO, I'M GONNA GO NOW.
'CUZ A DEAL IS A DEAL.
AND WHO'S AT THE WHEEL THESE DAYS? YOU, HARLEY--OR IS THAT THE ANNOYING, BORING DR. HARLEEN QUINZEL?
JUST GOOD OL' HARLEY.
AND HERE I THOUGHT WE DIDN'T HAVE ANY SECRETS FROM ONE ANOTHER.
A GIRL ALWAYS HAS A SECRET OR TWO, MISTER J.

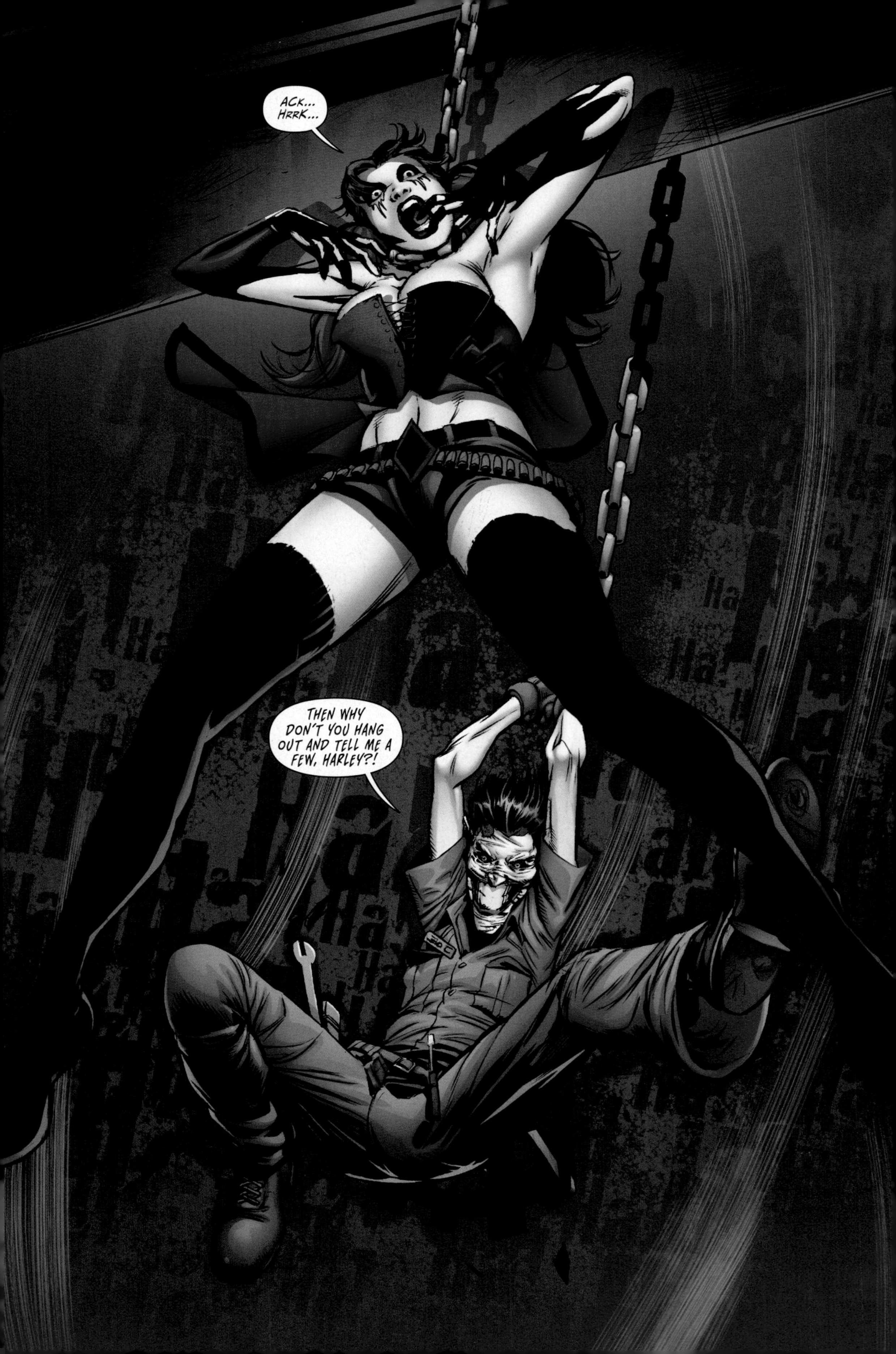
ACK... HRRK...
THEN WHY DON'T YOU HANG OUT AND TELL ME A FEW, HARLEY?!

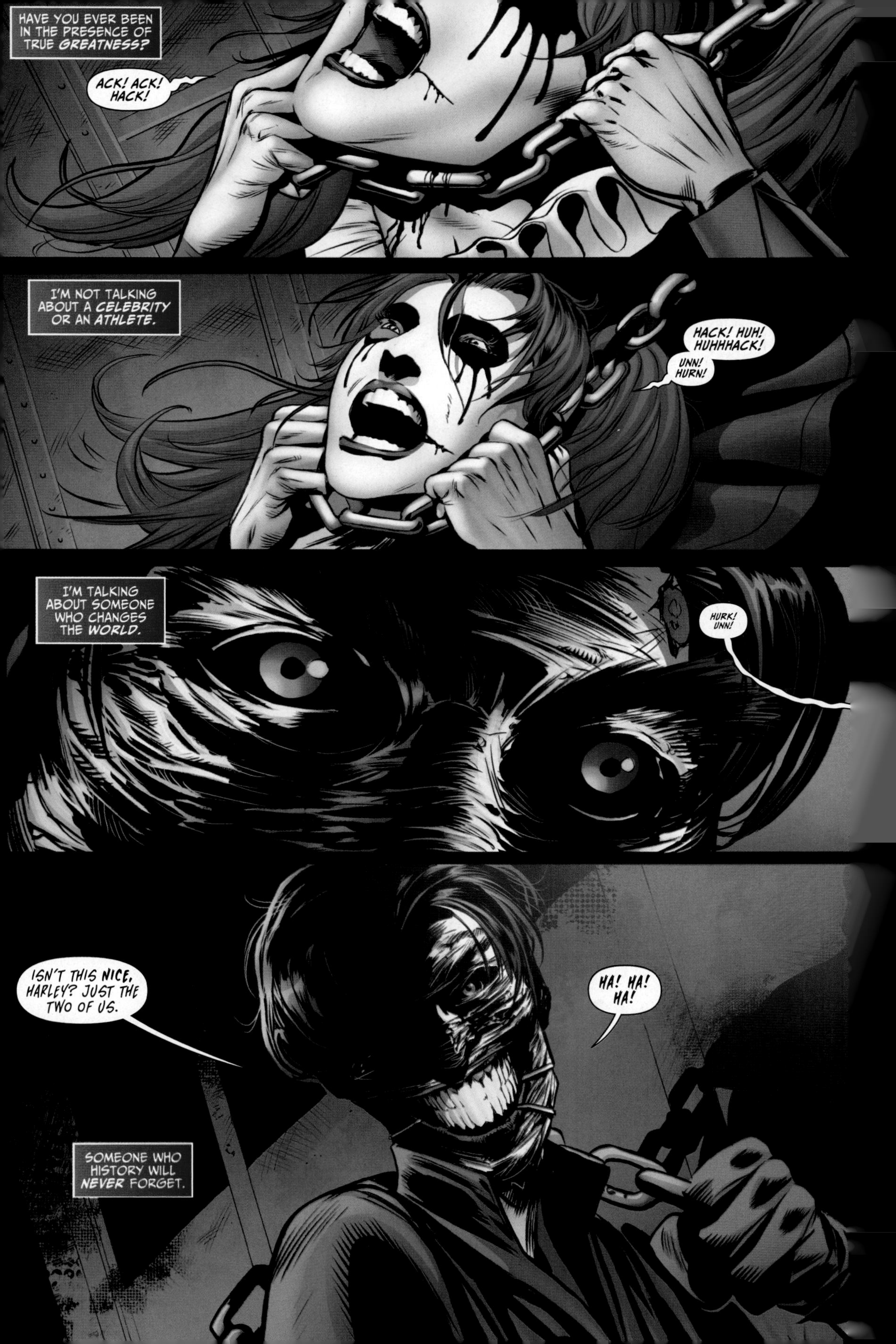
HAVE YOU EVER BEEN IN THE PRESENCE OF TRUE GREATNESS?
ACK! ACK! HACK!
I'M NOT TALKING ABOUT A CELEBRITY OR AN ATHLETE.
HACK! HUH! HUHHHACK!
UNN! HURN!
I'M TALKING ABOUT SOMEONE WHO CHANGES THE WORLD.
HURK! UNN!
ISN'T THIS NICE, HARLEY? JUST THE TWO OF US.
HA! HA! HA!
SOMEONE WHO HISTORY WILL NEVER FORGET.

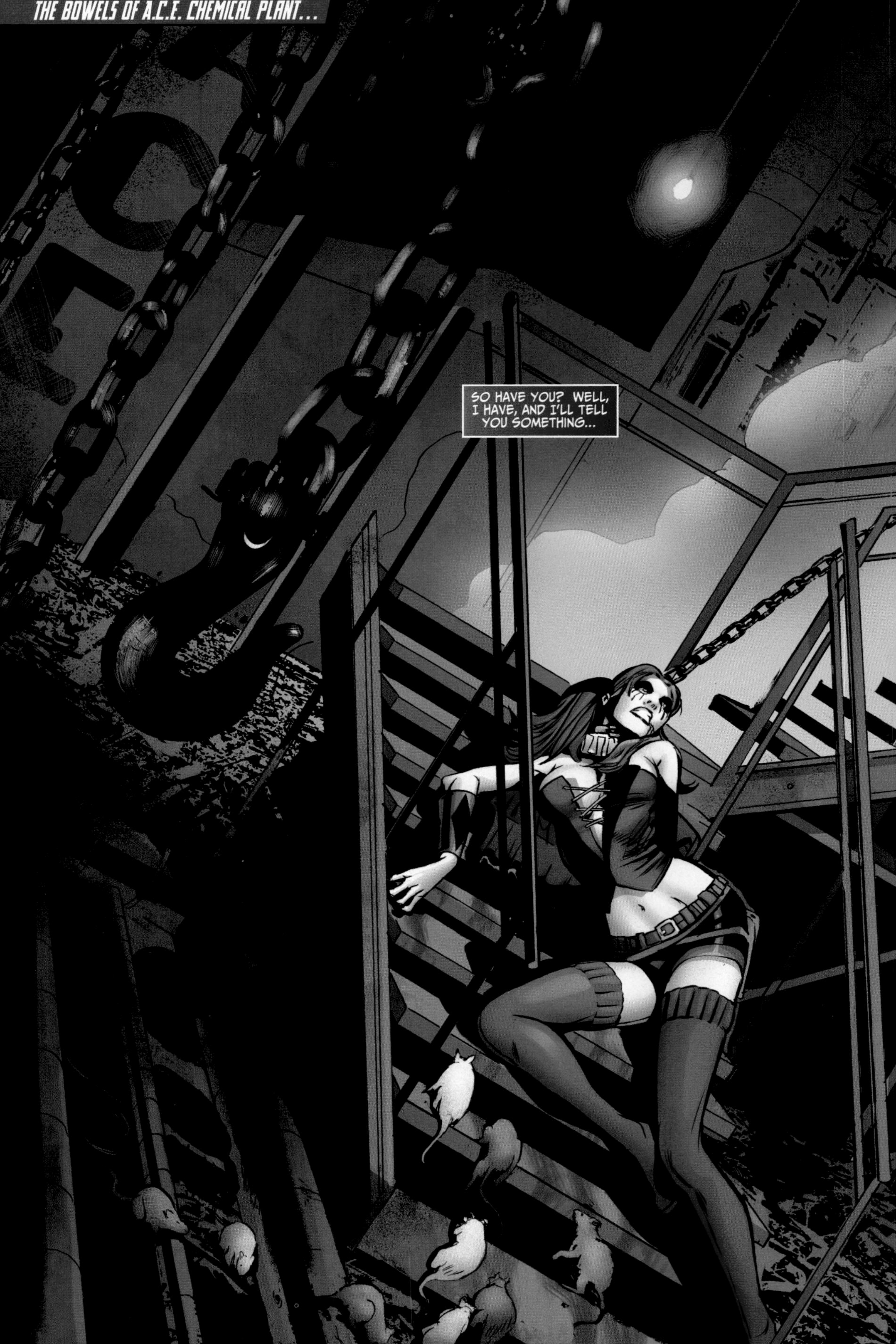
THE BOWELS OF A.C.E. CHEMICAL PLANT...
SO HAVE YOU? WELL, I HAVE, AND I'LL TELL YOU SOMETHING...

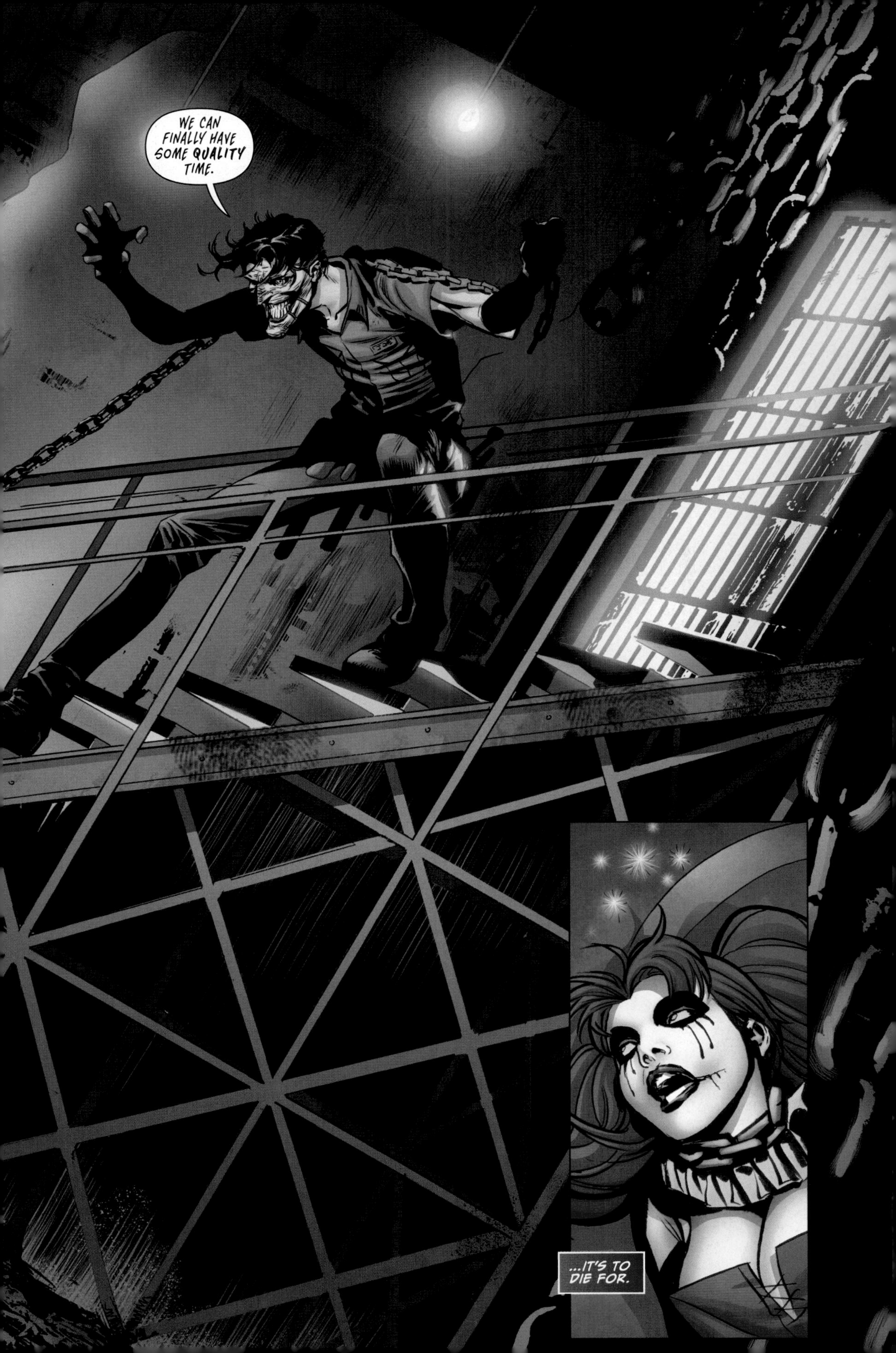
WE CAN FINALLY HAVE SOME QUALITY TIME.
...IT'S TO DIE FOR.

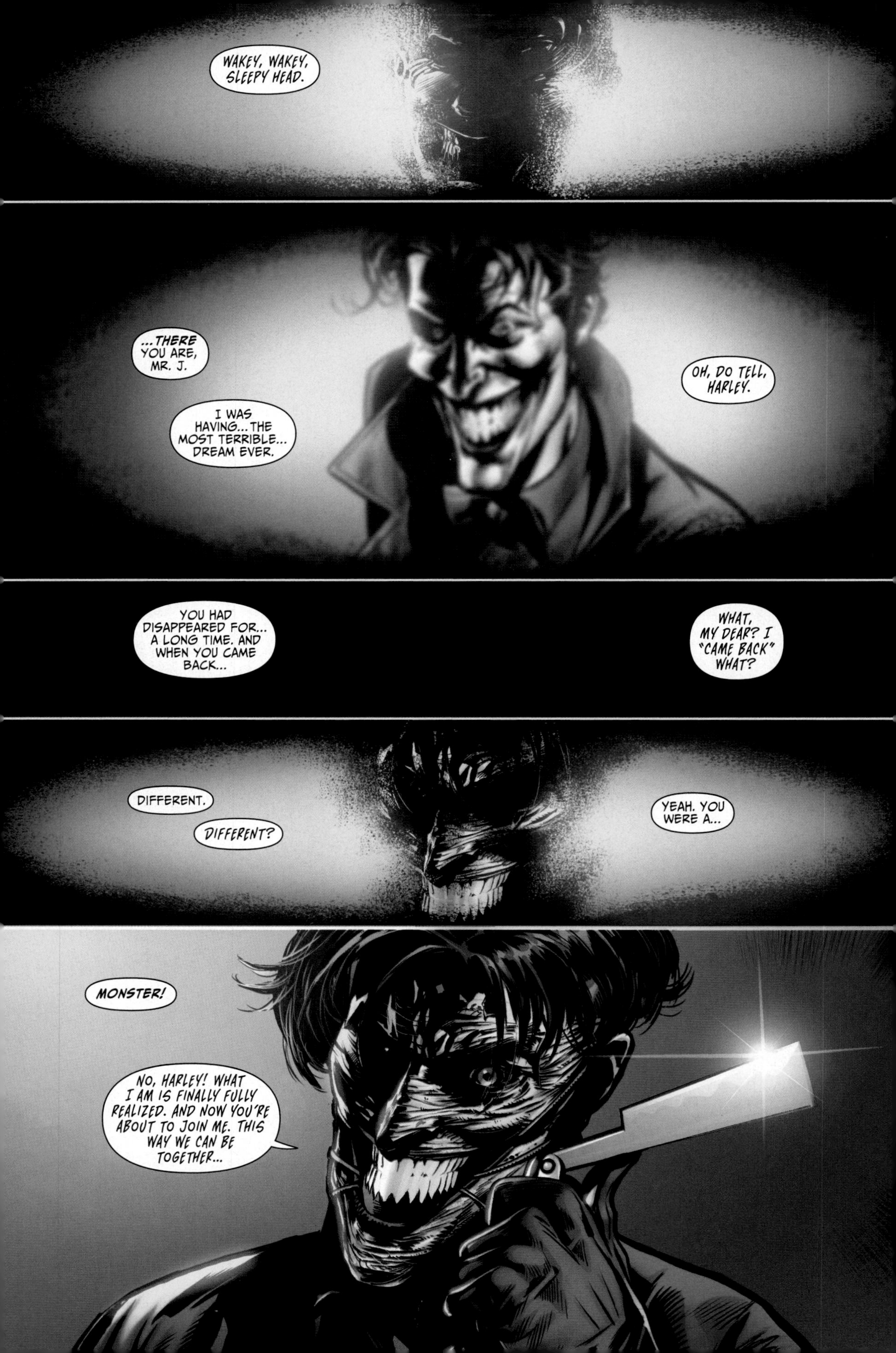
WAKEY, WAKEY, SLEEPY HEAD.
...THERE YOU ARE, MR. J.
I WAS HAVING...THE MOST TERRIBLE... DREAM EVER.
OH, DO TELL, HARLEY.
YOU HAD DISAPPEARED FOR... A LONG TIME. AND WHEN YOU CAME BACK...
WHAT, MY DEAR? I "CAME BACK" WHAT?
DIFFERENT.
DIFFERENT?
YEAH. YOU WERE A...
MONSTER!
NO, HARLEY! WHAT I AM IS FINALLY FULLY REALIZED. AND NOW YOU'RE ABOUT TO JOIN ME. THIS WAY WE CAN BE TOGETHER...

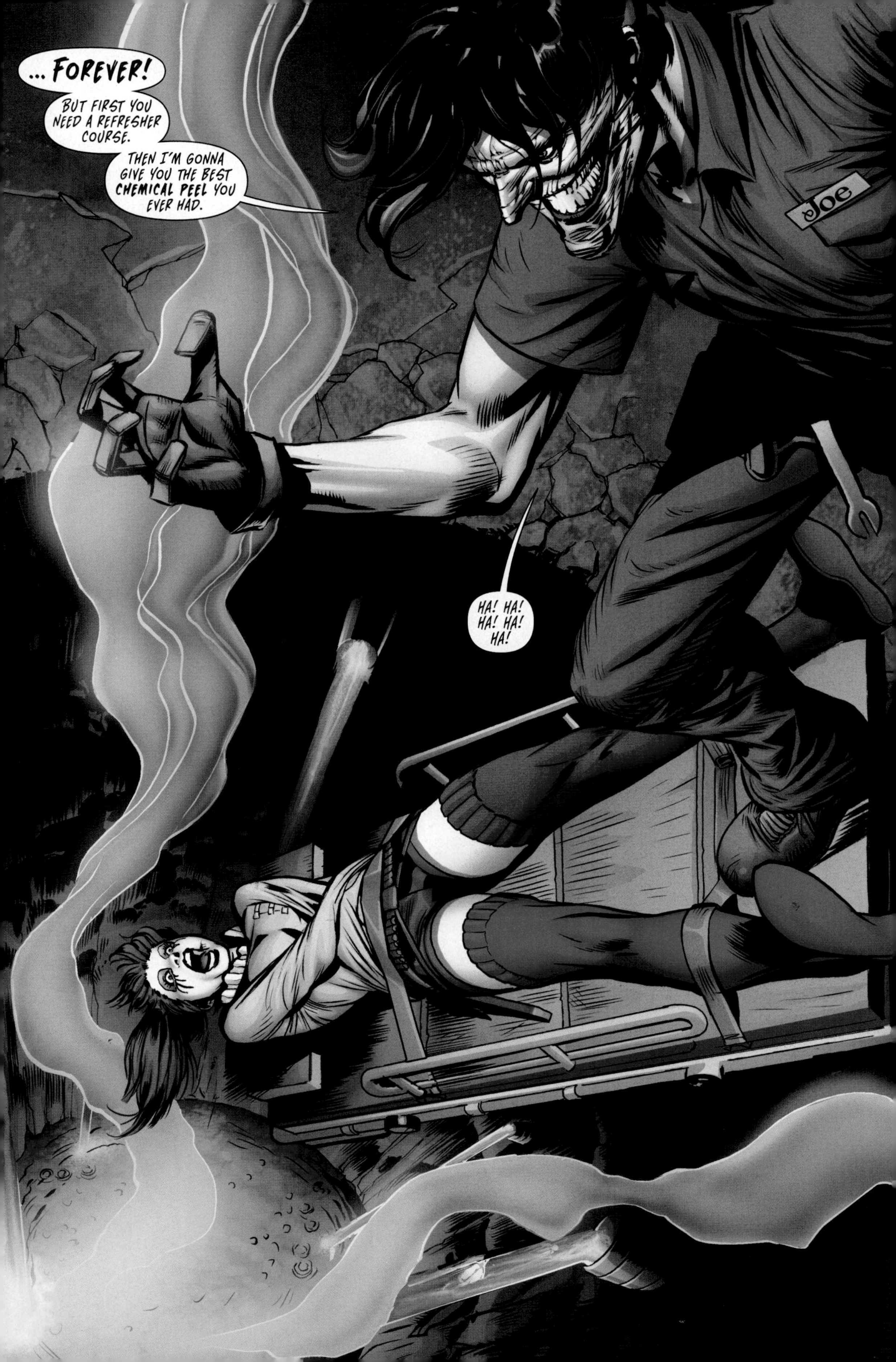
... FOREVER!
BUT FIRST YOU NEED A REFRESHER COURSE.
THEN I'M GONNA GIVE YOU THE BEST **CHEMICAL PEEL** YOU EVER HAD.
Joe
HA! HA! HA! HA! HA!

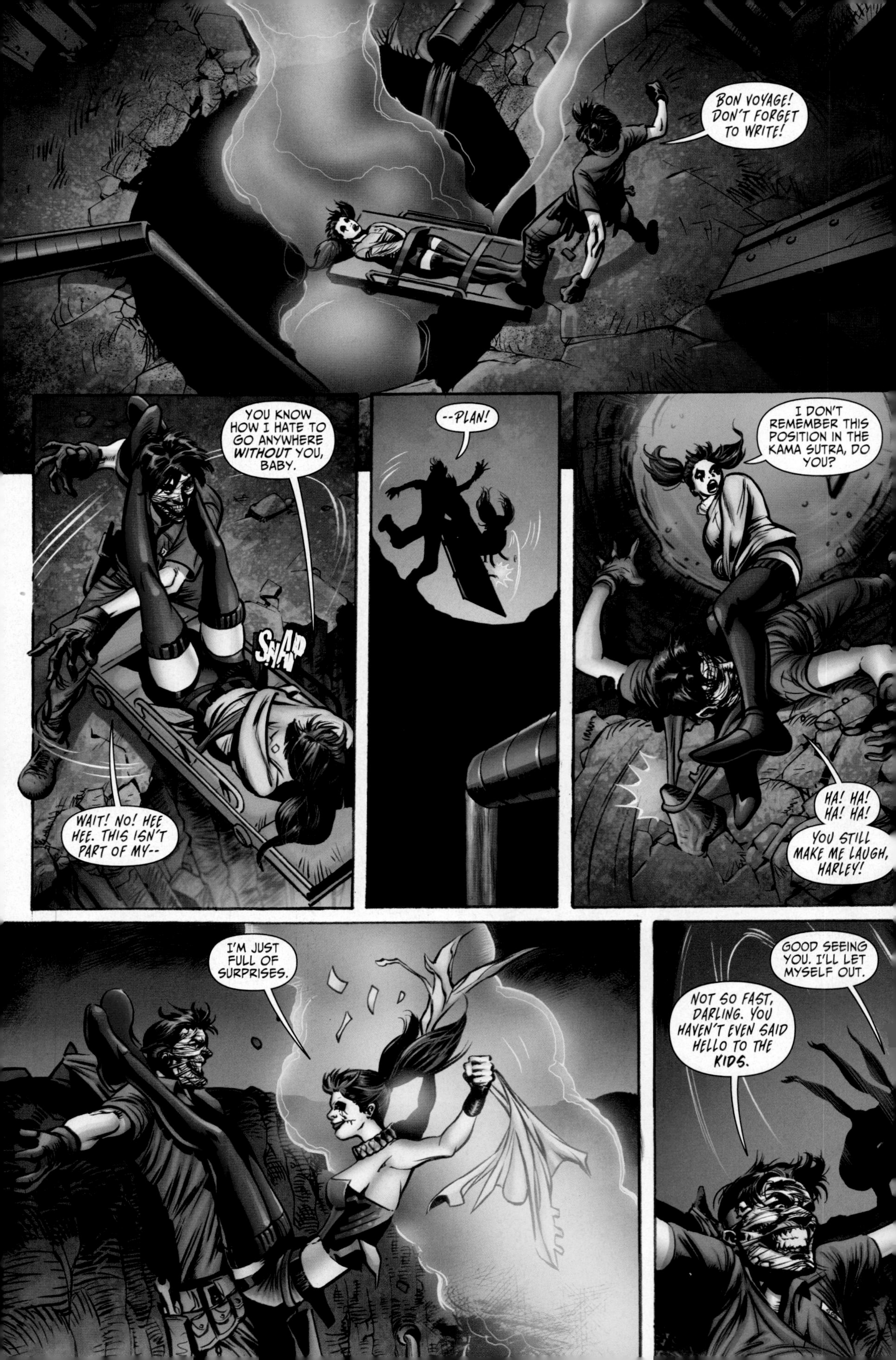
BON VOYAGE! DON'T FORGET TO WRITE!
YOU KNOW HOW I HATE TO GO ANYWHERE WITHOUT YOU, BABY.
SNAP
WAIT! NO! HEE HEE. THIS ISN'T PART OF MY--
--PLAN!
I DON'T REMEMBER THIS POSITION IN THE KAMA SUTRA, DO YOU?
HA! HA! HA! HA!
YOU STILL MAKE ME LAUGH, HARLEY!
I'M JUST FULL OF SURPRISES.
GOOD SEEING YOU. I'LL LET MYSELF OUT.
NOT SO FAST, DARLING. YOU HAVEN'T EVEN SAID HELLO TO THE KIDS.

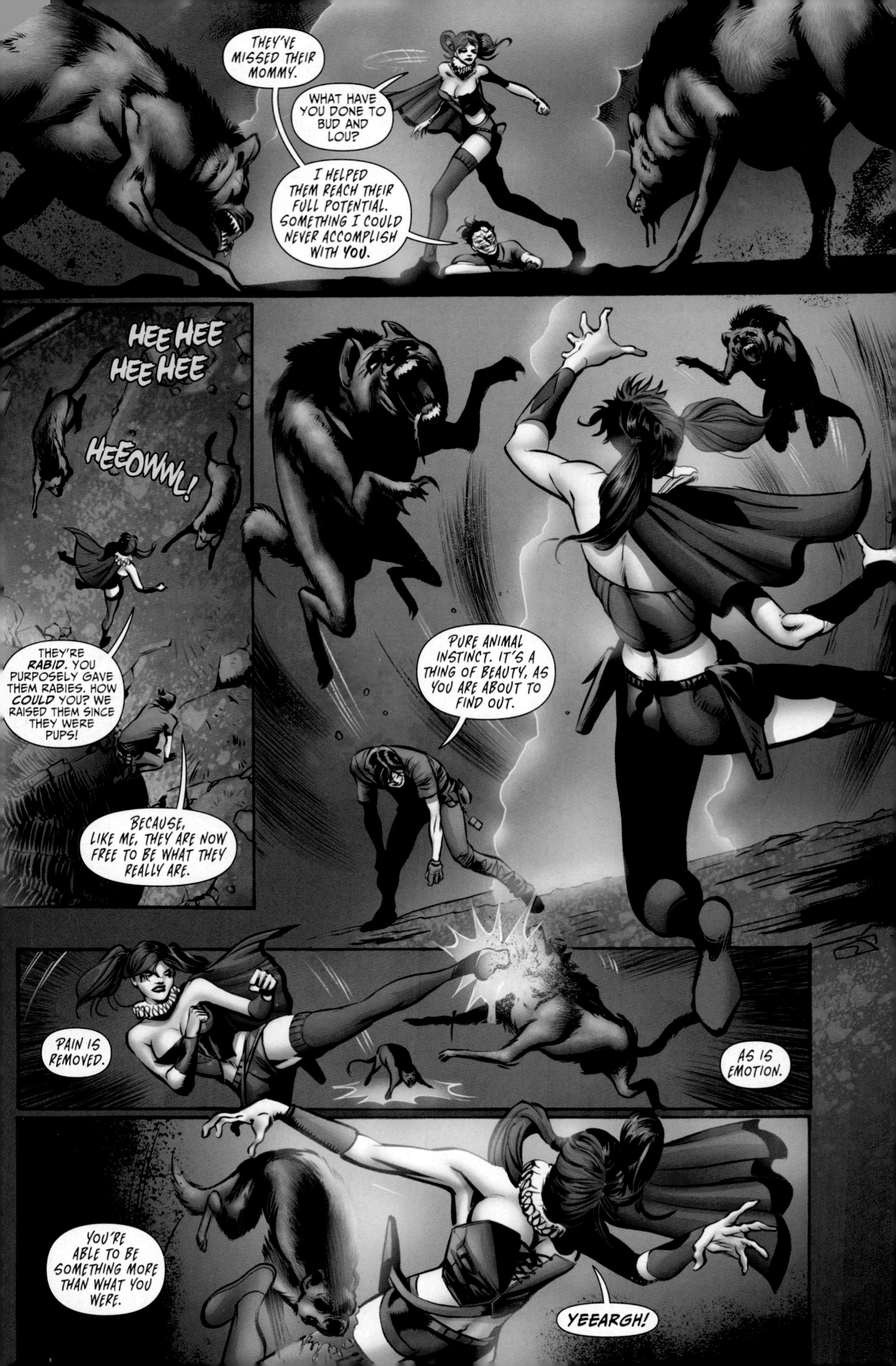
THEY'VE MISSED THEIR MOMMY.
WHAT HAVE YOU DONE TO BUD AND LOU?
I HELPED THEM REACH THEIR FULL POTENTIAL. SOMETHING I COULD NEVER ACCOMPLISH WITH YOU.
HEE HEE HEE HEE
HEEOWWL!
THEY'RE RABID. YOU PURPOSELY GAVE THEM RABIES. HOW COULD YOU? WE RAISED THEM SINCE THEY WERE PUPS!
BECAUSE, LIKE ME, THEY ARE NOW FREE TO BE WHAT THEY REALLY ARE.
PURE ANIMAL INSTINCT. IT'S A THING OF BEAUTY, AS YOU ARE ABOUT TO FIND OUT.
PAIN IS REMOVED.
AS IS EMOTION.
YOU'RE ABLE TO BE SOMETHING MORE THAN WHAT YOU WERE.
YEEARGH!

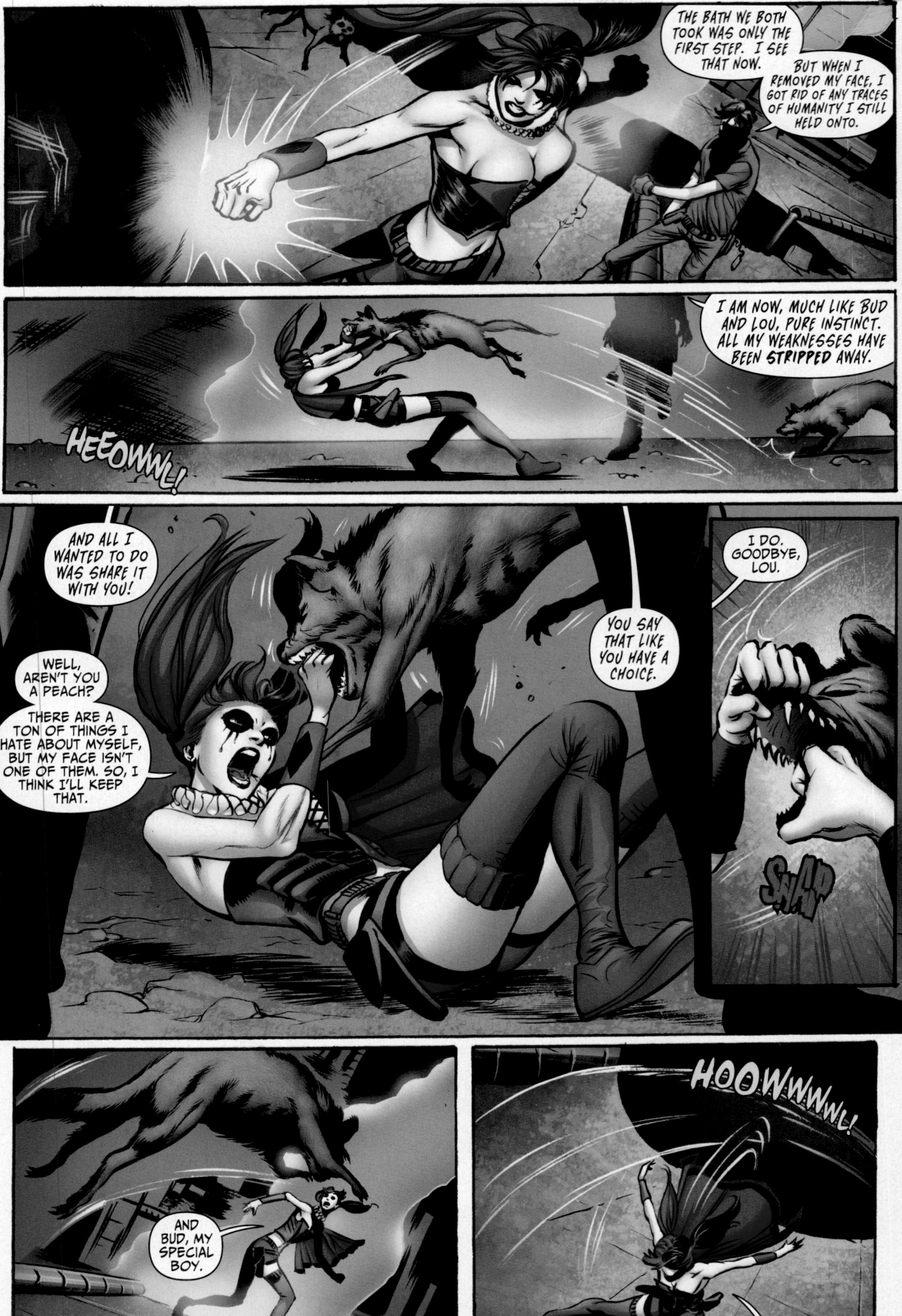
THE BATH WE BOTH TOOK WAS ONLY THE FIRST STEP. I SEE THAT NOW.
BUT WHEN I REMOVED MY FACE, I GOT RID OF ANY TRACES OF HUMANITY I STILL HELD ONTO.
I AM NOW, MUCH LIKE BUD AND LOU, PURE INSTINCT. ALL MY WEAKNESSES HAVE BEEN STRIPPED AWAY.
HEEOWWL!
AND ALL I WANTED TO DO WAS SHARE IT WITH YOU!
WELL, AREN'T YOU A PEACH?
THERE ARE A TON OF THINGS I HATE ABOUT MYSELF, BUT MY FACE ISN'T ONE OF THEM. SO, I THINK I'LL KEEP THAT.
YOU SAY THAT LIKE YOU HAVE A CHOICE.
I DO. GOODBYE, LOU.
SNAP
AND BUD, MY SPECIAL BOY.
HOOWWWWL!
I'M SORRY.

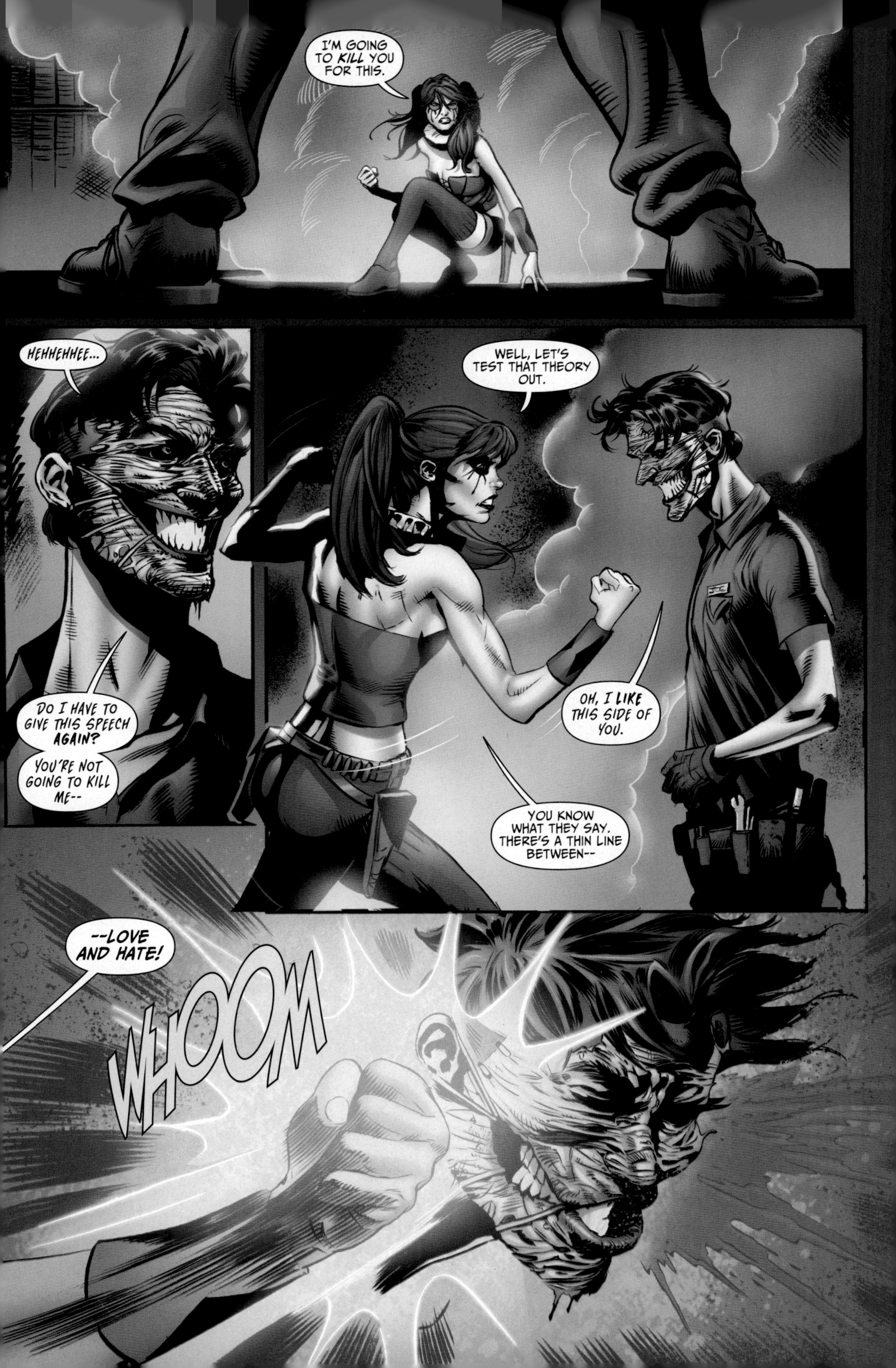
I'M GOING TO KILL YOU FOR THIS.
HEHHEHHEE...
DO I HAVE TO GIVE THIS SPEECH AGAIN?
YOU'RE NOT GOING TO KILL ME--
WELL, LET'S TEST THAT THEORY OUT.
OH, I LIKE THIS SIDE OF YOU.
YOU KNOW WHAT THEY SAY. THERE'S A THIN LINE BETWEEN--
--LOVE AND HATE!
WHOOM

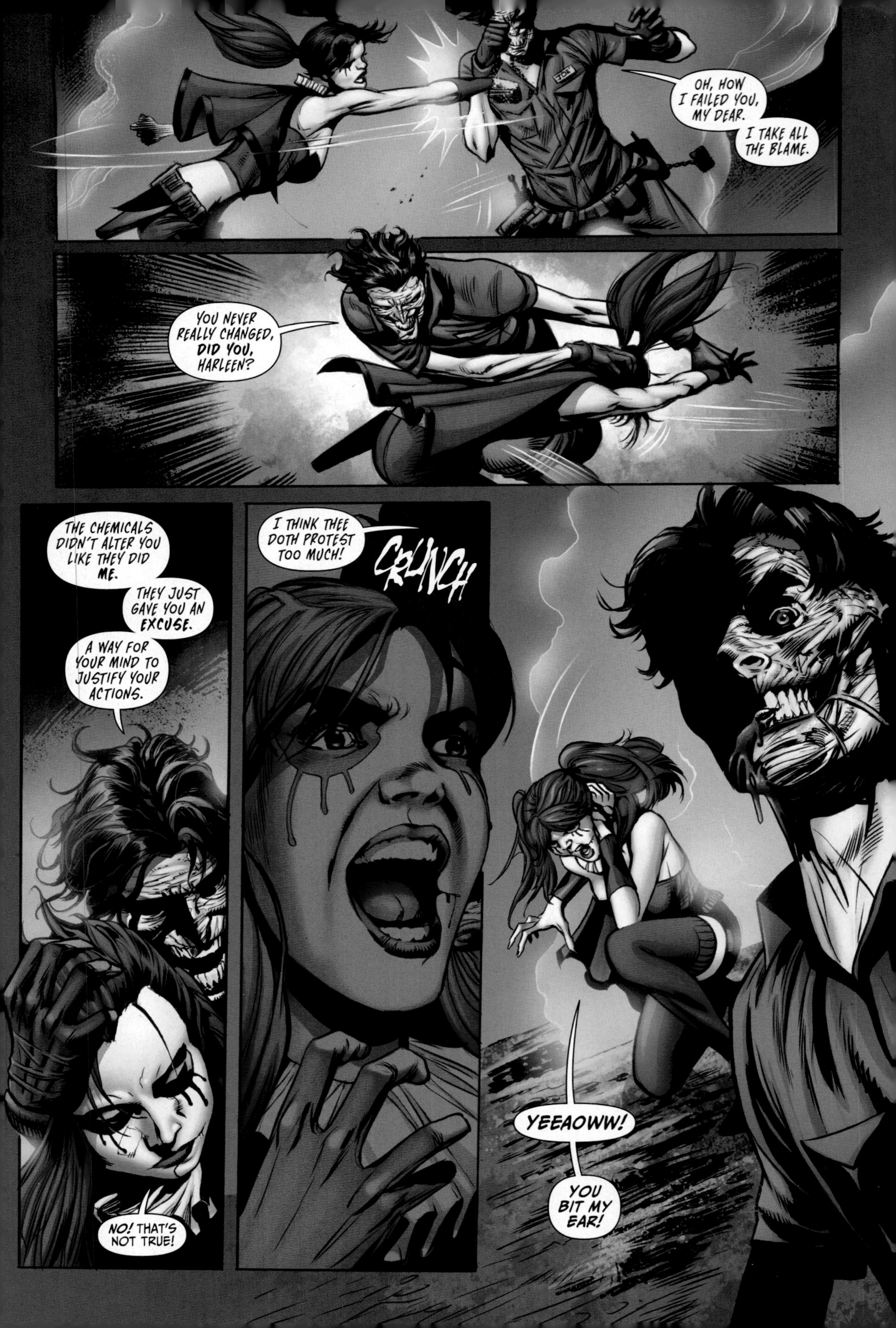
OH, HOW I FAILED YOU, MY DEAR.
I TAKE ALL THE BLAME.
YOU NEVER REALLY CHANGED, DID YOU, HARLEEN?
THE CHEMICALS DIDN'T ALTER YOU LIKE THEY DID ME.
THEY JUST GAVE YOU AN EXCUSE.
A WAY FOR YOUR MIND TO JUSTIFY YOUR ACTIONS.
NO! THAT'S NOT TRUE!
I THINK THEE DOTH PROTEST TOO MUCH!
CRUNCH
YEEAOWW!
YOU BIT MY EAR!

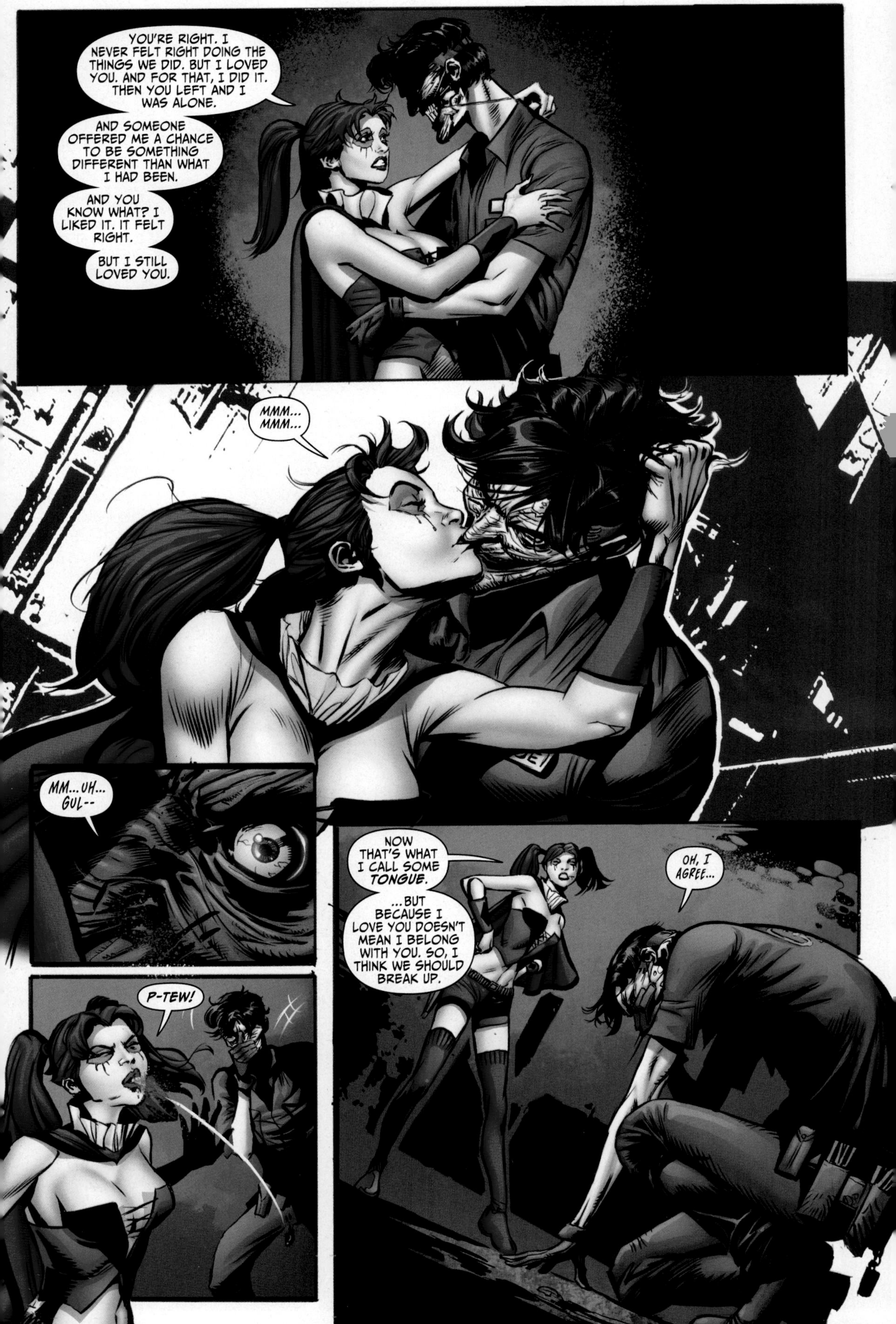
YOU'RE RIGHT. I NEVER FELT RIGHT DOING THE THINGS WE DID. BUT I LOVED YOU. AND FOR THAT, I DID IT. THEN YOU LEFT AND I WAS ALONE.
AND SOMEONE OFFERED ME A CHANCE TO BE SOMETHING DIFFERENT THAN WHAT I HAD BEEN.
AND YOU KNOW WHAT? I LIKED IT. IT FELT RIGHT.
BUT I STILL LOVED YOU.
MMM... MMM...
MM...UH... GUL--
P-TEW!
NOW THAT'S WHAT I CALL SOME *TONGUE*.
...BUT BECAUSE I LOVE YOU DOESN'T MEAN I BELONG WITH YOU. SO, I THINK WE SHOULD BREAK UP.
OH, I AGREE...

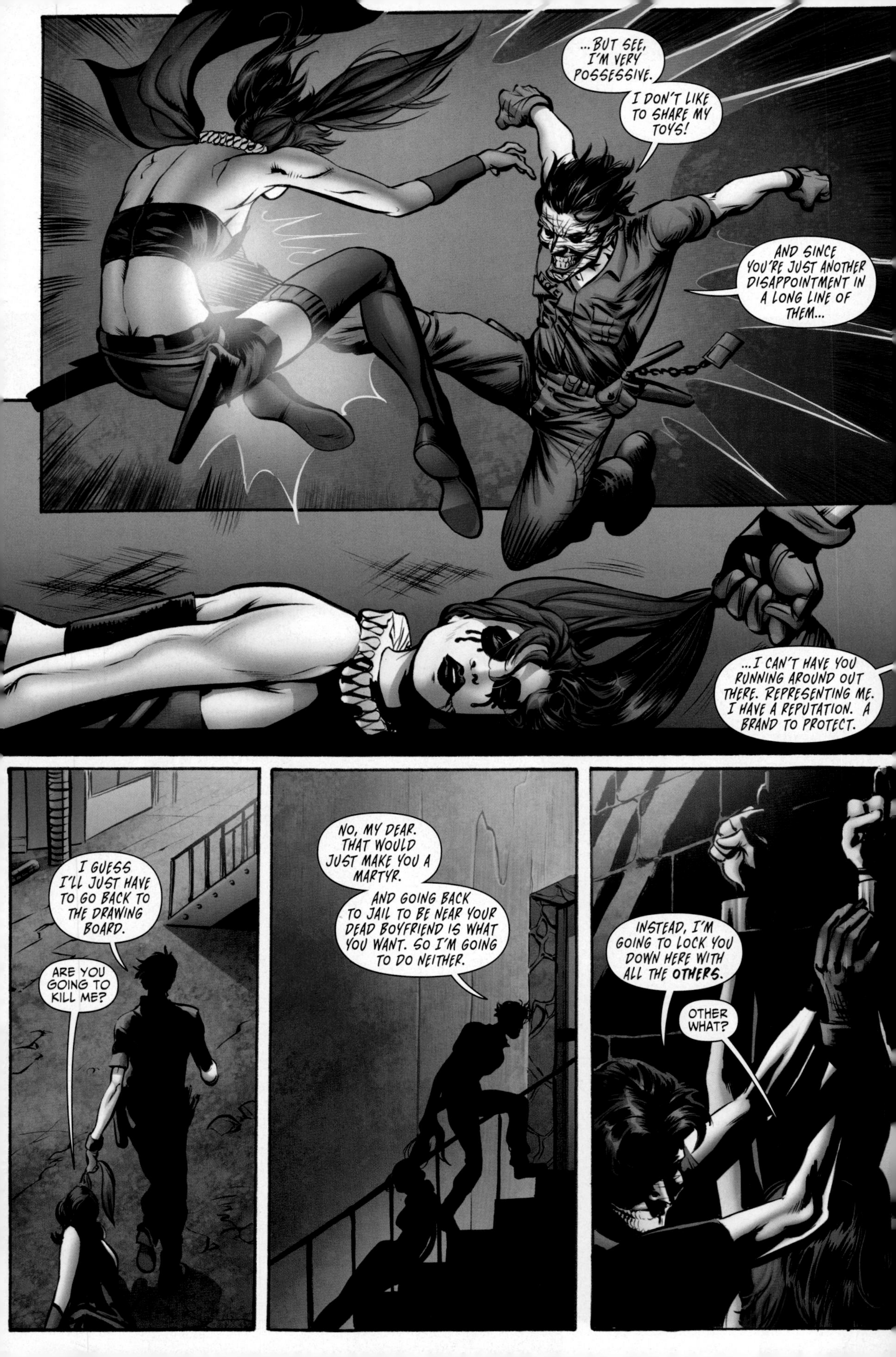
...BUT SEE, I'M VERY POSSESSIVE.
I DON'T LIKE TO SHARE MY TOYS!
AND SINCE YOU'RE JUST ANOTHER DISAPPOINTMENT IN A LONG LINE OF THEM...
...I CAN'T HAVE YOU RUNNING AROUND OUT THERE. REPRESENTING ME. I HAVE A REPUTATION. A BRAND TO PROTECT.
I GUESS I'LL JUST HAVE TO GO BACK TO THE DRAWING BOARD.
ARE YOU GOING TO KILL ME?
NO, MY DEAR. THAT WOULD JUST MAKE YOU A MARTYR.
AND GOING BACK TO JAIL TO BE NEAR YOUR DEAD BOYFRIEND IS WHAT YOU WANT. SO I'M GOING TO DO NEITHER.
INSTEAD, I'M GOING TO LOCK YOU DOWN HERE WITH ALL THE OTHERS.
OTHER WHAT?

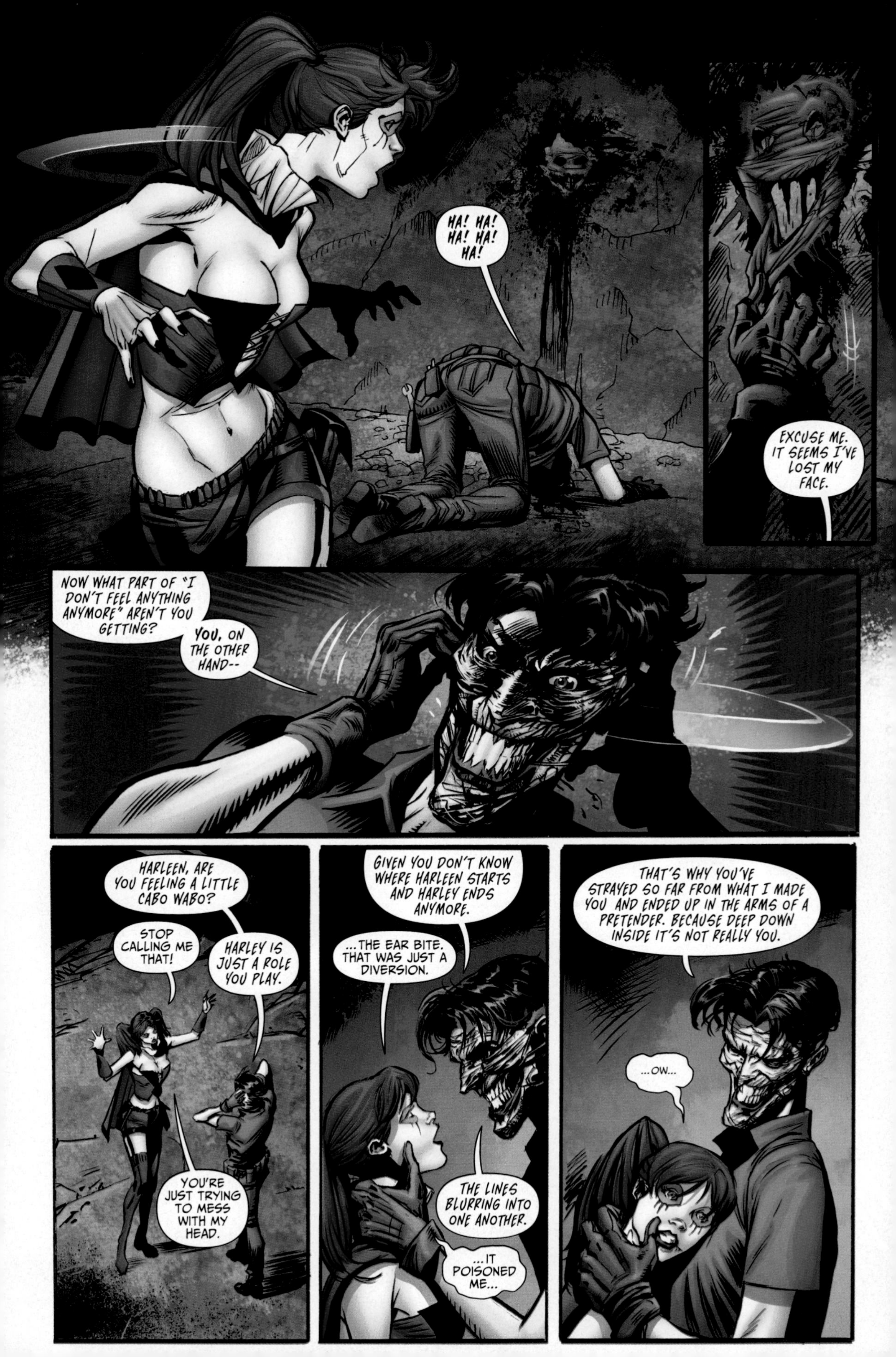
HA! HA! HA! HA! HA!
EXCUSE ME. IT SEEMS I'VE LOST MY FACE.
NOW WHAT PART OF "I DON'T FEEL ANYTHING ANYMORE" AREN'T YOU GETTING?
YOU, ON THE OTHER HAND--
HARLEEN, ARE YOU FEELING A LITTLE CABO WABO?
STOP CALLING ME THAT!
HARLEY IS JUST A ROLE YOU PLAY.
YOU'RE JUST TRYING TO MESS WITH MY HEAD.
GIVEN YOU DON'T KNOW WHERE HARLEEN STARTS AND HARLEY ENDS ANYMORE.
...THE EAR BITE. THAT WAS JUST A DIVERSION.
THE LINES BLURRING INTO ONE ANOTHER.
...IT POISONED ME...
THAT'S WHY YOU'VE STRAYED SO FAR FROM WHAT I MADE YOU AND ENDED UP IN THE ARMS OF A PRETENDER. BECAUSE DEEP DOWN INSIDE IT'S NOT REALLY YOU.
...OW...

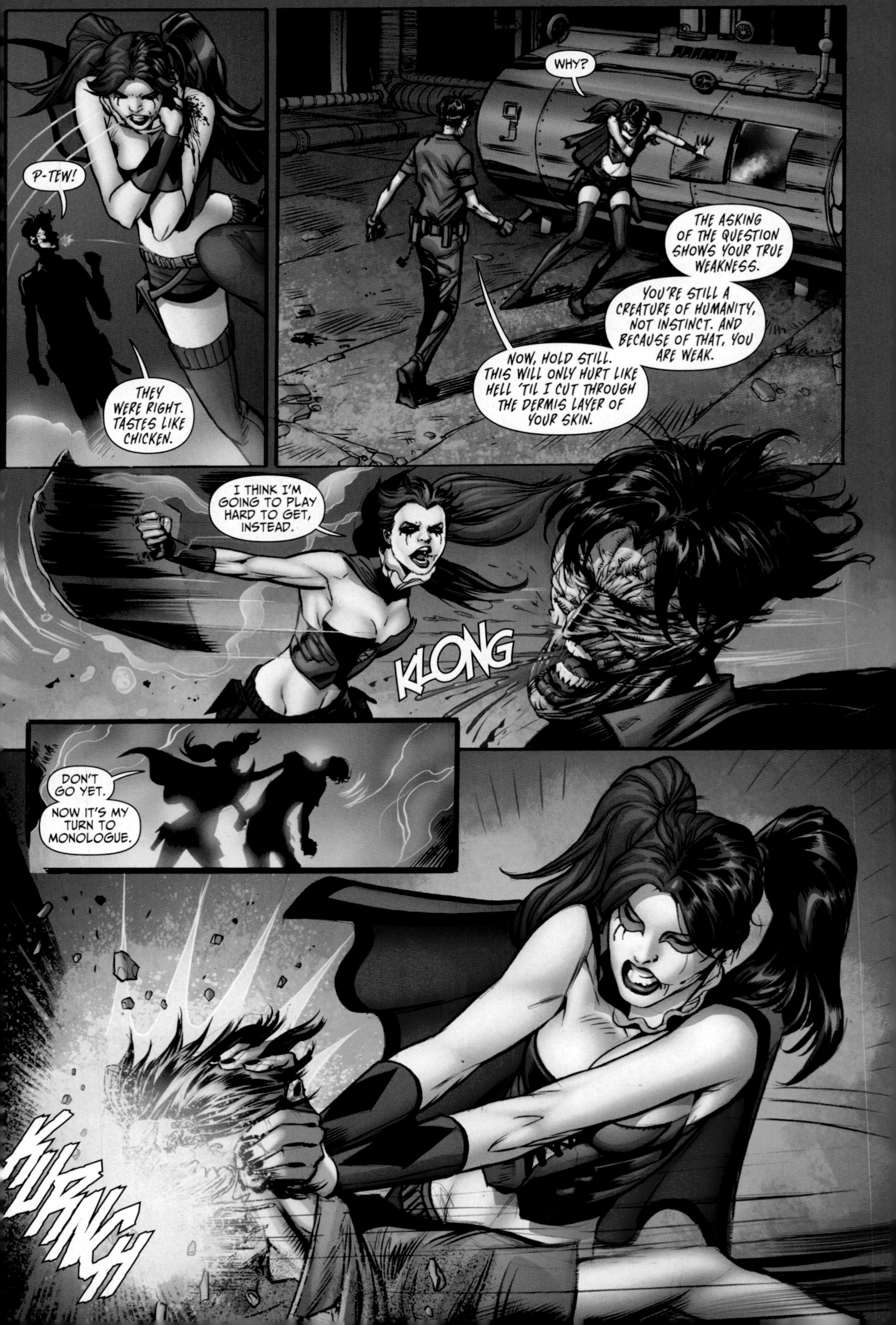
P-TEW!
THEY WERE RIGHT. TASTES LIKE CHICKEN.
WHY?
THE ASKING OF THE QUESTION SHOWS YOUR TRUE WEAKNESS.
YOU'RE STILL A CREATURE OF HUMANITY, NOT INSTINCT. AND BECAUSE OF THAT, YOU ARE WEAK.
NOW, HOLD STILL. THIS WILL ONLY HURT LIKE HELL 'TIL I CUT THROUGH THE DERMIS LAYER OF YOUR SKIN.
I THINK I'M GOING TO PLAY HARD TO GET, INSTEAD.
KLONG
DON'T GO YET.
NOW IT'S MY TURN TO MONOLOGUE.
KKRNCH

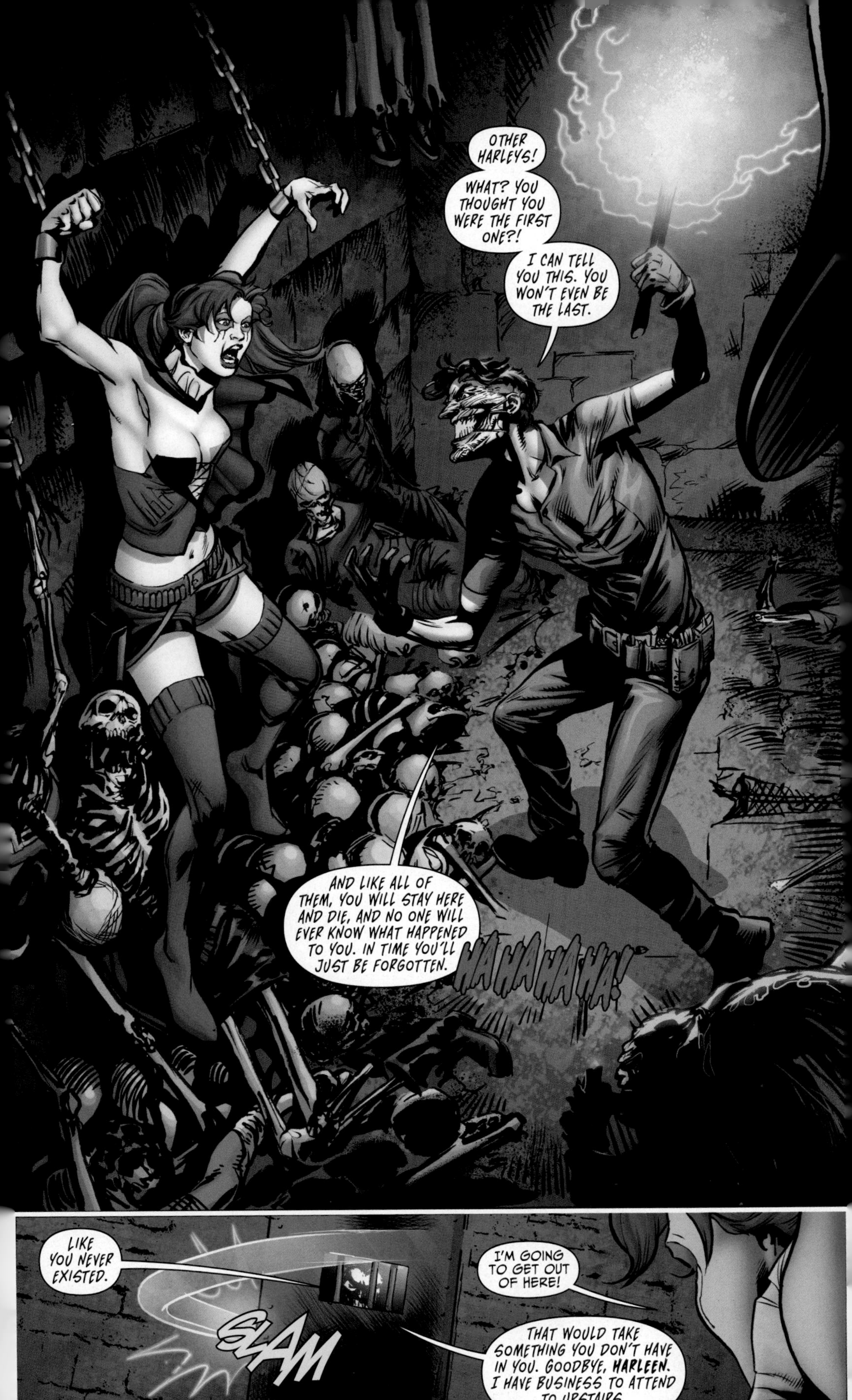
OTHER HARLEYS!
WHAT? YOU THOUGHT YOU WERE THE FIRST ONE?!
I CAN TELL YOU THIS. YOU WON'T EVEN BE THE LAST.
AND LIKE ALL OF THEM, YOU WILL STAY HERE AND DIE, AND NO ONE WILL EVER KNOW WHAT HAPPENED TO YOU. IN TIME YOU'LL JUST BE FORGOTTEN.
HA HA HA HA HA!
LIKE YOU NEVER EXISTED.
SLAM
I'M GOING TO GET OUT OF HERE!
THAT WOULD TAKE SOMETHING YOU DON'T HAVE IN YOU. GOODBYE, HARLEEN. I HAVE BUSINESS TO ATTEND TO UPSTAIRS.

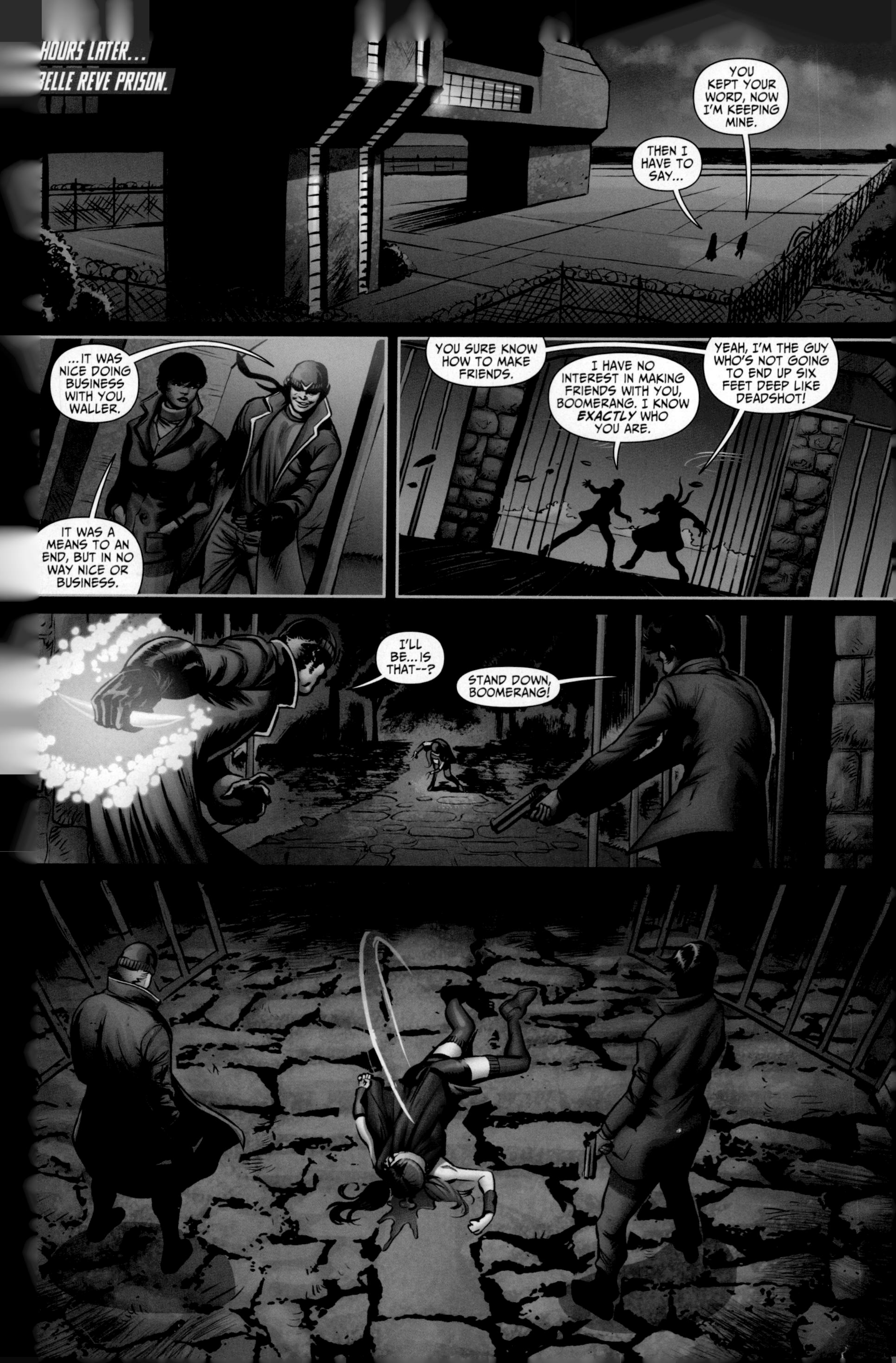
HOURS LATER...
BELLE REVE PRISON.
YOU KEPT YOUR WORD, NOW I'M KEEPING MINE.
THEN I HAVE TO SAY...
...IT WAS NICE DOING BUSINESS WITH YOU, WALLER.
IT WAS A MEANS TO AN END, BUT IN NO WAY NICE OR BUSINESS.
YOU SURE KNOW HOW TO MAKE FRIENDS.
I HAVE NO INTEREST IN MAKING FRIENDS WITH YOU, BOOMERANG. I KNOW EXACTLY WHO YOU ARE.
YEAH, I'M THE GUY WHO'S NOT GOING TO END UP SIX FEET DEEP LIKE DEADSHOT!
I'LL BE...IS THAT--?
STAND DOWN, BOOMERANG!

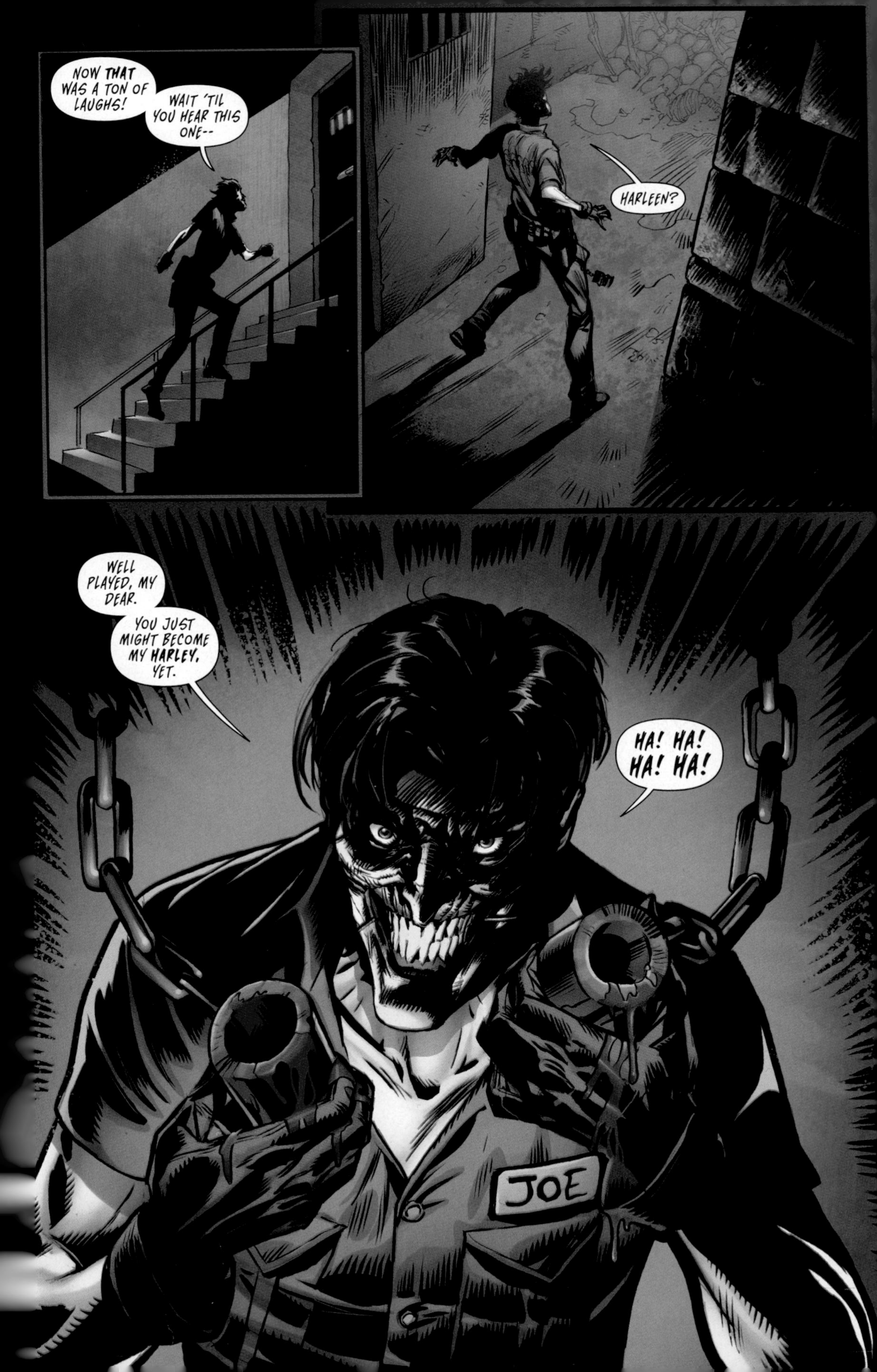

NOW THAT WAS A TON OF LAUGHS!
WAIT 'TIL YOU HEAR THIS ONE--
HARLEEN?
WELL PLAYED, MY DEAR.
YOU JUST MIGHT BECOME MY HARLEY, YET.
HA! HA! HA! HA!
JOE

PART FOUR

BATGIRL

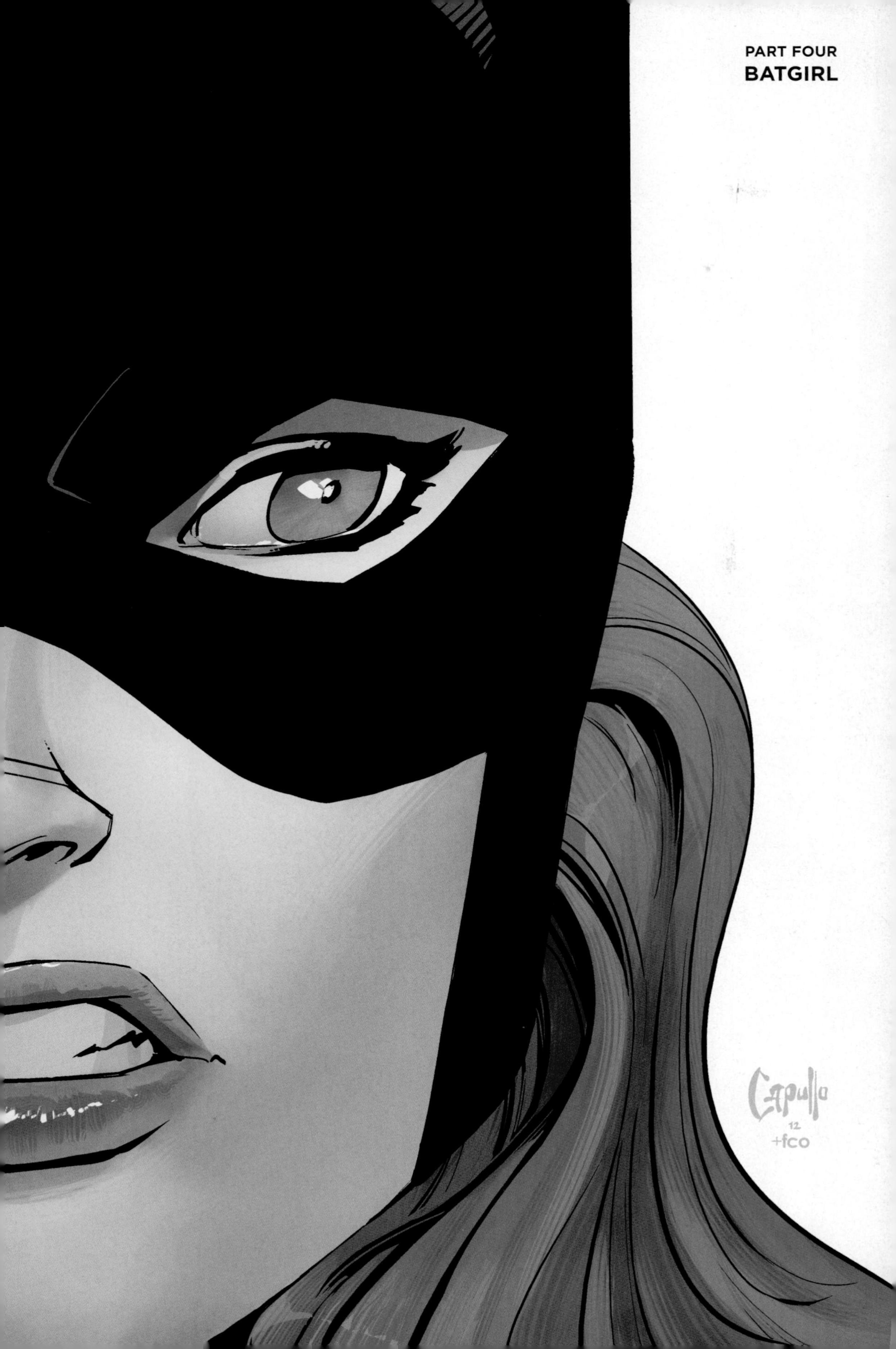
Capullo
12
+fco

ULISES ARREOLA KYLE RITTER colorists DAVE SHARPE letterer

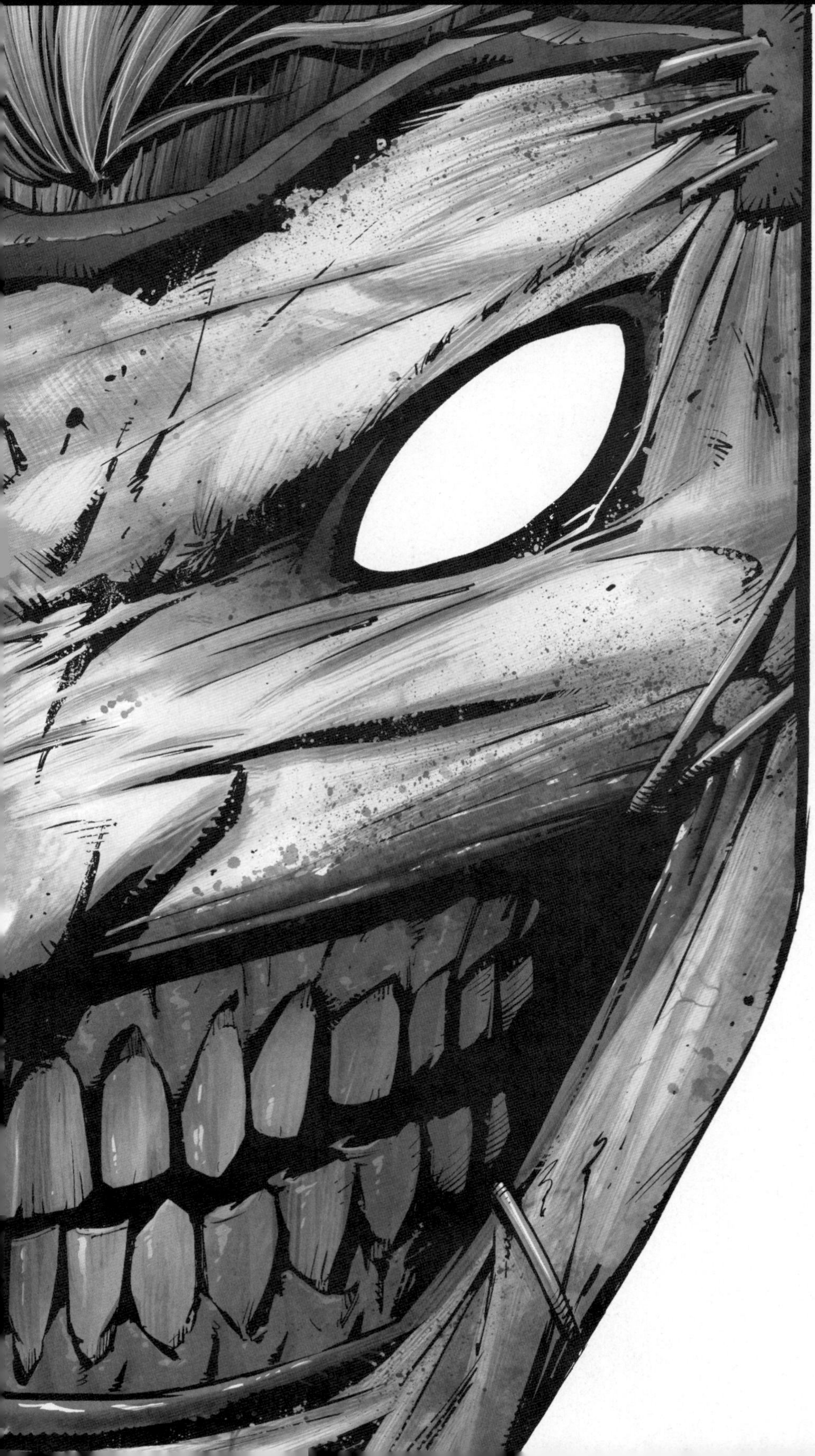

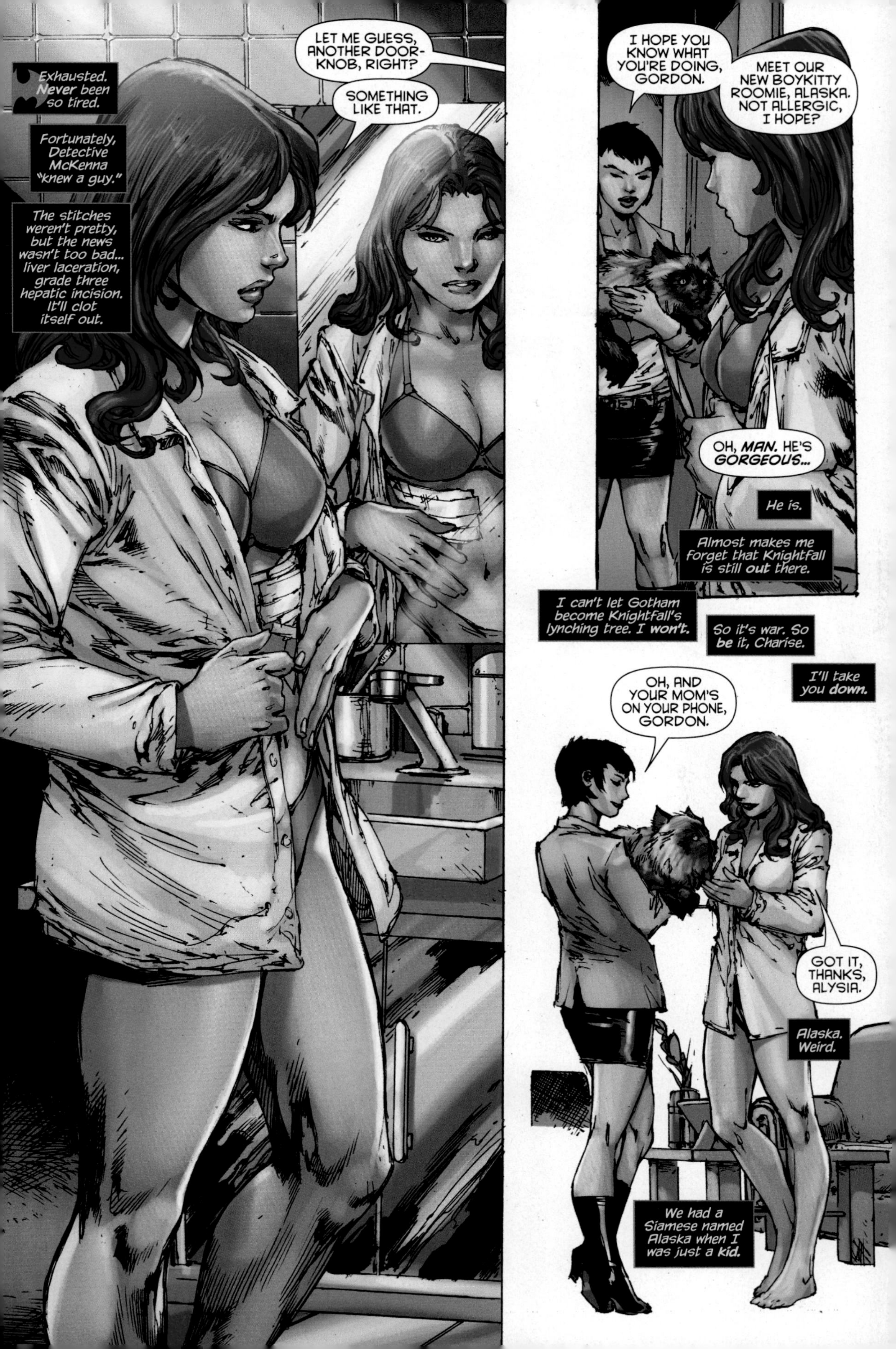

Exhausted. Never been so tired.
Fortunately, Detective McKenna "knew a guy."
The stitches weren't pretty, but the news wasn't too bad... liver laceration, grade three hepatic incision. It'll clot itself out.
LET ME GUESS, ANOTHER DOOR-KNOB, RIGHT?
SOMETHING LIKE THAT.
I HOPE YOU KNOW WHAT YOU'RE DOING, GORDON.
MEET OUR NEW BOYKITTY ROOMIE, ALASKA. NOT ALLERGIC, I HOPE?
OH, MAN. HE'S GORGEOUS...
He is.
Almost makes me forget that Knightfall is still out there.
I can't let Gotham become Knightfall's lynching tree. I won't.
So it's war. So be it, Charise.
I'll take you down.
OH, AND YOUR MOM'S ON YOUR PHONE, GORDON.
GOT IT, THANKS, ALYSIA.
Alaska. Weird.
We had a Siamese named Alaska when I was just a kid.

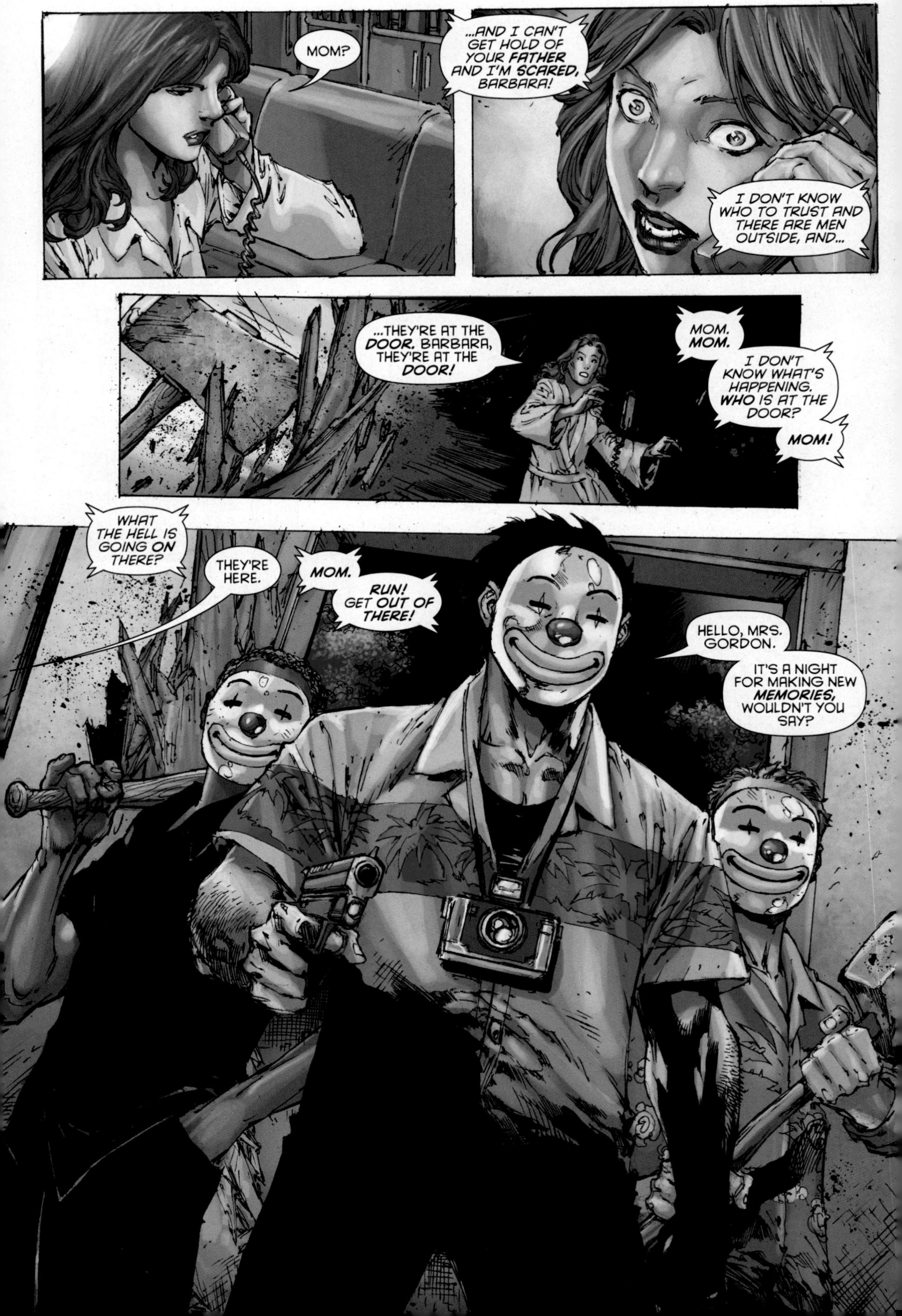
MOM?
...AND I CAN'T GET HOLD OF YOUR FATHER AND I'M SCARED, BARBARA!
I DON'T KNOW WHO TO TRUST AND THERE ARE MEN OUTSIDE, AND...
...THEY'RE AT THE DOOR. BARBARA, THEY'RE AT THE DOOR!
MOM. MOM.
I DON'T KNOW WHAT'S HAPPENING. WHO IS AT THE DOOR?
MOM!
WHAT THE HELL IS GOING ON THERE?
THEY'RE HERE.
MOM.
RUN! GET OUT OF THERE!
HELLO, MRS. GORDON.
IT'S A NIGHT FOR MAKING NEW MEMORIES, WOULDN'T YOU SAY?

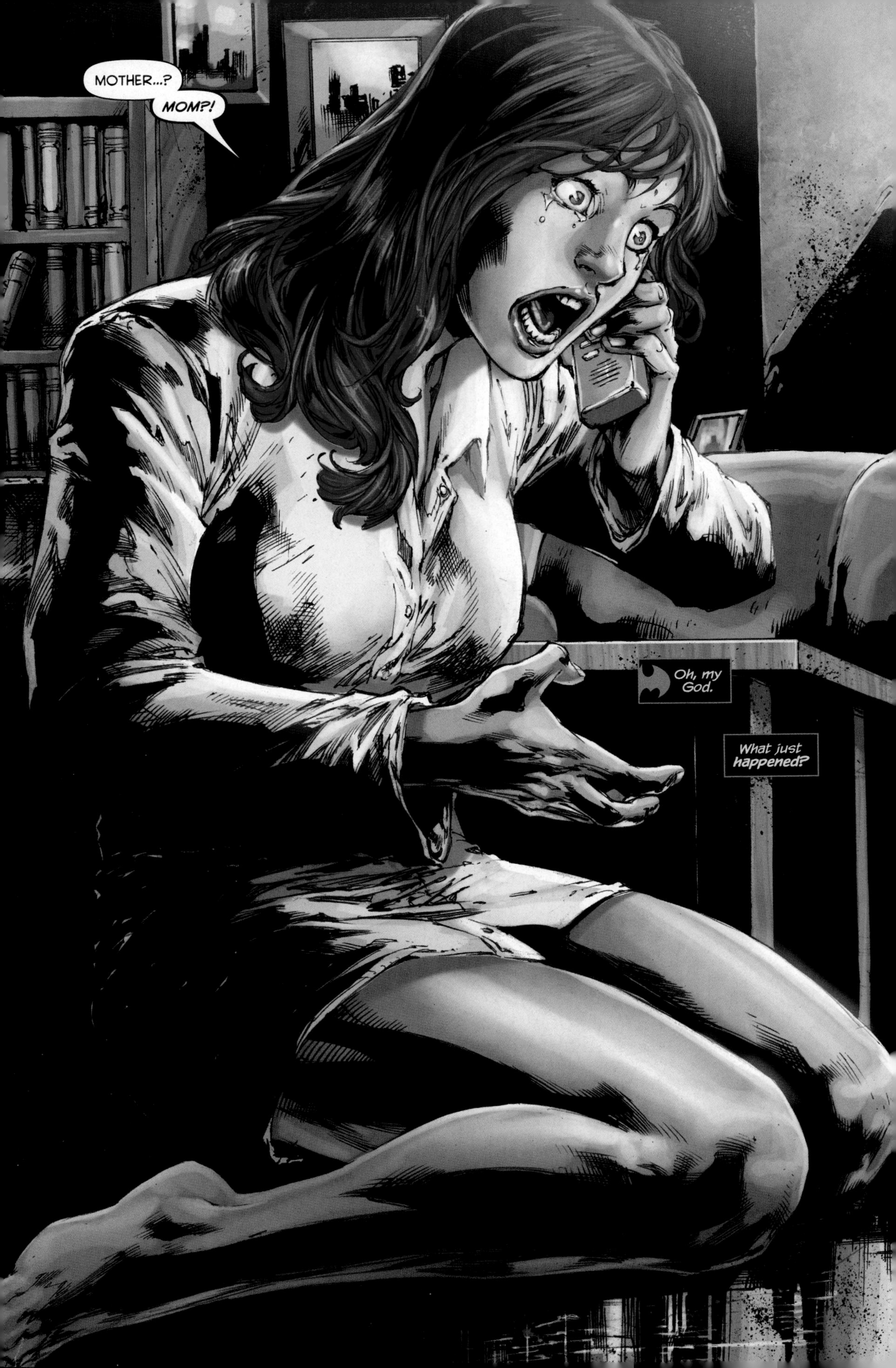
MOTHER...?
MOM?!
Oh, my God.
What just happened?

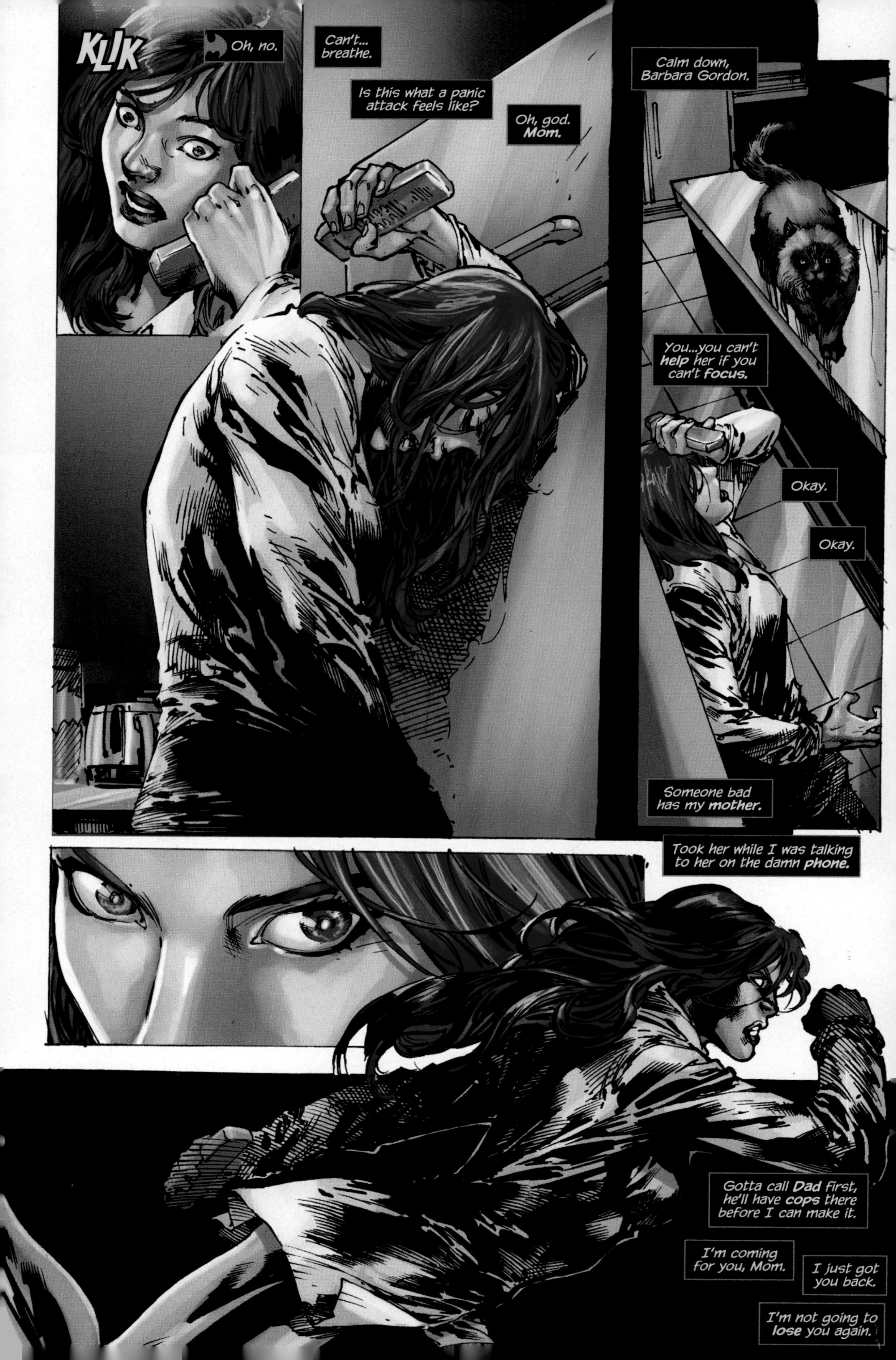
KLIK
Oh, no.
Can't... breathe.
Is this what a panic attack feels like?
Oh, god. **Mom.**
Calm down, Barbara Gordon.
You...you can't **help** her if you can't **focus.**
Okay.
Okay.
Someone bad has my **mother.**
Took her while I was talking to her on the damn **phone.**
Gotta call **Dad** first, he'll have **cops** there before I can make it.
I'm coming for you, Mom.
I just got you back.
I'm not going to **lose** you again.

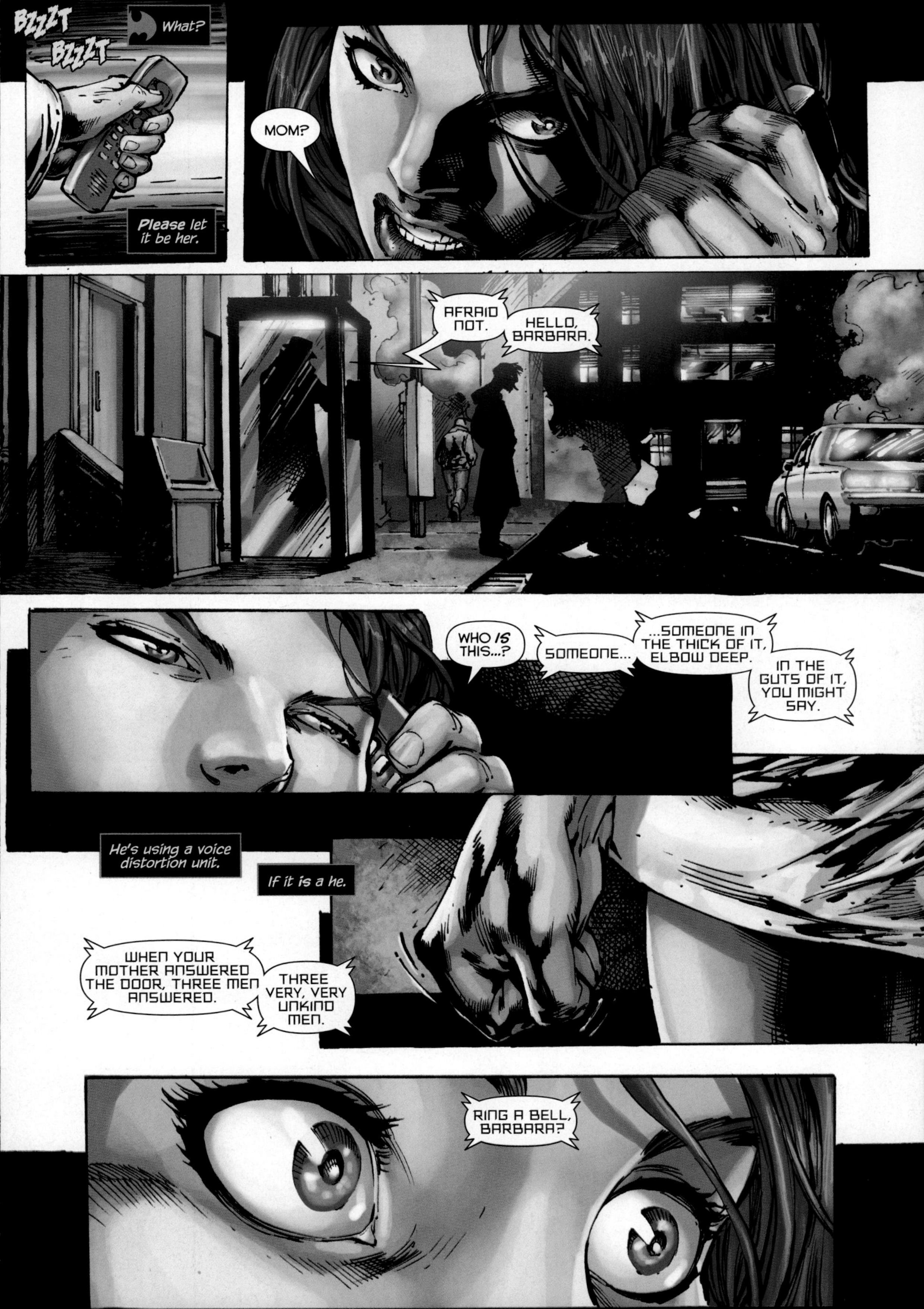
BZZZT
BZZZT
What?
Please let it be her.
MOM?
AFRAID NOT.
HELLO, BARBARA.
WHO IS THIS...?
SOMEONE...
...SOMEONE IN THE THICK OF IT, ELBOW DEEP.
IN THE GUTS OF IT, YOU MIGHT SAY.
He's using a voice distortion unit.
If it is a he.
WHEN YOUR MOTHER ANSWERED THE DOOR, THREE MEN ANSWERED.
THREE VERY, VERY UNKIND MEN.
RING A BELL, BARBARA?

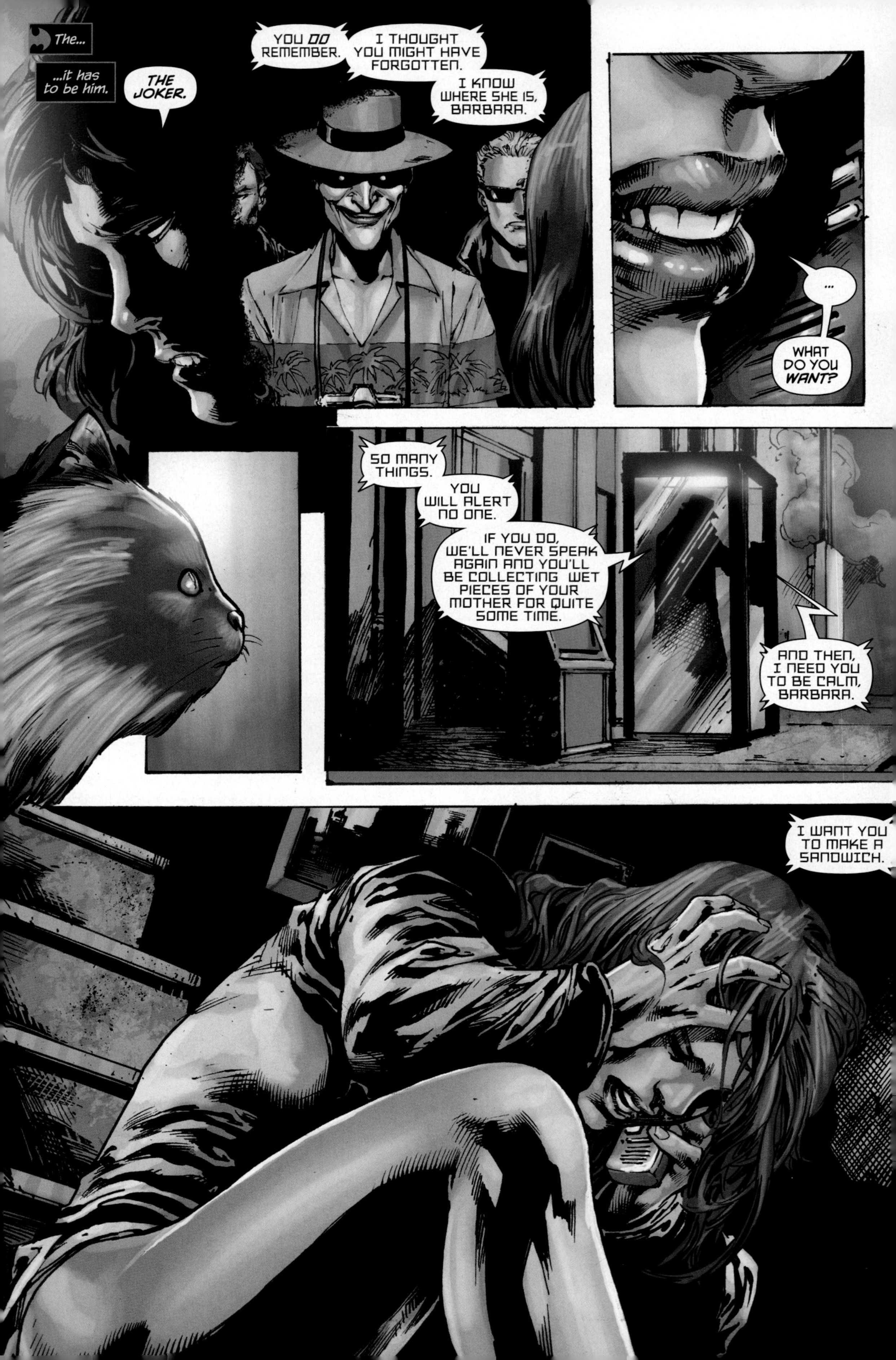
The...
...it has to be him.
THE JOKER.
YOU DO REMEMBER.
I THOUGHT YOU MIGHT HAVE FORGOTTEN.
I KNOW WHERE SHE IS, BARBARA.
...
WHAT DO YOU WANT?
SO MANY THINGS.
YOU WILL ALERT NO ONE.
IF YOU DO, WE'LL NEVER SPEAK AGAIN AND YOU'LL BE COLLECTING WET PIECES OF YOUR MOTHER FOR QUITE SOME TIME.
AND THEN, I NEED YOU TO BE CALM, BARBARA.
I WANT YOU TO MAKE A SANDWICH.

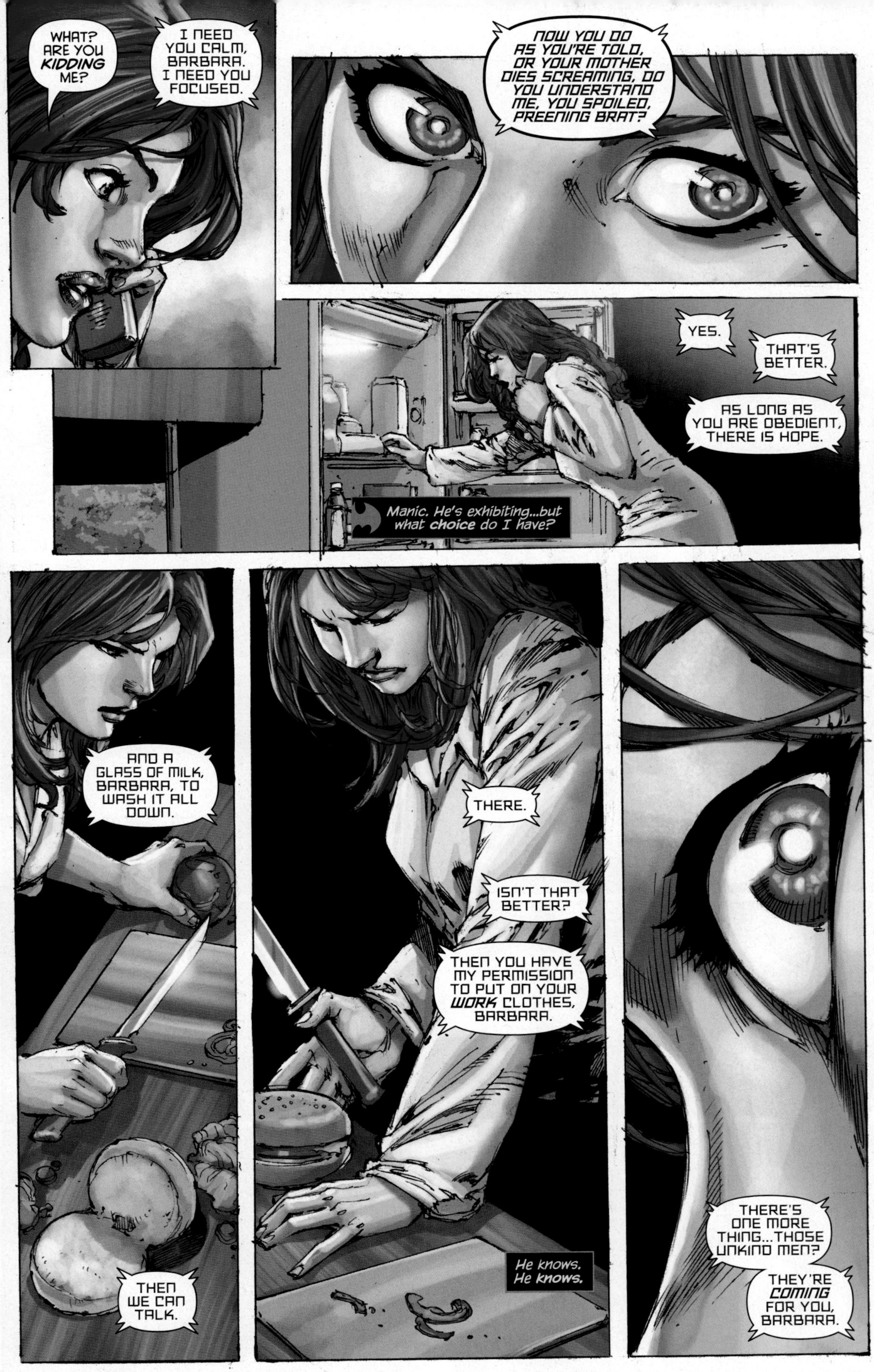
WHAT? ARE YOU *KIDDING* ME?
I NEED YOU CALM, BARBARA. I NEED YOU FOCUSED.
NOW YOU DO AS YOU'RE TOLD, OR YOUR MOTHER DIES SCREAMING, DO YOU UNDERSTAND ME, YOU SPOILED, PREENING BRAT?
YES.
THAT'S BETTER.
AS LONG AS YOU ARE OBEDIENT, THERE IS HOPE.
*Manic. He's exhibiting...but what **choice** do I have?*
AND A GLASS OF MILK, BARBARA, TO WASH IT ALL DOWN.
THEN WE CAN TALK.
THERE.
ISN'T THAT BETTER?
THEN YOU HAVE MY PERMISSION TO PUT ON YOUR ***WORK*** CLOTHES, BARBARA.
*He knows. He **knows.***
THERE'S ONE MORE THING...THOSE UNKIND MEN?
THEY'RE ***COMING*** FOR YOU, BARBARA.

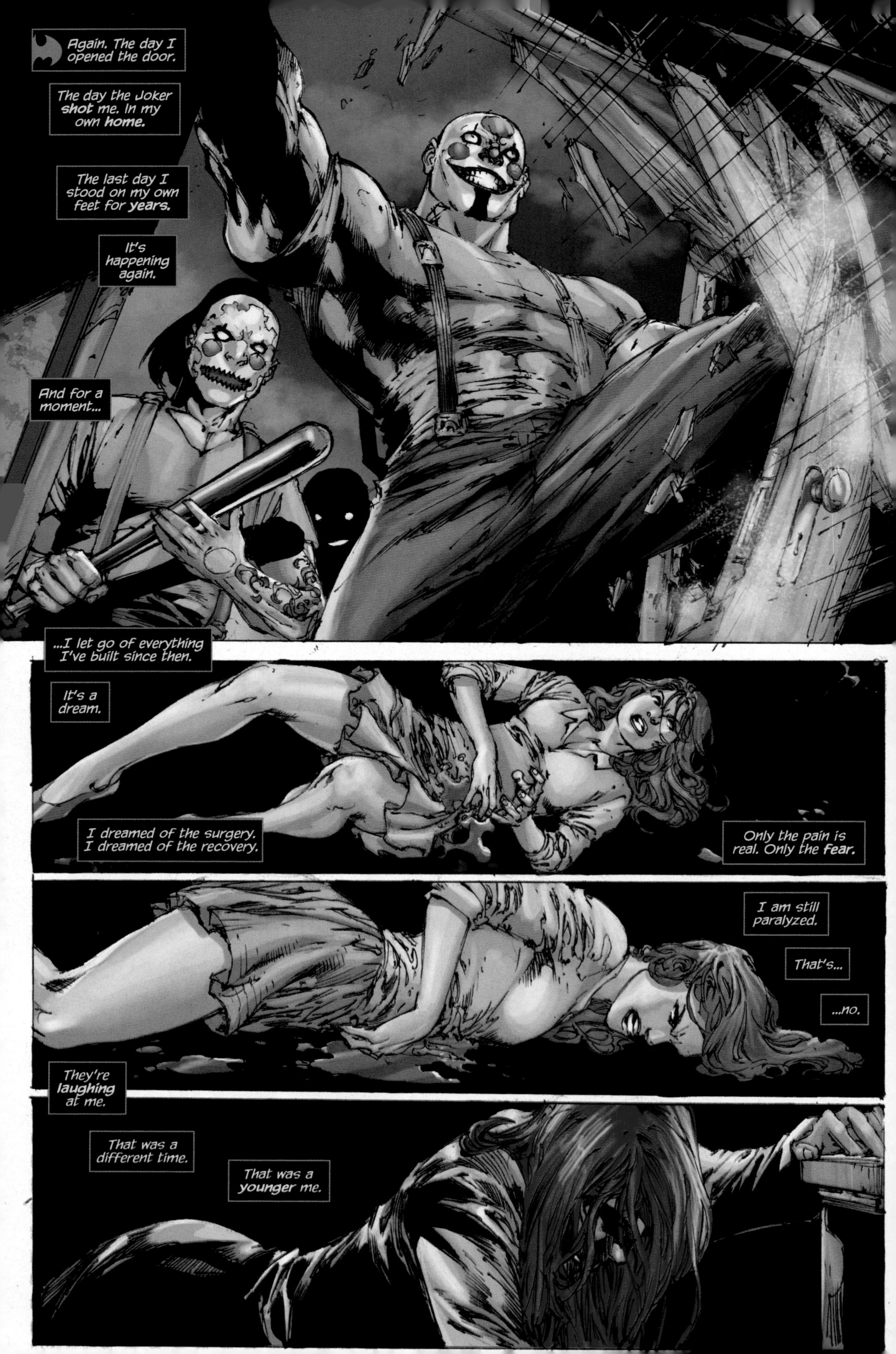

Again. The day I opened the door.
The day the Joker shot me. In my own home.
The last day I stood on my own feet for years.
It's happening again.
And for a moment...
...I let go of everything I've built since then.
It's a dream.
I dreamed of the surgery. I dreamed of the recovery.
Only the pain is real. Only the fear.
I am still paralyzed.
That's...
...no.
They're laughing at me.
That was a different time.
That was a younger me.

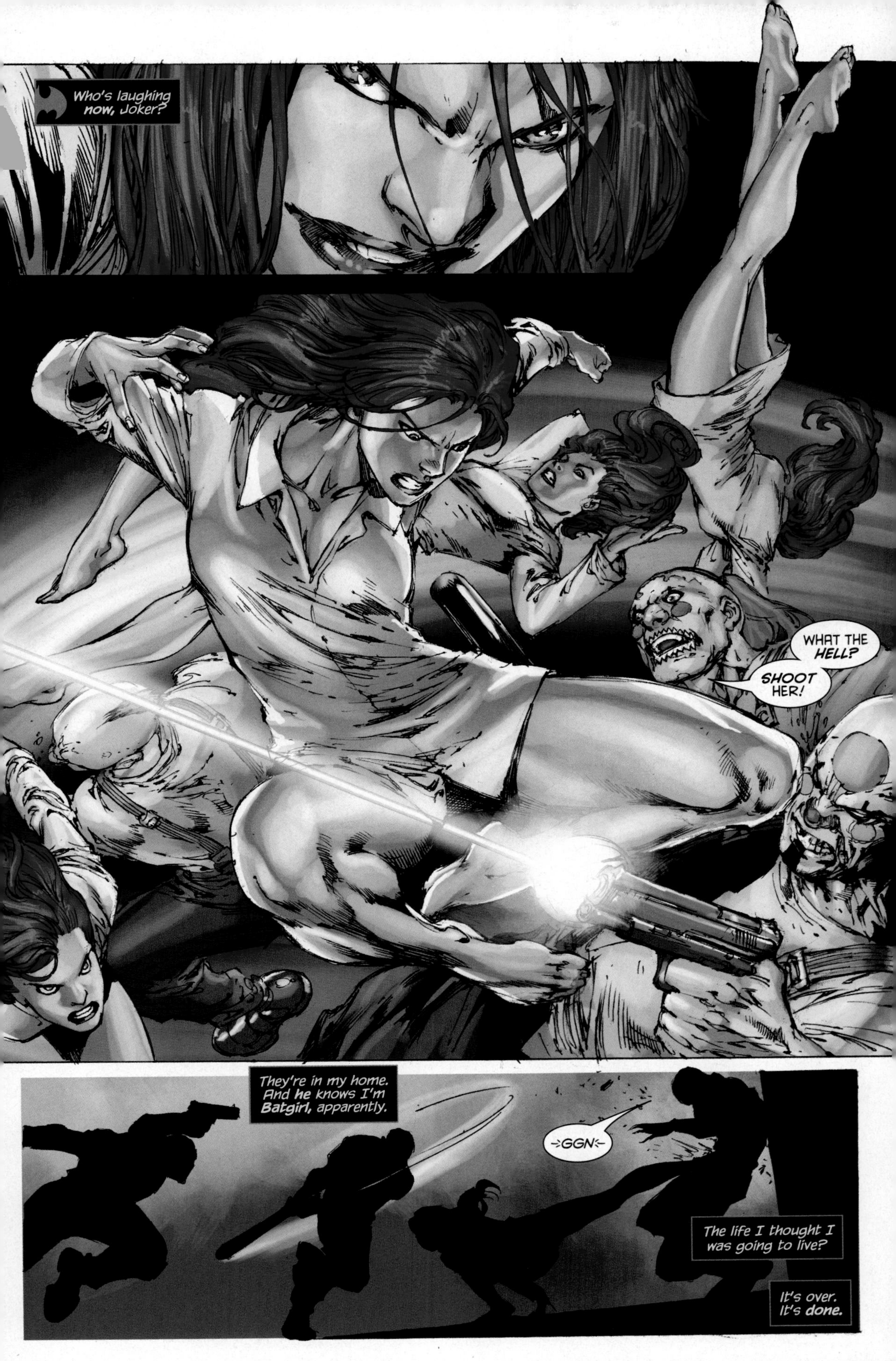
Who's laughing now, Joker?
WHAT THE HELL?
SHOOT HER!
They're in my home. And he knows I'm Batgirl, apparently.
-GGN-
The life I thought I was going to live?
It's over. It's done.

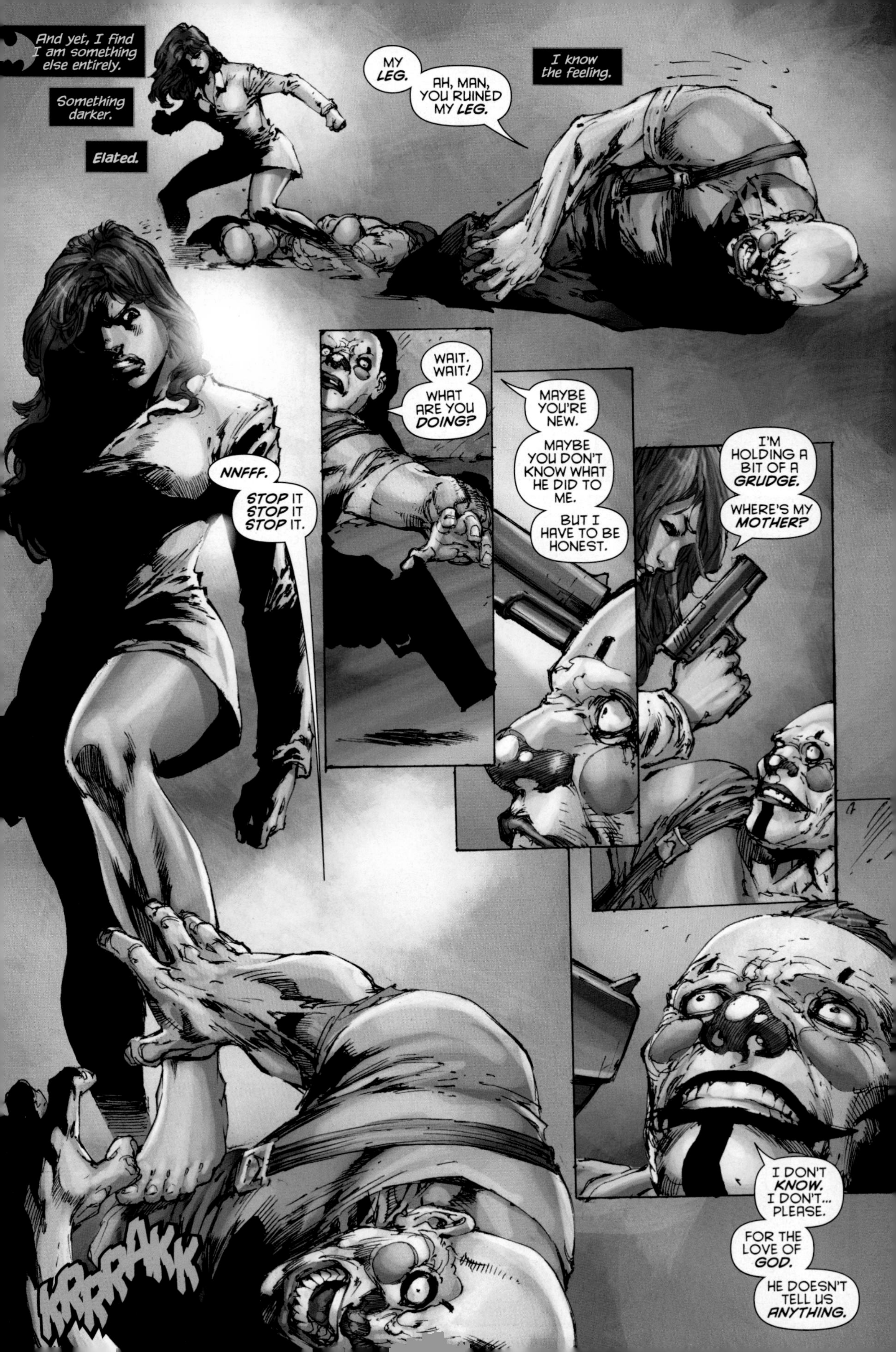

And yet, I find I am something else entirely.
Something darker.
Elated.
MY LEG.
AH, MAN, YOU RUINED MY LEG.
I know the feeling.
NNFFF.
STOP IT STOP IT STOP IT.
WAIT. WAIT!
WHAT ARE YOU DOING?
MAYBE YOU'RE NEW.
MAYBE YOU DON'T KNOW WHAT HE DID TO ME.
BUT I HAVE TO BE HONEST.
I'M HOLDING A BIT OF A GRUDGE.
WHERE'S MY MOTHER?
I DON'T KNOW. I DON'T... PLEASE.
FOR THE LOVE OF GOD.
HE DOESN'T TELL US ANYTHING.
KRRRAKK

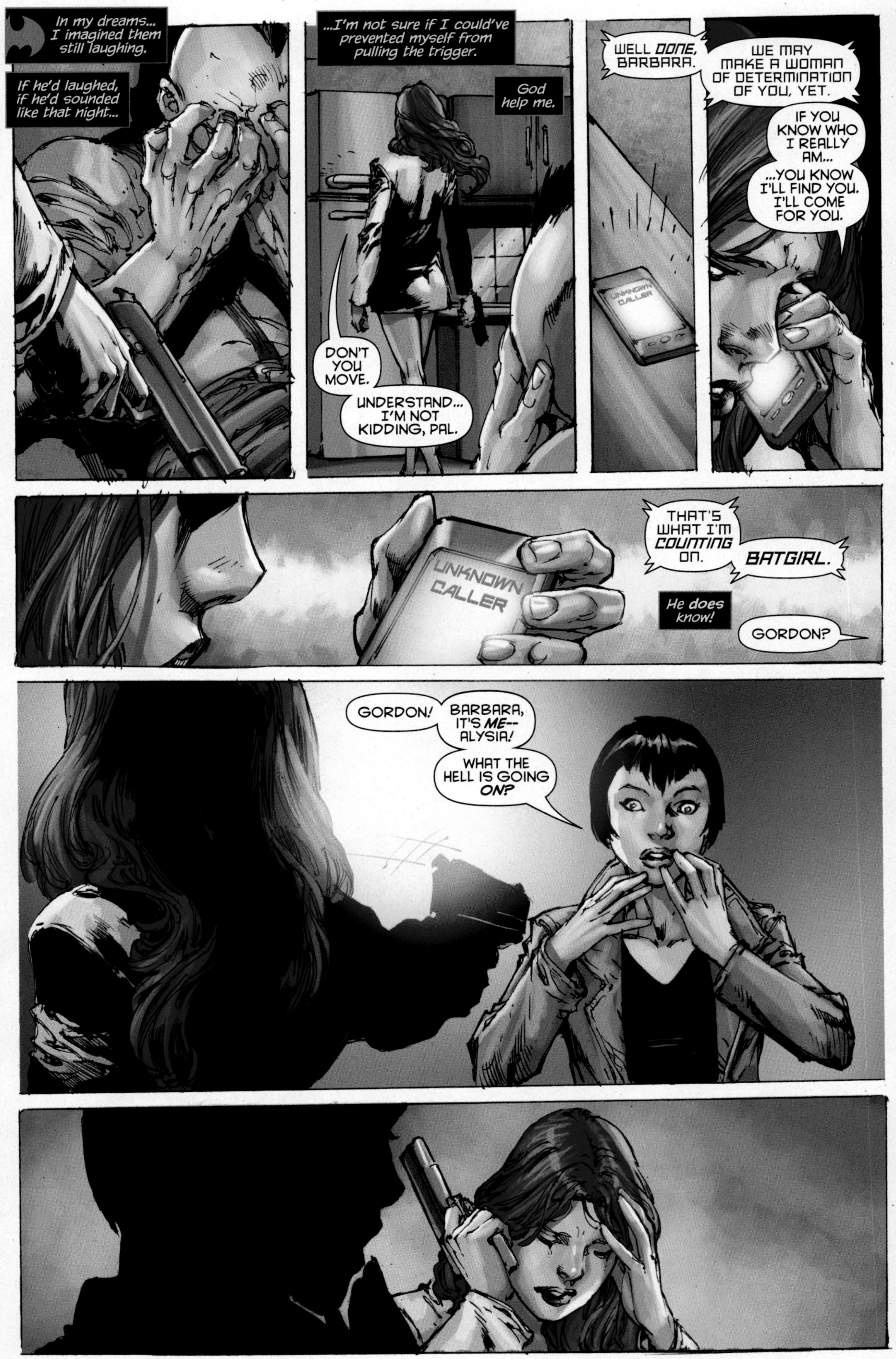

In my dreams... I imagined them still laughing.
If he'd laughed, if he'd sounded like that night...
...I'm not sure if I could've prevented myself from pulling the trigger.
God help me.
DON'T YOU MOVE.
UNDERSTAND... I'M NOT KIDDING, PAL.
WELL DONE, BARBARA.
WE MAY MAKE A WOMAN OF DETERMINATION OF YOU, YET.
UNKNOWN CALLER
IF YOU KNOW WHO I REALLY AM...
...YOU KNOW I'LL FIND YOU. I'LL COME FOR YOU.
UNKNOWN CALLER
THAT'S WHAT I'M COUNTING ON.
BATGIRL.
He does know!
GORDON?
GORDON!
BARBARA, IT'S ME-- ALYSIA!
WHAT THE HELL IS GOING ON?

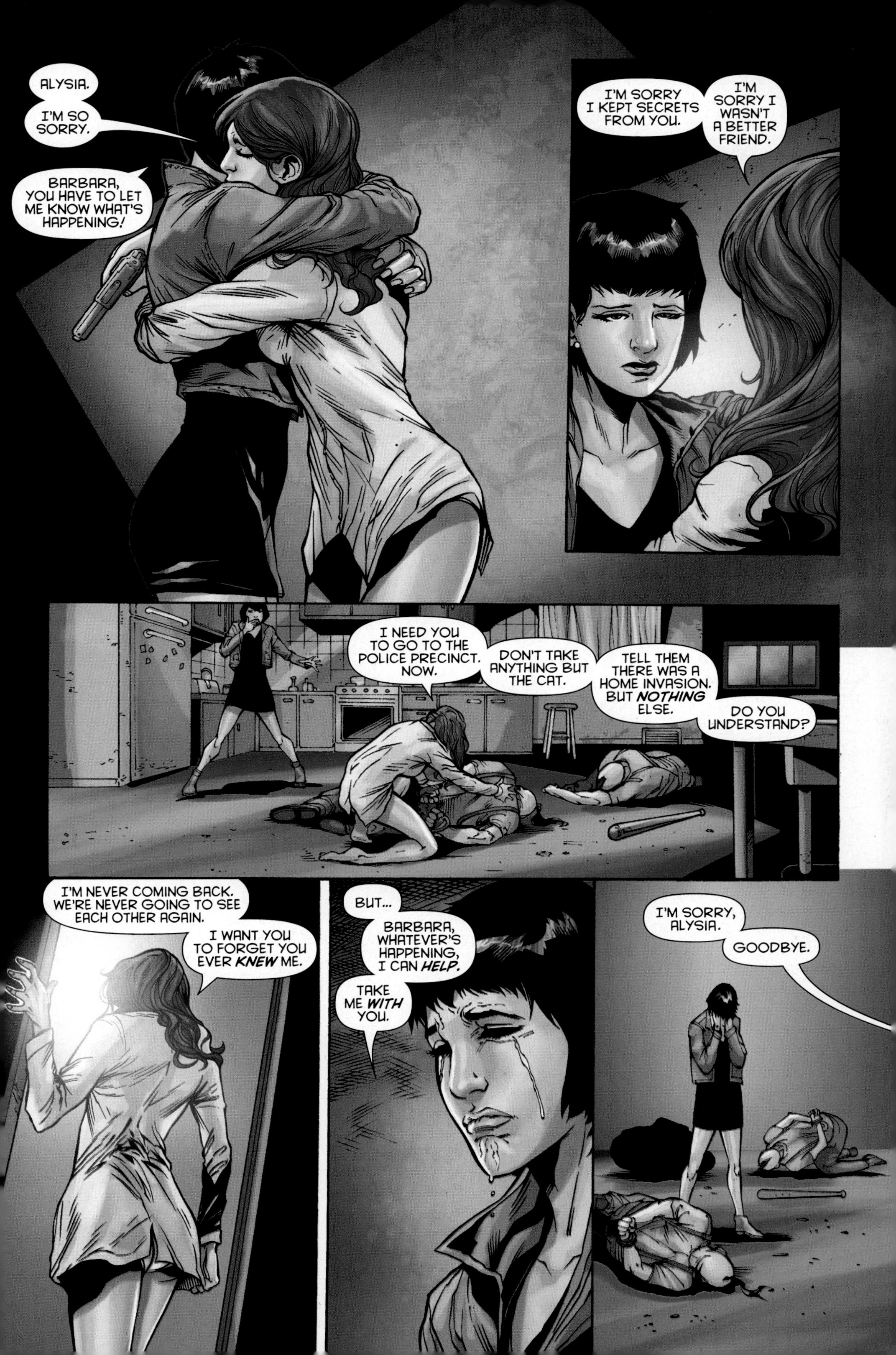
ALYSIA.
I'M SO SORRY.
BARBARA, YOU HAVE TO LET ME KNOW WHAT'S HAPPENING!
I'M SORRY I KEPT SECRETS FROM YOU.
I'M SORRY I WASN'T A BETTER FRIEND.
I NEED YOU TO GO TO THE POLICE PRECINCT. NOW.
DON'T TAKE ANYTHING BUT THE CAT.
TELL THEM THERE WAS A HOME INVASION. BUT *NOTHING* ELSE.
DO YOU UNDERSTAND?
I'M NEVER COMING BACK. WE'RE NEVER GOING TO SEE EACH OTHER AGAIN.
I WANT YOU TO FORGET YOU EVER *KNEW* ME.
BUT...
BARBARA, WHATEVER'S HAPPENING, I CAN *HELP*.
TAKE ME *WITH* YOU.
I'M SORRY, ALYSIA.
GOODBYE.

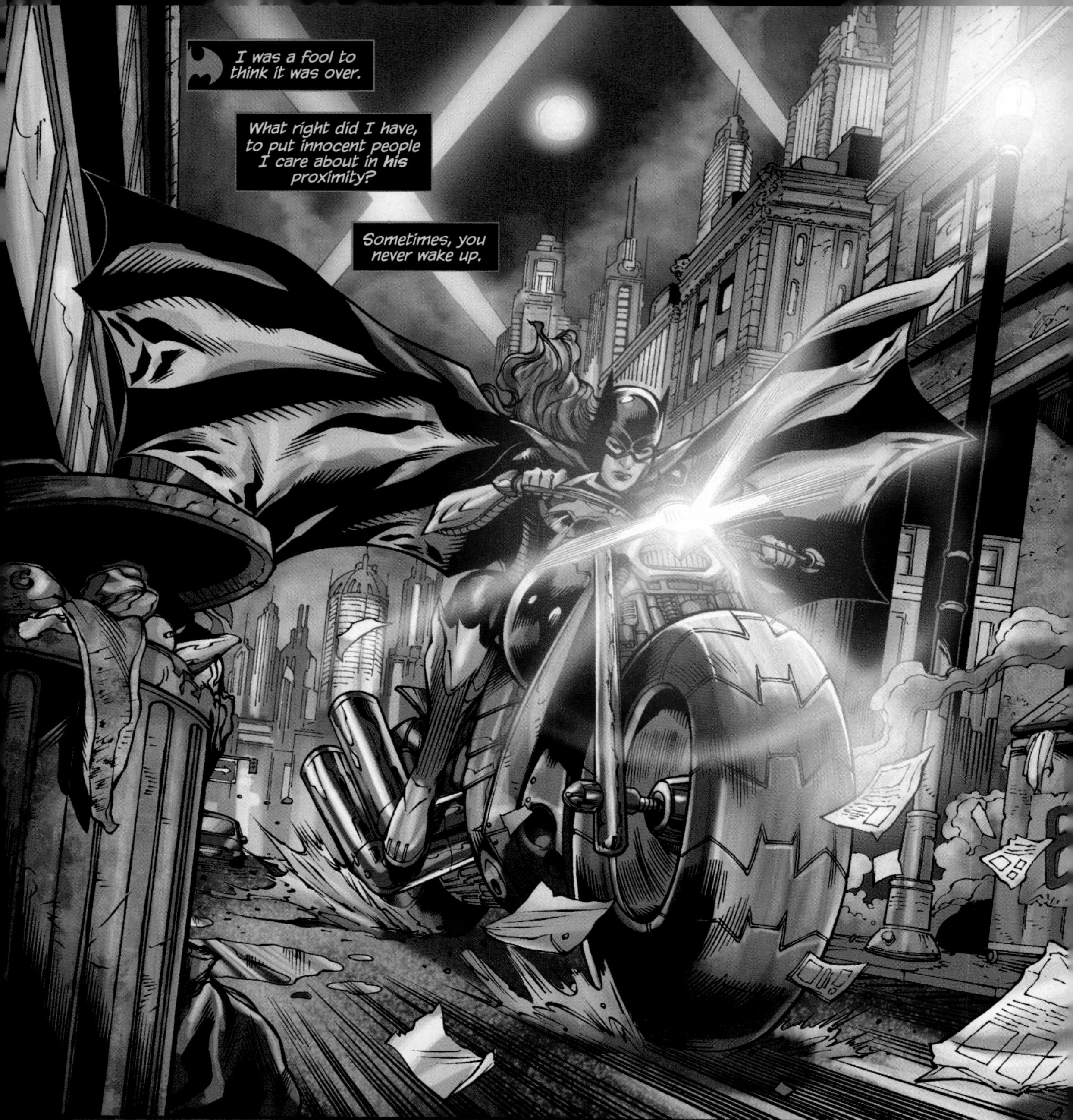
I was a fool to think it was over.
What right did I have, to put innocent people I care about in his proximity?
Sometimes, you never wake up.

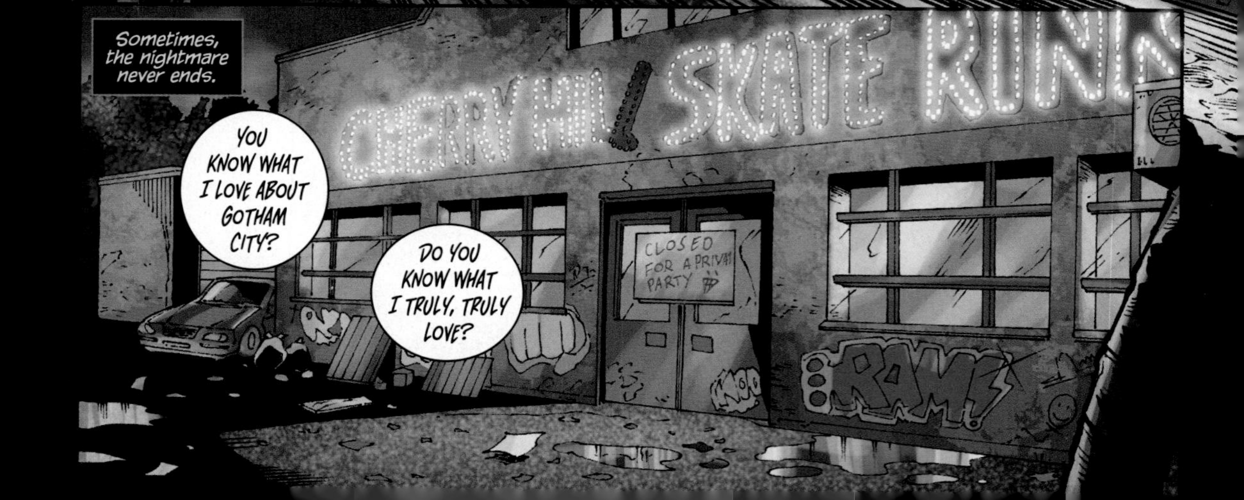
Sometimes, the nightmare never ends.
CHERRY HILL SKATE RINK
YOU KNOW WHAT I LOVE ABOUT GOTHAM CITY?
DO YOU KNOW WHAT I TRULY, TRULY LOVE?
CLOSED FOR A PRIVAT PARTY
RAM!

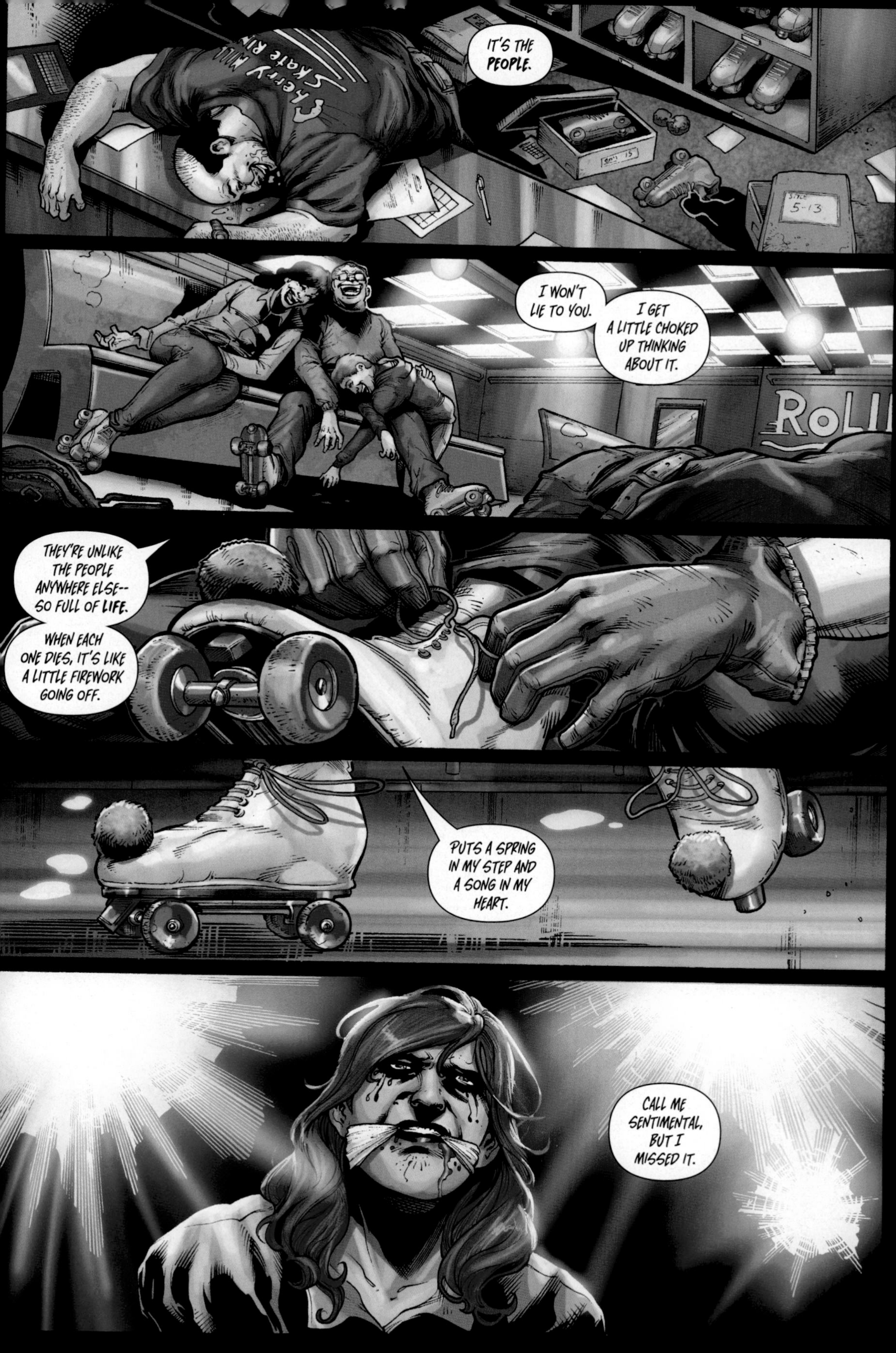
Cherry Hill Skate Rink
IT'S THE PEOPLE.
SIZE 5-13
I WON'T LIE TO YOU.
I GET A LITTLE CHOKED UP THINKING ABOUT IT.
ROLL
THEY'RE UNLIKE THE PEOPLE ANYWHERE ELSE-- SO FULL OF LIFE.
WHEN EACH ONE DIES, IT'S LIKE A LITTLE FIREWORK GOING OFF.
PUTS A SPRING IN MY STEP AND A SONG IN MY HEART.
CALL ME SENTIMENTAL, BUT I MISSED IT.

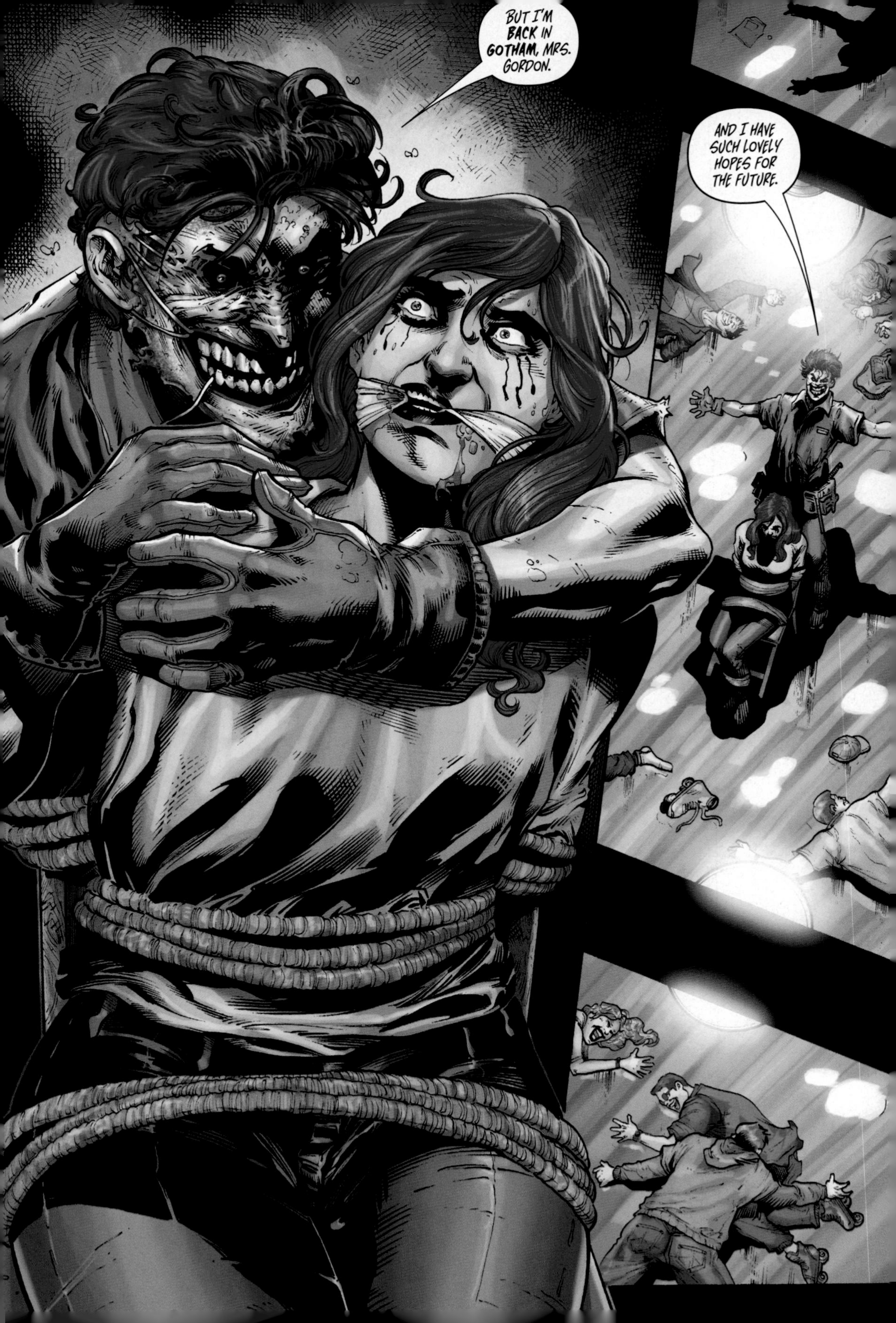
BUT I'M BACK IN GOTHAM, MRS. GORDON.
AND I HAVE SUCH LOVELY HOPES FOR THE FUTURE.

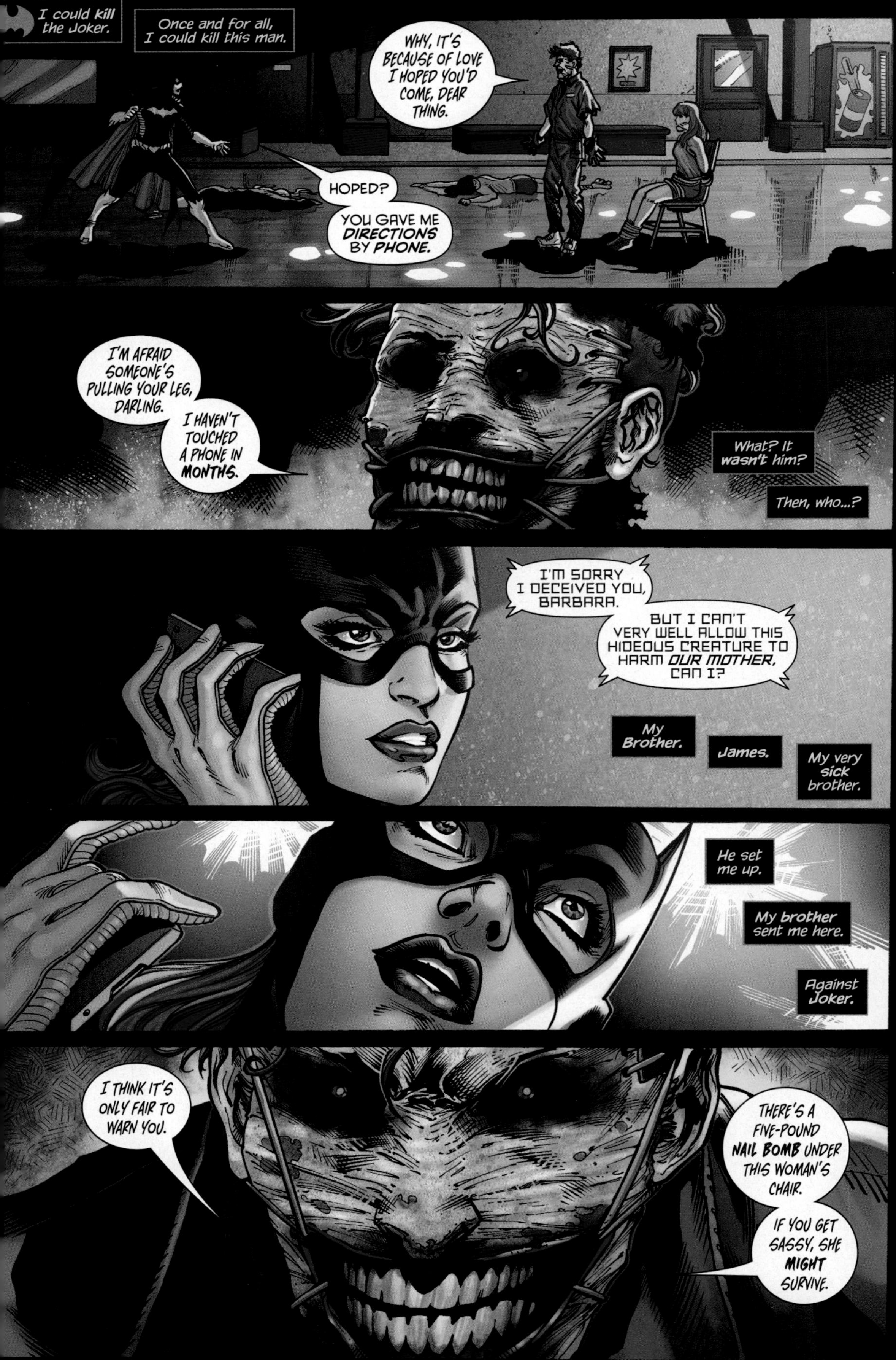

I could kill the Joker.
Once and for all, I could kill this man.
WHY, IT'S BECAUSE OF LOVE I HOPED YOU'D COME, DEAR THING.
HOPED?
YOU GAVE ME DIRECTIONS BY PHONE.
I'M AFRAID SOMEONE'S PULLING YOUR LEG, DARLING.
I HAVEN'T TOUCHED A PHONE IN MONTHS.
What? It wasn't him?
Then, who...?
I'M SORRY I DECEIVED YOU, BARBARA.
BUT I CAN'T VERY WELL ALLOW THIS HIDEOUS CREATURE TO HARM OUR MOTHER, CAN I?
My Brother.
James.
My very sick brother.
He set me up.
My brother sent me here.
Against Joker.
I THINK IT'S ONLY FAIR TO WARN YOU.
THERE'S A FIVE-POUND NAIL BOMB UNDER THIS WOMAN'S CHAIR.
IF YOU GET SASSY, SHE MIGHT SURVIVE.

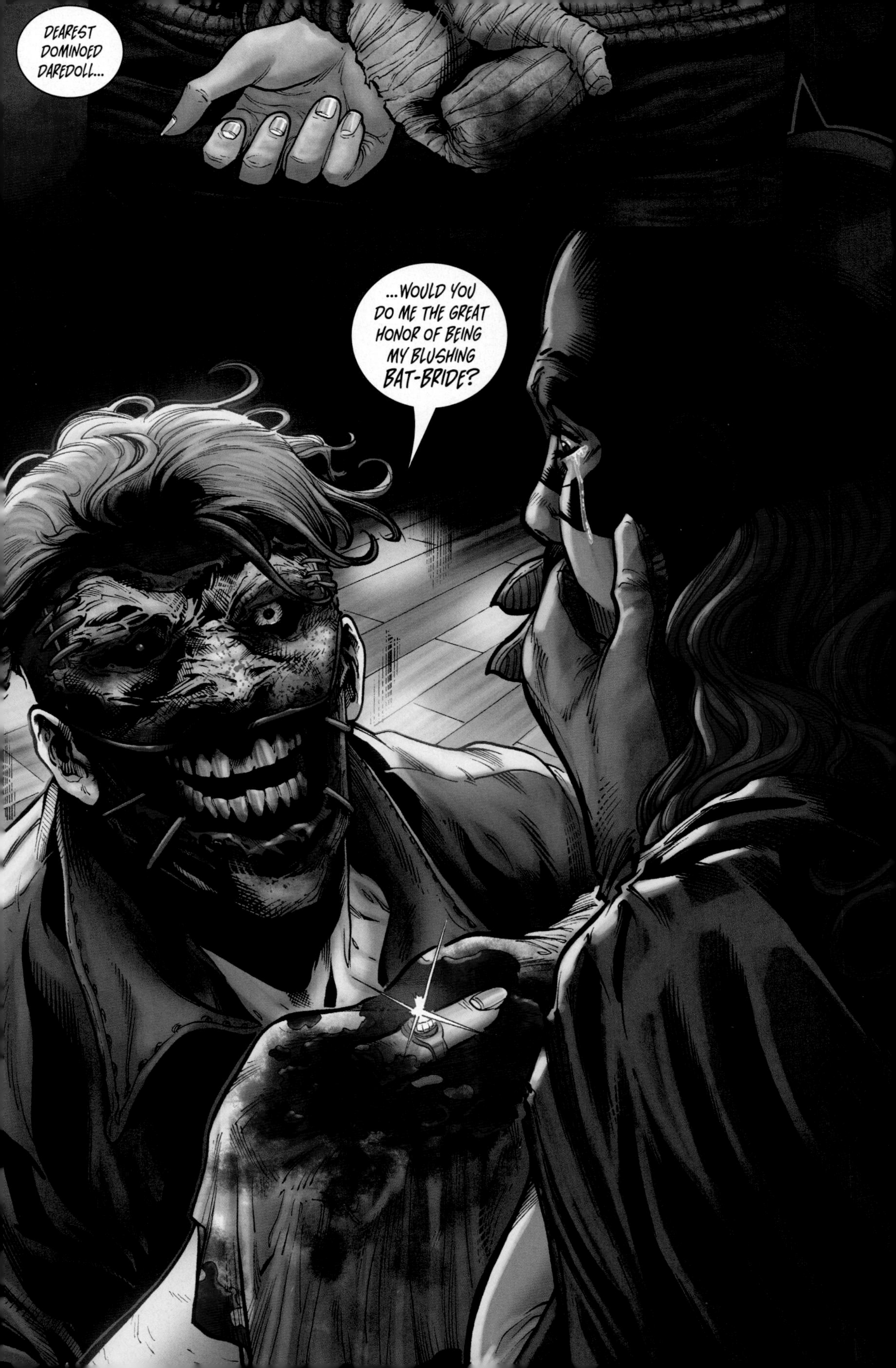
DEAREST DOMINOED DAREDOLL...
...WOULD YOU DO ME THE GREAT HONOR OF BEING MY BLUSHING BAT-BRIDE?

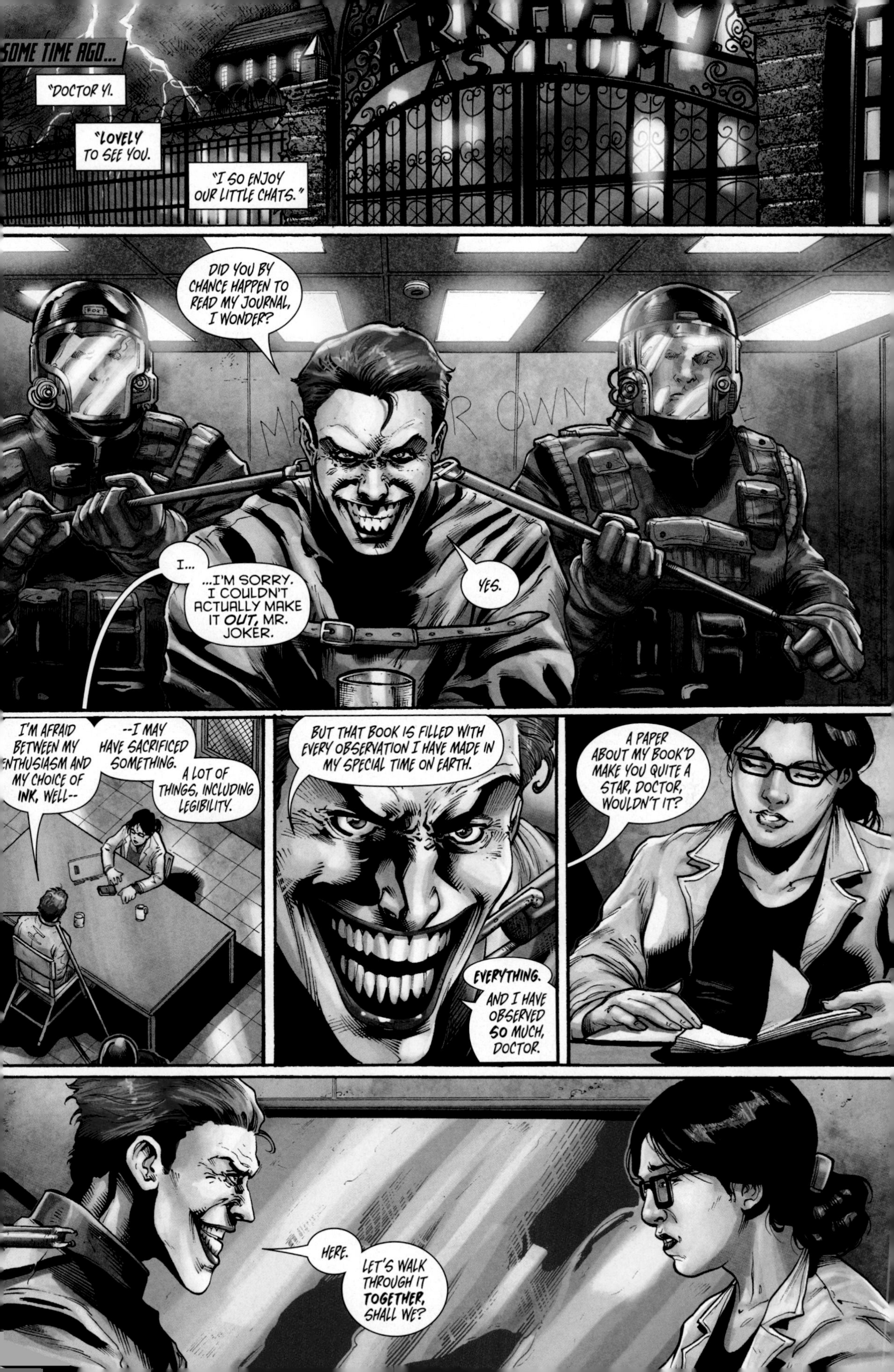
SOME TIME AGO...
"DOCTOR YI.
"LOVELY TO SEE YOU.
"I SO ENJOY OUR LITTLE CHATS."
ARKHAM ASYLUM
DID YOU BY CHANCE HAPPEN TO READ MY JOURNAL, I WONDER?
I...
...I'M SORRY. I COULDN'T ACTUALLY MAKE IT OUT, MR. JOKER.
YES.
I'M AFRAID BETWEEN MY ENTHUSIASM AND MY CHOICE OF INK, WELL--
--I MAY HAVE SACRIFICED SOMETHING.
A LOT OF THINGS, INCLUDING LEGIBILITY.
BUT THAT BOOK IS FILLED WITH EVERY OBSERVATION I HAVE MADE IN MY SPECIAL TIME ON EARTH.
EVERYTHING.
AND I HAVE OBSERVED SO MUCH, DOCTOR.
A PAPER ABOUT MY BOOK'D MAKE YOU QUITE A STAR, DOCTOR, WOULDN'T IT?
HERE.
LET'S WALK THROUGH IT TOGETHER, SHALL WE?

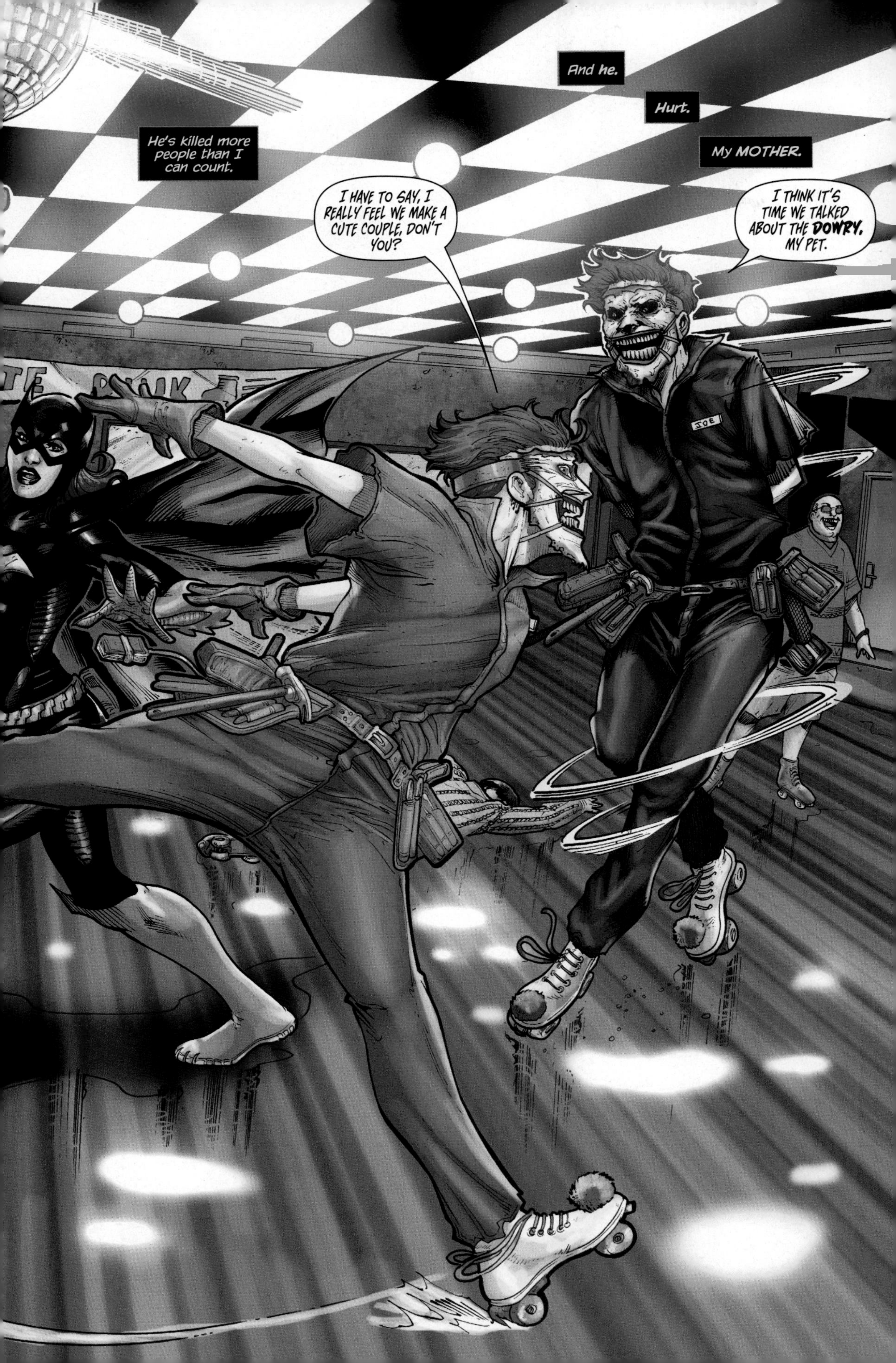
He's killed more people than I can count.
I HAVE TO SAY, I REALLY FEEL WE MAKE A CUTE COUPLE, DON'T YOU?
And he.
Hurt.
My MOTHER.
I THINK IT'S TIME WE TALKED ABOUT THE DOWRY, MY PET.
JOE

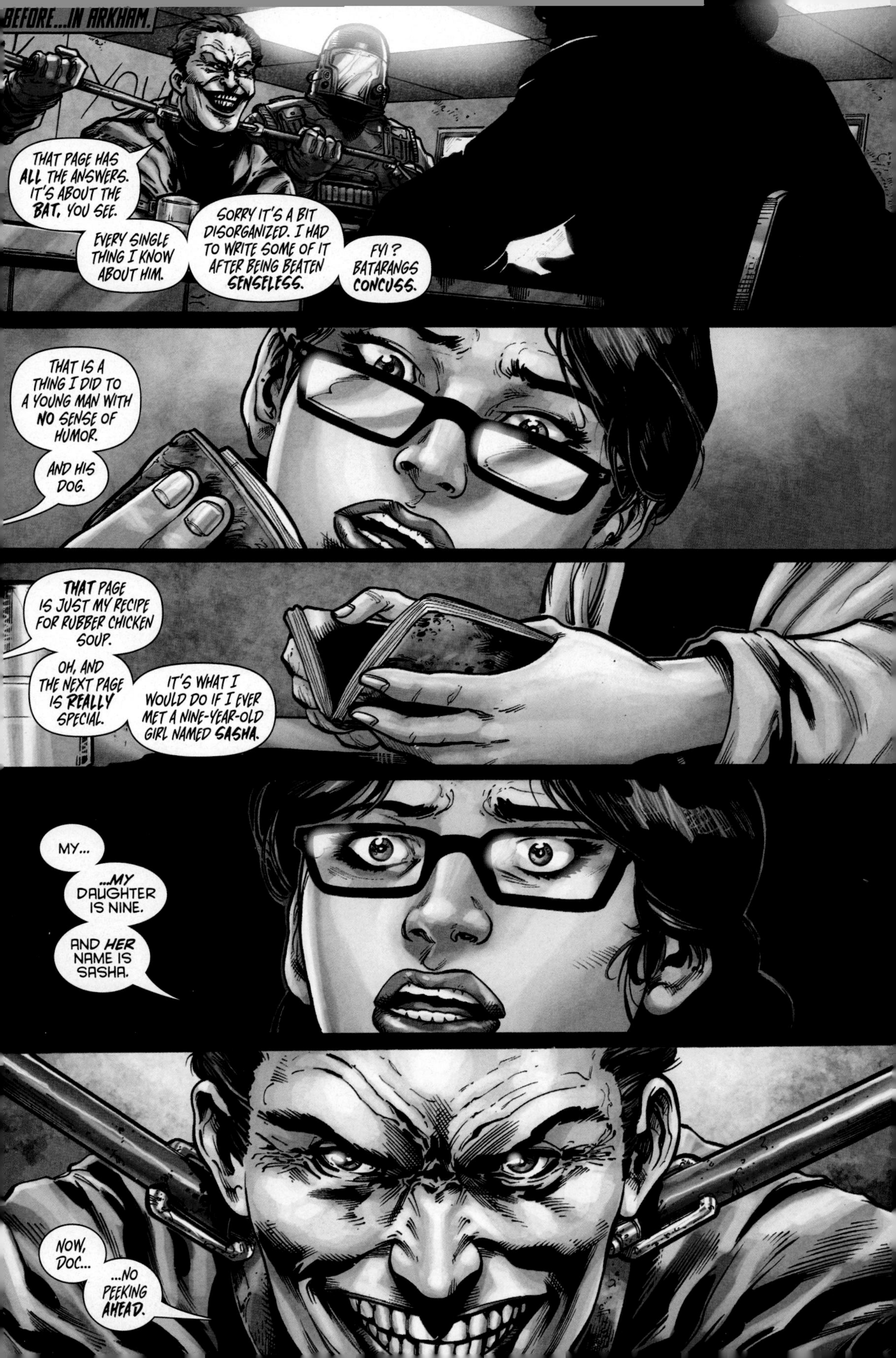
BEFORE...IN ARKHAM.
YOU
THAT PAGE HAS ALL THE ANSWERS. IT'S ABOUT THE BAT, YOU SEE.
EVERY SINGLE THING I KNOW ABOUT HIM.
SORRY IT'S A BIT DISORGANIZED. I HAD TO WRITE SOME OF IT AFTER BEING BEATEN SENSELESS.
FYI? BATARANGS CONCUSS.
THAT IS A THING I DID TO A YOUNG MAN WITH NO SENSE OF HUMOR.
AND HIS DOG.
THAT PAGE IS JUST MY RECIPE FOR RUBBER CHICKEN SOUP.
OH, AND THE NEXT PAGE IS REALLY SPECIAL.
IT'S WHAT I WOULD DO IF I EVER MET A NINE-YEAR-OLD GIRL NAMED SASHA.
MY...
...MY DAUGHTER IS NINE.
AND HER NAME IS SASHA.
NOW, DOC...
...NO PEEKING AHEAD.

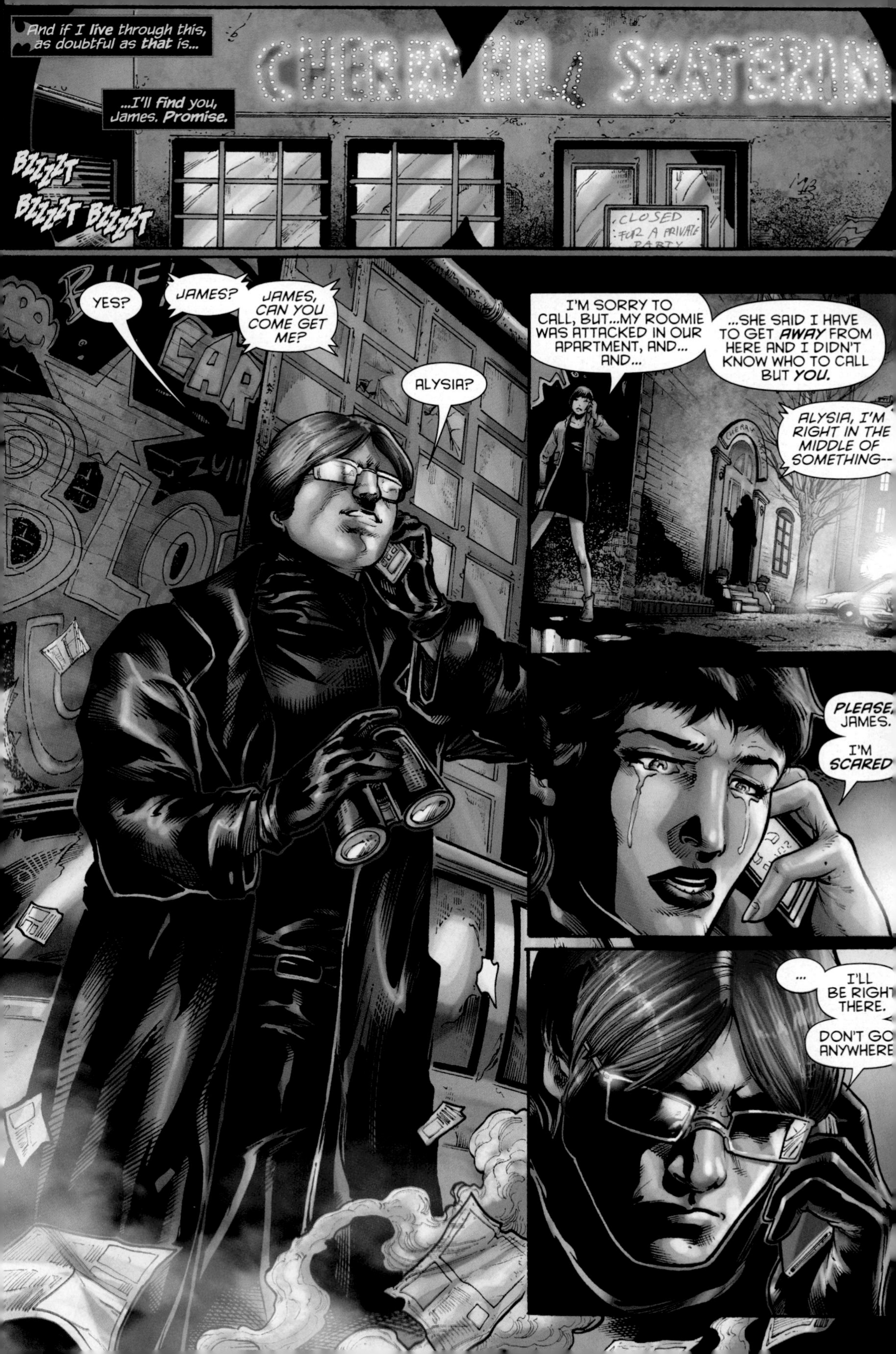
And if I live through this, as doubtful as that is...
...I'll find you, James. Promise.
CHERRY HILL SKATERAMA
CLOSED FOR A PRIVATE PARTY
BZZZZZT BZZZZZT BZZZZZT
YES?
JAMES?
JAMES, CAN YOU COME GET ME?
ALYSIA?
I'M SORRY TO CALL, BUT...MY ROOMIE WAS ATTACKED IN OUR APARTMENT, AND... AND...
...SHE SAID I HAVE TO GET AWAY FROM HERE AND I DIDN'T KNOW WHO TO CALL BUT YOU.
ALYSIA, I'M RIGHT IN THE MIDDLE OF SOMETHING--
PLEASE, JAMES.
I'M SCARED
...
I'LL BE RIGHT THERE.
DON'T GO ANYWHERE

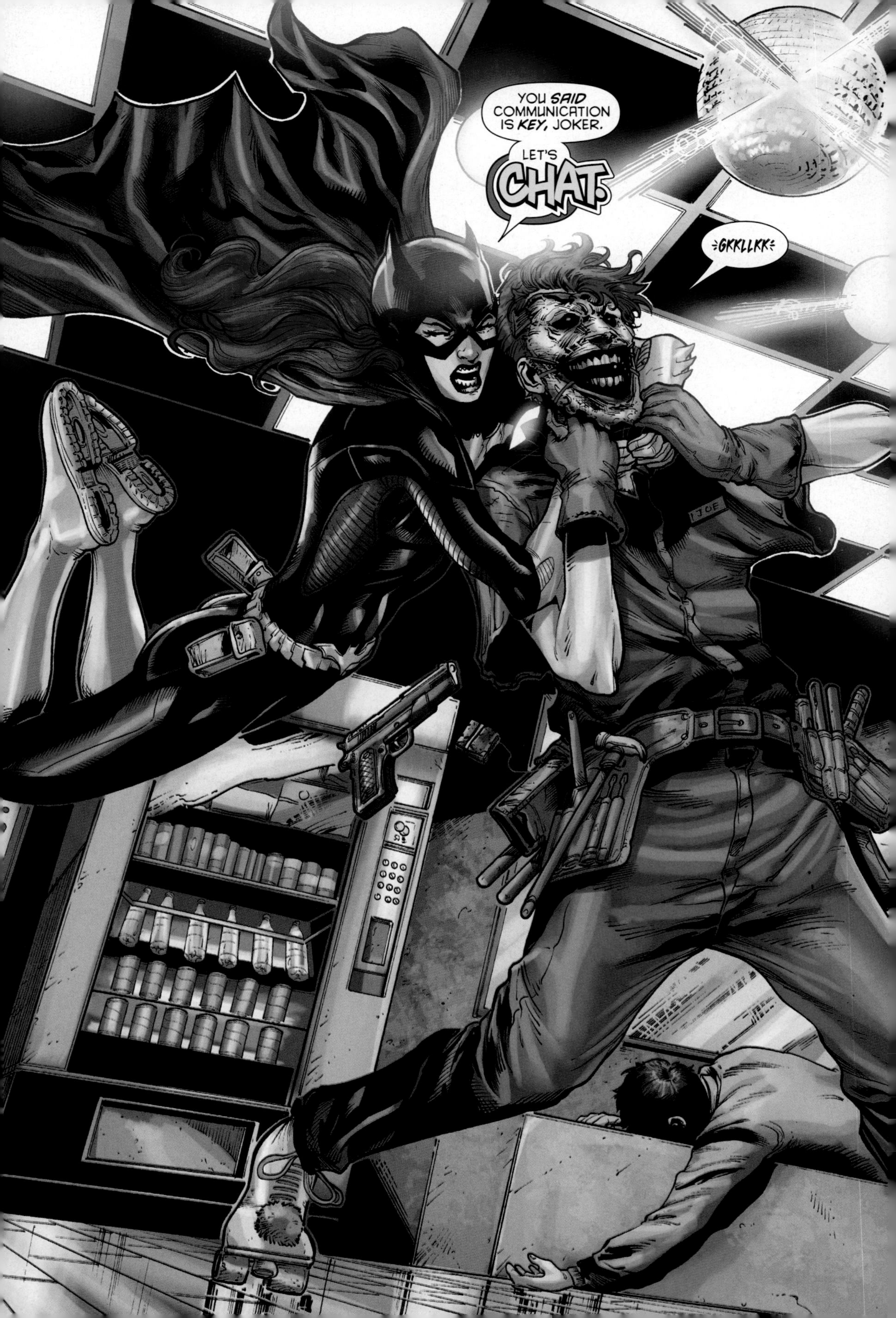
YOU SAID COMMUNICATION IS KEY, JOKER.
LET'S CHAT.
GKKLLKK

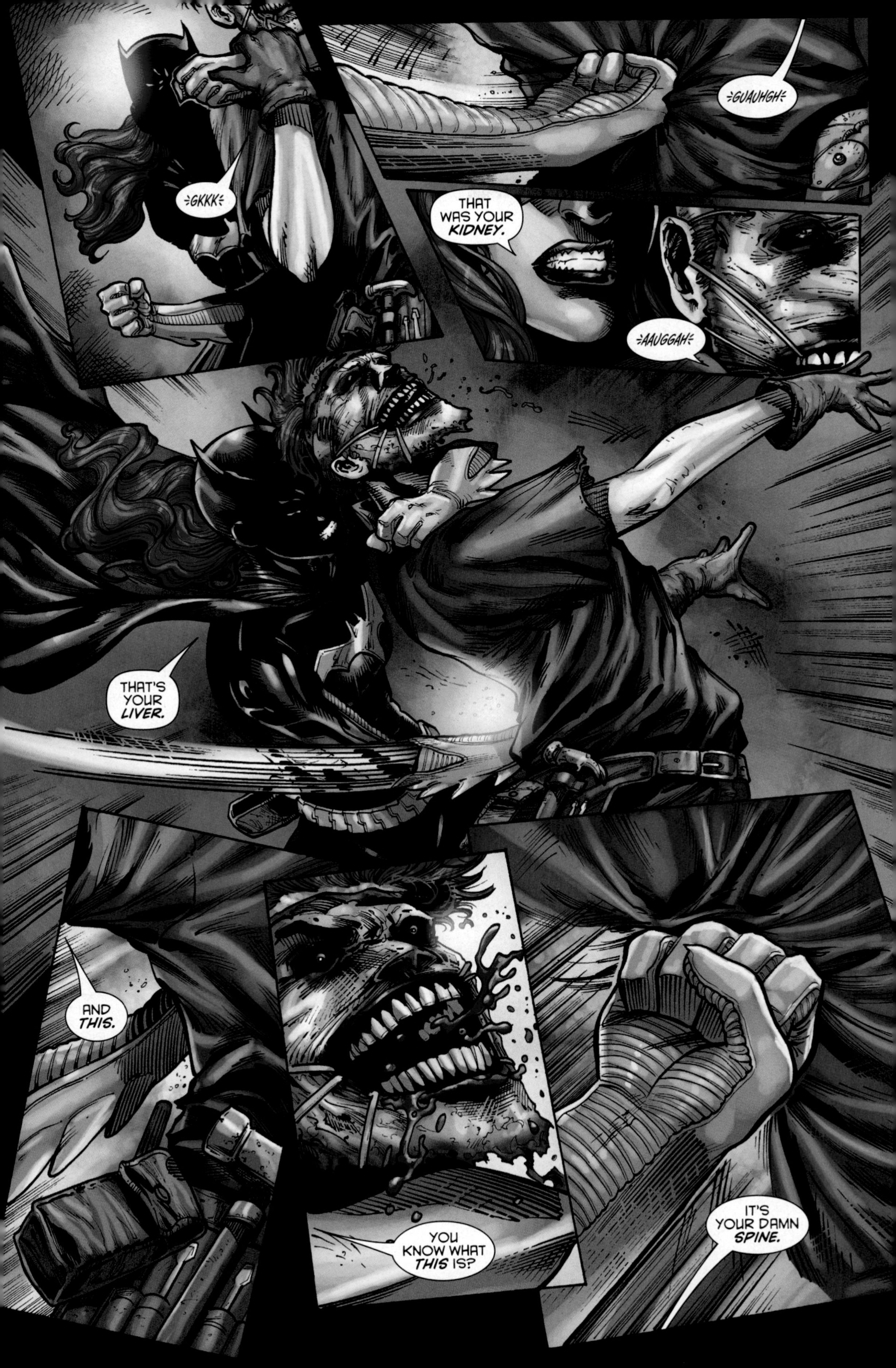
GKKK
GUAUHGH
THAT WAS YOUR KIDNEY.
AAUGGAH
THAT'S YOUR LIVER.
AND THIS.
YOU KNOW WHAT THIS IS?
IT'S YOUR DAMN SPINE.

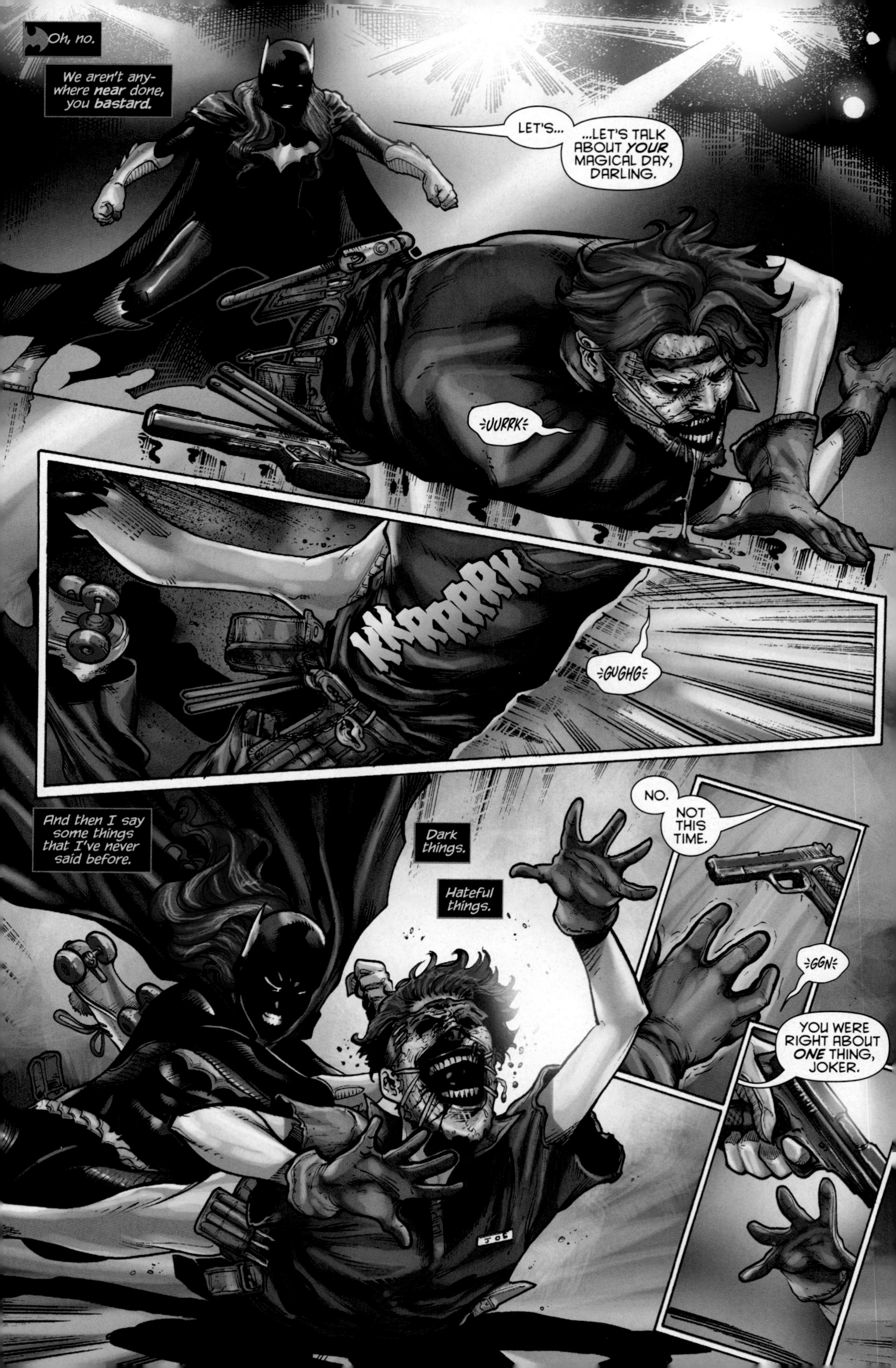
Oh, no.
We aren't any-where near done, you bastard.
LET'S...
...LET'S TALK ABOUT YOUR MAGICAL DAY, DARLING.
UURRK
KKRRRRK
GUGHG
And then I say some things that I've never said before.
Dark things.
Hateful things.
NO.
NOT THIS TIME.
GGN
YOU WERE RIGHT ABOUT ONE THING, JOKER.

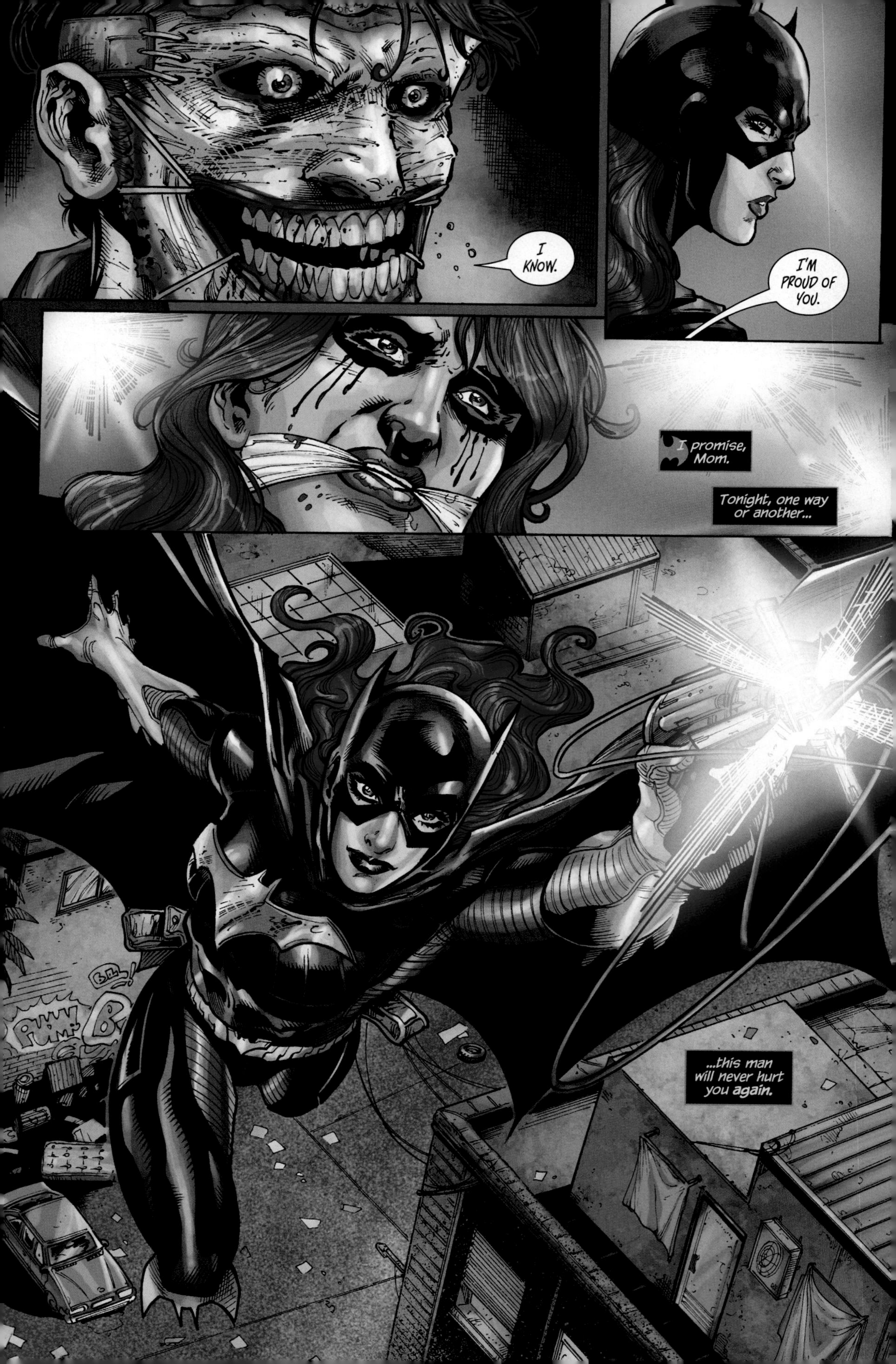
I KNOW.
I'M PROUD OF YOU.
I promise, Mom.
Tonight, one way or another...
...this man will never hurt you again.

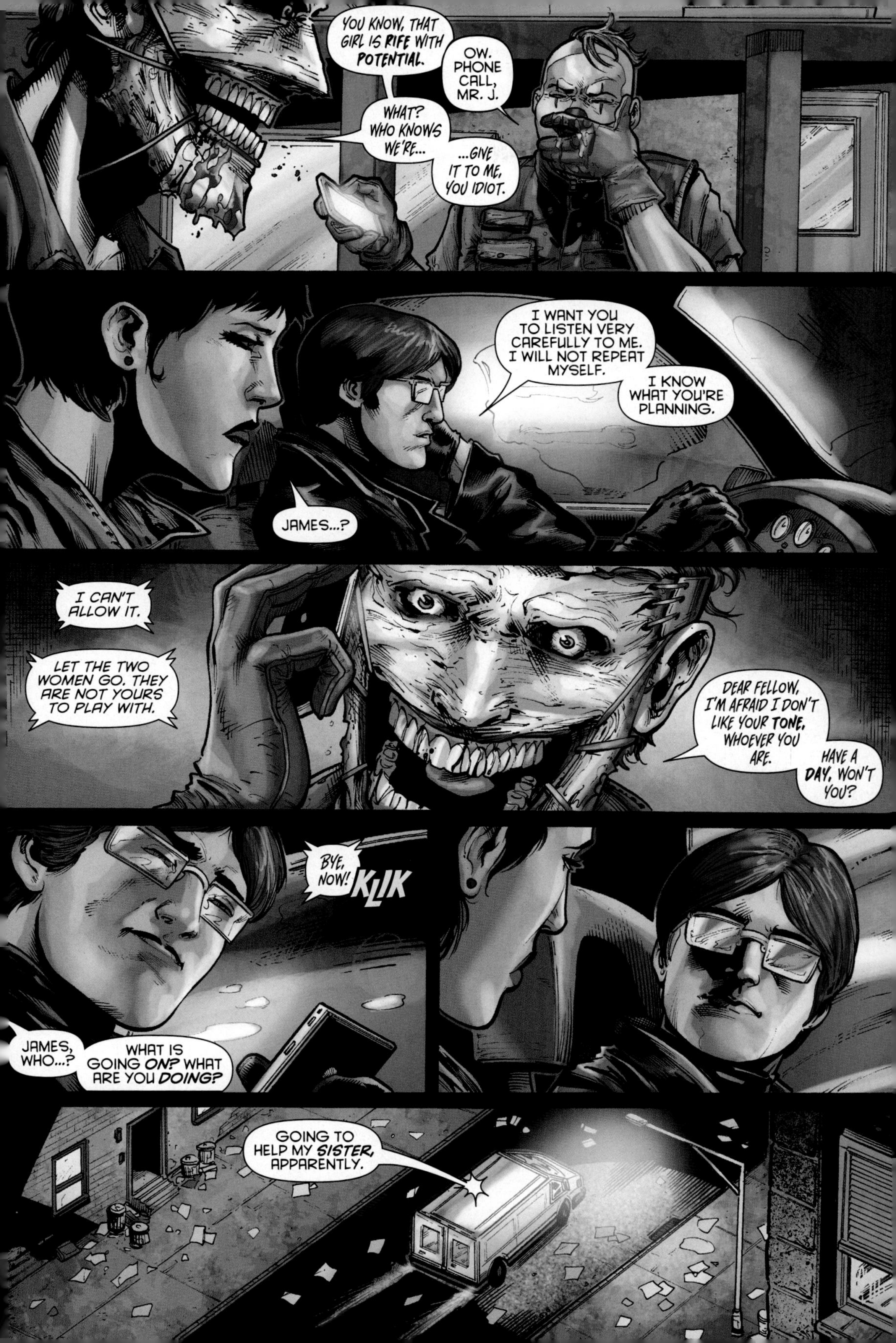

YOU KNOW, THAT GIRL IS RIFE WITH POTENTIAL.
OW. PHONE CALL, MR. J.
WHAT? WHO KNOWS WE'RE...
...GIVE IT TO ME, YOU IDIOT.
I WANT YOU TO LISTEN VERY CAREFULLY TO ME. I WILL NOT REPEAT MYSELF.
I KNOW WHAT YOU'RE PLANNING.
JAMES...?
I CAN'T ALLOW IT.
LET THE TWO WOMEN GO. THEY ARE NOT YOURS TO PLAY WITH.
DEAR FELLOW, I'M AFRAID I DON'T LIKE YOUR TONE, WHOEVER YOU ARE.
HAVE A DAY, WON'T YOU?
BYE, NOW!
KLIK
JAMES, WHO...?
WHAT IS GOING ON? WHAT ARE YOU DOING?
GOING TO HELP MY SISTER, APPARENTLY.

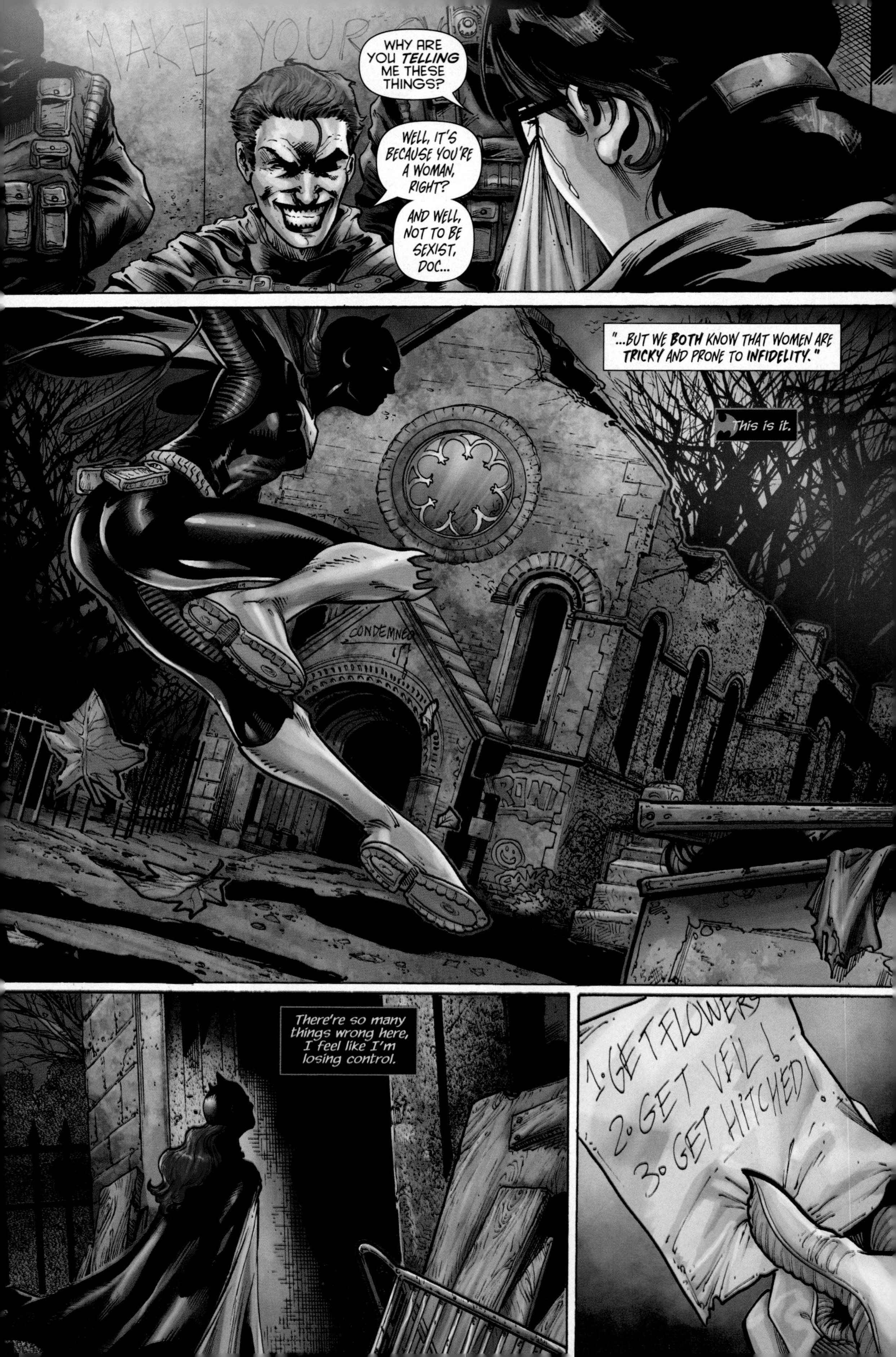
WHY ARE YOU **TELLING** ME THESE THINGS?
WELL, IT'S BECAUSE YOU'RE A WOMAN, RIGHT?
AND WELL, NOT TO BE SEXIST, DOC...
"...BUT WE **BOTH** KNOW THAT WOMEN ARE **TRICKY** AND PRONE TO **INFIDELITY.**"
This is it.
CONDEMNED
There're so many things wrong here, I feel like I'm losing control.
1. GET FLOWERS
2. GET VEIL!
3. GET HITCHED!

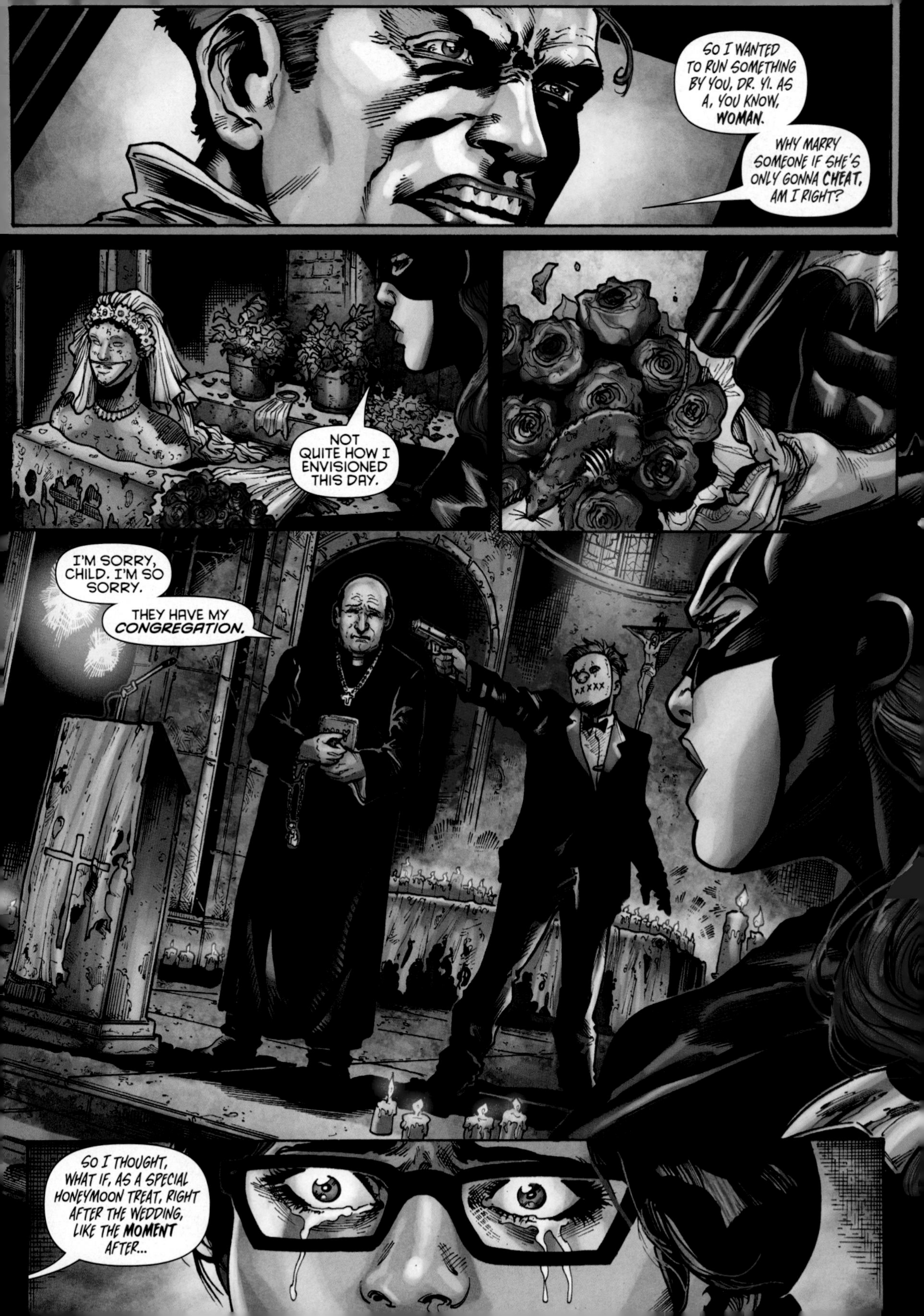
SO I WANTED TO RUN SOMETHING BY YOU, DR. YI. AS A, YOU KNOW, **WOMAN.**
WHY MARRY SOMEONE IF SHE'S ONLY GONNA **CHEAT,** AM I RIGHT?
NOT QUITE HOW I ENVISIONED THIS DAY.
I'M SORRY, CHILD. I'M SO SORRY.
THEY HAVE MY ***CONGREGATION.***
SO I THOUGHT, WHAT IF, AS A SPECIAL HONEYMOON TREAT, RIGHT AFTER THE WEDDING, LIKE THE **MOMENT** AFTER...

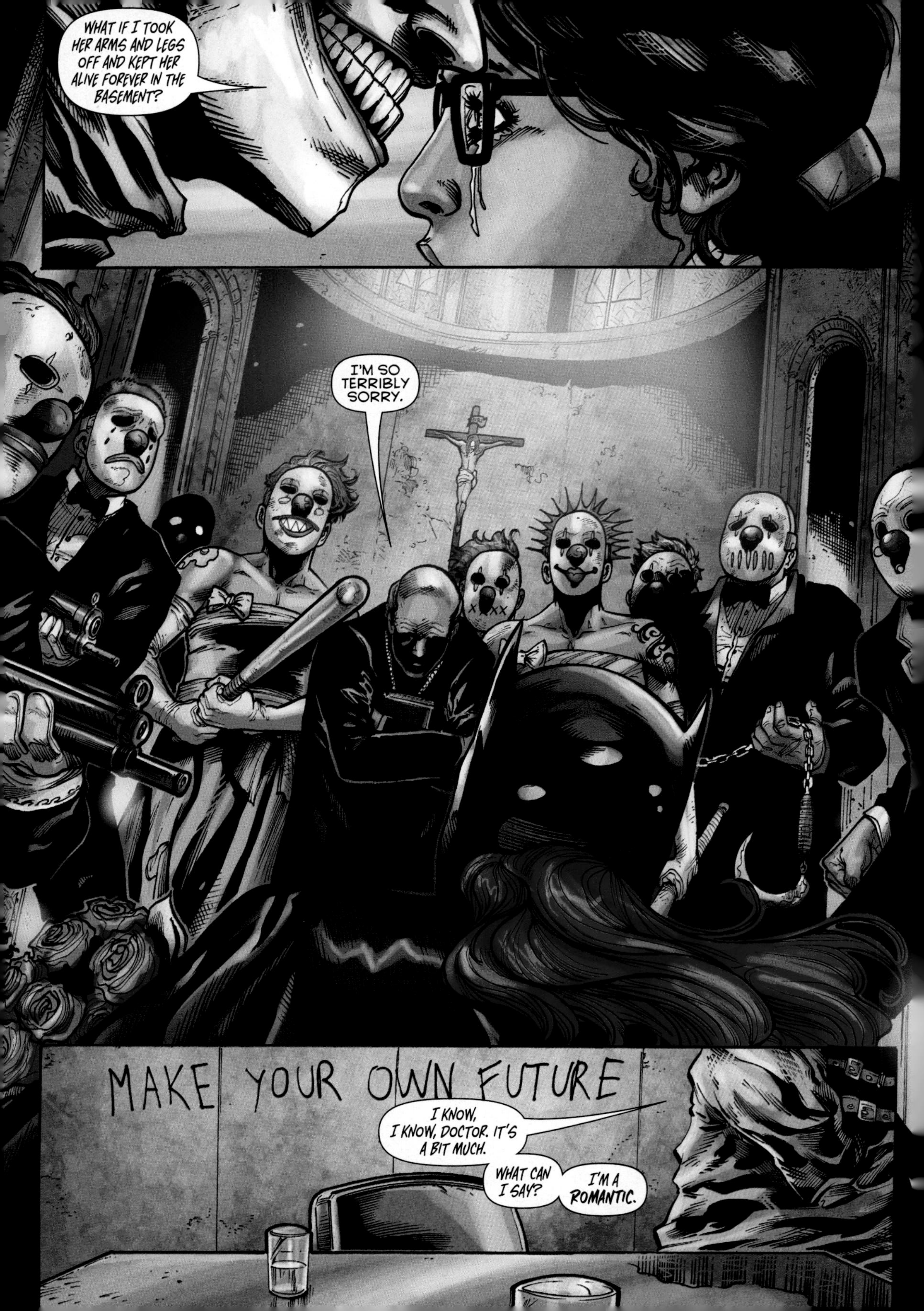
WHAT IF I TOOK HER ARMS AND LEGS OFF AND KEPT HER ALIVE FOREVER IN THE BASEMENT?
I'M SO TERRIBLY SORRY.
MAKE YOUR OWN FUTURE
I KNOW, I KNOW, DOCTOR. IT'S A BIT MUCH.
WHAT CAN I SAY?
I'M A ROMANTIC.

I was reborn in the fire of a muzzle flash.

I wanted to lead a normal life.

So that's what I did. I rolled the dice.

And I lost.

As a seventeen-year-old girl, I was shot and left to die by the worst man who ever walked the streets of this city.

→SNIFF!←

There is no amount of pain that will ever sate him. When you think he's taken everything you have?

He says something your mind can't even process.

He wants my hand in *marriage.*

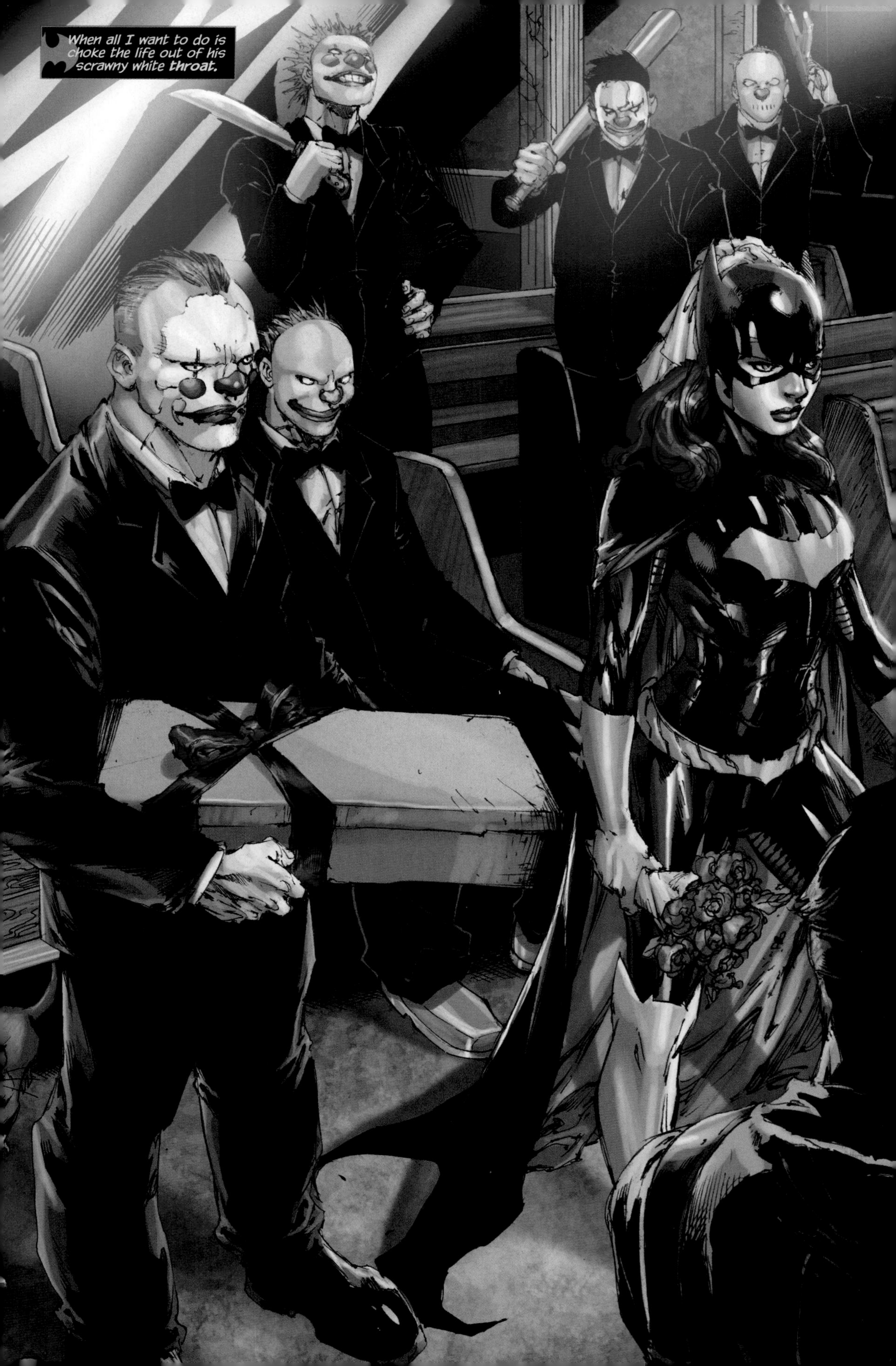
When all I want to do is choke the life out of his scrawny white throat.

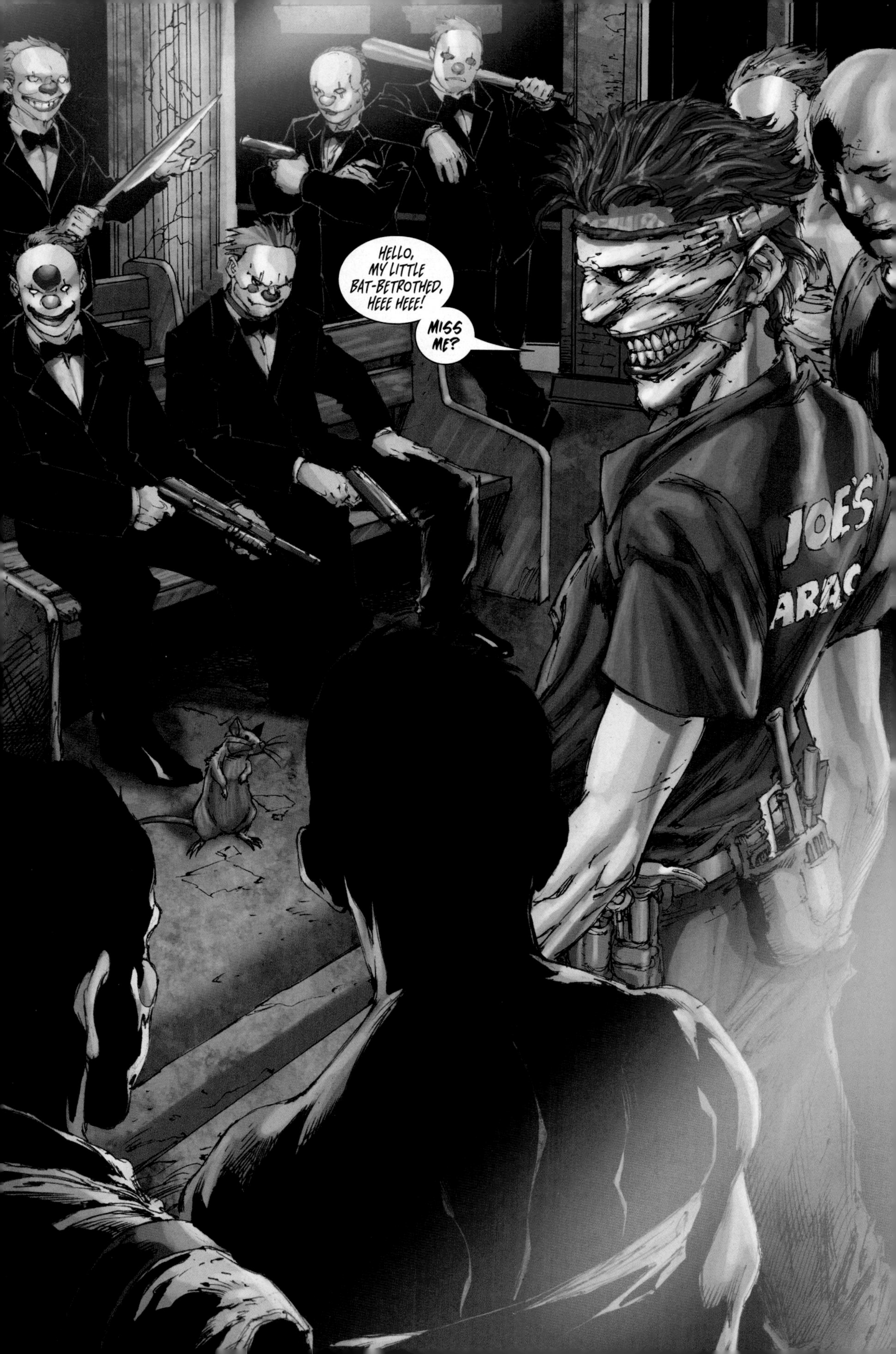
HELLO, MY LITTLE BAT-BETROTHED, HEEE HEEE!
MISS ME?
JOE'S

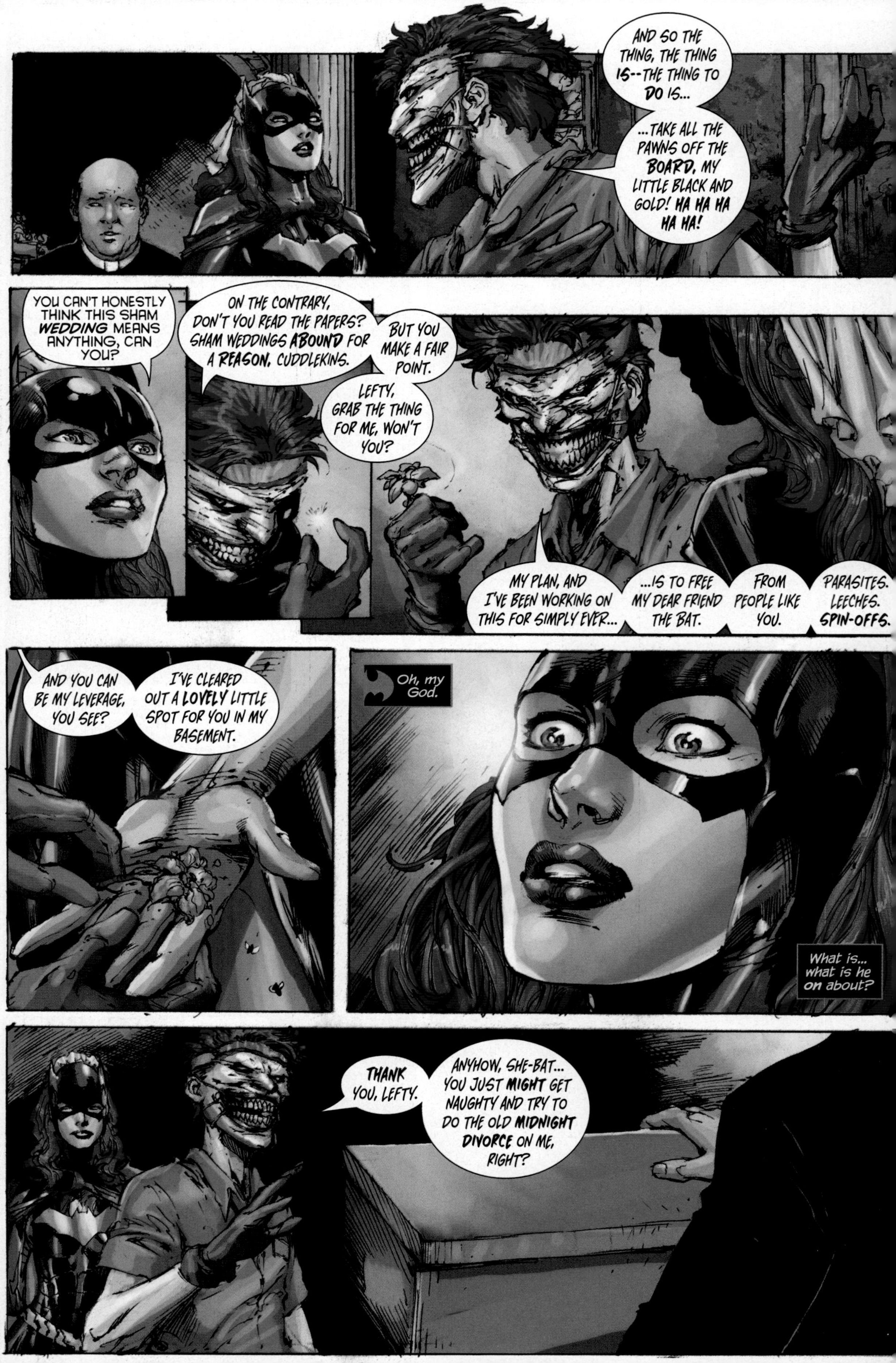
AND SO THE THING, THE THING IS--THE THING TO DO IS...
...TAKE ALL THE PAWNS OFF THE BOARD, MY LITTLE BLACK AND GOLD! HA HA HA HA HA!
YOU CAN'T HONESTLY THINK THIS SHAM WEDDING MEANS ANYTHING, CAN YOU?
ON THE CONTRARY, DON'T YOU READ THE PAPERS? SHAM WEDDINGS ABOUND FOR A REASON, CUDDLEKINS.
BUT YOU MAKE A FAIR POINT.
LEFTY, GRAB THE THING FOR ME, WON'T YOU?
MY PLAN, AND I'VE BEEN WORKING ON THIS FOR SIMPLY EVER...
...IS TO FREE MY DEAR FRIEND THE BAT.
FROM PEOPLE LIKE YOU.
PARASITES. LEECHES. SPIN-OFFS.
AND YOU CAN BE MY LEVERAGE, YOU SEE?
I'VE CLEARED OUT A LOVELY LITTLE SPOT FOR YOU IN MY BASEMENT.
Oh, my God.
What is... what is he on about?
THANK YOU, LEFTY.
ANYHOW, SHE-BAT... YOU JUST MIGHT GET NAUGHTY AND TRY TO DO THE OLD MIDNIGHT DIVORCE ON ME, RIGHT?

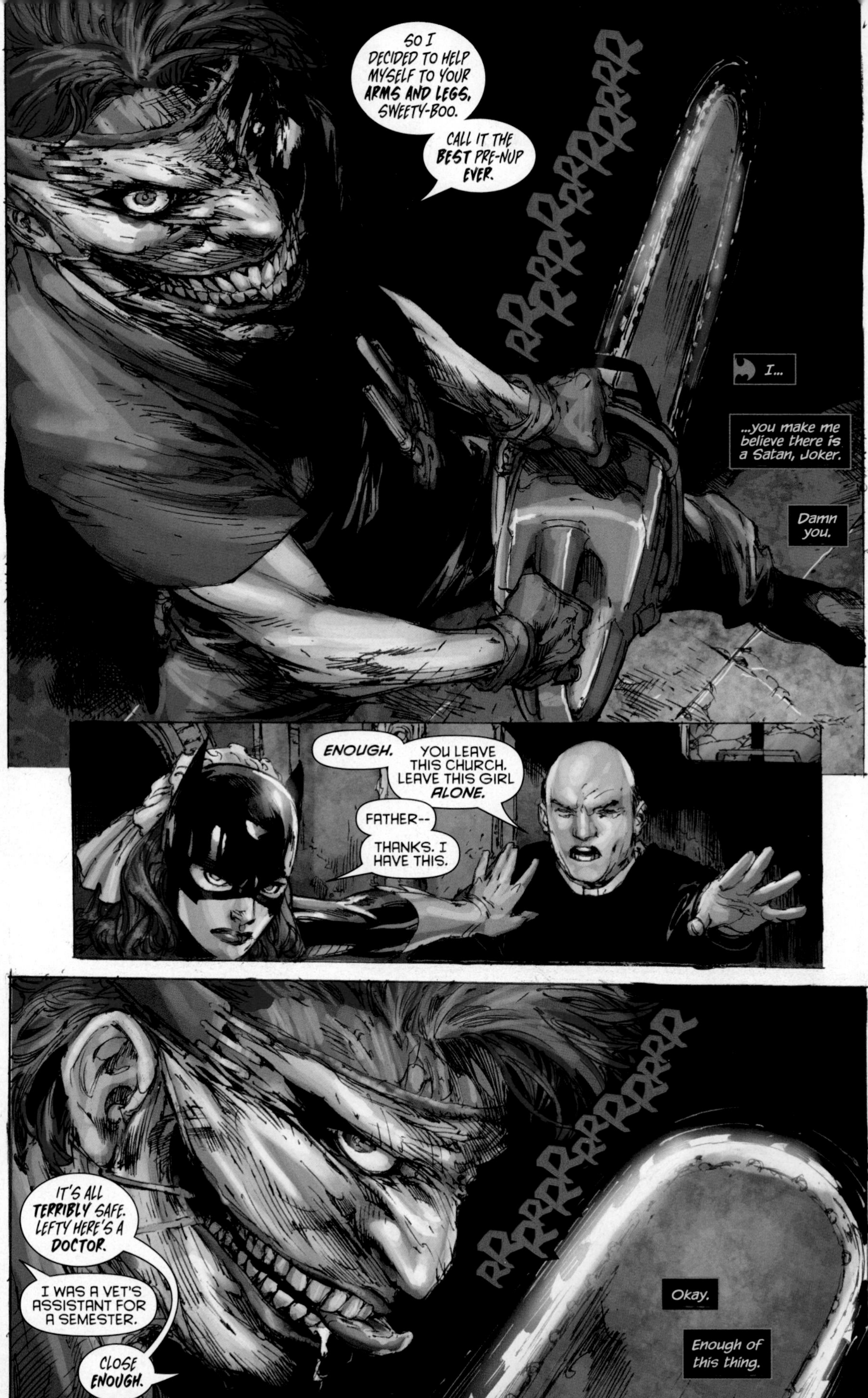
SO I DECIDED TO HELP MYSELF TO YOUR ARMS AND LEGS, SWEETY-BOO.
CALL IT THE BEST PRE-NUP EVER.
RRRRRRRRRRRRRRR
I...
...you make me believe there is a Satan, Joker.
Damn you.
ENOUGH.
YOU LEAVE THIS CHURCH. LEAVE THIS GIRL ALONE.
FATHER--
THANKS. I HAVE THIS.
RRRRRRRRRRRRRRR
IT'S ALL TERRIBLY SAFE. LEFTY HERE'S A DOCTOR.
I WAS A VET'S ASSISTANT FOR A SEMESTER.
CLOSE ENOUGH.
Okay.
Enough of this thing.

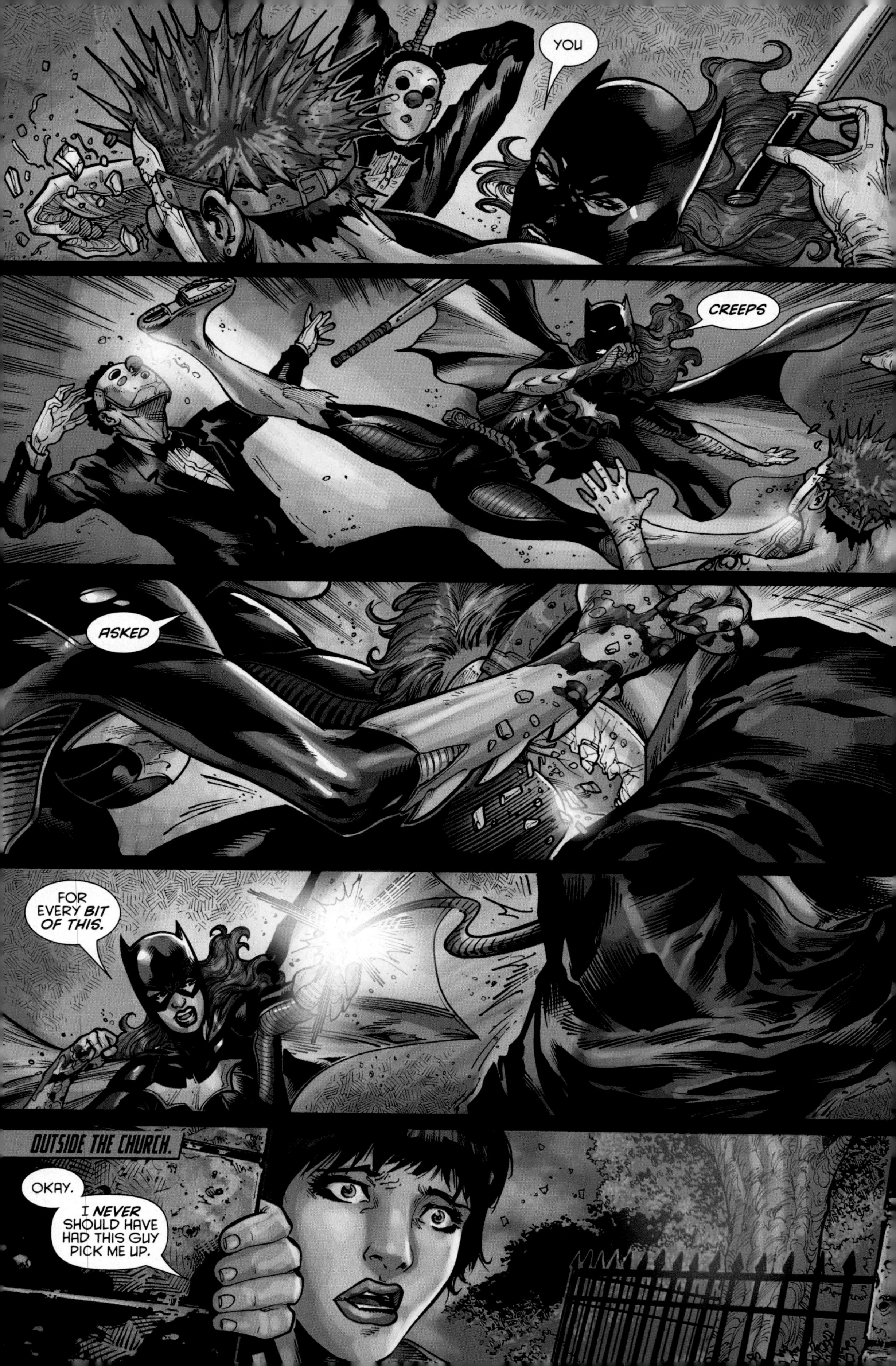

YOU
CREEPS
ASKED
FOR EVERY BIT OF THIS.
OUTSIDE THE CHURCH.
OKAY.
I NEVER SHOULD HAVE HAD THIS GUY PICK ME UP.

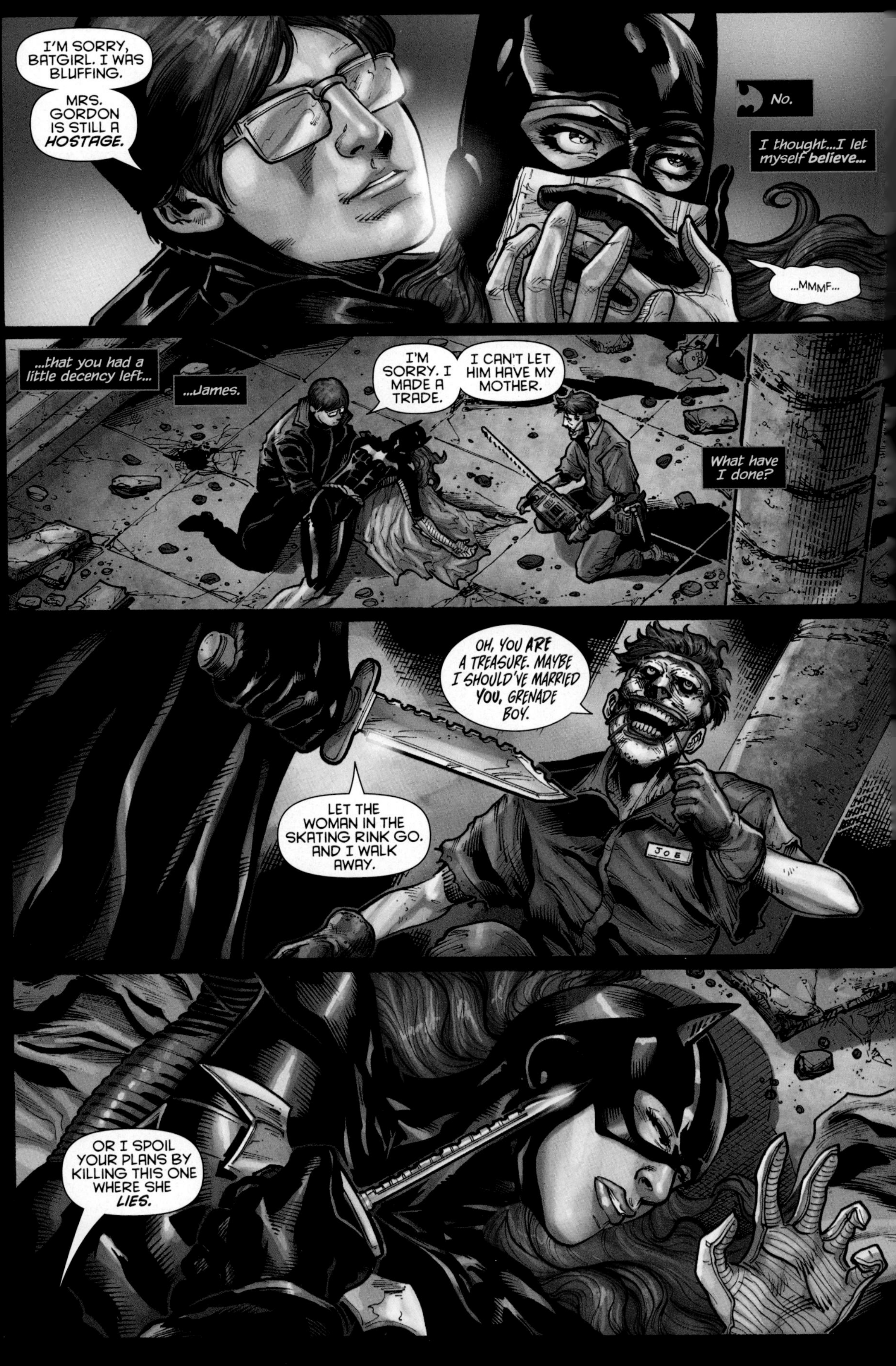
I'M SORRY, BATGIRL. I WAS BLUFFING.
MRS. GORDON IS STILL A *HOSTAGE.*
No.
I thought...I let myself **believe...**
...MMMF...
...that you had a little decency left...
...James.
I'M SORRY. I MADE A TRADE.
I CAN'T LET HIM HAVE MY MOTHER.
What have I done?
OH, YOU **ARE** A TREASURE. MAYBE I SHOULD'VE MARRIED **YOU**, GRENADE BOY.
LET THE WOMAN IN THE SKATING RINK GO. AND I WALK AWAY.
JOE
OR I SPOIL YOUR PLANS BY KILLING THIS ONE WHERE SHE *LIES.*

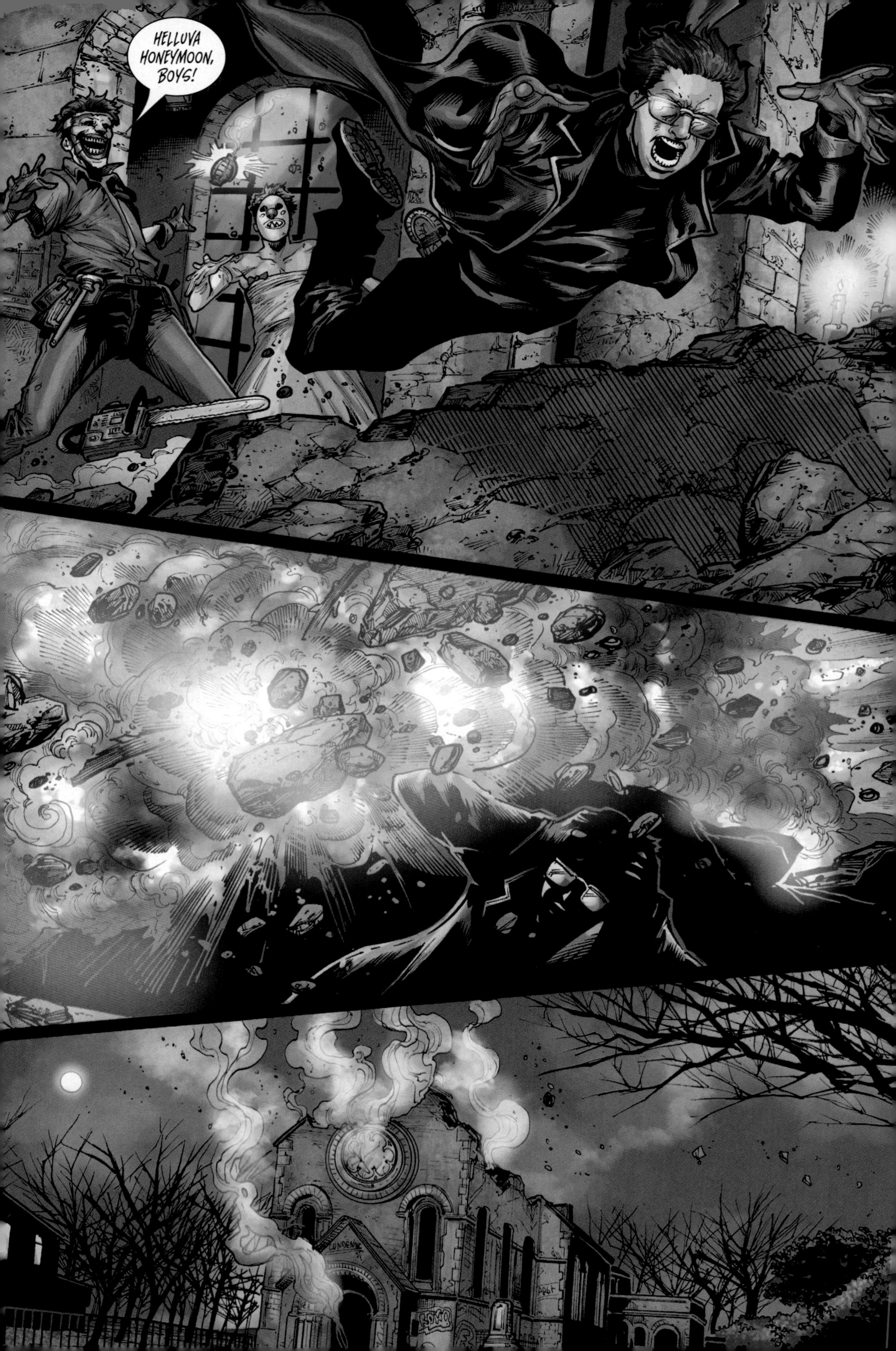
HELLUVA HONEYMOON, BOYS!

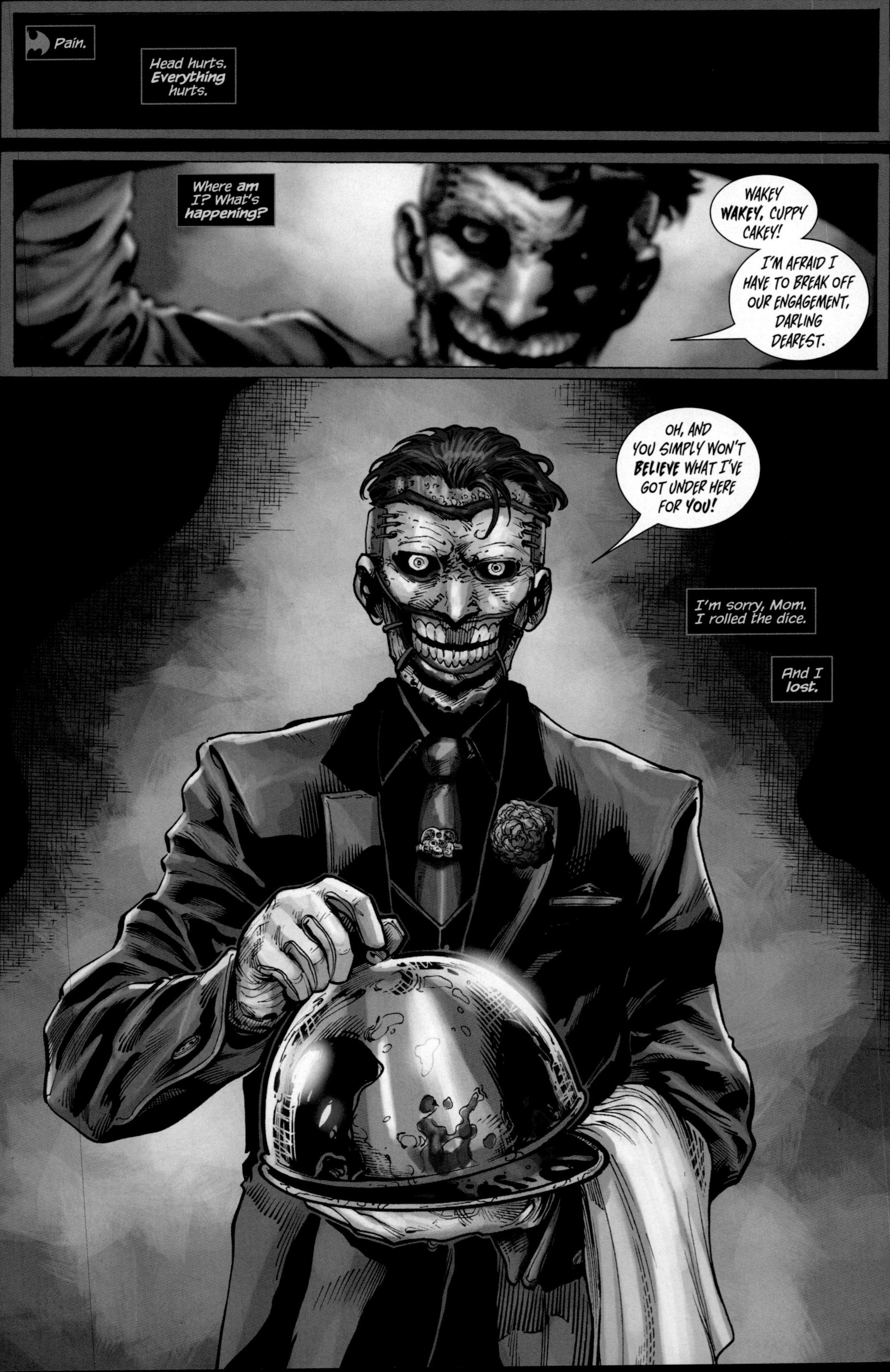
Pain.
Head hurts. Everything hurts.
Where am I? What's happening?
WAKEY WAKEY, CUPPY CAKEY!
I'M AFRAID I HAVE TO BREAK OFF OUR ENGAGEMENT, DARLING DEAREST.
OH, AND YOU SIMPLY WON'T BELIEVE WHAT I'VE GOT UNDER HERE FOR YOU!
I'm sorry, Mom. I rolled the dice.
And I lost.

PART FIVE

RED HOOD AND RED ROBIN

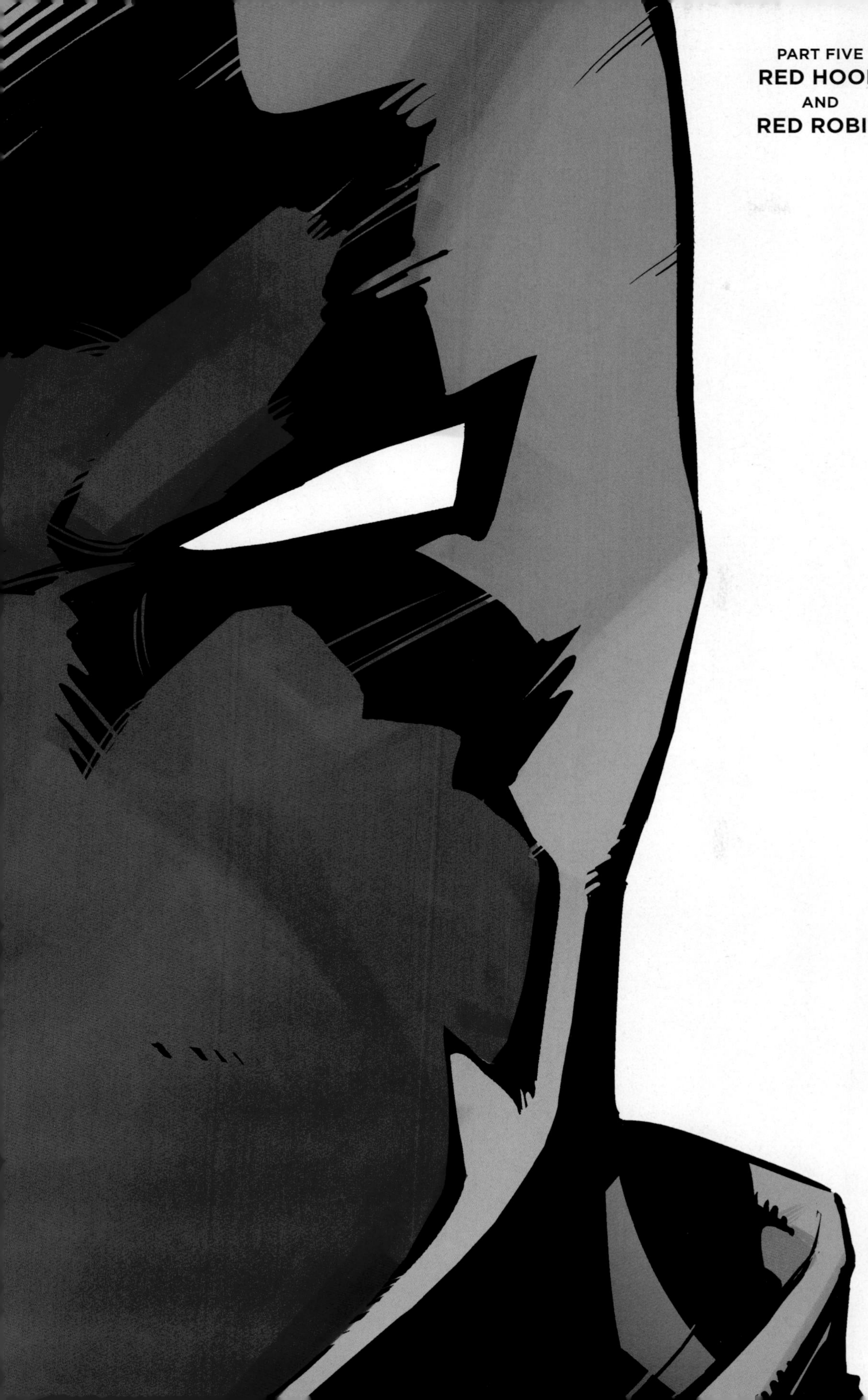

SCOTT LOBDELL FABIAN NICIEZA writers TIMOTHY GREEN II BRETT BOOTH NORM RAPMUND WAYNE FAUCHER PASCAL ALIXE ALE GARZA artists
ANDREW DALHOUSE BLOND colorists TRAVIS LANHAM DAVE SHARPE TAYLOR ESPOSITO letterers

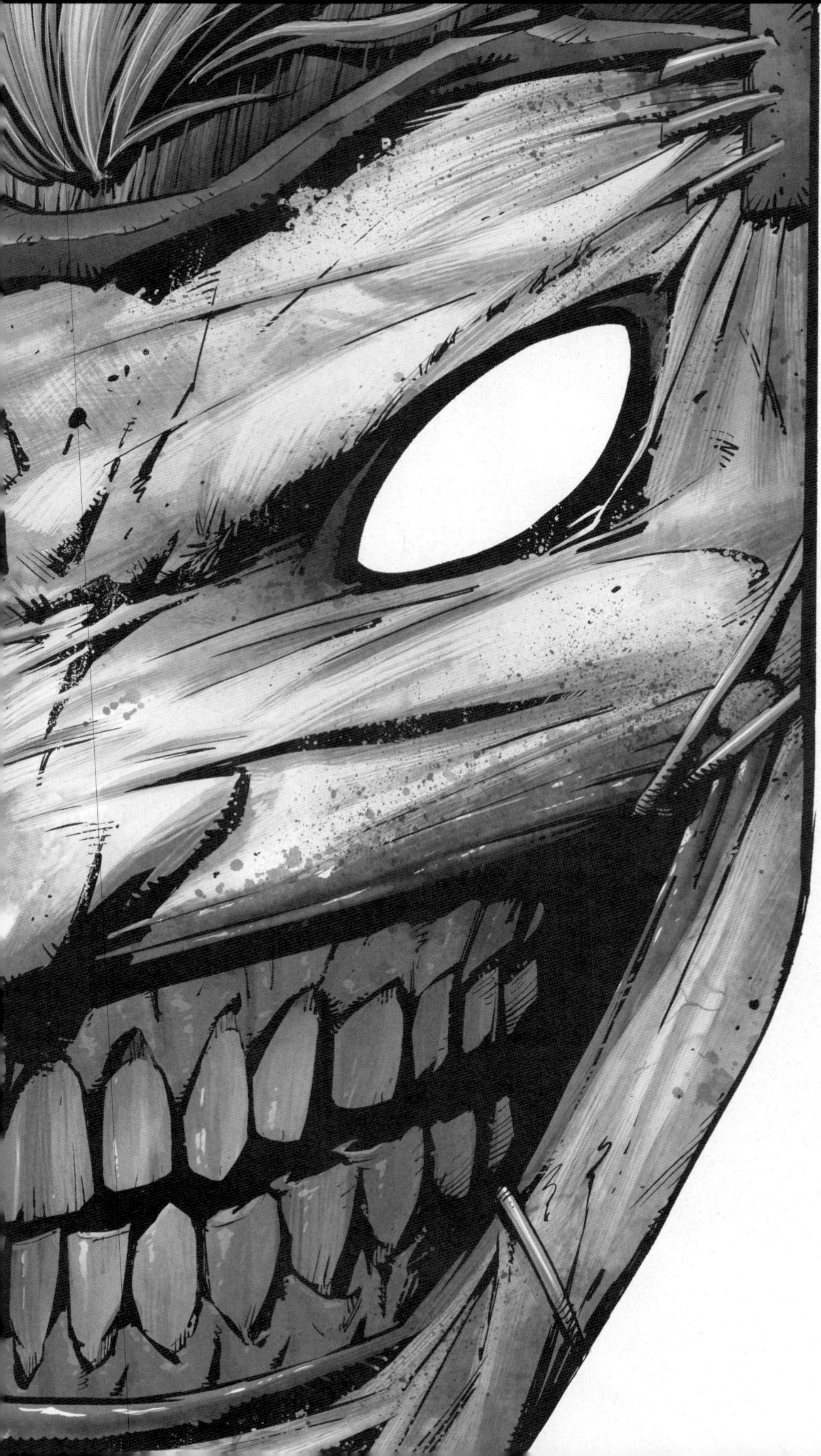

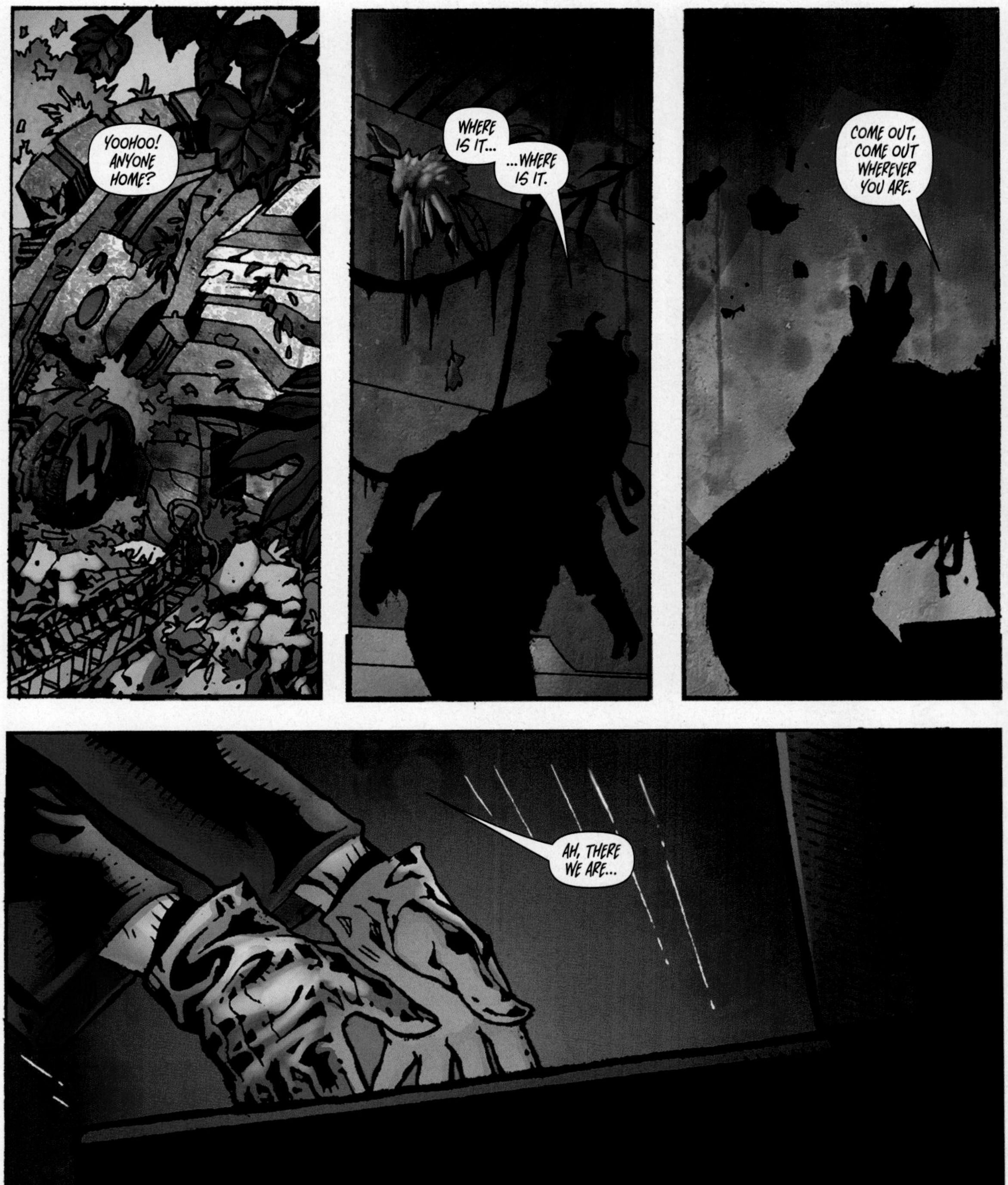

YOOHOO! ANYONE HOME?
WHERE IS IT...
...WHERE IS IT.
COME OUT, COME OUT WHEREVER YOU ARE.
AH, THERE WE ARE...

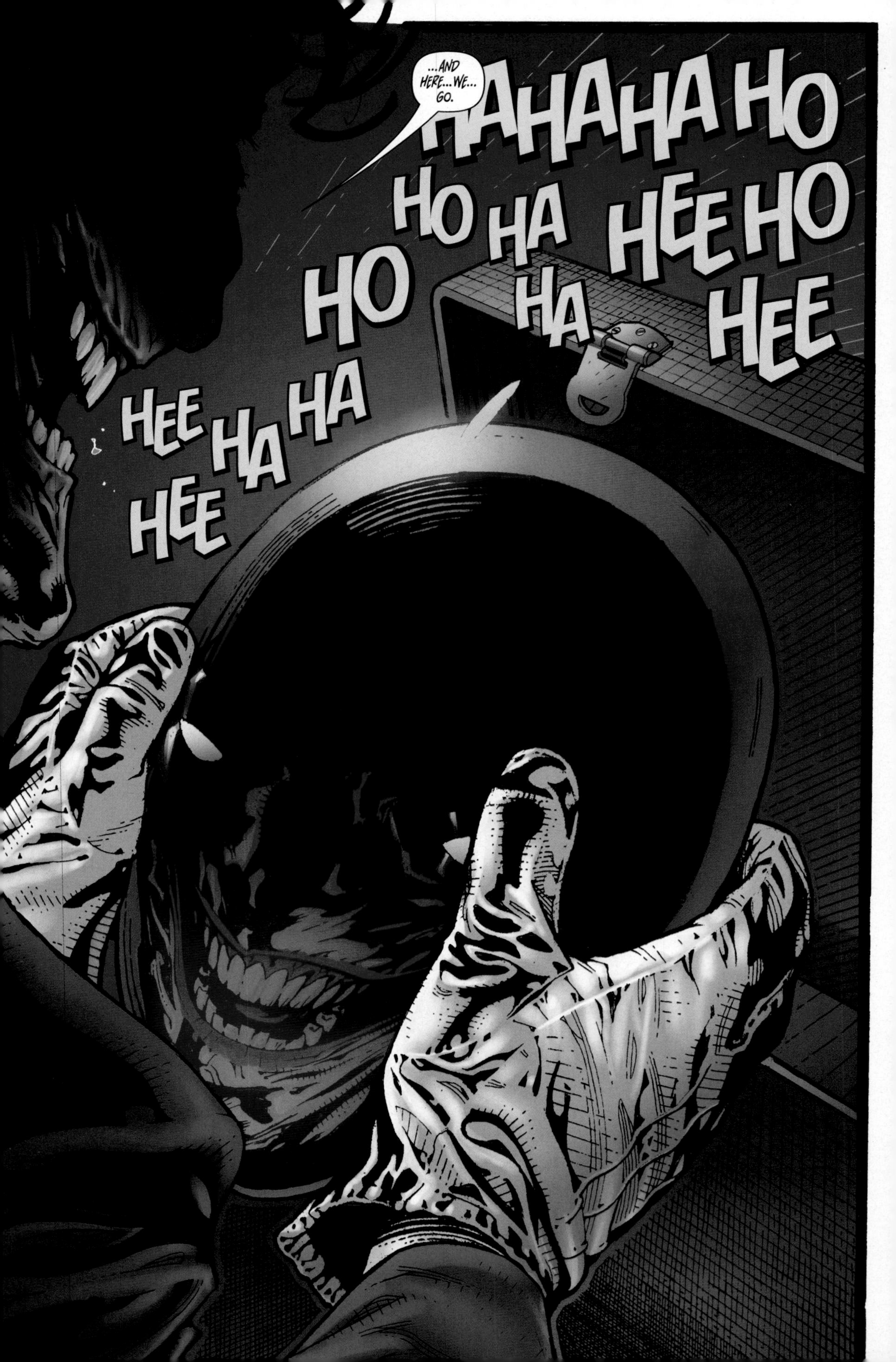
...AND HERE...WE... GO.
HAHAHA HO
HO HO HA HEE HO
HA HEE
HEE HA HA
HEE HA

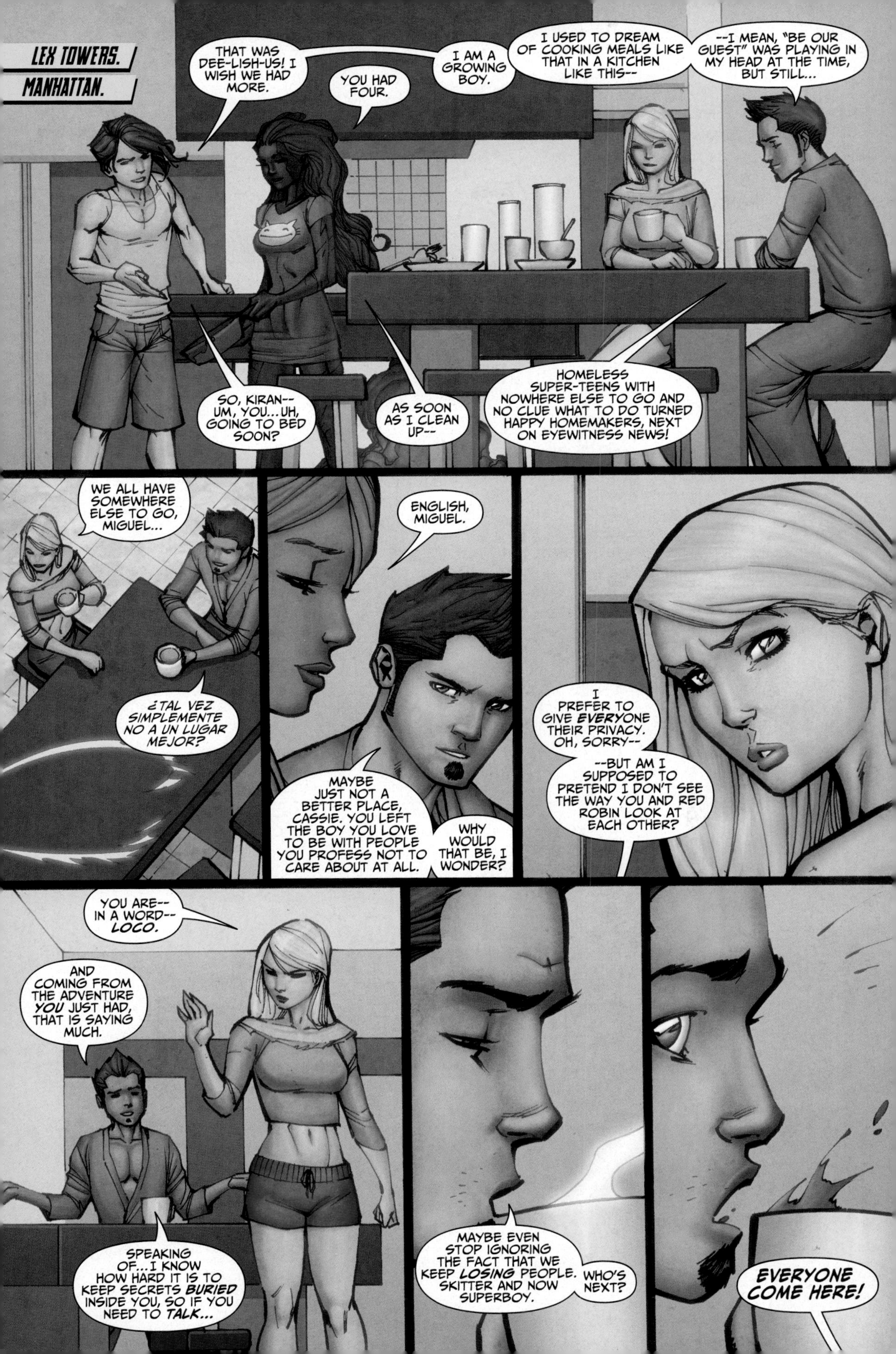
LEX TOWERS.
MANHATTAN.
THAT WAS DEE-LISH-US! I WISH WE HAD MORE.
YOU HAD FOUR.
I AM A GROWING BOY.
I USED TO DREAM OF COOKING MEALS LIKE THAT IN A KITCHEN LIKE THIS--
--I MEAN, "BE OUR GUEST" WAS PLAYING IN MY HEAD AT THE TIME, BUT STILL...
SO, KIRAN--UM, YOU...UH, GOING TO BED SOON?
AS SOON AS I CLEAN UP--
HOMELESS SUPER-TEENS WITH NOWHERE ELSE TO GO AND NO CLUE WHAT TO DO TURNED HAPPY HOMEMAKERS, NEXT ON EYEWITNESS NEWS!
WE ALL HAVE SOMEWHERE ELSE TO GO, MIGUEL...
¿TAL VEZ SIMPLEMENTE NO A UN LUGAR MEJOR?
ENGLISH, MIGUEL.
MAYBE JUST NOT A BETTER PLACE, CASSIE. YOU LEFT THE BOY YOU LOVE TO BE WITH PEOPLE YOU PROFESS NOT TO CARE ABOUT AT ALL.
WHY WOULD THAT BE, I WONDER?
I PREFER TO GIVE EVERYONE THEIR PRIVACY. OH, SORRY--
--BUT AM I SUPPOSED TO PRETEND I DON'T SEE THE WAY YOU AND RED ROBIN LOOK AT EACH OTHER?
YOU ARE--IN A WORD--LOCO.
AND COMING FROM THE ADVENTURE YOU JUST HAD, THAT IS SAYING MUCH.
SPEAKING OF...I KNOW HOW HARD IT IS TO KEEP SECRETS BURIED INSIDE YOU, SO IF YOU NEED TO TALK...
MAYBE EVEN STOP IGNORING THE FACT THAT WE KEEP LOSING PEOPLE. SKITTER AND NOW SUPERBOY.
WHO'S NEXT?
EVERYONE COME HERE!

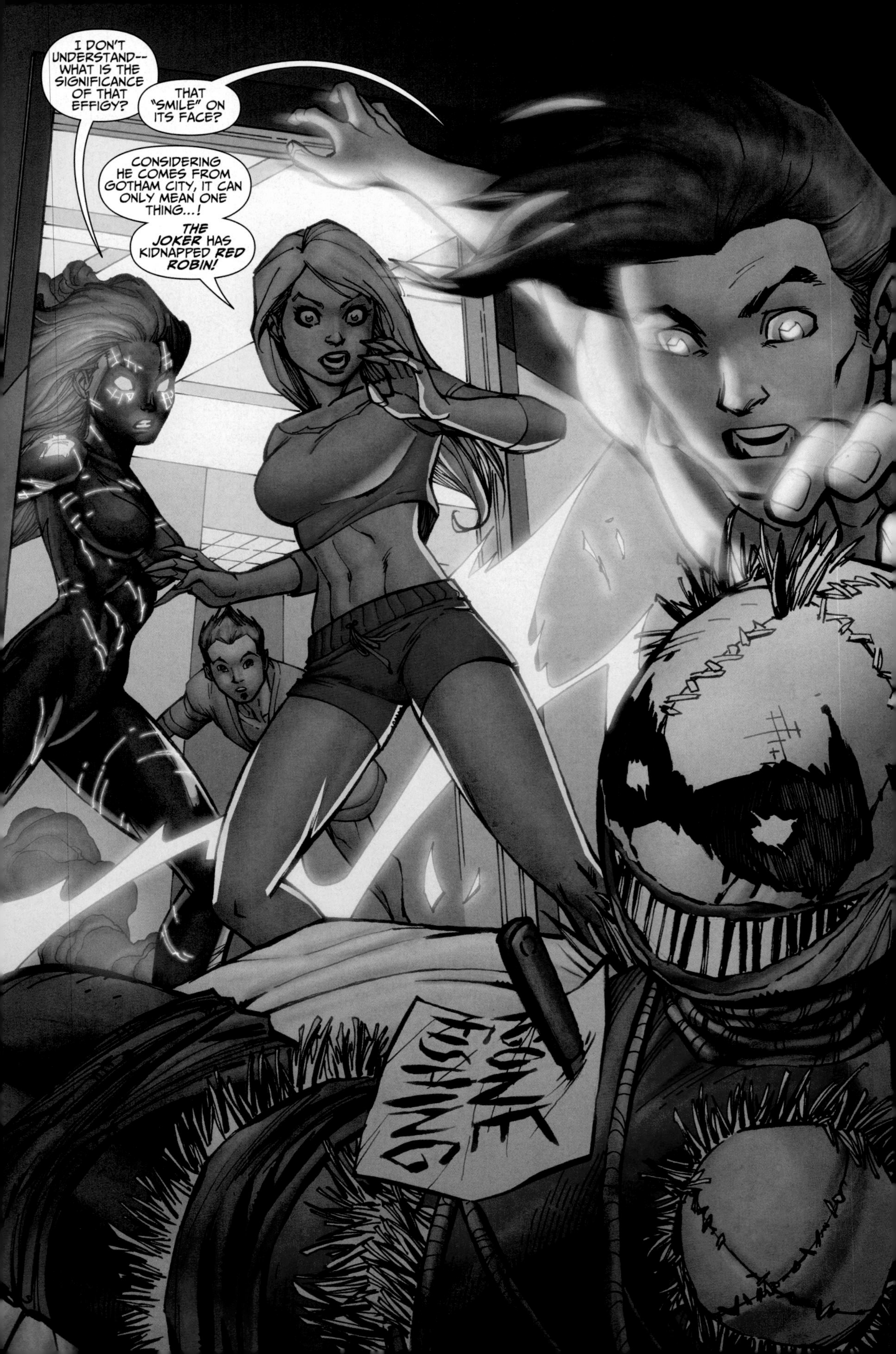
I DON'T UNDERSTAND-- WHAT IS THE SIGNIFICANCE OF THAT EFFIGY?
THAT "SMILE" ON ITS FACE?
CONSIDERING HE COMES FROM GOTHAM CITY, IT CAN ONLY MEAN ONE THING...!
THE JOKER HAS KIDNAPPED RED ROBIN!

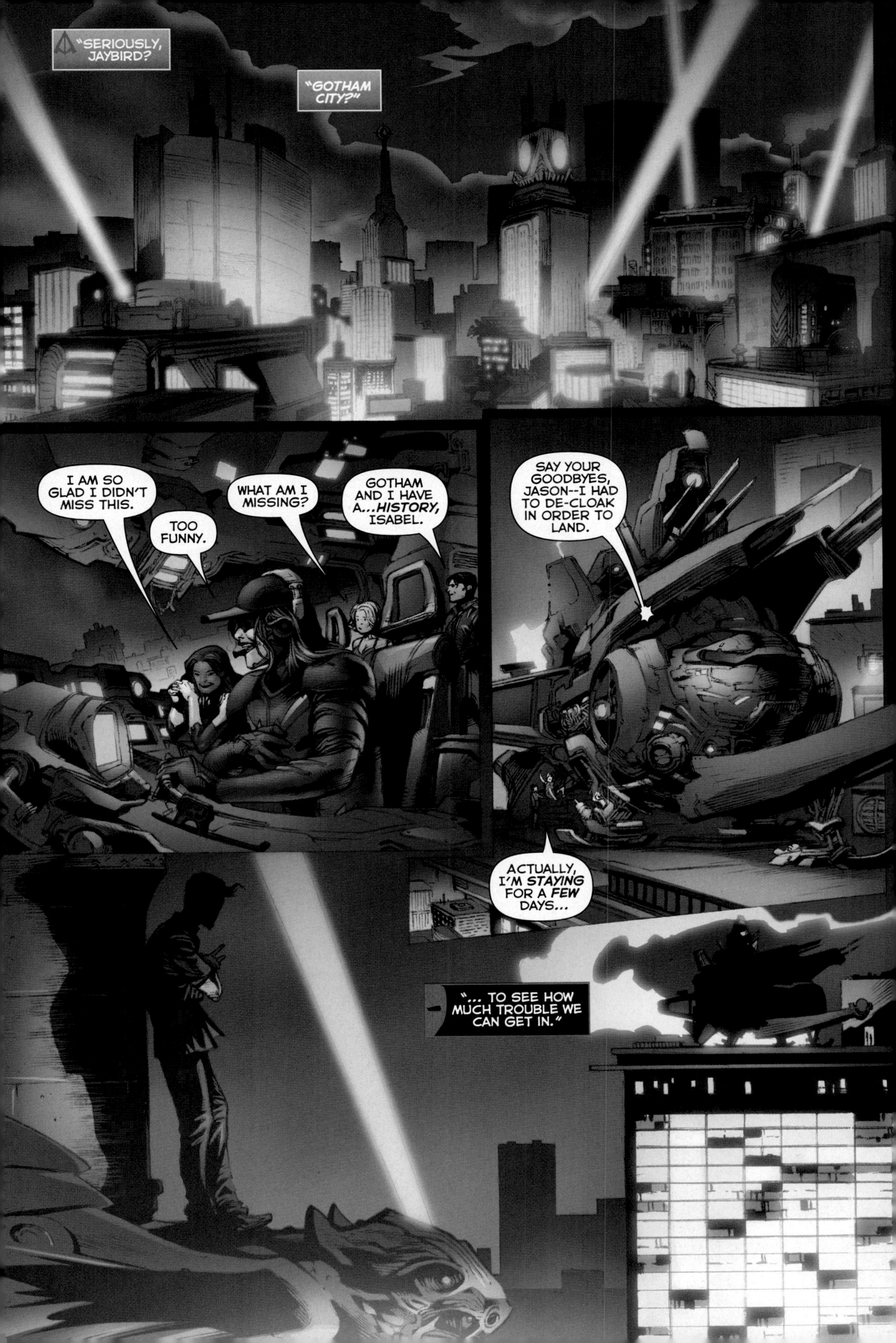
"SERIOUSLY, JAYBIRD?
"GOTHAM CITY?"
I AM SO GLAD I DIDN'T MISS THIS.
TOO FUNNY.
WHAT AM I MISSING?
GOTHAM AND I HAVE A...HISTORY, ISABEL.
SAY YOUR GOODBYES, JASON--I HAD TO DE-CLOAK IN ORDER TO LAND.
ACTUALLY, I'M STAYING FOR A FEW DAYS...
"... TO SEE HOW MUCH TROUBLE WE CAN GET IN."

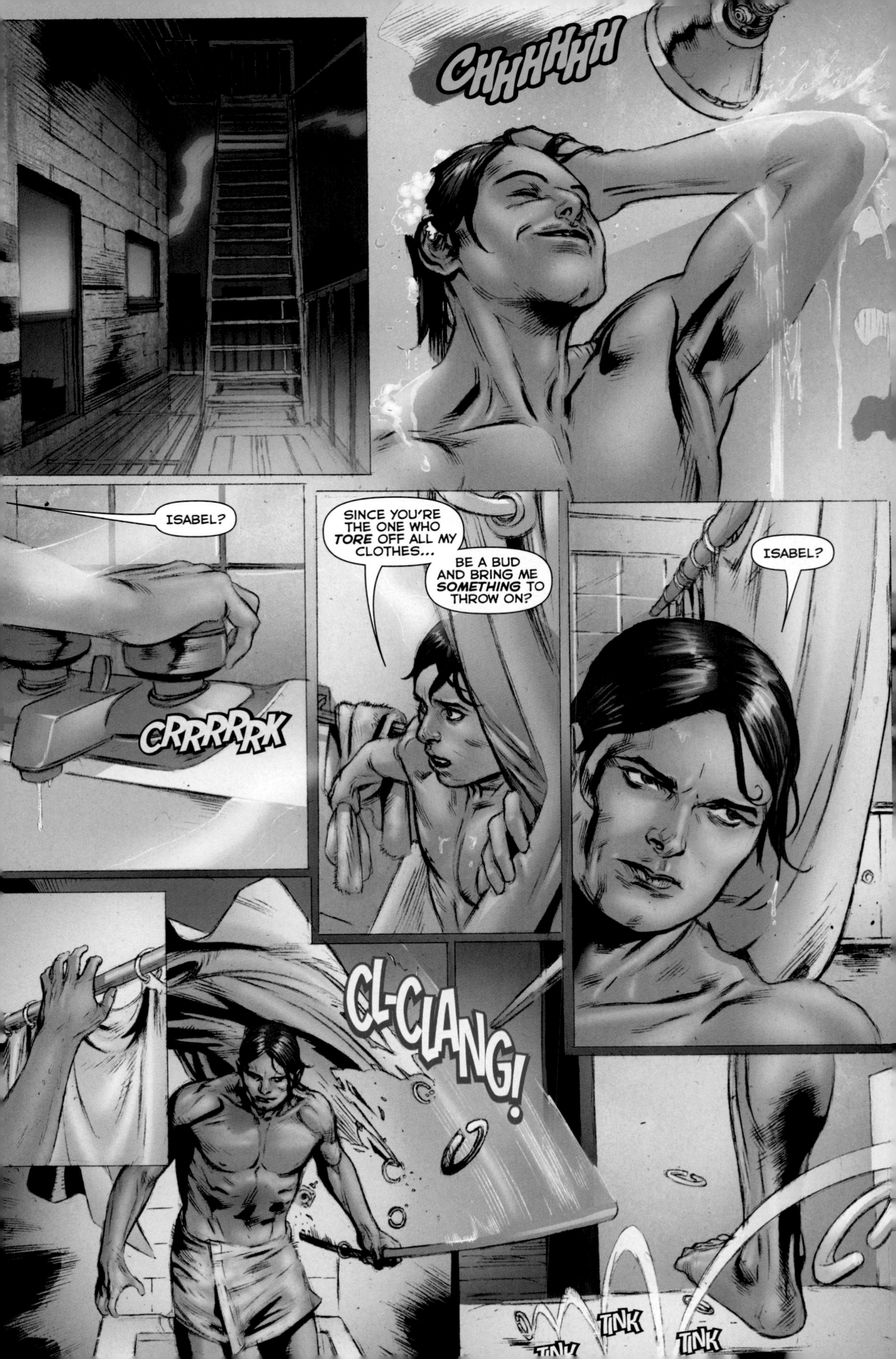
CHHHHHH
ISABEL?
CRRRRRK
SINCE YOU'RE THE ONE WHO TORE OFF ALL MY CLOTHES...
BE A BUD AND BRING ME SOMETHING TO THROW ON?
ISABEL?
CL-CLANG!
TINK
TINK
TINK

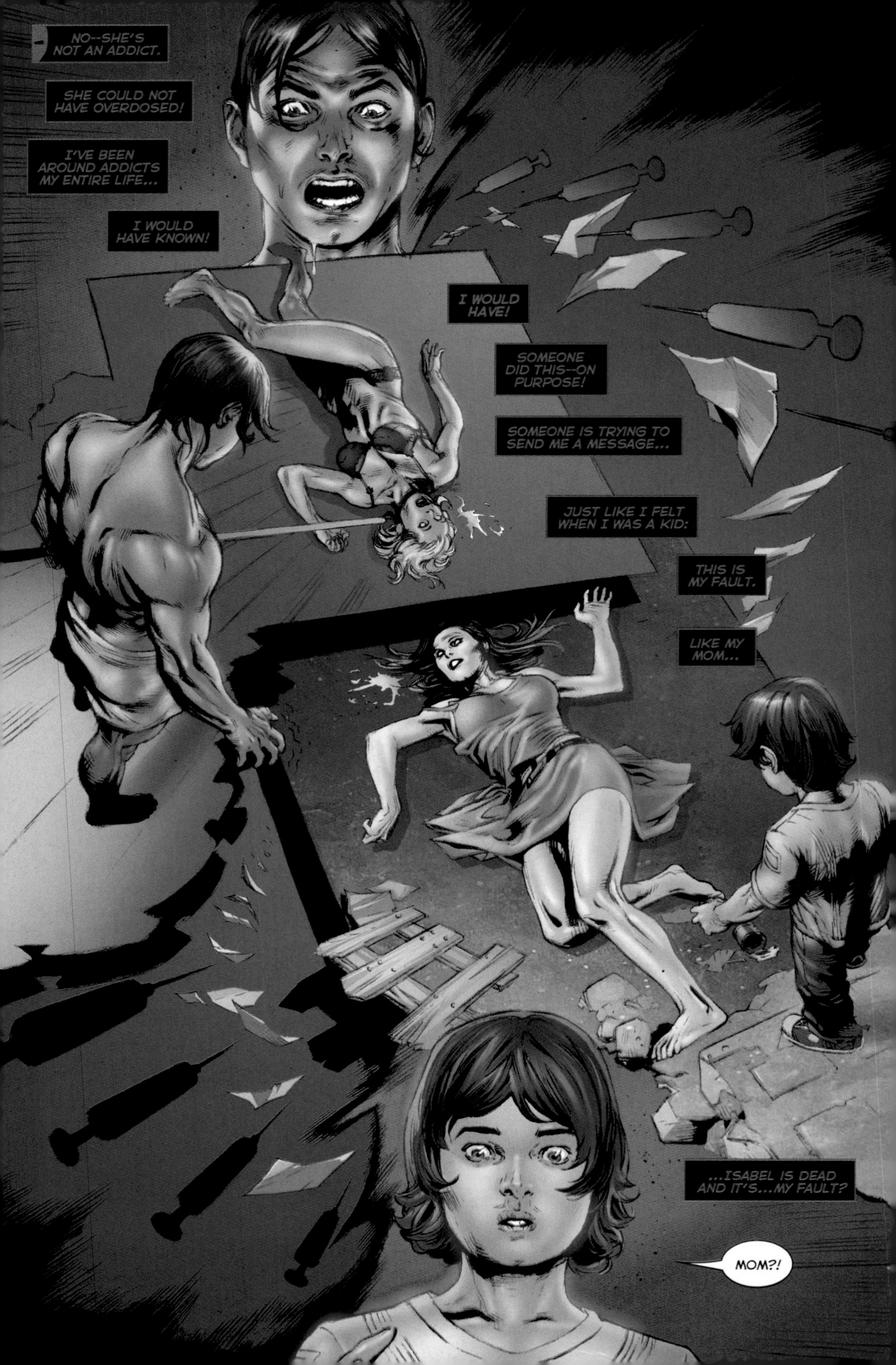
NO--SHE'S NOT AN ADDICT.
SHE COULD NOT HAVE OVERDOSED!
I'VE BEEN AROUND ADDICTS MY ENTIRE LIFE...
I WOULD HAVE KNOWN!
I WOULD HAVE!
SOMEONE DID THIS--ON PURPOSE!
SOMEONE IS TRYING TO SEND ME A MESSAGE...
JUST LIKE I FELT WHEN I WAS A KID:
THIS IS MY FAULT.
LIKE MY MOM...
...ISABEL IS DEAD AND IT'S...MY FAULT?
MOM?!

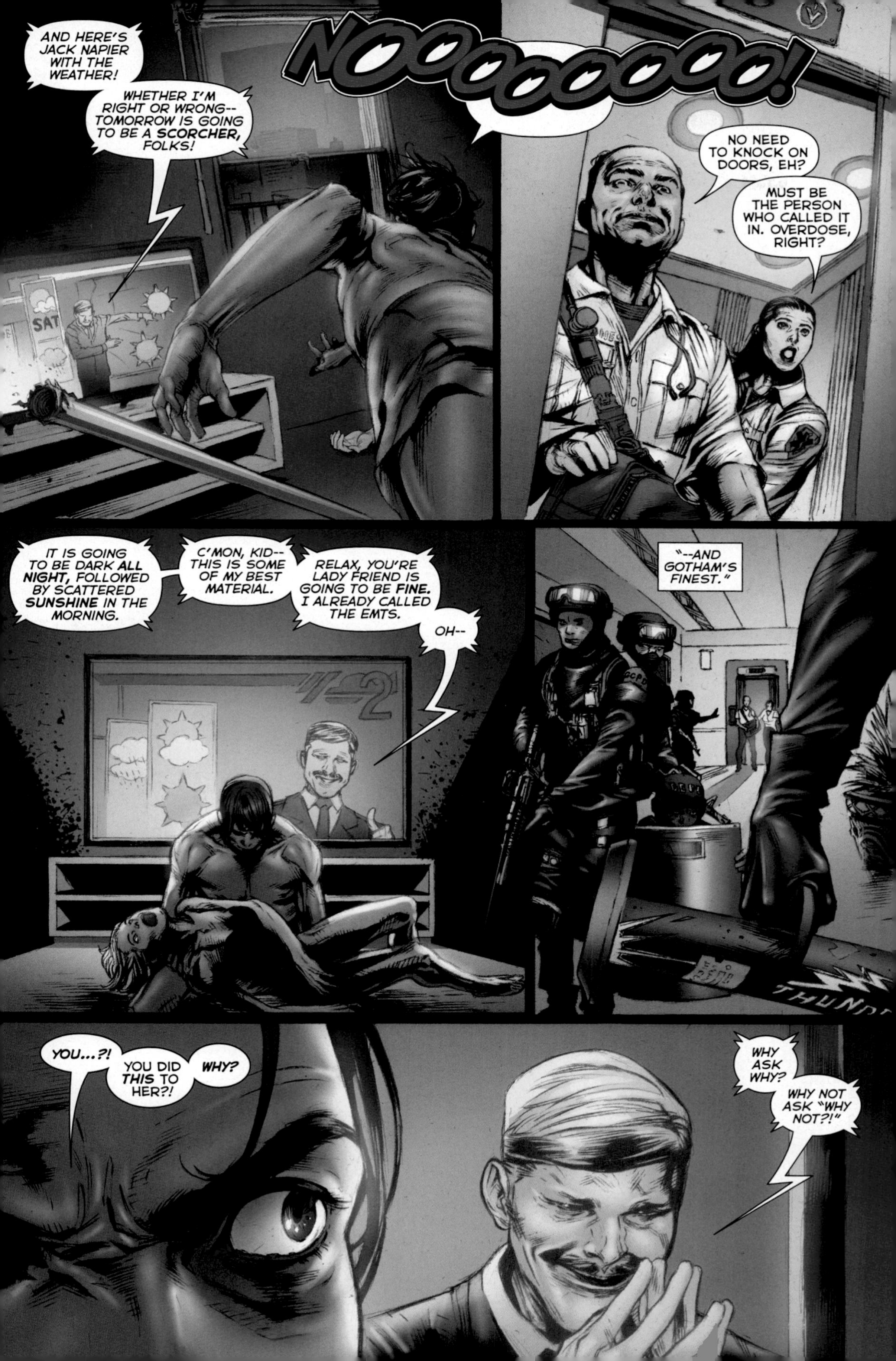
AND HERE'S JACK NAPIER WITH THE WEATHER!
WHETHER I'M RIGHT OR WRONG-- TOMORROW IS GOING TO BE A **SCORCHER,** FOLKS!
SAT
NOOOOOOOOOO!
NO NEED TO KNOCK ON DOORS, EH?
MUST BE THE PERSON WHO CALLED IT IN. OVERDOSE, RIGHT?
IT IS GOING TO BE DARK **ALL NIGHT,** FOLLOWED BY SCATTERED **SUNSHINE** IN THE MORNING.
C'MON, KID-- THIS IS SOME OF MY BEST MATERIAL.
RELAX, YOU'RE LADY FRIEND IS GOING TO BE **FINE.** I ALREADY CALLED THE EMTS.
OH--
2
"--AND GOTHAM'S FINEST."
GCPD
YOU...?!
YOU DID **THIS** TO HER?!
WHY?
WHY ASK WHY?
WHY NOT ASK "WHY NOT?!"

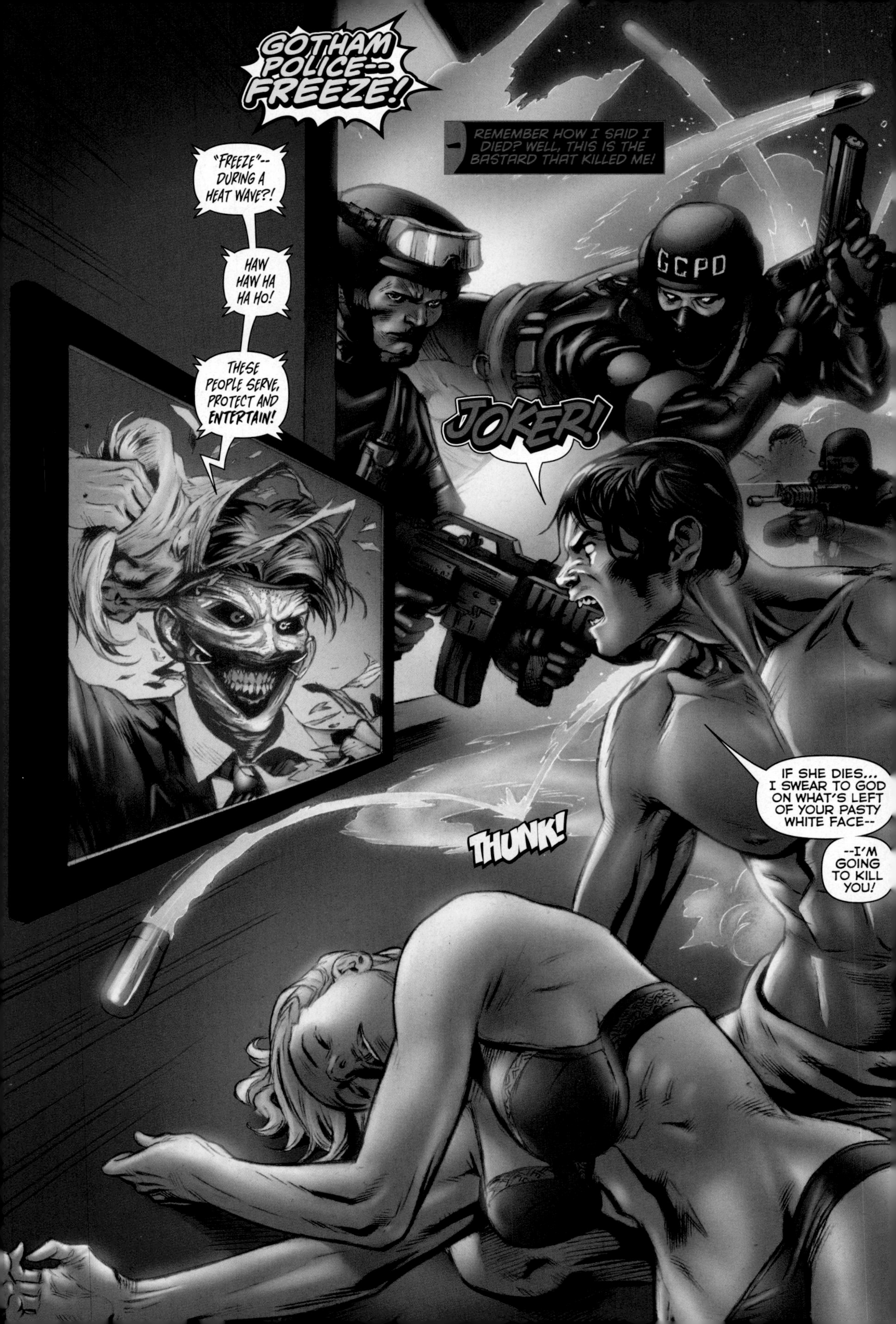
GOTHAM POLICE-- FREEZE!
REMEMBER HOW I SAID I DIED? WELL, THIS IS THE BASTARD THAT KILLED ME!
"FREEZE"-- DURING A HEAT WAVE?!
HAW HAW HA HA HO!
THESE PEOPLE SERVE, PROTECT AND ENTERTAIN!
GCPD
JOKER!
THUNK!
IF SHE DIES... I SWEAR TO GOD ON WHAT'S LEFT OF YOUR PASTY WHITE FACE--
--I'M GOING TO KILL YOU!

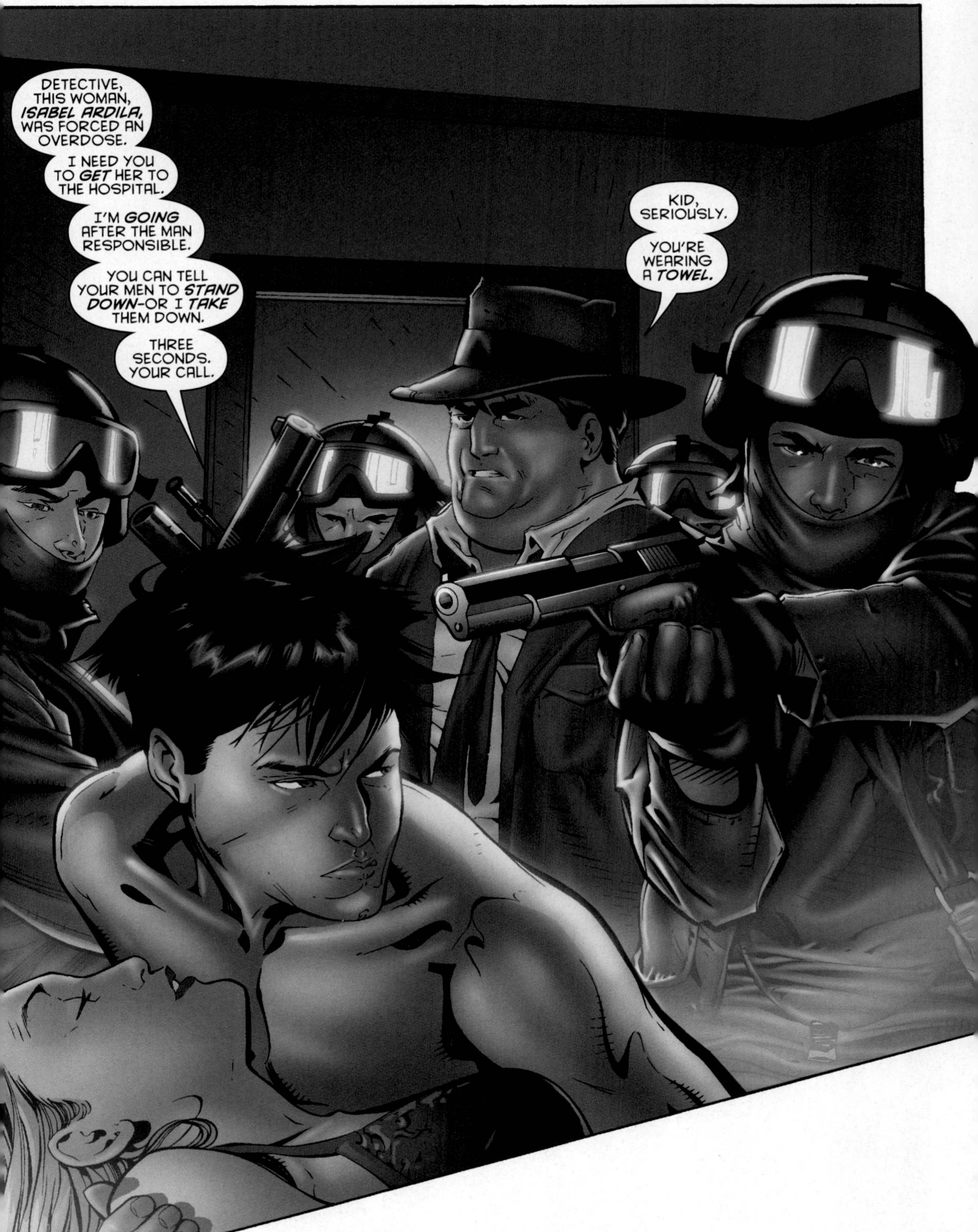
DETECTIVE, THIS WOMAN, *ISABEL ARDILA,* WAS FORCED AN OVERDOSE.
I NEED YOU TO *GET* HER TO THE HOSPITAL.
I'M *GOING* AFTER THE MAN RESPONSIBLE.
YOU CAN TELL YOUR MEN TO *STAND DOWN*–OR I *TAKE* THEM DOWN.
THREE SECONDS. YOUR CALL.
KID, SERIOUSLY.
YOU'RE WEARING A *TOWEL.*

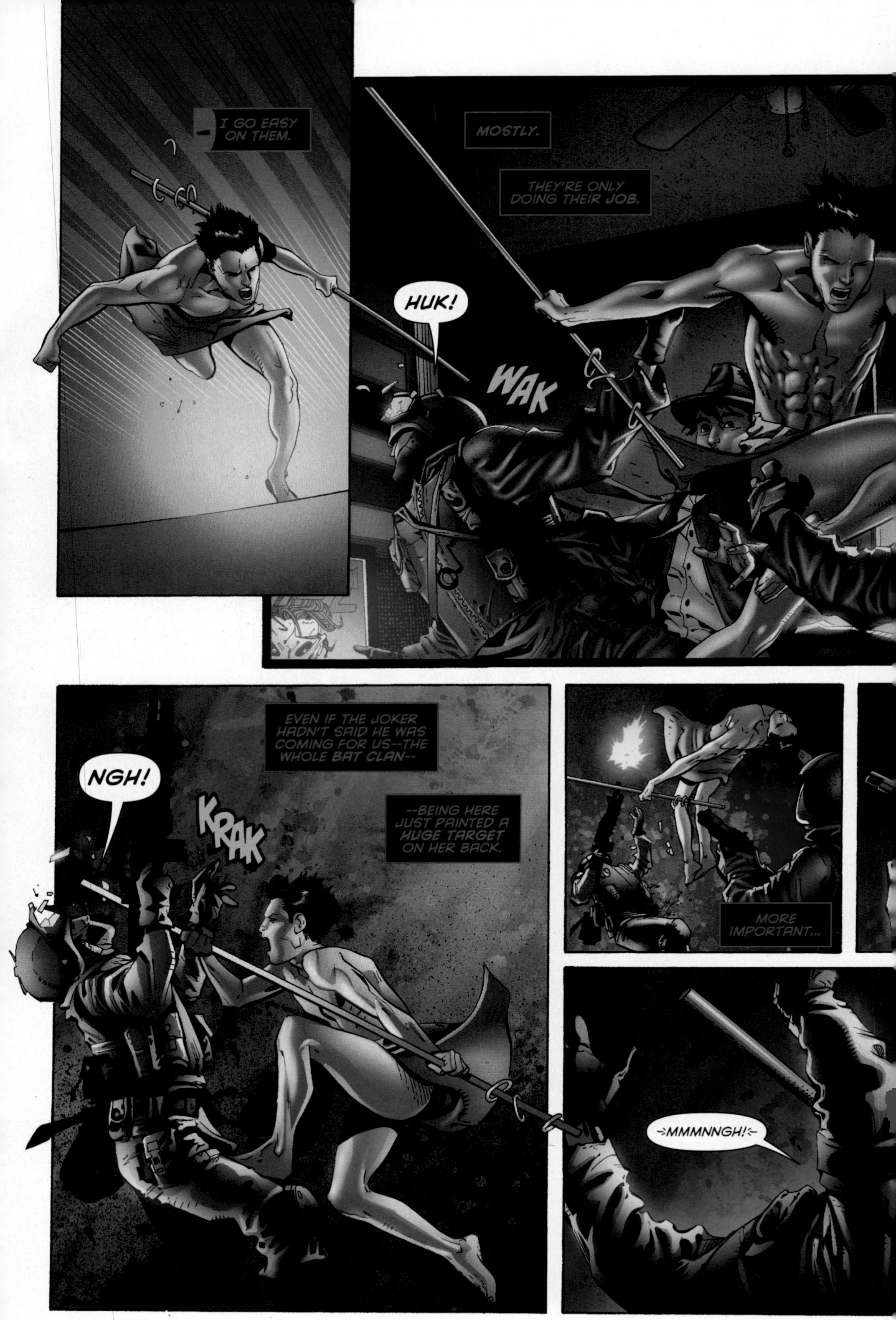
I GO EASY ON THEM.
MOSTLY.
THEY'RE ONLY DOING THEIR JOB.
HUK!
WAK
EVEN IF THE JOKER HADN'T SAID HE WAS COMING FOR US--THE WHOLE BAT CLAN--
NGH!
KRAK
--BEING HERE JUST PAINTED A HUGE TARGET ON HER BACK.
MORE IMPORTANT...
MMMNNGH!

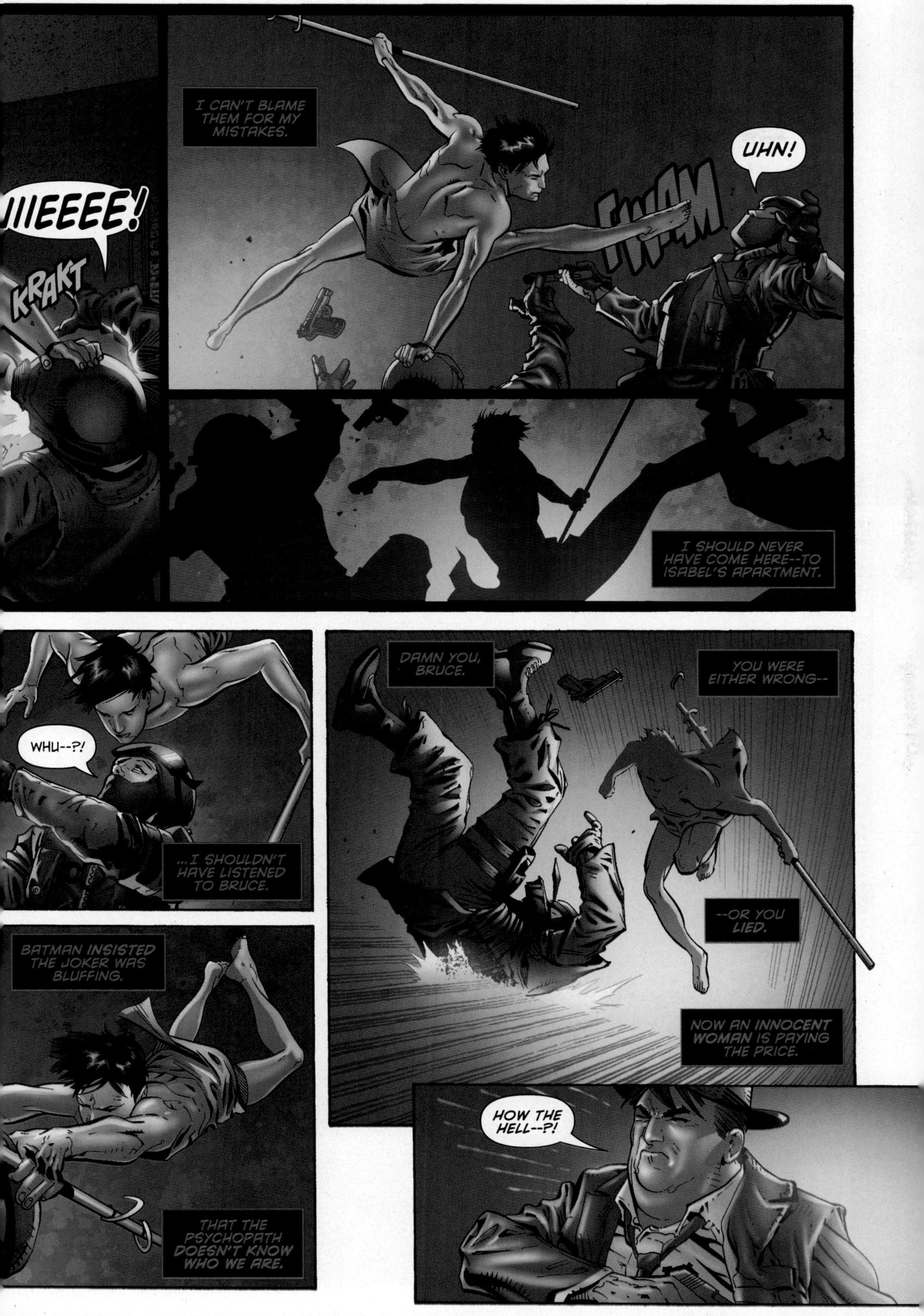

IIIEEEEE!
KRAKT
I CAN'T BLAME THEM FOR MY MISTAKES.
UHN!
WHAM
I SHOULD NEVER HAVE COME HERE--TO ISABEL'S APARTMENT.
WHU--?!
...I SHOULDN'T HAVE LISTENED TO BRUCE.
BATMAN INSISTED THE JOKER WAS BLUFFING.
THAT THE PSYCHOPATH DOESN'T KNOW WHO WE ARE.
DAMN YOU, BRUCE.
YOU WERE EITHER WRONG--
--OR YOU LIED.
NOW AN INNOCENT WOMAN IS PAYING THE PRICE.
HOW THE HELL--?!

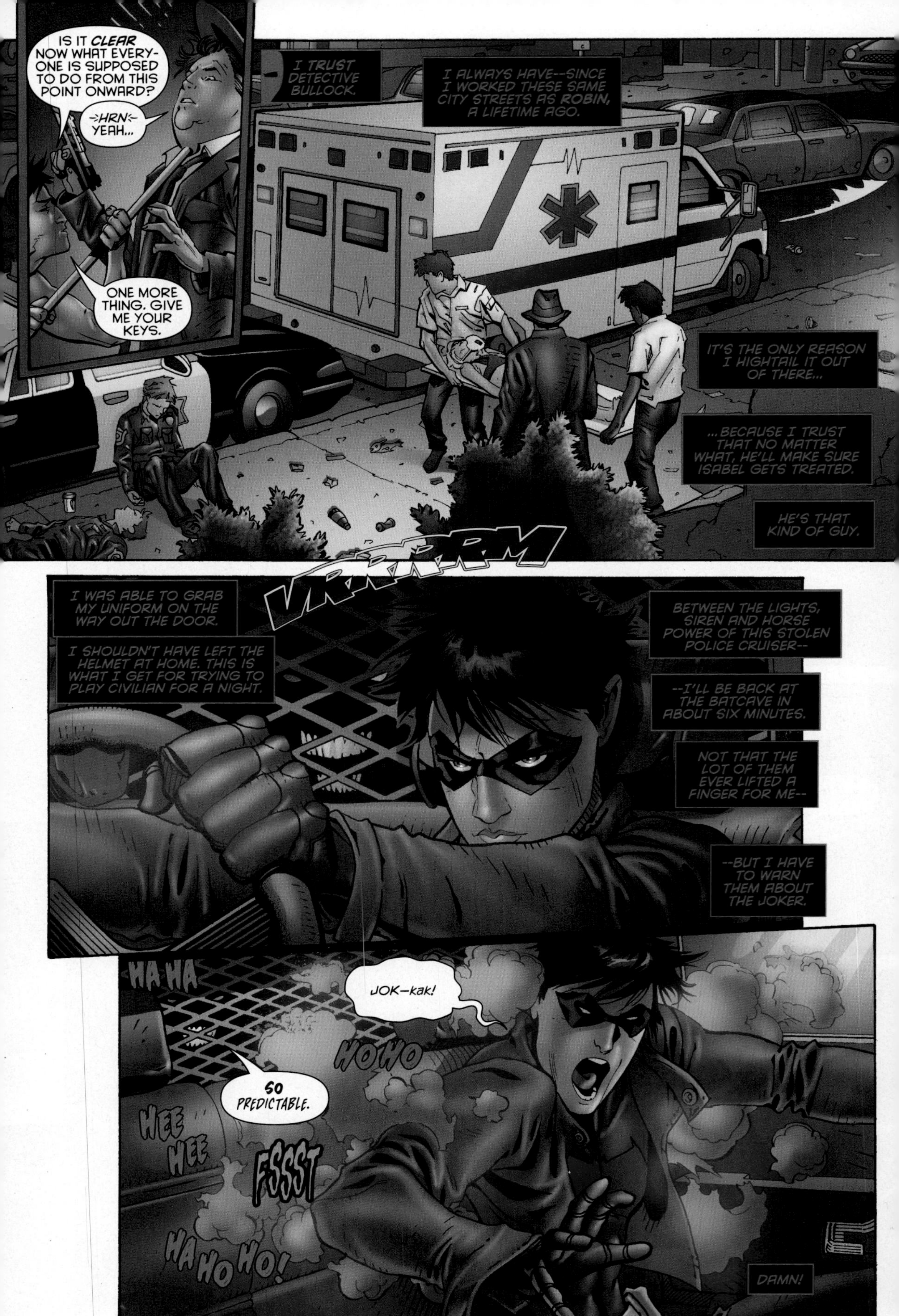

IS IT CLEAR NOW WHAT EVERY-ONE IS SUPPOSED TO DO FROM THIS POINT ONWARD?
-HRN- YEAH...
ONE MORE THING. GIVE ME YOUR KEYS.
I TRUST DETECTIVE BULLOCK.
I ALWAYS HAVE--SINCE I WORKED THESE SAME CITY STREETS AS ROBIN, A LIFETIME AGO.
IT'S THE ONLY REASON I HIGHTAIL IT OUT OF THERE...
...BECAUSE I TRUST THAT NO MATTER WHAT, HE'LL MAKE SURE ISABEL GETS TREATED.
HE'S THAT KIND OF GUY.
VRRRROOM
I WAS ABLE TO GRAB MY UNIFORM ON THE WAY OUT THE DOOR.
I SHOULDN'T HAVE LEFT THE HELMET AT HOME. THIS IS WHAT I GET FOR TRYING TO PLAY CIVILIAN FOR A NIGHT.
BETWEEN THE LIGHTS, SIREN AND HORSE POWER OF THIS STOLEN POLICE CRUISER--
--I'LL BE BACK AT THE BATCAVE IN ABOUT SIX MINUTES.
NOT THAT THE LOT OF THEM EVER LIFTED A FINGER FOR ME--
--BUT I HAVE TO WARN THEM ABOUT THE JOKER.
HA HA
JOK-kak!
HO HO
SO PREDICTABLE.
HEE HEE
FSSST
HA HO HO!
DAMN!

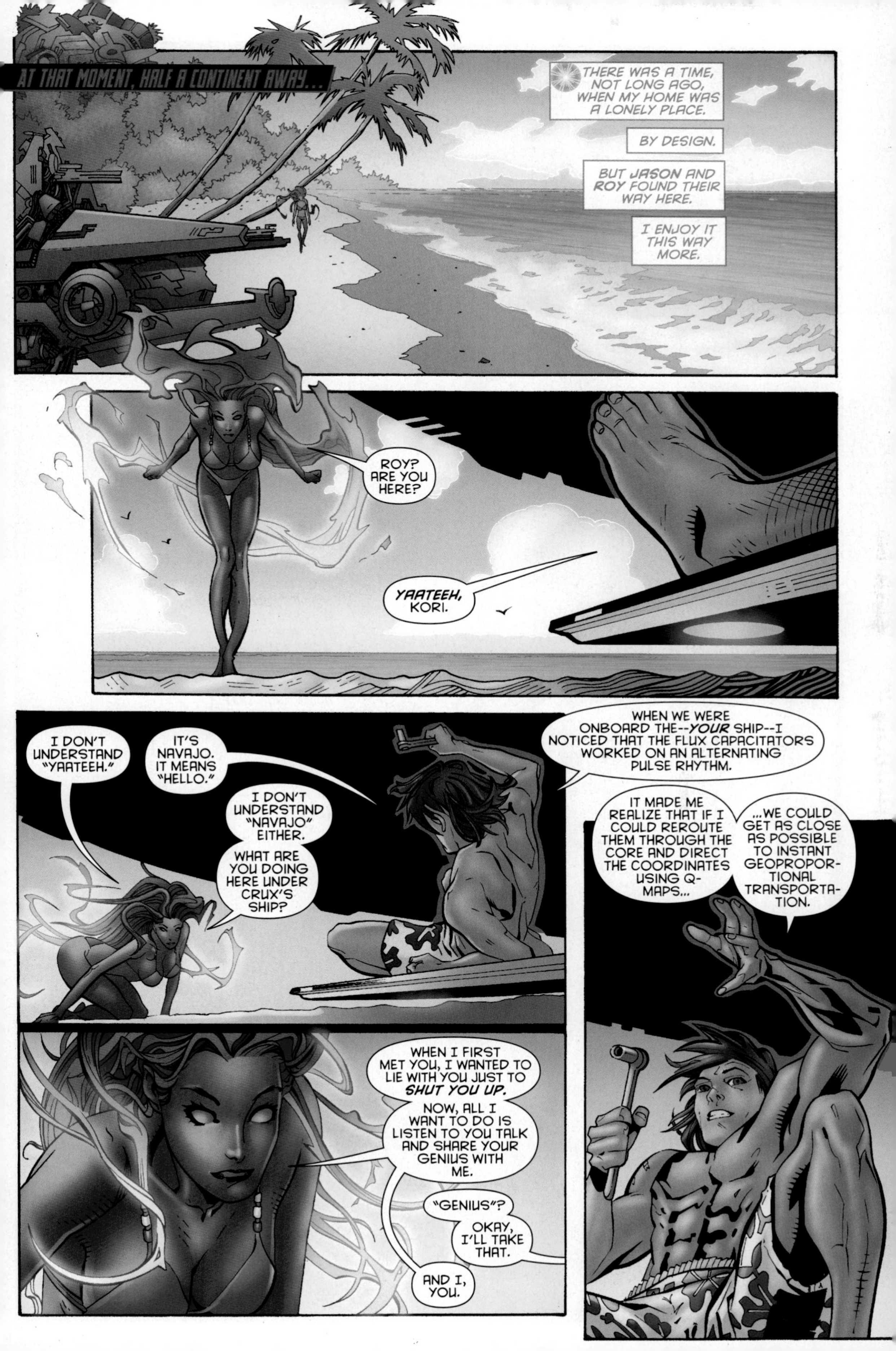
AT THAT MOMENT, HALF A CONTINENT AWAY...
THERE WAS A TIME, NOT LONG AGO, WHEN MY HOME WAS A LONELY PLACE.
BY DESIGN.
BUT JASON AND ROY FOUND THEIR WAY HERE.
I ENJOY IT THIS WAY MORE.
ROY? ARE YOU HERE?
YAATEEH, KORI.
I DON'T UNDERSTAND "YAATEEH."
IT'S NAVAJO. IT MEANS "HELLO."
I DON'T UNDERSTAND "NAVAJO" EITHER.
WHAT ARE YOU DOING HERE UNDER CRUX'S SHIP?
WHEN WE WERE ONBOARD THE--YOUR SHIP--I NOTICED THAT THE FLUX CAPACITATORS WORKED ON AN ALTERNATING PULSE RHYTHM.
IT MADE ME REALIZE THAT IF I COULD REROUTE THEM THROUGH THE CORE AND DIRECT THE COORDINATES USING Q-MAPS...
...WE COULD GET AS CLOSE AS POSSIBLE TO INSTANT GEOPROPORTIONAL TRANSPORTATION.
WHEN I FIRST MET YOU, I WANTED TO LIE WITH YOU JUST TO SHUT YOU UP.
NOW, ALL I WANT TO DO IS LISTEN TO YOU TALK AND SHARE YOUR GENIUS WITH ME.
"GENIUS"?
OKAY, I'LL TAKE THAT.
AND I, YOU.

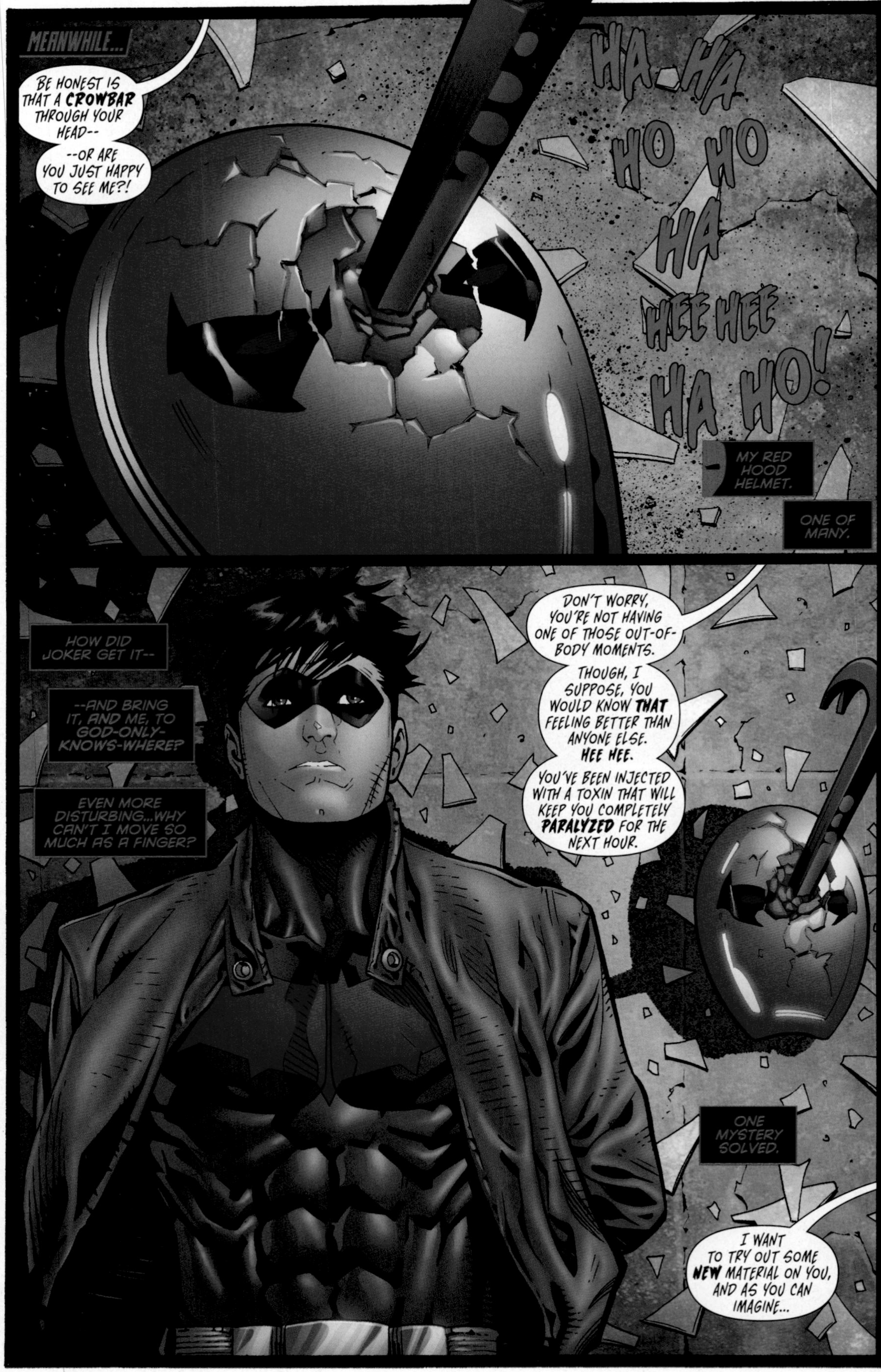

MEANWHILE...
BE HONEST IS THAT A CROWBAR THROUGH YOUR HEAD--
--OR ARE YOU JUST HAPPY TO SEE ME?!
HA HA HO HO HA HEE HEE HA HO!
MY RED HOOD HELMET.
ONE OF MANY.
HOW DID JOKER GET IT--
--AND BRING IT, AND ME, TO GOD-ONLY-KNOWS-WHERE?
EVEN MORE DISTURBING...WHY CAN'T I MOVE SO MUCH AS A FINGER?
DON'T WORRY, YOU'RE NOT HAVING ONE OF THOSE OUT-OF-BODY MOMENTS.
THOUGH, I SUPPOSE, YOU WOULD KNOW THAT FEELING BETTER THAN ANYONE ELSE. HEE HEE.
YOU'VE BEEN INJECTED WITH A TOXIN THAT WILL KEEP YOU COMPLETELY PARALYZED FOR THE NEXT HOUR.
ONE MYSTERY SOLVED.
I WANT TO TRY OUT SOME NEW MATERIAL ON YOU, AND AS YOU CAN IMAGINE...

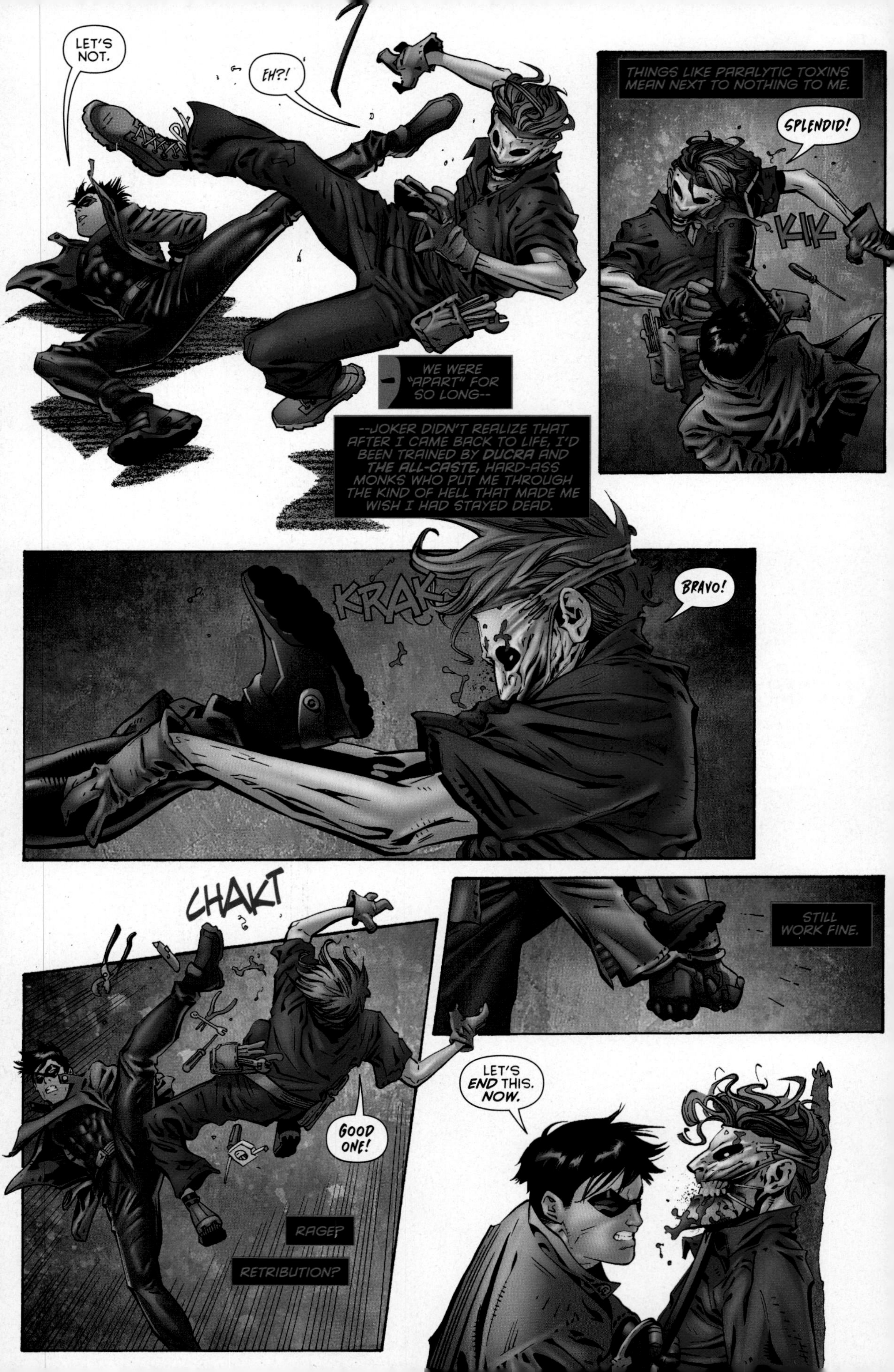

LET'S NOT.
EH?!
THINGS LIKE PARALYTIC TOXINS MEAN NEXT TO NOTHING TO ME.
SPLENDID!
KIK
WE WERE "APART" FOR SO LONG--
--JOKER DIDN'T REALIZE THAT AFTER I CAME BACK TO LIFE, I'D BEEN TRAINED BY DUCRA AND THE ALL-CASTE, HARD-ASS MONKS WHO PUT ME THROUGH THE KIND OF HELL THAT MADE ME WISH I HAD STAYED DEAD.
KRAK
BRAVO!
CHAKT
GOOD ONE!
RAGE?
RETRIBUTION?
STILL WORK FINE.
LET'S END THIS. NOW.

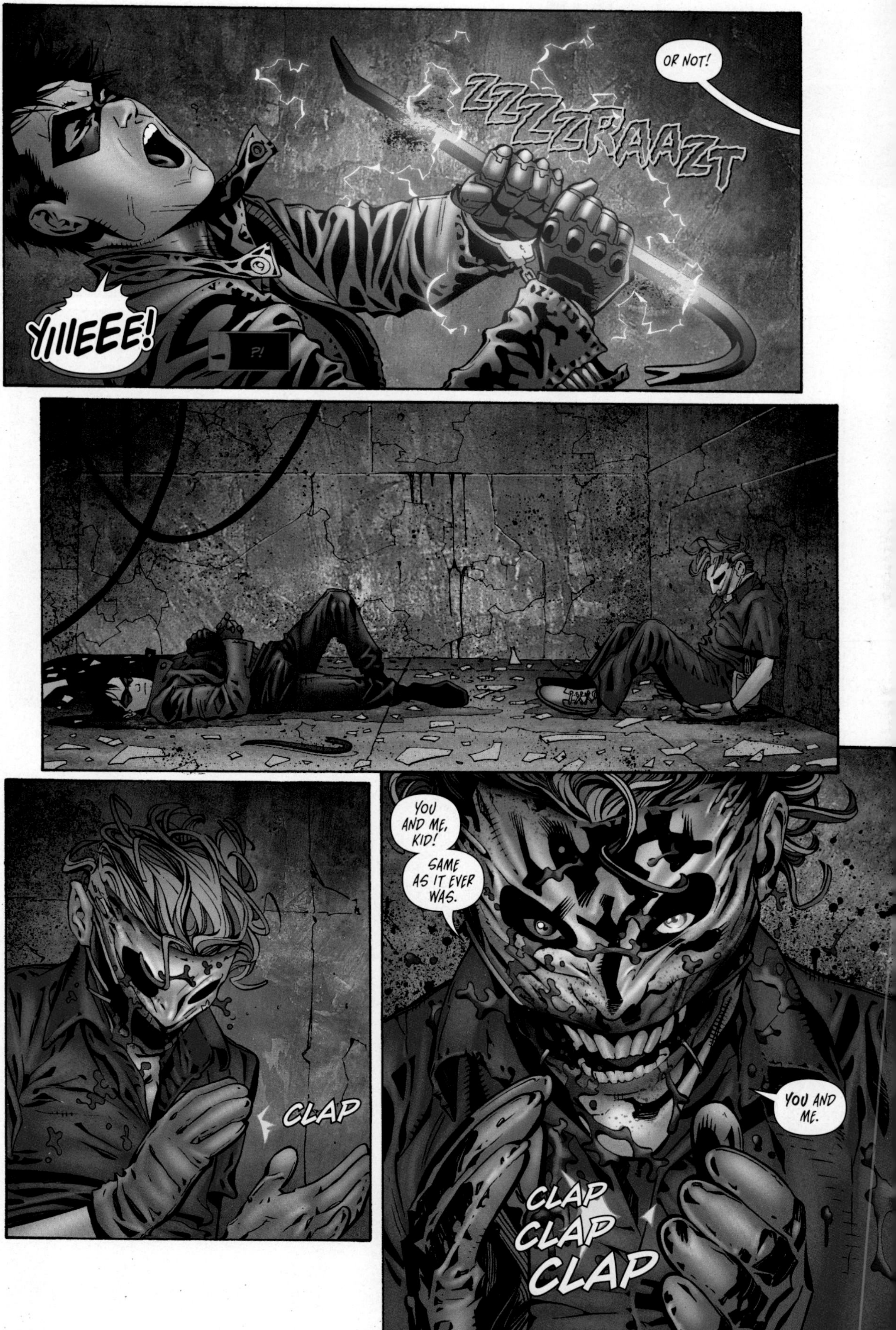
OR NOT!
ZZZZRAAZT
YIIIEEE!
?!
YOU AND ME, KID!
SAME AS IT EVER WAS.
CLAP
YOU AND ME.
CLAP
CLAP
CLAP

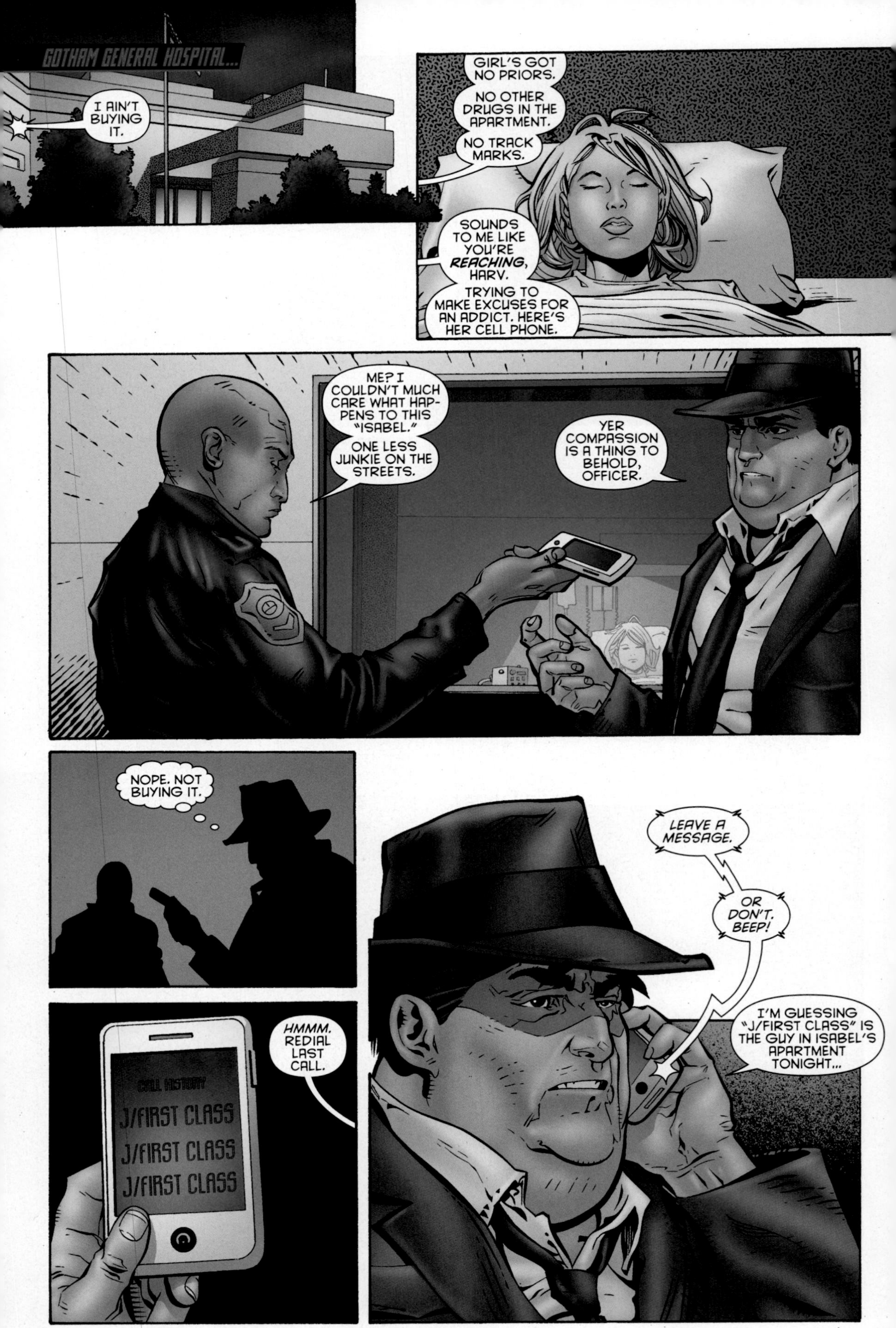
GOTHAM GENERAL HOSPITAL...
I AIN'T BUYING IT.
GIRL'S GOT NO PRIORS.
NO OTHER DRUGS IN THE APARTMENT.
NO TRACK MARKS.
SOUNDS TO ME LIKE YOU'RE *REACHING*, HARV.
TRYING TO MAKE EXCUSES FOR AN ADDICT. HERE'S HER CELL PHONE.
ME? I COULDN'T MUCH CARE WHAT HAPPENS TO THIS "ISABEL."
ONE LESS JUNKIE ON THE STREETS.
YER COMPASSION IS A THING TO BEHOLD, OFFICER.
NOPE. NOT BUYING IT.
CALL HISTORY
J/FIRST CLASS
J/FIRST CLASS
J/FIRST CLASS
HMMM. REDIAL LAST CALL.
LEAVE A MESSAGE.
OR DON'T. BEEP!
I'M GUESSING "J/FIRST CLASS" IS THE GUY IN ISABEL'S APARTMENT TONIGHT...

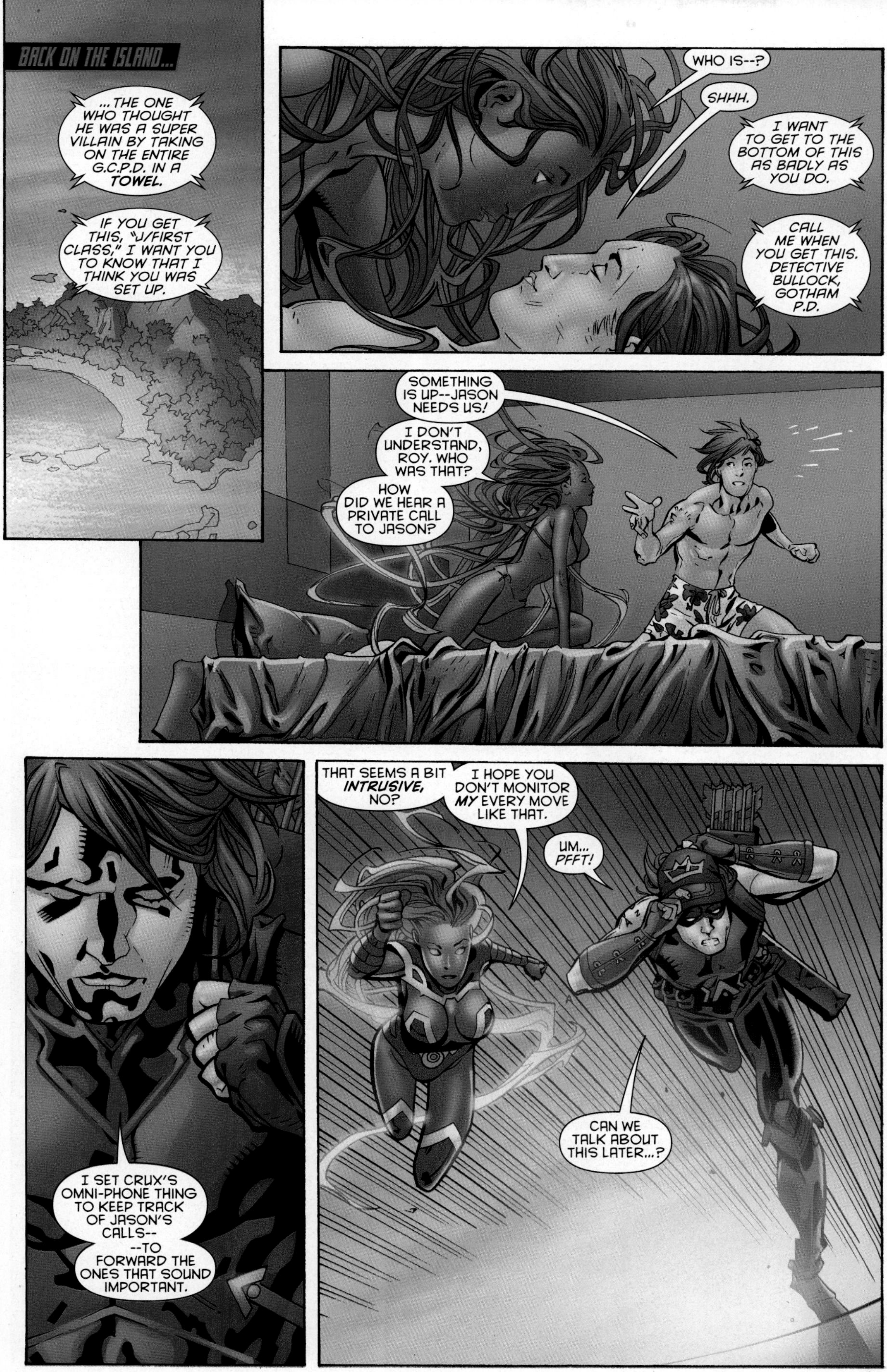
BACK ON THE ISLAND...
...THE ONE WHO THOUGHT HE WAS A SUPER VILLAIN BY TAKING ON THE ENTIRE G.C.P.D. IN A TOWEL.
IF YOU GET THIS, "J/FIRST CLASS," I WANT YOU TO KNOW THAT I THINK YOU WAS SET UP.
WHO IS--?
SHHH.
I WANT TO GET TO THE BOTTOM OF THIS AS BADLY AS YOU DO.
CALL ME WHEN YOU GET THIS. DETECTIVE BULLOCK, GOTHAM P.D.
SOMETHING IS UP--JASON NEEDS US!
I DON'T UNDERSTAND, ROY. WHO WAS THAT?
HOW DID WE HEAR A PRIVATE CALL TO JASON?
I SET CRUX'S OMNI-PHONE THING TO KEEP TRACK OF JASON'S CALLS--
--TO FORWARD THE ONES THAT SOUND IMPORTANT.
THAT SEEMS A BIT INTRUSIVE, NO?
I HOPE YOU DON'T MONITOR MY EVERY MOVE LIKE THAT.
UM... PFFT!
CAN WE TALK ABOUT THIS LATER...?

OW.

WAKEY WAKEY, SON.

YOU'LL MISS THE FIRST REEL AND THEN YOU'LL BE **LOST!**

WHERE THE HELL AM I?

COME OUT HERE AND SHOW WHAT'S LEFT OF YOUR FACE!

ARE YOU KIDDING, BOY?

THIS IS **PERSONAL!** AND I'VE GOT AN EVEN **BETTER** SURPISE FOR YOU.

"BOY."

"SON."

IF THIS IS **PERSONAL**--LIKE YOU SAY--WHY DON'T YOU CALL ME BY MY NAME?

MY **REAL** NAME?

SO CLEVER YOU ARE, HEE HEE!

EVEN IF I DIDN'T **BEAT YOU TO DEATH** LAST TIME, YOU'D **STILL** BE MY FLAVOR FAVE!

YOU WANT TO KNOW HOW MUCH I **REALLY** KNOW?

THE ANSWER IS RIGHT IN FRONT OF YOU.

...A BULLET FRAGMENT?

THIS IS OF NO SIGNIFICANCE TO ME. AT ALL.

NOW WHO IS BLUFFING?

IT...CAN'T BE.

THAT WOULD BE...

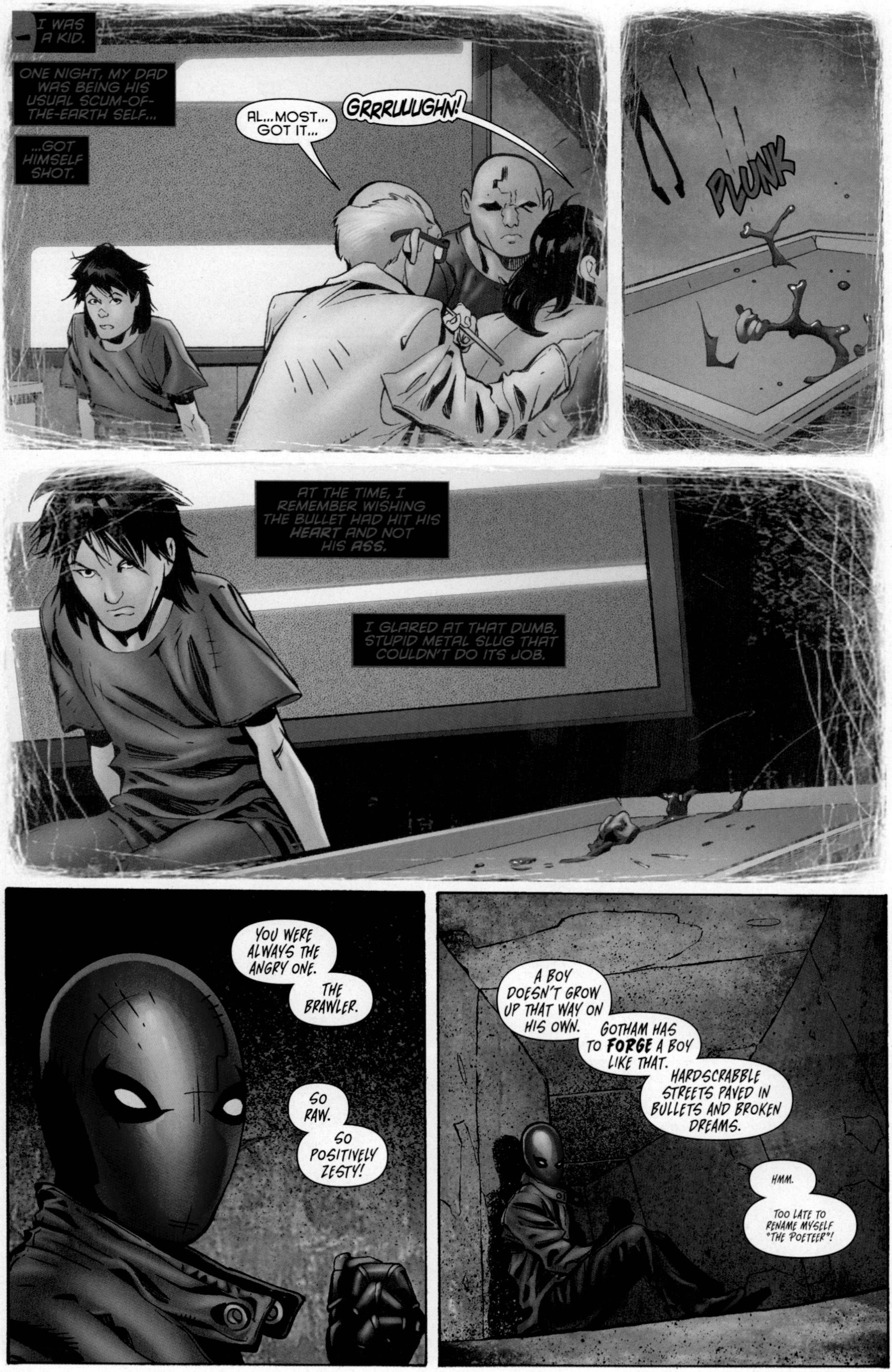

I WAS A KID.
ONE NIGHT, MY DAD WAS BEING HIS USUAL SCUM-OF-THE-EARTH SELF...
...GOT HIMSELF SHOT.
AL...MOST... GOT IT...
GRRRUUUGHN!
PLUNK
AT THE TIME, I REMEMBER WISHING THE BULLET HAD HIT HIS HEART AND NOT HIS ASS.
I GLARED AT THAT DUMB, STUPID METAL SLUG THAT COULDN'T DO ITS JOB.
YOU WERE ALWAYS THE ANGRY ONE.
THE BRAWLER.
SO RAW.
SO POSITIVELY ZESTY!
A BOY DOESN'T GROW UP THAT WAY ON HIS OWN.
GOTHAM HAS TO **FORGE** A BOY LIKE THAT.
HARDSCRABBLE STREETS PAVED IN BULLETS AND BROKEN DREAMS.
HMM.
TOO LATE TO RENAME MYSELF "THE POETEER"?

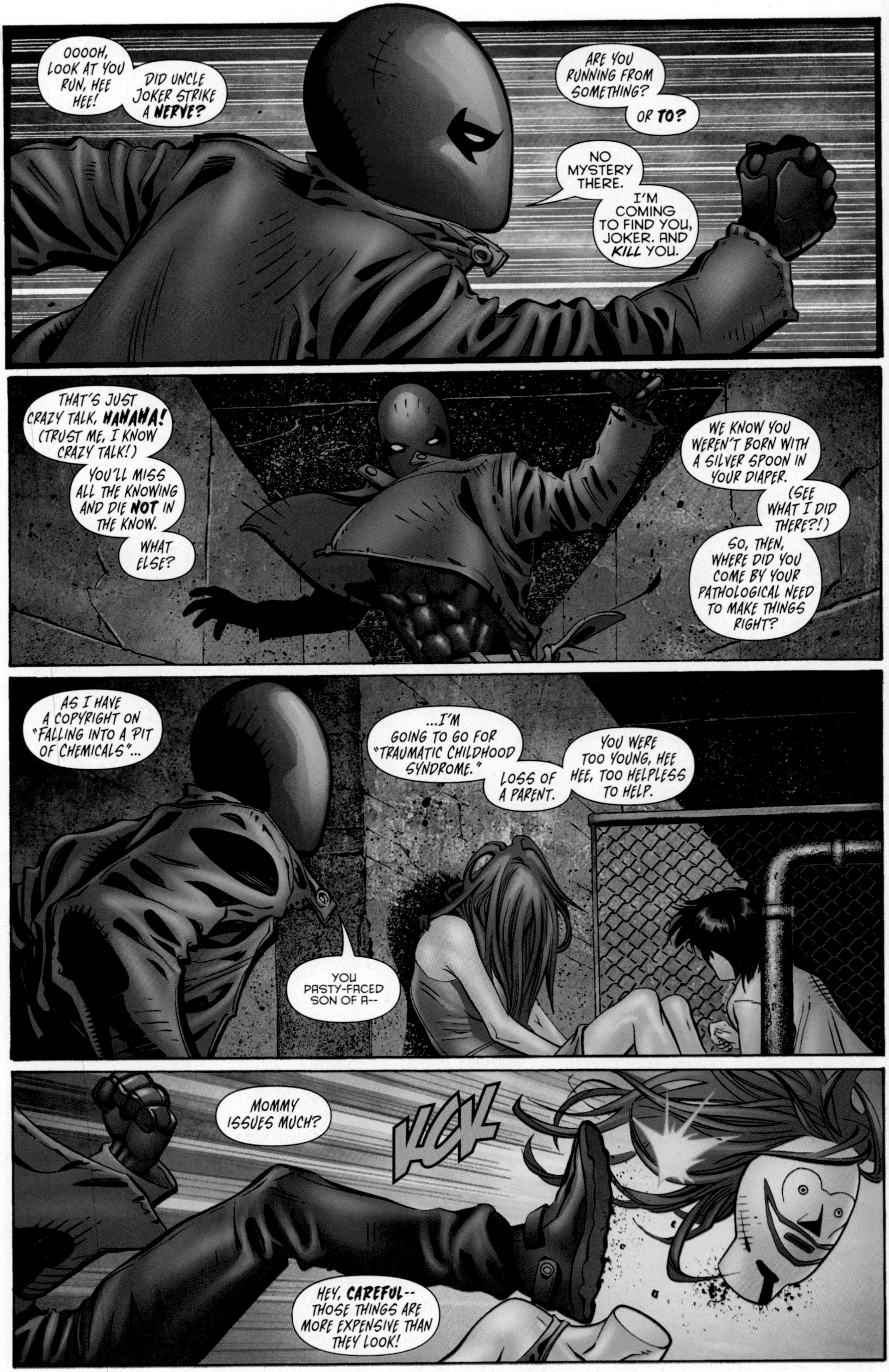
OOOOH, LOOK AT YOU RUN, HEE HEE!
DID UNCLE JOKER STRIKE A NERVE?
ARE YOU RUNNING FROM SOMETHING?
OR TO?
NO MYSTERY THERE.
I'M COMING TO FIND YOU, JOKER. AND KILL YOU.
THAT'S JUST CRAZY TALK, HAHAHA! (TRUST ME, I KNOW CRAZY TALK!)
YOU'LL MISS ALL THE KNOWING AND DIE NOT IN THE KNOW.
WHAT ELSE?
WE KNOW YOU WEREN'T BORN WITH A SILVER SPOON IN YOUR DIAPER.
(SEE WHAT I DID THERE?!)
SO, THEN, WHERE DID YOU COME BY YOUR PATHOLOGICAL NEED TO MAKE THINGS RIGHT?
AS I HAVE A COPYRIGHT ON "FALLING INTO A PIT OF CHEMICALS"...
...I'M GOING TO GO FOR "TRAUMATIC CHILDHOOD SYNDROME."
LOSS OF A PARENT.
YOU WERE TOO YOUNG, HEE HEE, TOO HELPLESS TO HELP.
YOU PASTY-FACED SON OF A--
MOMMY ISSUES MUCH?
KICK
HEY, CAREFUL-- THOSE THINGS ARE MORE EXPENSIVE THAN THEY LOOK!

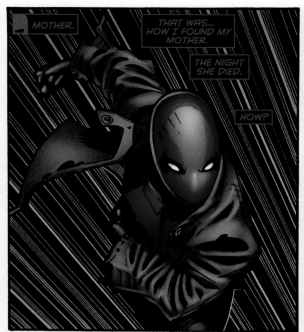

MOTHER.

THAT WAS... HOW I FOUND MY MOTHER.

THE NIGHT SHE DIED.

HOW?

HOW COULD JOKER--

CHUK-T

BUT IT DIDN'T TAKE.

YOU STRAYED OFF THE BEATEN NARROW.

DARE I SAY STUMBLED?

SLAMM

WHERE DID IT GO?

ALL THAT COMPASSION?

DID YOU LEAVE IT IN THE GRAVE?

OR DID YOU JUST LOCK IT UP IN A BOX SOMEWHERE: ONLY OPEN IN CASE OF EMERGENCY?

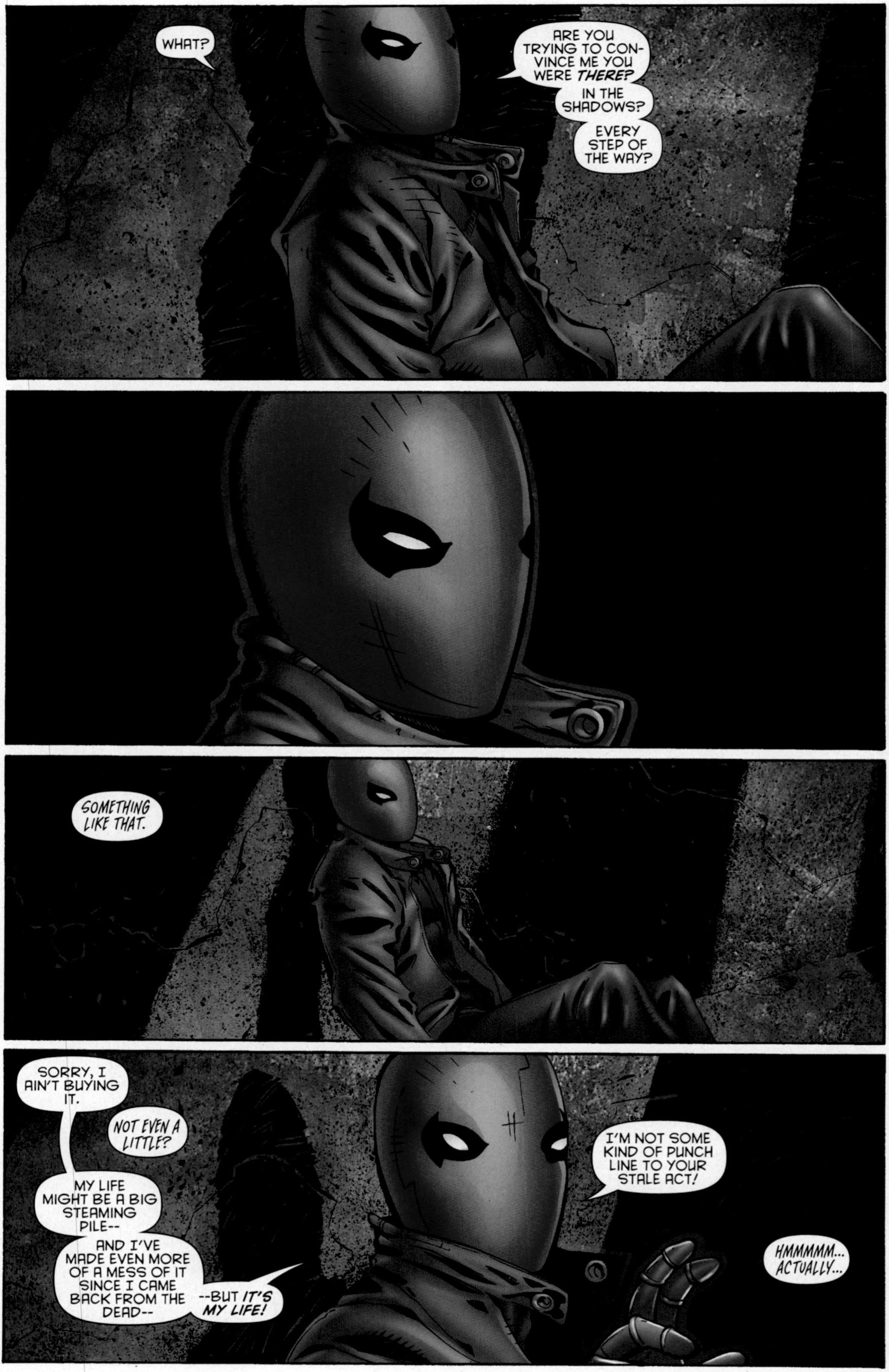
WHAT?
ARE YOU TRYING TO CONVINCE ME YOU WERE THERE?
IN THE SHADOWS?
EVERY STEP OF THE WAY?
SOMETHING LIKE THAT.
SORRY, I AIN'T BUYING IT.
NOT EVEN A LITTLE?
MY LIFE MIGHT BE A BIG STEAMING PILE--
AND I'VE MADE EVEN MORE OF A MESS OF IT SINCE I CAME BACK FROM THE DEAD--
--BUT IT'S MY LIFE!
I'M NOT SOME KIND OF PUNCH LINE TO YOUR STALE ACT!
HMMMMM... ACTUALLY...

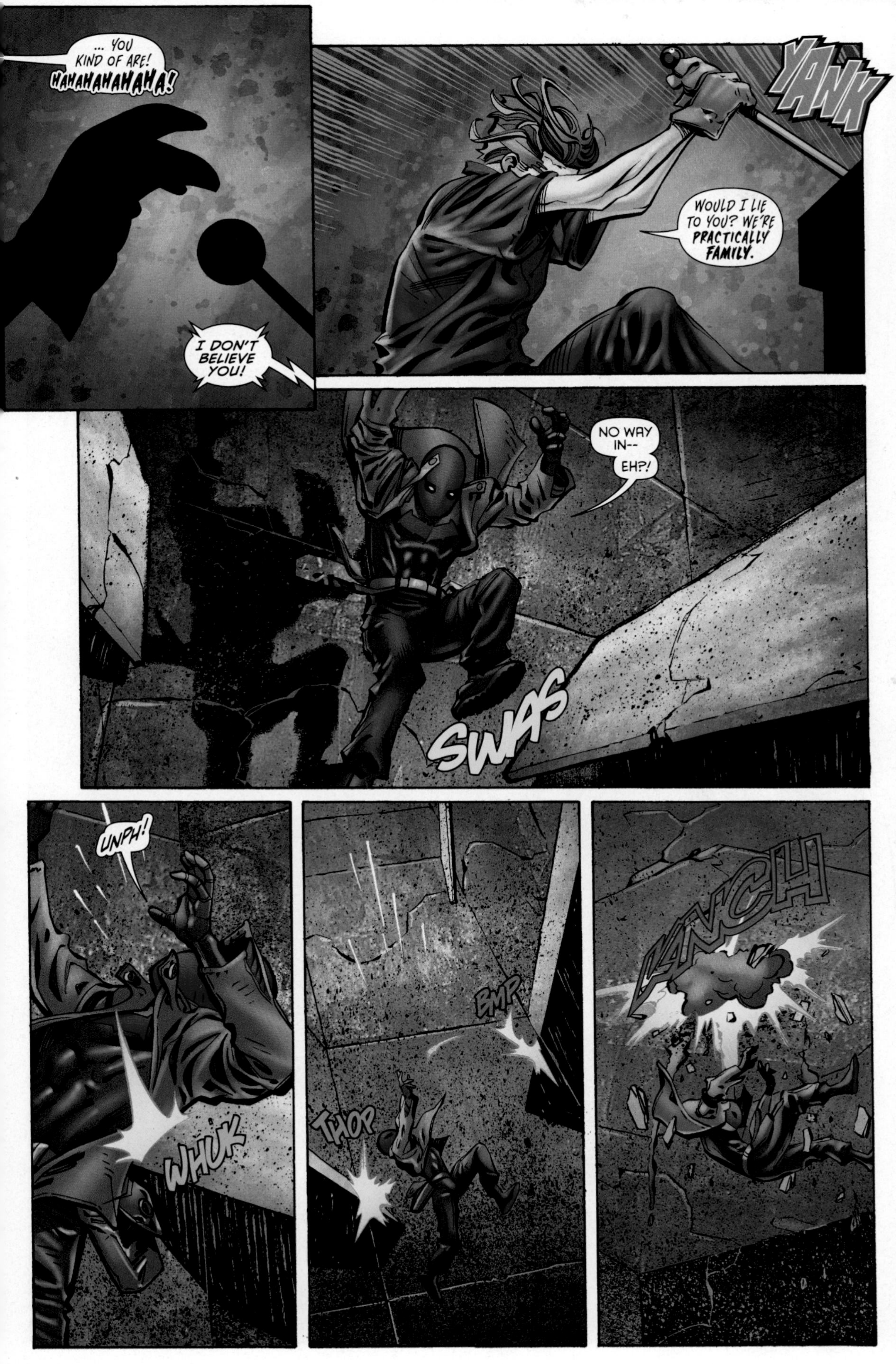
... YOU KIND OF ARE! HAHAHAHAHAHA!
I DON'T BELIEVE YOU!
YANK
WOULD I LIE TO YOU? WE'RE PRACTICALLY FAMILY.
NO WAY IN--
EH?!
SWAS
UNPH!
WHUK
BMP
THOP
CH

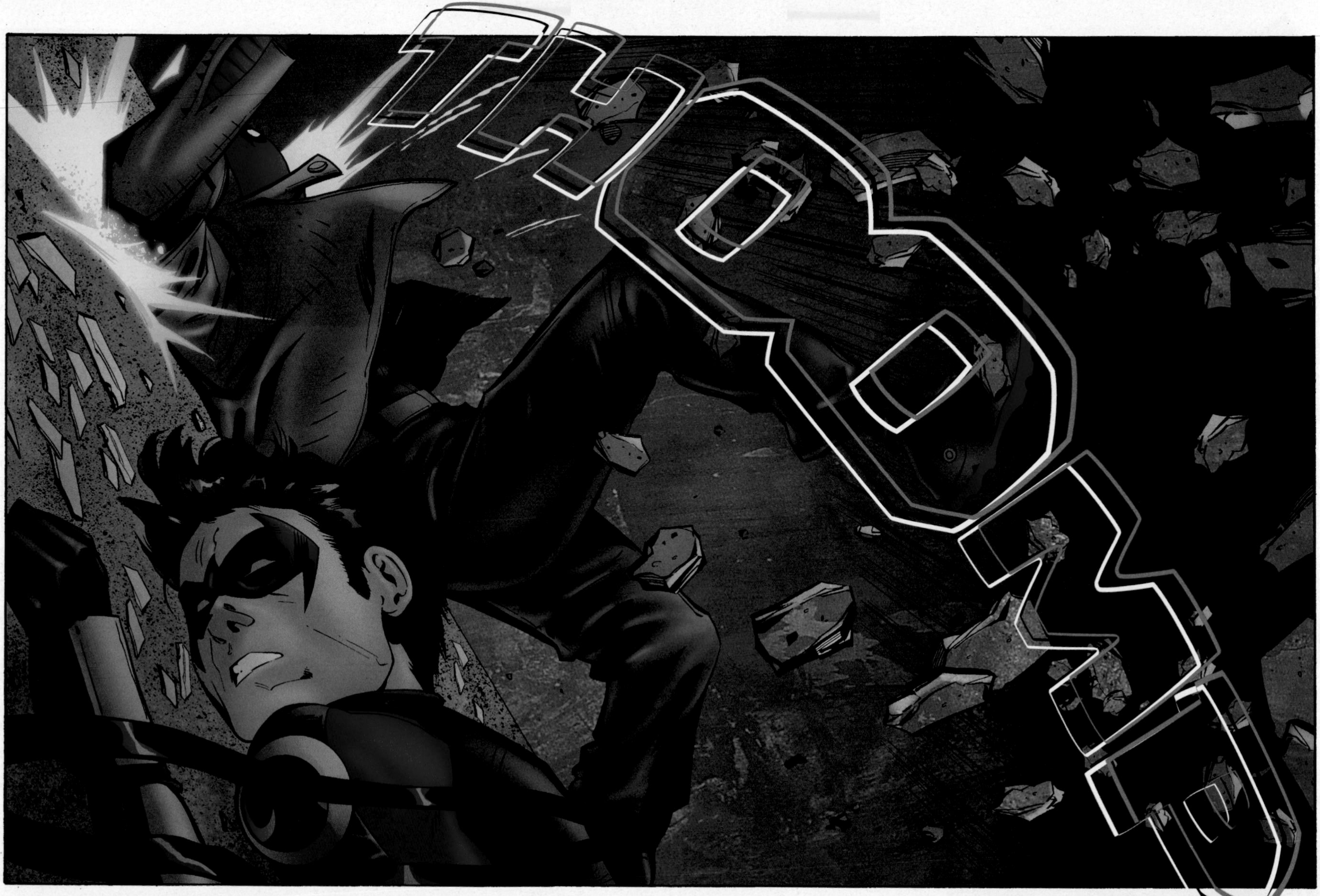
THOOMP

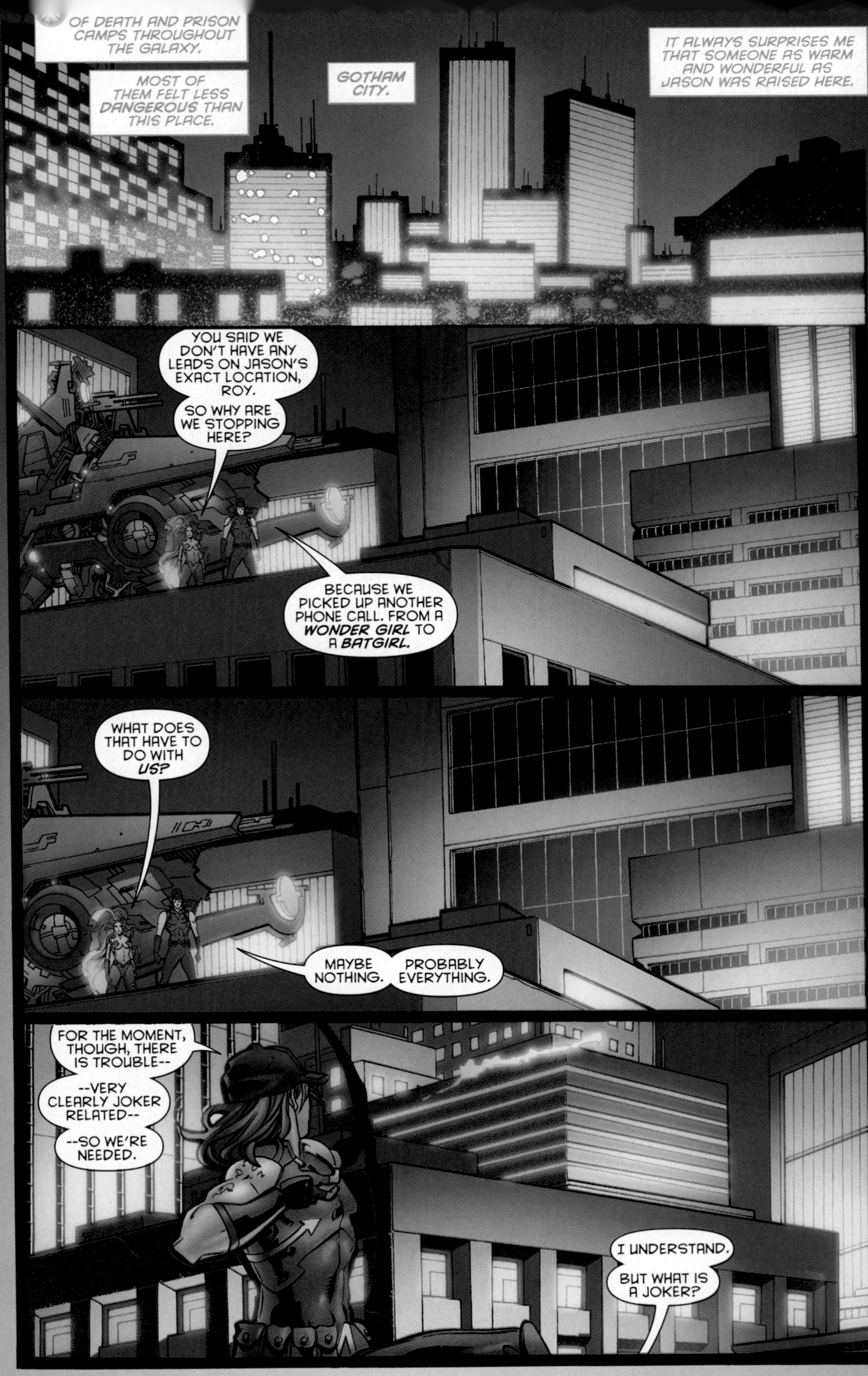
OF DEATH AND PRISON CAMPS THROUGHOUT THE GALAXY.
MOST OF THEM FELT LESS DANGEROUS THAN THIS PLACE.
GOTHAM CITY.
IT ALWAYS SURPRISES ME THAT SOMEONE AS WARM AND WONDERFUL AS JASON WAS RAISED HERE.
YOU SAID WE DON'T HAVE ANY LEADS ON JASON'S EXACT LOCATION, ROY.
SO WHY ARE WE STOPPING HERE?
BECAUSE WE PICKED UP ANOTHER PHONE CALL. FROM A WONDER GIRL TO A BATGIRL.
WHAT DOES THAT HAVE TO DO WITH US?
MAYBE NOTHING.
PROBABLY EVERYTHING.
FOR THE MOMENT, THOUGH, THERE IS TROUBLE--
--VERY CLEARLY JOKER RELATED--
--SO WE'RE NEEDED.
I UNDERSTAND.
BUT WHAT IS A JOKER?

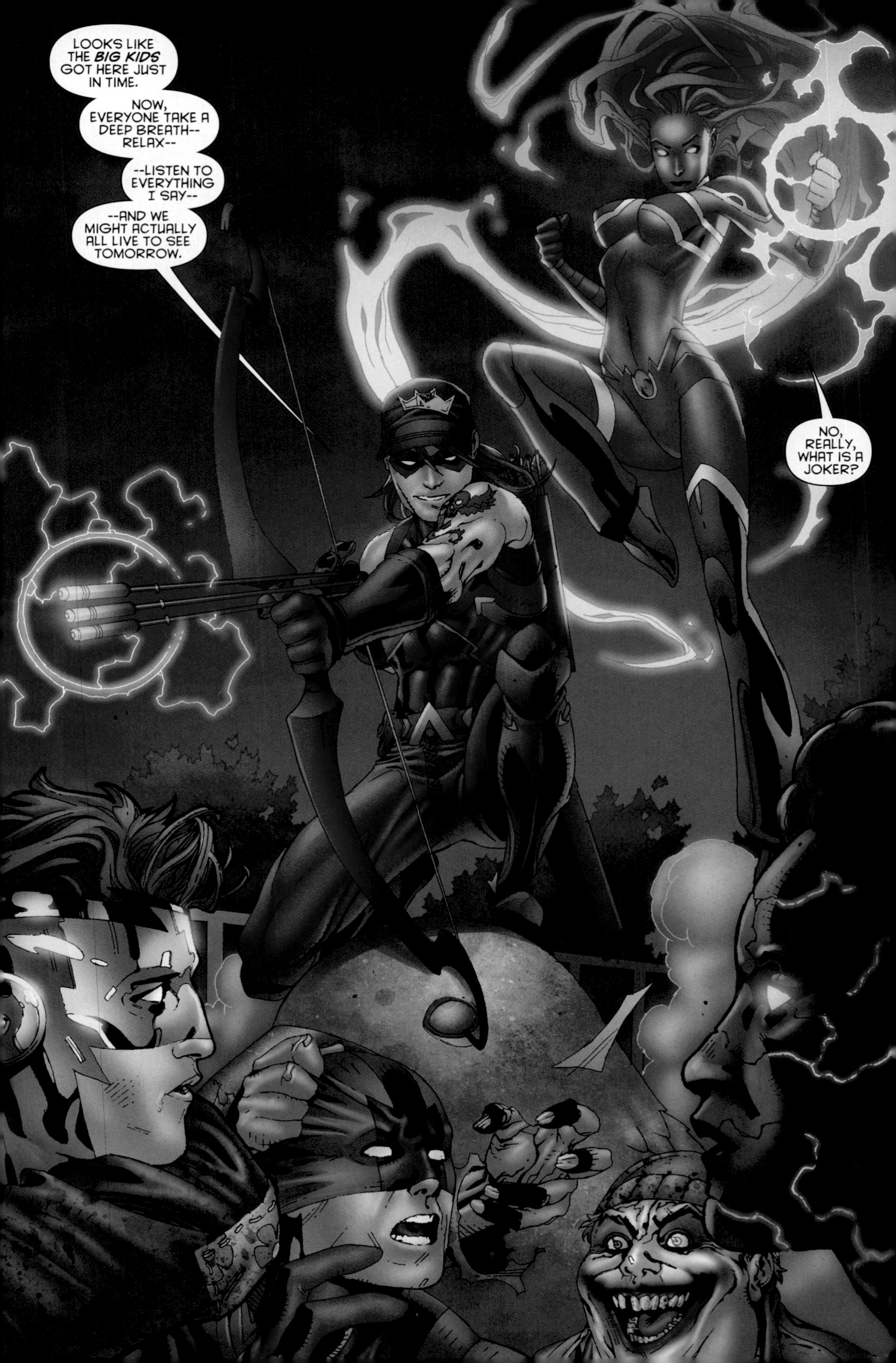

LOOKS LIKE THE *BIG KIDS* GOT HERE JUST IN TIME.
NOW, EVERYONE TAKE A DEEP BREATH-- RELAX--
--LISTEN TO EVERYTHING I SAY--
--AND WE MIGHT ACTUALLY ALL LIVE TO SEE TOMORROW.
NO, REALLY, WHAT IS A JOKER?

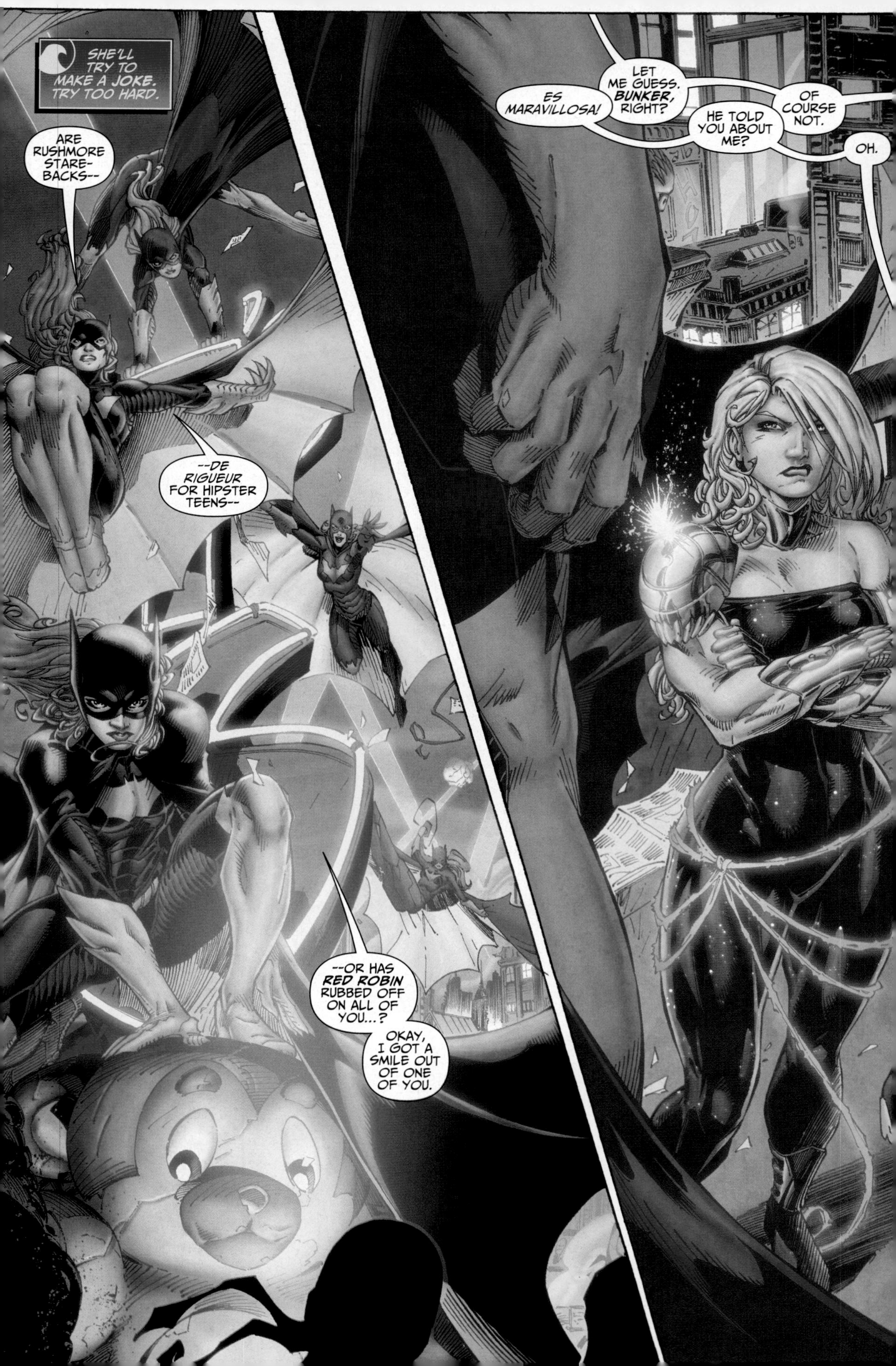
SHE'LL TRY TO MAKE A JOKE. TRY TOO HARD.
ARE RUSHMORE STARE-BACKS--
--DE RIGUEUR FOR HIPSTER TEENS--
--OR HAS RED ROBIN RUBBED OFF ON ALL OF YOU...?
OKAY, I GOT A SMILE OUT OF ONE OF YOU.
ES MARAVILLOSA!
LET ME GUESS. BUNKER, RIGHT?
HE TOLD YOU ABOUT ME?
OF COURSE NOT.
OH.

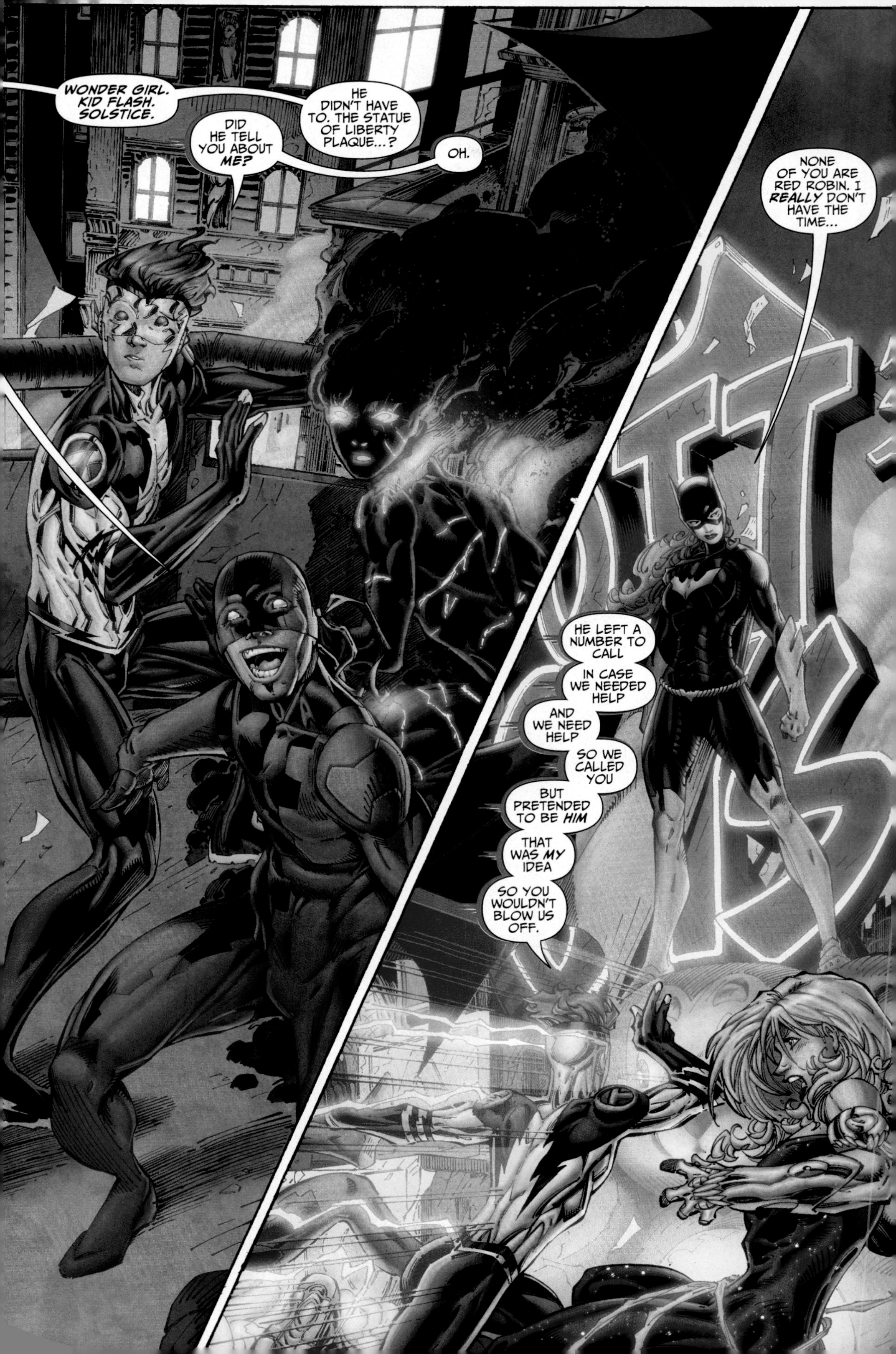
WONDER GIRL. KID FLASH. SOLSTICE.
HE DIDN'T HAVE TO. THE STATUE OF LIBERTY PLAQUE...?
DID HE TELL YOU ABOUT *ME?*
OH.
NONE OF YOU ARE RED ROBIN. I *REALLY* DON'T HAVE THE TIME...
HE LEFT A NUMBER TO CALL
IN CASE WE NEEDED HELP
AND WE NEED HELP
SO WE CALLED YOU
BUT PRETENDED TO BE *HIM*
THAT WAS *MY* IDEA
SO YOU WOULDN'T BLOW US OFF.

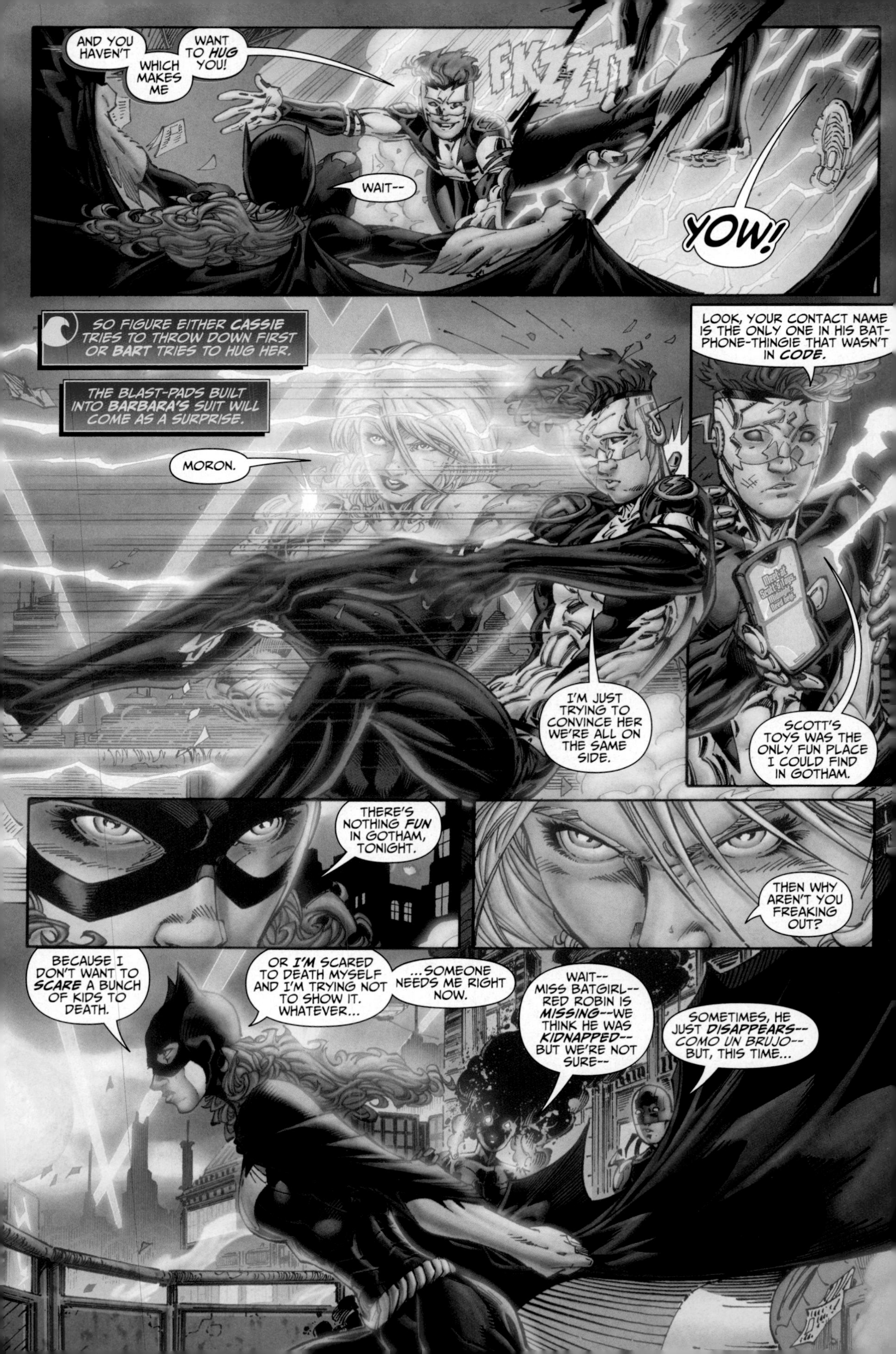
AND YOU HAVEN'T
WHICH MAKES ME
WANT TO HUG YOU!
FKZZTT
WAIT--
YOW!
SO FIGURE EITHER CASSIE TRIES TO THROW DOWN FIRST OR BART TRIES TO HUG HER.
THE BLAST-PADS BUILT INTO BARBARA'S SUIT WILL COME AS A SURPRISE.
MORON.
I'M JUST TRYING TO CONVINCE HER WE'RE ALL ON THE SAME SIDE.
LOOK, YOUR CONTACT NAME IS THE ONLY ONE IN HIS BAT-PHONE-THINGIE THAT WASN'T IN CODE.
SCOTT'S TOYS WAS THE ONLY FUN PLACE I COULD FIND IN GOTHAM.
THERE'S NOTHING FUN IN GOTHAM, TONIGHT.
THEN WHY AREN'T YOU FREAKING OUT?
BECAUSE I DON'T WANT TO SCARE A BUNCH OF KIDS TO DEATH.
OR I'M SCARED TO DEATH MYSELF AND I'M TRYING NOT TO SHOW IT. WHATEVER...
...SOMEONE NEEDS ME RIGHT NOW.
WAIT-- MISS BATGIRL-- RED ROBIN IS MISSING--WE THINK HE WAS KIDNAPPED-- BUT WE'RE NOT SURE--
SOMETIMES, HE JUST DISAPPEARS-- COMO UN BRUJO-- BUT, THIS TIME...

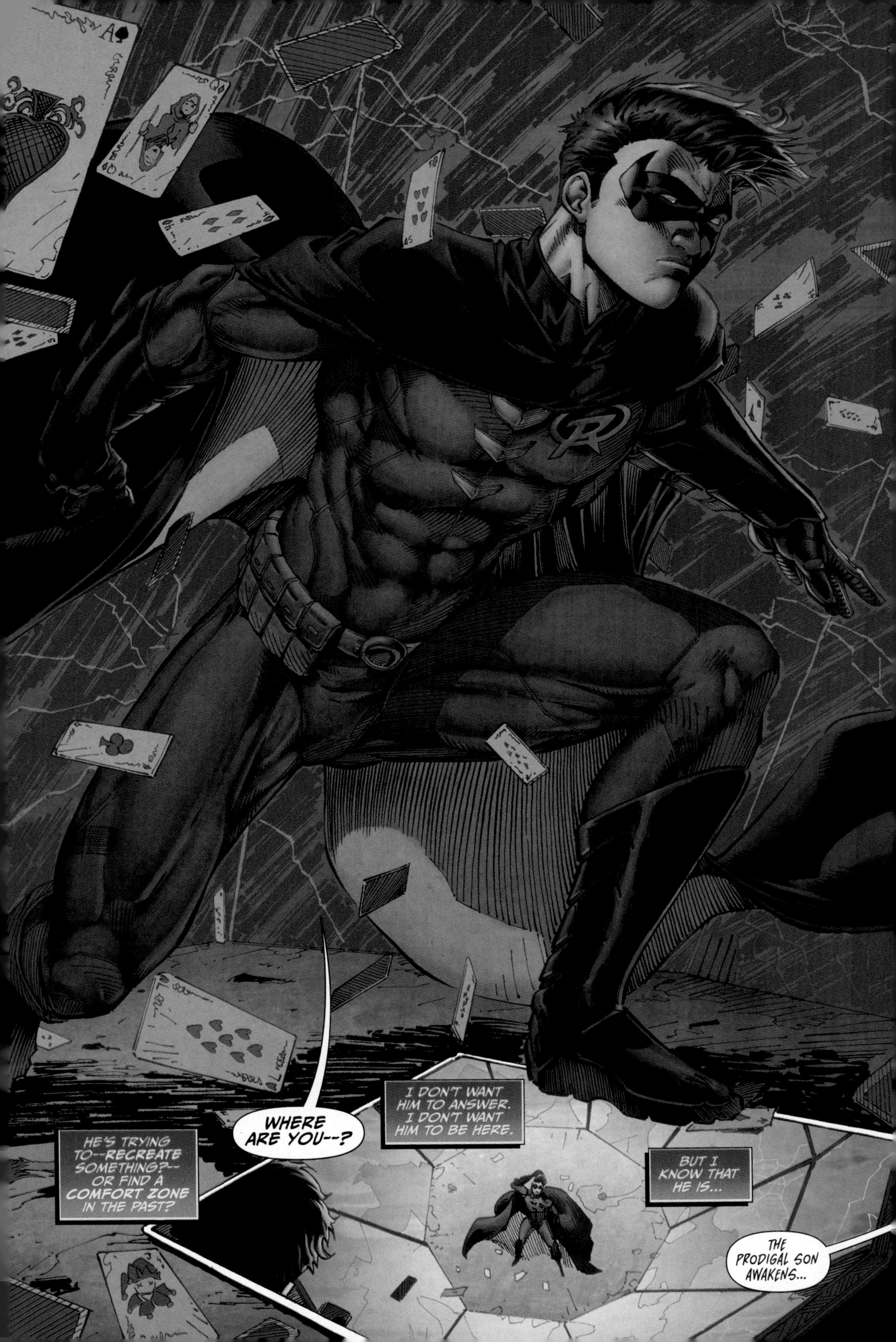
HE'S TRYING TO--RECREATE SOMETHING?-- OR FIND A COMFORT ZONE IN THE PAST?
WHERE ARE YOU--?
I DON'T WANT HIM TO ANSWER. I DON'T WANT HIM TO BE HERE.
BUT I KNOW THAT HE IS...
THE PRODIGAL SON AWAKENS...

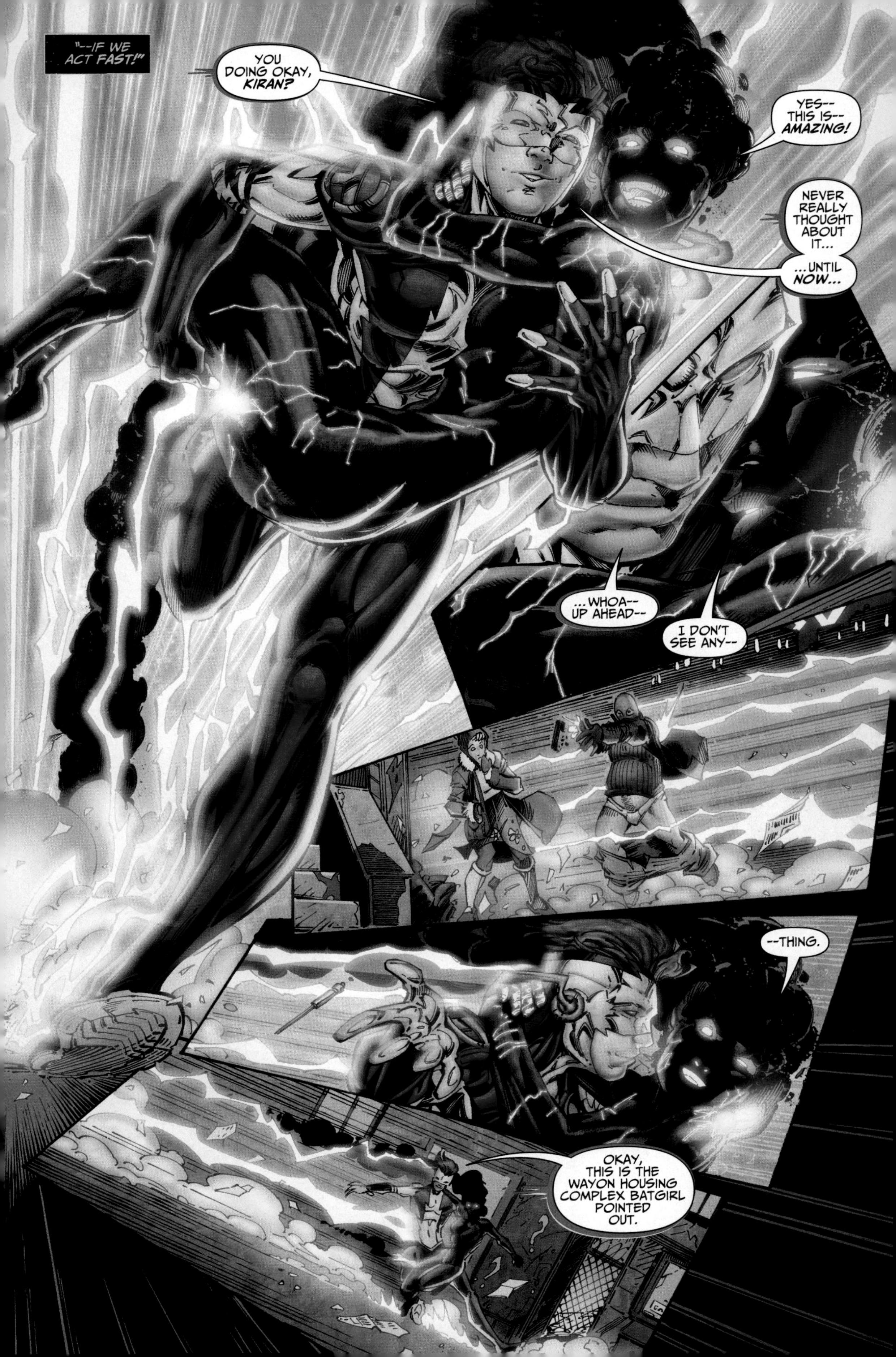
"--IF WE ACT FAST!"
YOU DOING OKAY, KIRAN?
YES-- THIS IS-- AMAZING!
NEVER REALLY THOUGHT ABOUT IT...
...UNTIL NOW...
...WHOA-- UP AHEAD--
I DON'T SEE ANY--
--THING.
OKAY, THIS IS THE WAYON HOUSING COMPLEX BATGIRL POINTED OUT.

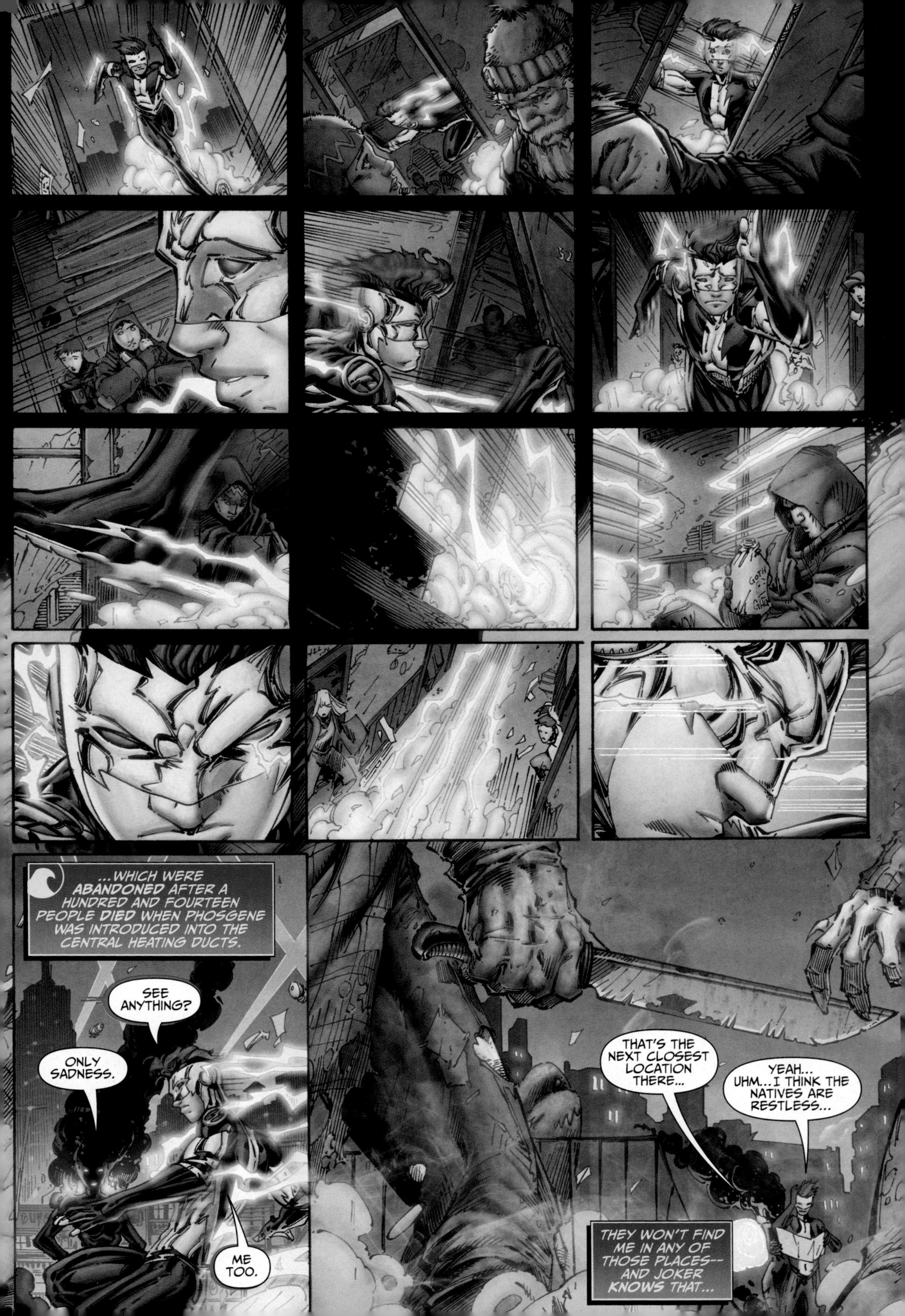

...WHICH WERE ABANDONED AFTER A HUNDRED AND FOURTEEN PEOPLE DIED WHEN PHOSGENE WAS INTRODUCED INTO THE CENTRAL HEATING DUCTS.
SEE ANYTHING?
ONLY SADNESS.
ME TOO.
THAT'S THE NEXT CLOSEST LOCATION THERE...
YEAH... UHM...I THINK THE NATIVES ARE RESTLESS...
THEY WON'T FIND ME IN ANY OF THOSE PLACES-- AND JOKER KNOWS THAT...

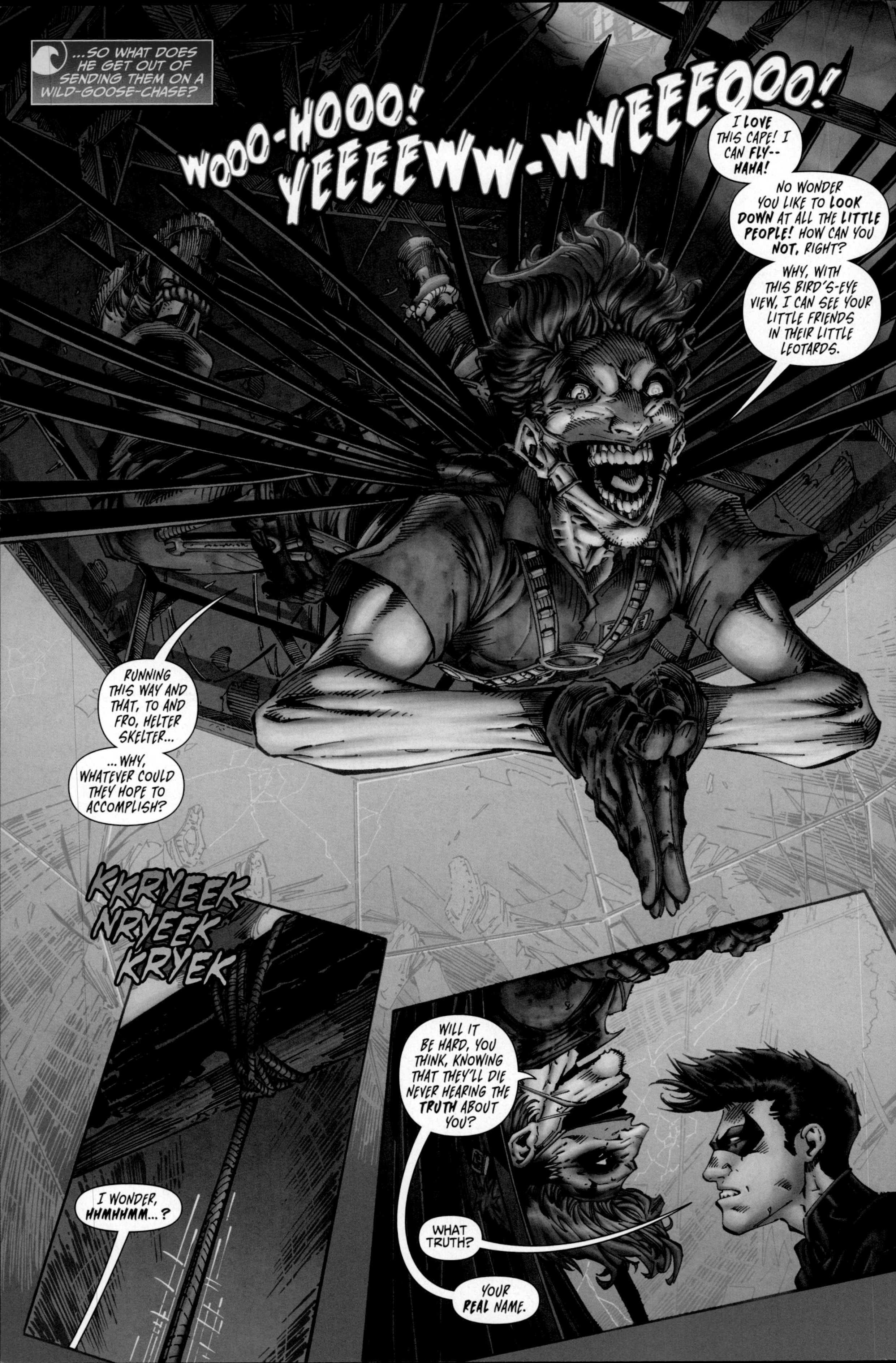
...SO WHAT DOES HE GET OUT OF SENDING THEM ON A WILD-GOOSE-CHASE?
WOOO-HOOO! YEEEEWW-WYEEEOOO!
I LOVE THIS CAPE! I CAN FLY-- HAHA!
NO WONDER YOU LIKE TO LOOK DOWN AT ALL THE LITTLE PEOPLE! HOW CAN YOU NOT, RIGHT?
WHY, WITH THIS BIRD'S-EYE VIEW, I CAN SEE YOUR LITTLE FRIENDS IN THEIR LITTLE LEOTARDS.
RUNNING THIS WAY AND THAT, TO AND FRO, HELTER SKELTER...
...WHY, WHATEVER COULD THEY HOPE TO ACCOMPLISH?
KKRYEEK NRYEEK KRYEK
I WONDER, HMMHMM...?
WILL IT BE HARD, YOU THINK, KNOWING THAT THEY'LL DIE NEVER HEARING THE TRUTH ABOUT YOU?
WHAT TRUTH?
YOUR REAL NAME.

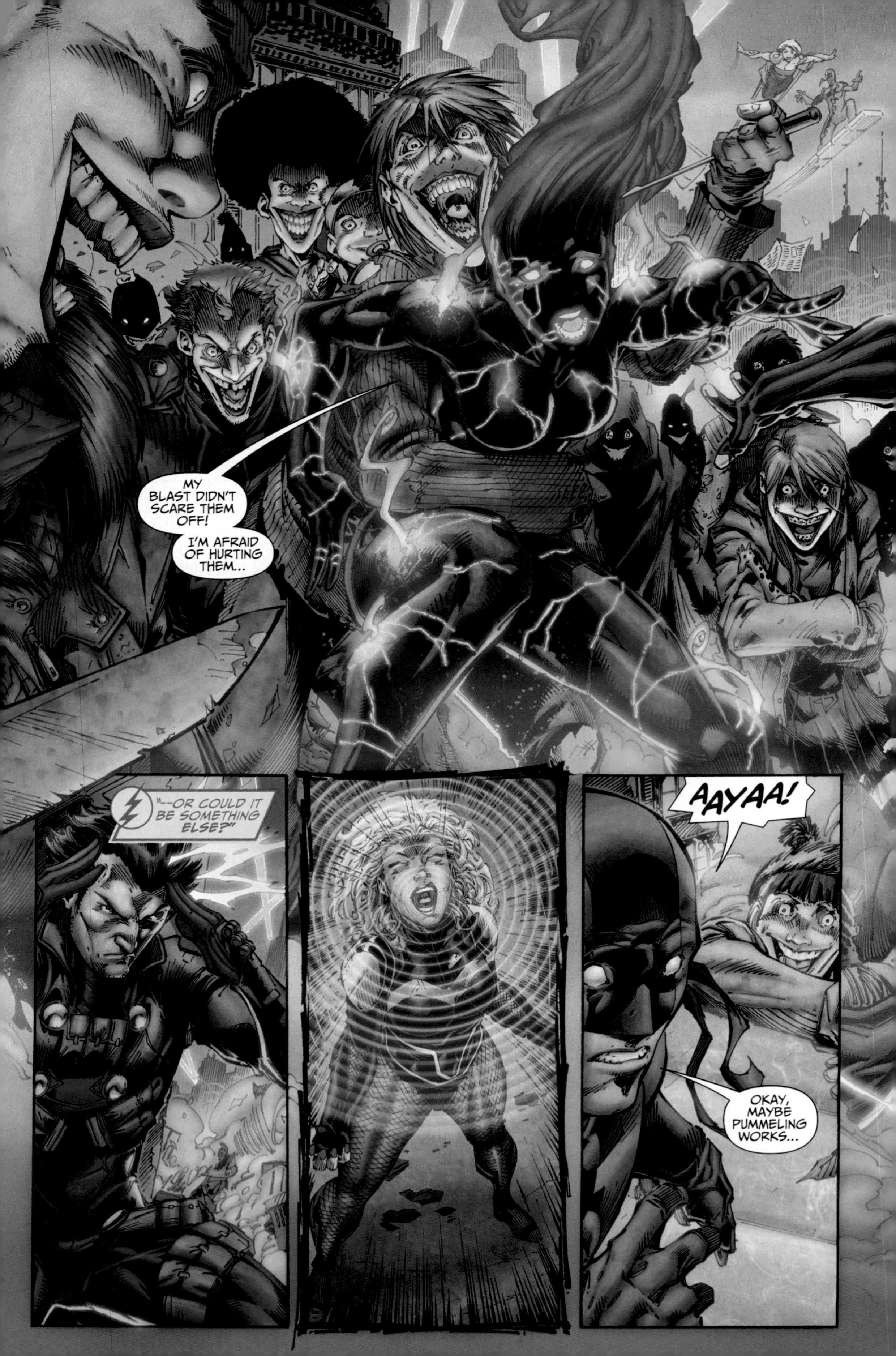

MY BLAST DIDN'T SCARE THEM OFF!
I'M AFRAID OF HURTING THEM...
"--OR COULD IT BE SOMETHING ELSE?"
AAYAA!
OKAY, MAYBE PUMMELING WORKS...

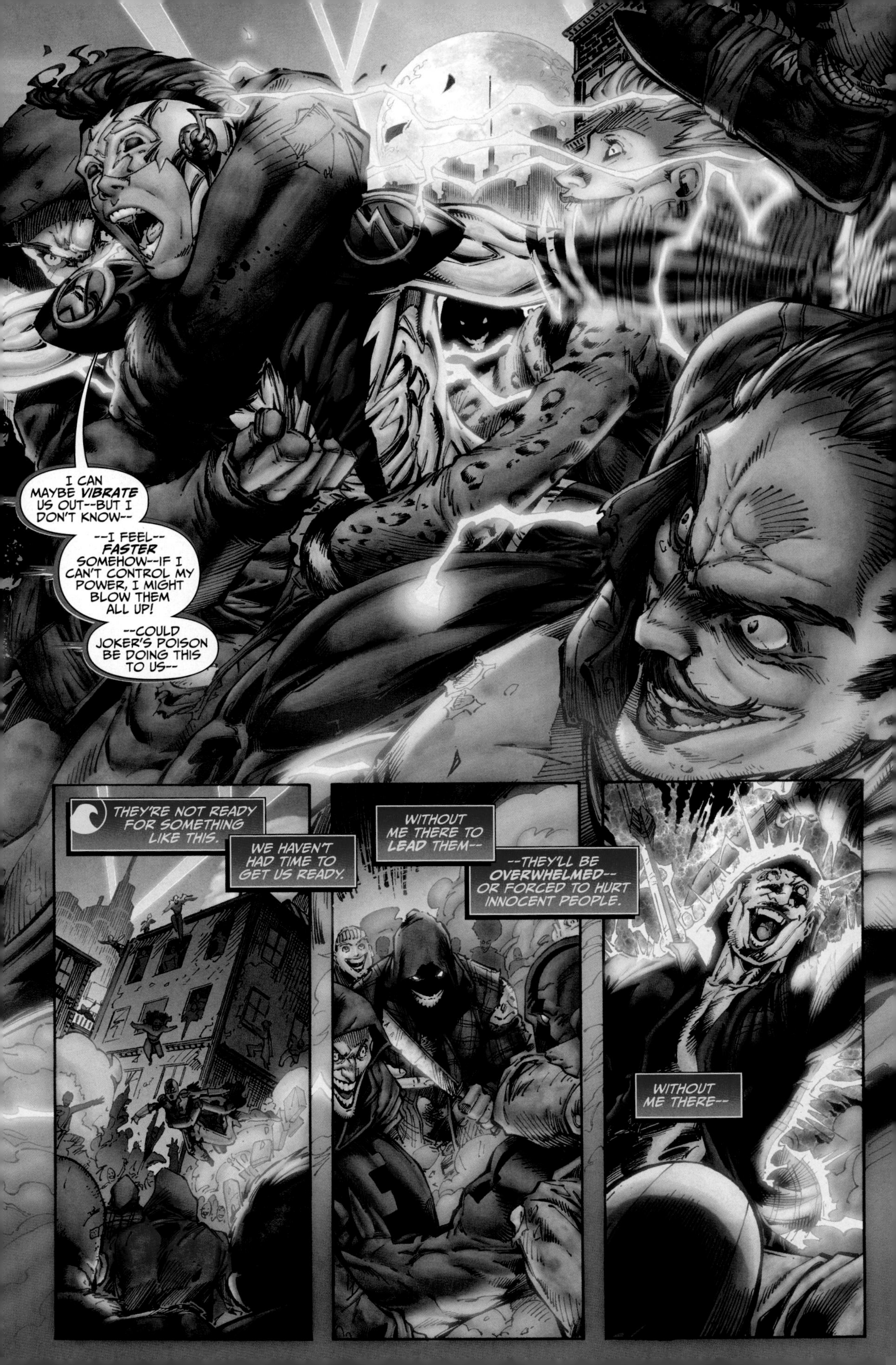
I CAN MAYBE VIBRATE US OUT--BUT I DON'T KNOW--
--I FEEL-- FASTER SOMEHOW--IF I CAN'T CONTROL MY POWER, I MIGHT BLOW THEM ALL UP!
--COULD JOKER'S POISON BE DOING THIS TO US--
THEY'RE NOT READY FOR SOMETHING LIKE THIS.
WE HAVEN'T HAD TIME TO GET US READY.
WITHOUT ME THERE TO LEAD THEM--
--THEY'LL BE OVERWHELMED-- OR FORCED TO HURT INNOCENT PEOPLE.
WITHOUT ME THERE--

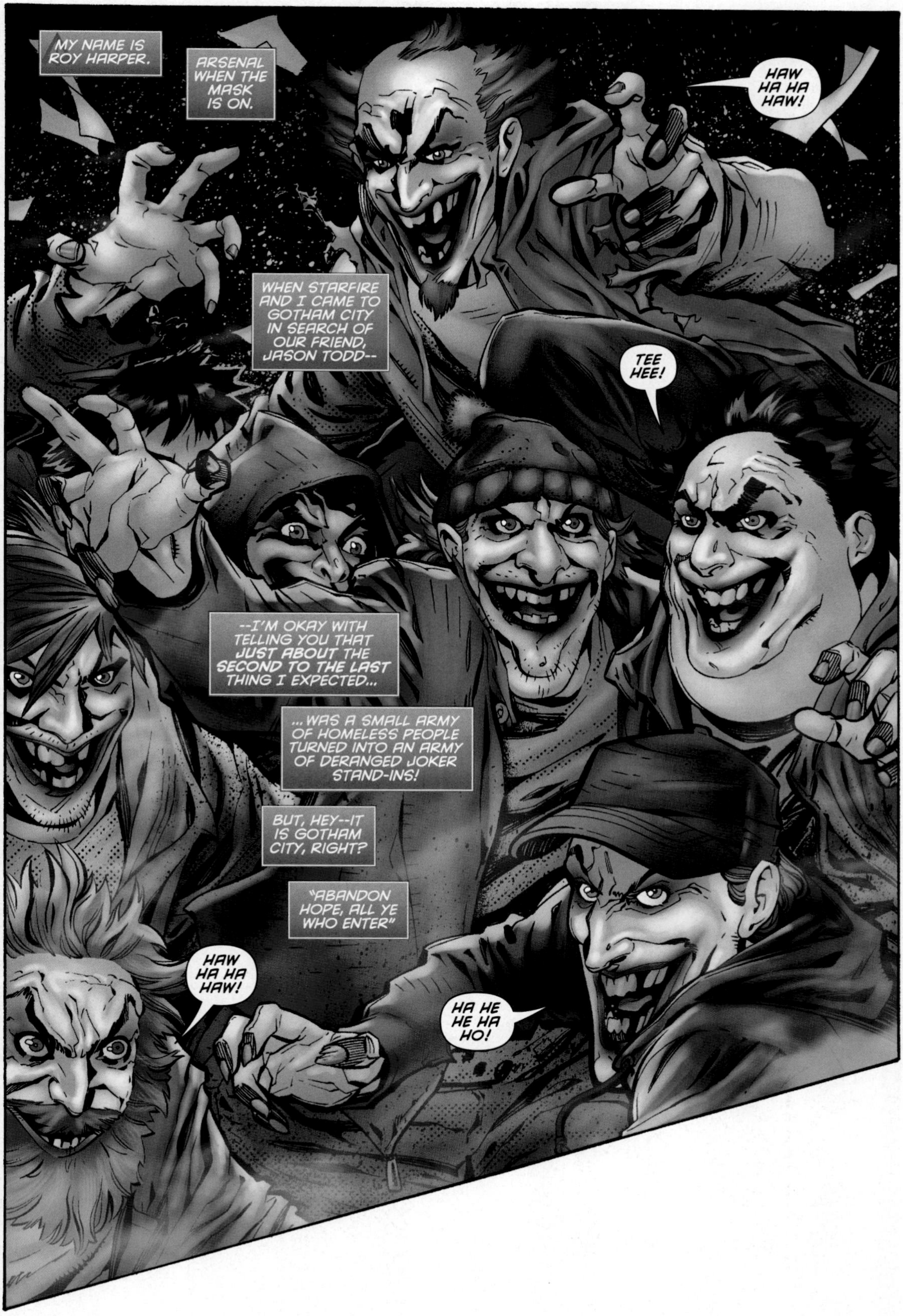
MY NAME IS ROY HARPER.
ARSENAL WHEN THE MASK IS ON.
HAW HA HA HAW!
WHEN STARFIRE AND I CAME TO GOTHAM CITY IN SEARCH OF OUR FRIEND, JASON TODD--
TEE HEE!
--I'M OKAY WITH TELLING YOU THAT JUST ABOUT THE SECOND TO THE LAST THING I EXPECTED...
...WAS A SMALL ARMY OF HOMELESS PEOPLE TURNED INTO AN ARMY OF DERANGED JOKER STAND-INS!
BUT, HEY--IT IS GOTHAM CITY, RIGHT?
"ABANDON HOPE, ALL YE WHO ENTER"
HAW HA HA HAW!
HA HE HE HA HO!

TURNS OUT THEY'RE LOOKING FOR THEIR OWN FEARLESS LEADER, RED ROBIN.

TELL ME WHY WE DO NOT SIMPLY INCINERATE THIS CREATURE.

BECAUSE I SAW THESE PEOPLE TRANSFORM.

ONLY A FEW MINUTES AGO!

WHAT IF THE JOKER'S GAS HASN'T *"SET"* YET?

MAYBE THERE'S A WAY TO *SAVE* THEM?

REAL BAD WITH NAMES.

SOLSTICE.

BUNKER.

AND, NO LIE--KID FLASH.

SO LISTEN, SPEEDY...

ARE YOU TALKING TO ME?

I AIN'T TALKING TO MYSELF!

THE NAME IS KID FLASH.

OH. WAS HOPING THAT WAS A JOKE.

EITHER WAY, YOU NEED TO USE WHAT IS *CLEARLY* YOUR SUPER SPEED TO CORRAL THESE PEOPLE.

WE CAN'T AFFORD LETTING EVEN ONE OF THEM GET AWAY UNTIL WE CAN FIND YOUR MIRACLE CURE!

WONDER GIRL?

WONDER GIRL, WHAT?

WAIT, WHAT--?! YOU'RE SERIOUSLY CHECKING IN WITH THIS GIRL BEFORE YOU LISTEN TO ME?

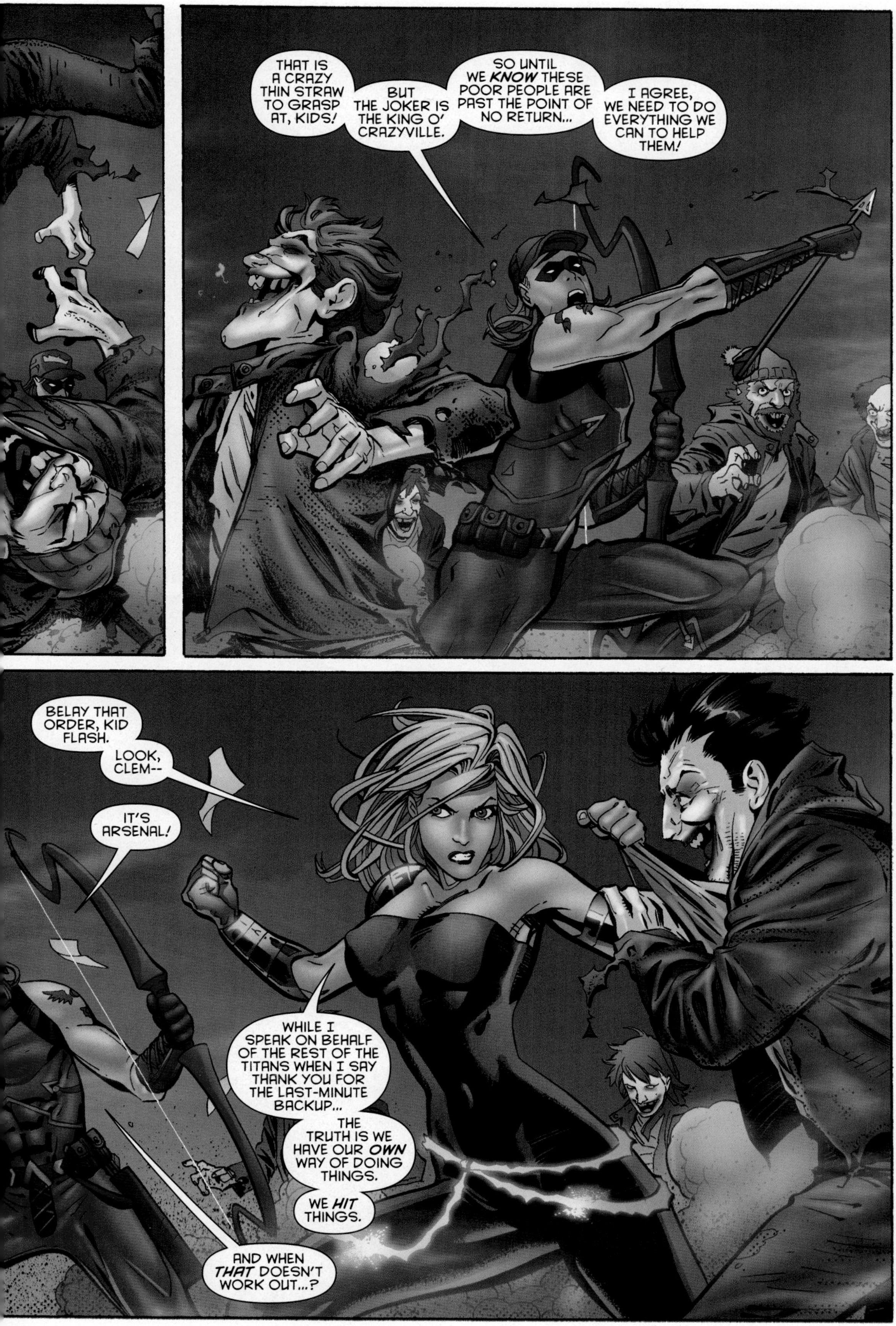
THAT IS A CRAZY THIN STRAW TO GRASP AT, KIDS!
BUT THE JOKER IS THE KING O' CRAZYVILLE.
SO UNTIL WE *KNOW* THESE POOR PEOPLE ARE PAST THE POINT OF NO RETURN...
I AGREE, WE NEED TO DO EVERYTHING WE CAN TO HELP THEM!
BELAY THAT ORDER, KID FLASH.
LOOK, CLEM--
IT'S ARSENAL!
WHILE I SPEAK ON BEHALF OF THE REST OF THE TITANS WHEN I SAY THANK YOU FOR THE LAST-MINUTE BACKUP...
THE TRUTH IS WE HAVE OUR *OWN* WAY OF DOING THINGS.
WE *HIT* THINGS.
AND WHEN *THAT* DOESN'T WORK OUT...?

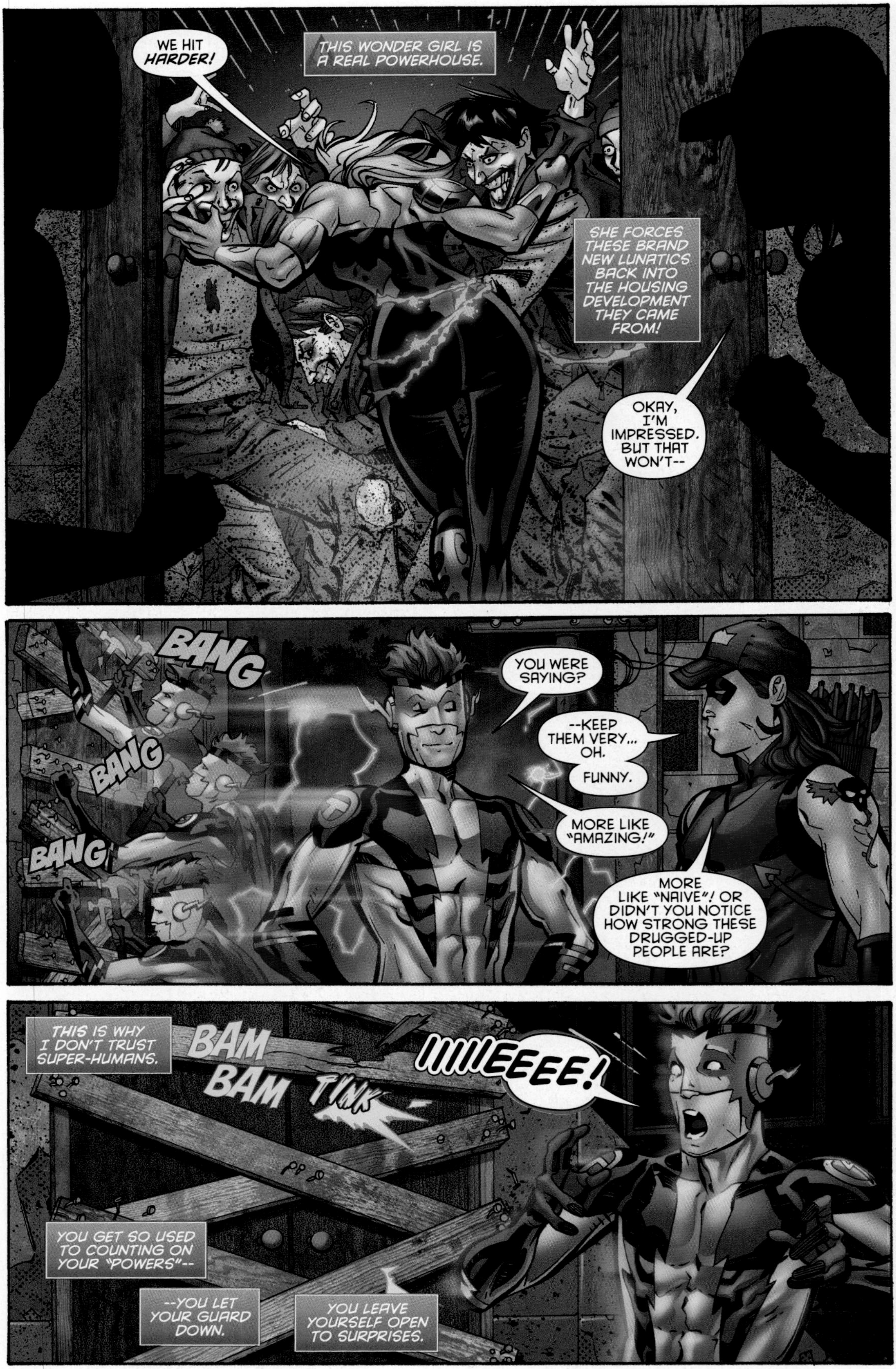

WE HIT HARDER!
THIS WONDER GIRL IS A REAL POWERHOUSE.
SHE FORCES THESE BRAND NEW LUNATICS BACK INTO THE HOUSING DEVELOPMENT THEY CAME FROM!
OKAY, I'M IMPRESSED. BUT THAT WON'T--
BANG
BANG
BANG
YOU WERE SAYING?
--KEEP THEM VERY... OH.
FUNNY.
MORE LIKE "AMAZING!"
MORE LIKE "NAIVE"! OR DIDN'T YOU NOTICE HOW STRONG THESE DRUGGED-UP PEOPLE ARE?
THIS IS WHY I DON'T TRUST SUPER-HUMANS.
BAM
BAM
TINK
IIIIIEEEEE!
YOU GET SO USED TO COUNTING ON YOUR "POWERS"--
--YOU LET YOUR GUARD DOWN.
YOU LEAVE YOURSELF OPEN TO SURPRISES.

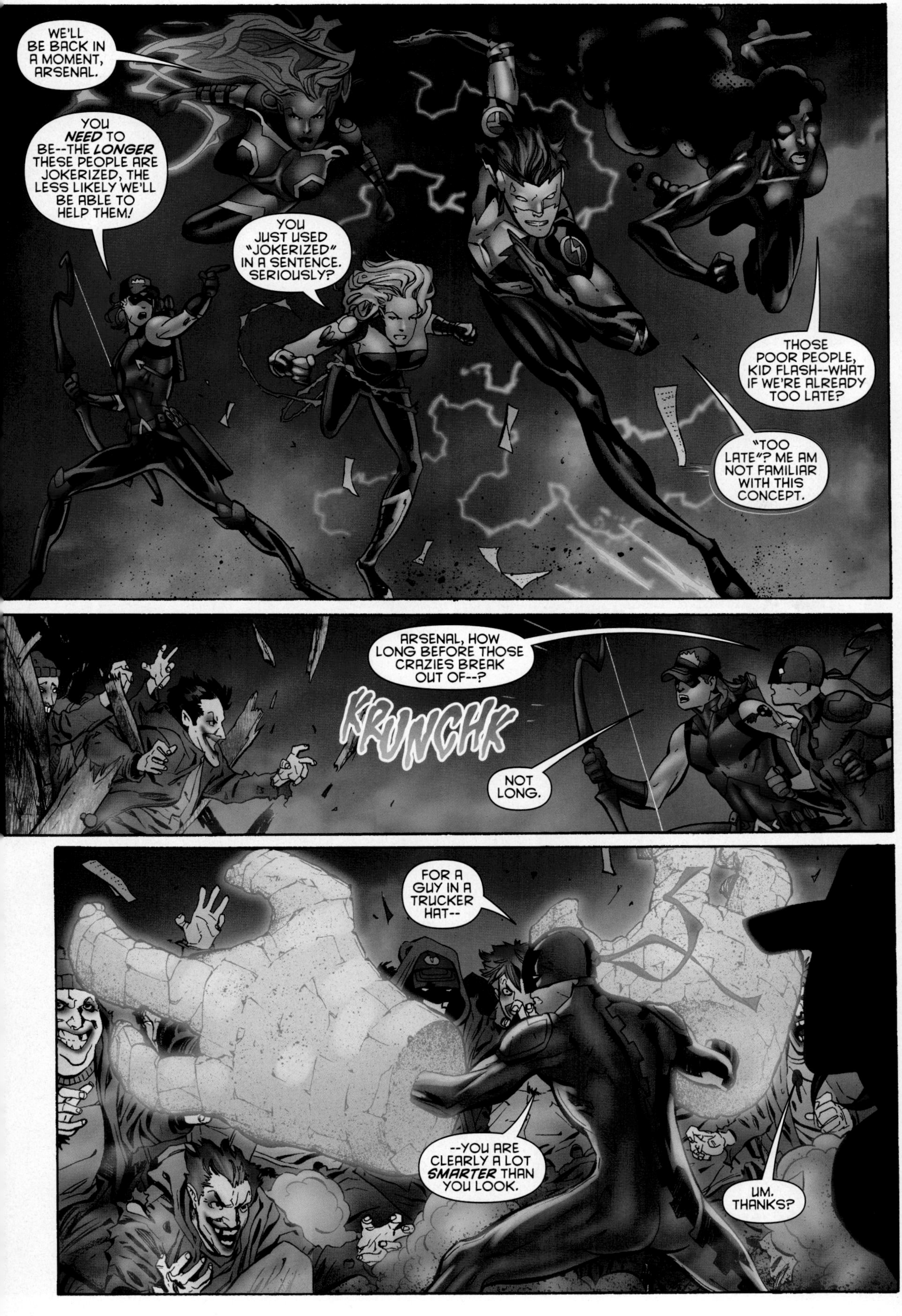
WE'LL BE BACK IN A MOMENT, ARSENAL.
YOU *NEED* TO BE--THE *LONGER* THESE PEOPLE ARE JOKERIZED, THE LESS LIKELY WE'LL BE ABLE TO HELP THEM!
YOU JUST USED "JOKERIZED" IN A SENTENCE. SERIOUSLY?
THOSE POOR PEOPLE, KID FLASH--WHAT IF WE'RE ALREADY TOO LATE?
"TOO LATE"? ME AM NOT FAMILIAR WITH THIS CONCEPT.
ARSENAL, HOW LONG BEFORE THOSE CRAZIES BREAK OUT OF--?
KRUNCHK
NOT LONG.
FOR A GUY IN A TRUCKER HAT--
--YOU ARE CLEARLY A LOT *SMARTER* THAN YOU LOOK.
UM. THANKS?

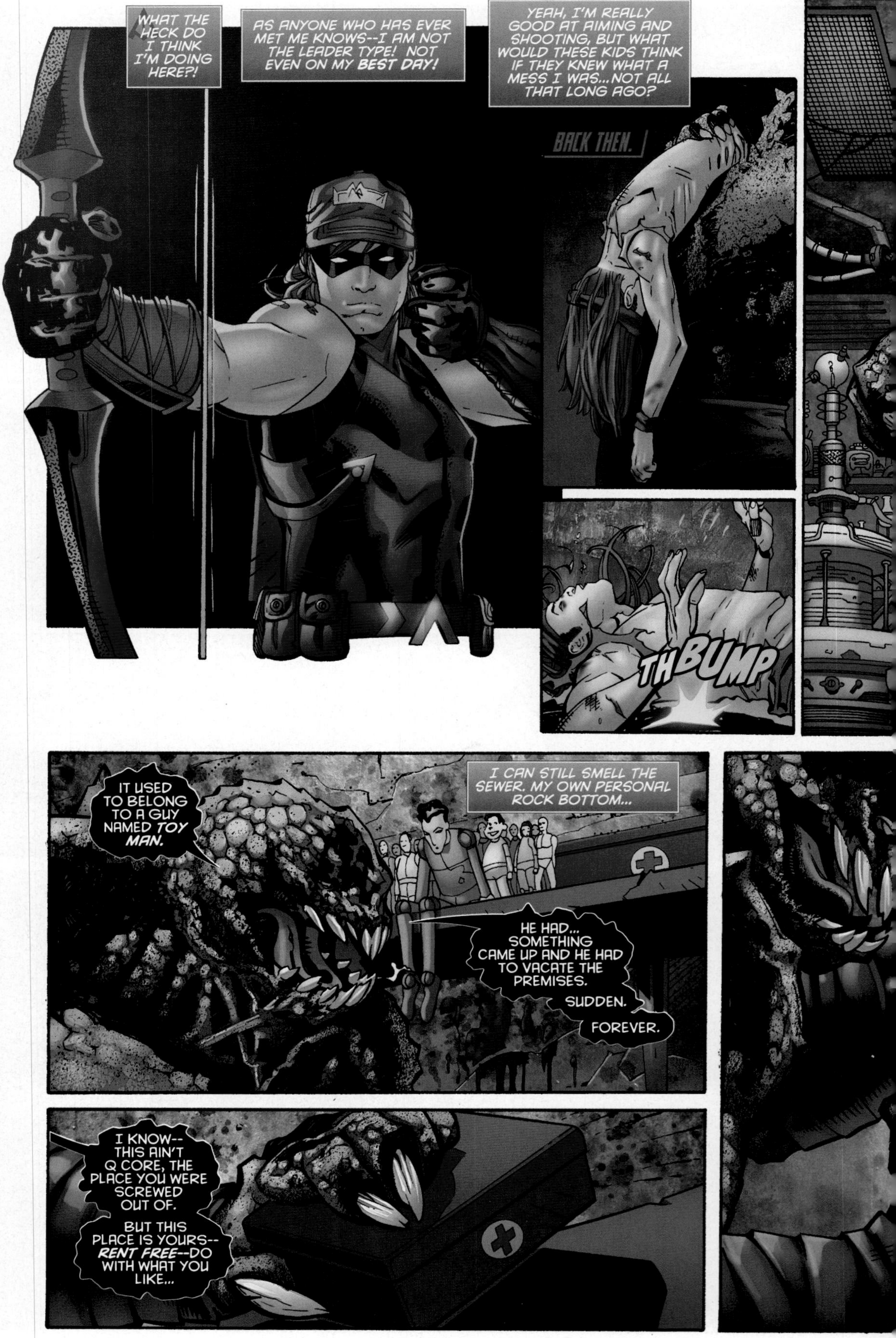
WHAT THE HECK DO I THINK I'M DOING HERE?!
AS ANYONE WHO HAS EVER MET ME KNOWS--I AM NOT THE LEADER TYPE! NOT EVEN ON MY BEST DAY!
YEAH, I'M REALLY GOOD AT AIMING AND SHOOTING, BUT WHAT WOULD THESE KIDS THINK IF THEY KNEW WHAT A MESS I WAS...NOT ALL THAT LONG AGO?
BACK THEN.
THBUMP
I CAN STILL SMELL THE SEWER. MY OWN PERSONAL ROCK BOTTOM...
IT USED TO BELONG TO A GUY NAMED TOY MAN.
HE HAD... SOMETHING CAME UP AND HE HAD TO VACATE THE PREMISES.
SUDDEN.
FOREVER.
I KNOW-- THIS AIN'T Q CORE, THE PLACE YOU WERE SCREWED OUT OF.
BUT THIS PLACE IS YOURS-- RENT FREE--DO WITH WHAT YOU LIKE...

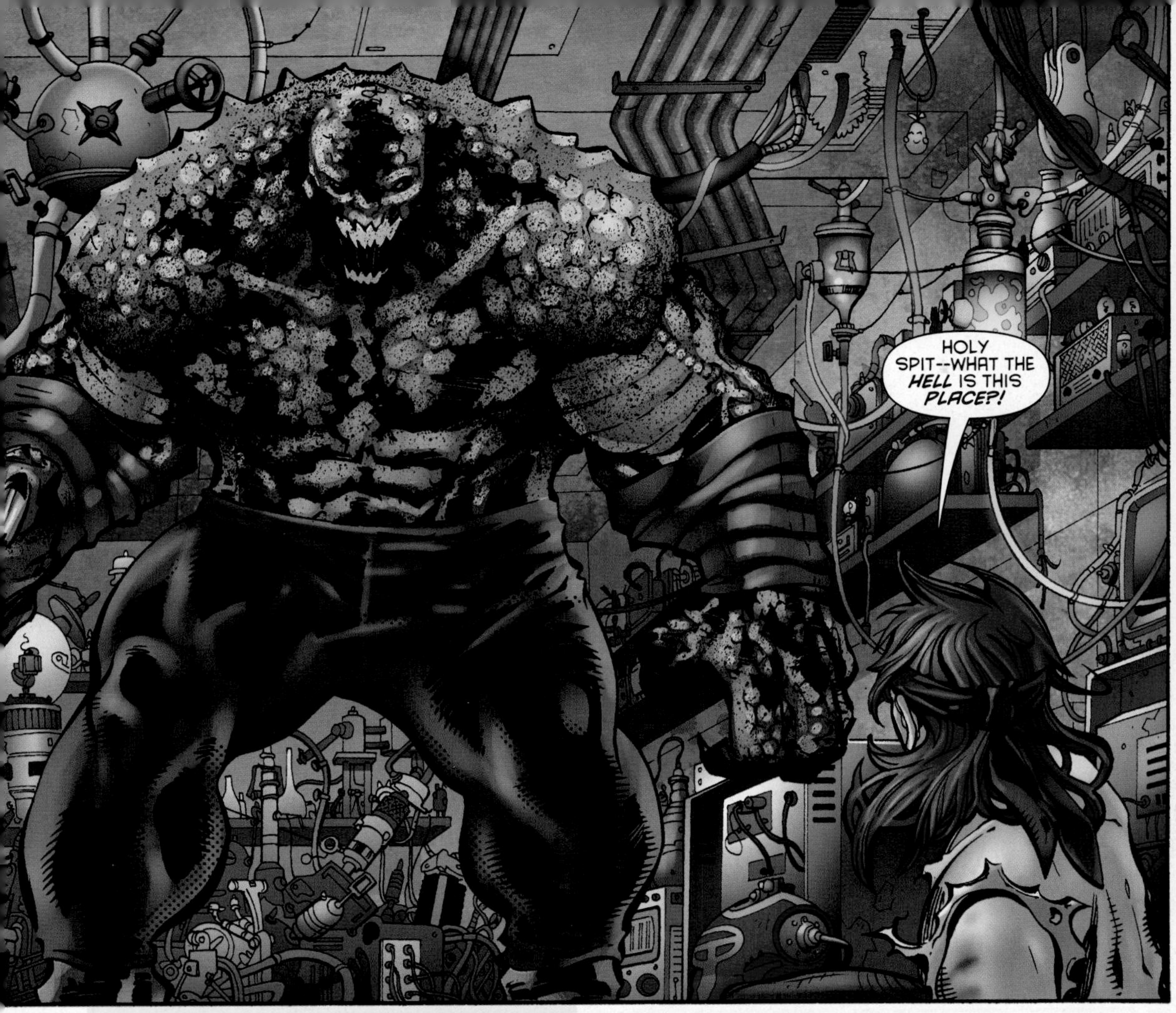
HOLY SPIT--WHAT THE *HELL* IS THIS *PLACE?!*

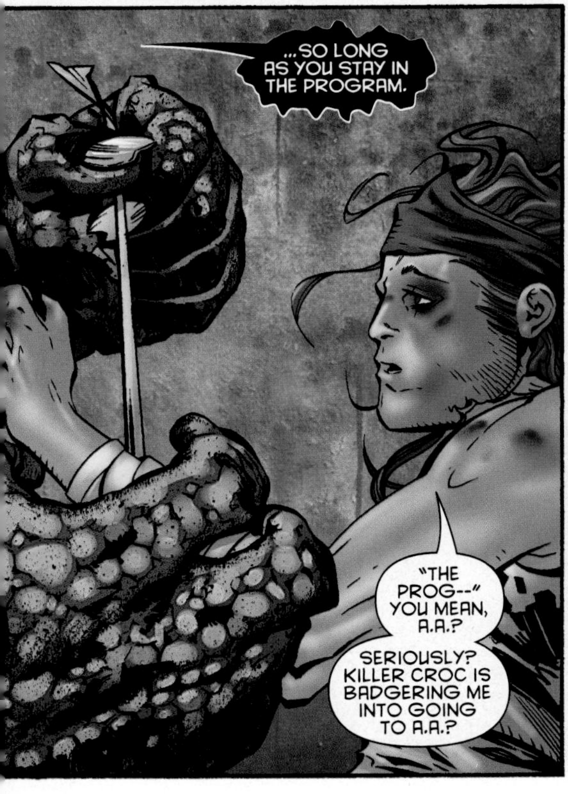
...SO LONG AS YOU STAY IN THE PROGRAM.
"THE PROG--" YOU MEAN, A.A.?
SERIOUSLY? KILLER CROC IS BADGERING ME INTO GOING TO A.A.?

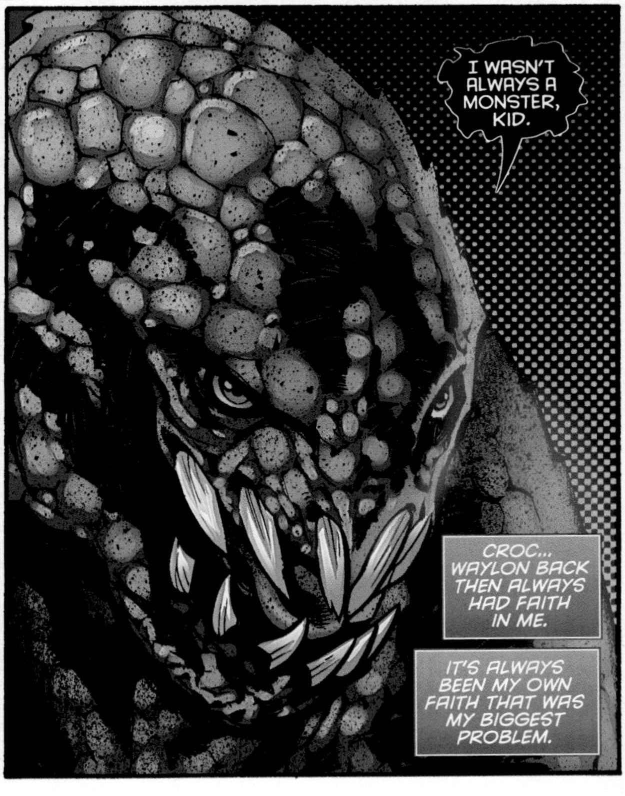
I WASN'T ALWAYS A MONSTER, KID.
CROC... WAYLON BACK THEN ALWAYS HAD FAITH IN ME.
IT'S ALWAYS BEEN MY OWN FAITH THAT WAS MY BIGGEST PROBLEM.

CAN I TELL YOU? I NEVER *MISSED* RED ROBIN UNTIL HE WAS GONE!

RIGHT. HOW CAN YOU MISS SOME--

THE GUY HAS NO POWERS AT ALL--NOT LIKE US-- BUT HE'S ALWAYS THE FIRST GUY THROUGH THE DOOR!

QUITE THE FRIENDS YOU HAVE THERE.

"FRIENDS" MIGHT BE TOO STRONG. WE'VE BARELY JUST MET.

BUT WE'RE GETTING THERE.

GROWING UP IN THIS TOILET OF TERROR MUST HAVE TAUGHT HIM NOT TO BE AFRAID OF ANYTHING.

HAVE YOU TOLD THEM?

NO.

DON'T YOU THINK THEY SHOULD BE ABLE TO MAKE THEIR OWN--EH?

I'LL TELL THEM, STARFIRE.

AT A TIME AND PLACE OF MY CHOOSING.

AND *NOT* A MOMENT BEFORE.

THOSE BOXES--THEY MUST BELONG TO THE JOKER!

OR A VERY POSSESSIVE SIX-YEAR-OLD BASED ON THE SCRAWLS.

BUT IF HE WROTE ON THEM...?

HE MUST HAVE THOUGHT *SOMEONE* WOULD EVENTUALLY FIND THIS PLACE--

TIC TIC TIC TIC

CURE! DO NOT TOUCH!

...BECAUSE HE LEFT A TWO-SECOND TRIGGER!

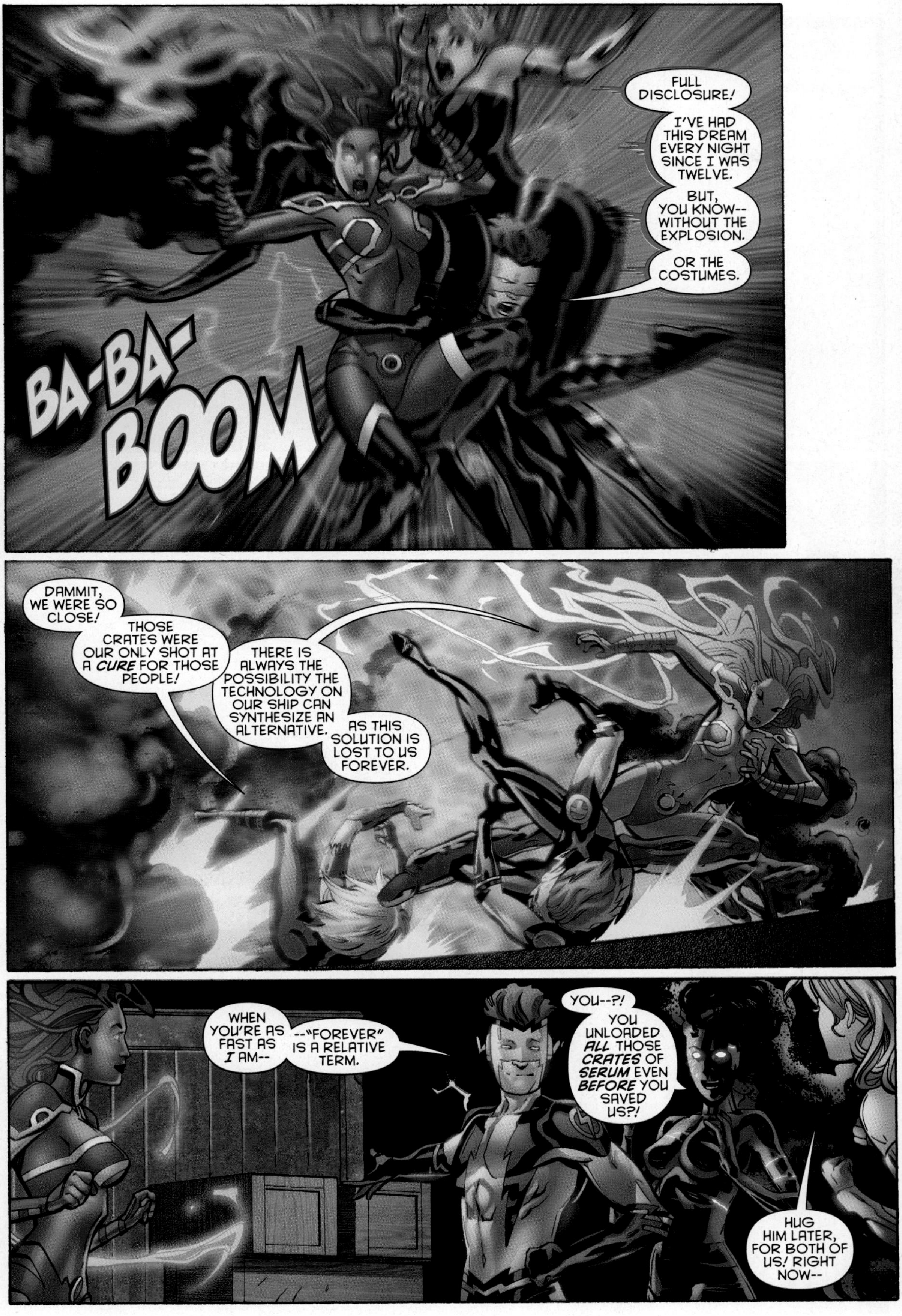
FULL DISCLOSURE!
I'VE HAD THIS DREAM EVERY NIGHT SINCE I WAS TWELVE.
BUT, YOU KNOW-- WITHOUT THE EXPLOSION.
OR THE COSTUMES.
BA-BA-BOOM
DAMMIT, WE WERE SO CLOSE!
THOSE CRATES WERE OUR ONLY SHOT AT A CURE FOR THOSE PEOPLE!
THERE IS ALWAYS THE POSSIBILITY THE TECHNOLOGY ON OUR SHIP CAN SYNTHESIZE AN ALTERNATIVE.
AS THIS SOLUTION IS LOST TO US FOREVER.
WHEN YOU'RE AS FAST AS I AM--
--"FOREVER" IS A RELATIVE TERM.
YOU--?!
YOU UNLOADED ALL THOSE CRATES OF SERUM EVEN BEFORE YOU SAVED US?!
HUG HIM LATER, FOR BOTH OF US! RIGHT NOW--

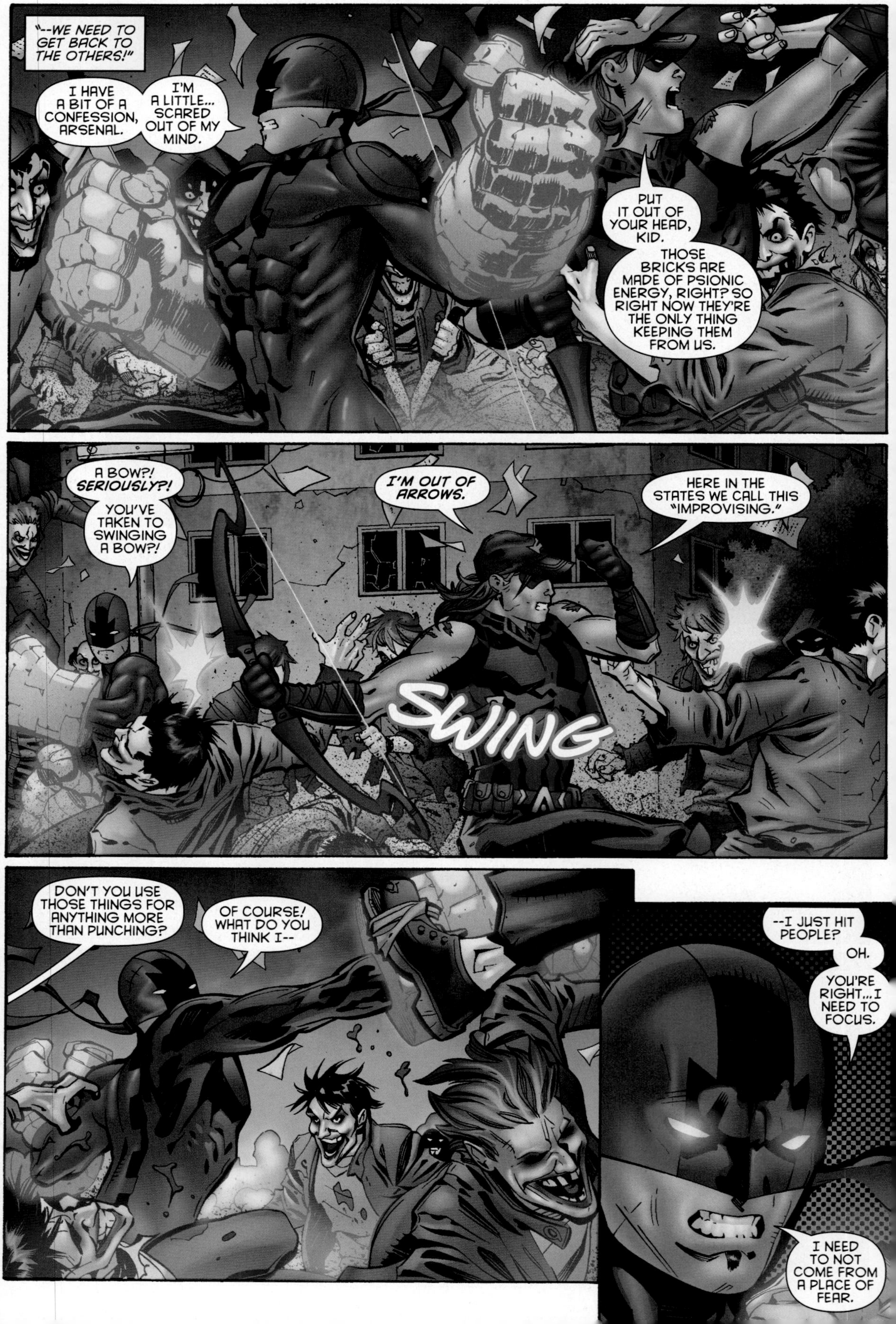
"--WE NEED TO GET BACK TO THE OTHERS!"
I HAVE A BIT OF A CONFESSION, ARSENAL.
I'M A LITTLE... SCARED OUT OF MY MIND.
PUT IT OUT OF YOUR HEAD, KID.
THOSE BRICKS ARE MADE OF PSIONIC ENERGY, RIGHT? SO RIGHT NOW THEY'RE THE ONLY THING KEEPING THEM FROM US.
A BOW?! SERIOUSLY?!
YOU'VE TAKEN TO SWINGING A BOW?!
I'M OUT OF ARROWS.
HERE IN THE STATES WE CALL THIS "IMPROVISING."
SWING
DON'T YOU USE THOSE THINGS FOR ANYTHING MORE THAN PUNCHING?
OF COURSE! WHAT DO YOU THINK I--
--I JUST HIT PEOPLE?
OH.
YOU'RE RIGHT...I NEED TO FOCUS.
I NEED TO NOT COME FROM A PLACE OF FEAR.

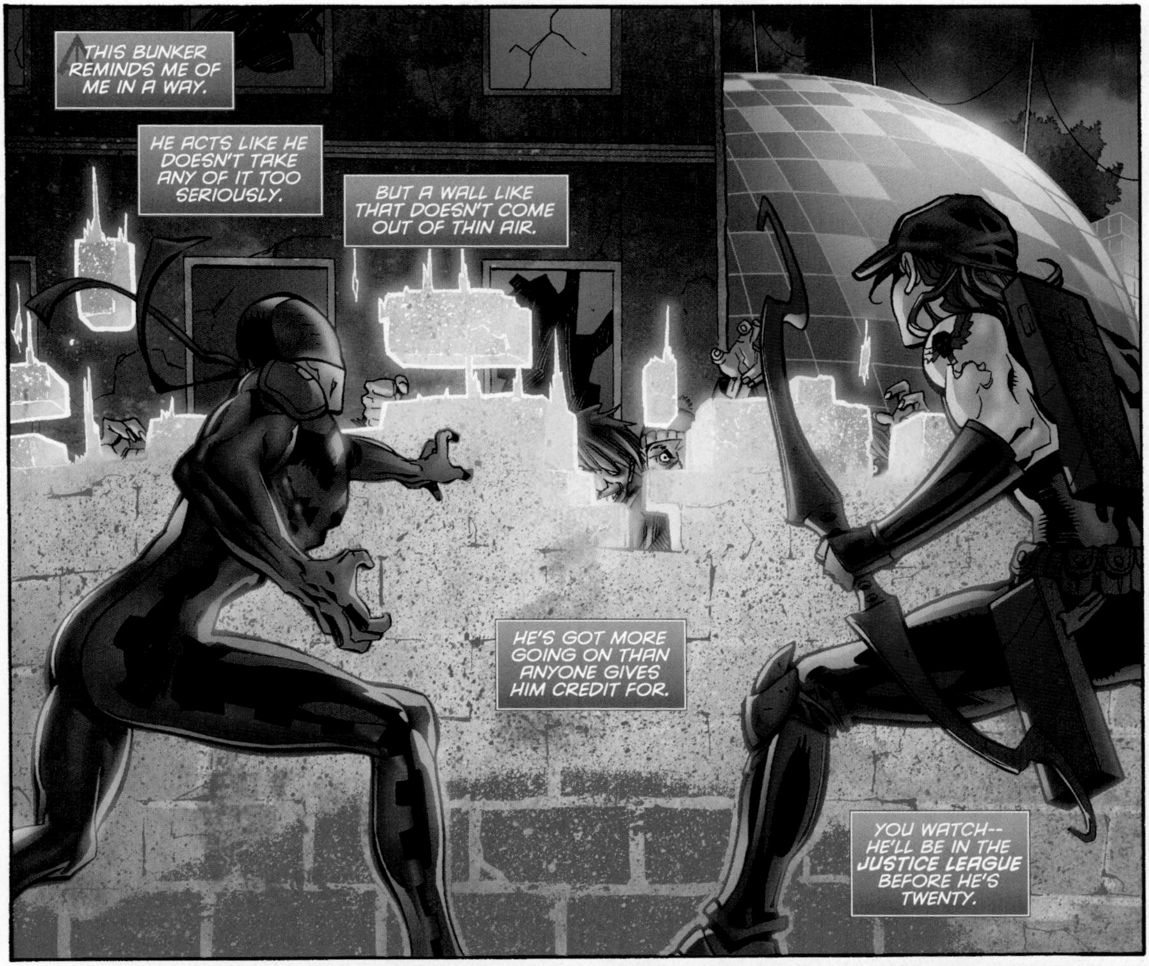
THIS BUNKER REMINDS ME OF ME IN A WAY.
HE ACTS LIKE HE DOESN'T TAKE ANY OF IT TOO SERIOUSLY.
BUT A WALL LIKE THAT DOESN'T COME OUT OF THIN AIR.
HE'S GOT MORE GOING ON THAN ANYONE GIVES HIM CREDIT FOR.
YOU WATCH-- HE'LL BE IN THE JUSTICE LEAGUE BEFORE HE'S TWENTY.

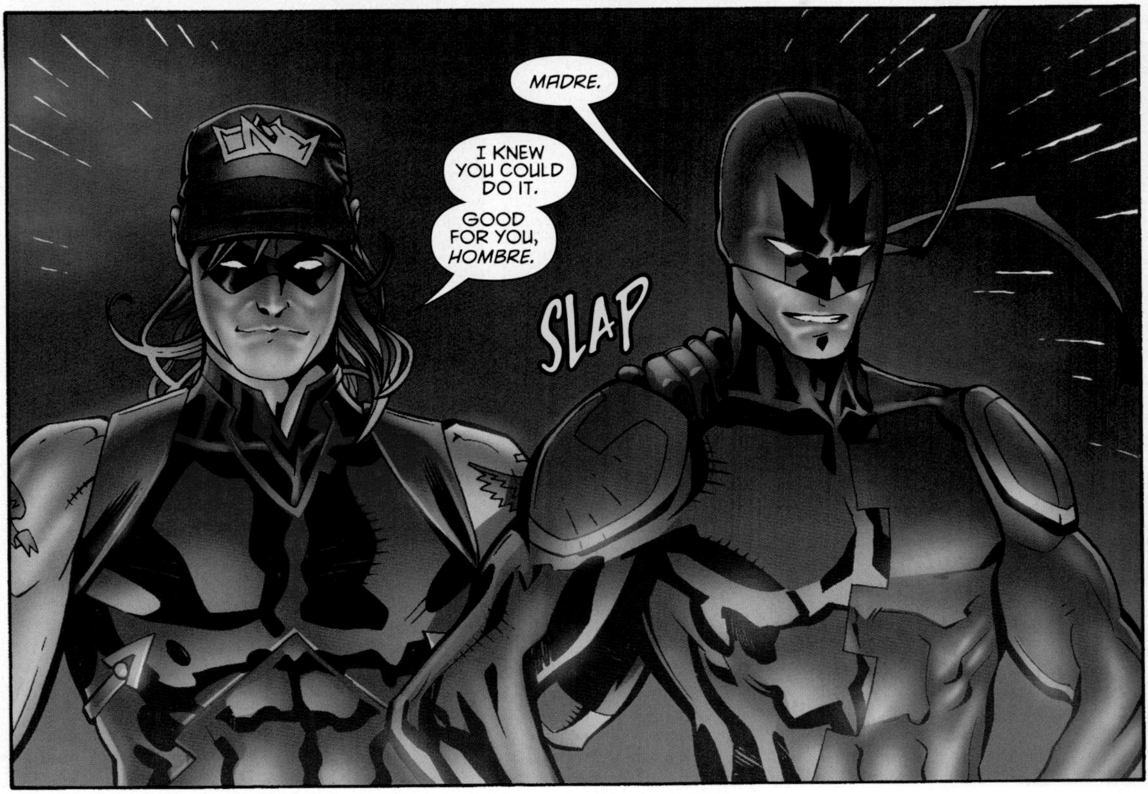
MADRE.
I KNEW YOU COULD DO IT.
GOOD FOR YOU, HOMBRE.
SLAP

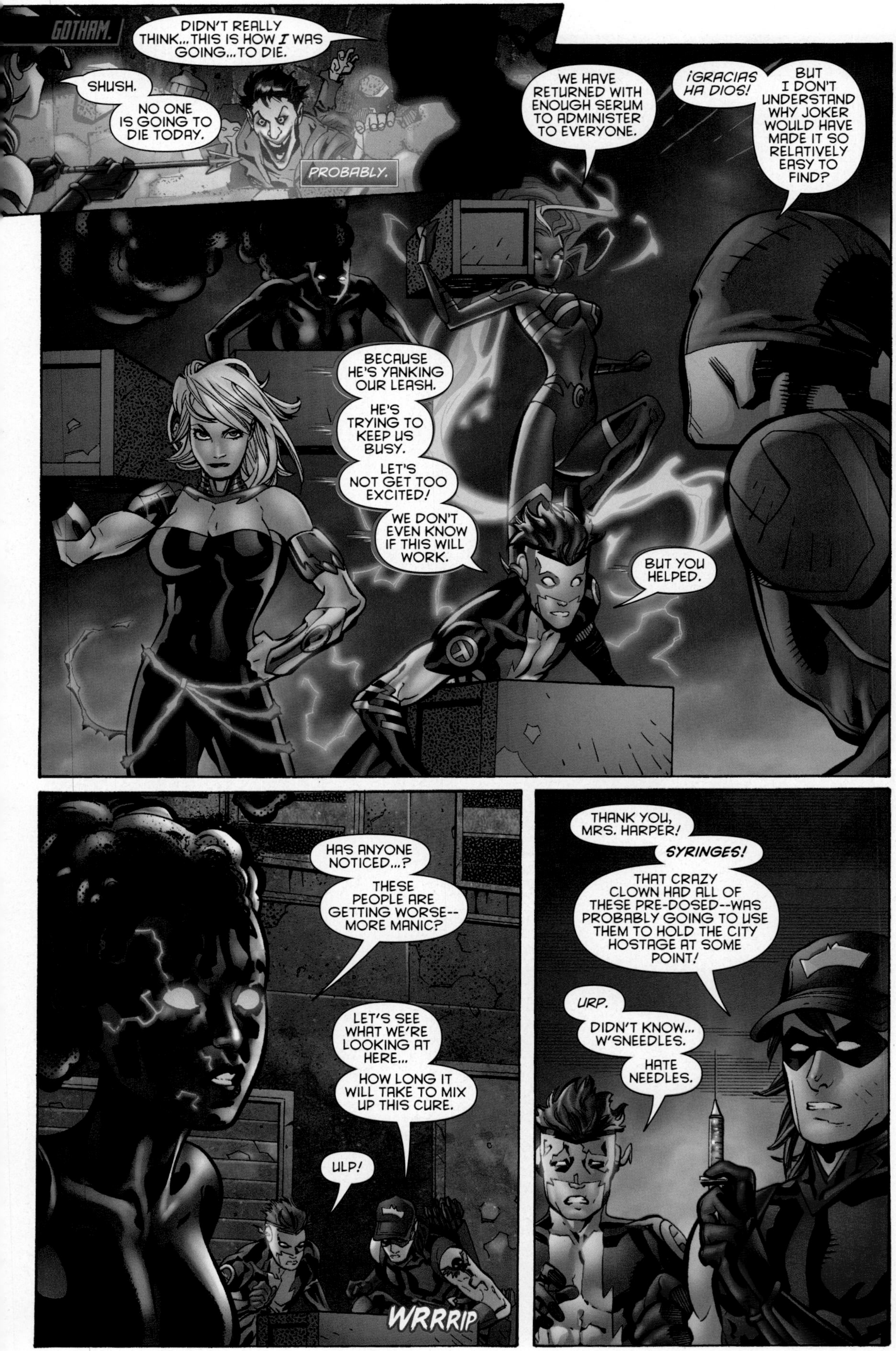
GOTHAM.
DIDN'T REALLY THINK...THIS IS HOW I WAS GOING...TO DIE.
SHUSH.
NO ONE IS GOING TO DIE TODAY.
PROBABLY.
WE HAVE RETURNED WITH ENOUGH SERUM TO ADMINISTER TO EVERYONE.
¡GRACIAS HA DIOS!
BUT I DON'T UNDERSTAND WHY JOKER WOULD HAVE MADE IT SO RELATIVELY EASY TO FIND?
BECAUSE HE'S YANKING OUR LEASH.
HE'S TRYING TO KEEP US BUSY.
LET'S NOT GET TOO EXCITED!
WE DON'T EVEN KNOW IF THIS WILL WORK.
BUT YOU HELPED.
HAS ANYONE NOTICED...?
THESE PEOPLE ARE GETTING WORSE-- MORE MANIC?
LET'S SEE WHAT WE'RE LOOKING AT HERE...
HOW LONG IT WILL TAKE TO MIX UP THIS CURE.
ULP!
WRRRIP
THANK YOU, MRS. HARPER!
SYRINGES!
THAT CRAZY CLOWN HAD ALL OF THESE PRE-DOSED--WAS PROBABLY GOING TO USE THEM TO HOLD THE CITY HOSTAGE AT SOME POINT!
URP.
DIDN'T KNOW... W'SNEEDLES.
HATE NEEDLES.

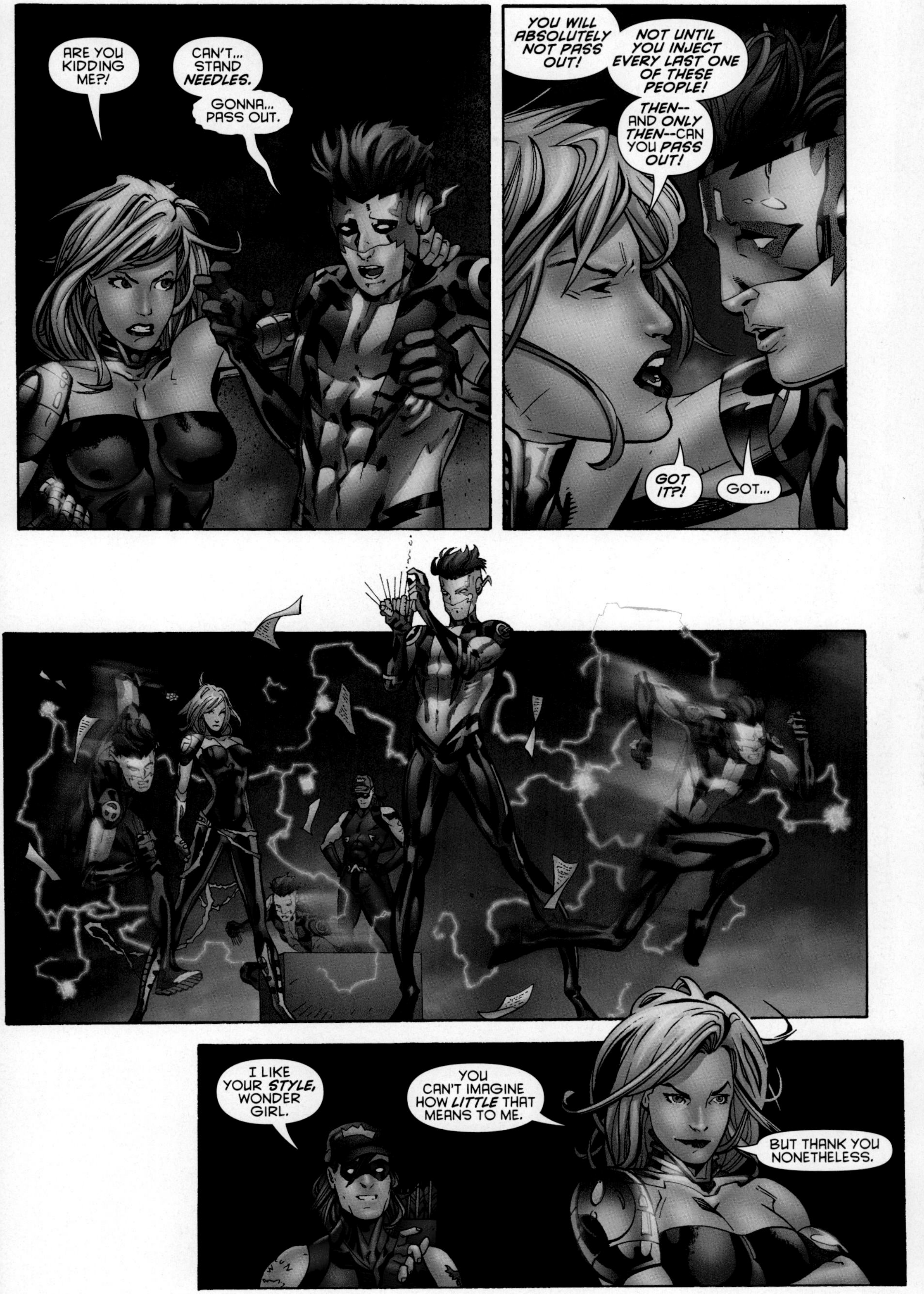
ARE YOU KIDDING ME?!
CAN'T... STAND NEEDLES.
GONNA... PASS OUT.
YOU WILL ABSOLUTELY NOT PASS OUT!
NOT UNTIL YOU INJECT EVERY LAST ONE OF THESE PEOPLE!
THEN--AND ONLY THEN--CAN YOU PASS OUT!
GOT IT?!
GOT...
I LIKE YOUR STYLE, WONDER GIRL.
YOU CAN'T IMAGINE HOW LITTLE THAT MEANS TO ME.
BUT THANK YOU NONETHELESS.

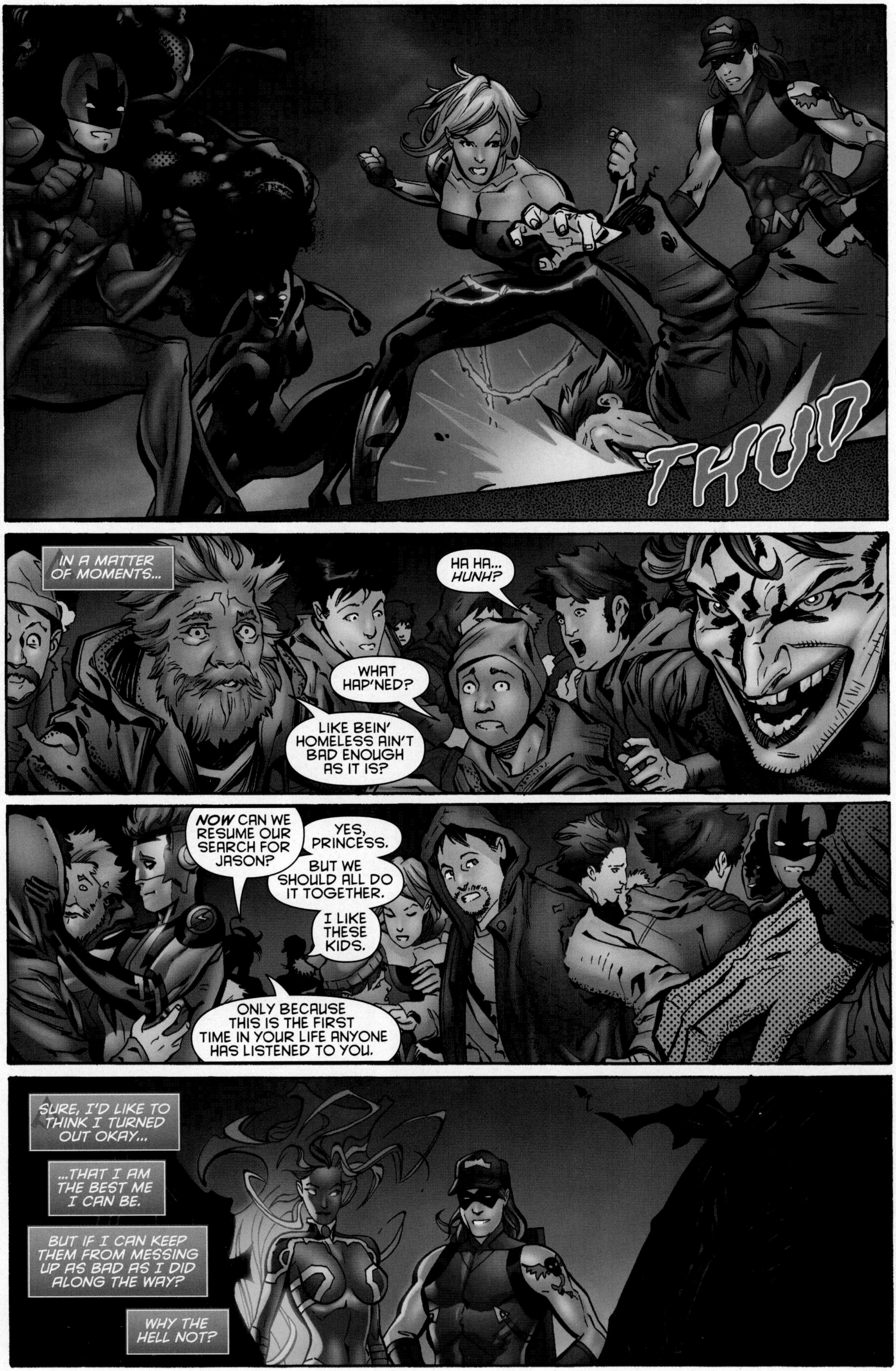
THUD
IN A MATTER OF MOMENTS...
HA HA... HUNH?
WHAT HAP'NED?
LIKE BEIN' HOMELESS AIN'T BAD ENOUGH AS IT IS?
NOW CAN WE RESUME OUR SEARCH FOR JASON?
YES, PRINCESS.
BUT WE SHOULD ALL DO IT TOGETHER.
I LIKE THESE KIDS.
ONLY BECAUSE THIS IS THE FIRST TIME IN YOUR LIFE ANYONE HAS LISTENED TO YOU.
SURE, I'D LIKE TO THINK I TURNED OUT OKAY...
...THAT I AM THE BEST ME I CAN BE.
BUT IF I CAN KEEP THEM FROM MESSING UP AS BAD AS I DID ALONG THE WAY?
WHY THE HELL NOT?

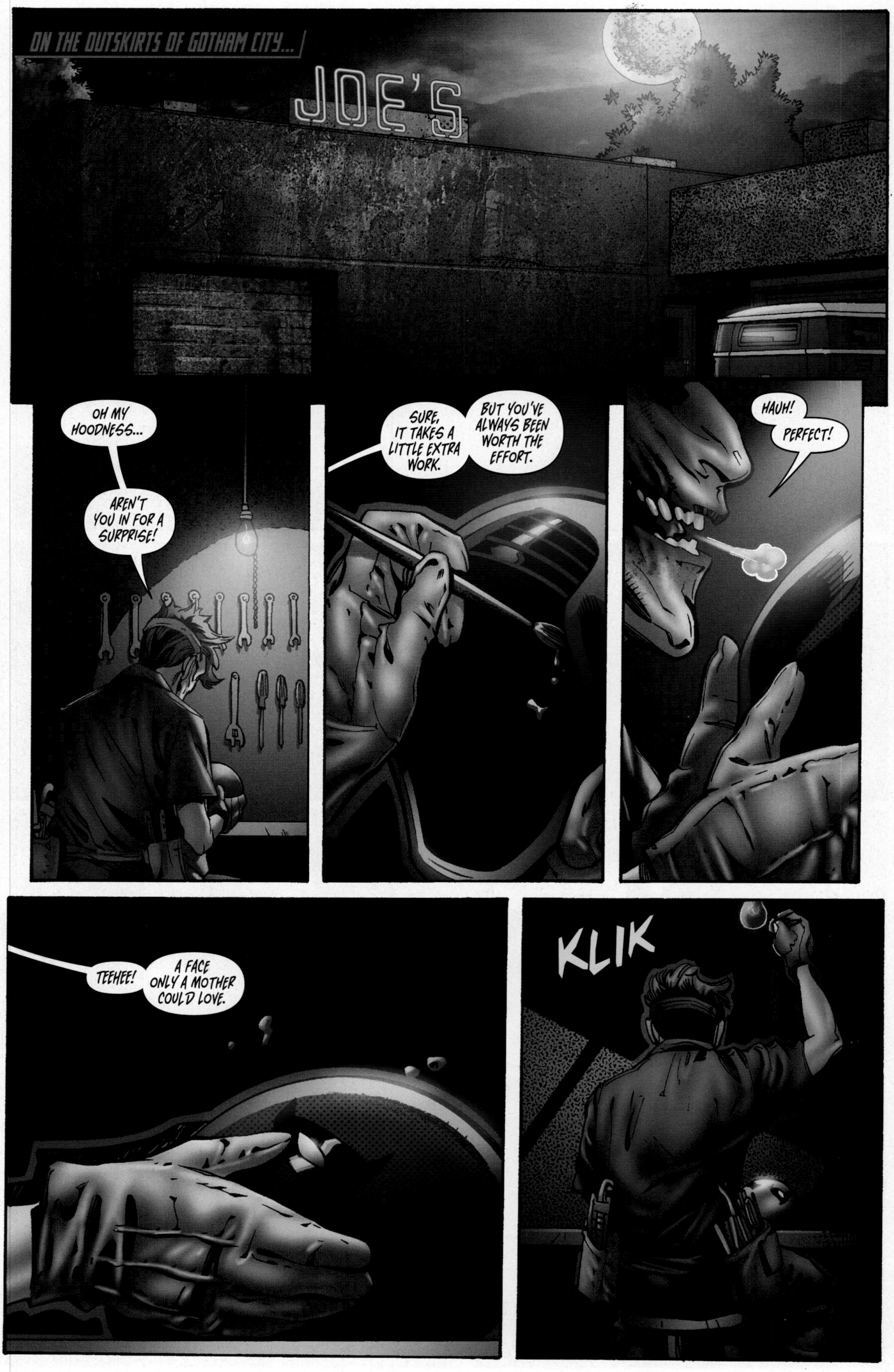
ON THE OUTSKIRTS OF GOTHAM CITY...
JOE'S
OH MY HOODNESS...
AREN'T YOU IN FOR A SURPRISE!
SURE, IT TAKES A LITTLE EXTRA WORK.
BUT YOU'VE ALWAYS BEEN WORTH THE EFFORT.
HAUH!
PERFECT!
TEEHEE!
A FACE ONLY A MOTHER COULD LOVE.
KLIK

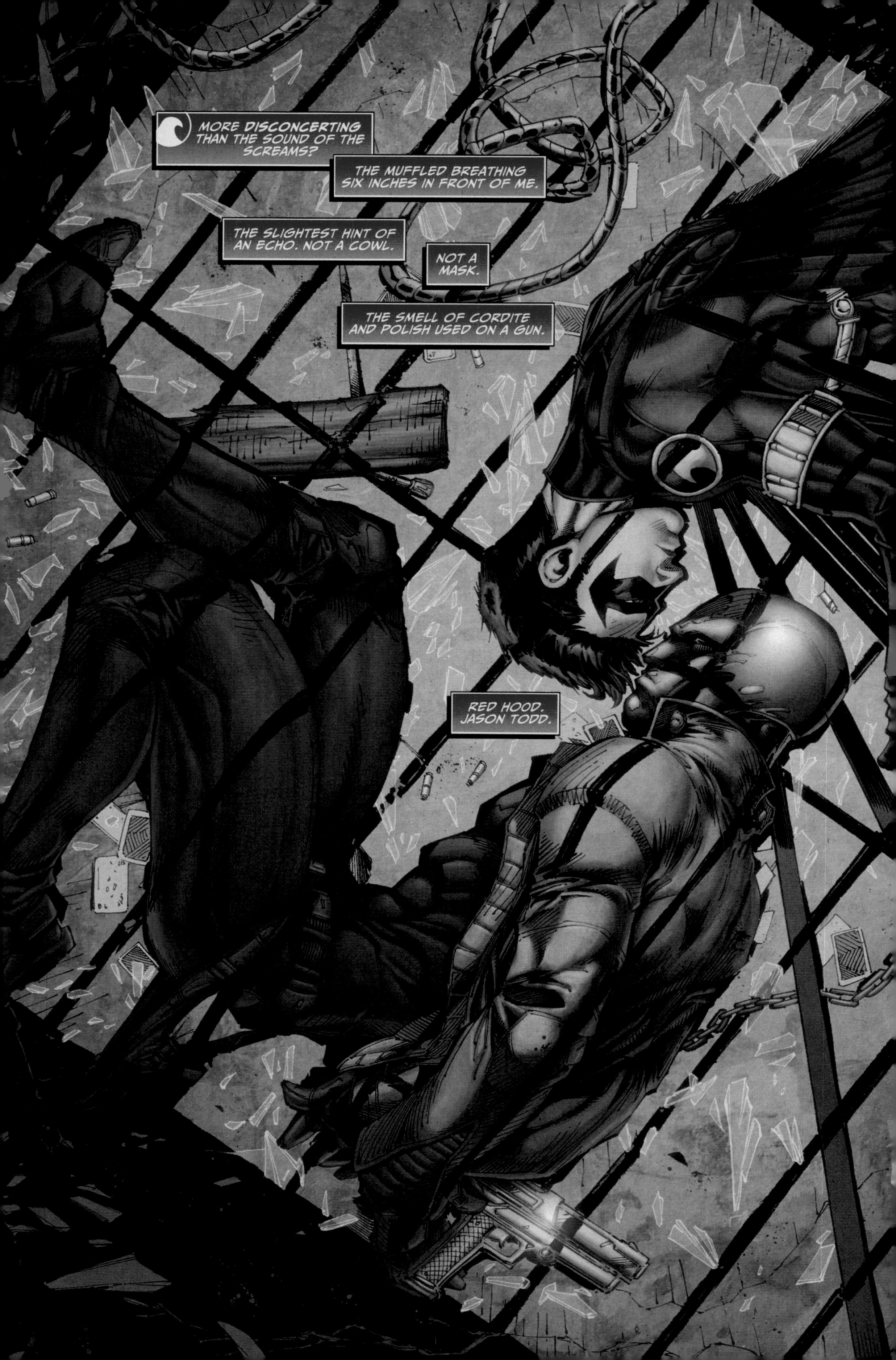
MORE DISCONCERTING THAN THE SOUND OF THE SCREAMS?
THE MUFFLED BREATHING SIX INCHES IN FRONT OF ME.
THE SLIGHTEST HINT OF AN ECHO. NOT A COWL.
NOT A MASK.
THE SMELL OF CORDITE AND POLISH USED ON A GUN.
RED HOOD. JASON TODD.

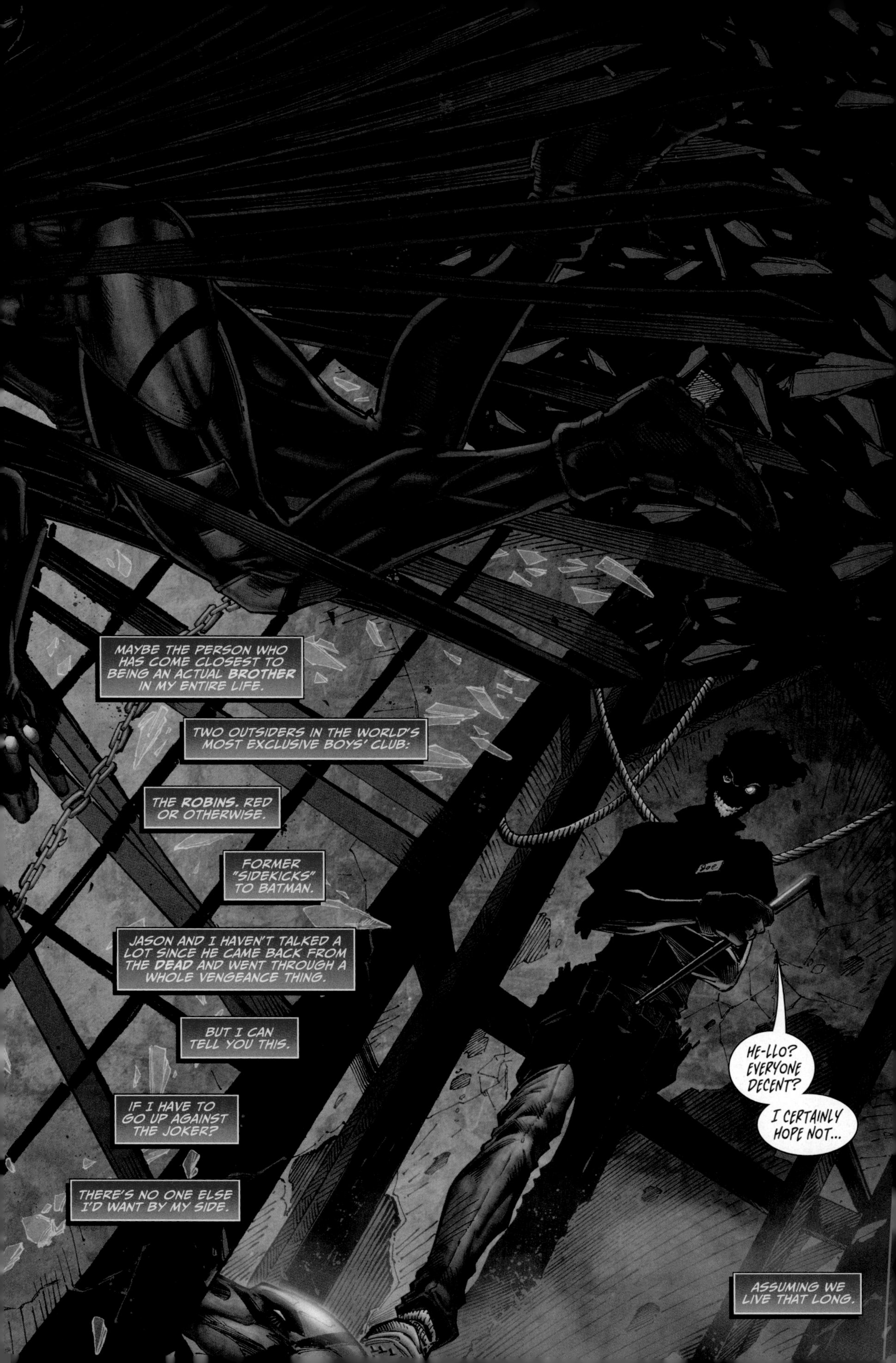
MAYBE THE PERSON WHO HAS COME CLOSEST TO BEING AN ACTUAL BROTHER IN MY ENTIRE LIFE.
TWO OUTSIDERS IN THE WORLD'S MOST EXCLUSIVE BOYS' CLUB:
THE ROBINS. RED OR OTHERWISE.
FORMER "SIDEKICKS" TO BATMAN.
JASON AND I HAVEN'T TALKED A LOT SINCE HE CAME BACK FROM THE DEAD AND WENT THROUGH A WHOLE VENGEANCE THING.
BUT I CAN TELL YOU THIS.
IF I HAVE TO GO UP AGAINST THE JOKER?
THERE'S NO ONE ELSE I'D WANT BY MY SIDE.
HE-LLO? EVERYONE DECENT?
I CERTAINLY HOPE NOT...
ASSUMING WE LIVE THAT LONG.

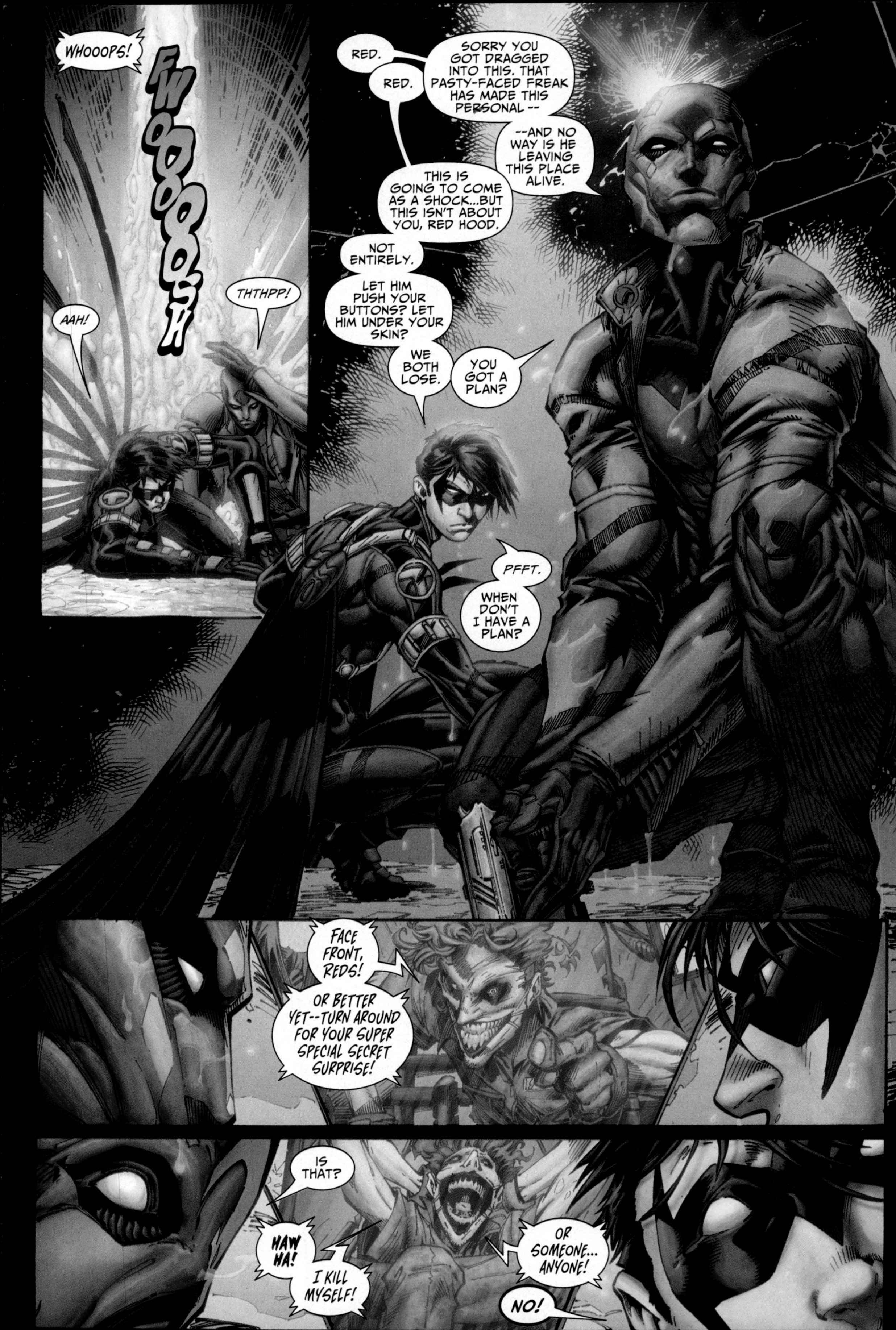
WHOOOPS!
FWOOOOSH
AAH!
THTHPP!
RED.
RED.
SORRY YOU GOT DRAGGED INTO THIS. THAT PASTY-FACED FREAK HAS MADE THIS PERSONAL --
--AND NO WAY IS HE LEAVING THIS PLACE ALIVE.
THIS IS GOING TO COME AS A SHOCK...BUT THIS ISN'T ABOUT YOU, RED HOOD.
NOT ENTIRELY.
LET HIM PUSH YOUR BUTTONS? LET HIM UNDER YOUR SKIN?
WE BOTH LOSE.
YOU GOT A PLAN?
PFFT.
WHEN DON'T I HAVE A PLAN?
FACE FRONT, REDS!
OR BETTER YET--TURN AROUND FOR YOUR SUPER SPECIAL SECRET SURPRISE!
IS THAT?
HAW HA!
I KILL MYSELF!
OR SOMEONE... ANYONE!
NO!

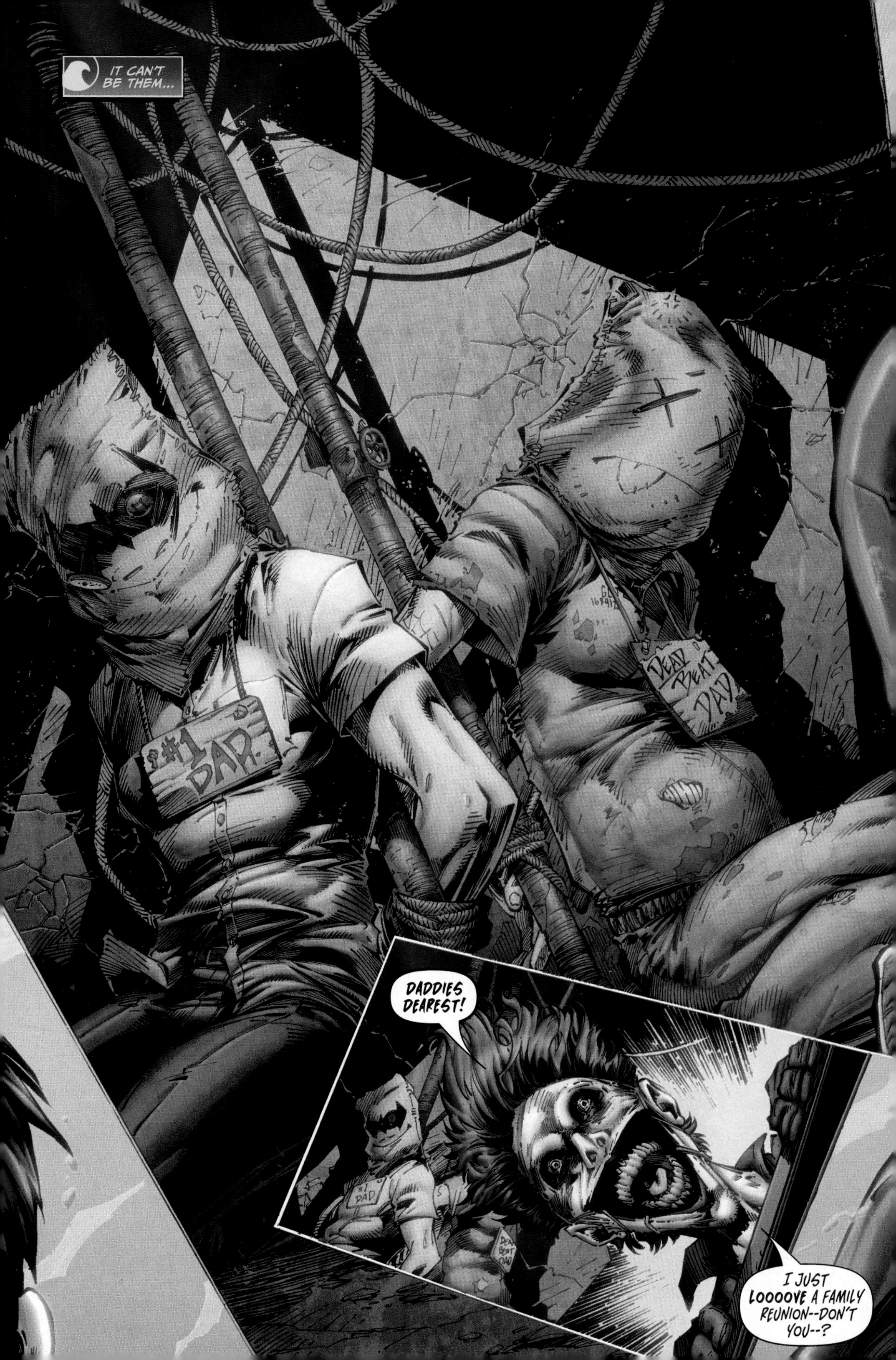
IT CAN'T BE THEM...
#1 DAD
DEAD BEAT DAD
DADDIES DEAREST!
I JUST LOOOOVE A FAMILY REUNION--DON'T YOU--?

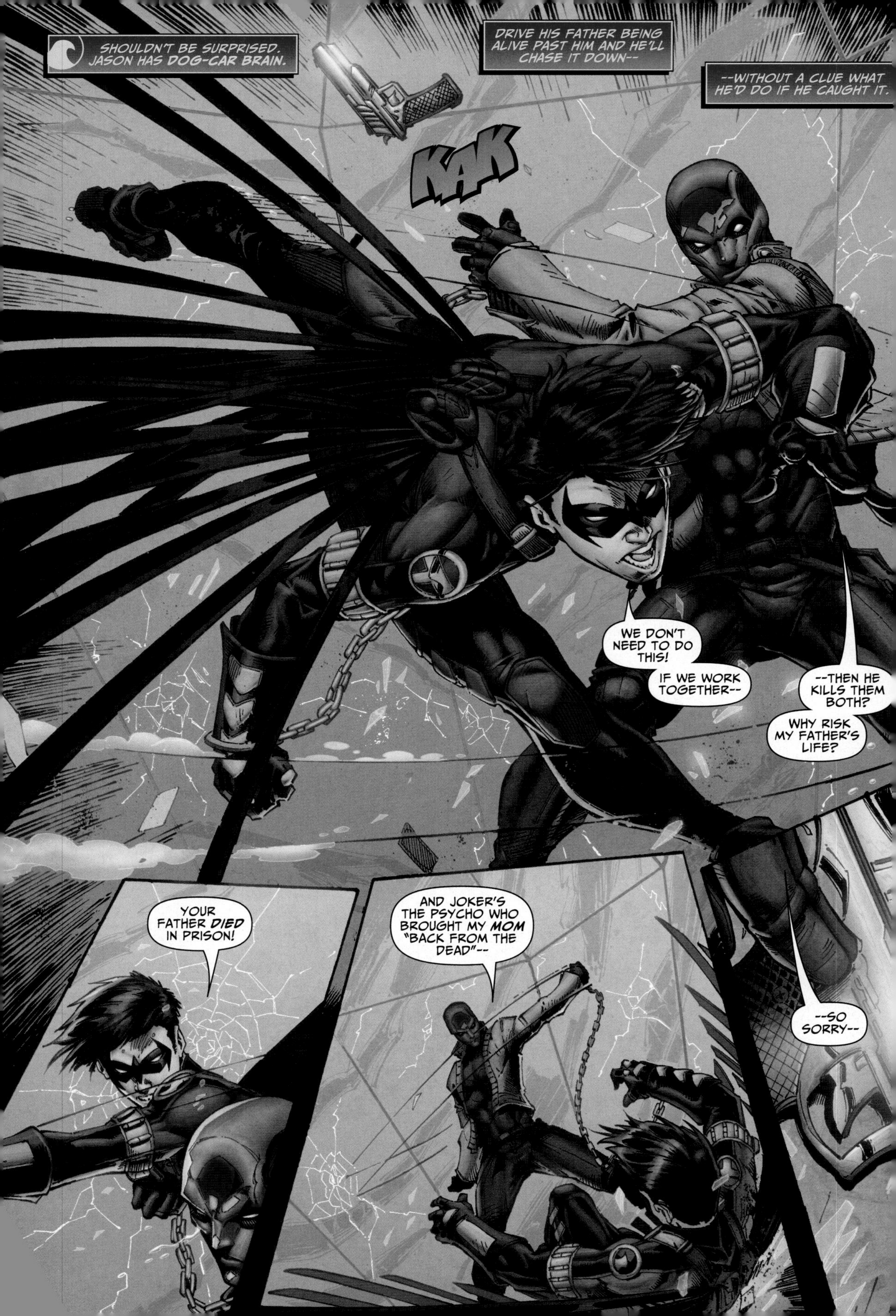

SHOULDN'T BE SURPRISED. JASON HAS DOG-CAR BRAIN.
DRIVE HIS FATHER BEING ALIVE PAST HIM AND HE'LL CHASE IT DOWN--
--WITHOUT A CLUE WHAT HE'D DO IF HE CAUGHT IT.
KAK
WE DON'T NEED TO DO THIS!
IF WE WORK TOGETHER--
--THEN HE KILLS THEM BOTH?
WHY RISK MY FATHER'S LIFE?
YOUR FATHER DIED IN PRISON!
AND JOKER'S THE PSYCHO WHO BROUGHT MY MOM "BACK FROM THE DEAD"--
--SO SORRY--

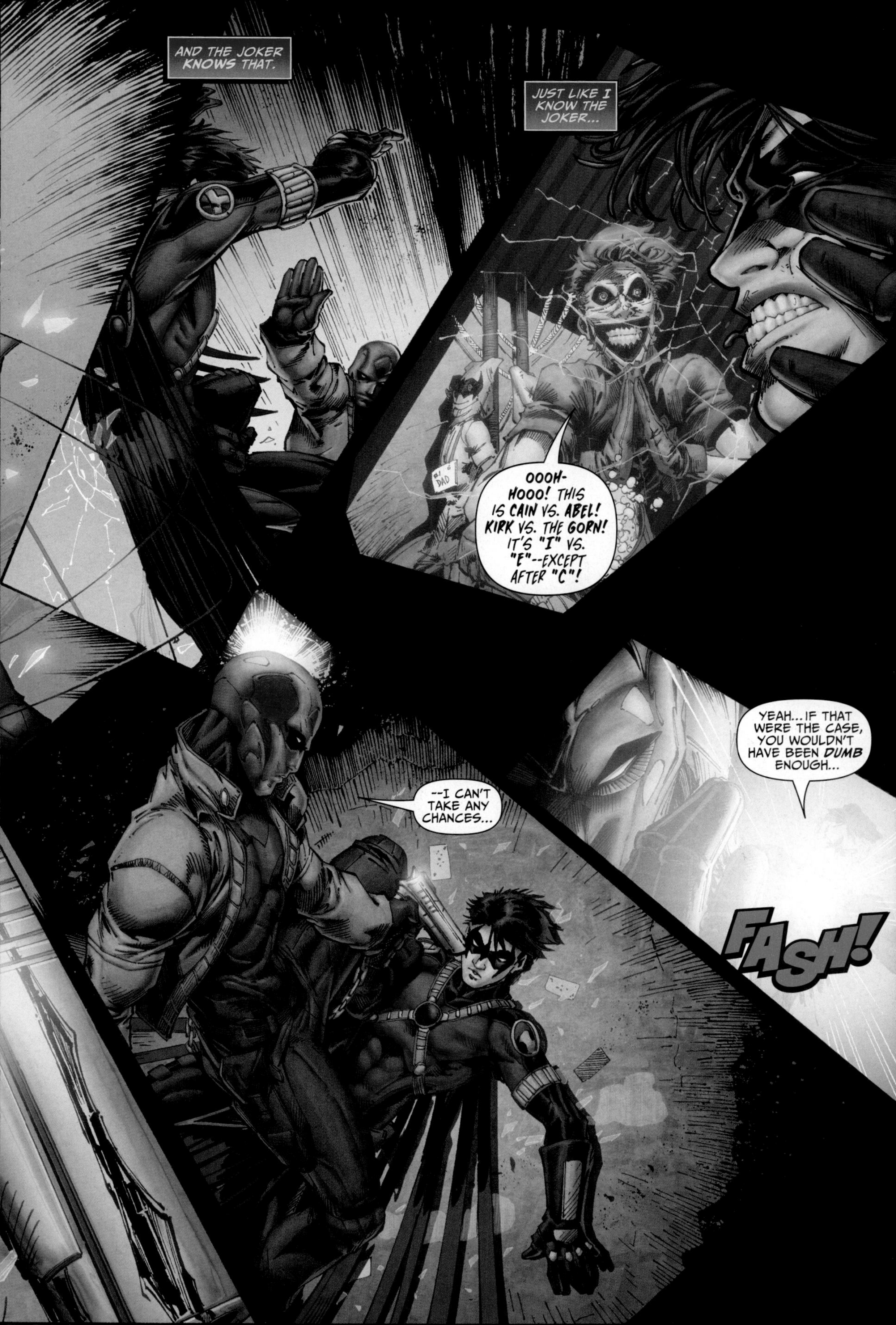
AND THE JOKER KNOWS THAT.
JUST LIKE I KNOW THE JOKER...
OOOH-HOOO! THIS IS CAIN VS. ABEL! KIRK VS. THE GORN! IT'S "I" VS. "E"--EXCEPT AFTER "C"!
#1 DAD
--I CAN'T TAKE ANY CHANCES...
YEAH...IF THAT WERE THE CASE, YOU WOULDN'T HAVE BEEN DUMB ENOUGH...
FASH!

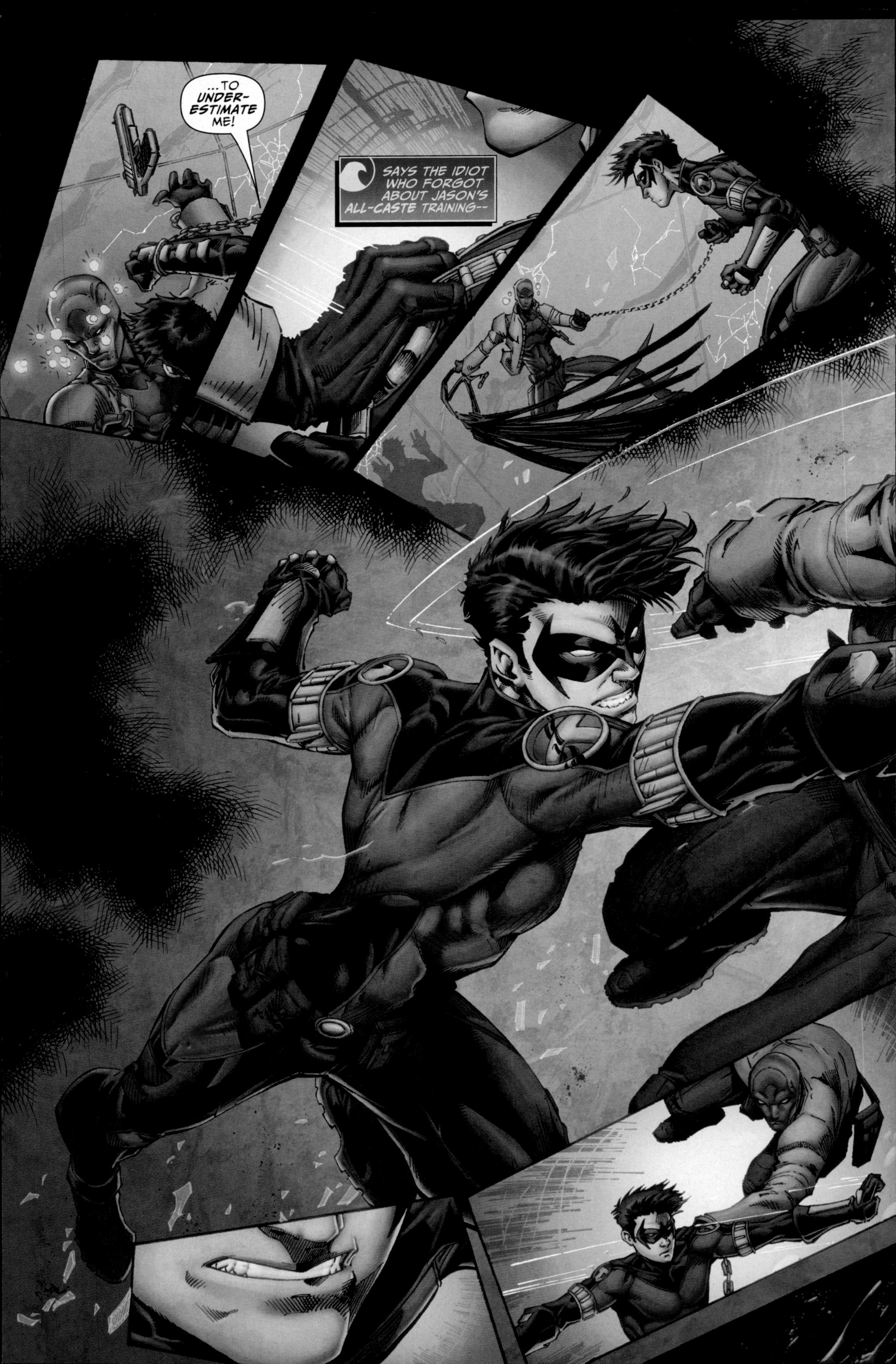
...TO UNDER-ESTIMATE ME!
SAYS THE IDIOT WHO FORGOT ABOUT JASON'S ALL-CASTE TRAINING--

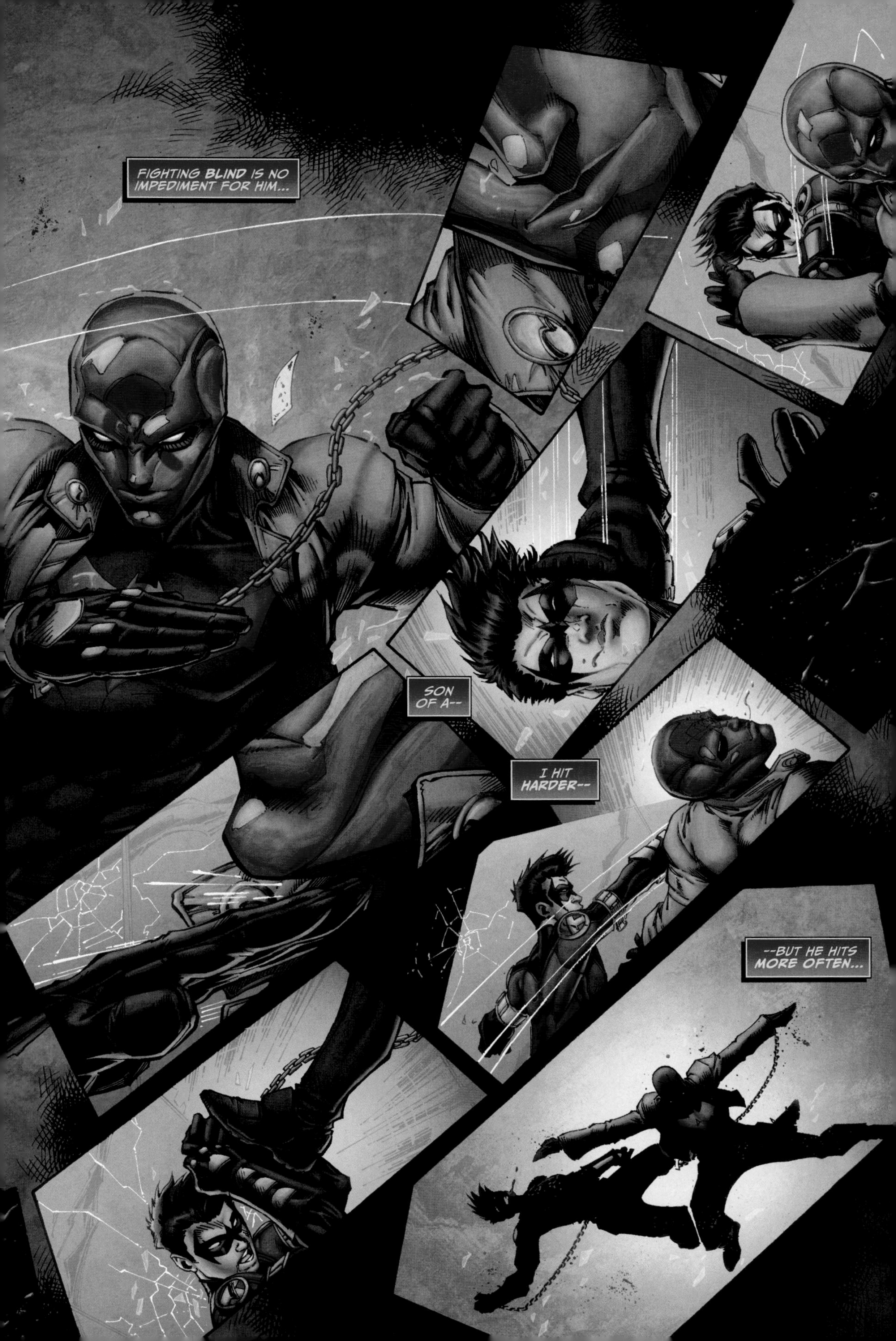

FIGHTING BLIND IS NO IMPEDIMENT FOR HIM...
SON OF A--
I HIT HARDER--
--BUT HE HITS MORE OFTEN...

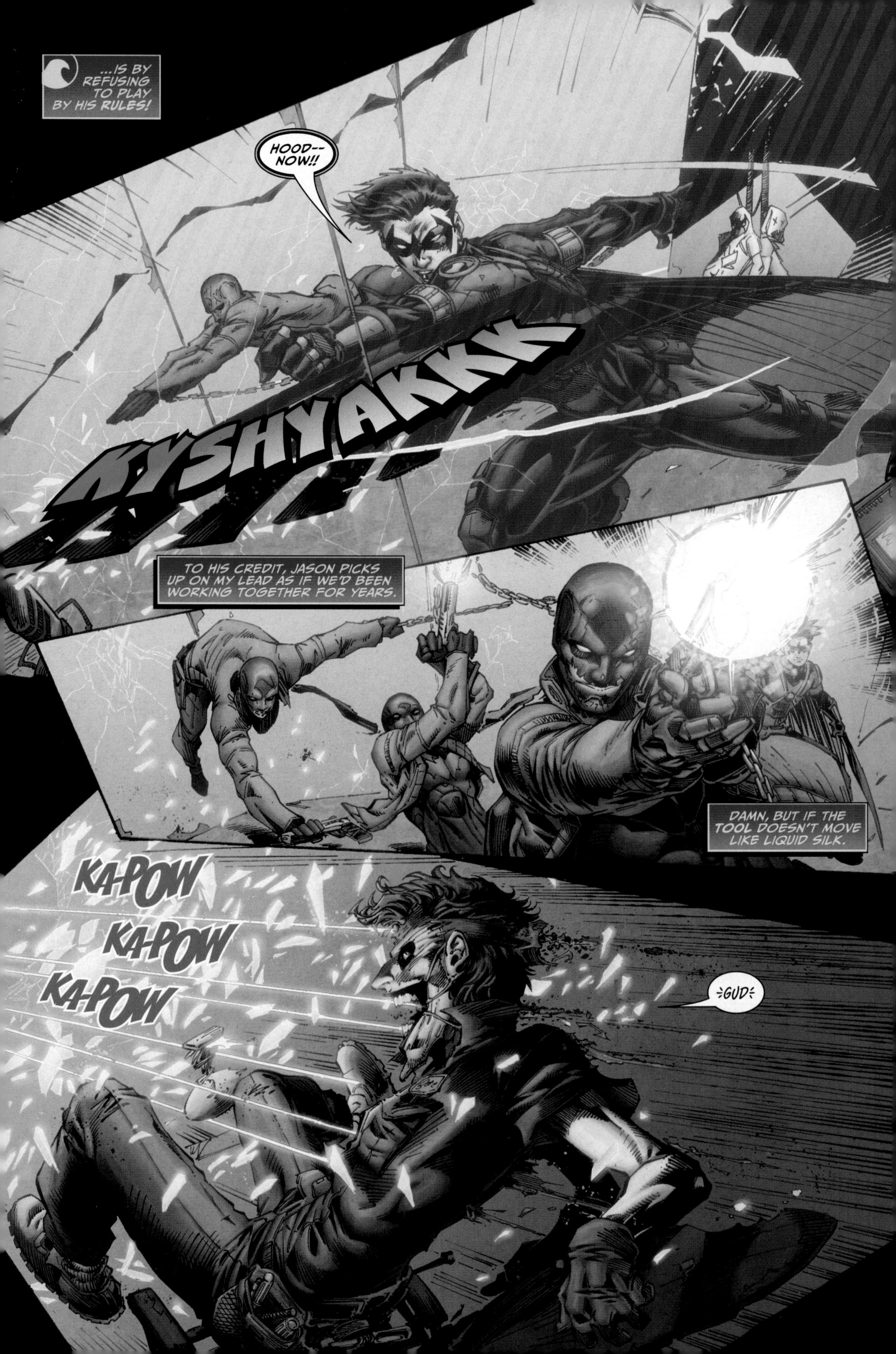
...IS BY REFUSING TO PLAY BY HIS RULES!
HOOD-- NOW!!
KYSHYAKKK
TO HIS CREDIT, JASON PICKS UP ON MY LEAD AS IF WE'D BEEN WORKING TOGETHER FOR YEARS.
DAMN, BUT IF THE TOOL DOESN'T MOVE LIKE LIQUID SILK.
KA-POW
KA-POW
KA-POW
GUD

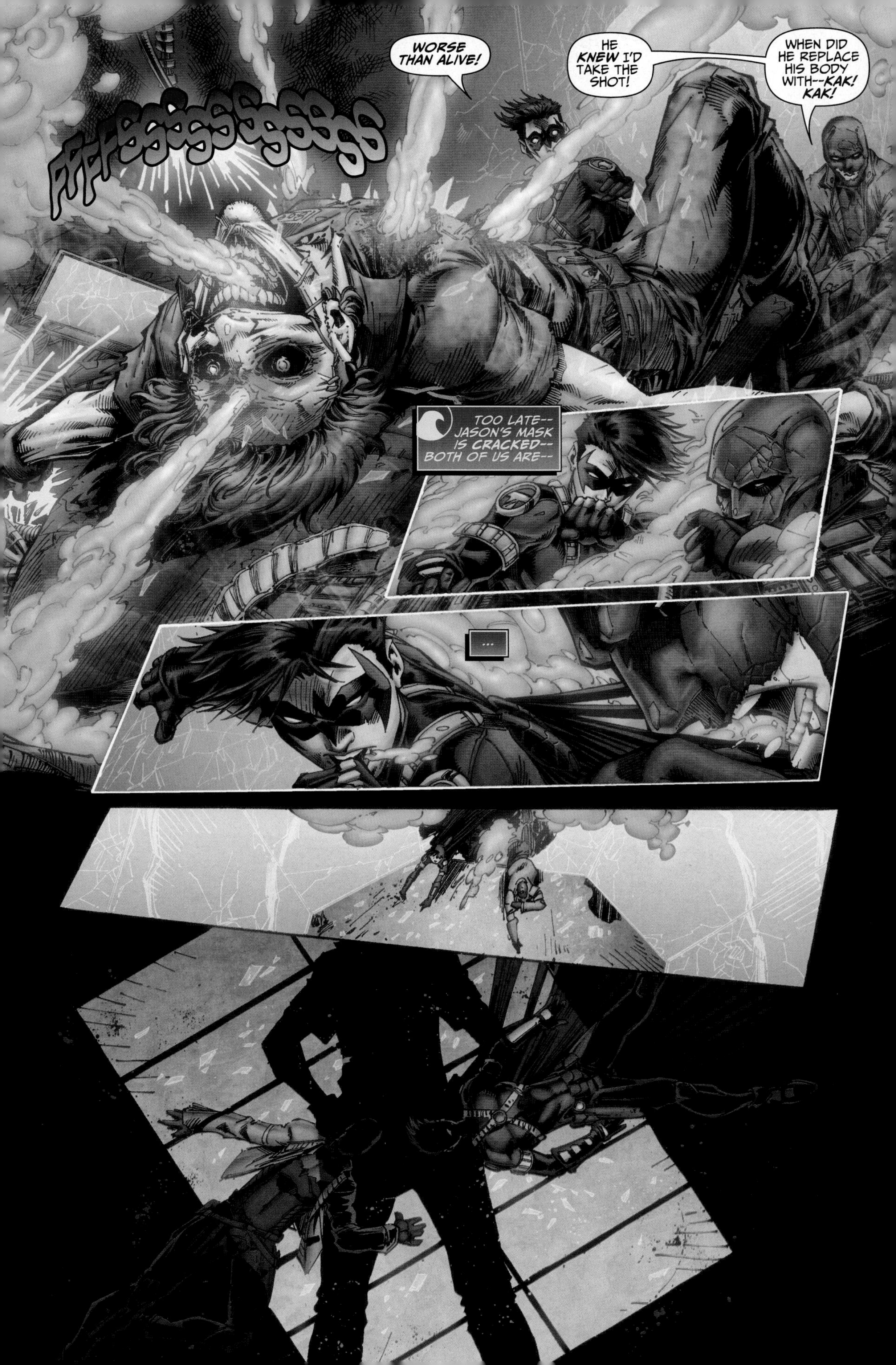
WORSE THAN ALIVE!
HE KNEW I'D TAKE THE SHOT!
WHEN DID HE REPLACE HIS BODY WITH--KAK! KAK!
FFFFSSSSSSSSSSSS
TOO LATE-- JASON'S MASK IS CRACKED-- BOTH OF US ARE--
...

PART SIX
NIGHTWING

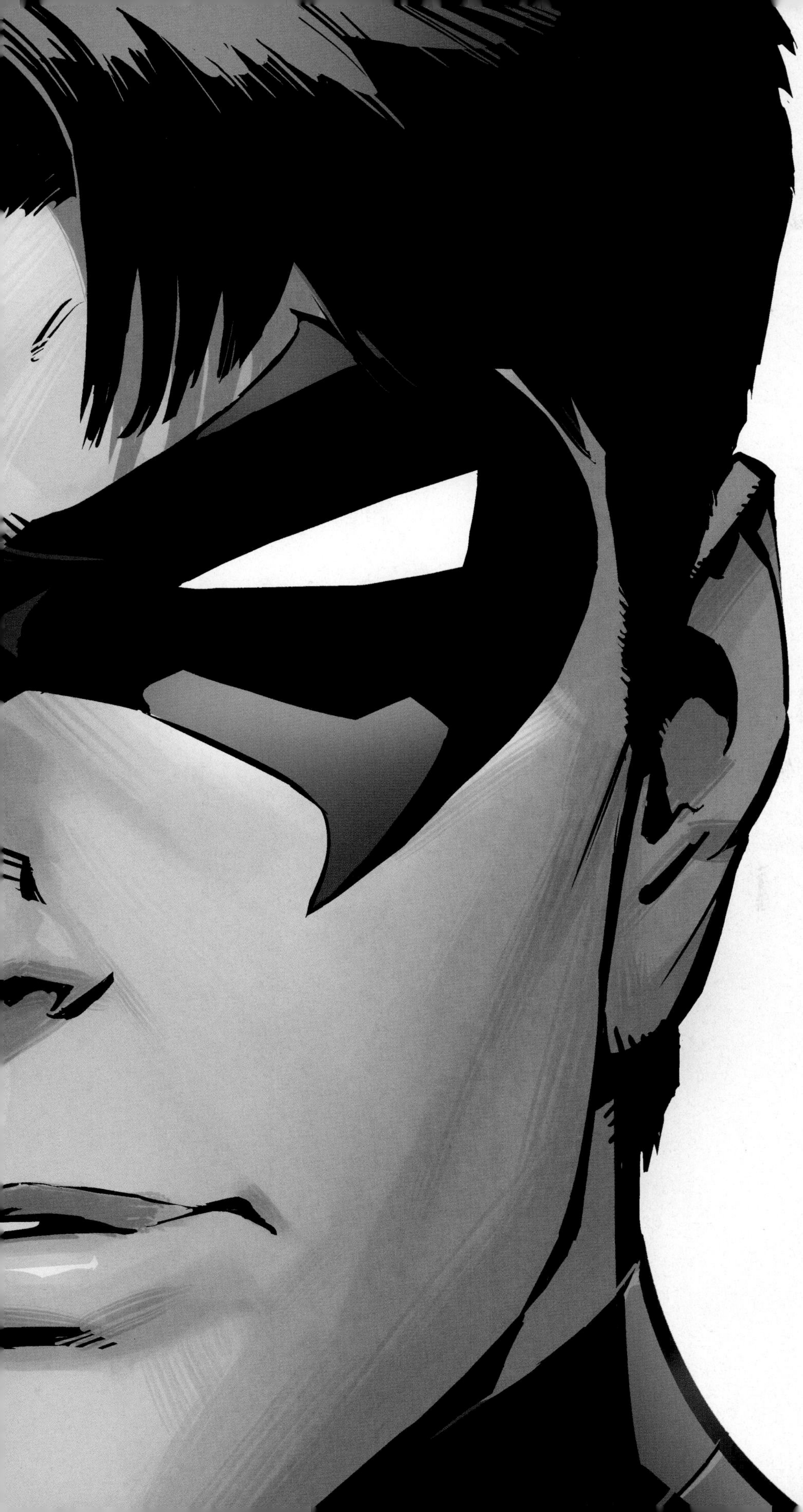

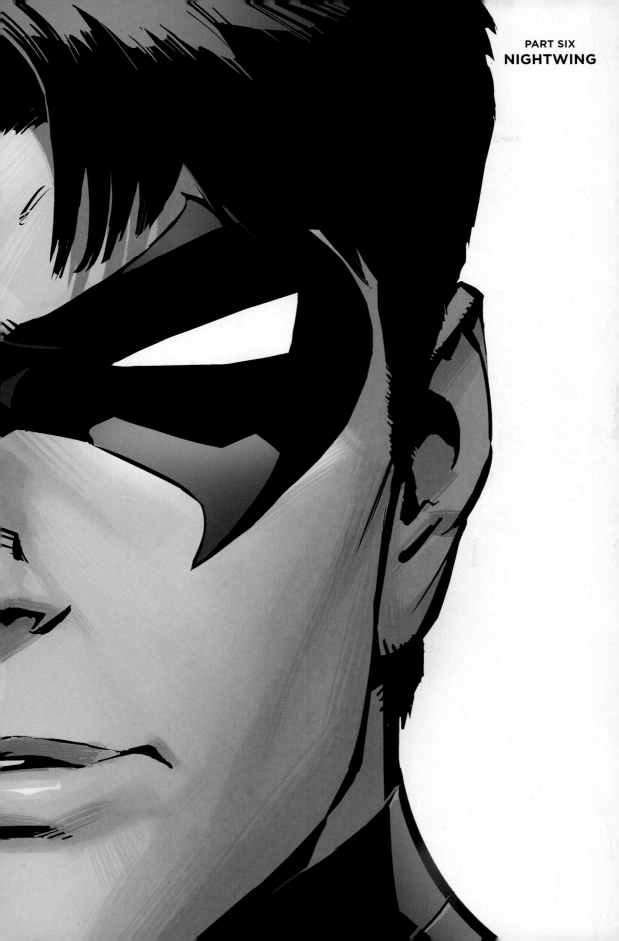

KYLE HIGGINS TOM DEFALCO writers EDDY BARROWS ANDRES GUINALDO pencillers EBER FERREIRA MARK IRWIN inkers
ROD REIS PETE PANTAZIS colorists CARLOS M. MANGUAL DAVE SHARPE letterers NIGHTWING created by MARV WOLFMAN and GEORGE PÉREZ

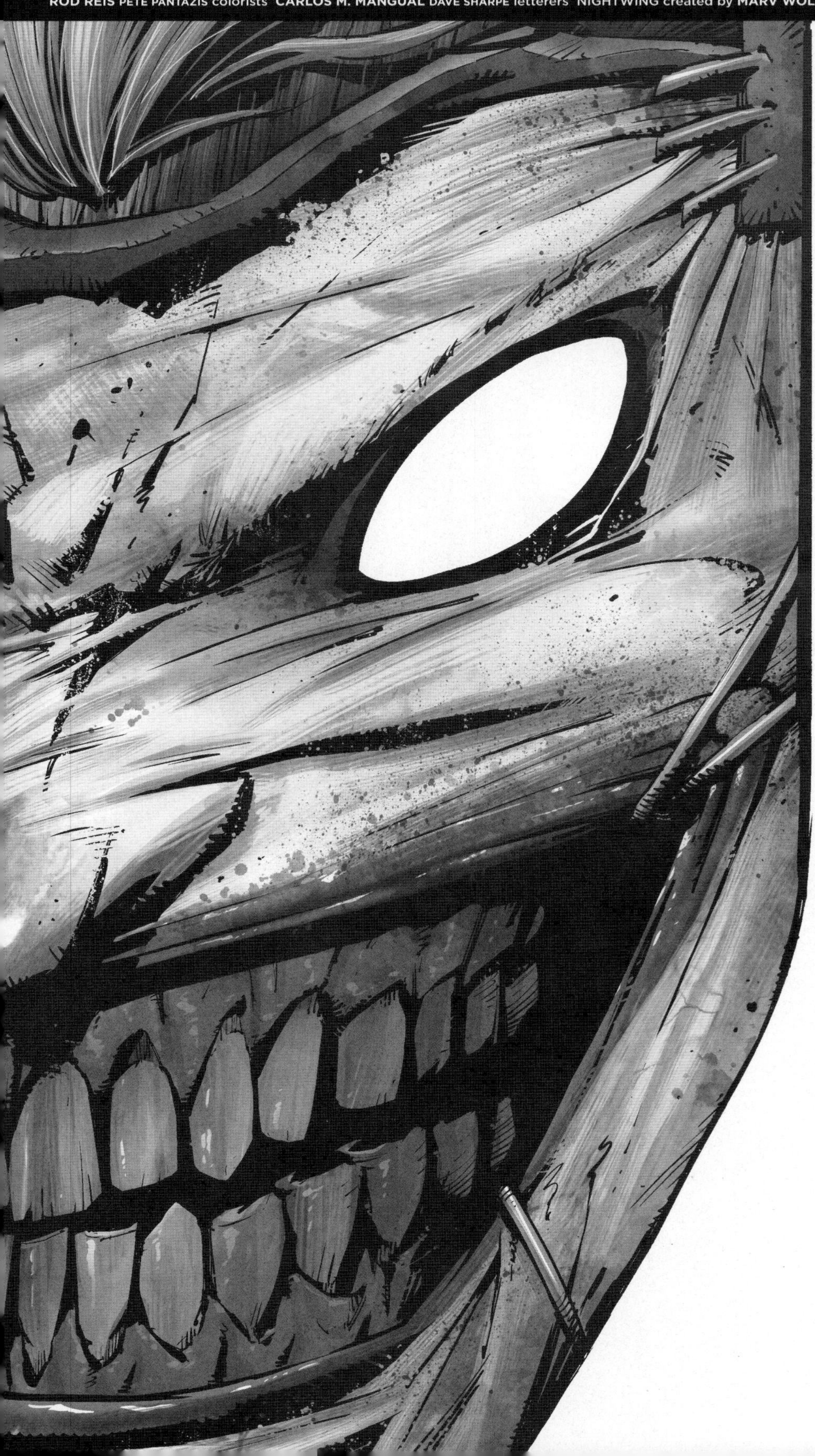

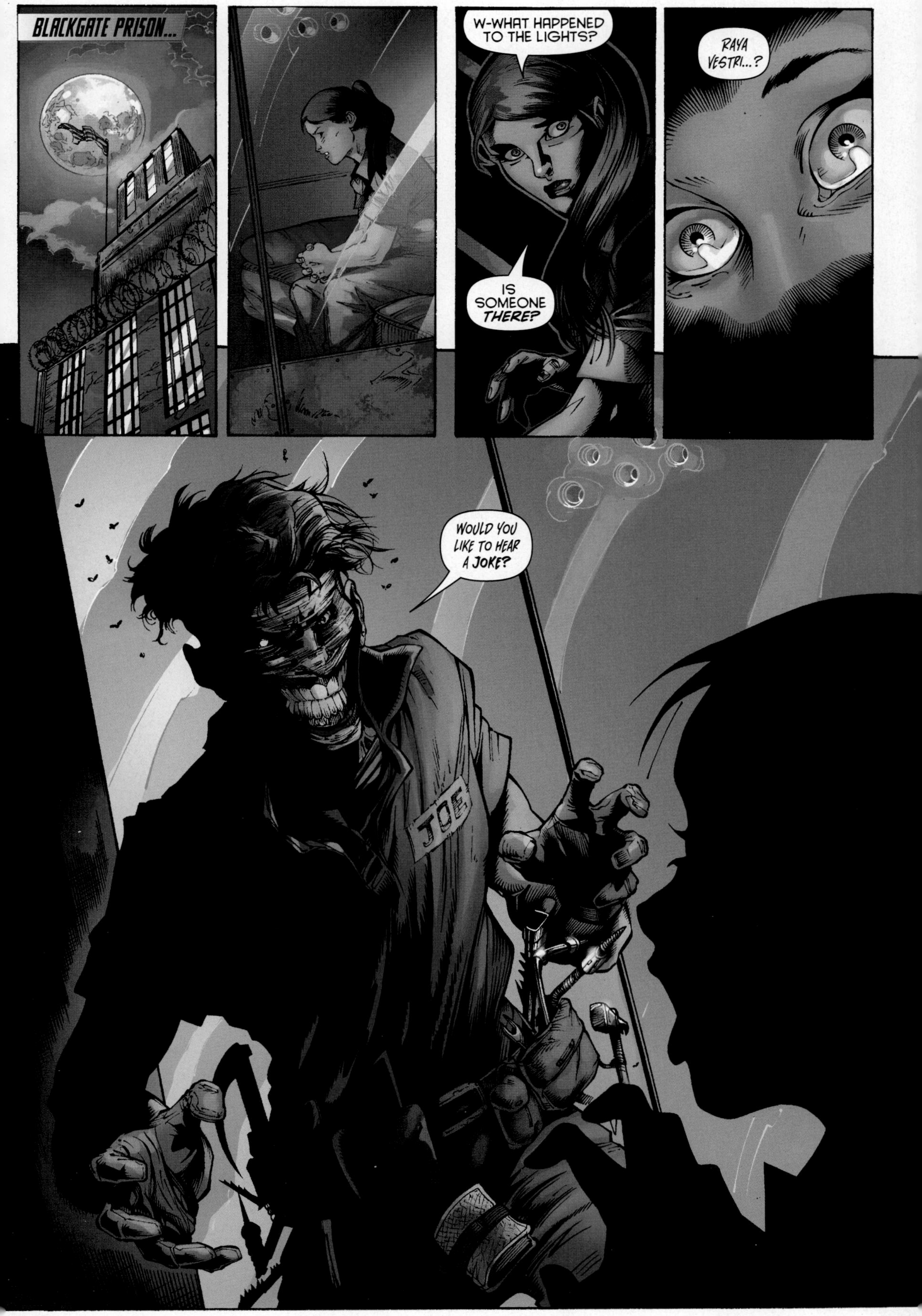
BLACKGATE PRISON...
W-WHAT HAPPENED TO THE LIGHTS?
IS SOMEONE THERE?
RAYA VESTRI...?
WOULD YOU LIKE TO HEAR A JOKE?
JOE

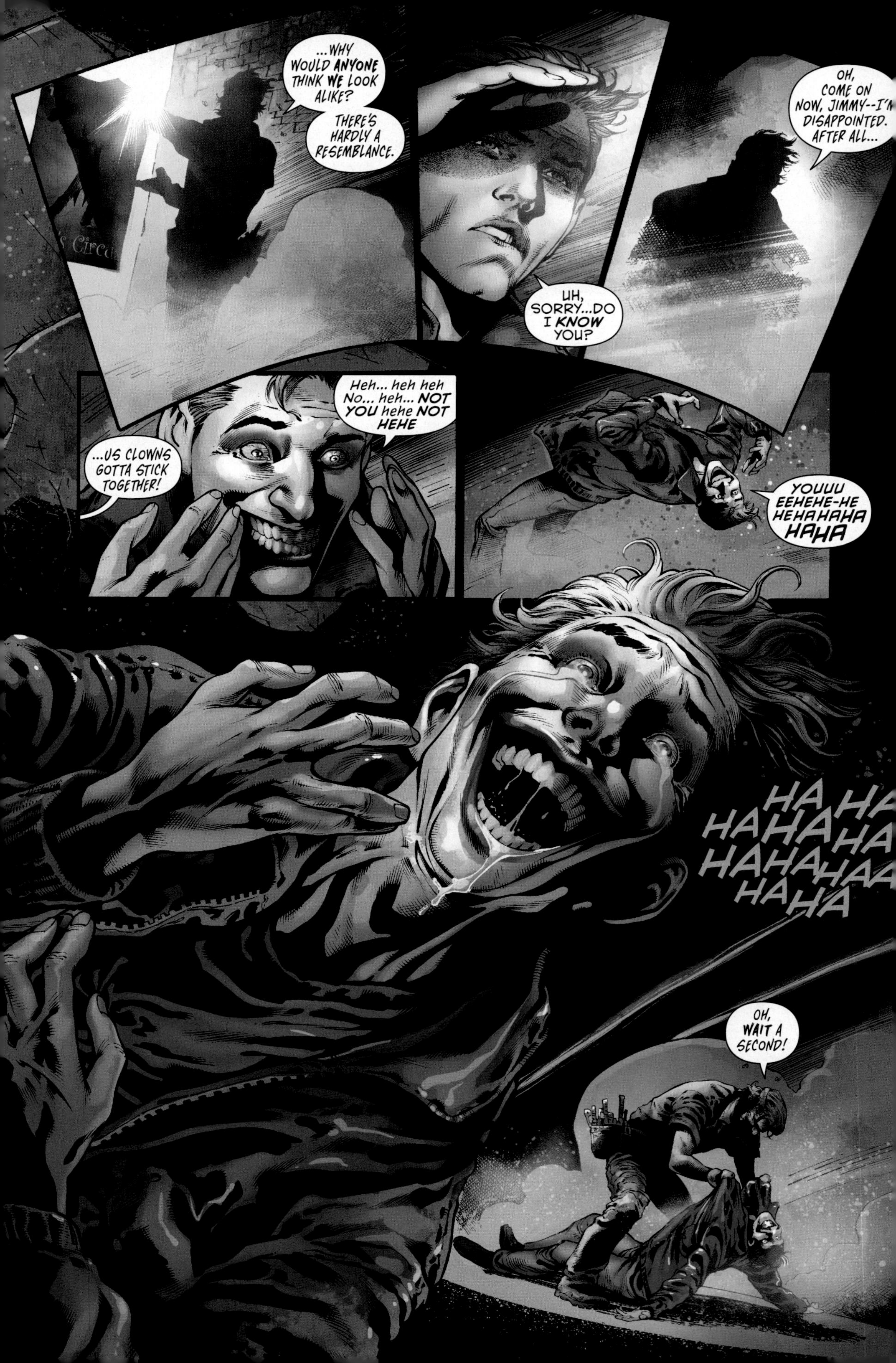
...WHY WOULD ANYONE THINK WE LOOK ALIKE?
THERE'S HARDLY A RESEMBLANCE.
UH, SORRY...DO I KNOW YOU?
OH, COME ON NOW, JIMMY--I'M DISAPPOINTED. AFTER ALL...
...US CLOWNS GOTTA STICK TOGETHER!
Heh... heh heh No... heh... NOT YOU hehe NOT HEHE
YOUUU EEHEHE-HE HEHAHAHA HAHA
HA HA HAHAHA HAHAHAA HAHA
OH, WAIT A SECOND!

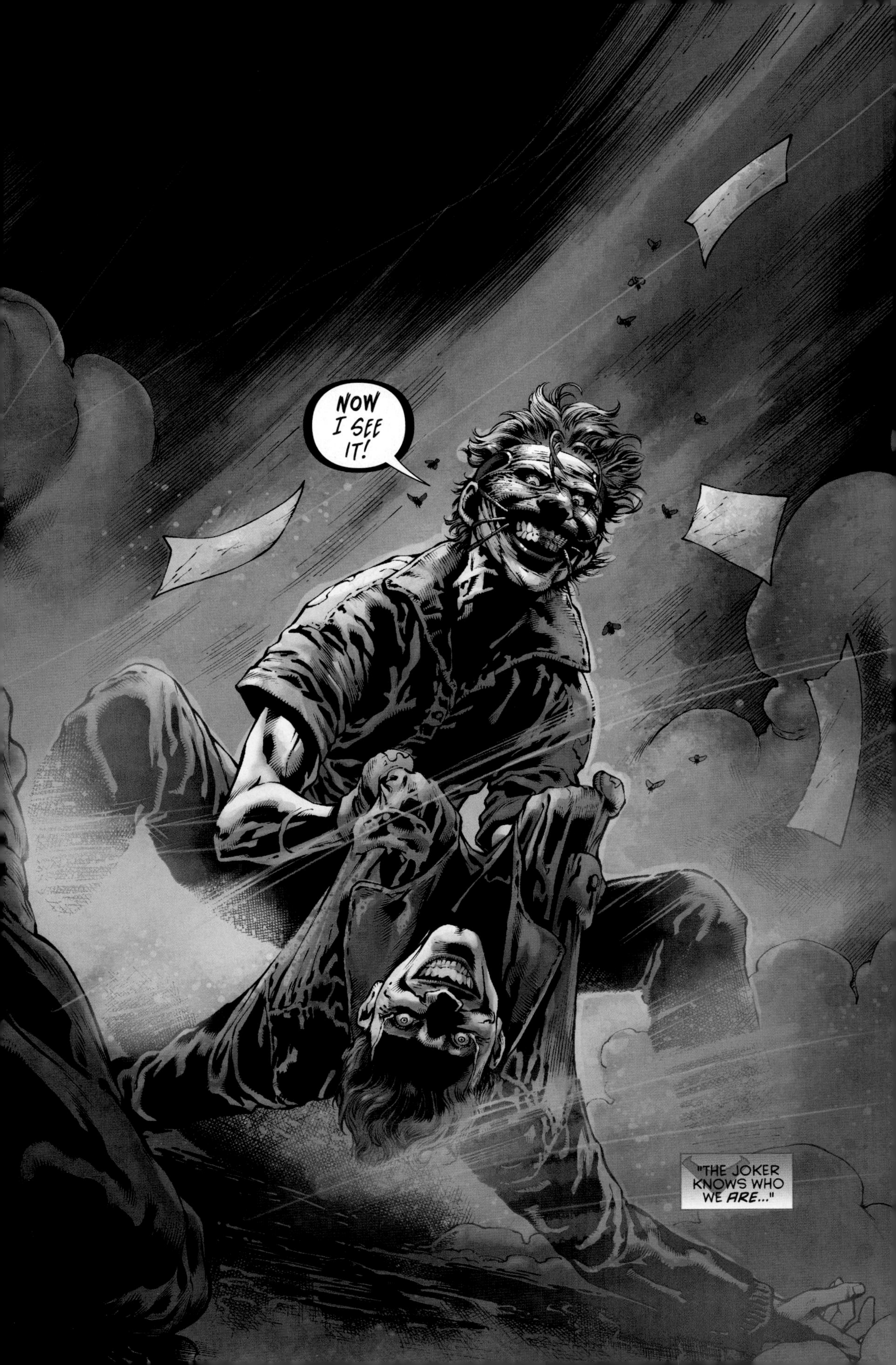
NOW I SEE IT!
"THE JOKER KNOWS WHO WE *ARE*..."

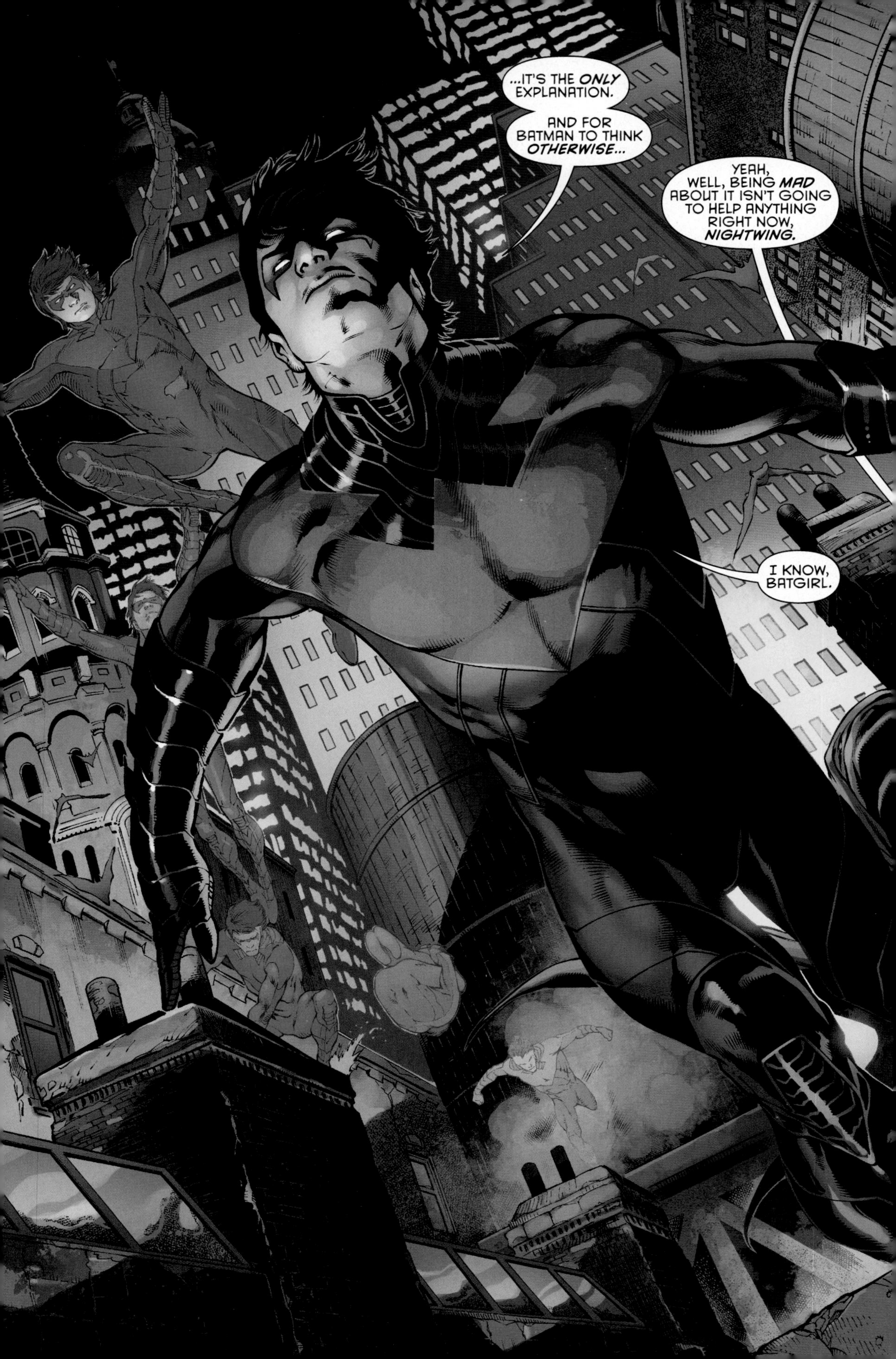
...IT'S THE ONLY EXPLANATION.
AND FOR BATMAN TO THINK OTHERWISE...
YEAH, WELL, BEING MAD ABOUT IT ISN'T GOING TO HELP ANYTHING RIGHT NOW, NIGHTWING.
I KNOW, BATGIRL.

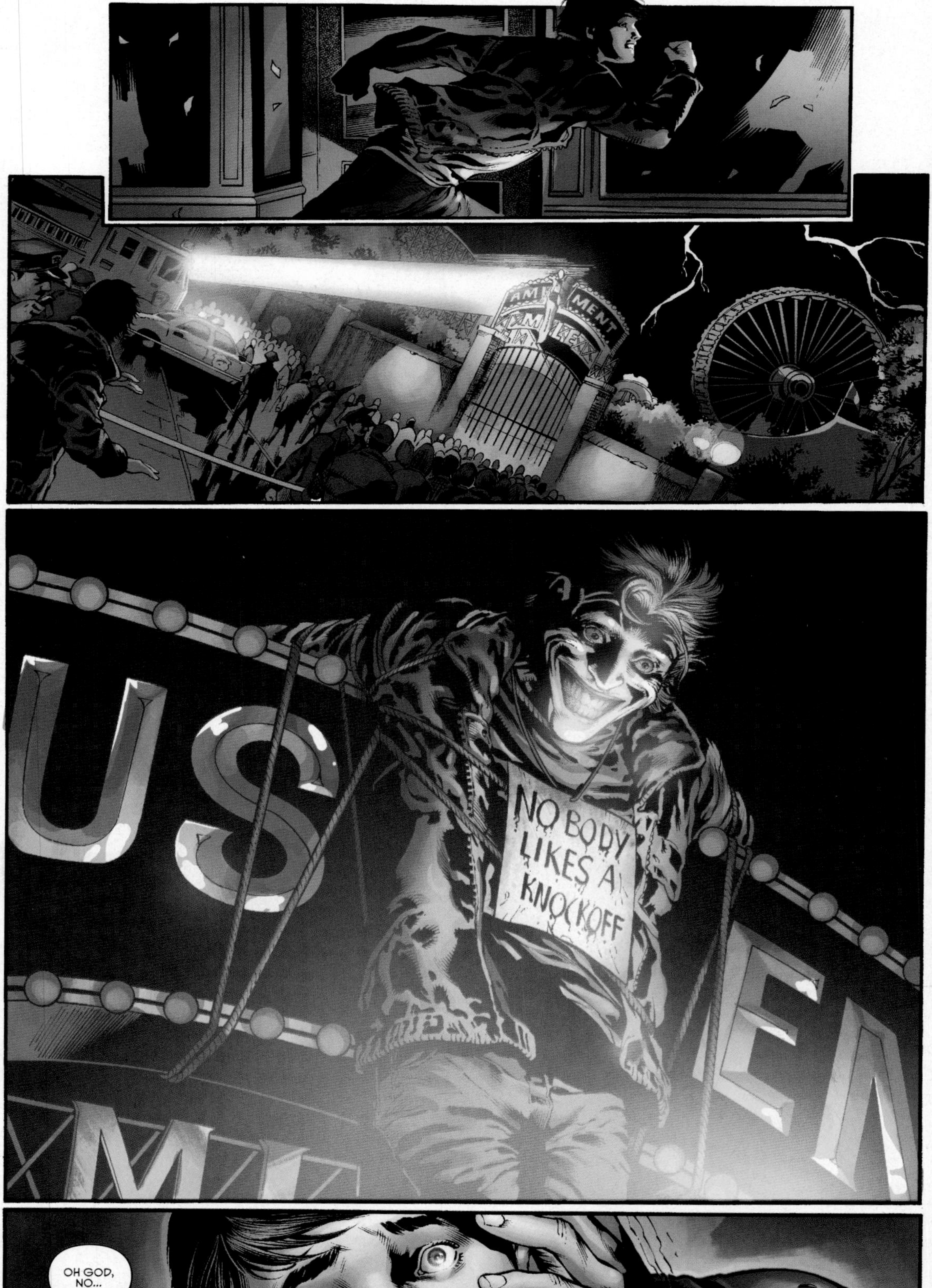
NO BODY LIKES A KNOCKOFF
OH GOD, NO...

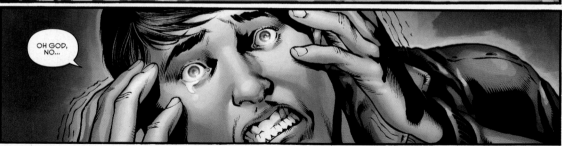

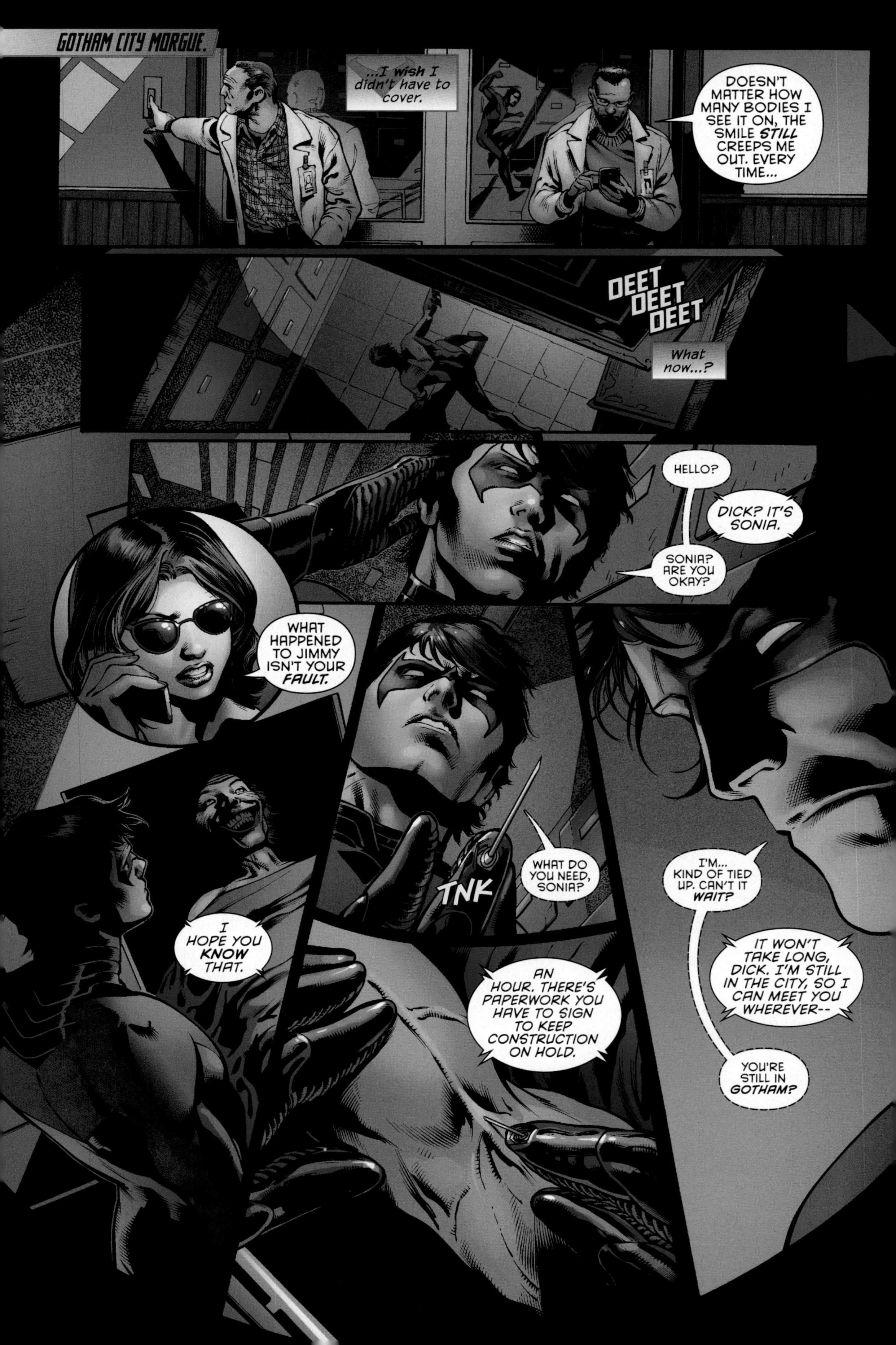
GOTHAM CITY MORGUE.
...I wish I didn't have to cover.
DOESN'T MATTER HOW MANY BODIES I SEE IT ON, THE SMILE STILL CREEPS ME OUT. EVERY TIME...
DEET DEET DEET
What now...?
HELLO?
DICK? IT'S SONIA.
SONIA? ARE YOU OKAY?
WHAT HAPPENED TO JIMMY ISN'T YOUR FAULT.
I HOPE YOU KNOW THAT.
TNK
WHAT DO YOU NEED, SONIA?
AN HOUR. THERE'S PAPERWORK YOU HAVE TO SIGN TO KEEP CONSTRUCTION ON HOLD.
I'M... KIND OF TIED UP. CAN'T IT WAIT?
IT WON'T TAKE LONG, DICK. I'M STILL IN THE CITY, SO I CAN MEET YOU WHEREVER--
YOU'RE STILL IN GOTHAM?

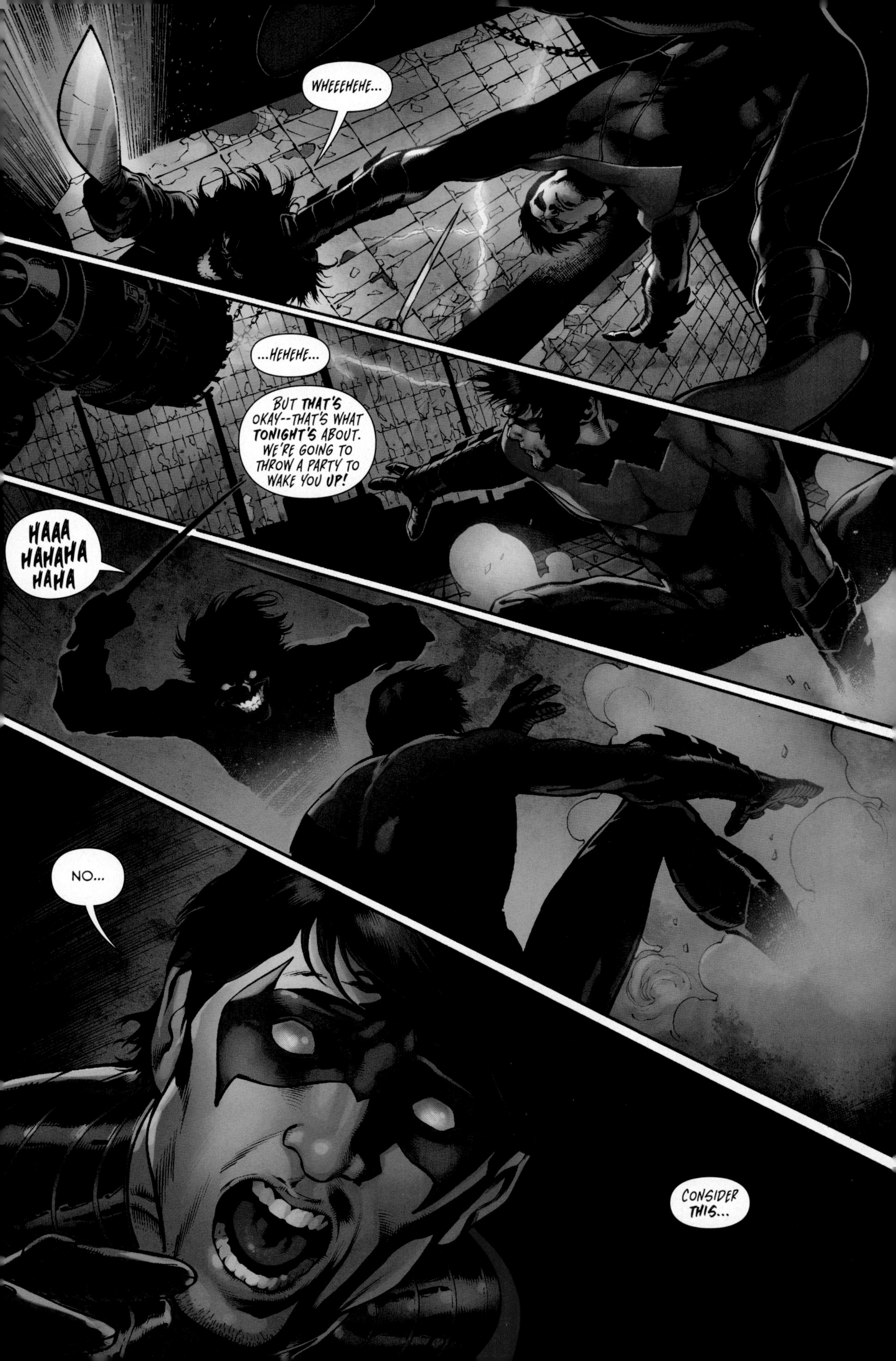
WHEEEHEHE...
...HEHEHE...
BUT THAT'S OKAY--THAT'S WHAT TONIGHT'S ABOUT. WE'RE GOING TO THROW A PARTY TO WAKE YOU UP!
HAAA HAHAHA HAHA
NO...
CONSIDER THIS...

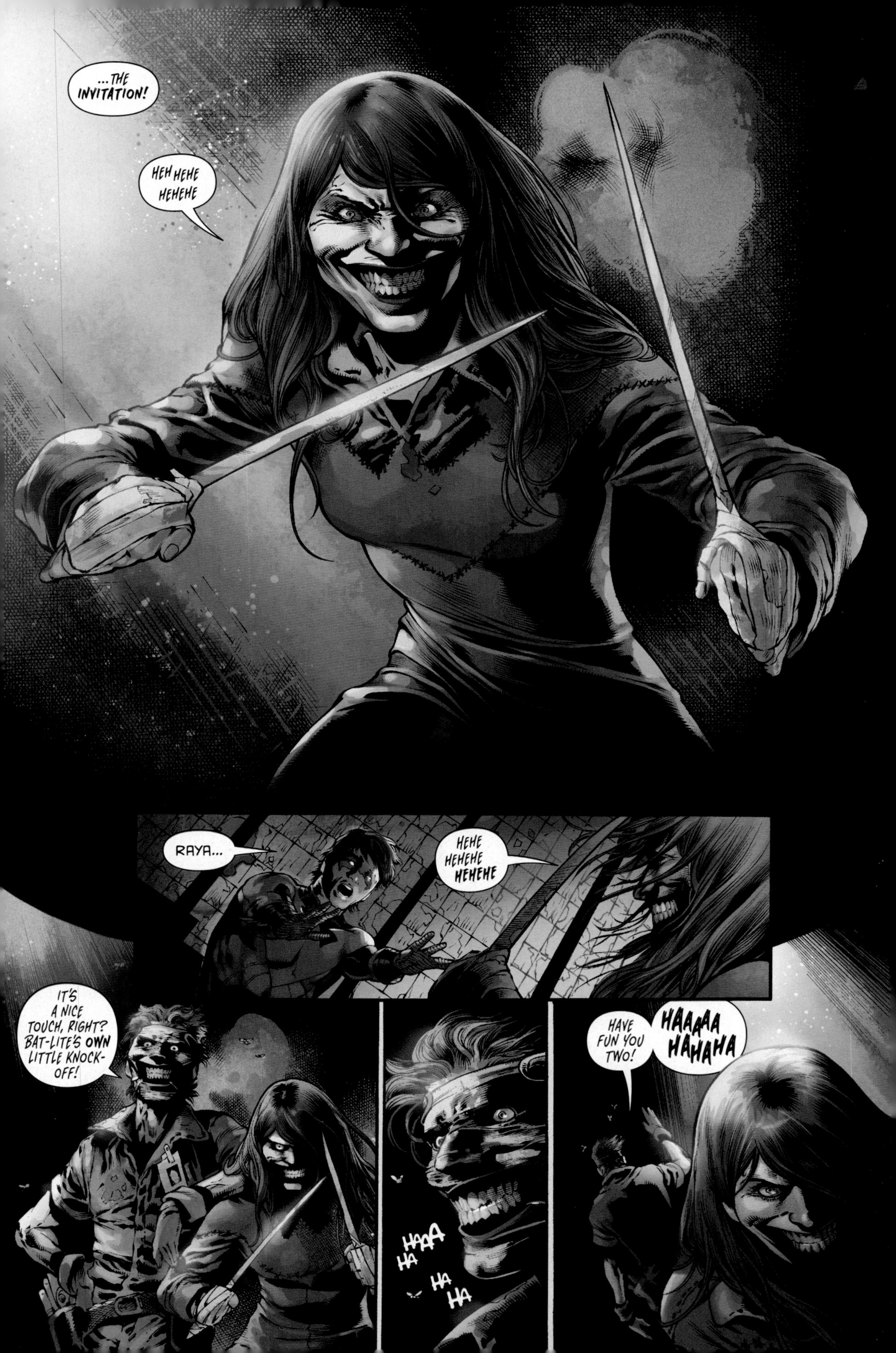
...THE INVITATION!
HEH HEHE HEHEHE
RAYA...
HEHE HEHEHE HEHEHE
IT'S A NICE TOUCH, RIGHT? BAT-LITE'S OWN LITTLE KNOCK-OFF!
HAAAA HA
HA HA
HAVE FUN YOU TWO!
HAAAAA HAHAHA

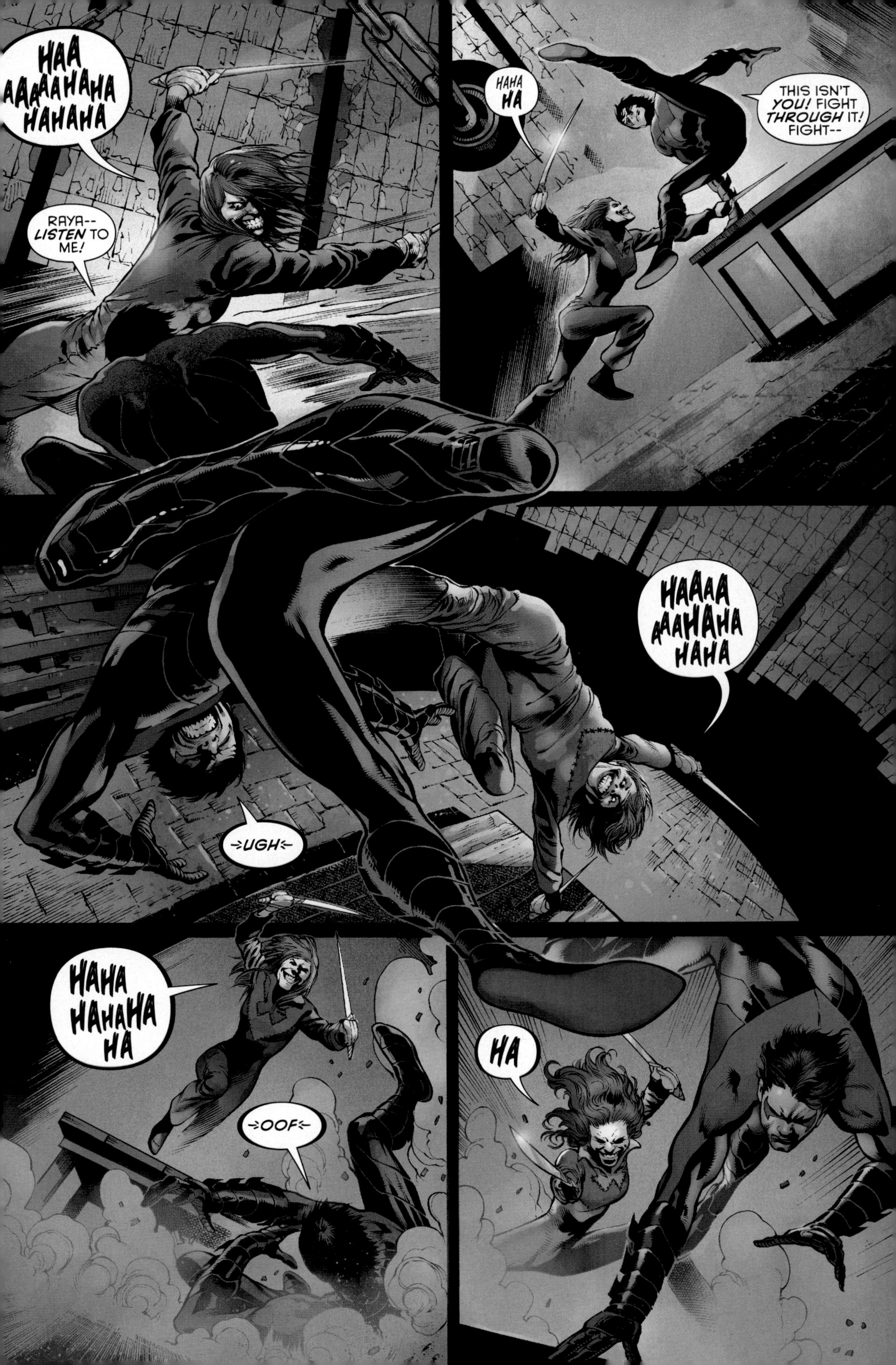
HAA AAAAAHAHA HAHAHA
RAYA-- LISTEN TO ME!
HAHA HA
THIS ISN'T YOU! FIGHT THROUGH IT! FIGHT--
HAAAA AAAHAHA HAHA
UGH
HAHA HAHAHA HA
OOF
HA

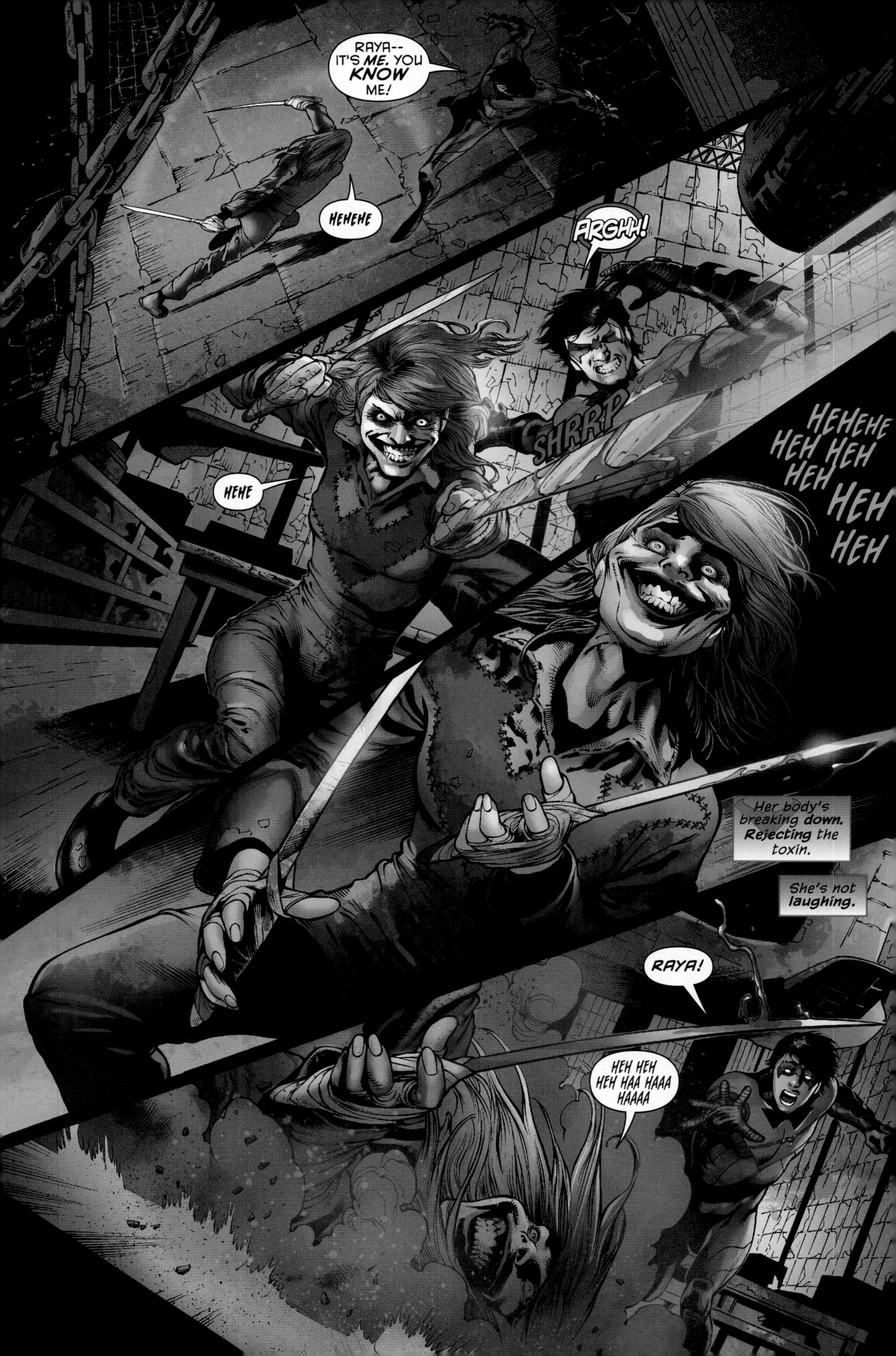

RAYA-- IT'S ME. YOU KNOW ME!
HEHEHE
ARGHH!
SHRRP
HEHE
HEHEHE HEH HEH HEH HEH HEH
Her body's breaking down. Rejecting the toxin.
She's not laughing.
RAYA!
HEH HEH HEH HAA HAAA HAAAA

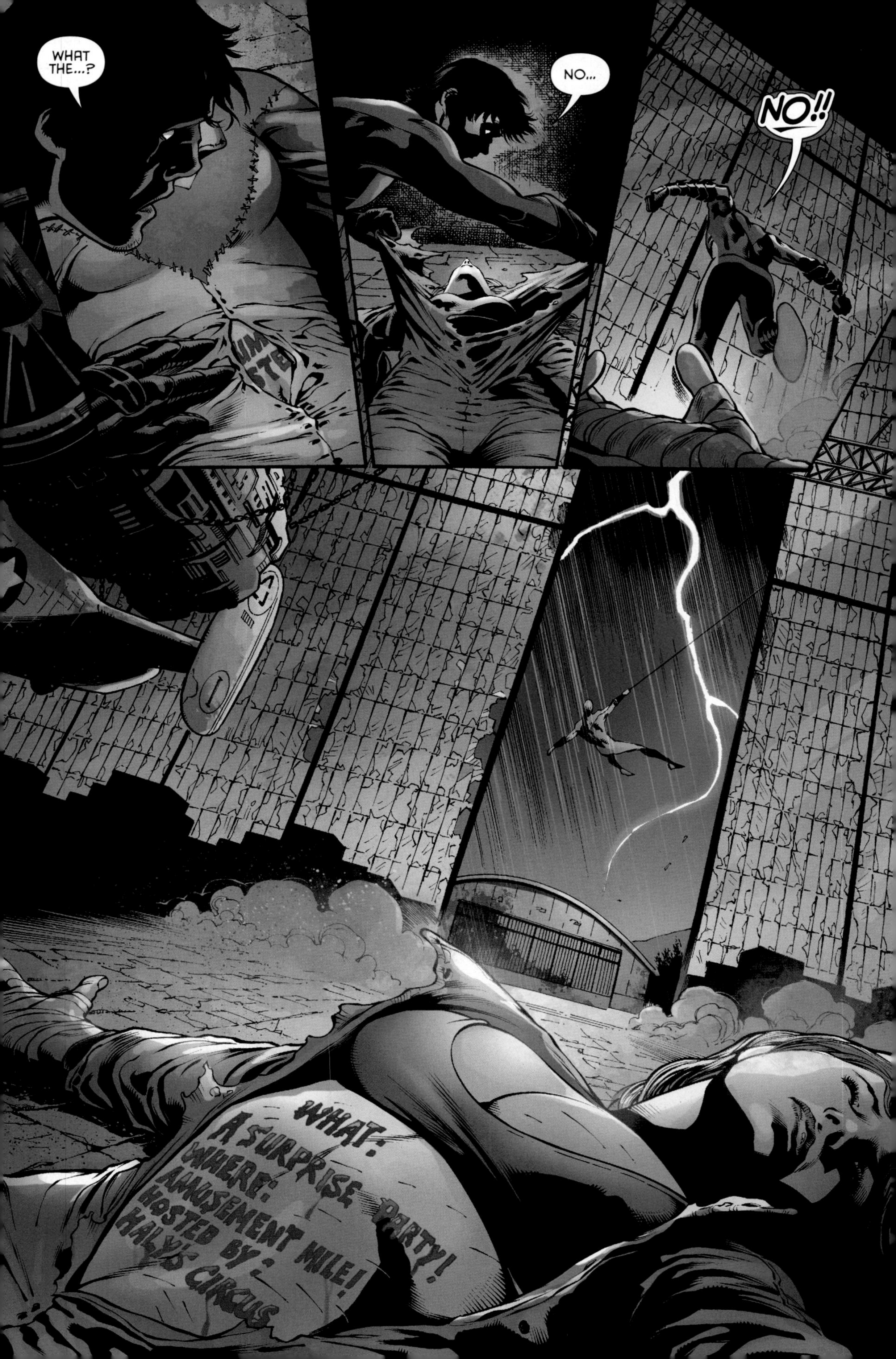
WHAT THE...?
NO...
NO!!
WHAT: A SURPRISE PARTY!
WHERE: AMUSEMENT MILE!
HOSTED BY: HALY'S CIRCUS

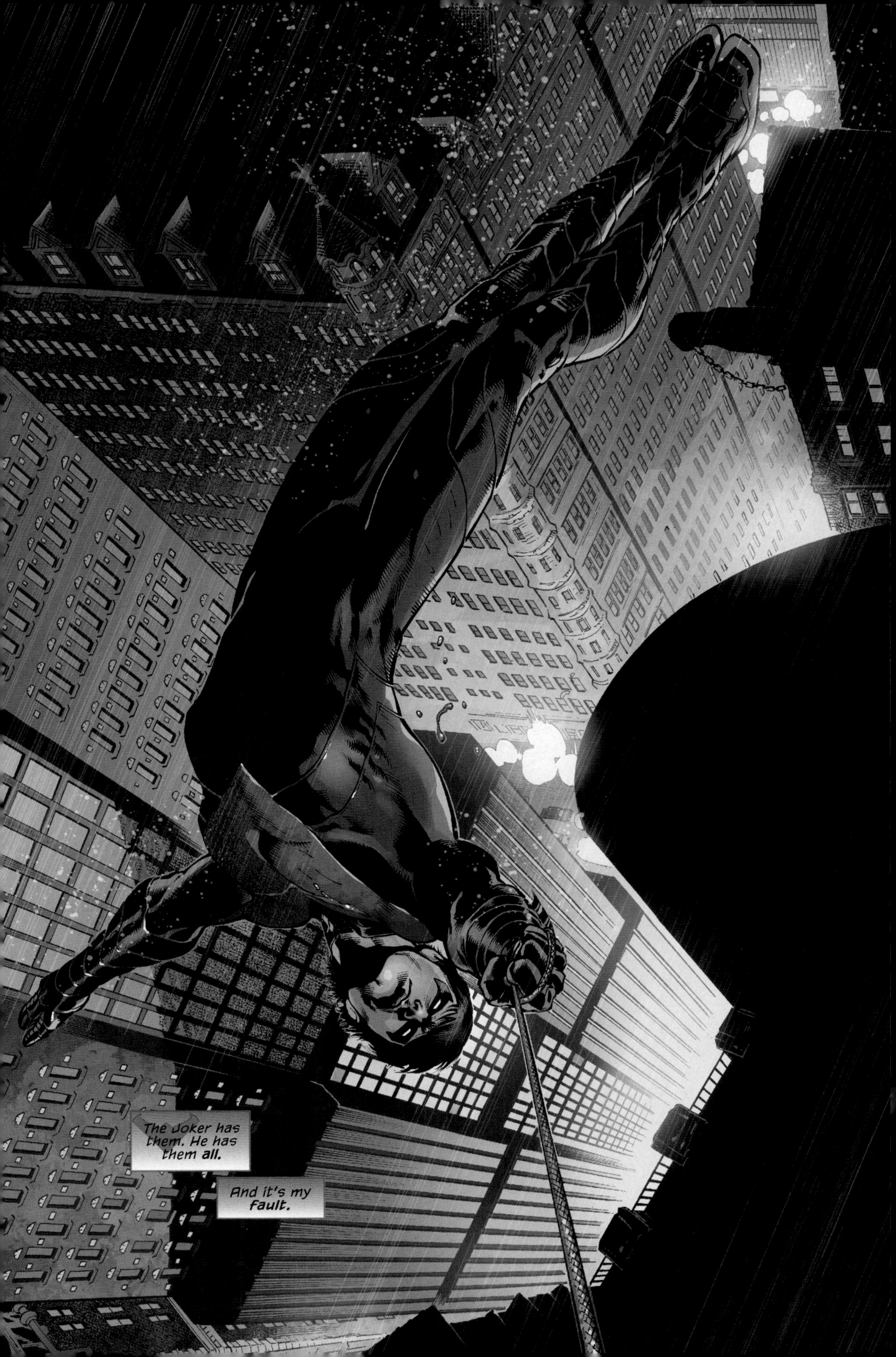
The Joker has them. He has them all.
And it's my fault.

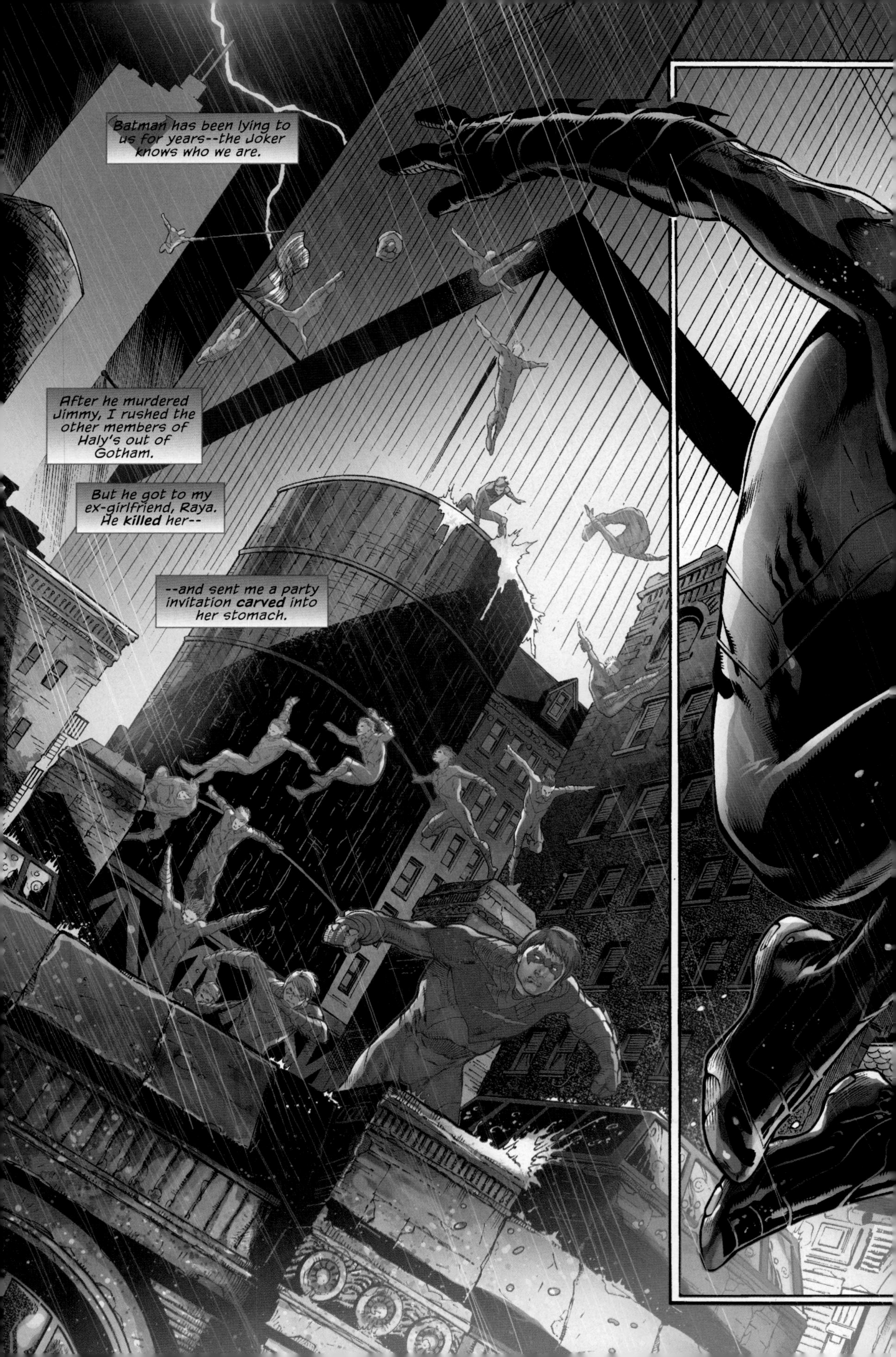
Batman has been lying to us for years--the Joker knows who we are.
After he murdered Jimmy, I rushed the other members of Haly's out of Gotham.
But he got to my ex-girlfriend, Raya. He **killed** her--
--and sent me a party invitation **carved** into her stomach.

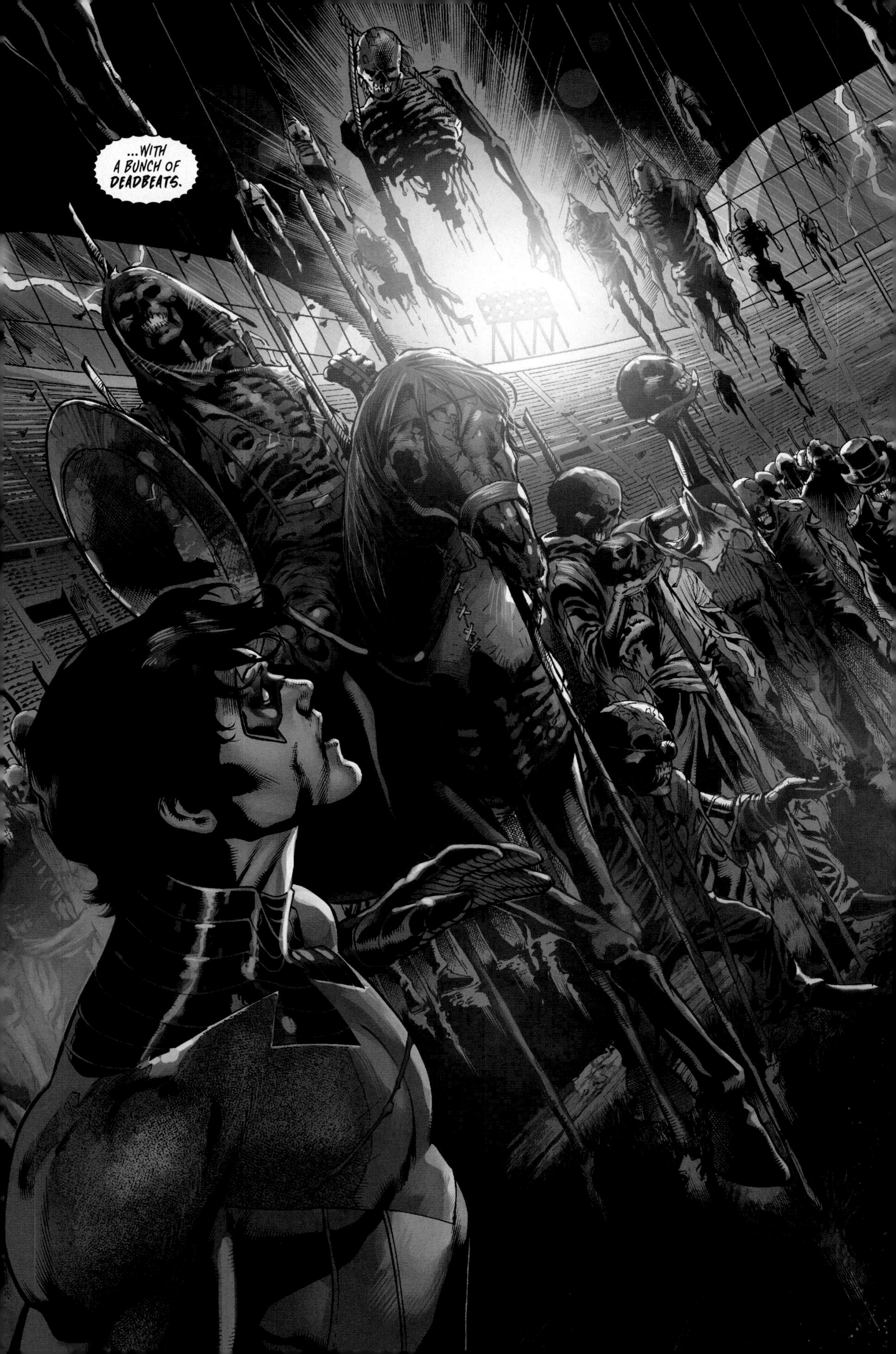
...WITH A BUNCH OF DEADBEATS.

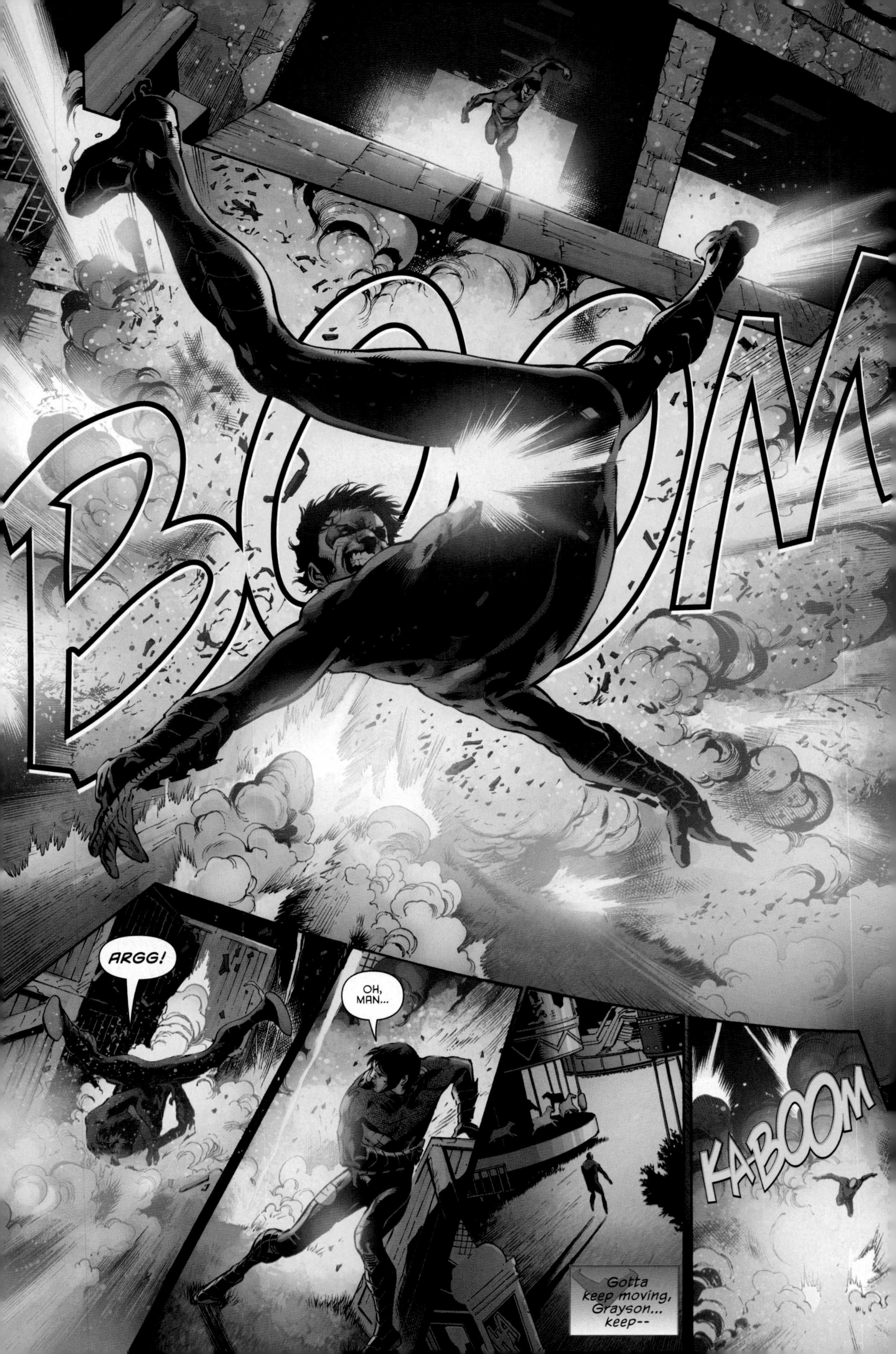
BOOM
ARGG!
OH, MAN...
KABOOM
Gotta keep moving, Grayson... keep--

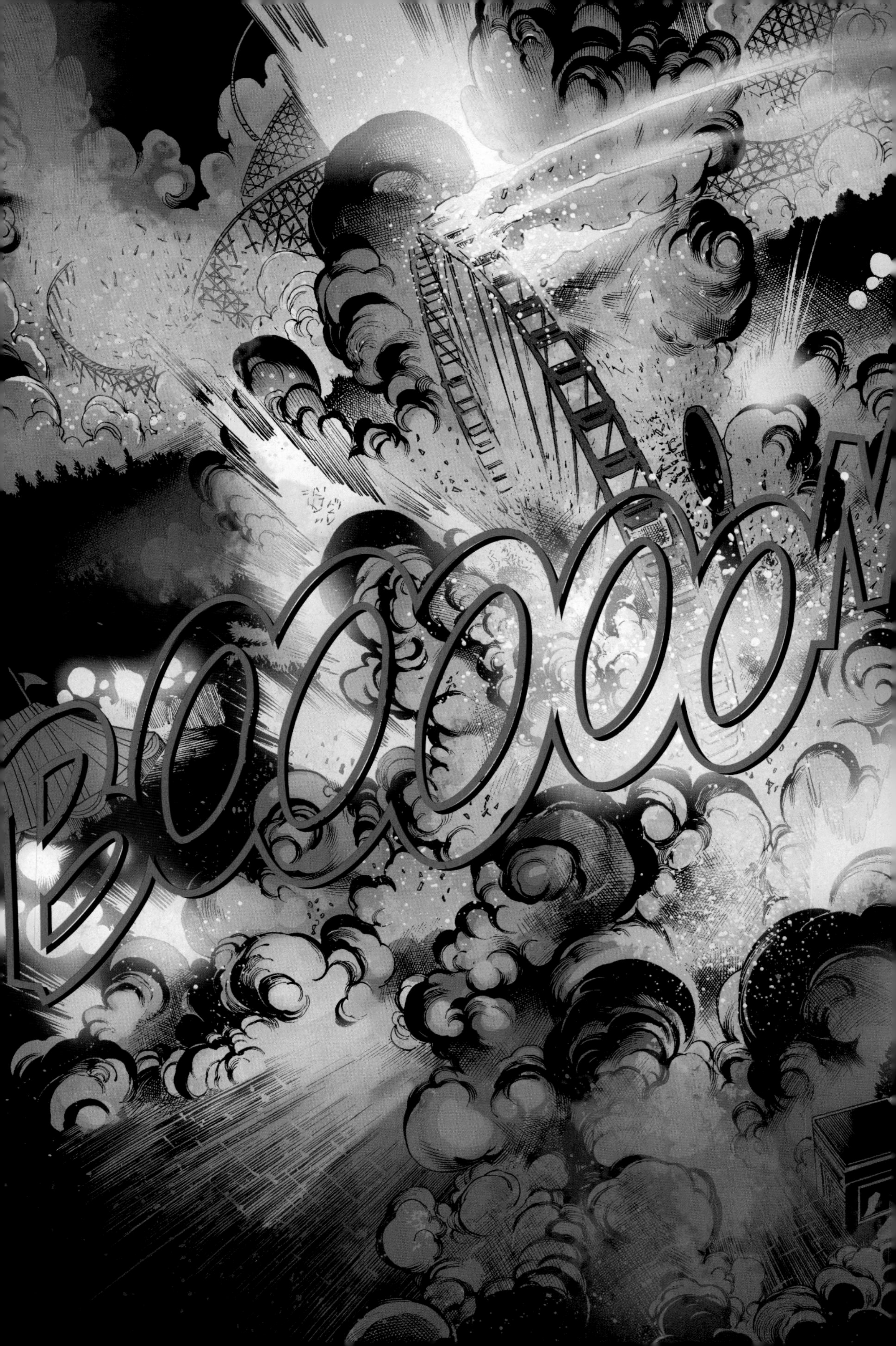
BOOOOOOOM

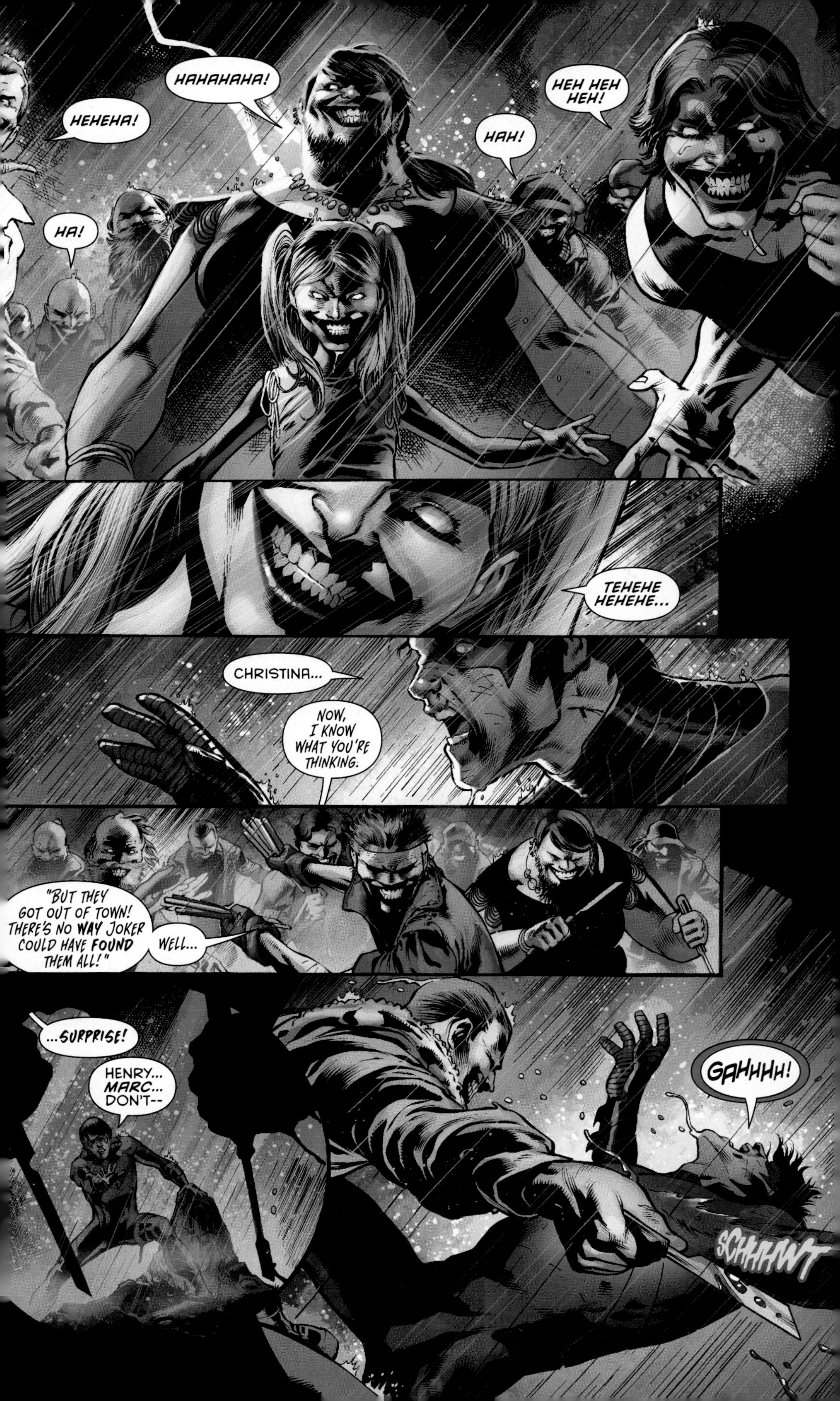
HEHEHA!
HAHAHAHA!
HAH!
HEH HEH HEH!
HA!
TEHEHE HEHEHE...
CHRISTINA...
NOW, I KNOW WHAT YOU'RE THINKING.
"BUT THEY GOT OUT OF TOWN! THERE'S NO WAY JOKER COULD HAVE FOUND THEM ALL!"
WELL...
...SURPRISE!
HENRY... MARC... DON'T--
GAHHHH!
SCHHHWT

PART SEVEN
ROBIN

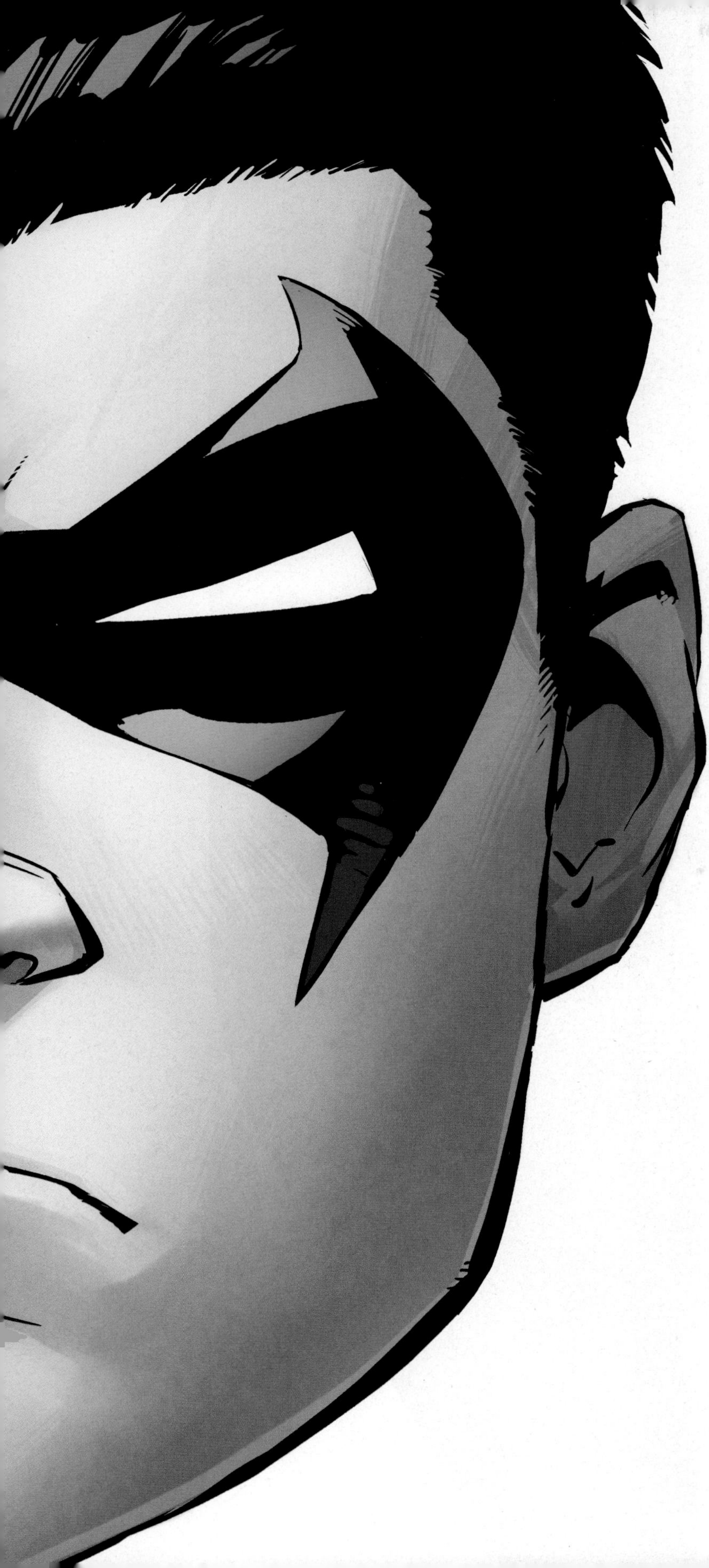

PETER J. TOMASI writer **PATRICK GLEASON** penciller **MICK GRAY** KEITH CHAMPAGNE inkers
JOHN KALISZ colorist **CARLOS M. MANGUAL** letterer

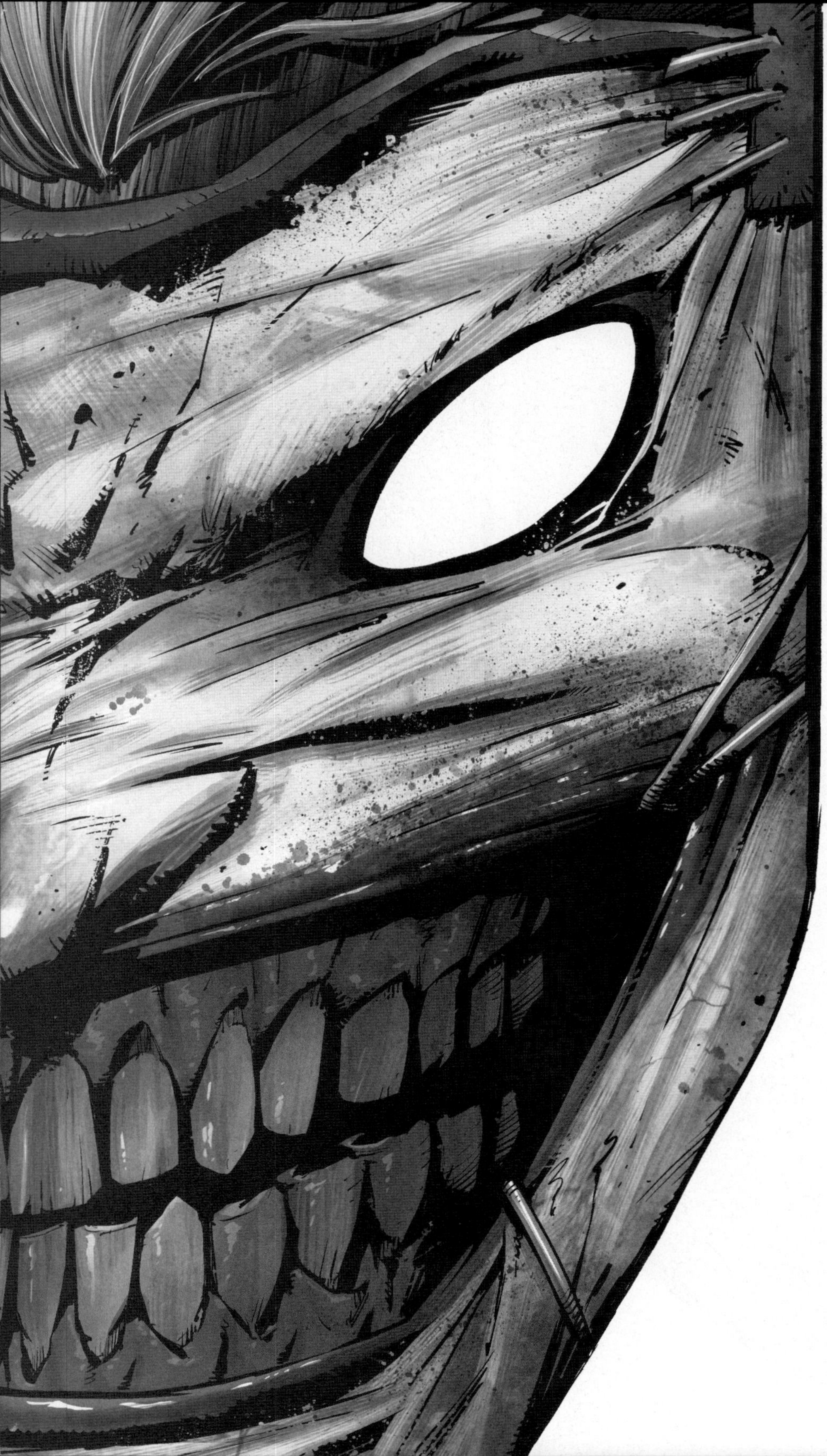

"...AND THE FIRST PLACE TO START IS THE SCENE OF ALFRED'S ABDUCTION."

WAYNE MANOR.

WE'VE COME UP EMPTY ON TIRE TREADS AND ANY PHYSICAL EVIDENCE, TITUS.

RRFF RRFF

NO FINGERPRINTS, HAIRS, OR EVEN SHOES WITH DISCERNIBLE SOLES...

...THE JOKER'S A TWISTED FREAK, NOT A GHOST...

SNURFF SNURFF

...URINE SAMPLE IS A MATCH FROM THE HYAENIDAE FAMILY OF SUBORDER FELIFORMS OF THE CARNIVORA.

AND THERE'S ONLY ONE PLACE THEY KEEP THOSE...

...HE HAD TO LEAVE SOMETHING BEHIND.

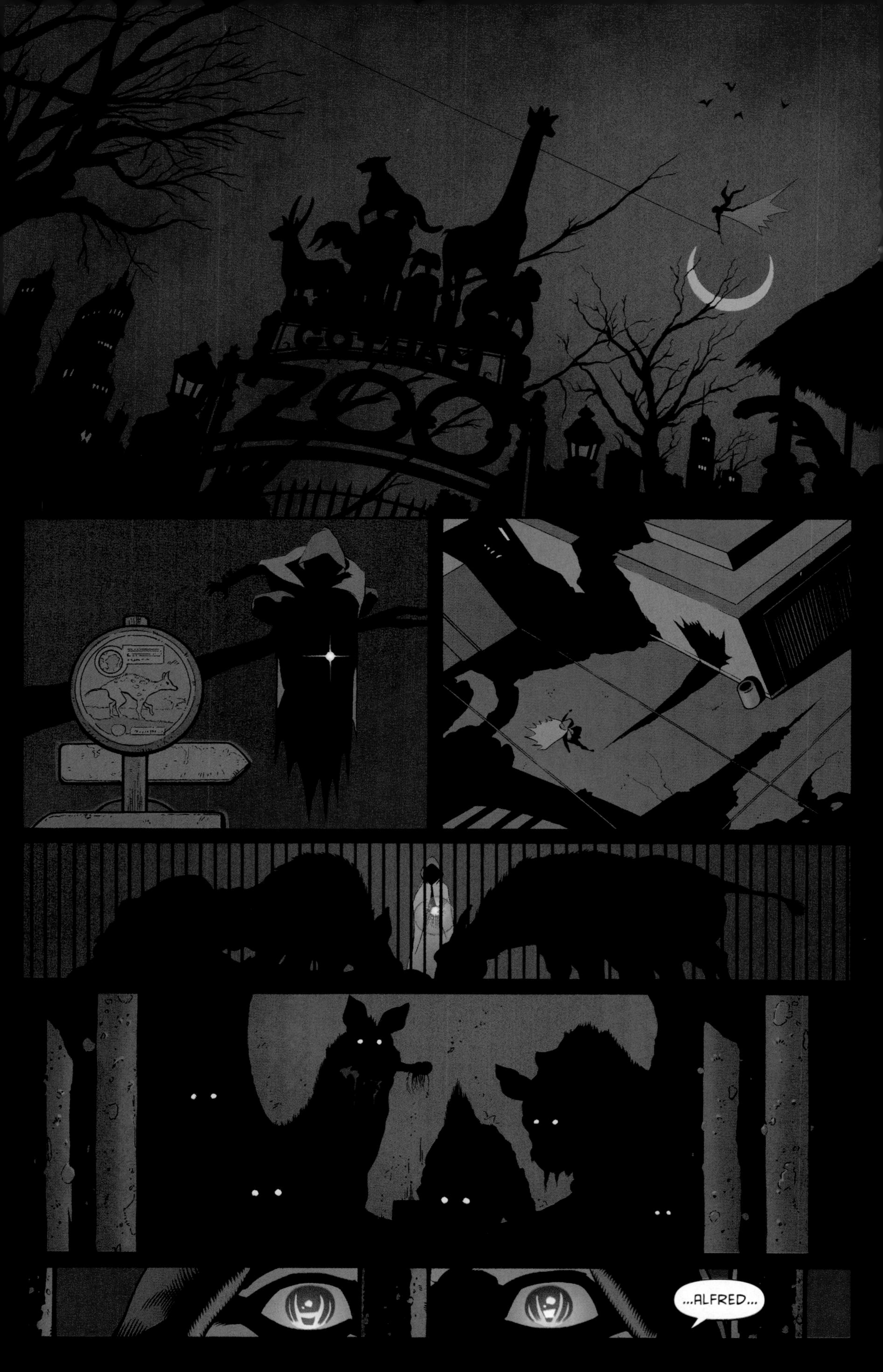
ZOO
...ALFRED...

...NO...THE GUARD...

KZZZt

RRARRR   FRAKK

KLANK

RRNN

RRARR

KRAK

RRARRR

KRAK

WHAK

KRAKSNAPP

RRARRR

RRARRR

KRAKK

POOM

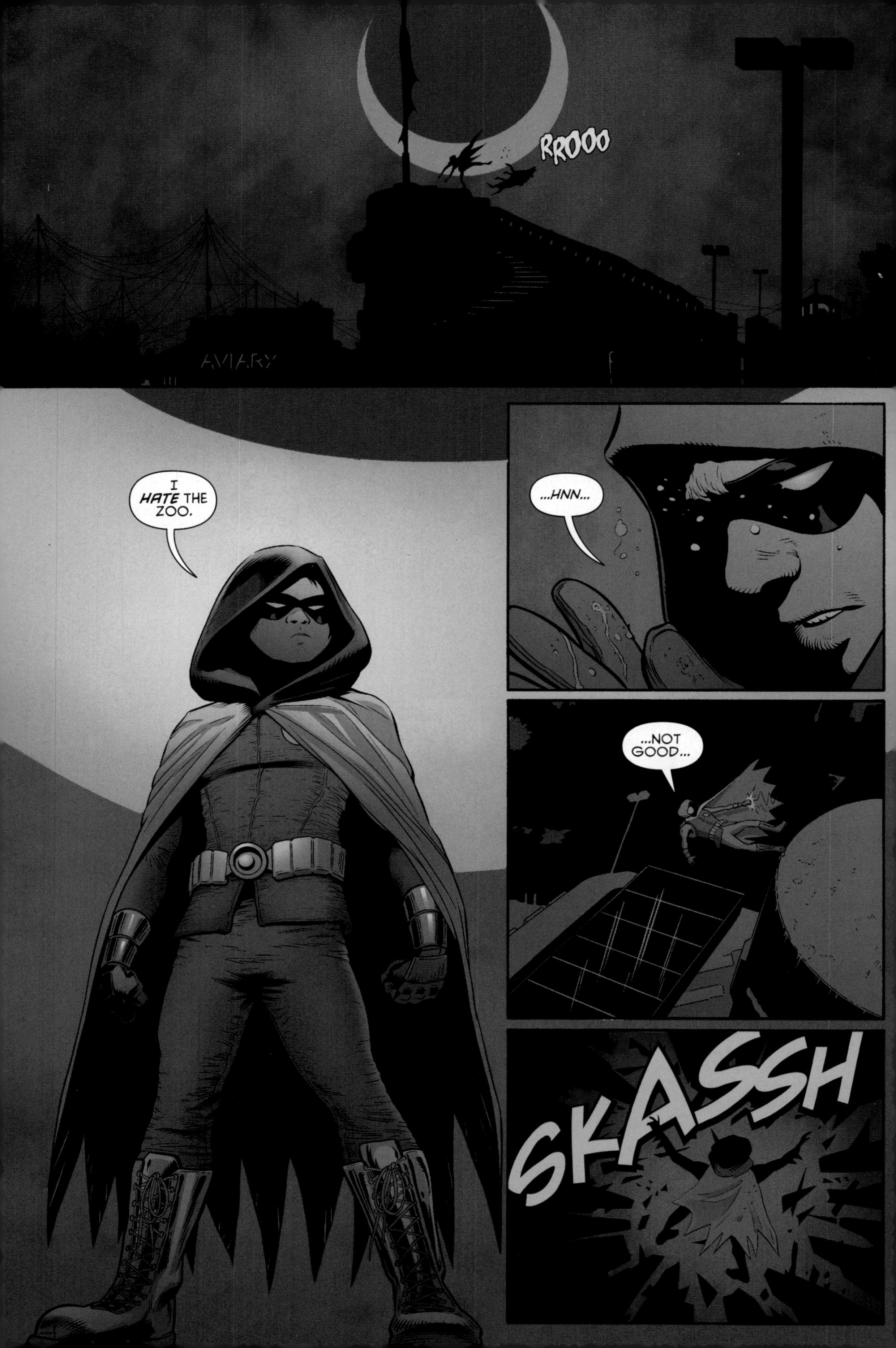

RROOO
AVIARY
I HATE THE ZOO.
...HNN...
...NOT GOOD...
SKASSH

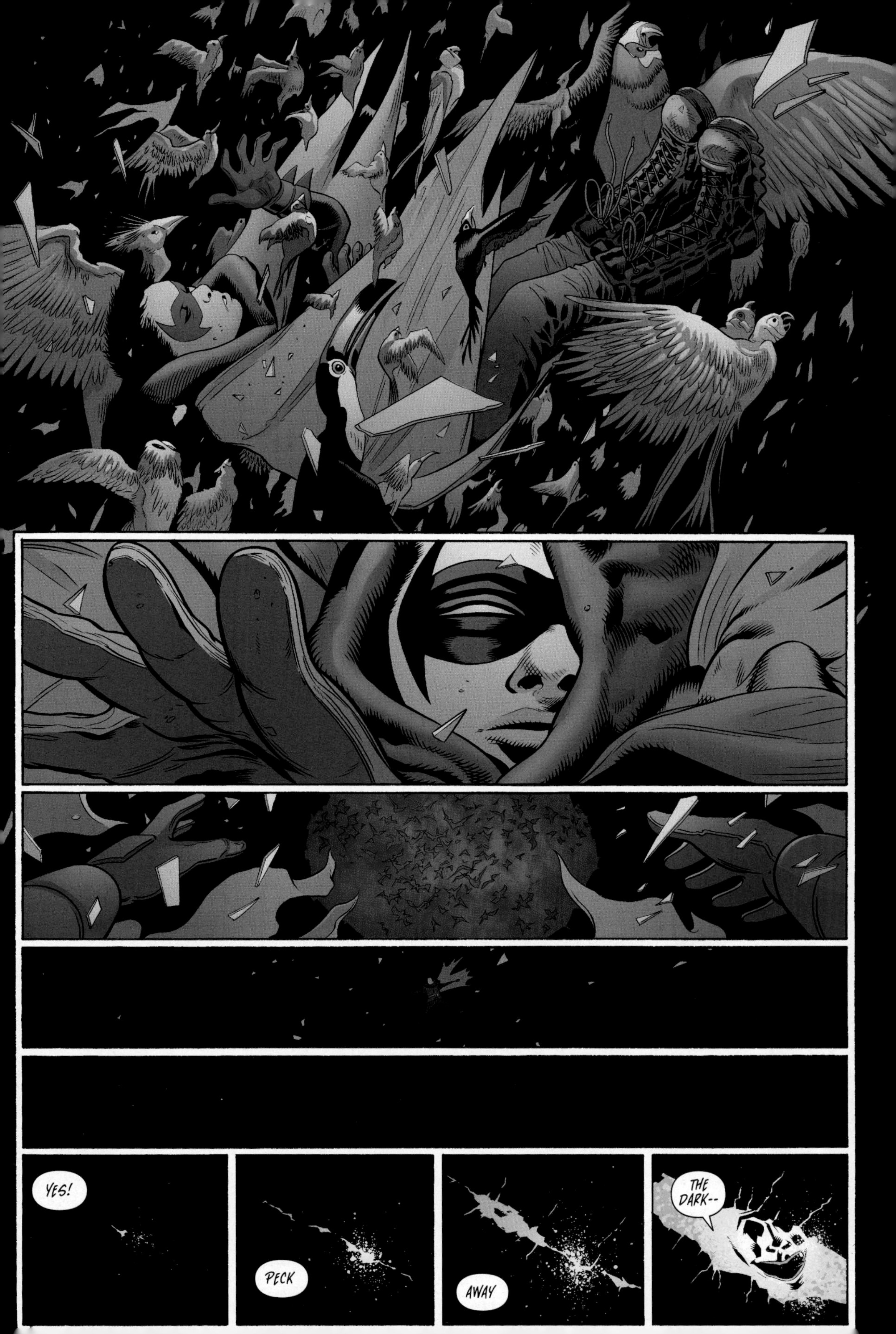
YES!
PECK
AWAY
THE DARK--

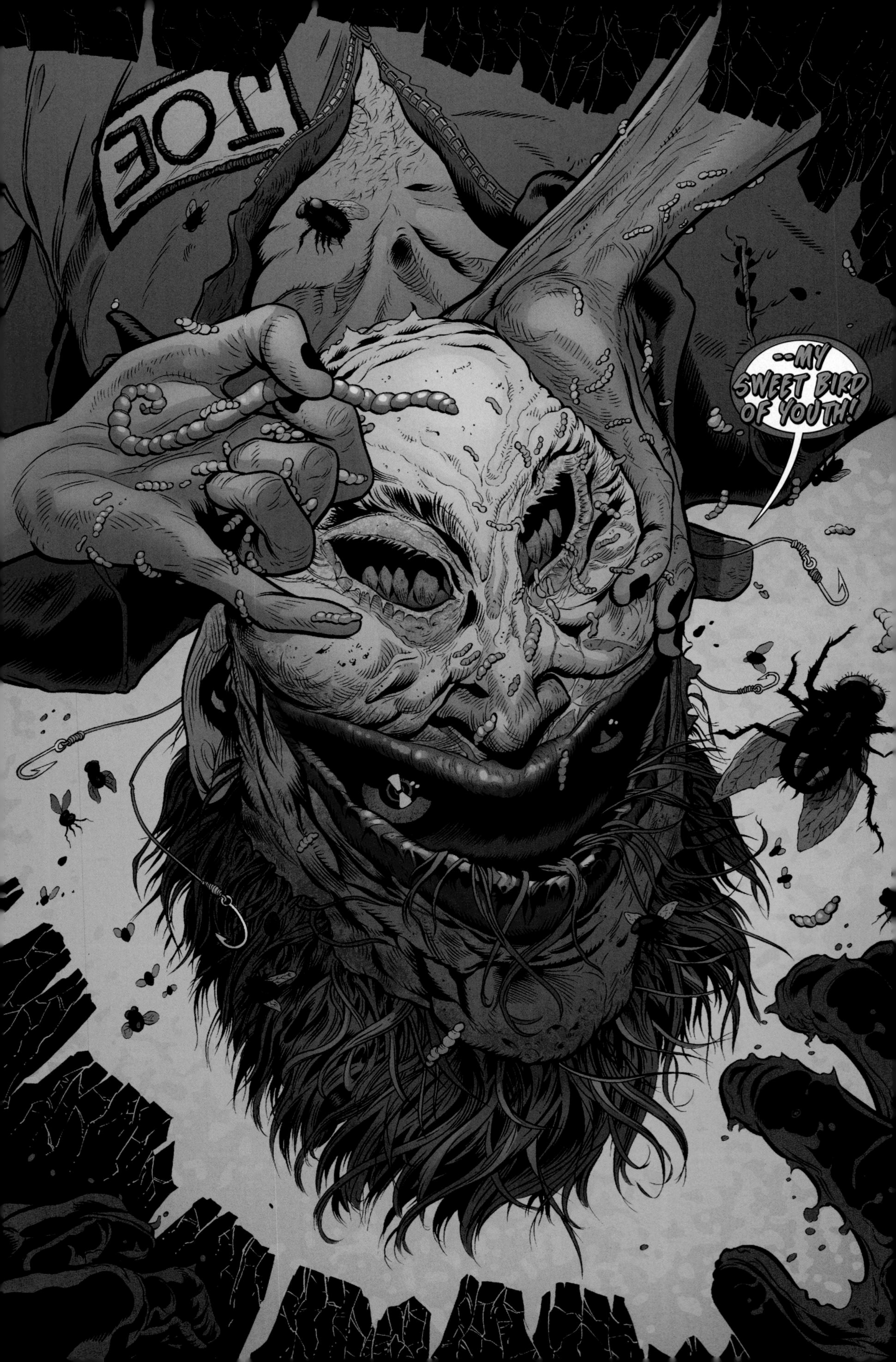
--MY SWEET BIRD OF YOUTH!

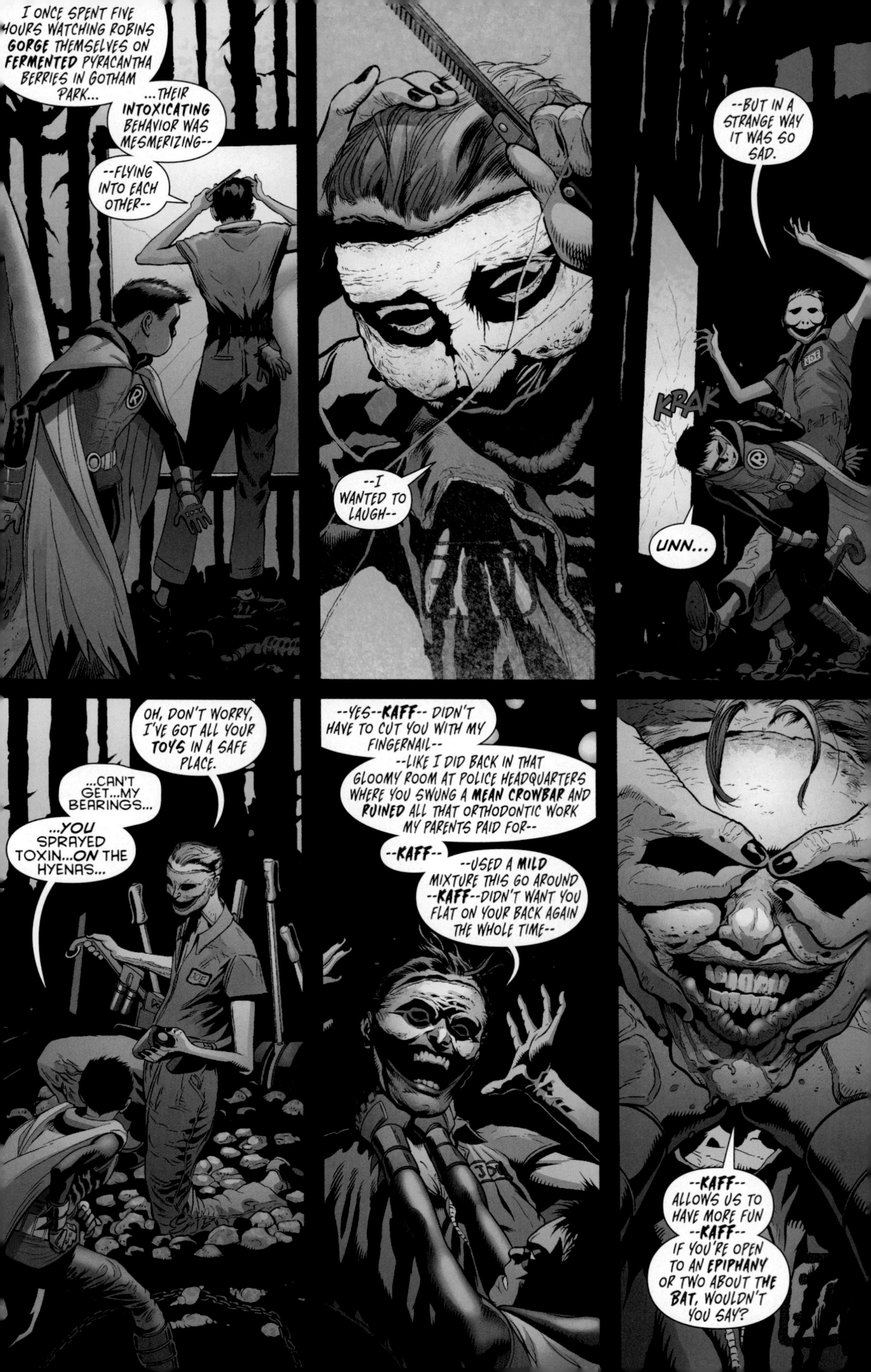
I ONCE SPENT FIVE HOURS WATCHING ROBINS GORGE THEMSELVES ON FERMENTED PYRACANTHA BERRIES IN GOTHAM PARK...
...THEIR INTOXICATING BEHAVIOR WAS MESMERIZING--
--FLYING INTO EACH OTHER--
--I WANTED TO LAUGH--
--BUT IN A STRANGE WAY IT WAS SO SAD.
KRAK
UNN...
OH, DON'T WORRY, I'VE GOT ALL YOUR TOYS IN A SAFE PLACE.
...CAN'T GET...MY BEARINGS...
...YOU SPRAYED TOXIN...ON THE HYENAS...
--YES--KAFF-- DIDN'T HAVE TO CUT YOU WITH MY FINGERNAIL--
--LIKE I DID BACK IN THAT GLOOMY ROOM AT POLICE HEADQUARTERS WHERE YOU SWUNG A MEAN CROWBAR AND RUINED ALL THAT ORTHODONTIC WORK MY PARENTS PAID FOR--
--KAFF--
--USED A MILD MIXTURE THIS GO AROUND --KAFF--DIDN'T WANT YOU FLAT ON YOUR BACK AGAIN THE WHOLE TIME--
--KAFF-- ALLOWS US TO HAVE MORE FUN --KAFF-- IF YOU'RE OPEN TO AN EPIPHANY OR TWO ABOUT THE BAT, WOULDN'T YOU SAY?

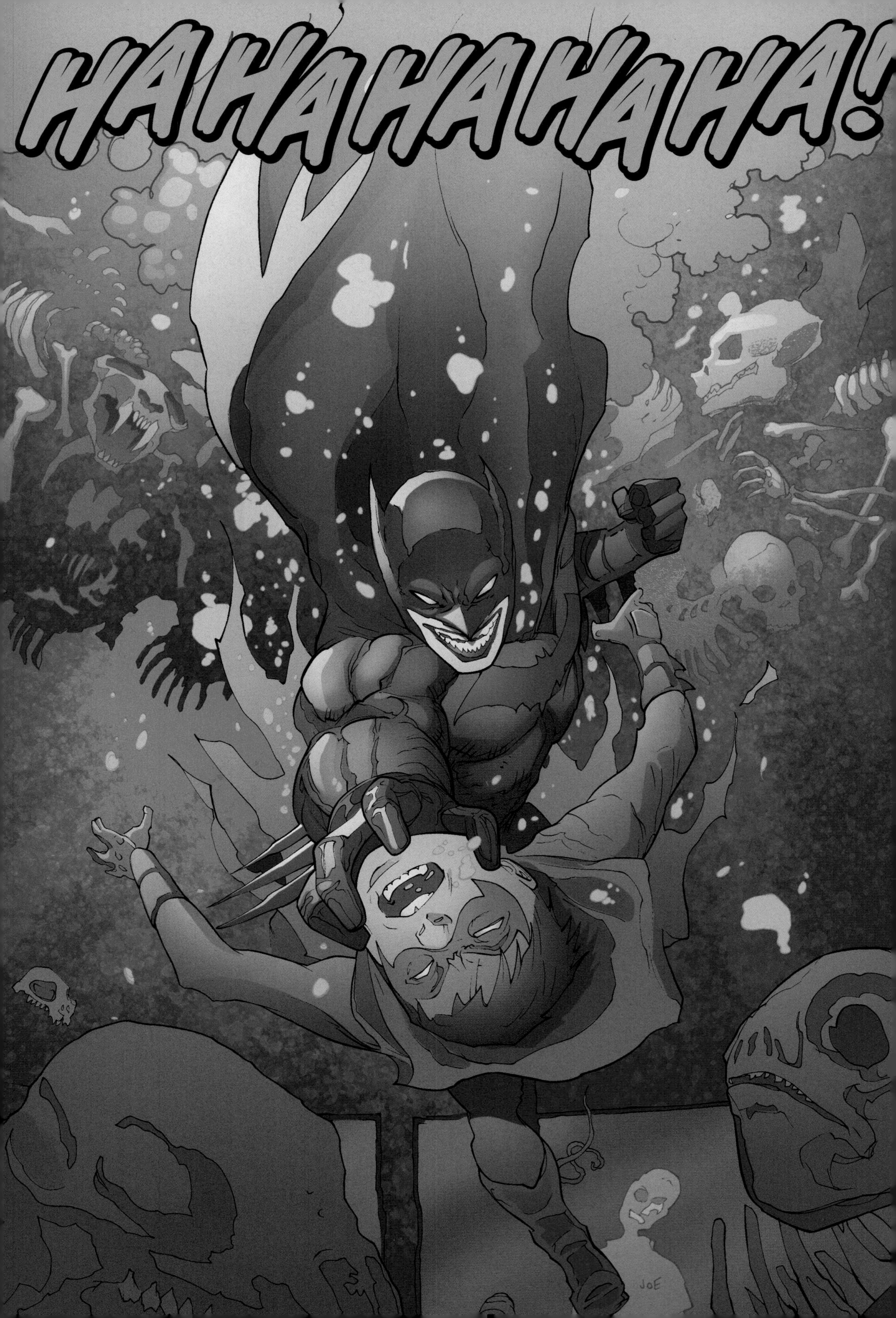
HAHAHAHAHAHAHA!
JOE

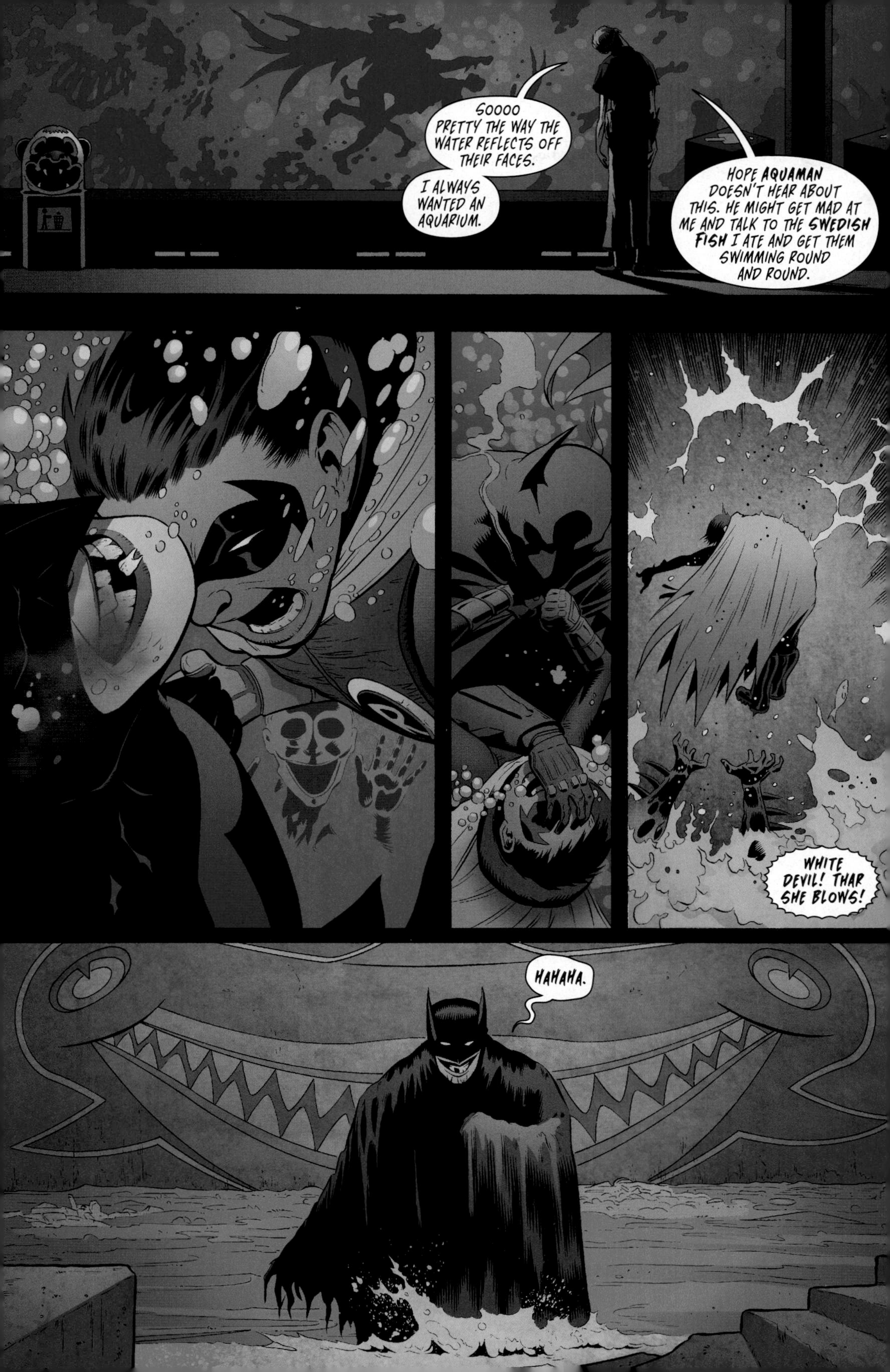
SOOOO PRETTY THE WAY THE WATER REFLECTS OFF THEIR FACES.
I ALWAYS WANTED AN AQUARIUM.
HOPE **AQUAMAN** DOESN'T HEAR ABOUT THIS. HE MIGHT GET MAD AT ME AND TALK TO THE **SWEDISH FISH** I ATE AND GET THEM SWIMMING ROUND AND ROUND.
WHITE DEVIL! THAR SHE BLOWS!
HAHAHA.

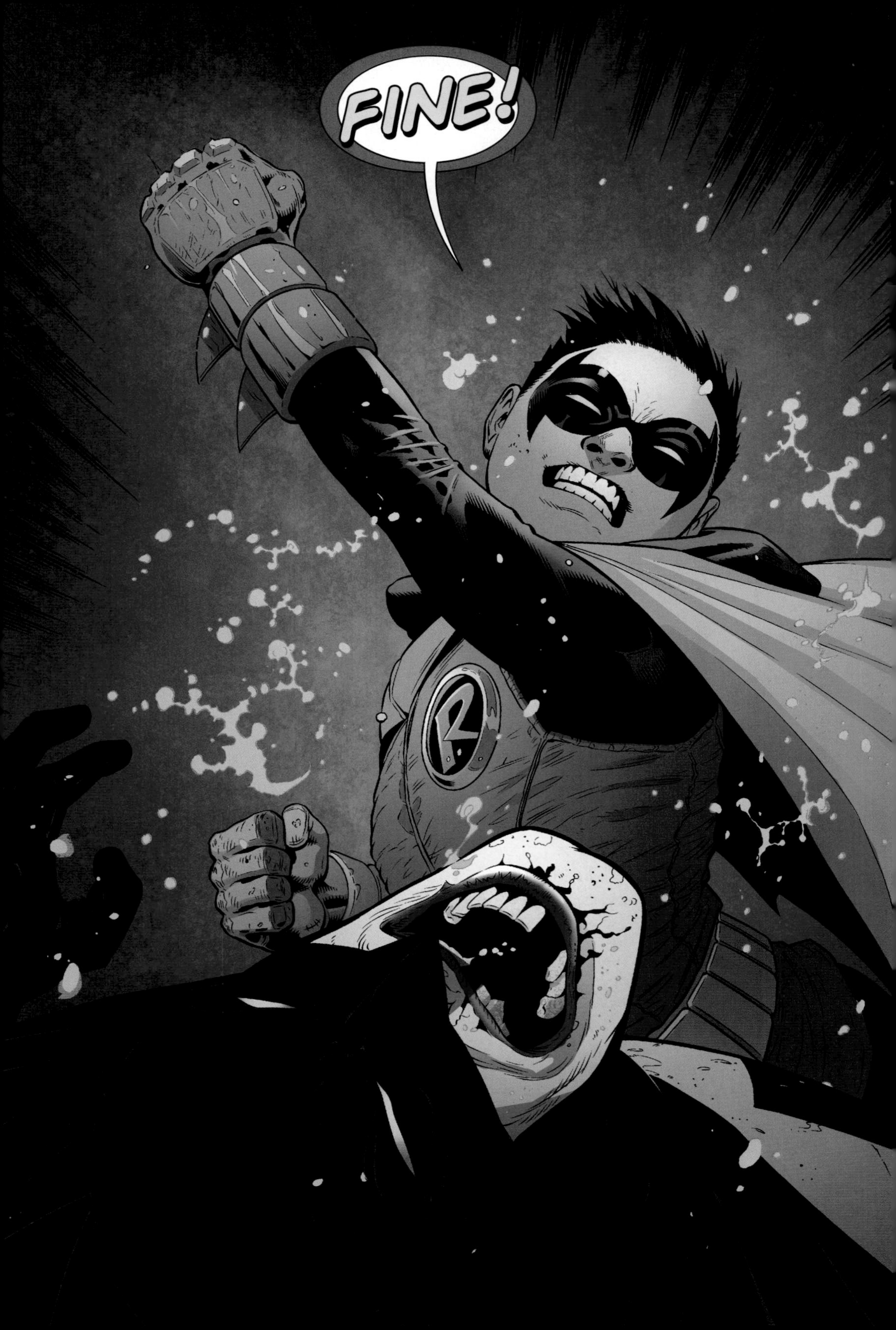
FINE!

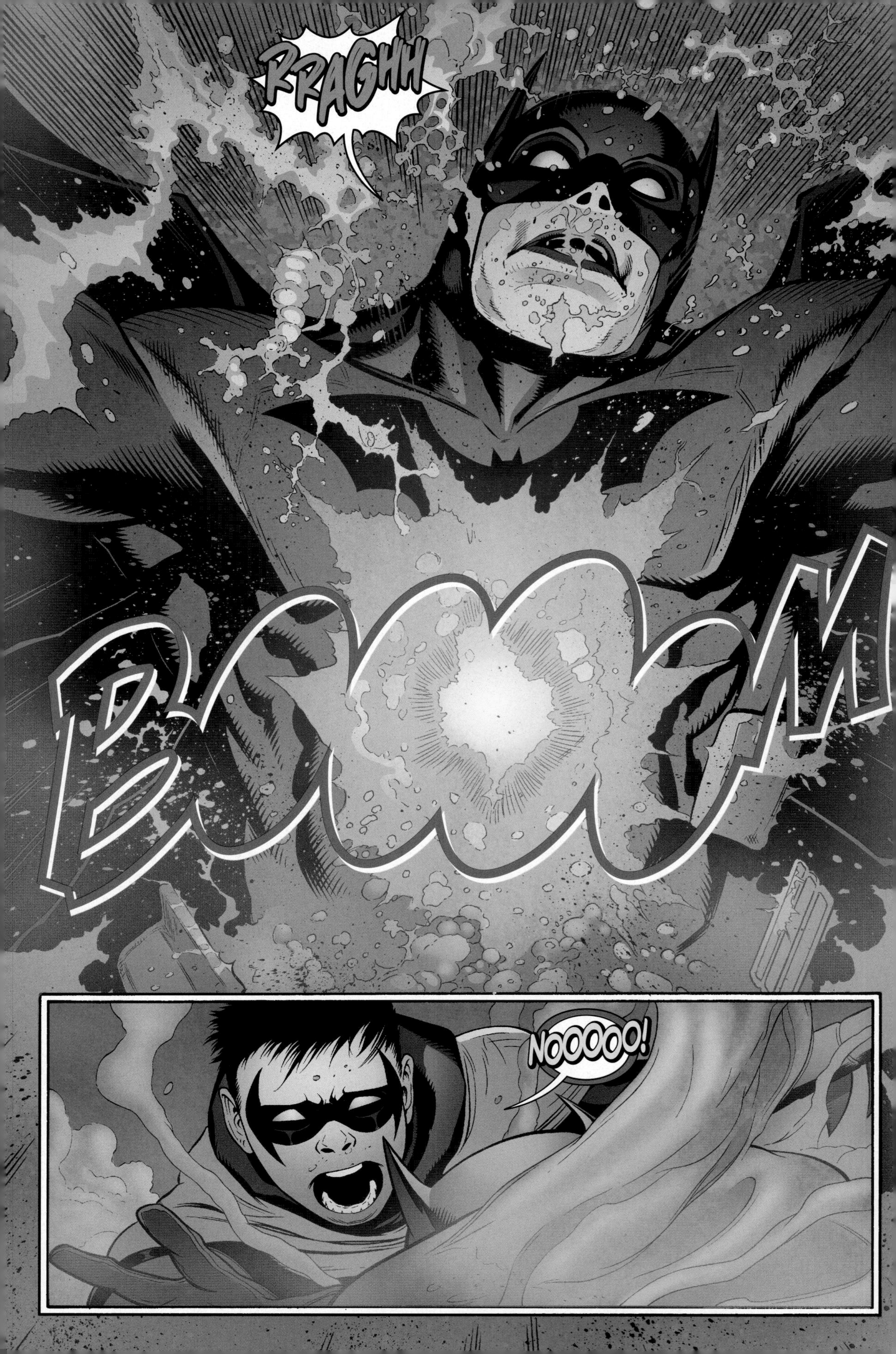
RRAGHH
BOOOOM
NOOOOO!

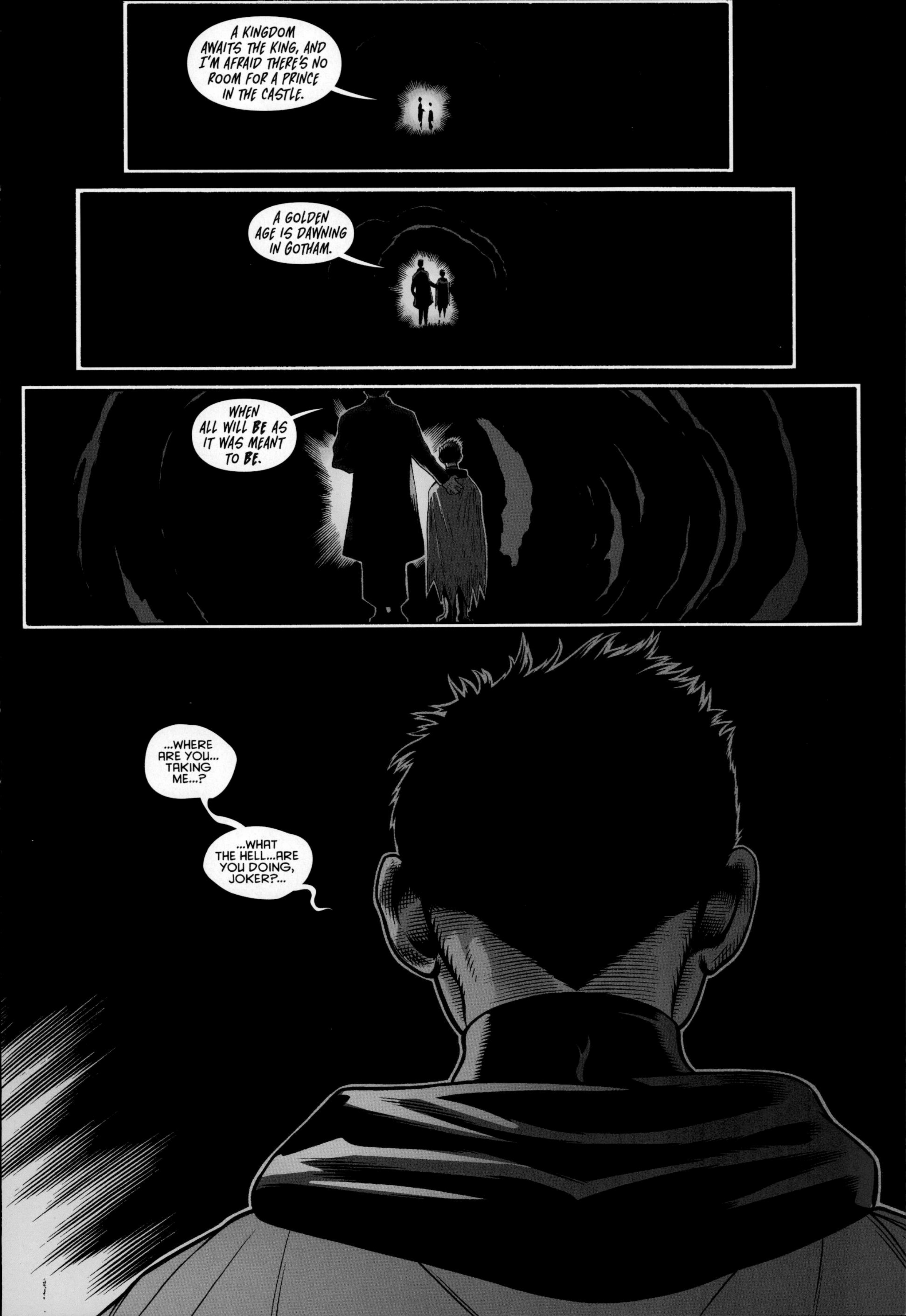
A KINGDOM AWAITS THE KING, AND I'M AFRAID THERE'S NO ROOM FOR A PRINCE IN THE CASTLE.
A GOLDEN AGE IS DAWNING IN GOTHAM.
WHEN ALL WILL BE AS IT WAS MEANT TO BE.
...WHERE ARE YOU... TAKING ME...?
...WHAT THE HELL...ARE YOU DOING, JOKER?...

CONCLUSION

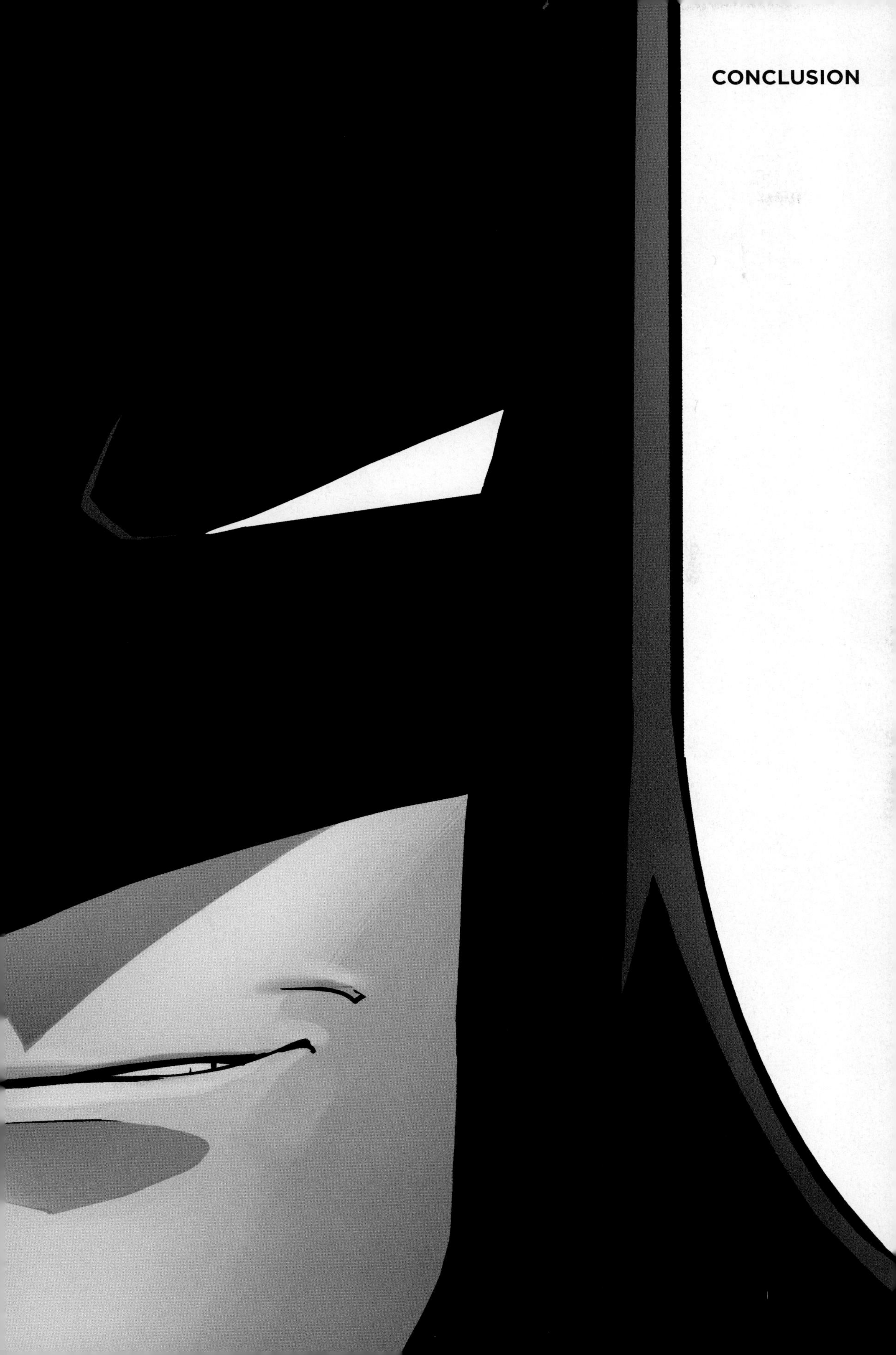

SCOTT SNYDER writer **GREG CAPULLO** penciller **JONATHAN GLAPION** inker
FCO PLASCENCIA colorist **RICHARD STARKINGS COMICRAFT'S JIMMY BETANCOURT** letterers

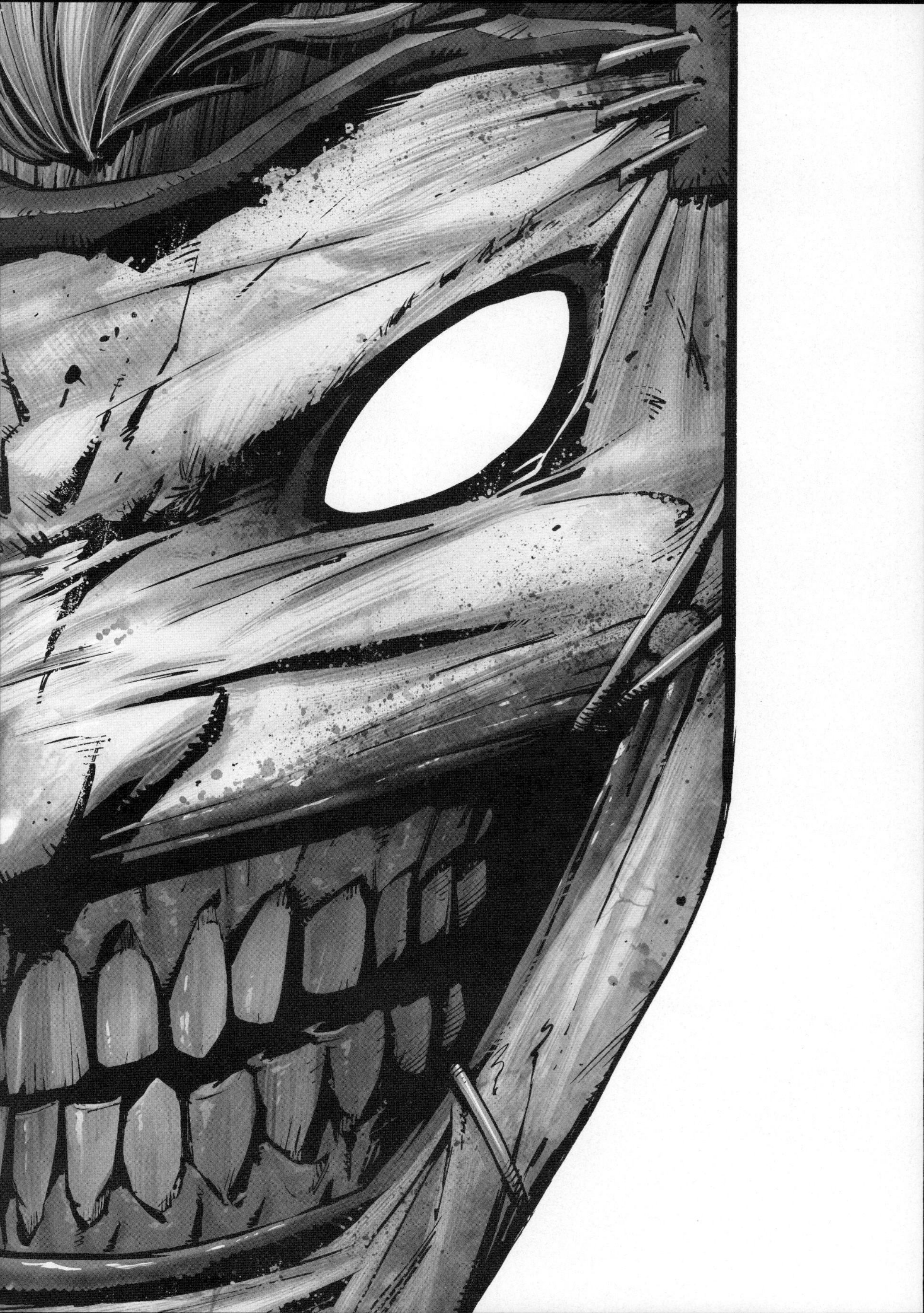

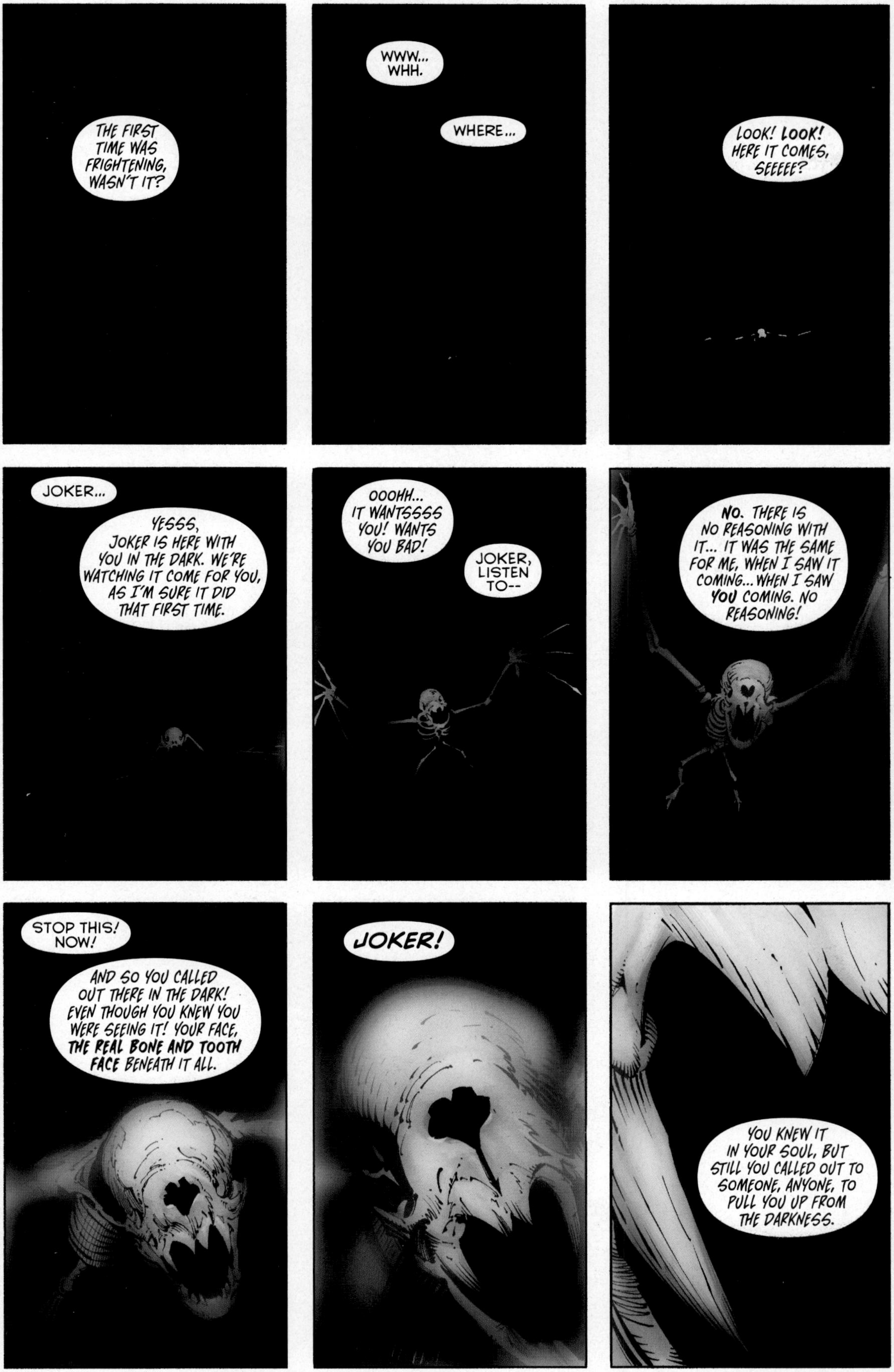
THE FIRST TIME WAS FRIGHTENING, WASN'T IT?
WWW... WHH.
WHERE...
LOOK! LOOK! HERE IT COMES, SEEEEE?
JOKER...
YESSS, JOKER IS HERE WITH YOU IN THE DARK. WE'RE WATCHING IT COME FOR YOU, AS I'M SURE IT DID THAT FIRST TIME.
OOOHH... IT WANTSSSS YOU! WANTS YOU BAD!
JOKER, LISTEN TO--
NO. THERE IS NO REASONING WITH IT... IT WAS THE SAME FOR ME, WHEN I SAW IT COMING... WHEN I SAW YOU COMING. NO REASONING!
STOP THIS! NOW!
AND SO YOU CALLED OUT THERE IN THE DARK! EVEN THOUGH YOU KNEW YOU WERE SEEING IT! YOUR FACE, THE REAL BONE AND TOOTH FACE BENEATH IT ALL.
JOKER!
YOU KNEW IT IN YOUR SOUL, BUT STILL YOU CALLED OUT TO SOMEONE, ANYONE, TO PULL YOU UP FROM THE DARKNESS.

...IT WAS *YOU*, BATS.

YOU WROTE THIS LITTLE LOVE LETTER, THIS BACKWARDS MAP, THIS HIT LIST...AND YOU WRITE IT AGAIN AND AGAIN, EVERY TIME YOU KEEP ONE OF *US* ALIVE, BUT LET ONE OF *THEM* FALL. AND THEY WILL FALL, MAYBE ONE BY ONE, MAYBE TOGETHER...BUT LOOK TO THE FUTURE, REALLY LOOK, AND YOU KNOW IT'S COMING...

...THAT DAY WHEN THEY'RE ALL DEAD AND BURIED, IN THEIR COLD BAT-GRAVES (HEE-HEE). BUT LOOK! THERE'S ME AND MY FRIENDS, AND...WHY, WE'RE STILL ALIVE AND KICKING! AND THERE YOU ARE, BATSSS...CHASING US, FOREVER CHASING!

AND WHY? BECAUSE IT'S WHAT YOU WANT TO HAPPEN. IT'S WHAT YOU NEEEED. BECAUSE YOU SEE, WITH *US* YOU'RE MORE! WITH *US*, YOU TRANSSSCEND! WITH *US*, YOU'RE ALWAYS.

BUT *THEM*, THEY MAKE YOU EVERYTHING YOU WANT TO FORGET THAT YOU ARE, EVERYTHING YOU'RE AFRAID OF. AND YOU WERE AFRAID, WHEN YOU TOOK *THEM* IN. I KNOW. IT'S OKAY, OLD FRIEND. IT WAS A MOMENT OF WEAK-NESSSSS...THE DIRT WAS PULLING.

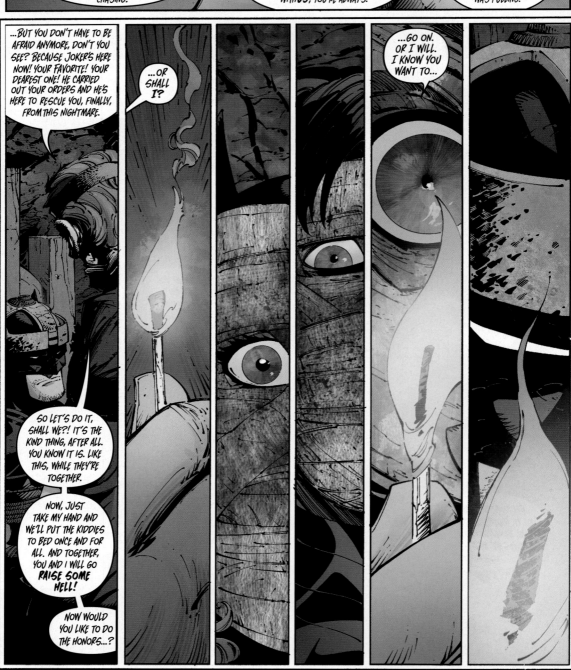

...BUT YOU DON'T HAVE TO BE AFRAID ANYMORE, DON'T YOU SEE? BECAUSE JOKER'S HERE NOW! YOUR FAVORITE! YOUR DEAREST ONE! HE CARRIED OUT YOUR ORDERS AND HE'S HERE TO RESCUE YOU, FINALLY, FROM THIS NIGHTMARE.

SO LET'S DO IT, SHALL WE?! IT'S THE KIND THING, AFTER ALL. YOU KNOW IT IS. LIKE THIS, WHILE THEY'RE TOGETHER.

NOW, JUST TAKE MY HAND AND WE'LL PUT THE KIDDIES TO BED ONCE AND FOR ALL. AND TOGETHER, YOU AND I WILL GO *RAISE SOME HELL!*

NOW WOULD YOU LIKE TO DO THE HONORS...?

...OR SHALL I?

...GO ON. OR I WILL. I KNOW YOU WANT TO...

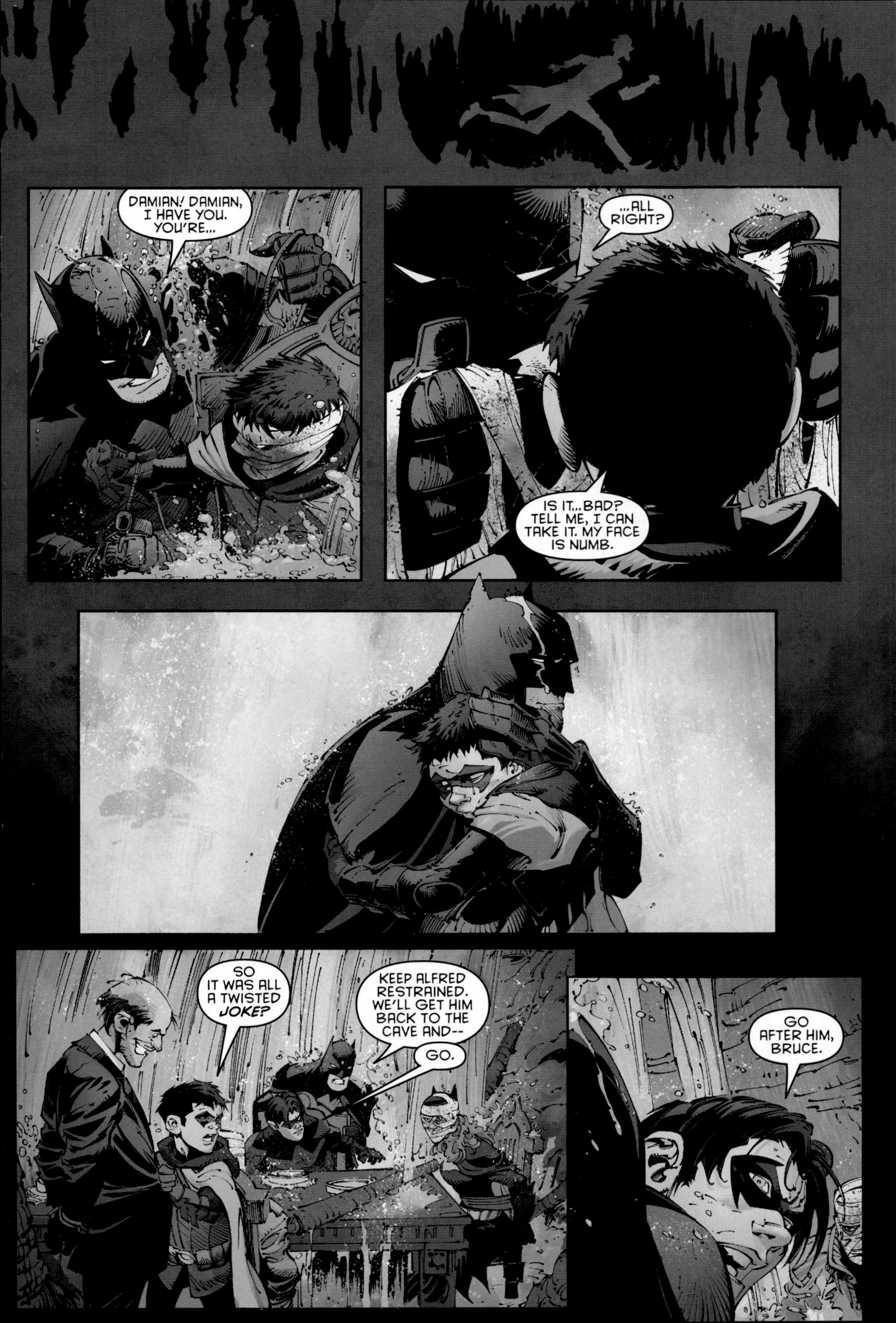
DAMIAN! DAMIAN, I HAVE YOU. YOU'RE...
...ALL RIGHT?
IS IT...BAD? TELL ME, I CAN TAKE IT. MY FACE IS NUMB.
SO IT WAS ALL A TWISTED JOKE?
KEEP ALFRED RESTRAINED. WE'LL GET HIM BACK TO THE CAVE AND--
GO.
GO AFTER HIM, BRUCE.

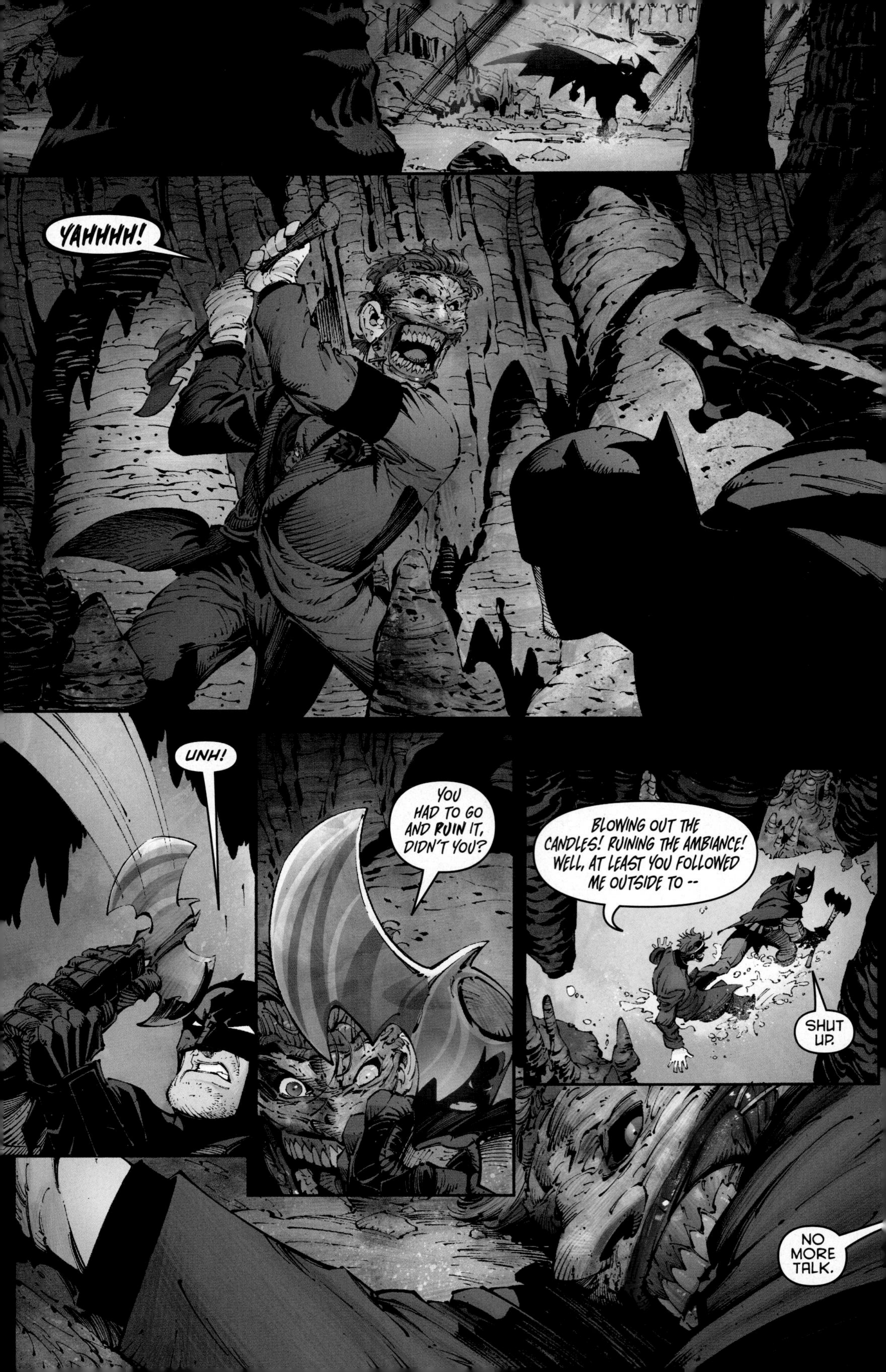
YAHHHH!
UNH!
YOU HAD TO GO AND RUIN IT, DIDN'T YOU?
BLOWING OUT THE CANDLES! RUINING THE AMBIANCE! WELL, AT LEAST YOU FOLLOWED ME OUTSIDE TO --
SHUT UP.
NO MORE TALK.

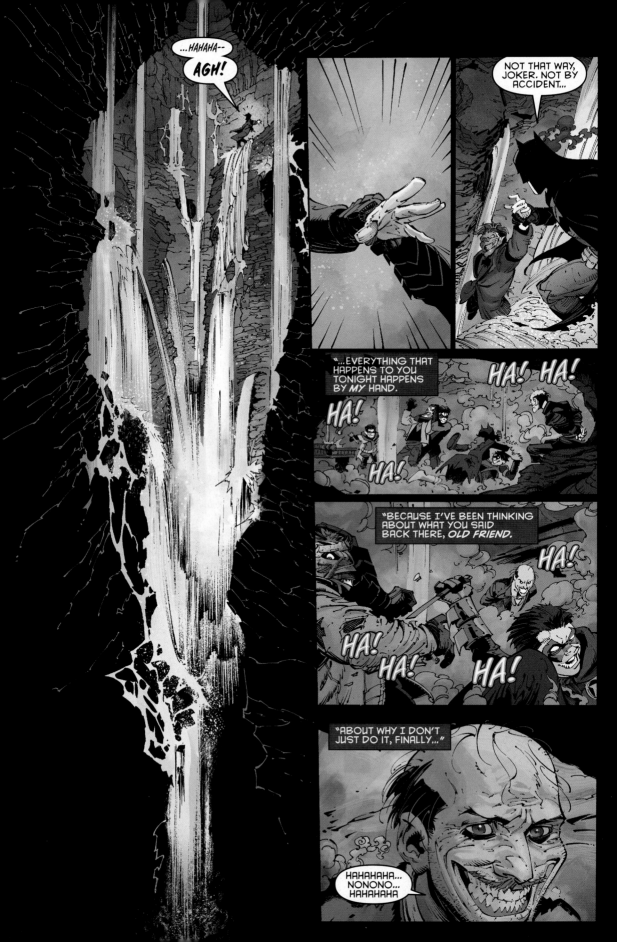

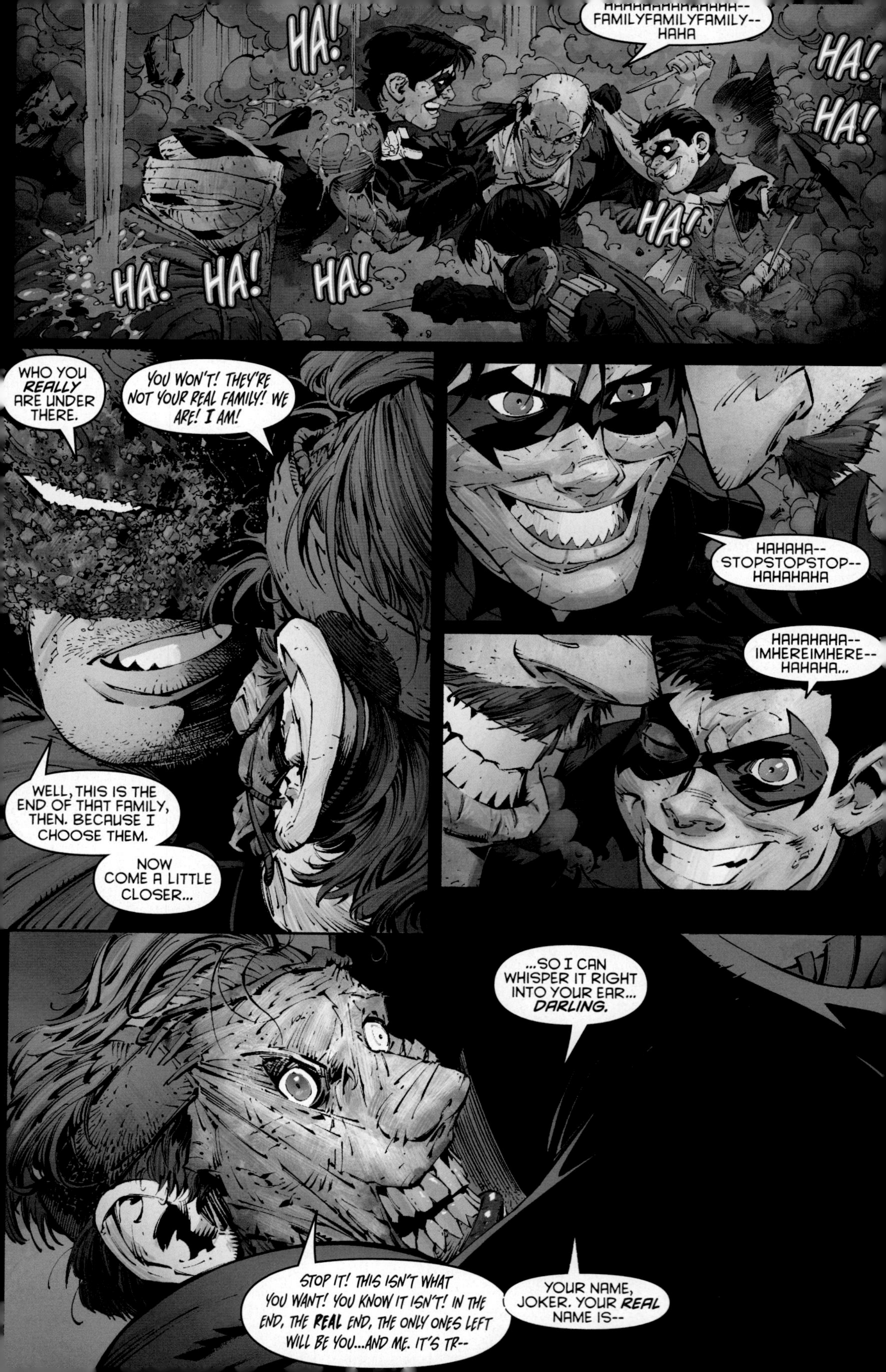
HA!
HAHAHAHAHAHAHAH-- FAMILYFAMILYFAMILY-- HAHA
HA! HA!
HA!
HA! HA! HA!
WHO YOU REALLY ARE UNDER THERE.
YOU WON'T! THEY'RE NOT YOUR REAL FAMILY! WE ARE! I AM!
HAHAHA-- STOPSTOPSTOP-- HAHAHAHA
HAHAHAHA-- IMHEREIMHERE-- HAHAHA...
WELL, THIS IS THE END OF THAT FAMILY, THEN. BECAUSE I CHOOSE THEM.
NOW COME A LITTLE CLOSER...
...SO I CAN WHISPER IT RIGHT INTO YOUR EAR... DARLING.
STOP IT! THIS ISN'T WHAT YOU WANT! YOU KNOW IT ISN'T! IN THE END, THE REAL END, THE ONLY ONES LEFT WILL BE YOU...AND ME. IT'S TR--
YOUR NAME, JOKER. YOUR REAL NAME IS--

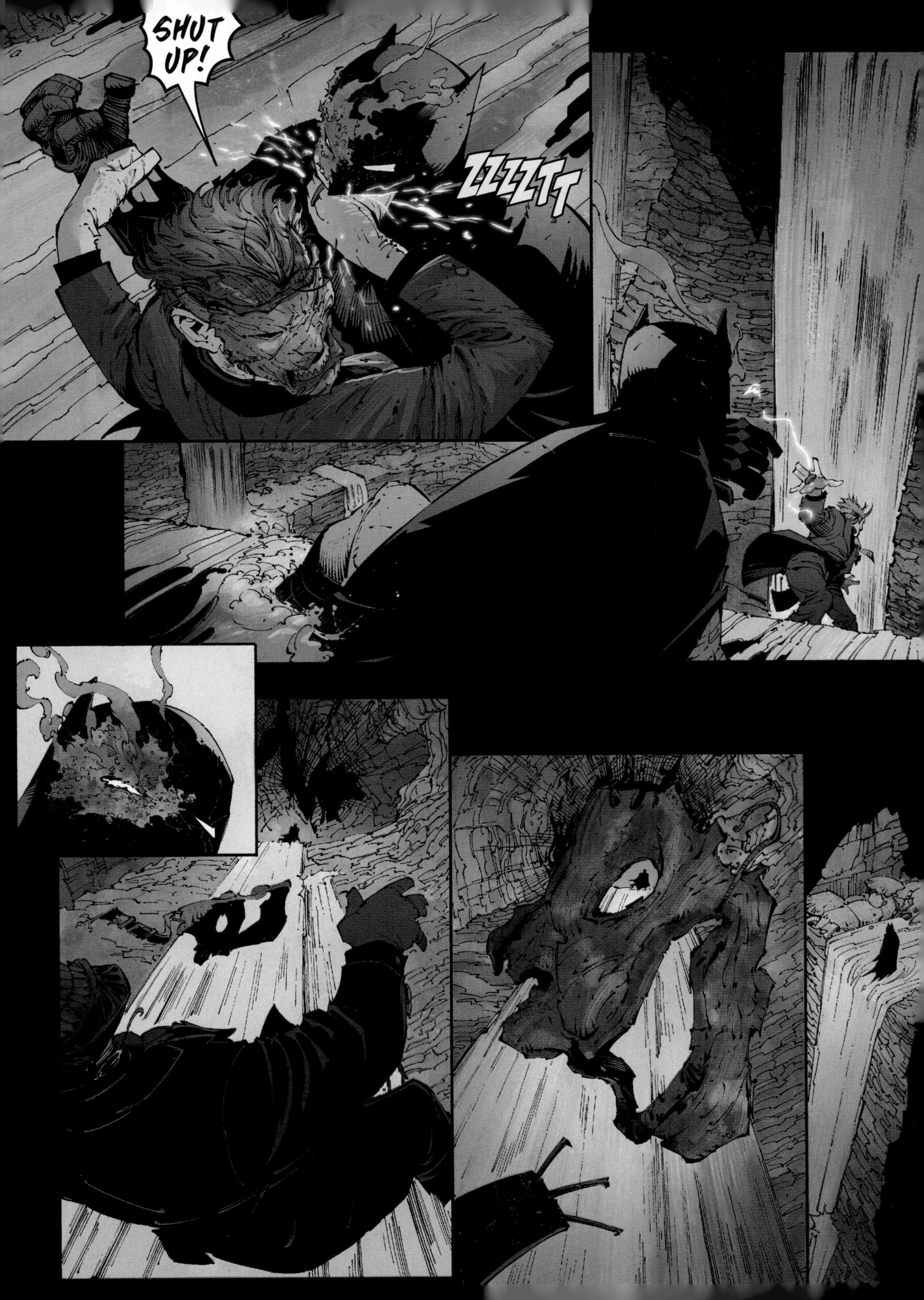
SHUT UP!
ZZZZTT

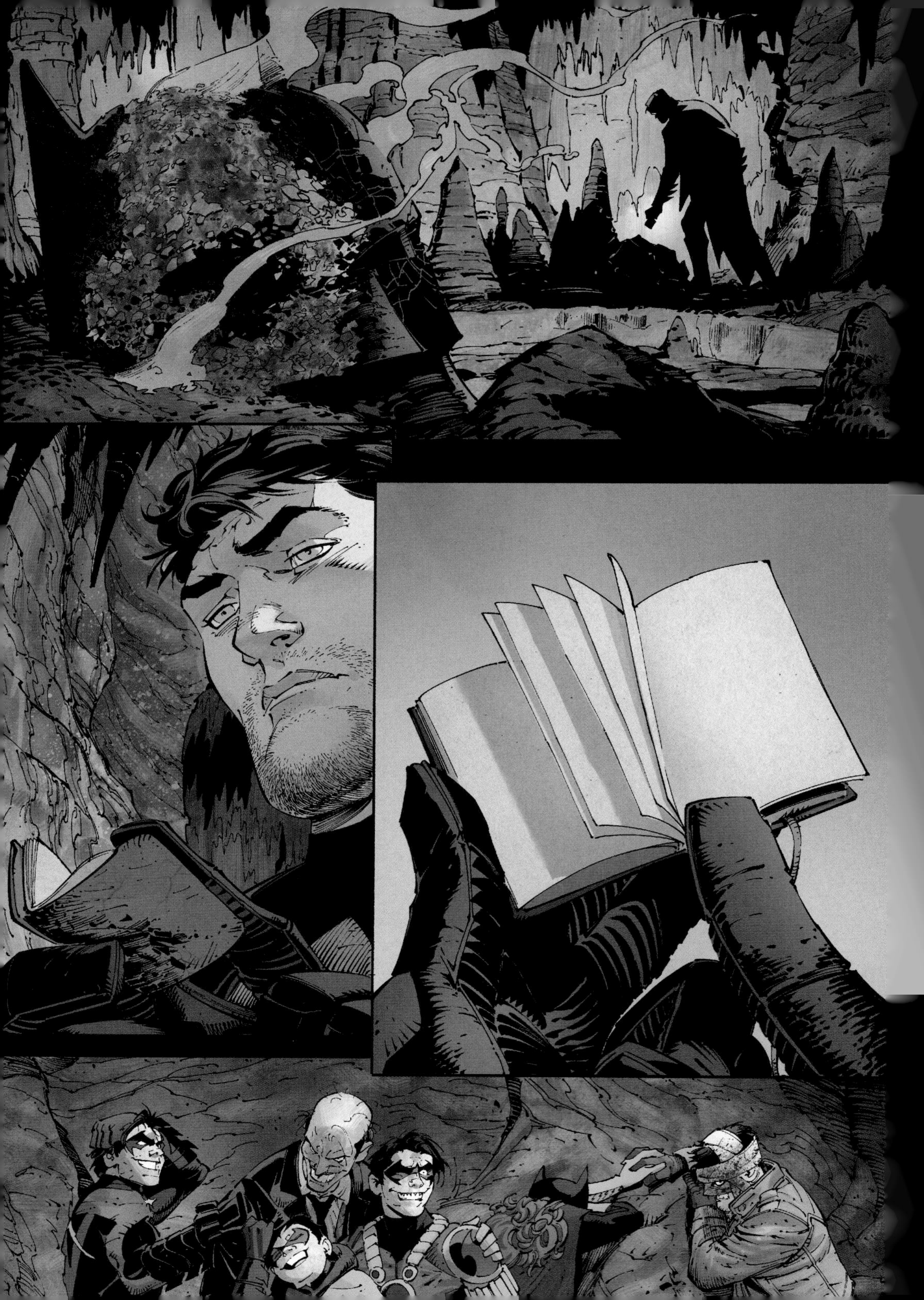

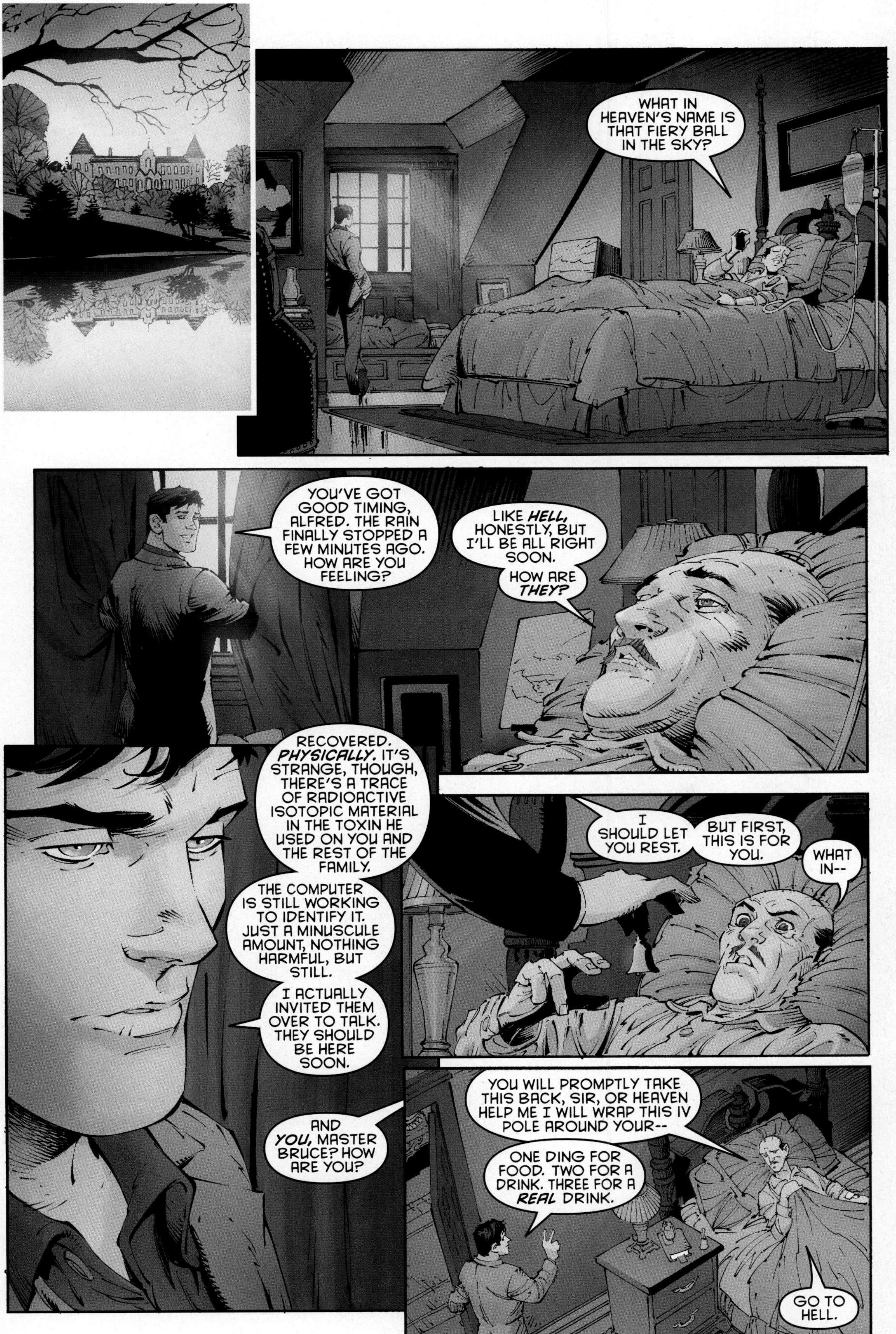
WHAT IN HEAVEN'S NAME IS THAT FIERY BALL IN THE SKY?
YOU'VE GOT GOOD TIMING, ALFRED. THE RAIN FINALLY STOPPED A FEW MINUTES AGO. HOW ARE YOU FEELING?
LIKE *HELL,* HONESTLY, BUT I'LL BE ALL RIGHT SOON.
HOW ARE *THEY?*
RECOVERED. *PHYSICALLY.* IT'S STRANGE, THOUGH, THERE'S A TRACE OF RADIOACTIVE ISOTOPIC MATERIAL IN THE TOXIN HE USED ON YOU AND THE REST OF THE FAMILY.
THE COMPUTER IS STILL WORKING TO IDENTIFY IT. JUST A MINUSCULE AMOUNT, NOTHING HARMFUL, BUT STILL.
I ACTUALLY INVITED THEM OVER TO TALK. THEY SHOULD BE HERE SOON.
AND *YOU,* MASTER BRUCE? HOW ARE YOU?
I SHOULD LET YOU REST.
BUT FIRST, THIS IS FOR YOU.
WHAT IN--
YOU WILL PROMPTLY TAKE THIS BACK, SIR, OR HEAVEN HELP ME I WILL WRAP THIS IV POLE AROUND YOUR--
ONE DING FOR FOOD. TWO FOR A DRINK. THREE FOR A *REAL* DRINK.
GO TO HELL.

SO YOU SEE, I KNEW THERE WAS NEVER ANY CHANCE THAT HE'D GOTTEN INTO THE CAVE. I KNEW IT BECAUSE I *KNOW* HIM. KNOW HIM BETTER THAN I WANT TO ADMIT. BUT THERE'S...THERE'S NO WAY TO TELL HIM THAT, ALFRED, IS THERE? NO WAY TO EXPLAIN THAT I *DID* LET HIM IN, BUT ONLY TO TRY TO END IT, TO TRY--

MASTER BRUCE.

NO, I'M JUST SAYING, ALFRED. THEY KNOW THAT HE'S WRONG, DON'T THEY? ABOUT WHY I NEVER DID IT BEFORE NOW. ABOUT ALL OF IT. BECAUSE HE *IS* WRONG. I'LL NEVER LET THAT HAPPEN, WHAT HE SAID. I'LL NEVER LET IT END UP LIKE THAT... EVERYONE GONE EXCEPT ME AND--

SIR, PLEASE. HE'S GONE NOW. IT'S OVER.

YES. I'LL RING YOU WHEN THE FAMILY ARRIVES. THAT'S *TIM* TEXTING NOW.

Tim:
Bruce. Something came up. Sorry, I won't be able to make it today.

HE...CAN'T MAKE IT. THERE'S SOMETHING FROM *BARBARA*, TOO.

Barbara:
BRUCE, Dad asked me to help him out with some th...
Rain...

"STILL NO WORD FROM *JASON*."

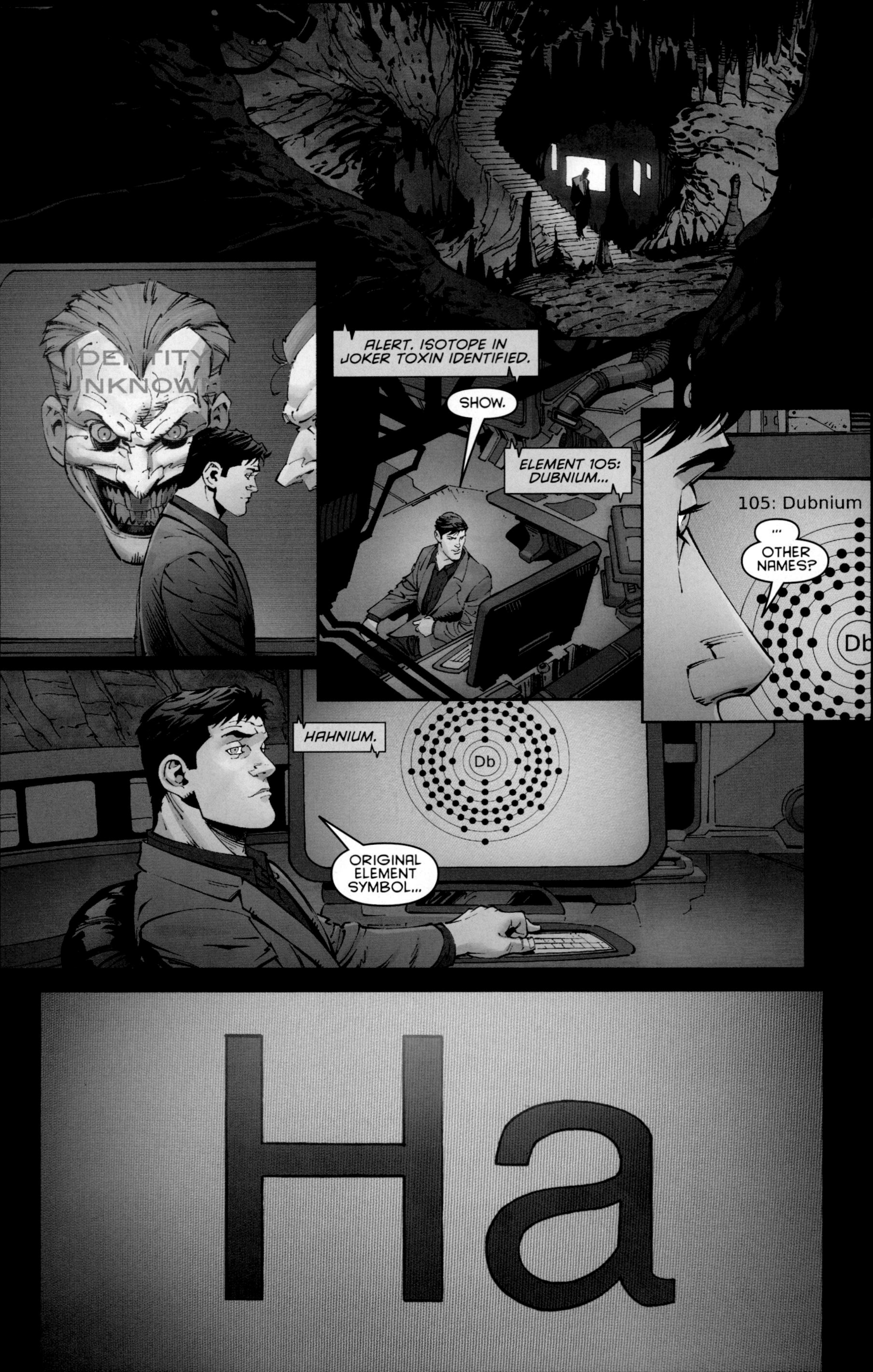
IDENTITY UNKNOWN
ALERT. ISOTOPE IN JOKER TOXIN IDENTIFIED.
SHOW.
ELEMENT 105: DUBNIUM...
105: Dubnium
Db
... OTHER NAMES?
HAHNIUM.
Db
ORIGINAL ELEMENT SYMBOL...
Ha

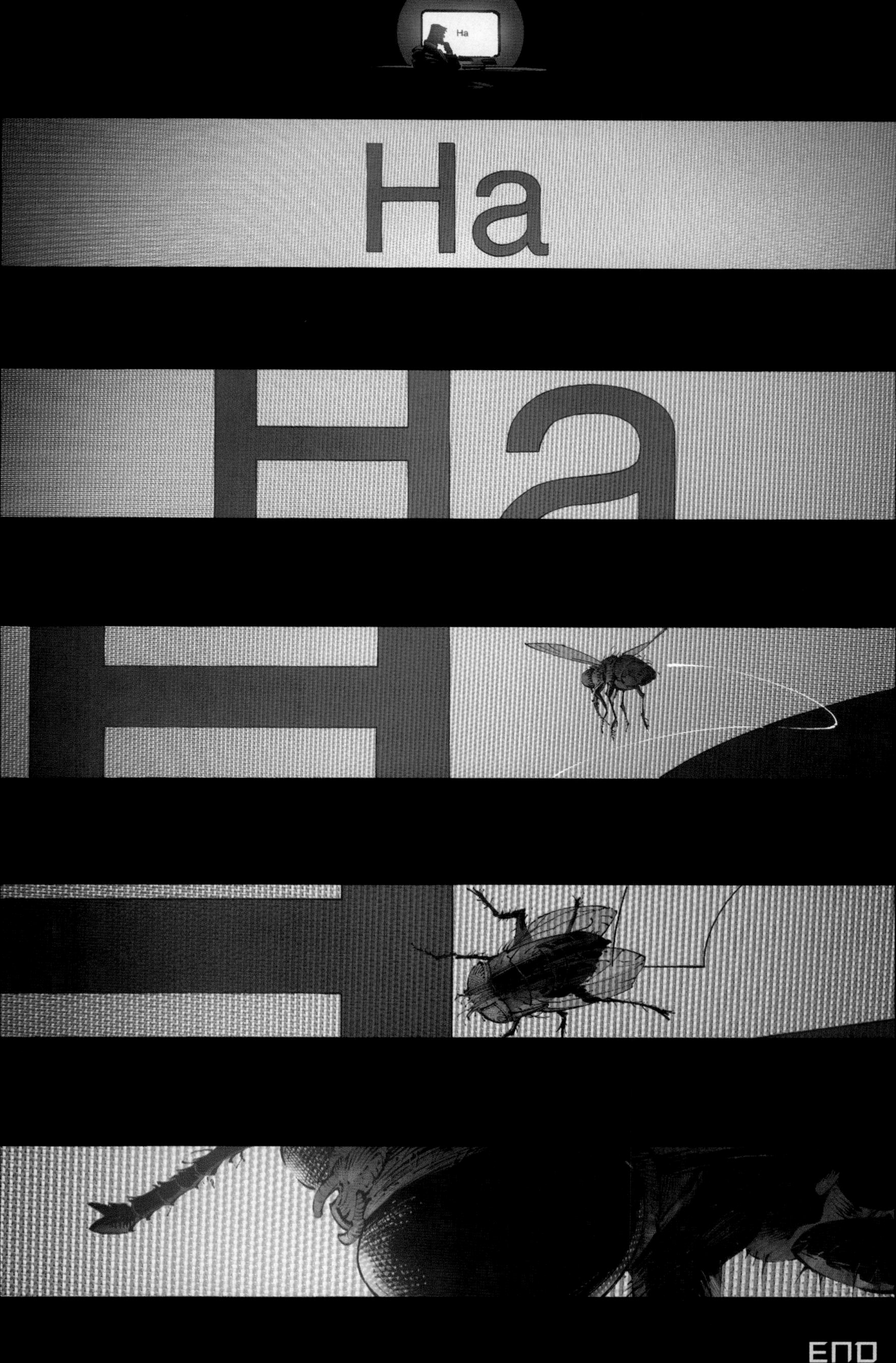
Ha
Ha
END

EPILOGUE

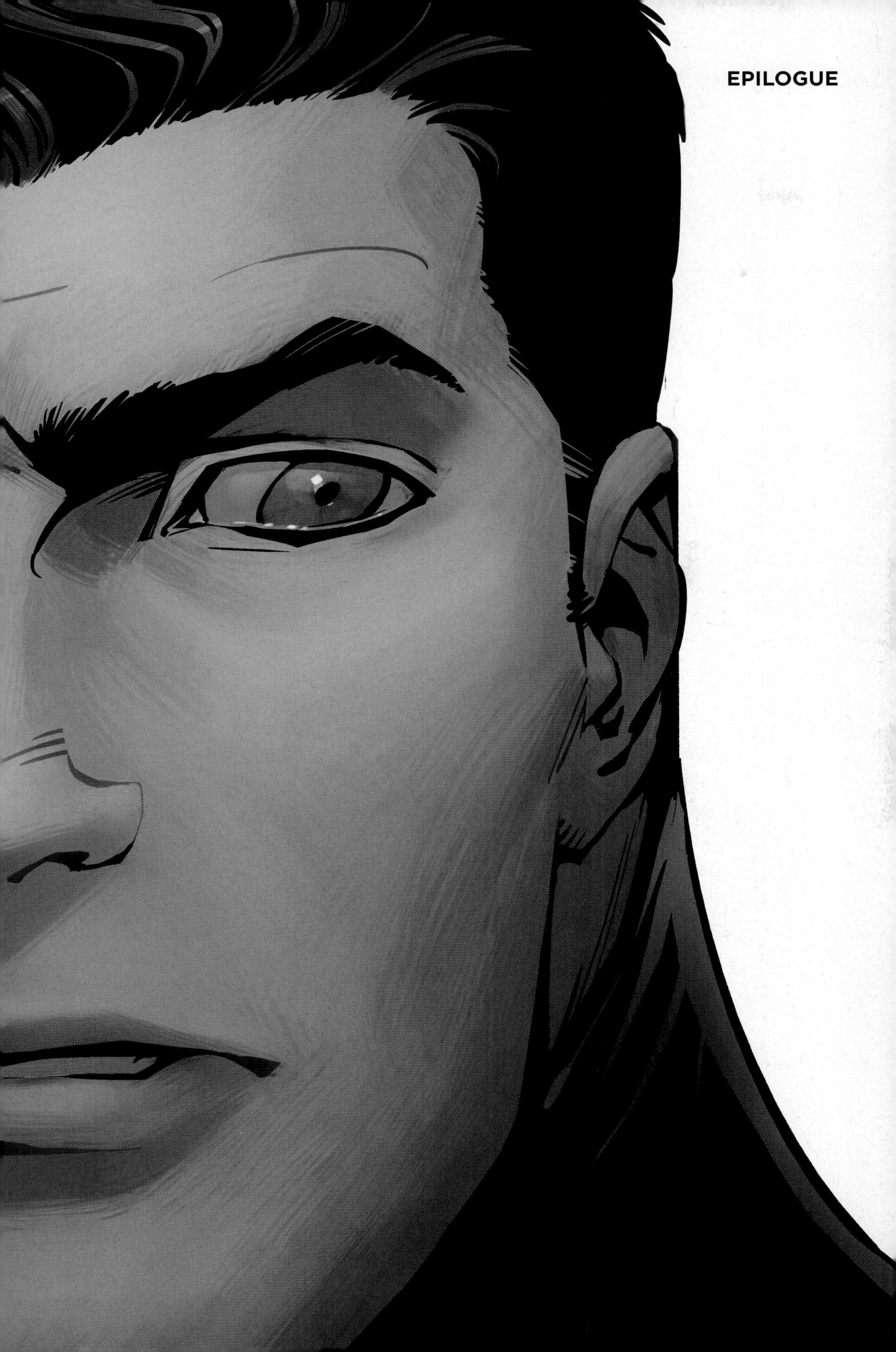

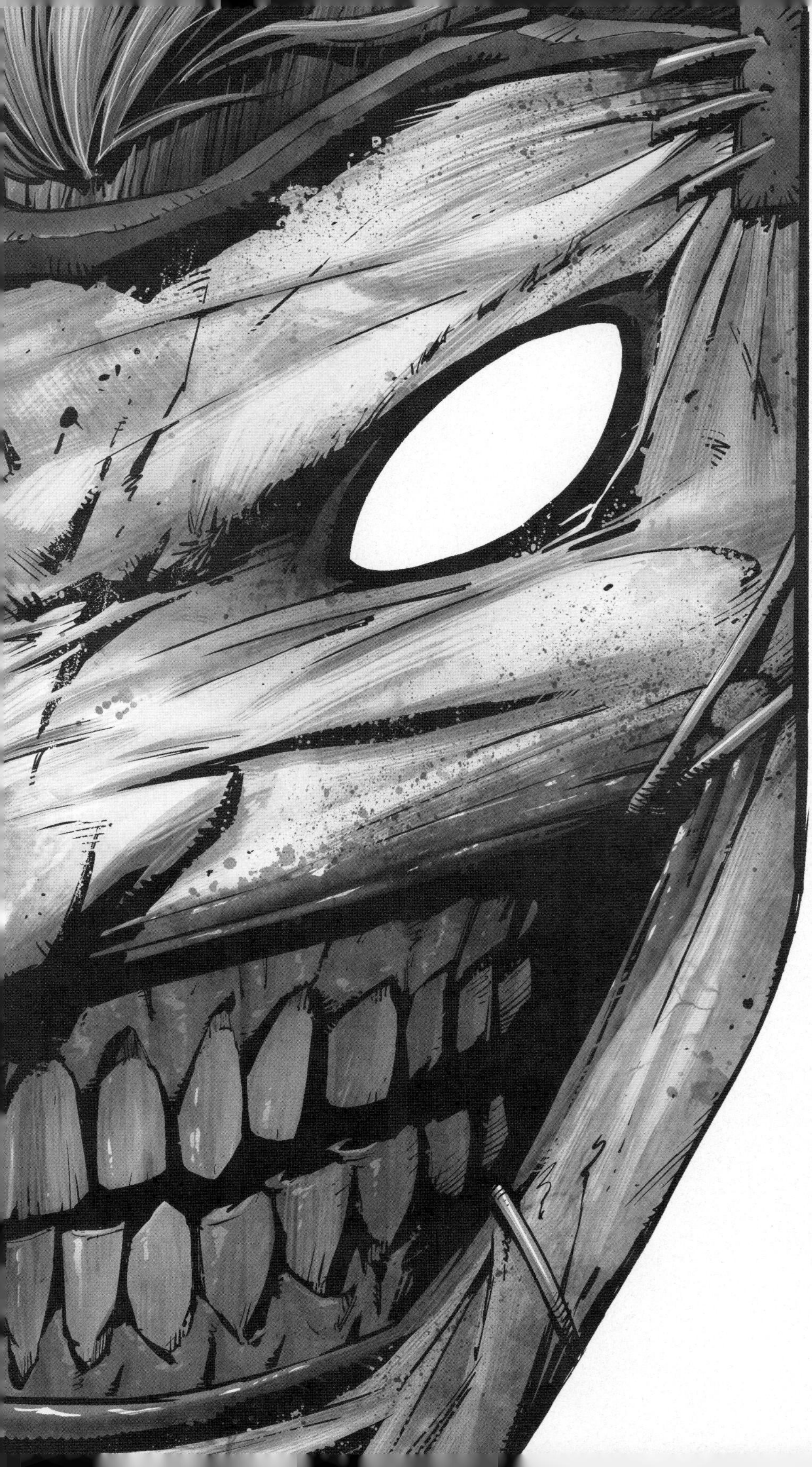

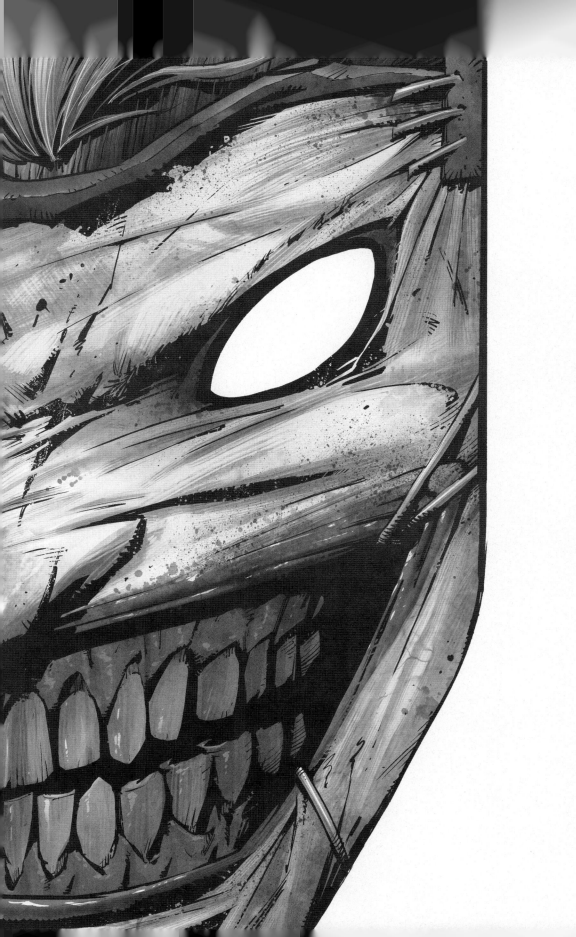

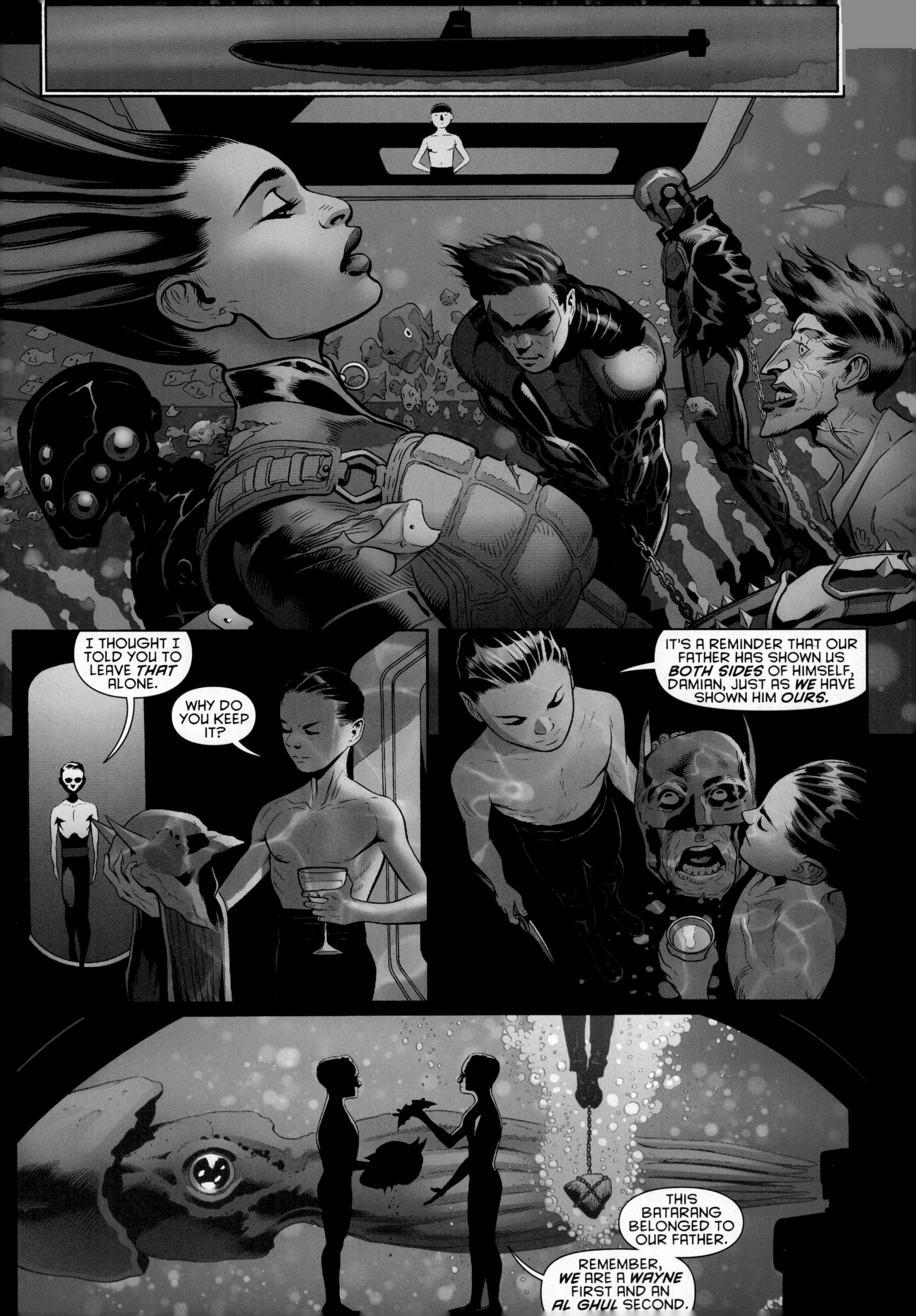
I THOUGHT I TOLD YOU TO LEAVE THAT ALONE.
WHY DO YOU KEEP IT?
IT'S A REMINDER THAT OUR FATHER HAS SHOWN US BOTH SIDES OF HIMSELF, DAMIAN, JUST AS WE HAVE SHOWN HIM OURS.
THIS BATARANG BELONGED TO OUR FATHER.
REMEMBER, WE ARE A WAYNE FIRST AND AN AL GHUL SECOND.

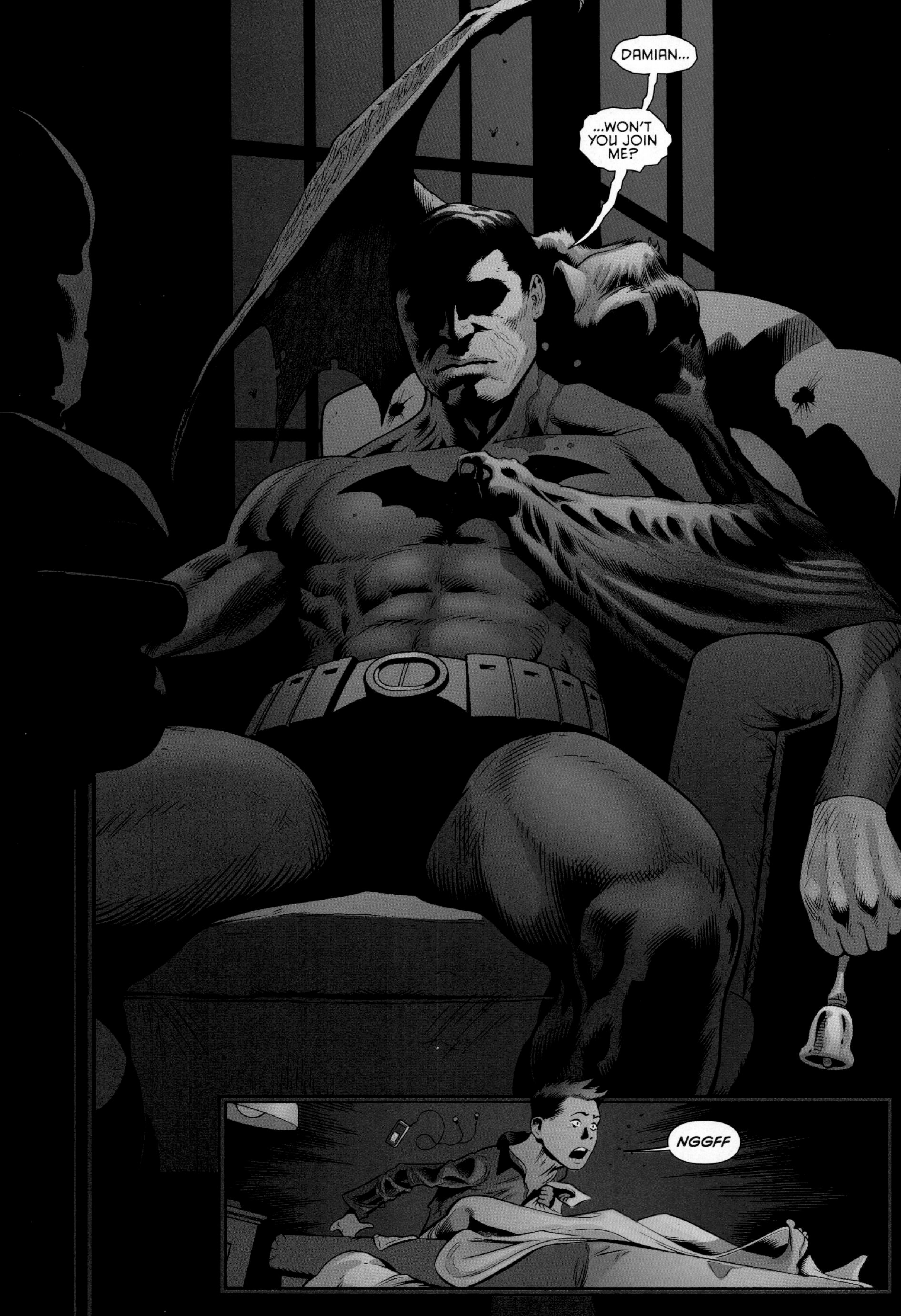
DAMIAN...
...WON'T YOU JOIN ME?
NGGFF

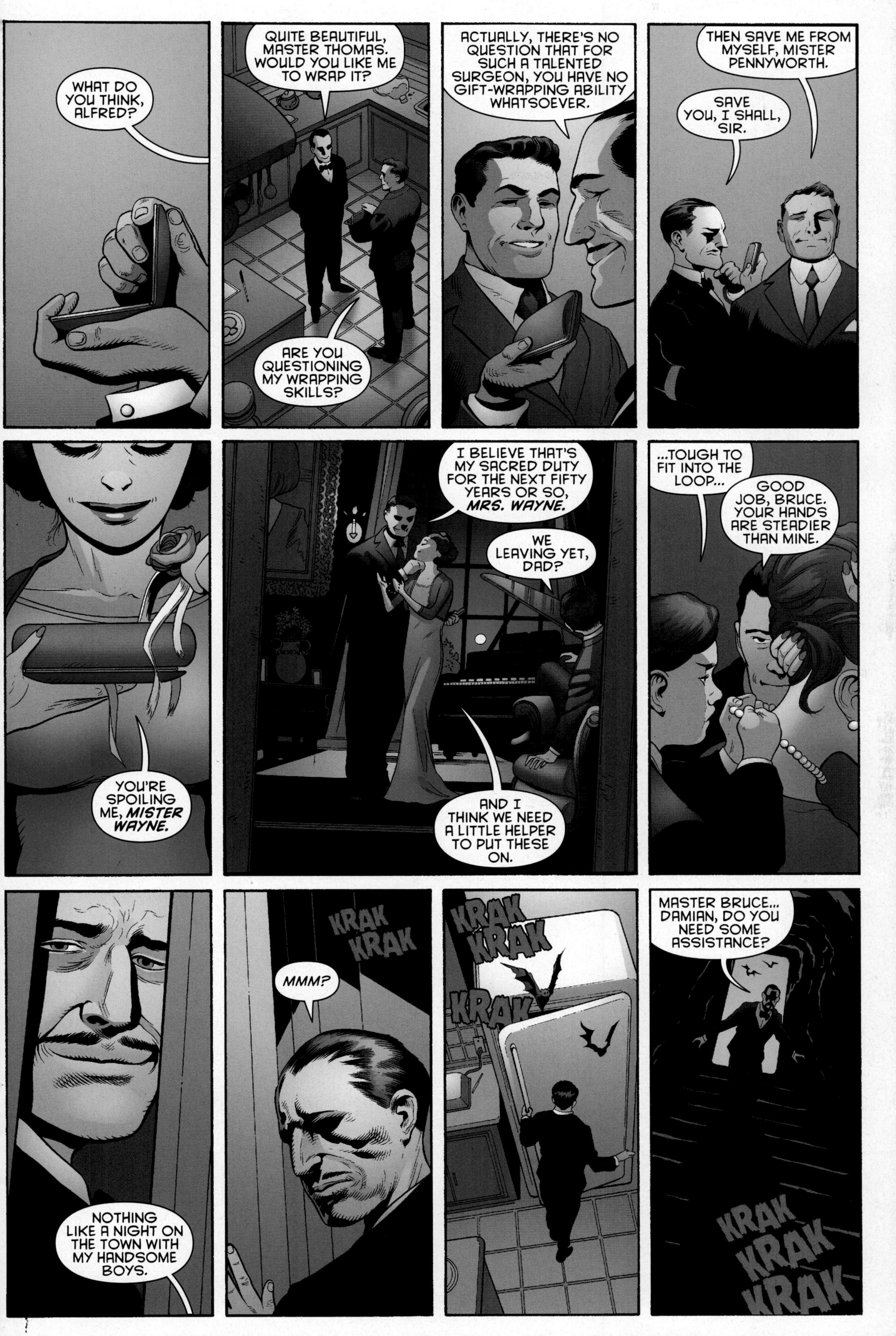
WHAT DO YOU THINK, ALFRED?
QUITE BEAUTIFUL, MASTER THOMAS. WOULD YOU LIKE ME TO WRAP IT?
ARE YOU QUESTIONING MY WRAPPING SKILLS?
ACTUALLY, THERE'S NO QUESTION THAT FOR SUCH A TALENTED SURGEON, YOU HAVE NO GIFT-WRAPPING ABILITY WHATSOEVER.
THEN SAVE ME FROM MYSELF, MISTER PENNYWORTH.
SAVE YOU, I SHALL, SIR.
YOU'RE SPOILING ME, MISTER WAYNE.
I BELIEVE THAT'S MY SACRED DUTY FOR THE NEXT FIFTY YEARS OR SO, MRS. WAYNE.
WE LEAVING YET, DAD?
AND I THINK WE NEED A LITTLE HELPER TO PUT THESE ON.
...TOUGH TO FIT INTO THE LOOP...
GOOD JOB, BRUCE. YOUR HANDS ARE STEADIER THAN MINE.
NOTHING LIKE A NIGHT ON THE TOWN WITH MY HANDSOME BOYS.
KRAK KRAK
MMM?
KRAK KRAK
KRAK
MASTER BRUCE... DAMIAN, DO YOU NEED SOME ASSISTANCE?
KRAK KRAK KRAK

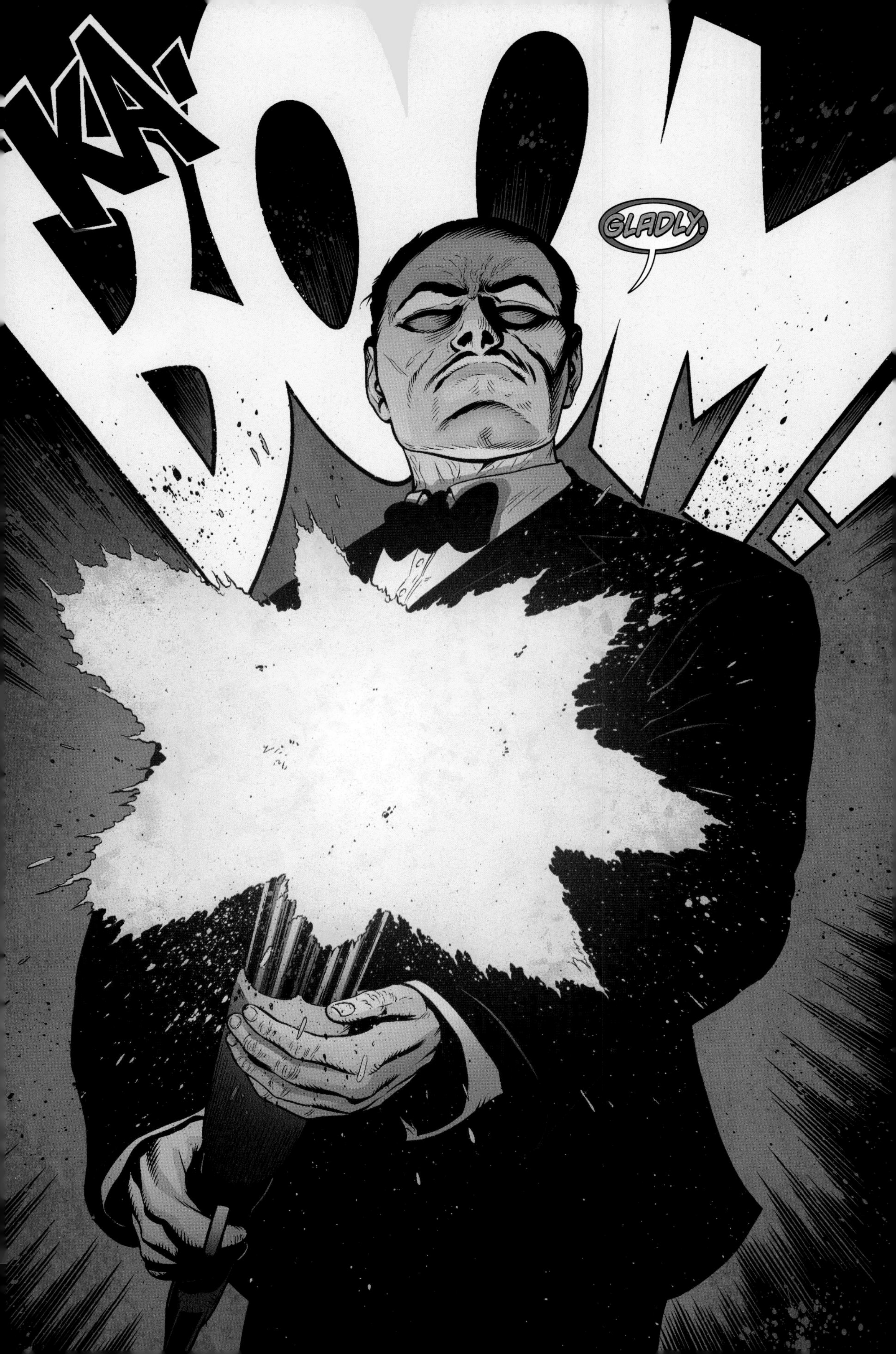
KA-BOOM!
GLADLY.

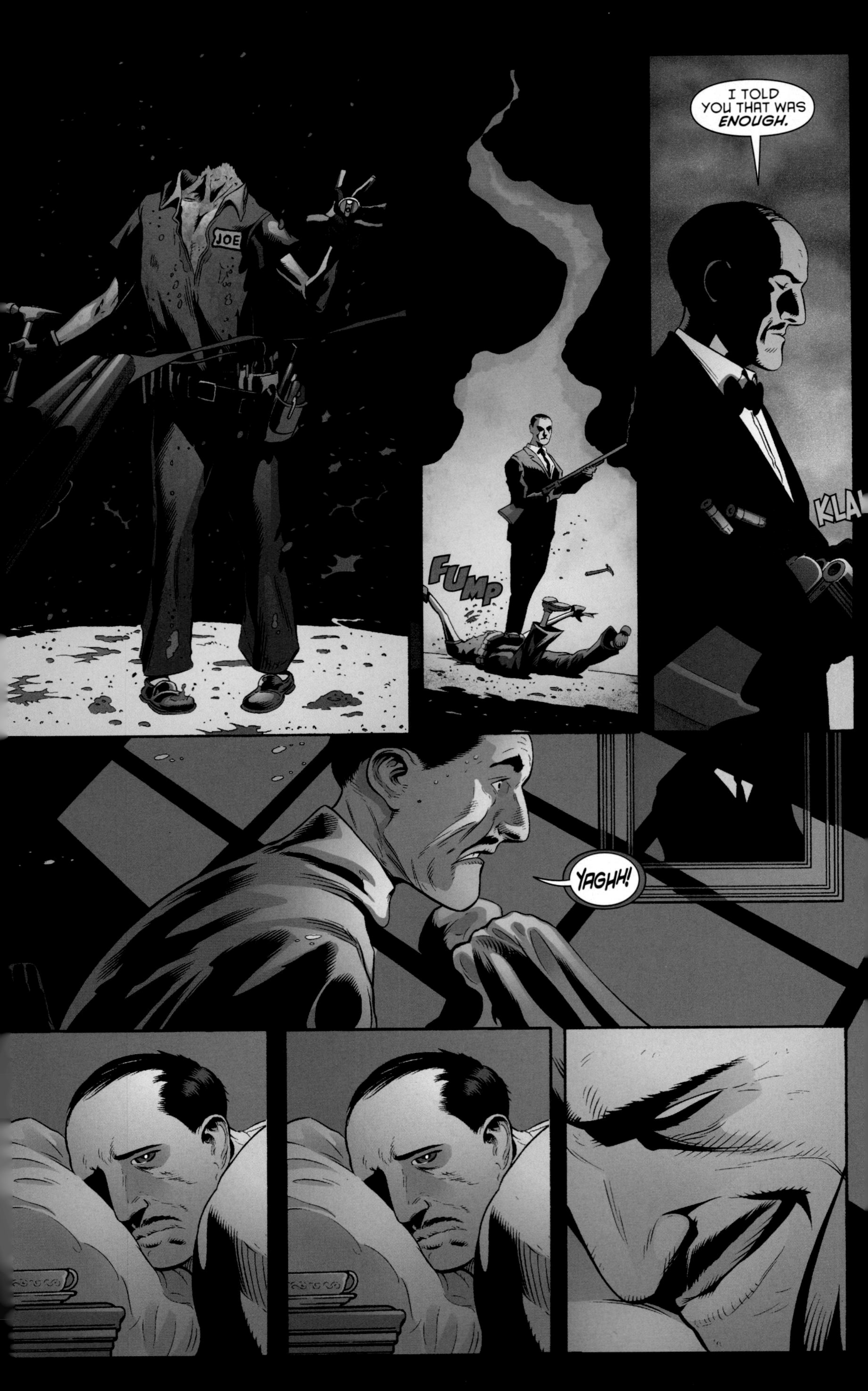
JOE
I TOLD YOU THAT WAS ENOUGH.
FUMP
KLA
YAGHH!

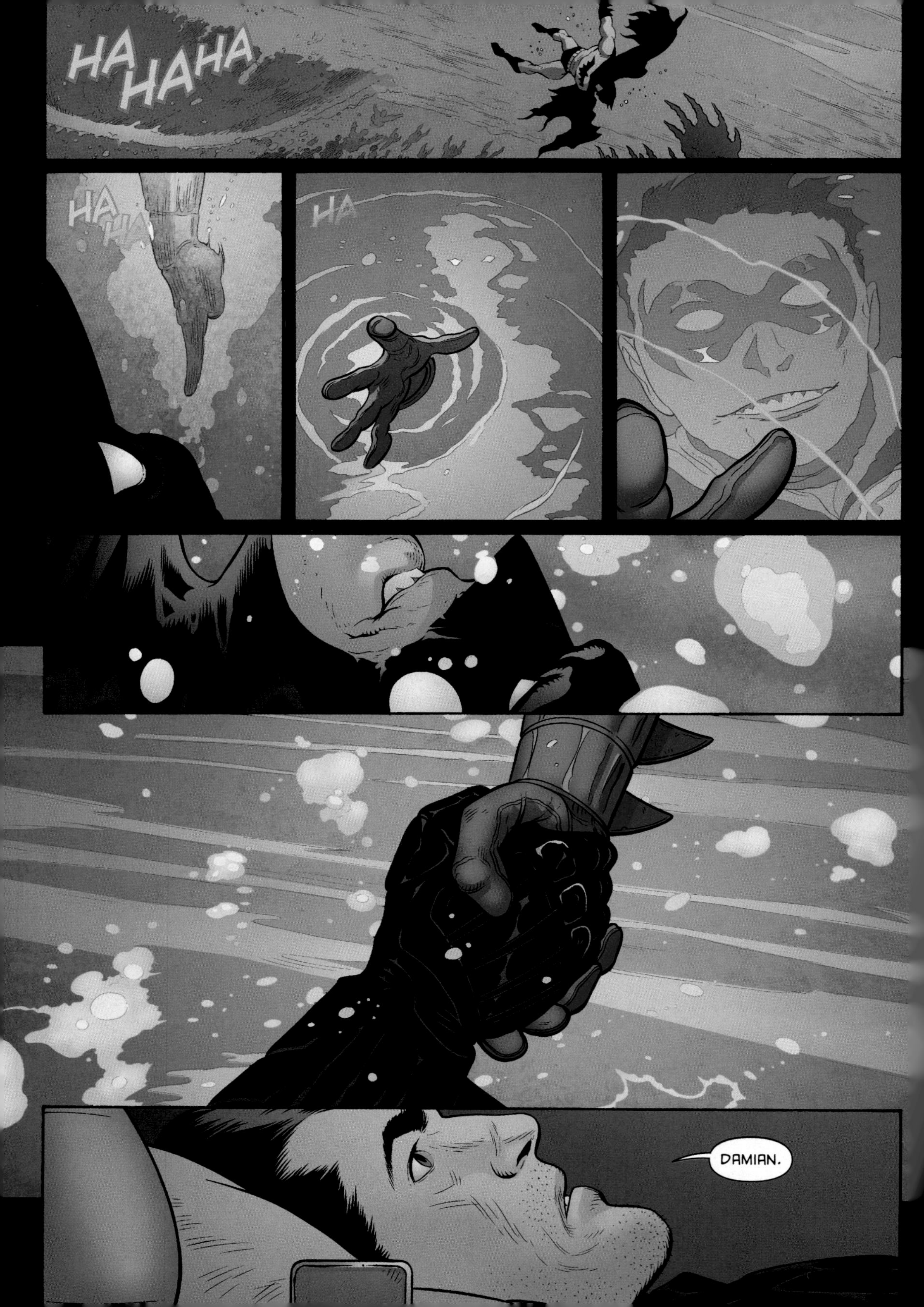
HA HAHA
HA HA
HA
DAMIAN.

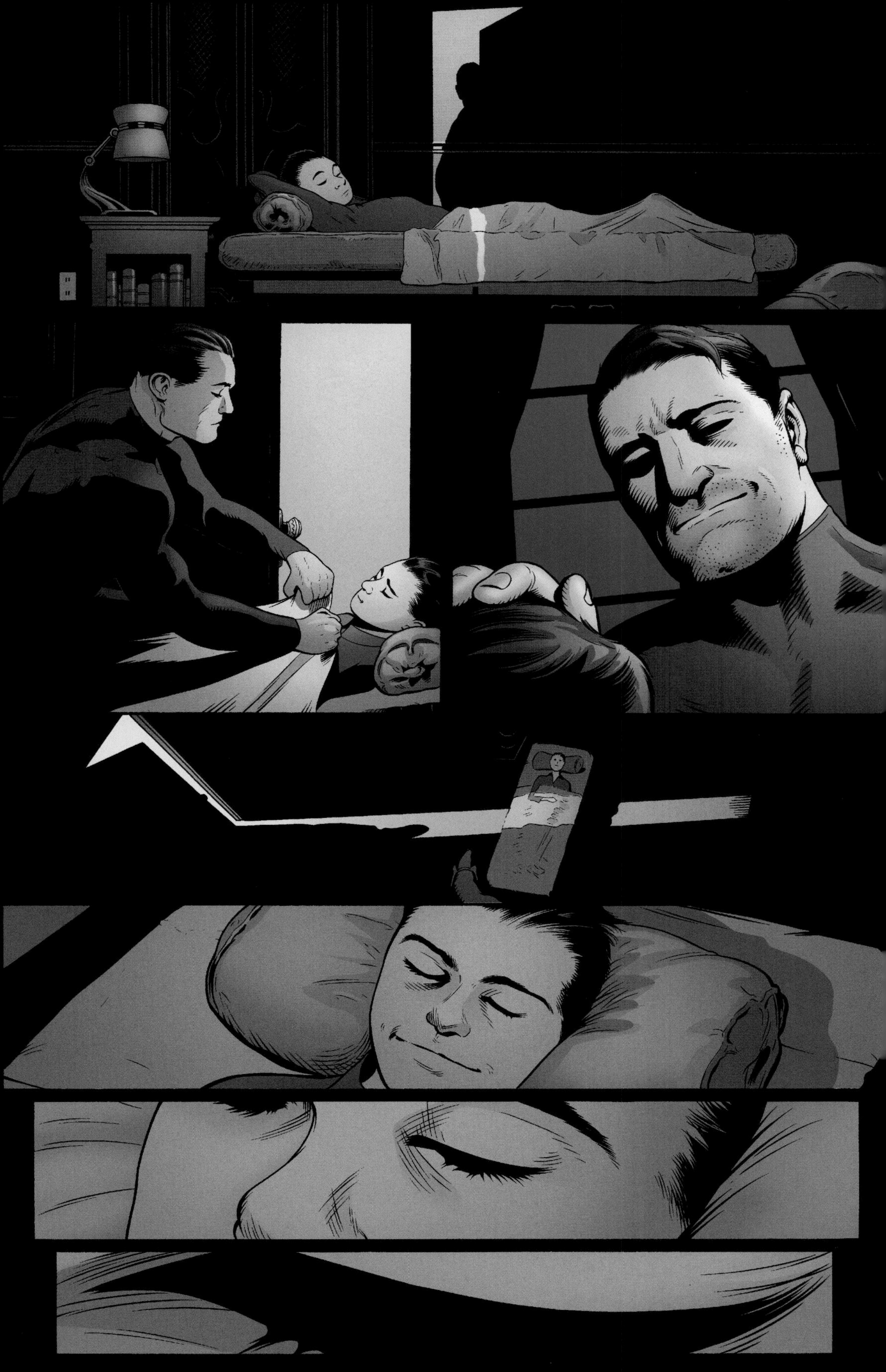

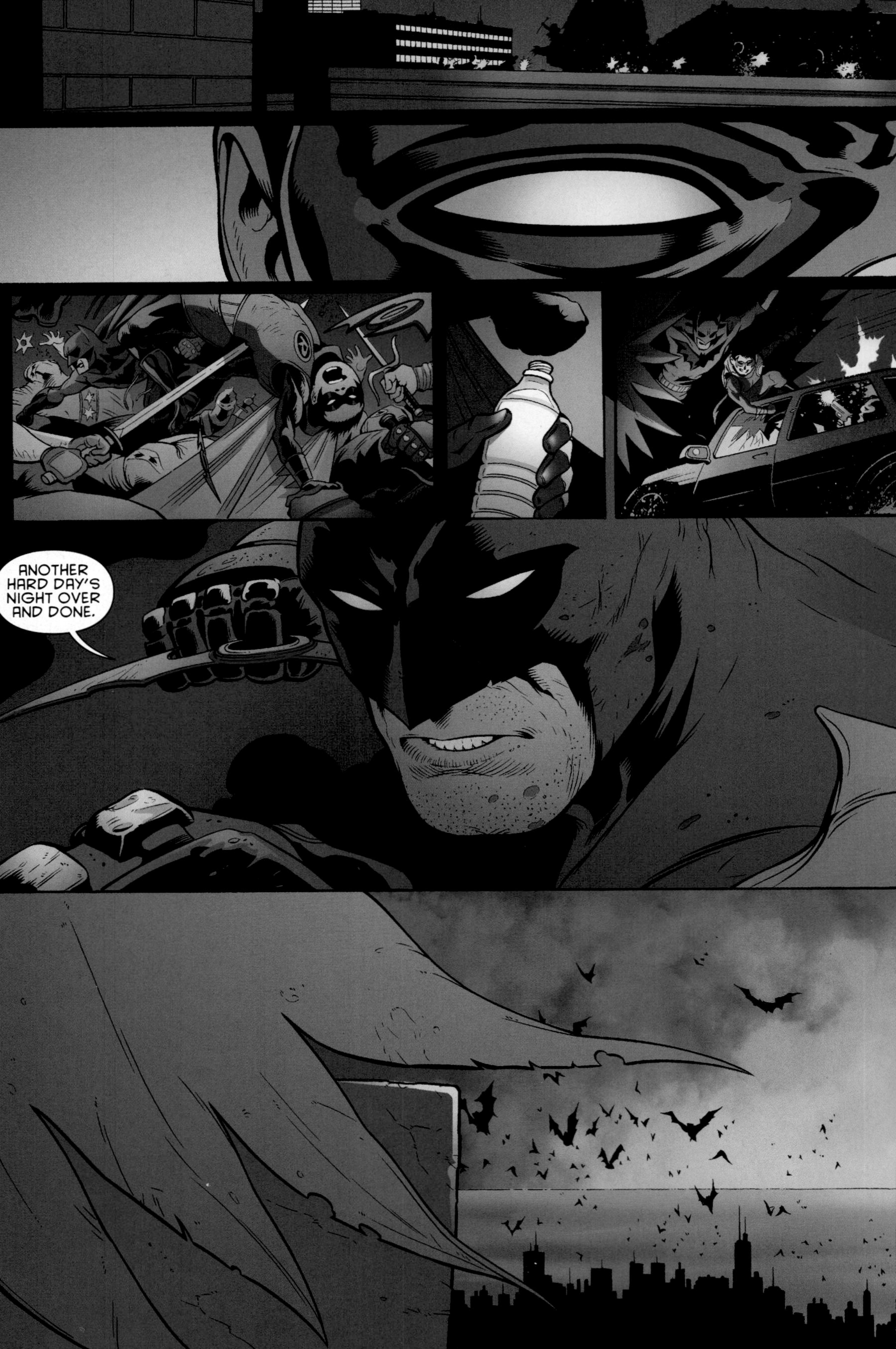
ANOTHER HARD DAY'S NIGHT OVER AND DONE.

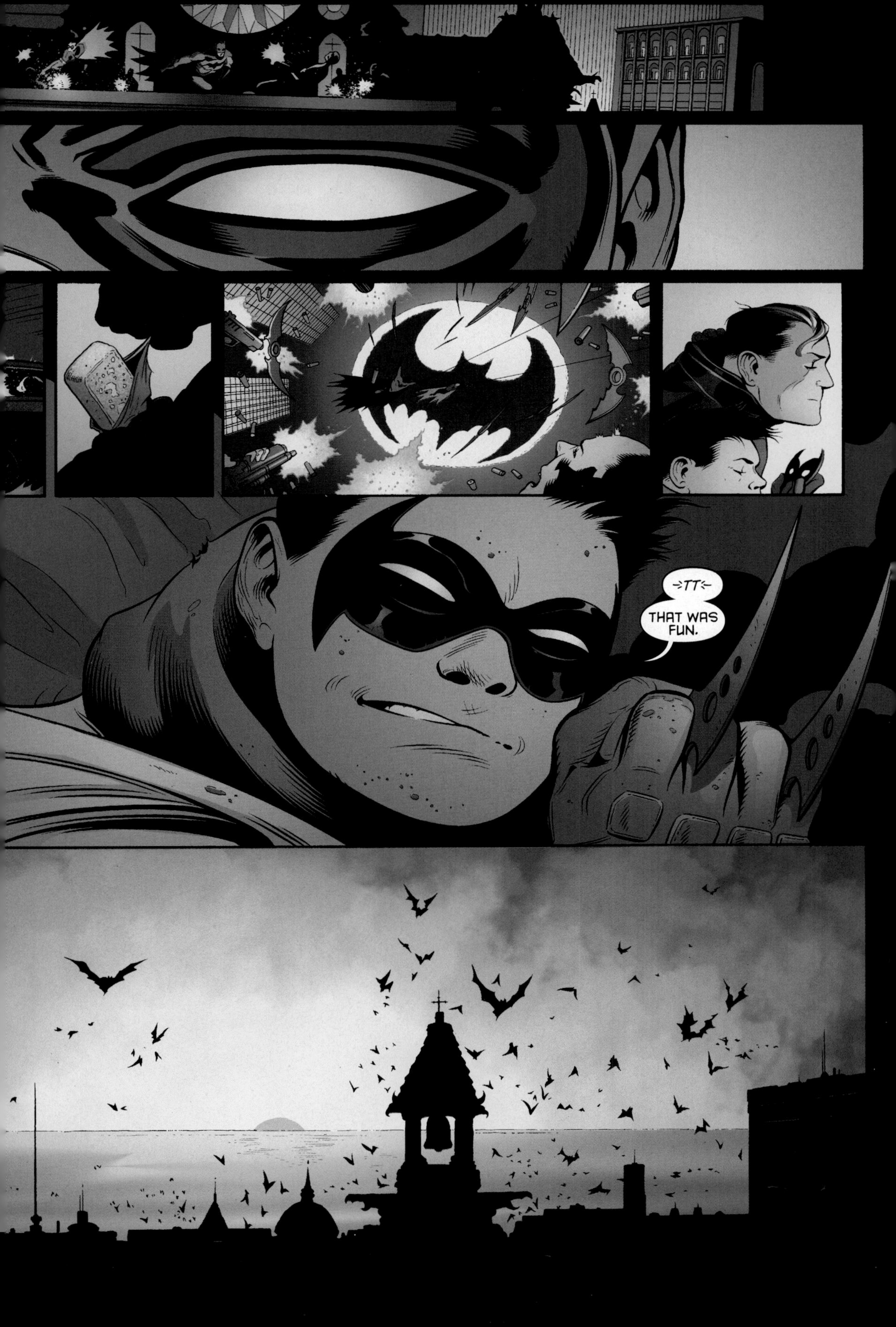
TT
THAT WAS FUN.

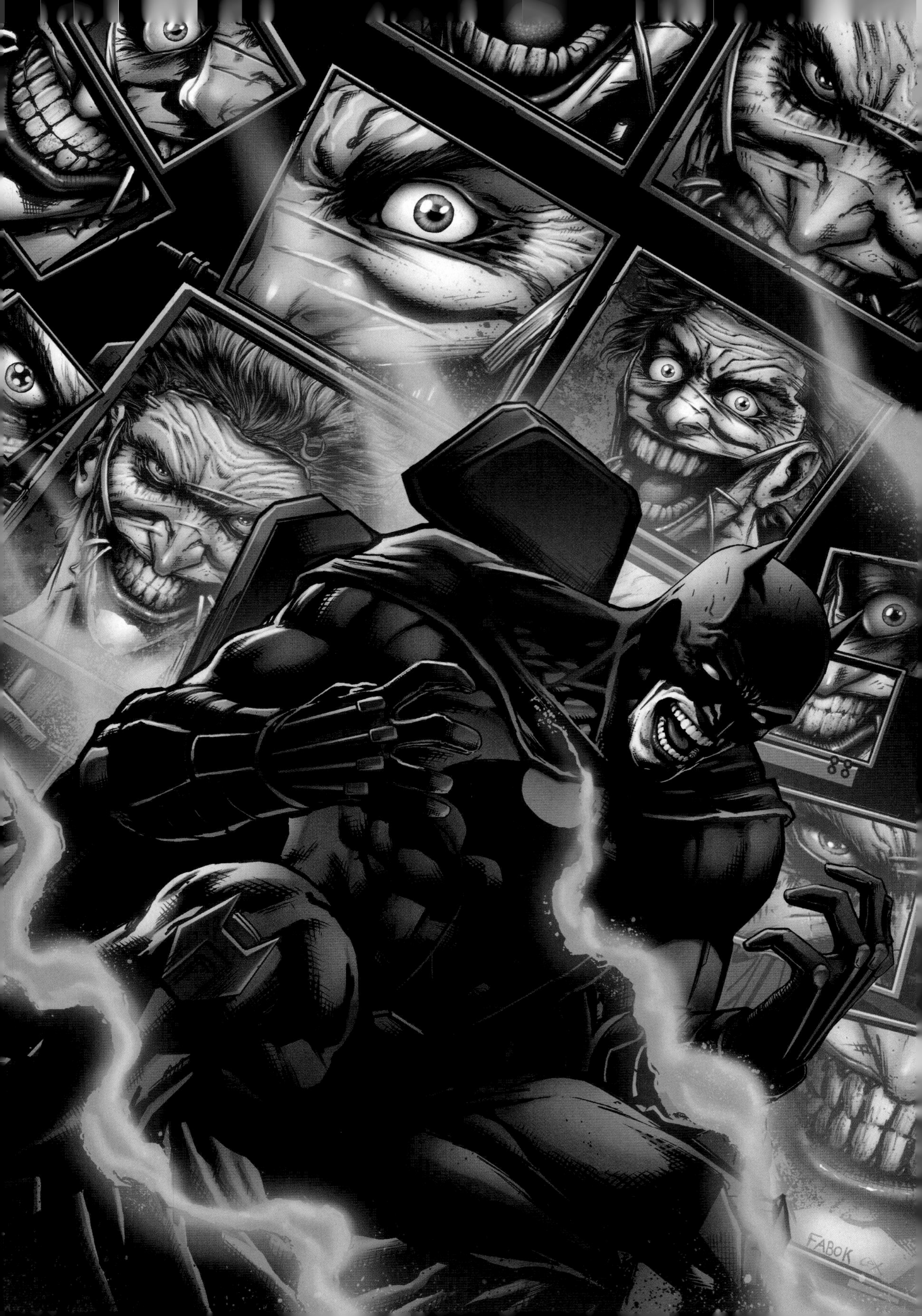
FABOK COX

DETECTIVE COMICS #17 cover by JASON FABOK & JEROMY COX

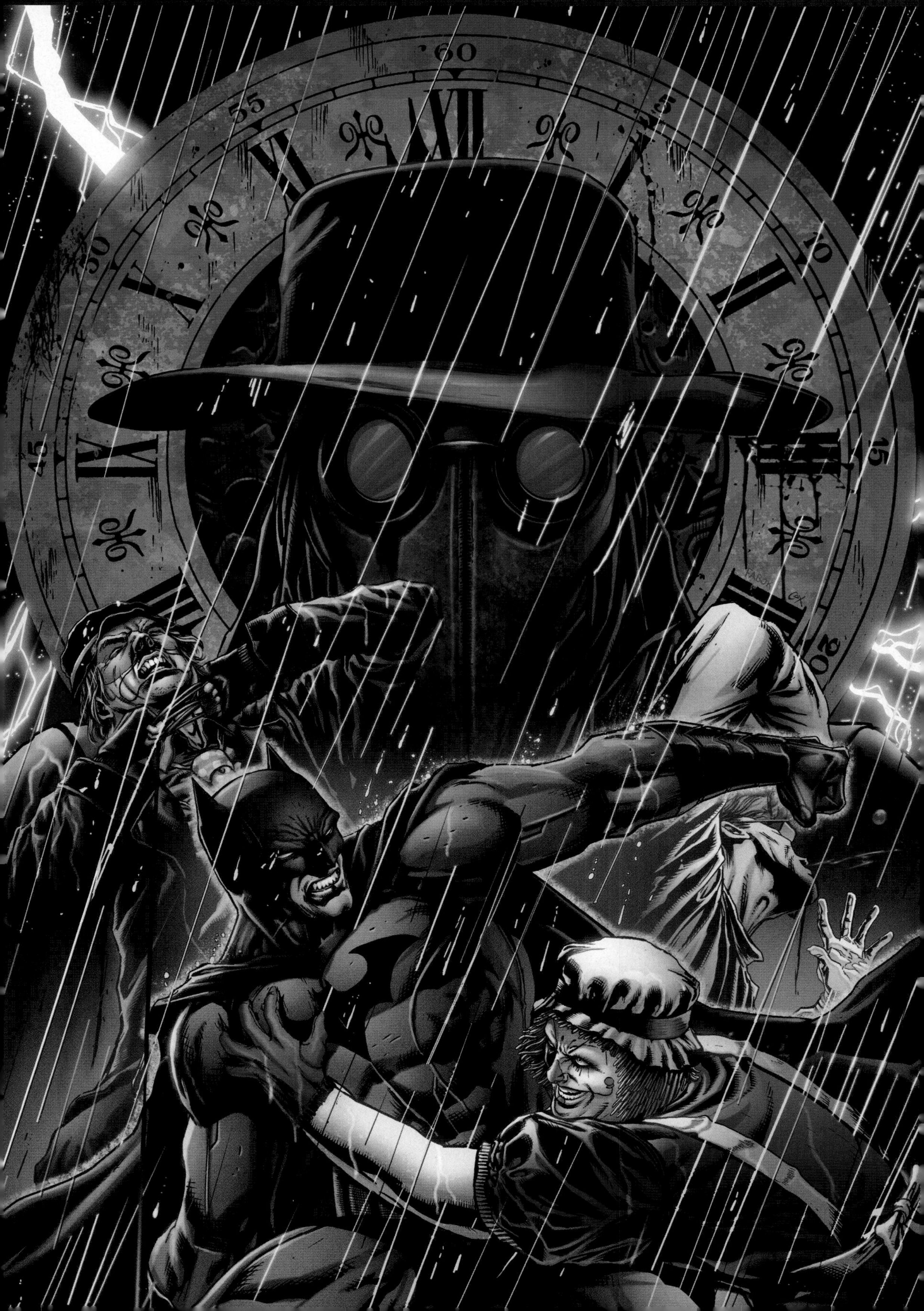

FABOK
COX

CATWOMAN #14 cover by TREVOR McCARTHY

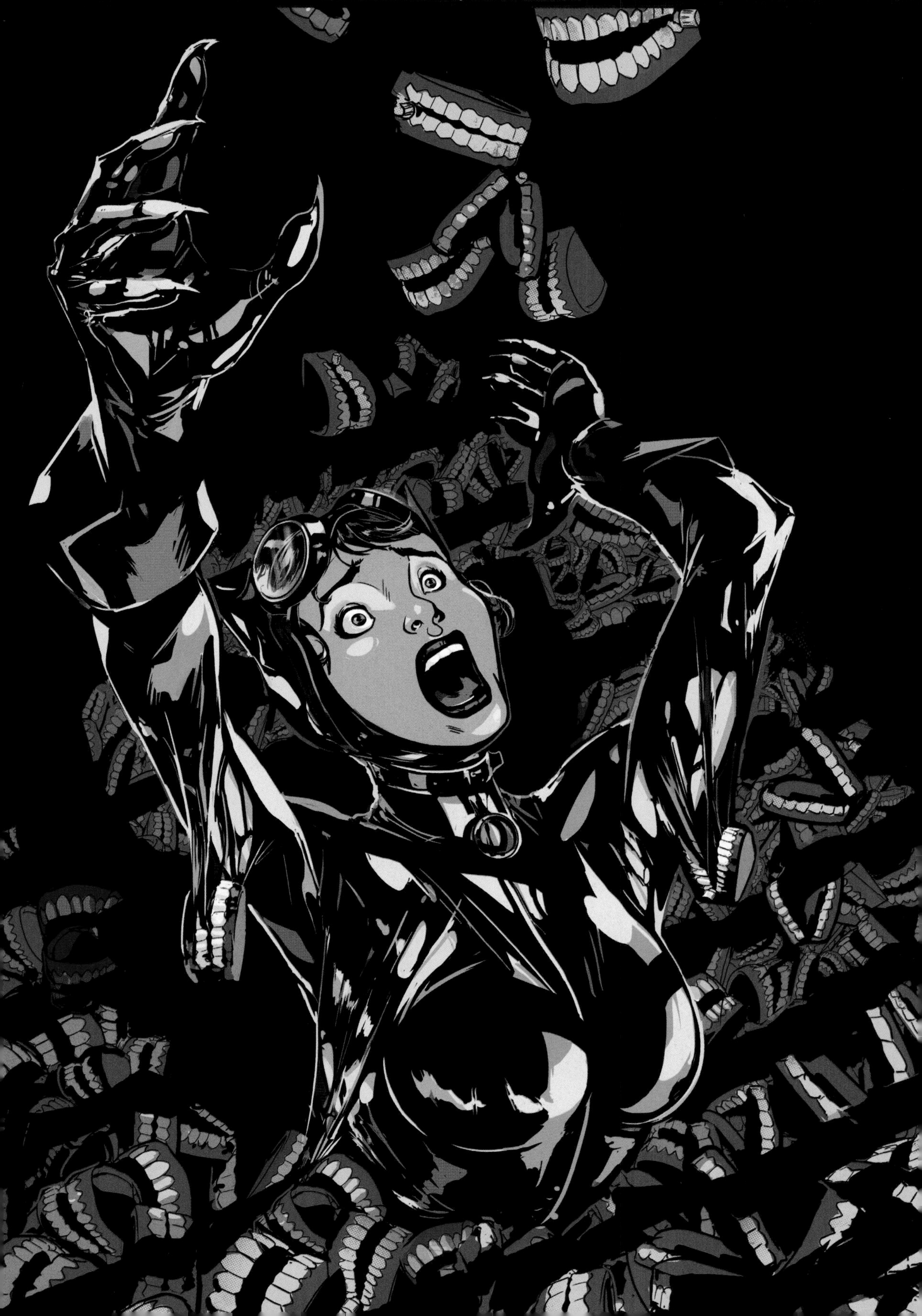

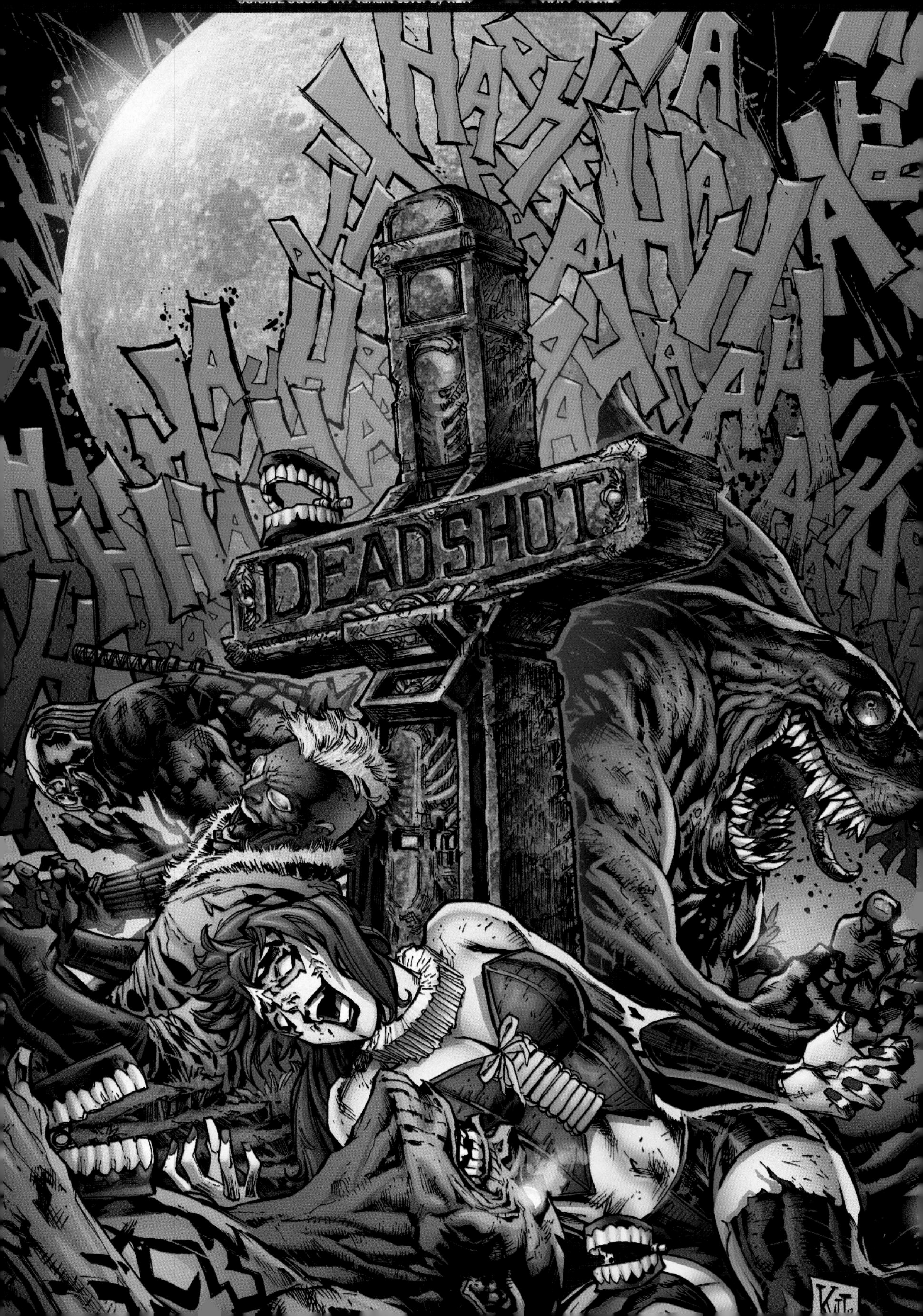
HA HA HA HA
DEADSHOT

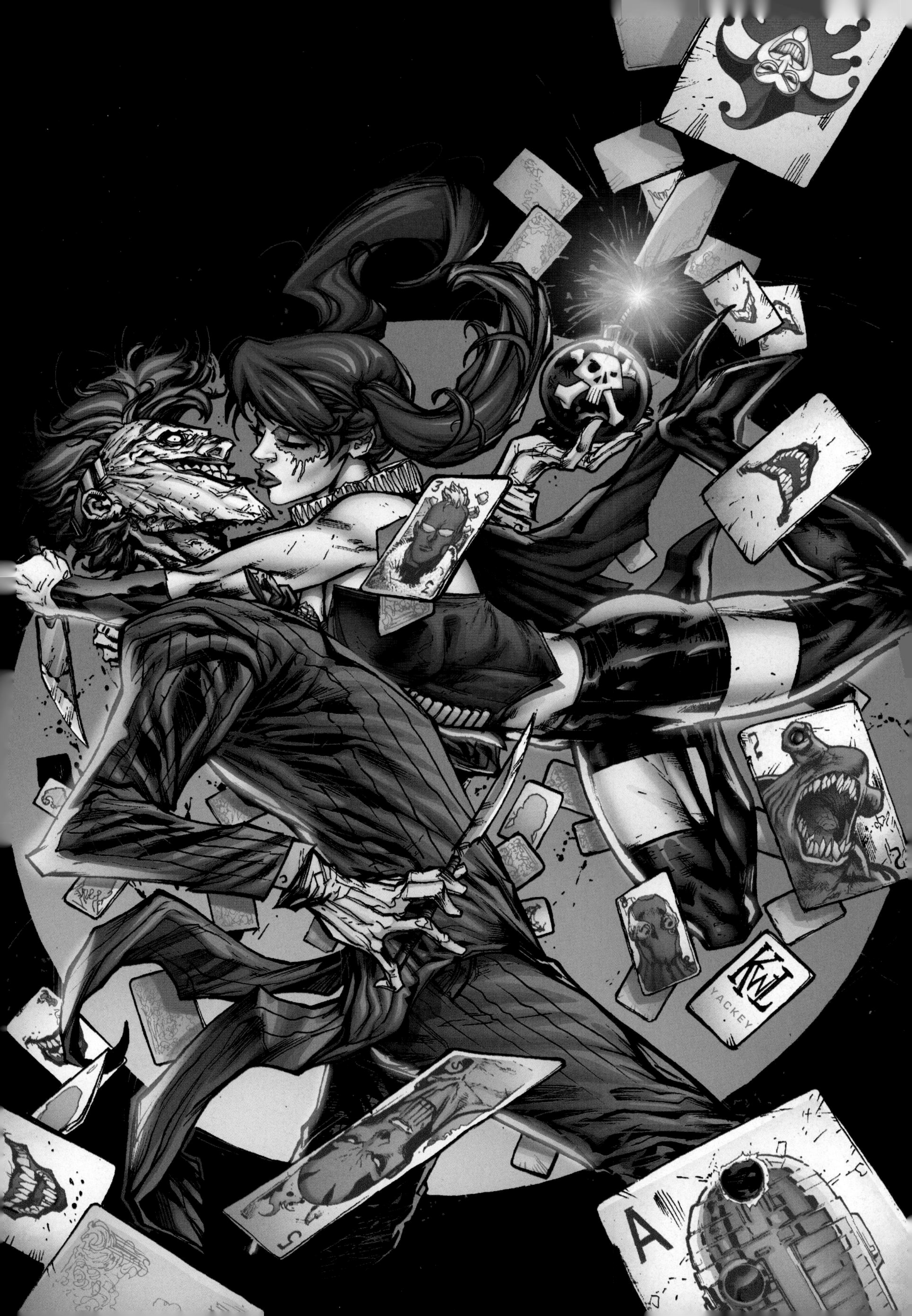
YACKEY

BATGIRL #14 cover by ED BENES & ULISES ARREOLA

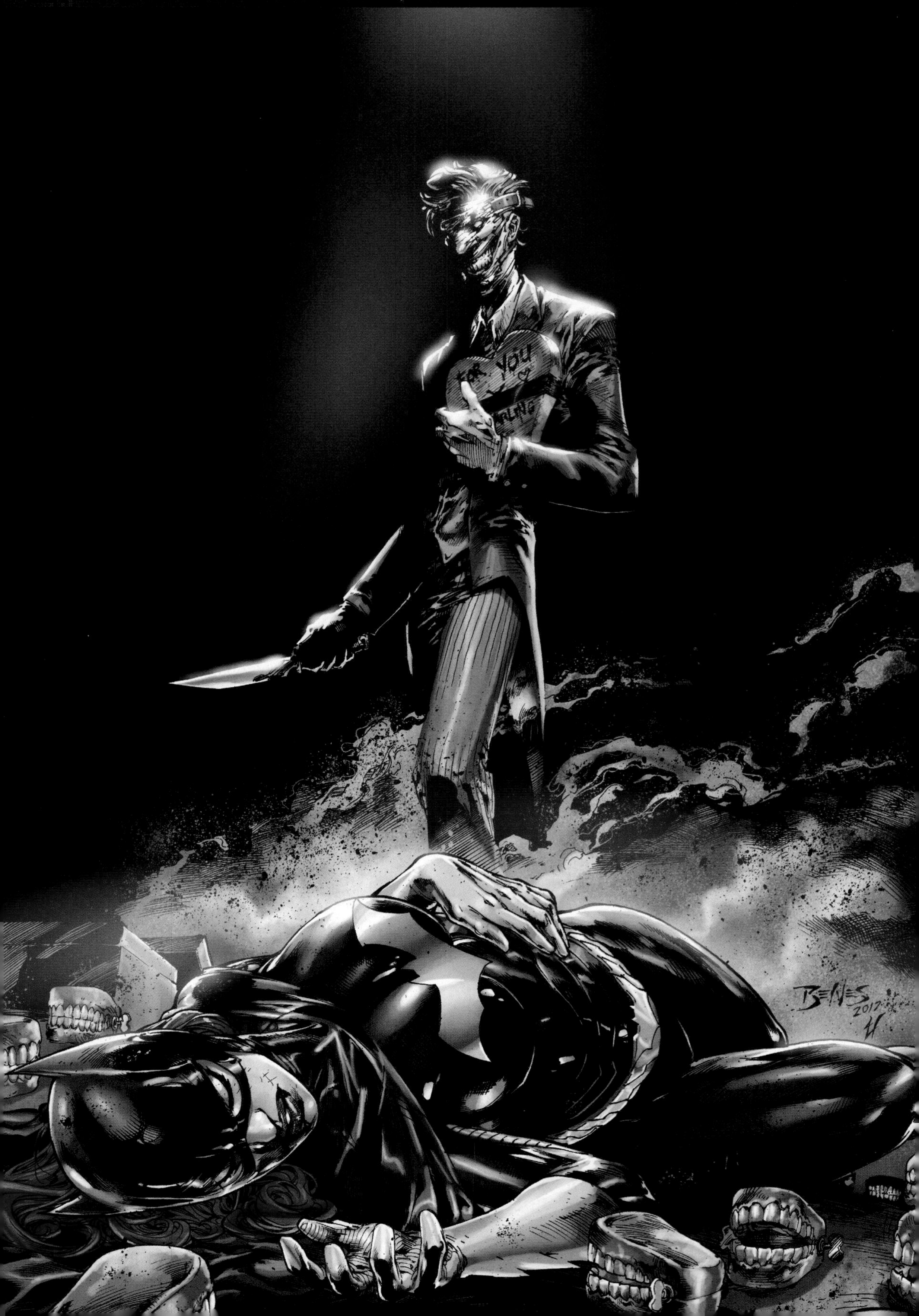
FOR YOU

BATGIRL #15 cover by **ED BENES** & **ULISES ARREOLA**

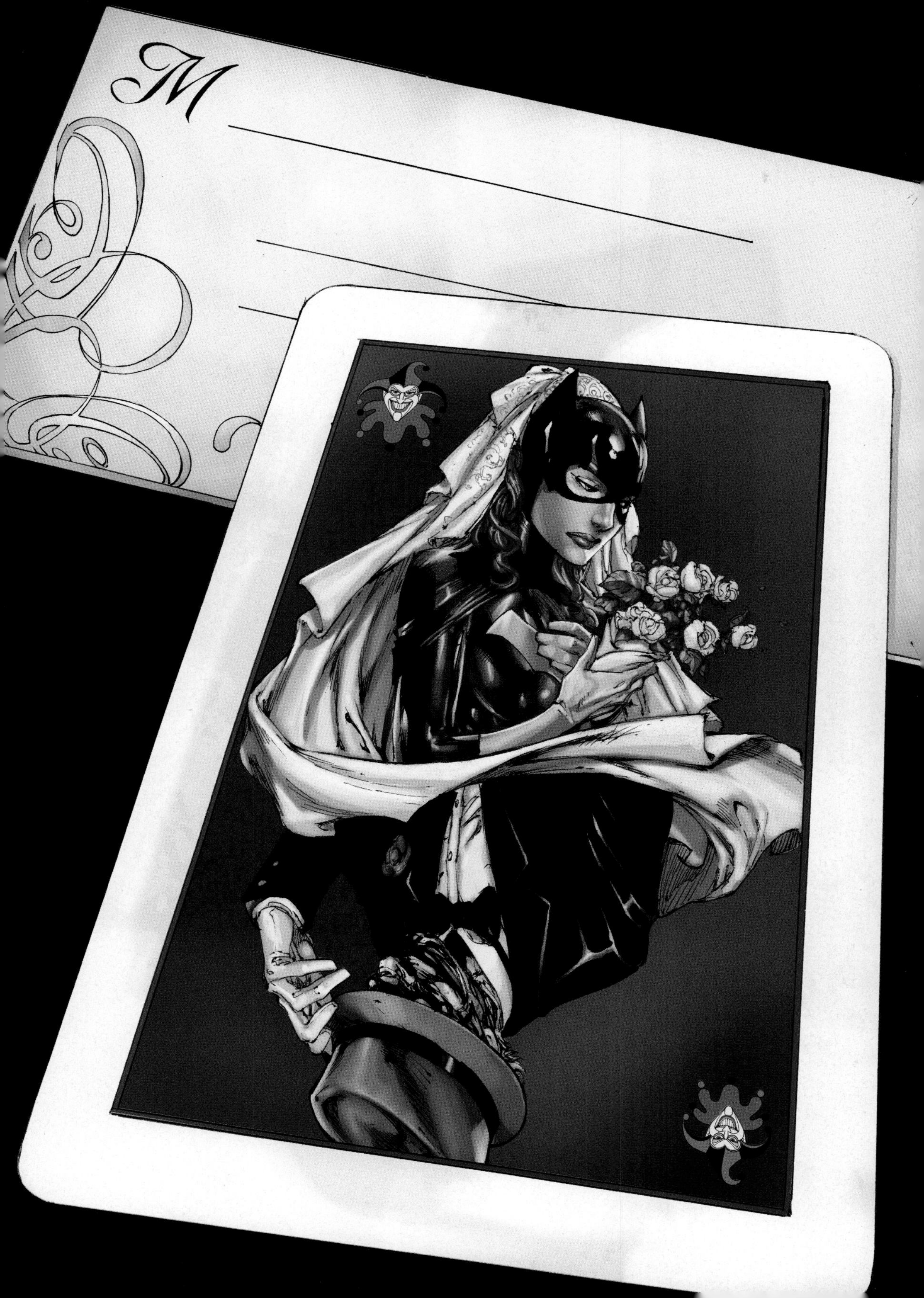
M

BATGIRL #16 cover by **ED BENES** & **ULISES ARREOLA**

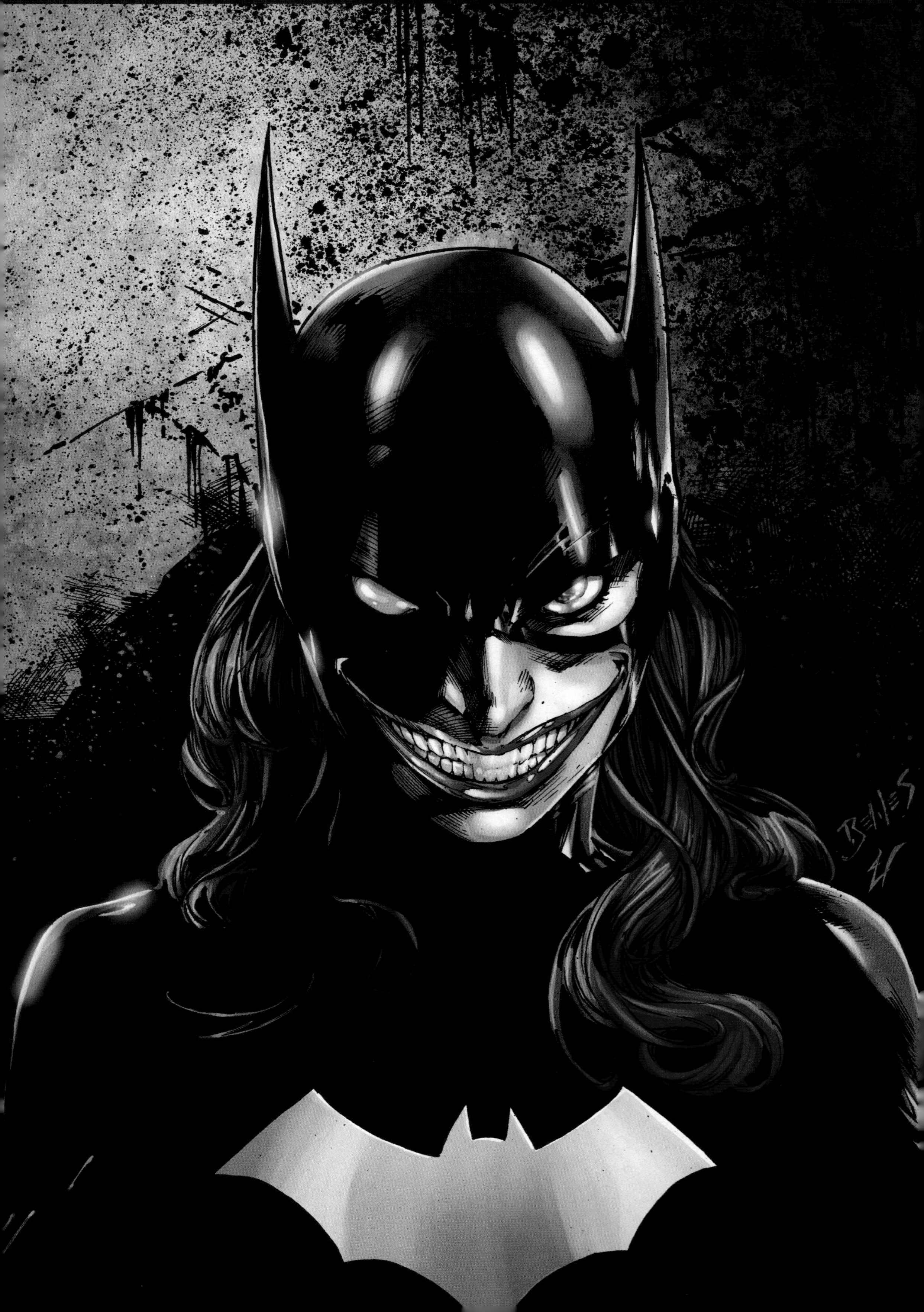

RED HOOD #15 unused cover by BRETT BOOTH, NORM RAPMUND & ROD REIS

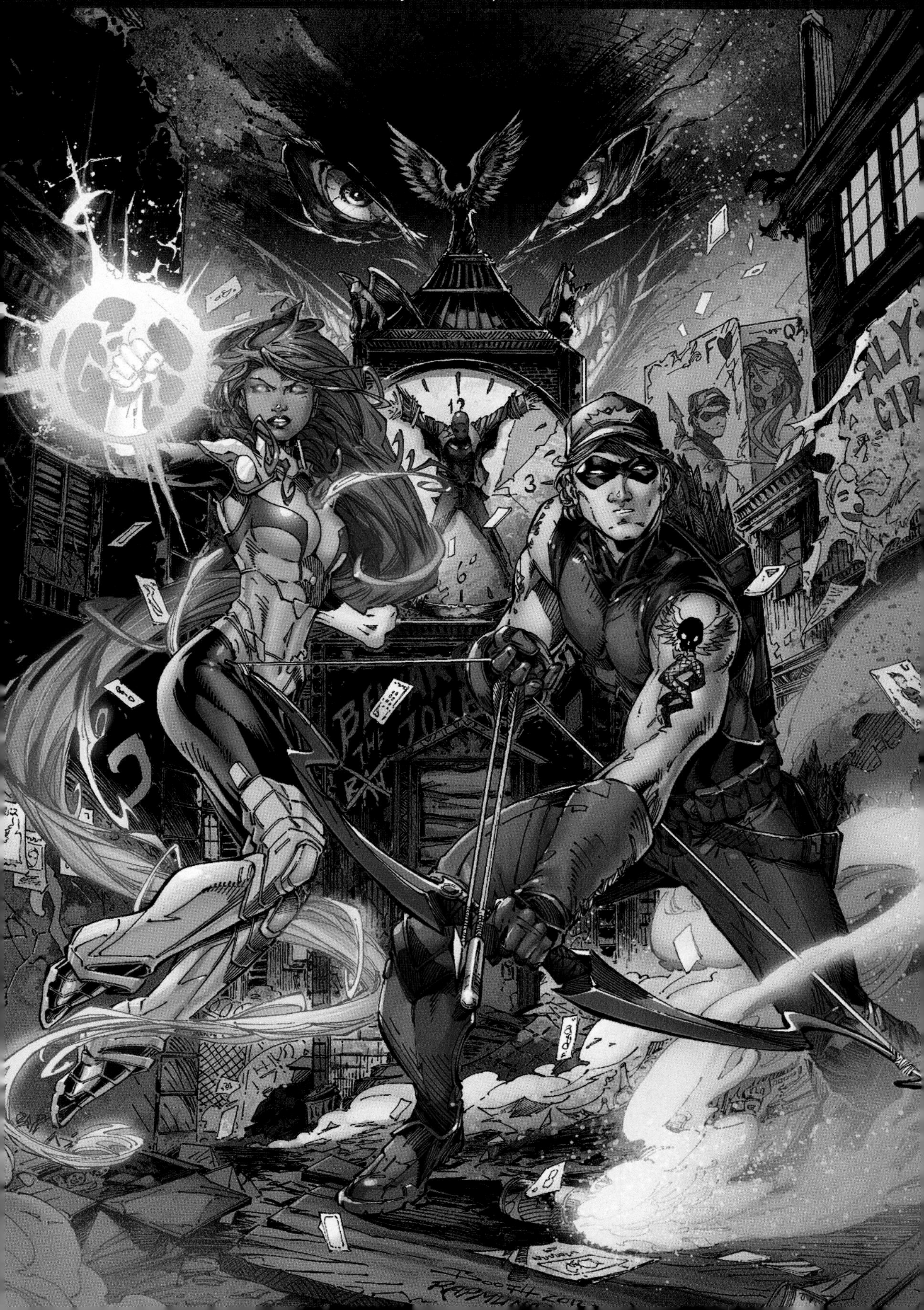

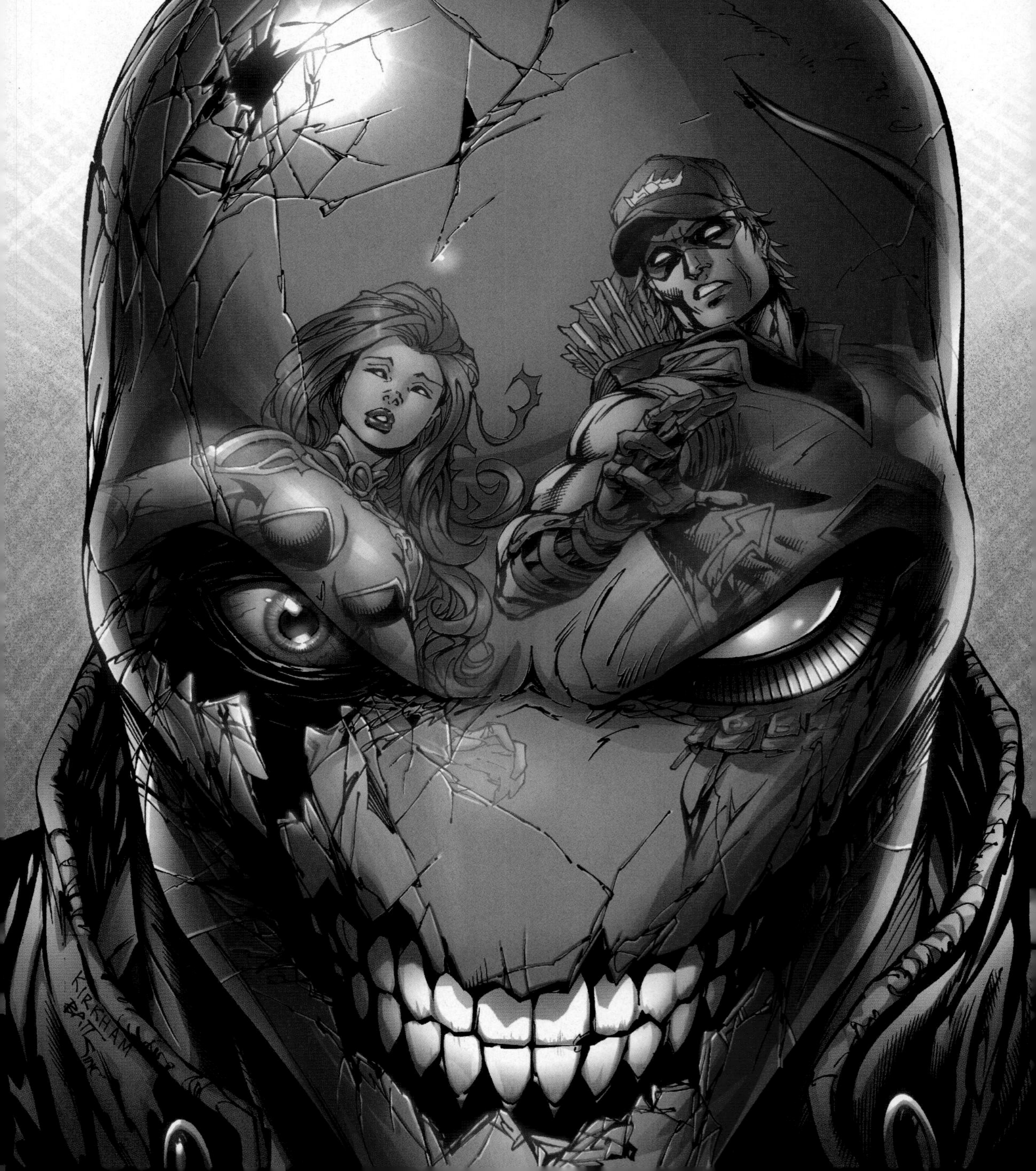

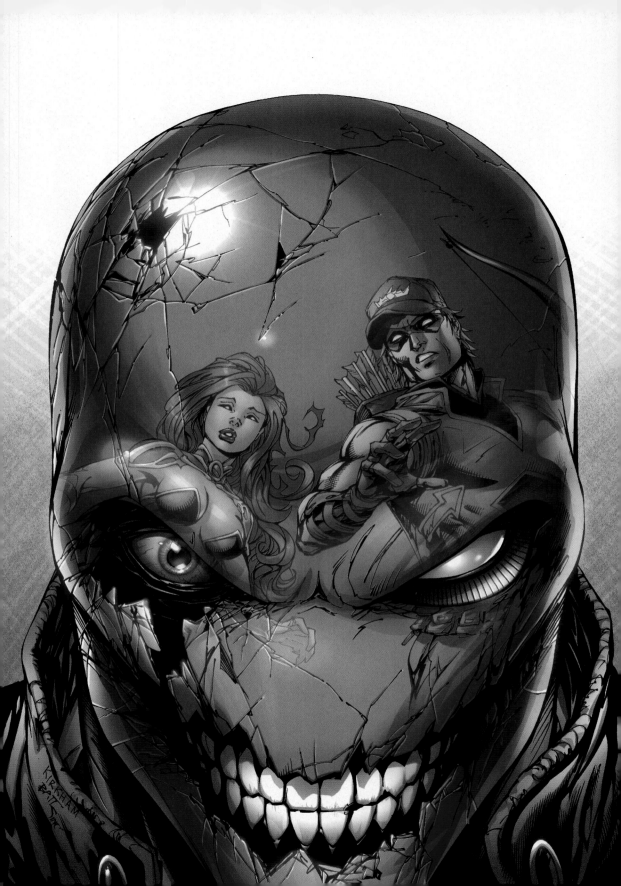

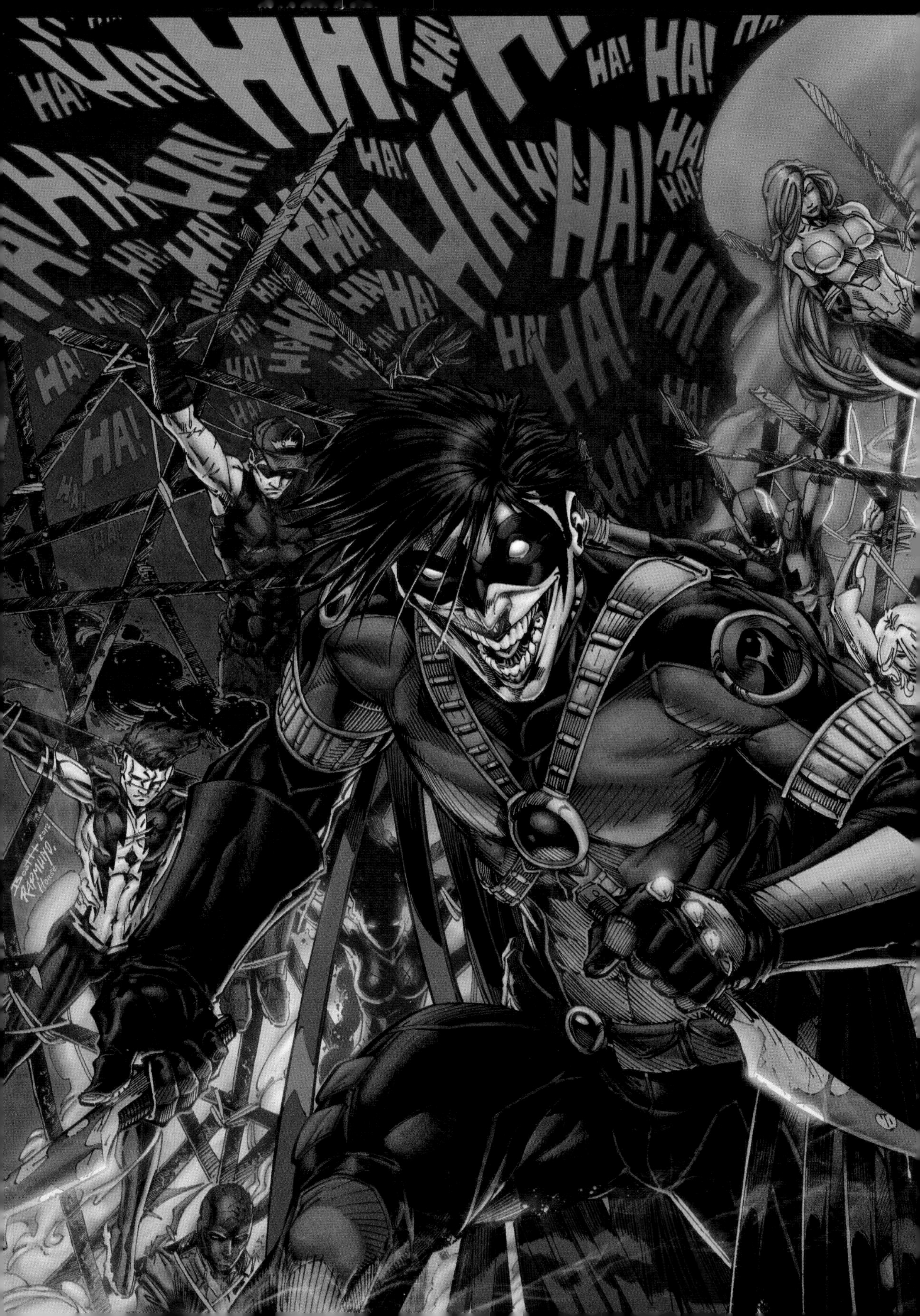
HA! HA! HA! HA! HA! HA! HA! HA! HA! HA!

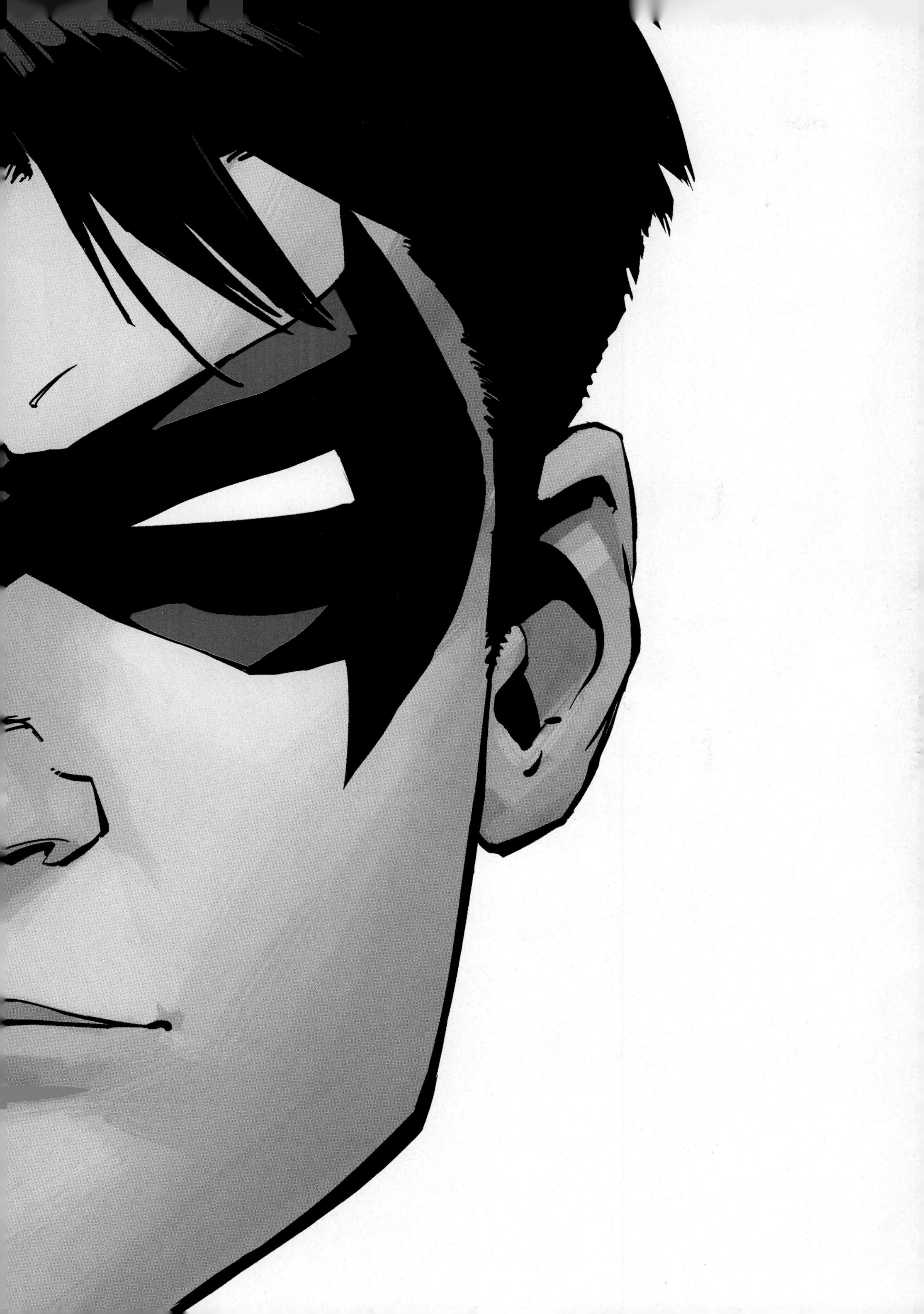

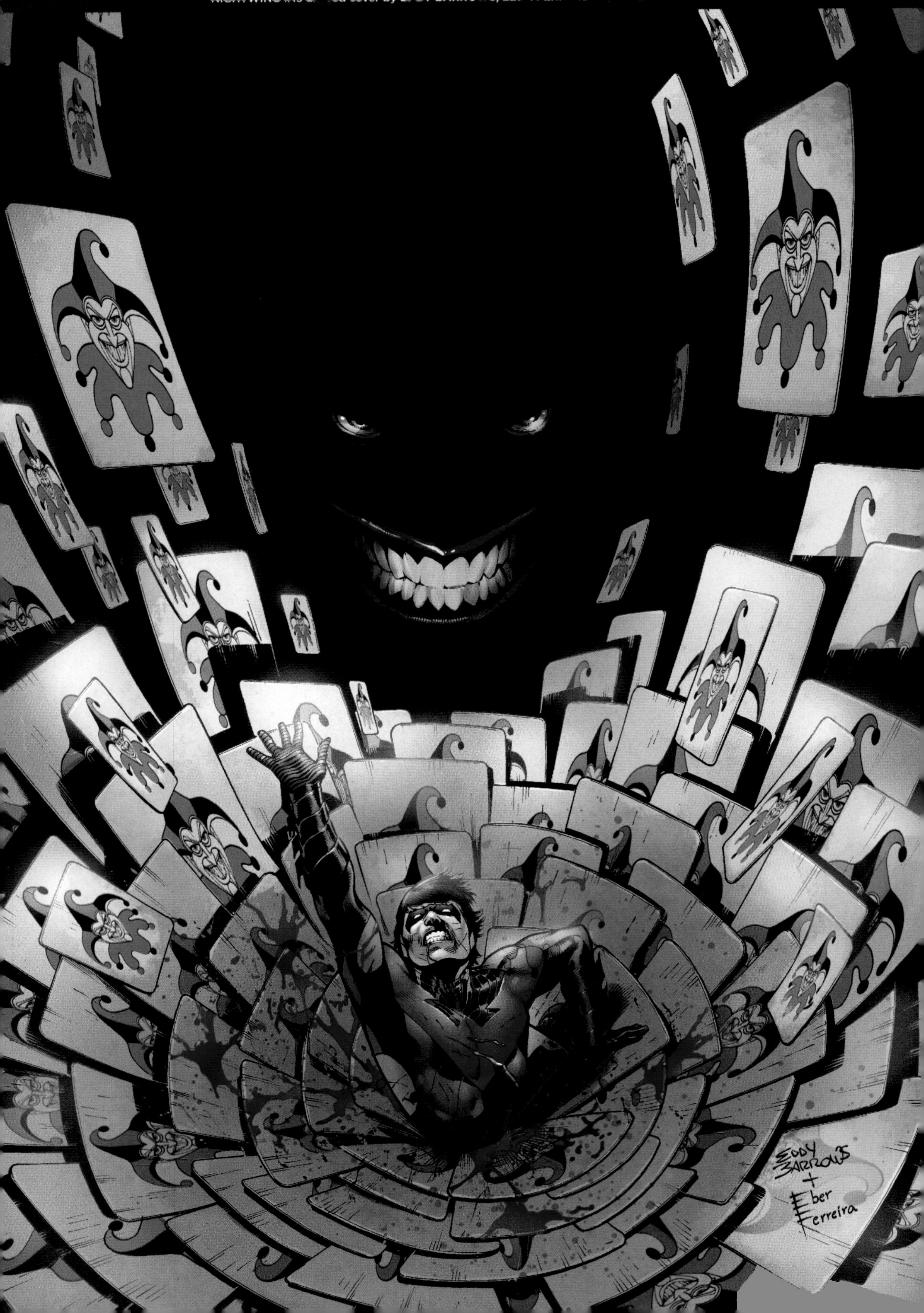
EDDY BARROWS
+
Eber Ferreira

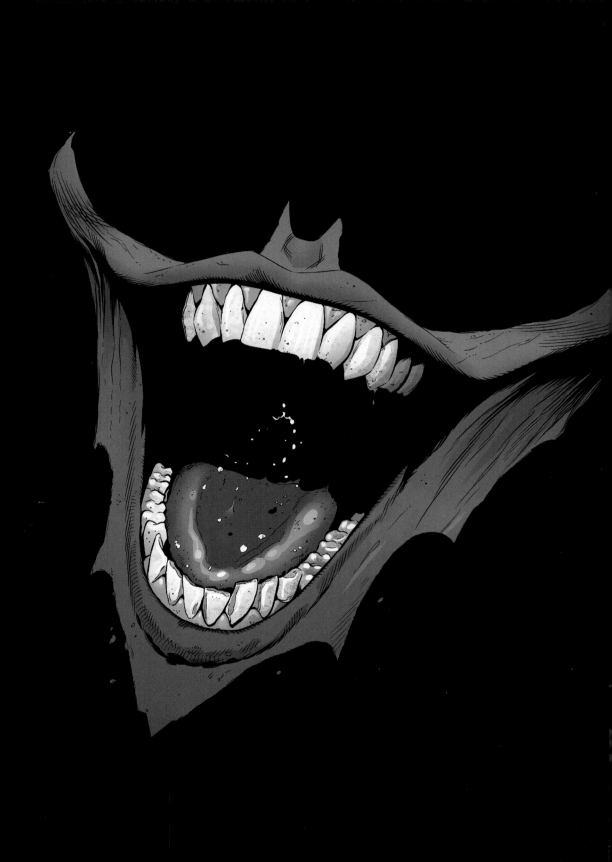